Better Homes and Gardens®

COMPLETE GUIDE TO FLOWER GARDENING

Susan A. Roth

BETTER HOMES AND GARDENS® BOOKS
Des Moines, Iowa

BETTER HOMES AND GARDENS® Books
An Imprint of Meredith® Books

COMPLETE GUIDE TO FLOWER GARDENING
Writer/Editor: Susan A. Roth
Senior Editor: Marsha Jahns
Art Director: Linda Vermie
Photographer: Susan A. Roth
Illustrator: Gary Palmer
Assistant Editor: Michele Burkhart
Editorial Assistant: Mary Jo Beeson
Indexer: Sharon Novotne O'Keefe
Researcher: Pamela K. Peirce
Consultants: Ball Seed Co., Virginia Blakelock, Paul Zimmerman

Vice President and Editorial Director: Elizabeth P. Rice
Executive Editor: Kay Sanders
Art Director: Ernest Shelton
Managing Editor: Christopher Cavanaugh

President, Book Group: Joseph J. Ward
Vice President, Retail Marketing: Jamie L. Martin
Vice President, Direct Marketing: Timothy Jarrell

Meredith Corporation
Chairman of the Executive Committee: E. T. Meredith III
Chairman of the Board and Chief Executive Officer: Jack D. Rehm
President and Chief Operating Officer: William T. Kerr

All of us at Meredith® Books are dedicated to providing you with
the information and ideas you need to garden successfully. We
guarantee your satisfaction with this book for as long as you own
it. If you have any questions, comments, or suggestions, please
write to us at:
MEREDITH® BOOKS, Garden Books
Editorial Department, RW 240
1716 Locust St.
Des Moines, IA 50309-3023

All photographs by Susan A. Roth, except for the following: Cathy Barash (page 339, top left), Derek Fell (page
377, bottom left), George Hale (page 316, top), Ellen
Henke (page 105, top), George Henke (page 105, bottom), Dency Kane (page 376, bottom right), J. Paul
Moore (page 9), Carole Ottesen (page 135, right), Pam
Peirce (pages 300, left; 315, top; 317, bottom; 326, right;
349, right); PHOTO NATS: (page 384, bottom right).

Special thanks to the garden designers whose work is
pictured on the following pages: Barbara Ashmun
Design, Portland, Oregon, pages: 56, 88, 114, 189T;
Duncan Callicot and Steve Snoddy, Nashville,
Tennessee, page: 95; Conni Cross, Cutchogue, New
York, pages: 39T, 54R, 55, 74B, 79, 81, 82, 107T, 107B,
134, 140, 142, 168B, 172, 188B; Creative Landscaping,
Easthampton, New York, page: 43; Donna Messina,
Cutchogue, New York, page: 38; Lucy Hardiman Design,
Portland, Oregon, pages: 40, 84L, 91; Kay McFadden-
Benecki, Portland, Oregon, (sculpture page 56); Tom
Pellet, Nashville, Tennessee, pages: 164B, 171

Special thanks to the following garden owners and pub-
lic gardens whose gardens are pictured in the book:
Robert C. Alexander, Moya Andrews, Barbara Ashmun,
Marsha Barriero, Marianne M. Byrd, Brookside Gardens,
Catnip Acres Herb Farm, Chicago Botanic Garden, Ellen
Costa and Morris Isaac, Conni and Jim Cross, Deepwood
Gardens, Dixon Galleries, Dumbarton Oaks, Susan Tyler
Eastman, Sydney Eddison, Isabel Fowlkes, Angela
Garguilo, Joyce Gillum-Koonce, Lucy L. Hardiman, Gail
Harrigan, Mary Jeanne Harris, Ellen and George Henke,
Pat Dixson Hoffman, Sharon and Bud Koehler, Richard
Kuisel, Dulcy Mahar, Mary McDonnell, Patty McGuigan,
Katherine Follin Maxwell, Martha McKeon, Minnesota
Landscape Arboretum, Louise and Wayne Mercer, Tony
Musto and Dennis Detralia, J. Paul Moore, New York
Botanic Gardens, Elaine Oaks, Old Westbury Gardens,
Carole Otteson, Darwin Otto, Carol and Dudley
Philhower, Barbara Paul Robinson, Jodi Slaymaker,
Becky Talbot, Kitty and Neil Taylor, United States
Botanic Garden, Penny Vogel and Millie Kiggens, Janette
Waltemath, Margaret Willoughby.

INTRODUCTION

Flowers bring joy to everyone who grows them, slows down to look at them, or buries a nose in their petals for a pleasant sniff. It is with the hope that we at Better Homes and Gardens® Books can bring more joy into the world that we offer you this book. Whether you're a beginning gardener who doesn't know which end of the seed is up or an experienced horticulturist with a moss-coated thumb, you'll find something of lasting value here.

If you've never grown a petunia or poppy before, the first chapter will get you growing. Once you've mastered the

basics of cultivating flowers and want to move beyond simply growing beautiful flowers to creating a beautiful flower garden, the second chapter will provide you with the design know-how. As you learn to look beyond individual flowers, to see them in the context of a garden setting, you'll find inspiration in the photographs and creative design ideas in Chapters 3–7. Every gardener will find the encyclopedia section at the end of the book to be a valuable reference for years to come. There you'll discover helpful identifying photographs and complete growing information for hundreds of lovely flowers.

CONTENTS

PART ONE

THE BASICS OF GARDEN FLOWERS 6–61

CHAPTER 1 FLOWER GROWING BASICS 8–39

CHAPTER 2 FLOWER GARDEN DESIGN BASICS.........................40–61

PART TWO

CREATING YOUR PERSONAL STYLE.......62–199

CHAPTER 3 DESIGNING COUNTRY GARDENS 64–97

CHAPTER 4 DESIGNING TRADITIONAL GARDENS 98–121

CHAPTER 5 DESIGNING NATURALISTIC GARDENS 122–151

CHAPTER 6 DESIGNING PROBLEM-SITE GARDENS 152–171

CHAPTER 7 DESIGNING COLOR-SCHEME GARDENS............172–199

PART THREE
THE FLORAL PALETTE

THE FLORAL PALETTE 200–386

CHAPTER 8 ENCYCLOPEDIA OF FLOWERS AND FOLIAGE ...202-386

PERENNIALS 202–291

ANNUALS..292–332

BULBS 333–363

ROSES 364–374

ORNAMENTAL GRASSES...375–382

FERNS..383–386

LIST OF BEST PLANTS BY REGION.............................387–392

MAIL-ORDER NURSERIES 393

HARDINESS ZONE MAP...394

FROST DATE MAPS...395

INDEX...396–408

The Basics of
Garden Flowers

CHAPTER ONE

FLOWER-GROWING BASICS

A Little Know-How Goes a Long Way Toward Cultivating a Beautiful Garden

Opposite: Spring gardens primarily count on hardy bulbs such as tulips for floral color because they sprout from the ground and begin growing and blooming during cool—even frosty—weather.

Left: A garden that uses large drifts of dependable flowering perennials for its backbone blooms lavishly year after year without demanding a great deal of attention or time-consuming upkeep.

Before you create a garden, you should first get to know the plants you'll be growing. Flowering annuals, perennials, bulbs, roses, ornamental grasses, and ferns—and perhaps some flowering shrubs and vines—are the stuff a flower garden is made of.

The garden designs in this book rely primarily on a core of perennials, bulbs, and ornamental grasses to create their backbones because these plants live for many years. Returning year after year to your garden, perennial plants give your design a long life with very little attention from you. Flowering annuals live only one growing season and demand a lot of care during that time. Most annuals, however, bloom nonstop, providing a welcome base of dependable color, so they do have an important place in almost any flower garden.

Below: Perennials, such as this spike gayfeather (*Liatris spicata*), die back to the ground and go dormant during winter, but regrow from their roots in spring. Flowers appear at the same time each year, lasting several weeks to a month or more, depending on the particular perennial.

Above right: Many perennials, such as this orange coneflower (*Rudbeckia fulgida* 'Goldsturm'), spread rapidly, forming larger clumps each year. To keep them from becoming invasive or losing vigor, coneflowers and other perennials should be dug up, divided, and replanted every few years.

UNDERSTANDING PERENNIALS

A perennial is any plant that lives for three or more years, and many live much longer. Technically, garden flowers termed perennials should be called herbaceous perennials because they lack the woody stems and branches of shrubs and trees, which are woody perennials. Most herbaceous perennials die to the ground during winter, but their roots remain alive and send up new growth in spring. The tall tops of

some perennials may die in fall, but the plants develop ground-hugging rosettes of leaves that survive the winter. A few perennials, such as bergenia and barrenwort, are herbaceous but have evergreen or semi-evergreen leaves. Other plants that are categorized as perennials, such as edging candytuft, are actually very low woody plants.

Most perennials bloom for two to three weeks at a specific time of the year, and their foliage remains until frost. Some cherished perennials, such as threadleaf coreopsis and purple loosestrife, are long blooming, producing flowers con-

tinuously for eight to 12 weeks. Others, such as garden phlox and delphinium, can be encouraged to rebloom later in summer by cutting back the first flush of flowers before they set seed.

Despite their short flowering period, many perennials contribute lovely foliage texture and color to the garden long after flowers fade. Some are grown just for their beautiful foliage alone. Many perennials spread, forming larger clumps every year. Some fast-growing plants need to be dug up and divided every few years or the plant loses vigor. Others must be continually hacked back or they spread so aggressively they take over the garden. A few perennials, such as peony and gas plant, grow happily for 10 to 50 years without needing division.

Perennials are cold hardy to different degrees; some can't make it through winters north of Washington, D.C., and others do just fine in Minnesota. Some thrive in the hot, humid summers of the South, while others wilt and flop under those same conditions. You'll find the perennials described in this book rated according to the USDA hardiness zones where they do best.

UNDERSTANDING ANNUALS

An annual plant completes its entire life cycle in a single growing season. It germinates, develops into a mature plant, blooms, sets seed, and finally dies, all in a span of several months. Most garden annuals keep on producing blossoms month after month with the aim of setting enough seed to perpetuate the species.

A hormonal trigger set off by seed formation or ripening signals many types of annuals to die. Gardeners can subvert this natural phenomenon, at least for a while, by continually removing faded flowers—a chore called deadheading. By preventing seed formation, the annuals usually keep right on furiously blooming.

Garden annuals hail from all over the world and from all kinds of climates, from rain forests to deserts, from meadows to seashores. Their origins dictate their preferred growing conditions. Some are cool-season annuals, blooming best during spring and fall conditions and slacking off during summer's heat. Others are warm-season annuals, flowering best in summer's hot sun.

As many as 70 percent of the plants that gardeners treat as annuals and are sold as annuals at your garden center are actually tender perennials. These are long-blooming perennials in their native habitats, but winter's cold, not their genetic makeup, kills them each year in your garden. Some are perennial in tropical or semitropical climates; others are perennial in temperate areas that receive only light frosts. Tender perennials, such as blue salvia and zonal geraniums, bloom quickly from seed and can be grown and treated much like annuals. Knowing which group a particular annual belongs to helps you understand how it will behave in your garden.

Warm-season annuals, such as zinnia, marigold, and cosmos, flourish in heat and make the best summer bloomers. Freezing temperatures kill the tender seedlings and sometimes the seeds. If sown outdoors, warm-season annuals need to be sown in spring after the soil has warmed; they take several months to mature and begin flowering. Because they grow so slowly, you are better off purchasing bedding plants instead of growing them from seed.

Cool-season annuals, such as nasturtiums, sweet alyssum, and pot marigolds (and some tender perennials), flower best during cool weather and wither or die during summer's heat. Freezing temperatures do not usually harm their seeds, which often self-sow and overwinter in the garden, sprouting in spring or summer.

Top left: Actually a tender perennial that can't survive winters in the North, mealy-cup sage (this white-flowered cultivar is *Salvia farinacea* 'Silver White') grows and blooms rapidly enough from seed to be treated as an annual in most gardens.

Center left: Sweet alyssum (*Lobularia maritima*) is a true annual, sprouting, flowering, and forming seeds all in a single growing season. It self-sows prolifically and may return to your garden year after year, germinating and flowering during cool weather.

Bottom left: China pinks (*Dianthus chinensis* 'Telstar Picotee') are hardy annuals whose blossoms tolerate a light frost unscathed.

Right: Zinnia (*Zinnia elegans*) is a warm-season annual, blooming best during summer's heat.

In temperate regions, early planting provides the best show from cool-season annuals, allowing them to bloom until summer's heat arrives. You can cut back heat-stressed annuals in midsummer to stimulate new growth and a new crop of flowers when cool weather returns. Cool-season annuals benefit from light shade or afternoon shade in the Southeast. Transplants or seeds of cool-season annuals can be planted outdoors in late summer or fall for late fall and winter bloom in warm climates, such as the desert Southwest or Florida.

Cool-season annuals may be hardy or half hardy. Hardy annuals can withstand the most cold. Sow their seeds in spring before frost danger has passed, or in late fall for spring germination. Half-hardy annuals, such as Madagascar periwinkle, spider flower, and cosmos, can withstand cold weather in spring and fall, but outright frost kills them. Sow their seeds outdoors in spring after all frost danger has passed, but you do not need to wait until the soil has warmed.

Below right: Shrub roses, such as this 'Mary Rose' English rose, make excellent additions to flower borders, providing year-round structure from their woody branches, handsome summer foliage, and spectacular fragrant blossoms.

Above: Hybrid tea roses produce elegant blossoms, but they grow best when separated in special rose gardens.

UNDERSTANDING ROSES

Roses are woody perennials that do not die to the ground in winter, although they lose all their foliage and go dormant in winter. There are many different types of roses—from large shrubs to small bushes and vining types—and some require specialized pruning to keep them blooming. Roses are indispensable additions to flower gardens and are so admired that they are often grown in separate gardens.

UNDERSTANDING BULBS

Not all plants we call bulbs are true bulbs. Some are corms, tubers, tuberous roots, or rhizomes. Whatever their true identity, bulbs are specialized underground storage structures that carry a plant through dormancy and contain the flower and leaf buds. Bulbs usually remain dormant most of the year, putting out leaves and flowers for only a few months.

Like annuals, bulbs can be tender or hardy. Tender bulbs survive winter only where the ground doesn't freeze as deep as the bulb. In cold climates, you can grow tender bulbs as annuals, discarding them at the end of the season, or you can dig them up before fall frost and store them in a cool, dry place over winter to be replanted when the soil warms up the next year.

Like perennials, hardy bulbs are cold hardy to different degrees and are recommended for certain hardiness zones. Most hardy bulbs do poorly in warm-climate areas, because they need a lengthy winter chill to break dormancy and get them growing in spring. In Florida and the Gulf Coast, you can plant cold-treated bulbs or dig up bulbs and store them in the refrigerator during winter, replanting them in spring. The Pacific Northwest's wet winters cause some bulbs to rot over winter unless they are planted with special care. Most hardy bulbs bloom in late winter or spring as their foliage emerges from the ground. After flowering, the foliage grows larger and in about six to 10 weeks begins to yellow and die to the ground. The plant disappears from the garden until the next spring.

Some summer- or fall-flowering bulbs produce leaves in spring, but these die back before flowering. Blossoms appear later in the season on naked stalks sent up from the underground bulb. These bulbs hail from regions with extreme summer drought and adapt by going dormant during the rainless seasons. Other bulbs (usually tuberous roots and rhizomes) sport foliage throughout the growing season. When grown in their preferred conditions, bulbs such as daffodils and crocus spread into large clumps. These won't need dividing or separating for many years, not until their flowering begins to diminish. Some bulbs, most notably tulips, bloom beautifully their first year in the garden but then fail to bloom well in subsequent years. Treat such bulbs as annuals, replanting and enjoying them each year.

UNDERSTANDING BIENNIALS

Living for only two years, biennials germinate from seed the first year and put all their energy into growing foliage and strong root systems. They often live through the winter as a rosette of ground-hugging leaves and then send up flowering shoots and set new seed the next growing season, dying once seeds ripen. Biennials can be unpredictable, however, not always adhering to this ideal life cycle. Some behave as short-lived perennials, flowering for perhaps two or three years in a row before dying.

Many biennials, such as foxgloves and hollyhocks, reseed themselves so successfully that they seem to be perennial in your garden. Usually seeds germinate the same season they ripen and fall to the ground, so flowers appear the next year, producing successive years of bloom. You can help the situation along by shaking seeds out on the ground where you want the plants to grow. Because they are often permanent additions to your garden, biennials are included with the perennials in this book.

Top left: Most bulbous plants, such as tulips, make but a brief appearance each year. They grow and bloom during spring and early summer, then go dormant, surviving summer's heat and drought and winter's cold underground.

Below: Hollyhock (*Alcea rosea*) lives only two years in the garden but often self-sows to perpetuate itself.

Left: Sweet William (*Dianthus barbatus*) is a biennial. It germinates from seed and grows leaves and stems its first year, dies to the ground in winter, then regrows and blooms the next summer before dying.

13

Left: Grown for the fabulous linear texture of their leaves and their feathery, late-season flowers, most ornamental grasses are clump-forming perennials that live for many years. Shown: *Miscanthus sinensis* 'Variegatus.'

UNDERSTANDING ORNAMENTAL GRASSES

Members of the huge grass family, ornamental grasses bring foliage and floral beauty to the garden for months on end. A few are evergreen, but most die back to the ground, leaving their bleached and dried leaves and fluffy seed heads to decorate the garden through winter. Ornamental grasses have recently enjoyed a resurgence in popularity and find a home in almost any style of garden.

Beware of the few ornamental grasses, some of which are dwarf bamboos, that spread by underground rhizomes. They can be very invasive. The best grasses to include in flower beds form well-behaved clumps that won't need dividing for 10 years.

UNDERSTANDING FERNS

Ferns are primitive, nonflowering plants much admired for their spectacular leaves. Most need shade and moisture to flourish, so they make perfect additions to shade gardens. Some, like hay-scented fern, spread by underground rhizomes and will colonize a large area. Others, such as Christmas fern, create beautiful clumps of dignified greenery.

Above: Ferns are nonflowering plants grown for their wonderful foliage. These long-lived perennial plants bring a myriad of textures and green hues to shady garden sites. Shown are Japanese painted fern (*Athyrium niponicum pictum*) and maidenhair fern (*Adiantum pedatum*).

IN THE BEGINNING

Your garden begins with the soil. And the better the soil, the better your flowers will grow. Most plants do best with a loose, fertile loam. Loam looks rich and dark brown and smells deliciously earthy. When you pick up a fistful of loam and squeeze it, the soil forms a loose, friable ball. Heavy soil has a high clay content and when squeezed into a ball forms a hard, rocklike mass. Light soil is sandy and won't form a ball at all, but trickles between your fingers.

You can make both heavy and light soil more loamlike by adding organic matter. Organic matter improves the soil's texture, helping heavy soil drain better and light soil hold more moisture, while adding nutrients. The amount of organic matter you need to add depends on the quality of the soil. If you already have loamy soil, you won't need to add much.

Excellent sources of organic matter are aged compost, leaf mold (composted leaves), or rotted manure. You usually can purchase it at low cost, or even get it free, from your community's yard waste recycling program. You can purchase aged manure, and sometimes compost, at most garden centers. A nearby farm may deliver a truckload of manure for a small fee. Be sure it is well aged because fresh manure burns plant roots; aged manure should not smell strong or offensive. Peat moss is a convenient source of organic matter, but it has very few nutrients and a short lasting power because it decomposes quickly. Peat should be a last-resort choice for improving soil. If you use it, be sure to wet it thoroughly before mixing it into the soil, because dry peat actually repels water.

Most plants do best in slightly acidic (pH 6 to 7) soil. If a soil test—you can have one performed by your county's agricultural extension service—shows that your soil is more acid than this, you can make it more neutral by adding ground limestone, following the soil test's recommendations. Usually 5 pounds of lime are needed for every 100 square feet of soil to raise the pH by one point. Slightly alkaline soil—higher than the neutral pH of 7—can be made neutral or slightly acidic by adding wettable ground sulfur at the rate of 5 pounds per 100 square feet or by working acidic organic matter such as leaf mold or sphagnum peat moss into the soil. Follow soil test recommendations if your soil is highly alkaline because it will require a great deal of sulphur. Test it each year because alkaline ground water tends to turn back the pH once you've lowered it.

WORKING THE SOIL

If you're beginning a new garden in an area that is now lawn, you'll first need to eliminate the grass. Don't power-till the grass into the soil, or the grass roots will return as weeds in your

When starting or enlarging a flower bed in a lawn area, strip off the sod rather than tilling it in, to prevent grass roots from returning later as garden weeds. You can strip the sod off by hand using a spade, or rent a power sodstripper.

flower bed. It's better to remove the sod entirely, using a rented power sod-stripper or a spade. Be sure the soil is moist, but not wet or soggy, when you begin working.

First mark the contours of the new bed with a clothesline or garden hose. Rearrange the hose until you are happy with the garden's shape, then sprinkle garden lime along the hose to make a more permanent marker. Use a spade or a half-moon edger to cut down into the sod along the lime marker. Then begin to strip off the sod with a spade by angling the flat end of the spade's blade just under the grass roots and pushing with your foot. Slice off the sod in easy-to-handle sections. You can add the sod to your compost heap, where it will quickly rot, or replant it elsewhere. After the sod is gone, dig into the soil as deeply as you can—one spade depth or 1½ feet—using a power tiller or a shovel or spade to turn it over. Loosening the soil creates a fluffy soil that's easy for roots to penetrate. With clay soil, you might want to loosen the soil down deeper with a garden fork. Push the fork into the subsoil and rock it back and forth without turning the soil over. Spread organic matter in a 2- to 6-inch-deep layer over the surface of the loosened soil, and apply lime or sulphur as needed. You might also want to add superphosphate, at 5 pounds per 100 square feet, because most soils are low in phosphorous. Then mix it all into the top 1 foot of soil, and smooth the soil with a garden rake.

Well-prepared soil gives perennial plants the best start possible—they'll send down deep roots and grow into healthy specimens that will bring you pleasure for years to come. Because perennials live so long, you won't get another chance to work the soil this deeply unless you renovate the entire bed, so take this opportunity to create the best soil possible.

PLANT ACQUISITION

In the old days, folks traded plants with one another, passing along seeds, cuttings, or divisions of their favorites with their friends and neighbors. Plant sharing like this is part of the joy of gardening. While you might be able to start an entire garden from slips of plants acquired from friends, few people start off that way. Most likely, you will purchase plants at a garden center or order them from a catalog.

PURCHASING PERENNIAL PLANTS

Perennials—including ornamental grasses, roses, and ferns—are often grown in quart, 1-gallon, or 2-gallon containers and set out for display and sale when in full bloom. While spring and fall are the best planting times, container-grown plants can be planted safely even during the height of summer if kept watered. Gallon containers can be expensive, and they create just a single clump in the garden. Even though they are smaller, several quart-size plants for about the price of a single large one make a better choice, because

Your garden center sells perennials, annuals, roses, and bulbs in all types and sizes of containers. Choose plants with dark green leaves and those whose roots aren't trailing out of the pot's drainage holes as assurance that they are healthy and have been well cared for.

you'll be able to arrange them into an attractive drift. Keep in mind that once released from the container the plants spread and grow much taller.

Shop wisely, choosing a reputable nursery over a discount garden center if you are after quality. Improperly trained personnel often neglect plants, allowing them to wilt repeatedly, which stresses them. Look for plants with healthy, dark green foliage, indicating that the plant has been properly watered and fed. Also check to see that a mat of roots isn't growing from the drainage holes in the pot. A trail of roots warns of a rootbound plant that may not transplant well.

Mail-order perennials may be very small plants—essentially year-old seedlings—in small pots or bare, dormant roots of more mature plants. Small container-grown plants probably won't bloom the first year you plant them, but they make an economical choice. Generally, mail-order companies pledge to ship bare-root plants at the proper planting time for your region so you can plant them immediately.

SHOPPING FOR BULBS

Bulbs can be ordered successfully from mail-order suppliers. Bulb purveyors wisely send out their glossy catalogs in spring. Use the color pictures to select the best tulips or hyacinths to complete your spring color scheme and order early—the bulbs will be shipped at the proper planting time. Some garden centers create beautiful displays of spring-blooming bulbs at fall planting time. Select the bulbs by using the colored photo decorating the boxes, and be sure to place a little tag with a picture of the flower in the bag with the bulbs, so you'll know what you have when you get home. Beware of bargain bulbs, for they are often no bargain; they may be of inferior

quality or size and will not bloom well. Select large, firm bulbs without blemishes or rotten spots and store them in a cool, dry place until planting time.

BUYING ANNUALS

Annuals come in divided plastic trays called cell-packs, usually four or eight in a pack. The little plants can quickly get overgrown in these small containers, so select wisely. The seedlings should have healthy, dark green foliage and a few flower buds or open flowers. Avoid larger annuals that are tall and leggy with roots trailing from the drainage holes; they are stressed and will transplant poorly.

You also can start annuals from seeds sown indoors in winter or right in the garden at the proper planting time. Seed-starting is both an art and a science, but it brings great rewards to people who have the patience to try it. One major benefit of starting annuals from seeds is that you no longer have to limit your garden choices to those offered by your local nursery. If you grow your own, a whole world of wonderful, uncommon plants can be yours.

When purchasing annuals, such as the pansies shown here, look for short, stocky plants with healthy dark green foliage and a few flower buds or open flowers. Avoid tall, leggy, potbound plants and those with yellow, wilted, or damaged leaves.

SEED STARTING

You can start almost any kind of flower from seed—annuals are the easiest to succeed with, perhaps because by their very nature they are programmed toward regenerating themselves through seeds. If you're patient, you can grow perennials and ornamental grasses from seeds, although several years may pass before the young plants are substantial enough to bloom and make a garden statement.

Seedlings need moisture, warmth, nutrients, and light, which you can supply in a controlled environment indoors with simple equipment. It's best if you're a nurturing sort of person, because, although the procedures are simple, you have to pay close attention and administer a lot of loving care at the proper times.

LIGHTING UP

In most parts of the country, winter sun—even on a south-facing windowsill—doesn't supply enough light for young seedlings. You need to provide artificial light from fluorescent tubes. Select a 4-foot-long shop light with two 40-watt bulbs and a white reflector, using one cool-white and one warm-white bulb to provide the spectrum of light plants need. (Expensive specialized plant grow lights are not necessary.) Plug the fixture into a timer, setting it to provide 14 hours of light each day.

Suspend the lights from adjustable chains over your growing area. Each 4-foot, two-bulb fixture lights a 2x4-foot seed-starting area, so space multiple lights accordingly to avoid gaps of low light.

Any table with a waterproof surface—you can build one from plywood and sawhorses, covering it with a plastic tablecloth—works well. Place this setup in the kitchen, basement, spare room, or any place that doesn't get very hot or cold.

Light intensity falls off the farther the tubes are from the seedlings. Keep the lights 2 inches above the tops of the seedlings at all times. That's why you need the chains, so you can raise the lights as the seedlings grow taller. If some seedlings get taller than others, make adjustments by placing low plants on bricks.

You'll need to replace the fluorescent tubes before they burn out, because their intensity dwindles with age. Get new ones when black rings appear at the ends of the tubes.

To successfully grow plants from seedlings, you'll need to supply light from an artificial light source. Even sun from a south-facing window is seldom strong enough in winter to foster healthy seedlings. Adjustable fluorescent lights with reflectors provide the best light and give you the most flexibility.

SEED-STARTING SETUP

SOIL AND CONTAINERS

Seeds germinate best in a fine-textured, evenly moist growing medium. You can purchase bagged and sterilized growing mixes at most garden centers or order them from a catalog. Some types are better than others. The best for germination are mixes containing fine-textured sphagnum moss and vermiculite. The mix is lightweight and holds water well but provides good aeration for seedling roots.

You can germinate seeds and grow seedlings in almost any type of container as long as it is no more than 2 to 3 inches deep, has drainage holes, and is clean. Some gardeners like to use recycled materials such as egg cartons, cut-off plastic milk jugs, or yogurt cups. If you use these recycled materials, be sure to wash them first in hot, soapy water and then punch holes in their bottoms with an ice pick. You'll get the best drainage by punching from the inside out, so a dam doesn't form around the hole. You also can use flats, cell-packs, and pots recycled from nursery purchases or purchased new from catalogs. Fill your clean containers with dry growing medium and then water from the bottom up by placing the containers in a tray or pan of warm water. Let the pots sit in the water until the soil surface glistens with moisture, then drain off excess water from the tray. Peat-based mixes are sometimes hard to wet at first.

SOWING TECHNIQUE

Seeds of most flowering annuals should be sown anywhere from 12 to 16 weeks before the last frost date for your area. Count backward from that date to get the proper time to sow each type of seed.

If you like, large, easy-to-handle seeds can be sown directly into individual cell-packs, peat pots, or 4-inch plastic pots instead of community flats. Experienced seed sowers usually have their own technique for delivering just the right amount of seed to the container. One good way is to use a white 3x5 file card folded in the middle. Pour a few seeds through a cut-off corner of the seed packet into the crease of the file card, then with a toothpick gently push off the seeds one by one from the card onto the soil in the container. Put two or three seeds in each individual container because all may not germinate. Push the seeds into the soil with the eraser end of a pencil. The general rule of thumb is to bury seeds at a depth of two to three times their size.

You may find it easier to sow fine seeds in a community flat and after they germinate transplant the seedlings into individual pots. Sow the seeds in rows in the flats. Handle them by pouring the packet out onto a white card and then picking up individual seeds with the tip of a moistened, flat toothpick. Fine seeds need only a dusting of soil as a cover. You might want to sift a small amount of germination medium through a kitchen strainer and keep the sifted particles in a jar to use when needed. Use a pinch of the sifted mix to cover fine seed, then apply a gentle mist to moisten it.

Seeds need to be spaced out in a community flat so the seedlings won't be crowded. An effective way to sow small seeds is to pour them from the seed packet into a folded file card and then push individual seeds off the tip one at a time using a toothpick.

Many seeds need light to germinate; do not cover these with soil. After tapping them onto the soil surface, gently mist to nestle the seed into the mix.

After sowing seeds, cover the pots or flats with plastic film or a special clear plastic humidity dome and set them under the lights. Most seeds germinate best at 65° to 70°F. Some do best with bottom heat, which you can provide with a special heating mat, although it isn't absolutely necessary. The containers won't need water again until the seeds germinate, usually in one to two weeks. (Perennials can take two weeks to several months.)

Once you see the little green tops, gradually remove the cover, first opening it slightly one day, then a little more the next until you remove it completely. Water from beneath when the soil surface seems dry, usually several times a week.

When the seedlings develop their first set of true leaves—the leaves that form above the rounded seed leaves—they need to be transplanted or thinned. Transplant seedlings from community flats to individual 4-inch pots or cell-packs by picking them up by the leaves and lifting the roots with a wooden tongue depressor in which you have cut a notch—don't touch the fragile stems with your hands. Thin seedlings already in individual containers to one seedling by cutting out the weakest ones with small scissors to avoid disturbing the roots of your chosen seedling.

As the seedlings grow, they require regular watering and fertilizing. It's easy to do both at once. Mix up a balanced soluble fertilizer at one-quarter the recommended strength and use this each time you water.

TRANSPLANTING SEEDLINGS

Transplant young seedlings into less crowded quarters after they have their first set of true leaves. Gently hold onto a leaf—not the stem—and use a wooden tongue depressor or plastic spoon to lift the seedling.

Create a planting hole in the new container with a pencil or other small instrument.

Place the seedling into the planting hole, being careful not to crush the fragile stem.

Gently press the growing medium around the seedling, being sure to plant the seedling at the same level it was growing.

After transplanting all the seedlings, apply a gentle spray of water to settle the growing medium around the roots.

Every seedling grows best at a certain range of temperatures. Try to keep your seedlings at the cool end of their range, which makes them stockier and sturdier. Be careful, however, because cool, damp conditions may foster damping off fungus. The fungus shouldn't be a problem if you start with sterilized potting mix and clean equipment. If your growing quarters are a dank basement, you may want to use an oscillating fan set on low to keep air circulating around your seedlings to help ward off fungus.

HARDENING OFF

Come planting time—after the soil has warmed and the danger of frost has passed for tender annuals, sooner for hardy and half-hardy annuals—you can't just take the seedlings outside and pop them in the garden. They must be hardened off, a process that accustoms them to the bright light, wind, and fluctuating temperatures of the great outdoors.

Set the seedlings outside in the shade—full sun will burn the leaves—for a few hours each day, gradually leaving them out longer and longer. Progressively increase their sun exposure and their exposure to colder temperatures. After 10 days to two weeks of gradual adjustment, the seedlings are ready for the garden.

A PERENNIAL DIFFERENCE

Perennials usually need another year in the pot before going into the garden. Rather than transplanting them to the garden, plant them in a nursery bed, either in rows in the ground or in quart containers. Provide winter protection for container plants with a cold frame, pine boughs, or leaves.

PLANTING AND CARING FOR PERENNIALS AND ORNAMENTAL GRASSES

Perennials and ornamental grasses are easy-care plants, but they are not totally care-free. They'll bring you enjoyment year after year if you give them just a bit of attention.

Bare-root plants are usually shipped at the proper planting time in spring. Unpack them immediately and soak them in lukewarm water for about 30 minutes if they look dry. If you can't plant them right away, moisten their packing material (usually sphagnum moss or wood shavings), rewrap them, and seal them in a plastic bag. Store in a cool, dark place.

At planting time, be sure to protect bare-root plants from drying sun and air; keep them wrapped in a moist towel laid in the shade until you pop them into their prepared planting hole.

Bare-root plants can be tricky. Many a gardener has puzzled over the mess of roots discovered among the packing material and wondered which end is up. Careful inspection should reveal remnants of dried stalks or new little shoots marking the crown (growing point) where the stems will grow. Observe the plant's root system—does it want to spread out or go down deep?

Dig a hole twice as wide and deep as the roots. Hold the plant in the hole, fanning the roots outward or downward according to their growth habit while filling in soil under and around the roots. Position the crown at the same depth it was growing previously, usually with the bottom of the crown an inch below the soil surface. Build a ring of soil over the root ball to act as a dam, then flood it with water to give the plant a good drink and settle the soil around it.

Don't allow the unplanted roots of bare-root plants to sit out, as they are here, or the roots can dry out or become sunburned. Instead, wrap the roots in a moist towel and put them in the shade until you've prepared the planting hole.

When planting container-grown perennials, break up the surface tangle of roots by raking the root ball from top to bottom with a weeding claw. This won't damage the roots, but will encourage them to grow outward rather than in a strangling circle.

Container-grown plants can be planted any time of year they are available. To remove the plant, first water it, then turn it upside down, holding your spread-out hand over the root ball to catch the plant as it slides out. If the plant won't budge, whack the bottom and sides of the container with a trowel to loosen the roots.

Roots of container-grown plants frequently encircle the surface of the root ball and may keep growing round and round even after planting, unless you take action. Lay the plant on its side on the ground. Holding it at the top with one hand, firmly rake the root ball's surface with a handheld weeding tool around the entire root ball. The tongs of the weeding claw should cut deeply into the root ball, cutting the entangling roots. The cut roots will branch out and grow into the surrounding soil.

Dig a hole wider and deeper than the container. Refill with soil, positioning the root ball level with the soil surface and firm the soil. Build a dam around the plant and flood with water, as described above.

MAJOR STAKES

Some perennials need to be staked so they grow straight and tall, don't flop onto their neighbors, aren't broken in the wind and rain, or aren't weighted to the ground with heavy blossoms. The staking method varies according to the plants' form, with an assortment of commercially available or homemade devices solving most staking needs. Use stakes that are inconspicuous and easy to install; green or brown materials look best. It's a good idea to position stakes early, before the plants need them, so that the foliage grows up and around, camouflaging the stake.

Tall plants with slender, unbranched flower stalks, such as foxglove, delphinium, and lily, call for individual stakes to support each stem. Drive a bamboo or wooden stake into the ground alongside the stem and loosely tie the two together with a loop of green garden twine, strips of old pantyhose, or paper-wrapped twist-ties. As the plant grows, add more ties at 1-foot intervals. The stake should be about three-fourths of the plant's ultimate height. You also can purchase plastic-coated metal stakes with locking loops on their ends to quickly and easily support individual stems; although expensive, they last for years and are easy to use.

Clumps of plants with many bushy, branched stems, such as aster, shasta daisy, and chrysanthemum, can be supported with a ring of twine attached to three to five stakes around the clump's exterior. Add twine at 1-foot intervals as the plants grow. The stems and flowers bend outward and rest on the twine, covering it naturally. You also can purchase metal rings with legs to serve this purpose. Install them early so the plants grow up through the rings.

A superb metal support consists of a round grid of 3-inch mesh supported by three legs; these come in different sizes and heights. Place the support over floppy, bushy plants when they are young. The stems grow right up through the mesh and are held beautifully and inconspicuously apart to show off individual flowers.

STAKING METHODS

Below: Dahlias grow through a metal grid support, which effectively separates the stems while providing an underpinning for the heavy flowers.

Homemade cages made of five or more lengths of bamboo stakes encircled by twine help to keep floppy, bushy plants upright.

Individual tall bamboo stakes help flower spikes to grow straight and prevent them from breaking in the wind.

Metal stakes with locking loops are easy to put in place in an emergency when a heavy blossom threatens to topple.

A metal grid with legs provides convenient support for heavy flowers. Place the support early so stems can grow through it.

Metal stakes with locking arms can be arranged into whatever configuration you need to prevent tall plants from leaning.

Twiggy brush—called 'pea stakes'—placed so low, lightweight plants can grow up and over it looks natural and costs nothing.

Above: An individual locking metal stake holds lily flowers aloft, keeping the stems from bending in wind and rain.

23

CUTTING BACK AND DEADHEADING PERENNIALS

Cut tall, leafless flower stalks to the ground after flowers fade to neaten the plants and prevent seed formation.

To encourage repeat bloom, shear back bushy plants with many flowers. Use hedge shears after blooming stops.

Use hand shears to cut off faded flowers near the main branch. This may stimulate reblooming.

PINCHING PERENNIALS

To pinch out a plant's growing point, break off the stem tip just above a pair of leaves.

Pinching stimulates branching and increases flowers, while keeping plants full and compact.

CUTTING BACK AND PINCHING

You can help normally tall, lanky plants to grow more compactly and possibly avoid the need for staking by pinching them. In spring, when summer bloomers such as balloon flower or milky bellflower are about 8 inches tall, break off the growing tip of each stem by snapping it between your fingers or cutting it with handheld shears. Late-summer and fall-blooming plants, such as asters, can be cut back twice by half—first when 4 inches tall and again when 1⅓ feet tall—to make them bushier and lower growing. Chrysanthemums need to be pinched at two-week intervals until midsummer for the best fall blooms and to keep them compact.

You also may wish to cut back some perennials after blooming to neaten them up or reduce their height. If a plant's foliage looks shabby from mildew or exhausted after blooming, you can cut it back to its base as long as you see evidence of new growth at the bottom. The new stems will produce healthy, fresh foliage.

If you pinch or rub off side flower buds or branches of certain perennials, such as peony, delphinium, and hibiscus, you'll channel the plant's energy into only a few blossoms rather than numerous ones. By disbudding this way, the blossoms you leave behind grow larger and showier. Be sure to remove the extras while they are mere suggestions of buds.

DEADHEADS

After perennials bloom, cut off faded flowers or flower stalks unless they will go on to produce decorative seed heads. Deadheading this way keeps the garden tidy and channels the plant's energy into its roots and leaves rather than into seed formation. Cut leafy flower stems just above the foliage.

By removing spent flowers, you also may encourage more flowers. Pinching off individual faded blossoms of balloon flower and coreopsis, for example, encourages more and more flowers to keep on appearing on the same stems, lengthening the bloom period. Cutting off the entire spent flower head of a garden phlox encourages side branches with a flush of new flowers a month or so after the first; the same is true for delphinium. If you don't know that a plant will rebloom after deadheading, try it and see.

Left: You can turn one mature perennial into many by dividing the roots. Plants with woody root systems, such as astilbe, can be divided by using a spade to split the root ball into several sections containing crowns. The sections can be spaced out and replanted to increase the size of the planting, used elsewhere, or given to friends.

THE GREAT DIVIDE

After several years, the single daylily crown you started with has developed into a large clump with several crowns. You can split them in half and replant them near each other, where they will fill in to make a dramatic drift, or you can replant them in separate locations or even give them away. Most perennials, with a few notable exceptions, slowly decline in vigor unless rejuvenated by being divided every few years.

A general rule of thumb is to divide spring-blooming plants immediately after they flower, and summer and fall bloomers in early spring when they have about 3 inches of top growth. However, in the South, Southwest, and Midwest, you may want to divide spring and summer bloomers in fall so they can readjust during cool weather. Wherever you live, time division so the plant's root system can regrow before stressful weather arrives. It's best, wherever you live, to divide perennials at least four weeks before hot or freezing temperatures arrive.

Above: Some easy-care plants, such as peony (*Paeonea lactiflora*), form long-lived clumps that don't spread and won't need dividing for many years. Other, more demanding kinds become crowded, losing vigor unless divided every few years.

DIVIDING PERENNIALS

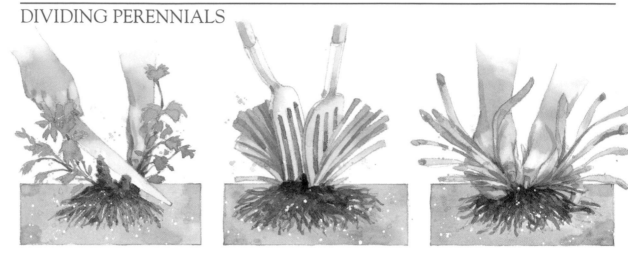

Perennials with tough, woody root systems may actually have to be cut apart with a kitchen knife.

Fleshy-rooted plants are safely divided by driving two garden forks into the middle of the clump and prying it into separate plants.

A sharp garden spade can be driven between two growing points, separating the clump into two plants.

Plants with fleshy roots, such as daylilies (this one is *Hemerocallis* 'Hot Ember'), form dense clumps with many crowns. The clumps can be separated into individual crowns to increase the number of plants.

Techniques vary according to a plant's growth habit. Some plants, such as chrysanthemum and shasta daisy, have shallow, fibrous root systems. Once the clump is dug up, you can easily pull it apart into many sections with your hands. Other plants, such as astilbe, have tough, woody roots growing in a tangled mass. Study the top growth to locate individual crowns, then drive the blade of a sharp spade between the crowns, dividing the clump into several sections.

You'll cause the least harm to the root systems of fleshy-rooted plants such as daylily and hosta if you divide them with two garden forks. Plunge the forks back-to-back into the middle of a clump, then press the handles outward, prying the clump in two. With your hands, pull apart individual crowns with their attached roots.

Large ornamental grasses, such as maiden grass and zebra grass, have such tough roots that you might have to use an ax or a chainsaw to divide them. Fortunately, this needs to be done only once every 10 years.

Fast-growing plants need more frequent division than slow growers. The encyclopedia sections of this book give the approximate timing, but your plants' appearance tells you when they need dividing. Clumps resembling doughnuts, with active growth on the outer edges and dead centers, need to be divided.

Use this occasion to replenish the soil before replanting the divisions. Fork over the soil and work in organic matter and superphosphate before replanting. Plant divisions as soon as possible, taking care to protect them from drying air and sun. If you can't replant immediately, "heal in" the divisions in a temporary location or in a pot of soil until you can. Water newly planted divisions, and mulch the soil well.

PLANTING AND CARING FOR ANNUALS

With a few notable exceptions, annuals require a lot more tending during the growing season than perennials. They also need to be replaced and the soil improved every year. Most annuals don't need staking, but a few tall types may be too floppy unless tied up. Follow the instructions given above for staking perennials.

PLANTING

You can start almost any annual from seed sown indoors (see above) or purchase them in cell-packs at the garden center. A few annuals—morning glory, nasturtium, and zinnia, for example—do best in most regions if sown right in the garden. Some garden centers rush the season a bit with annuals, getting them out and ready for sale before they are really safe from frost. If you wait too long to purchase the little plants, however, they will be bursting from their cell-packs and be so stressed that they may not adjust well.

Choose a cool, cloudy day to plant, when the weather is expected to remain moderate for at least a few more days. Water the cell-pack so the little plants will slide right out. If they need a little help, push the bottom of the cell with your thumb and the root ball should pop right out. Well-grown annuals will have visible roots, but you'll still be able to see soil. If a mat of roots forms a white network that obscures the soil, you'll need to break it apart to encourage the roots to grow outward, rather than going round and round as if they were still confined to the pot. Tear the bottom off the root ball, then gently split it up the middle by pulling with both hands in opposite directions.

Install each plant in a hole dug in prepared soil, spacing the plants so they'll fill in to form a beautiful mass. Be sure the transplant rests at the same level it was in the container. If it protrudes, it will dry out; if it's too low, it could rot. Apply mulch to discourage weeds and keep the soil moist and the plants clean.

Water right after planting. Because the plants are still small with relatively tiny root systems, you may need to water every day for several weeks, depending on the weather, until the plants get established. Wilting at this stage can cause serious setbacks for annuals.

IN A PINCH

You can help annuals branch and grow stronger, bushier, and more floriferous, by pinching out the growing tips of young plants. Use your thumb and forefinger to rub out the point between the top pair of leaves on all of the stems. Most annuals look and bloom best if regularly deadheaded, although some, notably impatiens, are self-cleaning. Individual annual flowers last only a few days, so pick off the dead flowers every few days. Pinch them off between thumb and forefinger, removing the entire flower and its ovary so seeds won't form. If you just pull off the petals, the remaining ovary may go on to fatten up and form seeds. If you notice this happening, pinch off the young seedpods, too.

For annuals such as flowering tobacco, which form tall flower stalks, or large-flowered annuals such as zinnia and marigold, remove the entire flowering stem, cutting just above a pair of leaves to encourage branching and blooming. Refresh plants with numerous small flower heads, such as verbena and sweet alyssum, by clipping them with pruning shears.

To remove annuals easily from their cell-packs, turn the well-watered container upside down and push on the bottom of the cell with your thumb to dislodge the seedling. If a thick network of white roots encircles the root ball, it's important to partially split it by carefully tearing up from the bottom. This encourages new roots to grow outward and helps the young plant establish itself quickly.

If annuals get tired by midsummer—this often happens with cool-season annuals—trim them back to reinvigorate them. Don't be afraid to cut stems back so they are only a few inches tall. As long as you leave enough leaves behind and water and fertilize when you do this, the plants should rebound vigorously for a beautiful late-summer and fall bloom.

ANNUAL APPETITES

Because annuals bloom so prolifically, most are heavy feeders. They need copious amounts of phosphorus, in particular, to feed their flowering. Too much nitrogen, however, may produce nothing but foliage.

You can fertilize annuals any number of ways. Work a granular fertilizer designed for annuals, such as 5-10-10, into the soil at planting time and replenish every month or according to package directions. An easy way to feed annuals is to apply timed-release fertilizer pellets to the soil around the plants at planting time. It slowly releases nutrients for three months, so you can forget about further fertilizing. In areas with long growing seasons you may want to apply the pellets a second time. If you prefer organic fertilizer, apply composted manure around the young plants every month, or water with a solution of commercial fish emulsion or seaweed extract.

PLANTING AND CARING FOR BULBS

Bulbs, especially spring-flowering ones, are about the easiest flowers to grow. As long as you follow a few simple rules, most types keep blooming year after year, getting better with each passing year.

Hardy bulbs look best planted in groups rather than individually. They work well in mixed borders, under deciduous shrubs, or naturalized in a woodland or lawn. (See Chapter 2 for design

Daffodils, and many other spring-blooming bulbs, go dormant in summer, leaving a bare space behind them in the garden. You can camouflage their unsightly dying foliage and avoid empty spaces by interplanting bulbs with perennials such as hostas, daylilies, and ferns.

FLOWERING BULBS

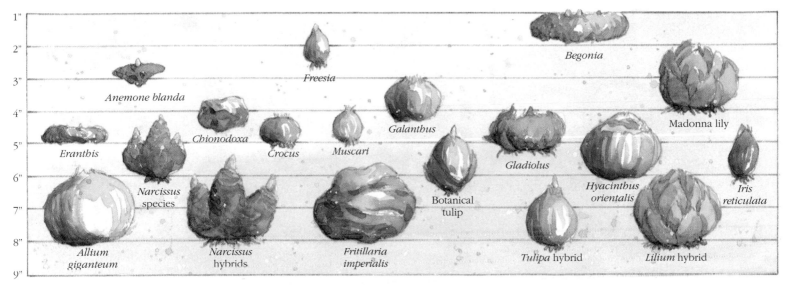

1"
2"
3" *Anemone blanda* — *Freesia* — *Begonia*
4" *Chionodoxa* — *Galanthus* — Madonna lily
5" *Eranthis* — *Crocus* — *Muscari* — *Gladiolus*
6" *Narcissus* species — *Hyacinthus orientalis* — *Iris reticulata*
7" Botanical tulip
8" *Allium giganteum* — *Narcissus* hybrids — *Fritillaria imperialis* — *Tulipa* hybrid — *Lilium* hybrid
9"

ideas.) Because their foliage becomes unsightly and then disappears by early summer, you'll need to decide when planting spring-blooming bulbs what will take their place in summer. They can share essentially the same garden place with later-blooming perennials. Good interplanting combinations include daylilies or hostas with narcissus, tulips, or crocus. You might tuck bulbs in the soil under ground covers such as lamb's-ears, whose gray foliage contrasts beautifully with spring-flowering bulbs. The perennial's foliage grows around the dying bulb foliage, providing a succession of foliage and flowers in the same spot in the garden.

PERFECT PLANTING

You can plant hardy bulbs anytime in fall before the soil freezes—right up until Thanksgiving or Christmas in some climates. It's best to plant bulbs early enough for their root systems to grow before really cold weather arrives. Late-planted bulbs grow roots in spring if need be, but may bloom later than normal. They'll get back on schedule in subsequent years. Be sure to water after planting to get the roots growing.

Positioning a bulb at its proper depth is one step in ensuring its longevity. Generally, bulbs should be positioned so the bottom of the bulb rests at a depth two and a half times the bulb's diameter. In well-drained or sandy soil, you can plant an inch or two deeper to increase longevity and discourage rodents.

Because bulbs look best planted in groups, you are better off using a garden spade instead of a bulb planter, which encourages you to plant bulbs singly. A spade allows you to plant bulbs side by side in large groups. Plant bulbs in big holes no smaller than a dinner plate; you may even want to dig wide, curving trenches and fill them with bulbs.

In general, bulbs should be planted with their bottoms at a depth two and a half times their diameters. Plant more deeply in light soil and more shallowly in heavy soil.

Layer different types of bulbs from top to bottom in the same hole to create nice companion plantings or a succession of bloom in the same location. For instance, you can dig an 8-inch-deep hole and place several Dutch hyacinths in the bottom, cover the Dutch hyacinths with soil, then plant a handful of grape hyacinths 5 inches deep. They bloom at the same time in spring, with the grape hyacinths creating a softening skirt beneath the more massive Dutch hyacinths.

To continue a succession of bloom and foliage, plant perennials around the bulb hole. This interplanting technique works in informal or formal gardens, providing the most flowers in the smallest space and hiding dying bulb leaves.

KNOW AND GROW

Be sure to remove spent flowers of large-flowered bulbs, such as daffodils, to channel their energy into forming large bulbs and offsets, not into seeds. Allow small bulbs, such as snowdrops, to set seed, so they self-sow and form large drifts.

Do not remove bulb foliage while it's green; the green leaves nourish the bulb and next year's flowers, whose buds form during summer. Cut or pull off leaves only after they yellow, or the bulb may not rebloom. You are safe mowing green leaves of crocus and snowdrops that are naturalized in a lawn if you wait at least six weeks after blooming.

Bulbs need fertilizer, but at the proper times. Work a high-phosphorous plant food, such as bonemeal or superphosphate, into the bottom of the hole when you plant. Use a balanced fertilizer in early spring when the shoots emerge and again after flowering to fuel foliage and bulb growth for next year's flowers.

Left: You can layer different types and sizes of bulbs in the same planting hole to create lovely floral combinations. Here, pink tulips and grape hyacinths bloom in a soft, springtime color combination.

Bulb foliage often suddenly pokes above ground during warm winter spells, causing gardeners to worry unnecessarily that later snow or freezing temperatures will kill the bulbs or destroy the flowers. Foliage and flower buds of spring-flowering bulbs can withstand temperatures in the 20s or even high teens. Not until the flower bud shows color will temperatures below 28°F harm spring bloomers. Late-winter bloomers, such as snow crocus and snowdrops, push right through snow to open their blossoms.

Above: Tender bulbs should be dug up in fall after light frost kills their leaves and stored over winter in a frost-free location. Some tubers, such as dahlias, are best kept slightly moist during storage. Store them in damp peat moss in a loosely sealed plastic bag.

DIVIDE AND CONQUER

Most bulbs won't need dividing for years. With the exception of hybrid tulips, bulbs (and corms, tubers, and such) multiply underground, forming offsets that in turn grow into blooming plants. You need to dig up and divide hardy bulbs only when the plant starts to peter out and flowering decreases. Save and replant the large bulbs in the garden, discarding small offsets or planting them in a nursery bed until they are large enough to bloom.

TENDER MOMENTS

In cold climates, dig up tender bulbs, such as gladiolus and dahlias, in fall after the first frost and before the ground freezes. Carefully lift them with a garden fork and shake off all soil. Cut top growth off at 2 inches. Set the bulbs to dry in a dim, airy place for two weeks before storing.

Separate large gladiolus corms and similar bulbs from their tiny offsets, saving them for the nursery bed. Place bulbs in a net bag or old stocking and hang in a cool (50° to 60°F), dark, airy place, such as a ventilated basement. Some gardeners like to dust corms with fungicide powder to ward off fungus attack.

Tubers and fleshy roots, such as dahlias, need to be kept moist during storage. Bury them in a container of slightly moist peat or vermiculite sealed in a plastic bag. Inspect from time to time to see that they haven't dried out.

If you're growing tender plants in a container, you don't have to dig them up. Cut off bulb tops and store the container in an unheated garage or shed that remains above freezing. Don't allow the soil to dry completely.

MODERN ROSE CARE

Unlike the other types of flowers, roses don't die to the ground. Their top growth is woody and permanent, although it can be injured in cold climates. Because they grow differently than other flowers, their care differs greatly. (Chapter 8 provides specifics for each rose type.)

BARE-ROOT BABIES

More often than not, roses arrive in your garden as dormant, bare-root plants. You can purchase bare-root roses at your nursery or order them by mail. The rose plant looks quite stark—a collection of stubby, thorny stems and stiff roots growing in opposite directions from a rough knob. The knob is the graft union where the roots and stems were grafted together.

Soak the entire plant in a bucket of water for no more than an hour before planting. Dig an 18-inch-deep and -wide planting hole. Mix a quart of organic matter, such as rotted compost or manure, in the soil from the hole, returning some to the hole to form a blunt mound. Place the rose on the mound so the graft union is 1 to 2 inches below soil level, where temperatures drop below 20°F, and just above it in warmer climates.

Position bare-root roses with their stiff roots spread out over a cone of soil in a deeply dug planting hole. The bud union, where stem is grafted to rootstock, should rest 1 or 2 inches below the soil surface in cold climates and just above it in warm climates. You can be sure of positioning the rose correctly by using a straight stick or shovel handle to indicate the soil level.

Refill the hole, firming the soil with your hands, and build a dam from a ring of soil over the roots. Fill the dam with water and allow it to soak in. Then mound soil up over the stems to form a dome about 6 inches high. The dome keeps the stems from drying out until the plant is rooted. Gradually remove the excess soil when the leaves open.

CARE AND FEEDING

Roses perform best in fertile, moist, heavy soil. Water them deeply several times a week during the growing season if rainfall is insufficient. They perform poorly if the soil dries out, so apply a heavy mulch to keep the soil cool and moist. Water with drip irrigation or a soaker hose to avoid wetting the foliage, because wet foliage encourages fungus disease. If you must use an overhead sprinkler, water in the morning so the foliage dries quickly.

Repeat-blooming roses feed heavily, so fertilize them regularly. First fertilize a newly planted rose a month after planting. Begin feeding established roses as soon as buds break in spring. Repeat applications every three to five weeks, most frequently in sandy soil.

Rose experts have their own secret fertilizer regimens. Some rely on lots of manure, others on regular dousings of fish emulsion, and still others on inorganic granular fertilizers designed especially for roses. In general, feed hybrid modern roses every two weeks from spring through summer to keep them growing and blooming. Although roses bloom in fall in cold climates, stop applying nitrogen fertilizer six weeks before the expected first frost so the bush stops growing and goes dormant. You can apply phosphorous and potassium, in the form of superphosphate and bonemeal, to help the roses harden up for winter.

32

KIND CUTS

Prune old garden roses and shrub roses the same way you prune most flowering shrubs, by thinning out the oldest stems. Modern bush roses, hybrid teas, and floribundas, however, require specialized pruning.

Prune dormant roses in late winter or early spring two weeks before your last expected frost. Shorten rose canes so they are 8 inches to 2 feet tall, depending on the particular cultivar's vigor, and cut out weak or damaged canes. Make cuts with lopping shears or handheld shears by cutting at an angle just above an outward-facing bud. Select the three to five most vigorous canes—these are the thickest and darkest green—and cut off the rest.

Keep in mind that although you perform the major pruning when roses are dormant, every time you cut off a fresh or faded flower you actually prune the bush and influence its growth. You must keep properly removing faded blossoms to stimulate new growth and more flowers.

When cutting a rose flower, use sharp handheld shears and cut at an angle just above the first large leaf, one with five leaflets. New growth emerges from the axil of this leaf and produces more blossoms. If you cut too high, weak growth results.

CUTTING CLIMBERS

Rambling roses, rampant climbers that bloom only once a year, bloom on old wood. They'll be most vigorous and floriferous if you cut off the canes entirely after they finish blooming. This encourages healthy new growth, which can reach

PRUNING MODERN BUSH ROSES

Prune modern roses in late winter while dormant. Most varieties are best pruned moderately by removing at ground level all but the five strongest canes (top) and shortening them to about 2 feet. Remove crossed and weak branches. Hard pruning (above), in which bushes are thinned to three canes and shortened to 8 inches to 1 foot, is best for very vigorous varieties.

PRUNING CUTS FOR ROSES

Every time you cut a rose for a bouquet you perform an act of pruning. To encourage reblooming, snip the rose stem just above the first large leaf with five leaflets.

New growth emerges from the bud at the base of the large leaf. Make your cut at an angle about ¼ inch above the bud so you don't damage the bud or leave an unsightly stub.

20 feet in a single season. Tie the new shoots to a trellis, fence, or arbor—wherever you want them to grow—using twine or strips of old pantyhose.

If you don't remove a rambler's year-old canes, they will rebloom on side branches the next year, but flowers may not be as lush. You might tie these canes off to the side to make room for the new canes; this also improves the lateral bloom. Without pruning, your rambler will turn into a thorny, impenetrable thicket with dead canes on the inside and flowers only on the edges.

Large-flowered climbers grow much less vigorously than ramblers and produce flowers throughout the growing season. They grow tall by adding height to the previous year's wood, so you should not prune them at all their first few years, except to remove spent flowers and damaged wood. Secure all the new growth to its support with twine or pantyhose strips. Only when the climber gets as tall as you want should you prune to guide its shape and remove old wood during the dormant season.

PRUNING CLIMBING ROSES

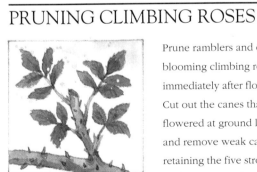

Prune ramblers and once-blooming climbing roses immediately after flowering. Cut out the canes that flowered at ground level and remove weak canes, retaining the five strongest new canes. Cut these back to five sets of large leaves and tie them to the support.

WINTER CARE

Although old garden roses and some shrub roses defy even the winters of the Far North, most modern bush roses are too tender to tolerate winter's worst. In Zone 5 or colder, you should protect rosebushes from winter cold; the graft union is especially sensitive to freezing. Cut back the rose to about 2 feet once freezing temperatures have blackened the foliage and make an insulating mound of soil, wood chips, or sawdust around the stems. If you use soil, don't dig it from the rose's roots, but bring it from elsewhere. Remove the protective mound in early spring and prune further as needed, because any part of the rose protruding above the mound may be dead.

Ramblers are usually cold hardy, but tender large-flowered climbers may be troublesome in northern climates. You must lower them from their trellis and insulate the entire length of their stems and the graft union. Usually, this means partially digging up the roots on one side of the plant so you can tip it all to the side. Then bury the stems under soil or wood chips until spring. It helps in handling the rose if you can loosely tie the canes into a bundle before lowering them.

Modern rosebushes need winter protection in cold climates. A chicken-wire cage filled with leaves, straw, or pine needles provides good insulation.

A traditional way to protect a rose from cold is to build a mound of insulating soil to cover the tender graft union and lower parts of the bush.

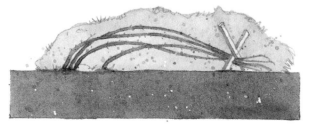

Rambling roses are cold hardy, but large-flowered climbers are not. Provide winter protection by carefully lowering climbers from their supports, partially digging up the roots if necessary, then burying them with soil or other insulation.

PRUNING SHRUB AND OLD GARDEN ROSES

Grown for their full, beautiful shapes and decorative flowers, shrub and old garden roses should be pruned only lightly, as you would other flowering shrubs. Prune repeat-flowering roses when dormant in late winter, and once-flowering shrubs after they finish blooming in early summer. Use lopping shears (not hedge shears) or a pruning saw to cut out the oldest, nonproductive wood and weak, flimsy canes at ground level. Old canes are thick and dark brown, often with split bark. Shorten the remaining canes by one-third to one-half of their length and clip back side shoots to two to five.

Try this pruning trick practiced by many rose aficionados to transform your shrub roses into head-to-toe blossoms: Cut the main canes back to different lengths, leaving the tallest ones in the middle and cutting the outer ones shorter. This gives the shrub a beautiful vase shape with blossom at all levels, not just at the top.

TENDING YOUR GARDEN

Most gardeners enjoy tending their gardens, believing that tending is part of the pleasure and satisfaction of gardening. Follow the easy-care methods described below and you'll eliminate some of the hard work and increase the pleasure.

MULCH MADNESS

If you don't do anything else for your garden, mulch it. Mulch—a layer of organic matter laid on top of the soil—has many advantages. It keeps the soil moist, slowly decays and releases nutrients to the soil, smothers weeds, improves soil texture, and prevents dirt from splashing onto leaves and flowers. It also provides a lovely finishing touch to any planting. In short, a well-mulched garden saves you work and keeps your plants healthier. The only disadvantage is that mulch can harbor slugs and snails in areas prone to infestations.

After planting, apply a 3- to 4-inch-deep layer of mulch around the plants, taking care to leave

Plants in a well-mulched garden grow with abandon because the soil is cool, moist, and nutrient rich. Mulched gardens also are easier to care for because mulch discourages weeds and ensures healthier plants.

35

space near the stems. Good choices are: shredded leaves, pine needles, shredded bark, pine bark mini-chips, and cocoa bean hulls. Do not use fresh sawdust or fresh wood chips because they rob the soil of nitrogen as they age. Do not use black plastic or fabric mulch, which are actually designed for vegetable gardens, because they do not allow perennials to spread. Add more mulch each year after dividing any plants that need it.

WORTHWHILE WEEDING

Weeds look unsightly, marring the beauty of your flower garden, but they also compete with flowers for water, nutrients, and light. A well-mulched garden won't need much weeding, and any weeds that do invade come out more easily. If you weed regularly, they'll never get the best of you. Don't hoe weeds in a flower garden as you would in a vegetable garden or you'll harm the perennials. Pull a weed with your hands, holding it at ground level and giving a long, slow, steady pull. Be sure to get out all of the root system so the weed won't regrow.

NEAT EDGES MAKE GOOD NEIGHBORS

Once you've designed the shape of your flower garden, keep it defined by installing an edging. The edging can be decorative or inconspicuous, but its main purpose should be to stop lawn grass from creeping into the flower garden and causing a weed problem and blurring its edges. An edging needs to extend at least 4 inches deep to stop grass roots from creeping into the garden. Edging also is an effective way to keep creeping garden flowers, such as sweet woodruff and bugleweed, from invading the lawn. The result is less maintenance work for you.

Left: Pine bark mini-chips make a decorative mulch, preventing soil from splashing plants and giving the garden a finished look. The chips also provide the other benefits of mulch—they smother weeds and keep the soil healthy.

Not all edgings reduce maintenance. Some types, such as little fences, angled bricks, and bricks laid on end rising halfway out of the ground, prevent close mowing. With these edgings, you'll have to return to hand edging with lawn shears or a string trimmer, which can harm your flowers and requires considerable effort. If an edging rises more than about ½ inch above the soil, it interferes with mower blades. The best edgings are the ones mower wheels can straddle so you leave no grass uncut.

You can purchase vinyl edging at most garden centers. Dark brown looks less conspicuous than

Above: Stone edging gives a country character to this garden, allowing plants to spill out over its surface to show off flowers and foliage. The stones are set low enough that mower wheels glide over them, allowing for a close cut and reducing trimming chores.

black or green. The best type has a tubular top edge that endures mower nicks and a bottom flap that grips the soil.

Install the edging using a spade to cut along the bed's edge, creating a straight-sided trench that follows the bed's contours. Position the edging against the outer side of the trough, with the tubular edge resting just above the soil line. (Grass blades should camouflage the edging.) Fill the trench with soil and firm it with your feet.

If you want a decorative edging, choose a mowing strip made of bricks or fieldstone. These are especially useful where a raised bed or wall makes mowing difficult. The mowing strip should be low enough and solid enough for the mower's wheels to run along it, cutting the edges of the grass. A mowing strip does not keep out wandering grass roots unless it is 4 inches deep. Bricks need to be set on end or sideways, not flat. A double row of staggered bricks is deep enough to stop grass roots and wide enough for the lawn mower.

COMMENDABLE COMPOSTING

Organic gardeners have always understood the value of transforming yard waste and kitchen scraps into a rich compost. Today most homeowners are well aware of the energy toll and expense it takes to haul away yard waste. Your community may no longer collect grass clippings and leaves, so you have to figure out how to get rid of them. Composting is the answer and also yields free fertilizer. Compost is made by microbes, not by you. You just have to figure out how to feed and house the microbes so they do their job efficiently. The microbes need moisture, air, and a proper diet. You can place your compost heap in a bin—homemade or purchased—to keep it neat, although that isn't necessary to the composting process.

A balanced diet consists of one-third high-nitrogen, two-thirds high-carbohydrate sources, and a bit of soil, arranged in a layered pile large enough to hold heat and moisture. Generally a 3-foot-square heap does the trick; it can be somewhat larger, however. High-nitrogen ingredients, such as grass clippings and kitchen scraps, are green and wet. High-carbohydrate materials, such as fallen leaves and newspaper, are dry and brown. If the ingredients in the compost pile are chopped up or shredded—a leaf shredder is a handy tool—they'll decay much faster. The green ingredients contain enough moisture to start things working. You should check the heap regularly, however, and give it an occasional spray from the hose as needed. Cover the heap with a tarpaulin to keep out drenching rain. If the compost is as moist as a wrung-out sponge, it is just right.

Turning over the pile once a week transforms the waste into compost in a few months. Use a lightweight pitchfork to mix the inside to the out-

An ideal composting system consists of three separate gated bins. One bin holds finished, ready-to-use compost. The other two are for compost in the process of decomposing. When turning the compost over, you can easily fork it from one bin to the other.

side and the top to the bottom. Mixing is easiest with two bins, so you can shift the compost from one to the other when you turn over the heap. As it decomposes, the compost heats up to about 150°F if all is well. If you don't turn it, the heap won't get very hot and it could take a year or two to decompose. Commercial compost tumblers, which turn over the ingredients with a cranked handle, make fast work of composting.

FREQUENT FERTILIZING

If you have it, spread a 1-inch-deep layer of well-rotted compost from your compost heap around your perennial plants every year in spring. This nourishes them and improves the soil. Cover the compost with fresh mulch and you won't need to fertilize the garden with chemical fertilizers.

Many gardeners like to boost their flowers with chemical plant foods. Fertilizers are rated according to the percentages of major nutrients they contain: nitrogen, phosphorous, and potassium, in that order. Common balanced fertilizers have ratings of 5-5-5 or 10-10-10. Compost is balanced, although low in nutrients, and would earn a ratio of 1-1-1 if so rated. Flowering plants usually benefit from having more phosphorous than nitrogen, so select a high-phosphorous fertilizer such as 5-10-5.

Carefully apply fertilizer, whether organic or inorganic, according to package directions or you could do more harm than good. Apply the plant food to perennials in early spring once you see new growth emerging. (Annuals and bulbs need a slightly different regimen; see above.) Reapply in midsummer, but never fertilize perennials and ornamental grasses in autumn because this stimulates plant growth at a time when you want the plants to begin to go dormant.

WATERING WELL

A well-prepared and well-mulched flower garden requires watering less frequently than one with poor, bare soil. Roots grow deeper and soil stays moist longer in the cool, deep soil of a mulched bed. That doesn't mean you won't have to water at all. Generally, garden plants need an inch of water a week during the growing season to perform their best.

It's best to apply water gently for a long period, so it soaks down at least 1½ feet. Supply this long drink once a week even during hot, dry weather, and plant roots will grow down to seek the deep water after surface water dries up.

Soaker hoses and drip irrigation systems (the kind with built-in emitters) are ideal ways to water flower beds. Lay the hoses out, spacing them 1½ feet apart.

Partially bury the tubing in the soil so just the top shows. That way, you won't nick it when planting or transplanting.

A mulch covering conceals the drip irrigation tubing or soaker hose and allows the water to flow freely.

These deep-rooted plants can survive drought better than shallowly watered plants whose roots remain near the soil's surface.

You can supply the water the sky does not in many ways. The best way is with a soaker hose laid under the mulch in the bed. Soaking rather than sprinkling prevents wet foliage, which can weigh plants down and encourage fungus disease. You can hook the soaker to a timer so it runs automatically.

GO AWAY, GARDEN PESTS

Well-grown flowers are less susceptible to insects and disease than those stressed by poor growing conditions. No matter how good you are in the garden, however, from time to time some plants will become infested with bugs or fungus. Knowledgeable personnel at your local nursery can usually help you figure out how to battle most plant pests. And they stock an arsenal of pesticides.

Before declaring chemical war on any insect or disease, try a few organic controls first. A strong spray from a hose, repeated daily, dislodges many insects, especially aphids. Soap sprays—those designed for plants—kill any soft-bodied insects they touch; so will sprays of horticultural oil, which coat and kill insect eggs. Sprays also can fight powdery mildew, a common fungus that coats the leaves of many plants with a white fuzz in late summer and fall.

Whether you choose organic or chemical pesticides, be sure to follow label directions. Any pesticide, if used improperly, can harm you or your plants.

CLEAN-UP CHORES

Fall cleanup gets rid of spores and eggs of pests that may spend the winter on garden debris, hanging around to reinfest your plants the next growing season. Begin your garden cleanup in fall, after frost kills off the annuals and demolishes the perennials' top growth. Pull the annuals out of the ground, shaking off as much soil as possible. Cut back the perennials' brown tops if you like, although you may want to leave those with pretty seedpods standing over winter. Most ornamental grasses look stunning in fall and well into winter—they bleach and dry into standing floral arrangements—so don't cut them back until very early spring. Cart all of the garden debris to your compost heap, cutting or shredding it to help it decay faster.

In cold, snowy climates, plant stems help hold an insulating blanket of snow over the flower garden. You might wait until early spring to cut back the perennials, or cut them back only part way, leaving a foot or two of dried stems to catch snow and keep plants snug.

WINTER PROTECTION

In climates where the soil alternately freezes and thaws in winter, perennials can be heaved from the soil. This frost heaving doesn't do them much good. Where a blanket of snow insulates the soil for months, this isn't as much of a problem as it is in more moderate climates.

You can protect perennials from frost heaving by covering them with evergreen boughs or oak leaves, or by applying a thick mulch in early winter after the soil freezes. The protective covering keeps the soil frozen and the plants anchored in the ground. Remove the covering in late winter.

The dried stems, leaves, and seed heads of many perennials and ornamental grasses look attractive throughout the winter and provide food and shelter for birds. Wait to cut the plants back until late spring so you can enjoy their naturalistic appearance.

CHAPTER TWO

FLOWER GARDEN DESIGN BASICS

Cultivate Your Artistic Talents Along with Your Flowers

Opposite: A garden designed to effectively combine various textures, colors, shapes, and sizes becomes a living work of art. Blooming together are dame's rocket (*Hesperis matronalis*), Argentine blue-eyed grass (*Sisyrinchium striatum*), yellow archangel (*Lamtastrum galeobdolon* 'Herman's Pride'), yellow lupine (*Lupinus* hybrid), and Jacob's-rod (*Asphodeline lutea*).

Left: A well-designed garden features not only plants that look good together but also ones that grow compatibly in the same sun, moisture, and soil conditions. Shown here are bearded iris (*Iris hybrida*), *Hosta* 'Albo-marginata,' columbine (*Aquilegia vulgaris*), and geum (*Geum chiloense*).

Although there are no right or wrong ways to design a flower garden, you'll probably be happiest with the results if you follow some basic design rules. By cultivating your innate artistic sense along with the flowers, you can create a garden that provides delightful viewing from spring through fall.

When positioning plants in your garden, try to use the colors, textures, and shapes of their flowers and foliage to create a beautiful picture that's in scale with its surroundings. Unlike a still life, however, your garden is alive with continually growing and changing plants. As a result, your design needs to take into account that plants will get larger, bloom in their appointed seasons, and die back. Your design also should reflect the type of soil and the amount of moisture and sunlight each plant requires for peak performance. Successfully choosing and combining plants that not only look good together but grow compatibly in the conditions your garden provides is the secret to successful flower gardening.

You also will want to plan your garden's overall style. How you combine flowers and other elements of your garden sets the mood and overall character of the garden. Chapters 3–7 present designs for many different garden styles—from cottage garden to formal English border—and describe how to create them. Before you begin, however, hone your design techniques here by learning how to transform the various elements of a garden into a beautiful and cohesive whole.

GARDEN OUTLINES

Your flower garden should be large enough to make a visual impact, small enough to care for in the time you have available, and fit attractively into the rest of your landscape. The garden's size, shape, and position are important design features and ought to be carefully thought through. If you carve a garden out of your lawn—either in its center or around its perimeter—be sure that whatever lawn is left has a pleasing shape, because the shape contributes to your landscape's overall design.

You can plant flowers almost anywhere in your yard as long as you have suitable growing conditions, but be sure to position the gardens where you'll be able to see and enjoy them throughout the day—from indoors and out. Don't feel bound by tradition, keeping the garden relegated to the backyard. Flowers look right anywhere—bordering a front walk, fronting the street, lining the driveway, or surrounding the front lawn. A flower border decorating a patio creates a pleasant setting for outdoor dining and entertaining.

BEDS AND BORDERS

A flower border is meant to be viewed from one side and is usually backed up against a garden wall, hedge, fence, or side of the house. A flower bed, on the other hand, lacks a structural background, although it may border a walkway or

Positioning your garden where it can be seen from both indoors and out brings you the most enjoyment from your efforts. This country garden borders a curving stone wall and lawn, bringing the flowers into full view from the patio and windows of the house.

patio and is often viewed from all sides. A bed in the middle of a lawn is called an island bed and poses some real design challenges. Borders are easier to design than beds because their background gives them a starting structure and serves as a solid backdrop to show off and silhouette the flowers.

To create an impact from spring through fall, a perennial or mixed flower garden should be at least 12 feet long and 3 feet wide. Unless you're an experienced gardener, you might want to start small and make the garden larger in subsequent years, as you become more accomplished. Keep the garden's width in proportion to its length. Generally, small garden plots should be three times as long as they are wide. Very long gardens may need to be only 8 to 12 feet wide.

When laying out your garden, consider how you're going to gain access to the plants in the rear when you need to tend them. Traditional borders have a 3-foot-wide path between the garden and the background hedge, which allows you to get at the tall plants in back. This 3 foot alley also helps air to circulate through the garden and prevents the hedge from shading plants at the rear, which would cause the plants to lean outward.

You can probably reach 3 or 4 feet into the garden from any side, so an 8-foot-wide bed or border is all you can tend without stepping directly in the garden. If you must step in the garden, it's a good idea to place stepping stones between the plants so you won't tromp on emerging growth or compact the soil.

CURVES AND ANGLES

Your garden can have straight sides and sharp corners or curving outlines, depending on its style. Curved shapes look more casual and informal than straight ones. Although intrinsically

Above: The curving edges of this mixed border give it a pleasant, informal appearance, in keeping with the billowing arrangements of flowers and foliage. Included with the flowers are two shrubs: butterfly bush (*Buddleia*) and bluebeard (*Caryopteris*). The grass is *Miscanthus sinensis* 'Morning Light.'

Left: The straight edges of this border of annuals and perennials give it a formal air, intensified by arranging the flowers in repeating drifts along the length of the border.

more formal, straight-sided beds and borders become less imposing if you arrange the plants within them in flowing drifts rather than rows.

Before digging up a new garden plot or redoing an old one, lay out the proposed border with a garden hose or flexible rope, rearranging the lines until you get a shape that looks right. Try making the front edge bend gently inward and then flare dramatically outward and perhaps back again. Avoid a lot of sharp curves in favor of fewer ones that sculpt gentle sweeps. Stand back and look at the result. As you transcribe the curves, be sure to create a pleasing overall outline, one that balances the out-curves with the in-curves. If your garden surrounds the yard's perimeter, avoid placing two out-curves opposite each other—this looks pinched. And if lawn borders the garden, make sure the curves aren't so sharp that they make it difficult to mow around them.

GIVING YOUR GARDEN AN EDGE

No matter what the shape and style of your flower garden, if it has a lawn edge, you'll want to carefully define that edge. This is often done by using an edging tool—usually a half-moon edger—to cut a sharp border between lawn and garden. The edge must be recut once or twice a year to keep it sharp and curtail grass roots. Without this labor-intensive maintenance or a physical barrier such as a vinyl lawn border or mowing strip, lawn grass can quickly creep into the garden and become a weedy mess.

Another option is to edge your garden with a decorative brick mowing strip, flagstone border, or gravel path. This works well when you want to sharply distinguish between green grass and the adjacent foliage of out-of-bloom plants. Stones and masonry used this way contrast effectively with flowers and foliage and give the garden a definite shape and structure, while allowing foreground plants to gently spill onto the stonework.

A third option is to edge the front of the border with low-growing plants whose foliage texture and color contrasts vividly with the green

Left: The sharp edge of this artfully angled mixed border of shrubs, old garden roses, and perennials comes from using a half-moon edger to make a sharp boundary between lawn and mulched garden.

grass. Lamb's-ears is a favorite edger; its broad, silver-furred leaves make flat rosettes that stand out boldly from the lawn. Other gray or silvery plants include dwarf lavender or blue fescue. For a different color contrast, consider the exquisite 'Palace Purple' coralbells, with its maple-shaped, reddish purple leaves. (Green-leaf forms of coralbells make good edgings along a stone border or gravel path.) Variegated lilyturf—either green-and-gold or green-and-white striped—makes a lovely foreground planting in shady sites. You also may want to edge the garden with long-

Above: A brick mowing strip sets off the flower bed while allowing the mower to closely trim the grass blades. Flowers include English daisy (*Bellis perennis*), forget-me-not (*Myosotis scorpioides*), lamb's-ears (*Stachys byzantina*), and silvermound mugwort (*Artemisia schmidtiana* 'Silvermound').

GET THE DRIFT

Once you've decided on colors and color combinations, try envisioning those colorful flowers in groups of several all-of-a-kind plants. The result is eye-catchingly beautiful. Avoid planting flowers singly in a one-of-a-kind fashion, even if carefully color-coordinated, because the result usually looks weak and amorphous. An exception to this rule is big, dramatic plants, which have so much character that they look fine planted alone as a focal point among contrasting forms.

Usually, you should group at least three of any one kind of flower together for impact. If space allows, use five or more of a kind. Arrange these groups of odd-numbered plants in a drift—an irregular, teardrop-shaped cluster that looks as if the flowers were planted by the wind, not by you. For the best effect, stagger the plants within the drift; don't plant them in lines or rows. Odd numbers of plants work better because even numbers too easily find themselves planted in straight lines.

Where there's room, repeat drifts of the same flowers throughout the garden to give it a sense of rhythm and continuity. This technique is especially important in formal gardens, where repetition creates a sense of calm and elegance.

Annuals and spring-flowering bulbs can be easily arranged in bold drifts, because you can purchase a lot of individual plants for very little money. When making large drifts of more costly perennials, you'll find it easier—and more affordable—to attractively arrange the plants if you use ones grown in quart-size containers rather than gallon pots. The smaller plants quickly spread and actually fill in the drift better than larger-size plants. Another cost saving technique is to purchase dormant roots from a mail-order company; these usually small plants are inexpensive and grow quickly.

Repeating drifts of the same flowers throughout a garden gives the design a sense of cohesion and restfulness. Shown here in a lovely monochromatic peachy-pink color combination are astilbe (*Astilbe* x *arendsii* 'Peach Blossom') and sweet William (*Dianthus barbatus* 'Newport Pink').

blooming, low annuals, such as sweet alyssum, wax begonias, or impatiens.

Edging plants may be planted as a continuous strip along the garden's front border for a formal effect. More pleasing, however, is a combination of various low-growing plants. Alternating clusters of one kind with clusters of another creates a more subtle edge, but one that nevertheless clearly says the garden begins here.

The cool-season annuals and flowering bulbs in this spring garden are neatly arranged according to height by creating a low foreground of pansies (*Viola* x *wittrockiana*), a midground of medium-height tulips (*Tulipa* x *hybrida*), and a background of taller tulips.

Create your garden by arranging selected plants in various-size, overlapping drifts. Keep the low plants in the front or foreground, the taller ones behind them in the midground, and the tallest ones in the background. Depending on your garden's style, however, avoid setting out plants by height in rigid rows. Instead, allow drifts of shorter and taller plants to wander about, weaving in and out in a casual display.

Remember that you'll be cutting off tall stalks of faded flowers so that a tall plant may become a short one after it finishes blooming. You might position a soaring plant in the midground as long as it blooms before, or after, the plants behind it.

Flowers with airy clusters of lacy flowers, such as gaura and coralbells, would be lost in the midground but work well in the foreground, despite their height. There they form a dainty, see-through scrim through which you can enjoy bolder flowers set behind them.

CREATING CONTRAST

The comparison between colors, textures, shapes, and sizes of the plants in your garden creates contrast. And contrast, whether strong or subtle, gives your garden its personality and allure. By grouping plants together to create pleasing contrasts, you have begun to design an effective flower garden.

TANTALIZING TEXTURE

A plant's texture depends somewhat on the roughness or smoothness of its leaves and petals, but even more on their size. Plants are usually described as being either bold, fine, or medium textured. Most plants fall into the medium category, so you need to concentrate on including the fine- and bold-textured ones when trying to create pleasing contrasts.

Plants with small leaves and flowers, such as sweet alyssum, cleome, threadleaf coreopsis, and woolly thyme, possess a fine texture that creates an airy, weightless effect. Fine-textured plants look smaller than they are and may seem to recede, giving the illusion of space.

Plants whose flowers are big and bold and whose leaves are wide and flat, such as rose mallow, castor-bean plant, and cannas, create a heavy, tropical look. Their dramatic texture seems insistent, grabbing your attention and creating excitement. Because they are so imposing, bold-textured plants work well seen from a distance and may make spaces appear smaller when used in quantity.

If planted in excess, bold plants may lose their allure and seem coarse and unwieldy. Too many fine-textured plants grouped together looks boring and restless, because your eye finds nowhere to land. Try to combine various textures, using bold plants as focal points among fine- or medium-textured ones, without overdoing the contrast.

Consider a combination of a carpet of sweet woodruff studded here and there with siebold hosta in a shade garden. This combination relies more on texture than color for its beautiful effect. The tiny woodruff leaves and starlike white flowers swirl beneath the wide, flat pads of hosta leaves, enhancing the innate character of each.

The way you blend fine-, bold-, and medium-textured plants gives your garden its character. Use texture poorly and the garden becomes disturbingly busy and jumbled or boring and uninteresting. Use texture well, and you can render your garden pleasantly stimulating, quietly serene, or jazzy and exciting.

Above left: Foliage alone can create garden excitement through contrasting colors and textures. Here, the arching blades of maiden grass (*Miscanthus sinensis* 'Gracillimus') stand out against the rounded leaves of a smokebush *(Cotinus* 'Royal Purple') shrub.

Above right: The cloudlike flowers of baby's breath (*Gypsophila paniculata*) help soften and blend bolder lilies (*Lilium*) and garden phlox (*Phlox paniculata*).

Left: This informal garden escapes busyness because the plants are artfully combined with an eye toward color and texture.

PLANTS WITH SPIKES OR SPIRES OF FLOWERS

These perennials add drama to a flower garden with the vertical accents of their tall flower spikes. A few clumps of vertical flowers scattered through the garden beautifully spice up the globes and clouds of other flowers.

Delphinium x *elatum*

SPRING-FLOWERING PERENNIALS

Ajuga reptans (bugleweed, carpet bugle)
Digitalis purpurea (foxglove)

SUMMER-FLOWERING PERENNIALS

Alcea rosea (hollyhock)
Asphodeline lutea (Jacob's-rod, king's-spear)
Baptisia australis (blue wild indigo)
Campanula persicifolia (peach-leaf bellflower)
Delphinium x *elatum* (delphinium)
Hosta spp. and hybrids (hostas)
Kniphofia uvaria (red-hot poker, torchlily)
Lavandula angustifolia (lavender,
    English lavender)
Liatris spicata (spike gayfeather, blazing star)
Ligularia spp. (golden rays)
Lupinus hybrids (lupine)
Malva alcea (hollyhock mallow)
Penstemon barbatus (beard-tongue)
Polygonum bistorta (knotweed, snakeweed,
    European bistort)
Salvia x *superba* (hybrid blue salvia, hybrid sage)
Sidalcea malviflora (checkerbloom, prairie mallow)
Stachys byzantina (lamb's-ears)
Thermopsis caroliniana (southern lupine,
    Carolina lupine)
Verbascum x *hybridum* (mullein)
Veronica longifolia (speedwell)
Veronica spicata (spiked speedwell)
Yucca filamentosa (Adam's needle, needle palm)

LATE-SUMMER- AND FALL-FLOWERING PERENNIALS

Aconitum spp. (monkshoods)
Astilbe taquetii 'Superba' (fall astilbe)
Cimicifuga spp. (bugbanes)
Hosta spp. and hybrids (hostas)
Lobelia cardinalis (cardinal flower)
Lobelia siphilitica (big-blue lobelia)
Perovskia atriplicifolia (Russian sage)
Physostegia virginiana (obedient plant, false
    dragonhead)
Salvia spp. (sages)

ANNUALS

Antirrhinum majus (snapdragon)
Campanula medium (Canterbury bells)
Celosia cristata (cockscomb)
Consolida ambigua (rocket larkspur)
Lavatera trimestris (tree mallow, annual mallow)
Lupinus texensis (Texas blue-bonnet)
Matthiola incana (stock)
Moluccella laevis (bells-of-Ireland)
Nicotiana alata (flowering tobacco)
Nicotiana sylvestris (great-flowering tobacco)
Nicotiania langsdorfii (green-flowered tobacco)
Salvia farinacea (mealy-cup sage)
Salvia splendens (red salvia, scarlet sage)
Salvia viridis (painted sage)

SPRING-FLOWERING BULBS

Camassia leichtlinii (camas)
Hyacinthus orientalis (Dutch hyacinth)
Muscari spp. (grape hyacinths)

SUMMER-FLOWERING BULBS

Canna x *generalis* (canna lily)
Crocosmia x *crocosmiiflora* (montbretia)
Gladiolus hybrids (gladiolus)
Polianthes tuberosa (tuberose)

LATE-SUMMER- AND FALL-FLOWERING BULBS

Canna x *generalis* (canna lily)

Here the round, speckled leaves and spurred orange flowers of nasturtium (*Tropaeolum majus* 'Alaska') make a pretty contrast of color and form with the blue flower spires of spiked speedwell (*Veronica spicata* 'Blue Charm').

THE SHAPE OF THINGS

Plants of different sizes and shapes grouped together create contrast. A garden of only daisy shapes seems redundant and boring, but could easily be enlivened with a few clumps of tall, spirelike flowers. Use combinations of daisies, globes, spikes, and billowy masses of various flowers to create a lively display.

Keep in mind that spikes and spires often dominate a scene, so use them judiciously. Cloudlike masses, such as crambe and baby's breath, soften more dramatic forms, making a pretty background for the bolder individual flowers of peonies, lilies, and Oriental poppies.

And while you're thinking about contrasting flower shapes, be sure to consider foliage shapes as well. Tall, sword-shaped leaves can create the same vertical drama that flower spires do. They make effective contrasts against rounded or feathery leaves and flowers.

You can maximize contrasts—and excitement—by placing plants with different colors, textures, and forms next to each other. Too much contrast, however, may become overpowering,

so you might want to create combinations in which only one or two of the ingredients differ.

Consider, for instance, a group of dwarf gayfeather arranged behind a sprawling mass of pink coreopsis. Gayfeather's upright, feathery spires contrast sharply with the tiny daisies of the coreopsis. The contrast, although subtle, is evident even though both perennials feature lavender-pink, fine-textured flowers. You could contrast color as well as form by pairing a white-flowered gayfeather with the pink coreopsis.

USING COLOR EFFECTIVELY

The first thing anyone notices about a flower invariably is its color, and you probably consider color first when selecting a flower for your garden. Therefore, it makes sense to choose and combine flower colors carefully.

Whether it's a tumultuous cottage garden or a stately double English border, your garden will look prettier and be more fun to create if you plan it around a color scheme. The color scheme can be a simple monochromatic theme, such as an all-white or all-pink garden; a festive multicolored affair such as a red, white, and blue garden; or a hot-colored garden of yellow, gold, orange, and scarlet flowers. Your garden's color scheme might even change through the seasons if it relies heavily on perennials, perhaps emphasizing yellows and whites in spring, pinks and blues in summer, and purples and violets in autumn.

Too much color in a garden can be as much of a problem as too little color. A riot of flower colors creates a restless look. Instead of creating a happy marriage, flowers of adjacent plants may constantly argue and nag at each other. By giving a little thought to choosing compatible colors, you can create a garden filled with flowers that complement one another and enhance the overall beauty of the garden.

With a little planning and observance of a few guidelines, you can learn to combine colors in a way that makes a beautiful flowery statement. Although your garden may wear an obvious color scheme, such as a blue-and-yellow theme, it also may seem to be a rainbow of colors without an obvious color plan. Only you will know that its beauty came from some very careful color choices.

THE COLOR WHEEL

Even though the flower colors in your garden rarely match the pure colors of the color wheel, by understanding how these 12 colors relate to one another you can begin to approach your garden's design with an artist's imagination. Red, yellow, and blue are the primary colors of the color wheel. These are pure, vibrant colors. When mixed in varying amounts, and with black or white, they create all the other colors of the universe. A half-and-half mixture of any of the three primary colors creates the three secondary colors: red and yellow creates orange, blue and

yellow makes green, and red and blue yields violet. Equal amounts of a primary color and one of its neighboring secondary colors creates an intermediate color: red-orange, yellow-orange, yellow-green, blue-green, blue-violet, and red-violet. These 12 colors form the palette of a basic color wheel. Sophisticated versions of the basic color wheel incorporate more intermediary colors and may include gradations in lightness and darkness of these colors.

Mix white with any color and you get a tint or pastel version of that color. Pastel colors, because they are paler, seem less commanding than the full hue. Add black and you create a shade, a darker version of that color. The darkness of a shade gives it a deep, rich hue. Add both white and black, or gray, and the result becomes a dusky version called a tone. Tones are subtle, subdued colors that help to blend darker and brighter hues. Because so many plant pigments contribute to a flower's color, rarely will you encounter a pure hue. You're more likely to find your garden's palette created of tints, shades, and tones of secondary and intermediate colors.

Colors also change with the lighting. When seen in overcast light, pastel colors intensify. In brilliant sunshine, pastels may seem to fade to nothingness; in shade, they light up the shadows. Intense colors become brilliant in full sun, but dark shades, such as burgundy or purple, become gloomy when seen in shade.

Neighboring colors affect one another. Yellow-green may look sickly next to blue but takes on a healthy glow beside orange. If you decide to use clashing colors in your garden, separate them with neutral ones. White flowers are time-honored peacekeepers, but pastels often work well, too. Foliage plants with gray or silver leaves add pizzazz to a garden while helping to harmonize clashing flower colors.

Consulting a color wheel helps you design pleasing floral color combinations when planning your garden design. The basic color wheel consists of 12 colors—three primary ones (red, yellow, and blue), three secondary ones (green, violet, and orange), and six intermediary ones (red-orange, yellow-orange, yellow-green, blue-green, blue-violet, and red-violet).

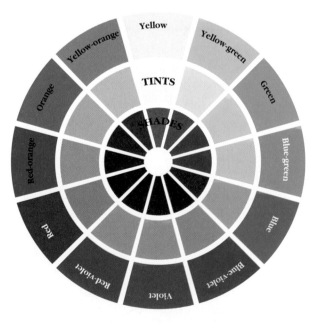

DESIGNING WITH COLOR

A flower garden's color scheme is probably the easiest part of the garden to design. All you need to do is think of flowers in terms of color combinations. Start by asking yourself which colors will be next door or in the neighborhood when each plant is in bloom.

While you'll certainly want to include your favorite colors, you'll obtain more successful results if you consider a few guidelines before deciding on a color scheme for your flower garden. Because you never see your garden in isolation, but within the context of your entire landscape, be sure it all comes together in a pleasing whole by choosing colors that:
- look good with the color of the siding and shutters on your house.
- complement colors of flowering trees and shrubs that figure prominently in your landscape.
- combine well with the foliage colors of prominent landscape shrubs and trees.
- combine well with the hardscape (bricks, stones, and wood) in your yard and garden.

Once you start thinking about what else provides color in your landscape, you might decide to forego yellow and red tulips, for instance, in favor of pastel pink and white ones, because they will look better with the hot-pink crab apple trees that dominate your front yard in May. If the bricks of your house are sandy yellow, you might like to play up the warm tones with yellow and orange flowers, rather than pink and lavender. Red, magenta, and scarlet are too dark for and clash with a red brick walkway or house, but pale blue, creamy white, or pastel pink complement and contrast with the bricks.

Colors have different effects on the eye, and some may work better in specific garden sites than others. Garden designers rely on the following guidelines to create successful designs:
- Hot, bright colors, like yellow and orange, advance and seem closer than they are, carrying well over a distant view. Hot colors are usually attention getting and exciting.
- Cool colors, like blue and lavender, recede, seeming farther away than they really are, and are not easy to see from a distance. Cool colors are usually restful and soothing.
- White and pastel colors lighten up shady areas and seem to pop right out of the shadows.
- Dark colors, like red and purple, look gloomy when planted in shade and are hard to see.
- Combinations of analogous colors (those side by side on the color wheel) are soothing and pleasing.
- Combinations of complementary colors (those opposite each other on the color wheel) are bold and exciting.
- Groups of plants with white or creamy white flowers or silver or gray foliage are neutral, effectively separating warring flower colors and enhancing harmonious ones.

Left: This annual garden's bold color scheme relies on masses of flowers and colorful foliage plants in shades of yellow, blue, and purple. Foliage plants include purple fountain grass (*Pennisetum setaceum* 'Rubrum') and coleus (*Coleus* 'Pineapple Beauty'). Shown are mealy-cup sage (*Salvia farinacea* 'Victoria') and lantana (*Lantana camara* 'Samantha').

Above top: Orange, red, and yellow are hot, attention-getting colors that are easy to see from a distance. Shown is columbine (*Aquilegia* x *hybrida*).

Above bottom: Cool colors—blue, violet, and green—are soothing but recede, so place them close up. Shown is delphinium (*Delphinium* x *elatum* 'Tom Thumb').

Once you decide on a color theme, you can approach the planning in a number of ways. You might sit down with this book's encyclopedia section, a dozen or so garden catalogs, and a pencil and paper, and start drawing your garden, carefully selecting perennials, annuals, and bulbs in the right colors so your scheme is carried out from spring through fall. Or, you might opt to simply purchase only those plants you see at the nursery with blossoms in your chosen colors. Because nurseries usually display only blooming annuals and perennials, relegating out-of-bloom specimens to the back lot, you might be wise to plant the garden over a period of months. Visit the garden center once a month, purchasing perennials as they go into bloom and leaving spots for later-blooming plants during the course of the year.

GREEN IS A COLOR, TOO

When considering garden color, most people think of flower color and overlook foliage. But green, the color of leaves, is a color, too, and a very important one in the garden. All too often green is relegated to the background and isn't given its due as a color in its own right.

Green foliage comes in many shades, tints, and hues, ranging from kelly green to blue-green to chartreuse to lime-green. These colors figure strongly in enhancing or detracting from flower color combinations. Foliage plants, such as hostas and ornamental grasses, can be used as strong color components among bright flowers. Yellow-green leaves look warm and cheerful with yellow, orange, and scarlet flowers, and blue-greens do a wonderful job enhancing pink and magenta flowers. And while flowers are often fleeting, foliage remains to beautify your garden month after month throughout the growing season.

Don't ignore the color impact foliage brings to the garden. Green leaves vary from emerald green to blue-green to yellow-green and gray-green, and some foliage may be silver or reddish purple. Shown here are two popular large hostas, 'Blue Mammoth' and 'Sun Power.'

A GARDEN SYMPHONY

Part of the art—and science—of designing a perennials garden is to achieve an ever-changing sequence of flowers that begins in spring and doesn't finish until the end of fall. Orchestrating this kind of bloom is not easy, but it can be done. Don't despair if your garden experiences a few dramatic pauses in bloom; most do.

You can help prevent such lulls by including a generous assortment of annuals along with the perennials. Their steady blossoming carries the day when perennials are temporarily out of bloom. The day-after-day sameness of most annuals makes an all-annuals garden, though colorful, a bit tedious. It's this very sameness, however, that makes annuals so useful in a mixed flower garden, because they provide a reliable source of blossoms to carry on between waves of flowering perennials and summer bulbs.

When planning your garden, try to select a balanced assortment of spring-, summer-, and fall-blooming perennials as garden mainstays, with bulbs, annuals, and ornamental grasses to accompany them. The lists of recommended perennials in this book are arranged by bloom season to make this goal easier. You can actually draw a plan for your proposed garden on graph paper, plugging in the selected plants to see how they'll work. If you do this, you might want to make three copies of the plan—one for spring, one for summer, and one for fall—coloring in drifts of blooming plants during their appropriate seasons. You also can simply list by season the flowers you want to include, checking to see that you have a good balance.

ACHIEVING IMPACT

To create impact in a small garden, choose long-blooming perennials because you'll get a flower-filled scene that changes from month to month. Although most perennials put on their floral show for only two or three weeks, some bloom for six, eight, or even 12 weeks.

Another way to achieve impact is to group plants of different heights and bloom seasons closely together, interplanting taller specimens to rise out of lower ones, and early bloomers to take the place of late bloomers. This way you'll get more weeks of color out of the same garden spot than you would if everything were planted in tidy, separate locations.

For the best effect, choose low-growing plants with a spreading habit to weave around the stems of more upright specimens. Snow-in-summer, for example, forms a frothy cascade of snowy white flowers in early summer and then remains quietly gray the rest of the year. A creeping plant, it could be allowed to weave around and under clusters of upright plants that also do well in poor, dry soil. Gayfeather and purple coneflower are other good choices; they bloom later in summer, giving additional color in the same location, while looking lovely emerging from the mat of gray leaves. Lilies, which bloom best with their roots in shade but their tops in full sun, can be planted with a skirt of ferns or astilbes. The tall stalks of fragrant lilies are counterbalanced by the lacy greenery around their feet, so the garden looks lush and beautiful both before and after the lily blossoms fade.

Interplanting works especially well with spring-flowering bulbs and perennials. Plant early blooming bulbs in the same space as later-blooming perennials and they happily cohabit, flowering in their respective seasons. The bulbs

Left: Wherever possible, but especially in small gardens, choose long-blooming perennials such as *Coreopsis verticillata* 'Moonbeam,' *Sedum* x *telephium* 'Autumn Joy,' and fountain grass (*Pennisetum alopecuroides*) to bring months of color to the garden.

usually rest deeper in the soil than the perennials' roots and, because their foliage dies back by early summer, they don't compete with the perennials for air space. Interplanting also allows perennials to fill in bare spots the dormant bulbs would otherwise leave behind when they retreat into the ground for the rest of the year.

Happy bulb-perennial combinations include daffodils and daylilies, glory-of-the-snow and dwarf daylilies, tulips and hostas, crocus and spotted nettle, and giant alliums and ornamental grasses.

Above left: To make the best use of space and create a natural feel, arrange tall plants to grow out of ground-covering ones. Shown are lamb's-ears (*Stachys byzantina*) and purple coneflower (*Echinacea purpurea* 'Magnus').

Above right: Interplanting tulips among perennials such as astilbe and hosta creates several seasons of flowers in the same space and hides the bulbs' dying leaves.

LONG-BLOOMING PERENNIALS

These perennials make noteworthy additions to any flower border, but especially to small ones, because they bloom for an exceptionally long time. Although most look and perform better if deadheaded, those with an * must be cut back or deadheaded after each flowering flush to promote reblooming.

Platycodon grandiflorus

PERENNIALS THAT BLOOM FOR 6 TO 8 WEEKS

Achillea x 'Coronation Gold' (fern-leaf yarrow)
Achillea x 'Moonshine' (moonshine yarrow)
Aquilegia x *hybrida* 'McKana Hybrid' (hybrid columbine)
Aster novi-belgii x *novae-angliae* 'Treasurer' (Michaelmas daisy, fall aster)
Aster x 'Alma Potschke' (Michaelmas daisy, fall aster)
Campanula carpatica (Carpathian bellflower)
Centaurea montana (mountain bluet) *
Centranthus ruber (red valerian, Jupiter's beard)
Ceratostigma plumbaginoides (leadwort, plumbago)
Cimicifuga spp. (bugbanes)
Coreopsis verticillata (threadleaf coreopsis)
Echinacea purpurea 'Bright Star' (purple coneflower)
Echinops ritro 'Taplow Blue' (globe-thistle)
Geranium endressii 'Wargrave Pink' (cranesbill)
Geranium sanguineum (bloody cranesbill)
Heliopsis helianthoides scabra (false sunflower)
Helleborus spp. (Christmas and Lenten roses)
Hemerocallis hybrids (daylilies)
Lavandula angustifolia 'Munstead' (lavender)
Linum perenne (blue flax)
Monarda didyma 'Cambridge Scarlet' (bee-balm, oswego tea)
Oenothera speciosa (showy evening primrose)
Oenothera 'Fireworks' (common sundrops)
Phlox maculata 'Miss Lingard' and 'Omega' (wild sweet William, spotted phlox) *
Phlox paniculata 'Mt Fuji' (garden phlox, summer phlox) *
Physostegia virginiana 'Vivid' (obedient plant, false dragonhead)
Rudbeckia fulgida 'Goldsturm' (orange coneflower)
Sidalcea malviflora (checkerbloom, prairie mallow)
Tradescantia x *andersoniana* (spiderwort)
Veronica longifolia 'Lavender Charm' (speedwell)
Veronica spicata 'Blue Peter' and 'Icicle'

PERENNIALS THAT BLOOM FOR 10 WEEKS

Armeria maritima (sea pink, thrift)
Aster x *frikartii* 'Monch' and 'Wonder of Staffa' (Frikart's aster)
Chrysanthemum parthenium (feverfew, matricaria)

Chrysogonum virginianum (goldenstar)
Dicentra eximia (fringed bleeding heart) *
Gaillardia x *grandiflora* 'Baby Cole' (blanket-flower)
Hemerocallis hybrids 'Happy Returns,' 'Lemon Lollipop,' 'Penny's Worth,' 'Stella de Oro' (daylilies)
Nepeta x *faassenii* 'Dropmore' (catmint)*
Perovskia atriplicifolia (Russian sage)
Phlox paniculata 'Sandra' (garden phlox, summer phlox)*
Platycodon grandiflorus (balloon flower) *
Rudbeckia laciniata 'Autumn Glory' (shining coneflower)
Salvia x *superba* 'May Night' (hybrid blue salvia, hybrid sage)
Scabiosa caucasica 'Blue Butterfly' (pincushion flower, scabious) *
Sedum x *telephium* 'Autumn Joy' (autumn joy stonecrop)
Stokesia laevis 'Bluestone' (Stokes' aster)

PERENNIALS THAT BLOOM FOR 12 WEEKS OR MORE

Achillea millefolium 'Fire King' and 'Appleblossom' (common yarrow)*
Anthemis tinctoria 'E. C. Buxton' (golden marguerite)
Aster x 'September Ruby'
Campanula poscharskyana (Serbian bellflower)
Campanula portenschlagiana (Dalmatian bellflower)
Chrysanthemum x *rubellum* (hybrid chrysanthemum) *
Coreopsis grandiflora 'Sunray' and 'Early Sunrise' (coreopsis, tickseed)*
Coreopsis verticillata 'Moonbeam' and 'Zagreb' (threadleaf coreopsis)
Corydalis lutea (yellow corydalis)
Dicentra eximia 'Luxuriant', 'Zestful, 'Bountiful' (fringed bleeding heart)
Gaura lindheimeri (white gaura)
Phlox paniculata 'Eva Cullum' and 'Franz Schubert' (garden phlox, summer phlox)*
Verbena bonariensis (Brazilian verbena)
Veronica longifolia 'Sunny Border Blue' (speedwell)*

A foliage garden is as lovely as any flower garden—the effects last longer, too. Grown for foliage are: purple-leaf coralbells (*Heuchera* 'Palace Purple'), lamb's-ears (*Stachys* 'Silver Carpet'), and dusty miller (*Centaurea* 'Silver Dust'). For flowers and foliage: Japanese anemone (*Anemone* x *hybrida*) and *Coreopsis* 'Moonbeam.'

FOLIAGE FIRST—OR MAYBE SECOND

How you use foliage in your garden is as important as how you use flowers. Many garden designers say that you should choose a perennial first for its foliage and secondarily for its flowers because the leaves contribute to your garden's picture a lot longer than the flowers. If you have a difficult time convincing yourself to do this, at least rank the leaves a close second. You might want to avoid plants with uninteresting or tattered-looking leaves, or locate them away from center stage.

Consider size, shape, texture, and color of both flowers and foliage when situating plants to devise winning combinations. Many perennials feature beautifully textured or colored leaves. Astilbe and columbine, for example, have lovely fernlike leaves that create a delicate, refined look. Others, such as hosta and rodgersia, offer big, bold leaves that create drama and dynamic contrast. Some are striped or splashed with gold or silver variegations, or washed all over with deep purple or steely blue-green. Others are loved for their felt-covered silvery leaves.

55

CREATING A STYLISH GARDEN

A garden's accessories add color and style to the scene, catching the eye as a focal point of solid structure among ever-changing waves of softer flowers. You can dress up your garden with a latticework fence, create a focal point from a rustic birdbath tucked among the ferns and wildflowers, or train roses to tumble over a gated arbor to create a romantic country setting. Whatever accessories you add to your garden, be sure they match your garden's personality.

Left: A stone wall provides a soft gray background and rugged texture that makes a pleasant contrast with tulips and pansies in a spring garden.

BACKGROUND CHECK

Your garden's background material contributes to its mood. Brick walls usually seem neat and formal. Tall walls create a sense of enclosure and privacy, setting an intimate mood. They stop air circulation and retain heat, however, creating a warm microclimate, which can be good or bad depending on where you live. A garden along the wall of the house could be positioned in baking sun or in day-long shade depending on the exposure; sometimes house walls create a rain shadow, shielding the ground from falling rain and creating dry conditions. Fieldstone walls lend a country air to a garden—the more tumbledown the wall, the more romantic the garden. Because they are usually lower, stone garden walls won't affect your garden's growing conditions.

Most people put up fences for privacy and to keep children and pets on one side or the other. Because fences act as a dominant landscape feature, you should choose the fence's style and color carefully to match your home and the style of garden you have in mind. Split-rail looks casual; lattice looks elegant. A 4-foot-tall fence serves as an adequate barrier, but an 8-foot-tall fence creates a dramatic sense of enclosure.

Most fences are less solid than a wall and allow air to flow through. Because tall fences can cast shade, you might want to avoid planting right up against them so the plants won't lean toward the light. You'll also want access to the fence for repairs and painting. Light-colored fences—those stained white or gray—reflect more light into shady gardens than ones stained dark green.

Above: A lattice fence gives this garden an effective backdrop without casting shade or impeding air circulation.

When planting a flower garden along a hedge, remember that the hedge is alive. It will grow taller and larger and need pruning and other attention. Take care to leave an access path between the flowers and the shrubs, so you can tend the hedge. Select noninvasive hedge shrubs to keep roots from invading the garden. Favorite choices include evergreens such as yew, boxwood, and Japanese holly, which can be sheared into formal wall-like hedges or pruned naturalistically into fluffy, free-form shapes.

Top Left: A hedge is a traditional garden backdrop in English gardens. The foliage stops the eye, focusing attention on the flowers while giving them a dark green background that makes them dramatically stand out.

Bottom left: This brilliantly colored garden becomes all the more extraordinary because of the distant view it frames. Similarly, the mountain view would be less beautiful without the flower-filled foreground.

INTIMATE AND BORROWED VIEWS

Sometimes the garden pictures we paint around our homes are cozy, secluded scenes made intimate by enclosures—fences, hedges, walls, and even tall screen plantings such as hemlocks or pines. You might choose such a backdrop for your flower garden to give you privacy or to camouflage unattractive views.

Where the view is worth emphasizing, you can enhance it further with a flower-filled garden as a frame. Keep in mind that any view—whether of a small fish pond or a rocky seashore—becomes more beautiful and alluring if you don't see all of it at once. Plant a garden or build a fence in front of a view, but do so judiciously, creating a glimpse of the view through an arbor, for instance, and allowing the view to unfold dramatically as you turn a corner.

Far left: Even if you never stroll on it, the apple-blossom-strewn path through this garden leads your eye into the scene, making it seem more intimate and inviting.

Near left: Stepping stones give structure to this naturalistic planting of California poppies (*Eschscholzia californica*), while serving the practical purpose of preventing the flowers from being crushed underfoot.

Opposite: Wood chips keep a garden path from becoming muddy and look earthy and natural. The chips are inexpensive when compared to the cost of paving, and they are not permanent enough to prohibit you from easily redesigning the garden when it comes time to renovate.

PATHS OF DISTINCTION

Both formal and informal gardens benefit from paths that direct viewers through the garden. Even if you don't walk on it, a path leads your eye, pointing the way and directing you toward the scene you have so carefully crafted. Formal gardens call for straight paths with sharp corners along the front of the border. The path provides a place to walk and allows foreground plants to spill forward. With a lawn border, edges have to be neater, and floppy plants are in danger of being mowed. Paths may intersect at right angles or lead to a strong focal point such as a bench or statue set in an alcove or cutout.

Informal gardens call for curving paths that might duck behind a large shrub or corner of the house, creating a bit of mystery. The path should meander in a seemingly unstudied fashion, but actually point the way to pretty focal points of intense color or interest.

Choose a path surface to match your garden's style. Mulch and wood chips look good in wildflower and naturalistic gardens, while more formal materials are called for in traditional settings. Choose quarried straight-edged flagstones for formal gardens and fieldstones for a country mood. Brick paths work in almost any style of garden as does dark-colored gravel. Avoid white gravel because its brightness captures your attention, detracting from the flowers. Be sure to give gravel an edging to hold it in place and lay an undercoating of landscape fabric beneath so the stones don't work their way into the soil and disappear.

Right: A large statue creates a dramatic focal point in a garden, drawing the eye and bringing cohesion to the garden's design.

Opposite: No matter how well-designed your garden, it will prosper only if you match plants to the site's growing conditions. Here, moisture-loving Japanese primroses (*Primula japonica*) and Christmas ferns (*Polystichum acrostichoides*) flourish in the boggy soil bordering a natural stream.

FOCAL POINTS

Anything that draws your eye and holds it is a focal point. Although plants or plant groupings often create focal points in a garden, structures and accessories such as birdbaths, benches, gates, and statues make strong, permanent focal points. Place focal points such as these judiciously, and don't use too many in one garden.

Benches should match your garden's style. Teak benches with wide or straight backs and armrests are traditional in English gardens, although the shape of the bench is more important than the type of wood. Less expensive versions may be made in oak or pine. Grapevine and cedar-log furniture possess a rustic charm that makes a perfect addition to a country flower or herb garden.

Statuary that seems cute in a cottage garden may look tacky in a more formal setting, so choose carefully. A stone bunny or frog peering out from beneath a hosta leaf adds whimsical charm that enhances the appeal of a country setting but looks ridiculous in a formal rose garden. In formal settings, avoid cuteness and opt for drama. Choose a large, graceful urn or tall figurine to make a grand statement.

A FINAL WORD

Whatever the style of your garden, or what types of plants you're growing, your garden will be most successful and easiest to care for if you match plants to their preferred growing conditions. Proper sun and moisture conditions are the most important factors determining whether a plant thrives or fails. If you know something about a plant's natural environment, you may be able to instinctively understand its needs. You needn't be a naturalist, however, to be a great gardener. Chapter 8 gives you all the information you need to successfully cultivate any flower you wish to grow. The rest is up to you.

The best way to go about flower gardening is to evaluate your site's growing conditions and then select plants adapted to them. If you do the opposite—decide what you want to grow and then set out to create the proper growing conditions—you may be in for a lot of work. The lists included in Chapters 3–7 will help you select flowers for particular conditions and garden styles.

One final piece of advice: If something in your garden displeases you, don't be afraid to rearrange or change it. You can easily repaint your garden picture with a shovel or trowel to make better combinations and vignettes. Although plants are best moved in spring or fall, most won't be set back by being dug up and replanted as long as you do it on a cool, damp day and move them with a hefty clump of soil surrounding their roots. Your shovel may become your best friend and your best design tool.

61

CREATING YOUR PERSONAL STYLE

CHAPTER THREE

DESIGNING COUNTRY GARDENS

Create a Garden Overflowing with Exuberant Flowers and Fragrant Herbs

Opposite: A white gazebo creates both a dramatic focal point and a romantic retreat in this flower- and herb-filled Oregon garden. Blooming in June and creating a vertical accent in the foreground are delphinium (*Delphinium* x *elatum*) and foxglove (*Digitalis purpurea*).

Left: A picket fence and gated arbor planted on both sides with flowers and roses defines this cottage garden. Long-blooming double-flowered balloon flowers (*Platycodon grandiflorus* 'Double Blue') flank the brick walk leading from the parking area to the gate.

You don't have to live in the country to enjoy a country-style garden. The informal gardens described here adapt as readily to the small lot of a city rowhouse as to the open expanse of a farmhouse property. Designed to overflow with an exuberant mix of colorful flowers, a country-style garden reflects today's relaxed lifestyle and love of home and outdoor living.

Your garden's country feel comes from informally arranging appropriate flowers and herbs in combination with rustic or romantic structures, and perhaps a whimsical sculpture or found objects, in a seemingly unstudied design. You'll want to plan the lines and bones of the garden to give it an appealing design, even though that design may not be apparent to the casual observer. Actually, if the garden's structure is not obvious, so much the better, for the garden's unplanned look gives it friendliness and invites you to enjoy its welcoming charm.

Whether in the city, suburbs, or country, you can lend a country feel to your garden by surrounding it with a picket or split-rail fence, rose-draped arbor, or fieldstone wall. A gazebo creates a romantic getaway where you can relax and enjoy the garden surrounded by perfumed flowers. Add a patio, perhaps planted with flowers and herbs that release their fragrances when brushed by passing feet, and your garden becomes an outdoor living room where you can relax among delightful sights and scents.

Traditionally, country gardens were practical gardens and the plants grown in them served first as food, medicines, dyes, and fibers. The beauty of their flowers and foliage came as an afterthought. The gardens described here, however, celebrate an abundance of flowers—their amazing colors, textures, and fragrances are the first consideration. You'll also find practical ideas and plants here, too. You can plant a cut-flower garden where you can grow extra flowers for fresh and dried arrangements to decorate your home. You'll discover you can grow culinary herbs side by side with cutting flowers in the cottage garden tradition or separate them into a pretty—and practical—herb garden. Either way, you'll find the herbs conveniently at hand to toss into your favorite recipes.

Above: Traditional herb gardens trace their roots back to monastery gardens, where medicinal herbs were grown. These gardens were tidy and orderly, relying on a geometrical structure and symmetry to give them interest and to organize the plants.

Left: A care-free country-style herb garden laid out in concentric circles brims with color in late June when the chives (*Allium schoenoprasum*), lavender (*Lavandula angustifolia*), and sage (*Salvia officinalis*) come into bloom.

HERBS STARTED IT ALL

Today's flower gardens trace their roots back to medieval European monasteries, where monks collected and tended medicinal herbs. In fact, all of the doctors of the Middle Ages were botanists whose primary medicines consisted of prescriptions of healing plants. They planted their herb collections, or apothecary gardens, in orderly fashion in rectangular beds with paths in between.

In the early Middle Ages, no one had the time or money to grow plants simply for enjoyment. Over the centuries, however, these utilitarian gardens evolved into more elaborate geometrical arrangements and began to include flowering plants gathered from exotic lands, which were appreciated for their beauty alone.

DESIGNING A TRADITIONAL HERB GARDEN

Valued for their scent, flavor, or medicinal properties, herbs are appreciated more for their practical uses than for their beauty. Although many herbs, such as chives, lavender, and bee-balm, are beautiful flowering plants, others pass hardly noticed when in bloom. Many herbs, especially those such as sage, woolly thyme, and rosemary that hail from the hot, dry Mediterranean region, have eye-catching gray or silvery leaves. Some, such as purple-leaf sage or golden oregano, feature brightly colored foliage that makes an eye-catching splash in the garden. Most herbs, however, exhibit a subtle beauty that needs enhancement to make a great-looking garden.

You can take a hint from the old cloister gardens and impose an orderly symmetry on your herb garden. This symmetry and the building materials you choose to outline the beds, pave the walks, and provide a background give the garden its main impact, providing a stage to set

ESSENTIAL HERBS FOR HERB GARDENS

These herbs include those most valued for flavoring food or scenting soaps and potpourri, or for their pretty flowers or foliage. Although many others are appropriate for herb gardens because of their medicinal (sometimes poisonous) properties or their connection to folklore, the following herbs are essential to almost any herb garden.

Lavandula angustifolia

PERENNIALS

Achillea millefolium (common yarrow)
Alchemilla mollis (lady's mantle)
Angelica archangelica (wild parsnip, cow parsnip, archangel)
Chamaemelum nobile (chamomile, Roman chamomile)
Galium odoratum (sweet woodruff)
Lavandula angustifolia (lavender, English lavender)
Mentha suaveolens 'Variegata' (variegated pineapple mint)
Mentha x *piperita* (peppermint)
Monarda didyma (bee-balm, oswego tea)
Nepeta x *faassenii* (catmint)
Origanum vulgare 'Aureum' (golden oregano, golden marjoram)
Ruta graveolens (rue)
Salvia officinalis (garden sage)
Stachys byzantina (lamb's-ears)
Thymus spp. (thymes)
Viola odorata (sweet violet)

ANNUALS

Anethum graveolens (dill)
Borago officinalis (borage)
Calendula officinalis (pot marigold)
Ocimum basilicum (sweet basil)
Pelargonium spp. (scented geraniums)
Petroselinum crispum (parsley)
Tropaeolum majus (nasturtium)

BULBS

Allium schoenoprasum (chives)
Crocus sativus (saffron crocus)

ROSES

Rosa gallica officinalis (apothecary rose)
Rosa rugosa (beach rose)
Rosa x *damascena* (damask rose)

off the herbs' subtle textures and colors and saving it from bleakness in winter.

Usually herb gardens have a formal layout, with paths or walks bisecting it into a repetitive pattern of beds. You can make a simple garden of four squares formed by two walks intersecting at right angles. If you want something more elaborate, give the beds curved edges where the walks meet to create a central circle where you can place a sculpture, birdbath, or traditional sundial. For a large garden, elongate the squares into rectangles rather than making larger squares that you won't be able to reach into to tend.

Herb gardens also might be based on concentric circles, ovals, or diamonds. A favorite design is a wagon wheel where the spaces between the spokes of the wheel contain different herbs. Just about any strong pattern or geometric arrangement works as long as you keep it balanced.

Paths may be paved with bricks, cobbles, or gravel. Beds look neatest if edged with timbers, low rock, or brick walls. A tidy mulch dresses the garden up and keeps the foliage clean. Favorite mulches include cocoa hulls, which have a beautiful reddish brown color and a chocolate aroma, and pea gravel, which keeps moisture-sensitive herbs from rotting.

Often a low, formally clipped hedge forms a backdrop or even an edging for the garden. The hedge may be made of aromatic plants, such as rosemary or lavender, or from traditional garden hedge plants. A backdrop of old garden roses makes an excellent choice, turning the garden into a bower of flowers in early summer. Especially suitable are gallica roses, which were included in apothecary gardens for their healing properties, and rugosa roses, whose ripe hips are rich in vitamin C and ideal for teas.

This dooryard herb garden seems a fitting companion to the austerely beautiful Colonial-style home. A dark-stained fence perfectly matches the clapboard, while a rough-hewn stone walk and stoop echoes the pioneer spirit embodied by both home and garden. Lamb's-ears (*Stachys byzantina*) forms a year-round silvery mat along the path defining the beds where culinary herbs grow right at hand. Garden ornaments and pots of flowers and tender herbs enhance the country feel.

HERB GARDEN

A brick path, a low boxwood hedge, and a silvery evergreen edging of fragrant lavender give year-round structure and color to this herb garden. An identical selection of culinary herbs in each of the four beds carries out the formal design. Try covering the soil with cocoa-hull mulch to add a beautiful finishing touch and a chocolate scent to the garden.

2 FEET

LOW BOXWOOD HEDGE

BRICK WALK

PERENNIALS AND BULBS

A   *Lavandula angustifolia* 'Munstead Dwarf' (lavender), 50
B   *Thymus pseudolanuginosus* (woolly thyme), 8
C   *Mentha* x *piperita* (peppermint), 4
D   *Allium schoenoprasum* (chives), 4
E   *Origanum vulgare* (oregano), 4
F   *Salvia officinalis* 'Tricolor' (garden sage), 8
G   *Monarda fistulosa* (wild bergamot), 4
H   *Borago officinalis* (borage), 12
I   *Achillea millefolium* (common yarrow), 4

ANNUALS

J   *Petroselinum crispum* (parsley), 40
K   *Tropaeolum majus* (nasturtium), 12
L   *Ocimum basilicum* 'Purple Ruffles' (sweet basil), 12
M   *Pelargonium tomentosum* (peppermint geranium), 1

ROSES

N   *Rosa gallica officinalis* (apothecary rose), 4

69

A variation of a classic four-square herb garden that she fell in love with at Colonial Williamsburg, Becky's 20x40-foot garden is laid out symmetrically with brick walks, brick-edged raised beds, and low boxwood hedges surrounding a central sundial. She designed and constructed the garden herself about 20 years ago, creating and planting one bed at a time and spending a year completing the project. The only help Becky had was from a mason who replaced the original slippery wood-chip paths with bricks.

AN HERB GARDENER

Becky Talbot and Rum-Tum-Tiger contemplate the joys of gardening from the bench in her southern herb garden. Rum-Tum-Tiger especially appreciates the catmint (*Nepeta mussinii*), which Becky grows as a pretty edging, and the more potent but weedy-looking catnip (*Nepeta cataria*), which she relegates to the garden's fringes.

A member of the Herb Society of America, Becky finds growing herbs more difficult in the South than elsewhere because hot, humid weather fosters fungus attacks on sage, thyme, catmint, and the other woolly, gray-leaved herbs she so loves. Becky defies these adverse conditions by planting in raised beds to improve drainage, avoiding crowded plantings to promote air circulation and to dry fungus-prone foliage, and using a layer of grit under creeping plants so they can dry off. Becky top-dresses the beds with an unlikely gritty substance—a fired-clay product used in auto shops to soak up oil spills. She purchases 50-pound bags of the stuff, applying it once a year as a mulch under the herbs. The particles soak up and bind moisture, and their sharp edges work better than sand to create a dry surface and break up the hard soil as they get worked in. The terra-cotta color looks smashing with the bricks and herbs, too.

THE BIRTH OF THE COTTAGE GARDEN

While monks were cultivating orderly plantings of vegetables and medicinal and culinary herbs, peasants tended their own less-sophisticated gardens just outside their cottage doors. In these patchwork gardens, they raised vegetables and fruits as a mainstay of their diets, including medicinal herbs to cure their ills, culinary herbs to season their food, and strewing herbs to combat odors and ward off evil spirits.

A cottager's garden usually grew right beside the dirt path that led from the lane to the door. A fence or stone wall enclosed the yard to keep domestic and wild animals away from the house and out of the garden. In England, flowers gathered from the roadsides or woodlands, or in later years secreted from the master's flower garden, found their way among the cabbages and turnips, and thus was born the beginnings of today's flower gardens.

With the Renaissance, commoners achieved independence from their villages' manor houses and became less poor. So, too, did their gardens evolve into richer assortments of plants, many of which they grew for pure enjoyment. Vegetables and fruits now grew behind the cottages, while herbs, flowers, and ornamental plants adorned front paths and twined over the fences and walls. All these plants had to be hardy: annuals that either self-seeded readily from year to year or perennials whose roots survived the winters to grow again the following year.

These humble cottage gardens, with their romantic collections of tumultuous flowers, inspired the huge, sophisticated flower borders of the English estates during the late 1800s and early 1900s. Charming vine-covered cottages with their romantic chaos of colorful flowers filling their front yards still enchant us today along roads and byways of the British Isles. And it is the English flower gardening tradition—both the cottage garden and the estate garden—that influences American gardeners today.

DESIGNING AN OLD-FASHIONED COTTAGE GARDEN

You can locate your cottage garden in the traditional manner along the walk to your home's front door, or place it anywhere else on your property where it receives full sun. Use the side of your house, garage, barn, or toolshed as one garden wall, enclosing the other sides with a rustic fence or stone wall. Embellish the garden's entrance with a gate or arbor.

A path leading from the gate through the garden is a must, whether it takes you to the kitchen, to the front door, or to a bench under an apple tree. Although tradition calls for a functional straight path, you can be creative and lay out a meandering walk with plants spilling over the edges if you wish. Just keep the paving simple.

Above: Everblooming polyantha roses (*Rosa* 'The Fairy'), sweet peas (*Lathyrus odorata*), and pansies (*Viola x wittrockiana* 'Mini Blue') decorate this picket fence in fine cottage-garden tradition.

Below: An exuberant mix of perennials and self-sowing annuals turns this mountain cottage into a riot of summer color.

Gravel or used bricks make suitable and inexpensive choices. Or you can lay down cobblestones or stepping stones snuggled among fragrant paving plants.

Cottage-garden flowers include perennials, bulbs, and self-seeding annuals, often planted together with herbs and vegetables. You can arrange perennials in random patches, if you want a bit of order in your garden, and surround them with self-sowing annuals. Each year, the annuals' serendipitous arrangements bring delightful surprises to the garden. Tuck culinary herbs and vegetables wherever you find spaces, or plant them to edge a path. Imagine a pretty frill of curly parsley creating a scalloped edging along the walk, or pastel green leaf lettuces thriving in the shade beneath the daisies.

Because disorder is synonymous with cottage gardening, you might even mix the seeds of your chosen annuals together and scatter them over prepared soil and wait for the results. So much for design! Just take care to select an assortment of spikes, daisies, and fluffy flower heads so the garden boasts a pleasing variety of contrasting shapes. Be sure to include flowers that bloom at different seasons, so the garden will be in constant bloom from spring through fall.

Your garden fence and gate demand to be embellished with flowering vines. Climbing roses—ramblers are traditional, but large-flowered climbers work wonderfully, too—add a romantic note and aren't so heavy that they'll topple the fence. Other cottage garden choices include honeysuckle, wisteria, and clematis, or annuals such as morning glories and moonflowers. You might even try your hand at training grapes, gourds, or cucumbers along the fence.

It's important to tame the chaos of flowers in your garden and give your eye a place to rest by creating a focal point in the garden. You might

Opposite: Whimsical garden ornaments create focal points among the tumult of cottage-garden flowers.

Top: No country garden would be complete without a climbing rose tumbling over an arbor—even if that country-style garden is in the city. This rose-clad arbor and bench marks the entrance from the sidewalk of a cottage-style garden that adorns the front yard of a house located on a busy city street. The arbor makes a perfect transition from street to garden, sending out the message to leave all your cares outside.

Bottom: This astonishing mix of annuals captures the magic of a cottage garden, without appearing jumbled, by combining an assortment of flowers in contrasting shapes and colors.

do this with a bench or a small tree placed in a prominent location. A crab apple or other fruit tree makes a good choice. Don't forget old-fashioned roses, the kinds that look as though they stepped off the canvas of a Victorian oil painting. They're a good choice where a shrub is called for.

Every cottage garden deserves a garden ornament to enhance its charm and provide a focal point among the flowers. Use a birdbath or gazing globe to create a strong focal point, but be cautious about your choice of statuary. Stone bunnies and frogs look cute peeking from beneath the leaves, but painted dwarfs and Snow-Whites might be a bit *too* whimsical.

CARING FOR YOUR COTTAGE GARDEN

Your cottage garden won't require as much maintenance as a more manicured formal flower garden. Don't be overly concerned about deadheading the flowers, at least late in the season, because the flowers in a cottage garden should be encouraged to self-sow. After seedpods have ripened, cut off the stalks and shake them over the garden to distribute the seeds. Mulch the garden only lightly so the self-sown flower and herb seeds can sprout. An inch of mini-bark chips or shredded leaves dresses up the garden and keeps dirt from splattering on the flowers, but it doesn't

deter self-sown plants from germinating. Hand-pull weeds cautiously in spring so you can distinguish the desirable seedlings from the pests. Because you won't be tilling the bed every year, weeds will not be a major problem after the first year or so, especially if you spread a light mulch. While you're weeding, do a little rearranging, transplanting flower seedlings that appear in odd locations to better spots. You can arrange similar plants in loose groups and also thin out seedlings that are too close.

SELF-SOWING FLOWERS AND HERBS FOR COTTAGE GARDENS

ANNUALS AND BIENNIALS

Antirrhinum majus (snapdragon)
Browallia speciosa (amethyst flower, star flower)
Calendula officinalis (pot marigold)
Centaurea cyanus (bachelor's button, cornflower)
Clarkia amoena (godetia, satin flower)
Cleome hasslerana (spider flower)
Consolida ambigua (rocket larkspur)
Cosmos bipinnatus (cosmos)
Eschscholzia californica (California poppy)
Euphorbia marginata (snow-on-the-mountain)
Impatiens wallerana (impatiens, busy lizzie)
Lobularia maritima (sweet alyssum)
Lunaria annua (money-plant, dollar-plant, honesty)
Mirabilis jalapa (four o'clock)
Moluccella laevis (bells-of-Ireland)
Myosotis sylvatica (woodland forget-me-not)
Nigella damascena (love-in-a-mist)
Papaver rhoeas (corn poppy, Shirley poppy, Flanders poppy)
Portulaca grandiflora (moss rose)
Torenia fournieri (wishbone flower)
Tropaeolum majus (nasturtium)
Viola tricolor (Johnny-jump-up)

These annual and biennial flowers and herbs readily self-sow to happily perpetuate themselves in your cottage garden.

Mirabilis jalapa

HERBS

Anethum graveolens (dill)
Borago officinalis (borage)
Ocimum basilicum (sweet basil)
Perilla frutescens (beefsteak plant)
Petroselinum crispum (parsley)

OLD-FASHIONED PERENNIALS AND BIENNIALS FOR COTTAGE GARDENS

Still popular today, these treasured cottage-garden flowers decorated the gardens of yesteryear. Use the time-honored beauties in your garden to create an irresistible and easy-care display.

SPRING

Aurinia saxatilis (basket-of-gold)
Bellis perennis (English daisy)
Dicentra spectabilis (common bleeding heart)
Digitalis purpurea (foxglove)
Galium odoratum (sweet woodruff)
Myosotis scorpioides (forget-me-not)
Phlox subulata (moss pink)
Primula veris (cowslip primrose)
Pulmonaria officinalis (common lungwort)
Viola tricolor (Johnny-jump-up)

SUMMER

Alcea rosea (hollyhock)
Aquilegia vulgaris (granny's bonnet)
Campanula glomerata (clustered bellflower)
Campanula persicifolia (peach-leaf bellflower)
Centaurea montana (mountain bluet)
Centranthus ruber (red valerian, Jupiter's beard)
Cerastium tomentosum (snow-in-summer)
Chamaemelum nobile (chamomile)
Chrysanthemum parthenium (feverfew, matricaria)

Dianthus barbatus (sweet William)
Dianthus deltoides (maiden pinks)
Hemerocallis fulva (tawny daylily)
Hemerocallis lilioasphedelus (lemon daylily)
Hesperis matronalis (dame's rocket, sweet rocket)
Lychnis coronaria (rose campion)
Lychnis chalcedonia (Maltese cross)
Monarda didyma (bee-balm, oswego tea)
Paeonia lactiflora (Chinese peony, garden peony)
Phlox paniculata (garden phlox, summer phlox)
Saponaria officinalis (bouncing Bet)
Stachys byzantina (lamb's-ears)

LATE SUMMER AND FALL

Aconitum spp. (monkshoods)
Anemone x *hybrida* (Japanese anemone)
Sedum spectabile (showy stonecrop)
Viola tricolor (Johhny-jump-up)

OLD-FASHIONED BULBS FOR COTTAGE GARDENS

Having stood the test of time, these old-fashioned bulbs are as popular today as they were a century or more ago. Use them generously to bring bouquets of charm to your cottage garden.

SPRING

Convallaria majalis (lily-of-the-valley)
Crocus x *vernus* (Dutch crocus)
Fritillaria imperalis (crown imperial)
Galanthus nivalis (snowdrop)
Hyacinthus orientalis (Dutch hyacinth)
Muscari botryoides (grape hyacinth)
Narcissus x *poeticus* (pheasant's-eye narcissus, poet's narcissus)
Scilla siberica (Siberian squill)
Tulipa clusiana (candystick tulip, lady tulip)
Tulipa sylvestris (Florentine tulip)
Tulipa x *hybrida* (hybrid tulips)

SUMMER

Lilium candidum (Madonna lily)
Lilium longifolium (tiger lily)
Polianthes tuberosa (tuberose)

LATE SUMMER AND FALL

Lycoris squamigera (resurrection lily, naked ladies, hurricane lily, magic lily)

COTTAGE GARDEN

Designed to overflow for months with flowers, this charming cottage garden will become more romantically chaotic over the years as its lines begin to blur. Blossoming starts in late winter when snowdrops decorate the lawn, disappearing just before the grass needs mowing. Spring bulbs bring life to the beds, followed by hordes of summer and fall flowers.

PERENNIALS AND BIENNIALS

A *Alcea rosea* (hollyhock), 12
B *Hemerocallis fulva* (tawny daylily), 5
C *Campanula persicifolia* (peach-leaf bellflower), 8
D *Centranthus ruber* (red valerian), 8
E *Phlox paniculata* (garden phlox), 6
F *Centaurea montana* (mountain bluet), 1
G *Anemone* x *hybrida* (Japanese anemone), 5
H *Dicentra spectabilis* (bleeding heart), 2
I *Stachys byzantina* (lamb's-ears), 12
J *Aquilegia vulgaris* (granny's bonnet, columbine), 3
K *Chrysanthemum parthenium* (feverfew), 8
L *Dianthus barbatus* (sweet William), 6
M *Bellis perennis* (English daisy), 17
N *Aconitum carmichaelii* (azure monkshood), 7
O *Lunaria annua* (money-plant), 8
P *Paeonia lactiflora* (Chinese peony), 1
Q *Digitalis purpurea* (foxglove), 3
R *Pulmonaria officinalis* (common lungwort), 14
S *Monarda didyma* (bee-balm), 2
T *Viola tricolor* (Johnny-jump-up), 24

BULBS

U *Fritillaria imperalis* (crown imperial), 12
V *Convallaria majalis* (lily-of-the-valley), 24
W *Galanthus nivalis* (snowdrop), 100
X *Crocus* x *vernus* (Dutch crocus), 125
Y *Narcissus* x *poeticus* (pheasant's-eye narcissus), 40
Z *Tulipa* 'Apeldoorn' (Darwin hybrid tulip), 40

ANNUALS

AA *Impatiens wallerana* (impatiens), 80
BB *Lobularia maritima* (sweet alyssum), 40
CC *Cosmos bipinnatus* (cosmos), 8
DD *Cleome hasslerana* (spider flower), 10

VINES

EE *Clematis* x *jackmanii* (Jackman clematis), 1
FF *Rosa* 'Lady Gay' (rambler rose), 2
GG *Clematis maximowiziana* (sweet autumn clematis), 2

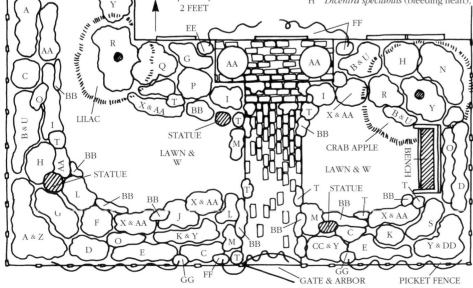

Joyce believes her love of gardening was passed down to her in her genes. She remembers being 3 years old—no taller than the flowers—and working alongside her mother in their Virginia garden. It has been only in the last few years, when she became semiretired and no longer needed to concentrate on her career, that Joyce began gardening in earnest. Her garden has become a very personal and spiritual place. In it she does exactly what she wants, claiming she didn't even realize she was a gardener until she recently ran into other gardeners. Now a member of a maverick garden club called The Dirty Ladies

A COTTAGE GARDENER

Joyce Gillum-Koonce, a semiretired mental health professional, says she salivates when visiting nurseries—an expensive problem—and jokes that she is considering starting a support group for plant addicts.

(members would rather trade seeds over the back fence than drink tea and wear white gloves), Joyce and her compatriots spend summer meetings relentlessly visiting gardens and winter meetings absorbing knowledge from the club's guest speakers. Joyce delights in the climate of the Pacific Northwest, where she lives, because it is closer to the British Isles than anywhere else in the United States. This means she can grow many of the tender plants that perform so well in England. In her own garden, Joyce tried to bring home the ambience of the cottage gardens she observed through their garden gates while wandering about the back roads of England and France.

This flower-filled cottage garden takes up the backyard of Joyce's city home. Once nothing more than lawn and shrubs, the garden gradually evolved as she added more and more beds and took out lawn. Joyce sculpted the 50-year-old rhododendrons in the rear to create a shade garden and added the arbor and garden house.

DESIGNING A CUTTING GARDEN

Part of the pleasure in growing a country garden brimming with flowers is being able to harvest blossoms from the garden to use as luxurious indoor bouquets. If you're a crafter, you can grow everlasting flowers for drying and fashioning into long-lasting wreaths and arrangements. You also might enjoy using the seedpods and fruits that ripen in fall as unusual additions to your creations. The major drawback in picking flowers from the garden for indoor use is that you rob your outdoor display of its beauty. You might have to choose between the pleasure of seeing the irises blooming at the curve of your front walk as you go to and from the house and enjoying them in a vase on the hall table. The ideal situation is not being forced to choose, but having enough blossoms to go around. The best way to assure this is to design a separate cutting garden intended to produce cut flowers.

There are two schools of thought on creating a cutting garden. One school favors setting out flowers in rows with paths in between, similar to the way you might lay out a vegetable garden.

A cut-flower garden laid out with rows of flowers and narrow paths in between—similar to a vegetable garden—makes flower growing and harvesting a simple matter. Locate such a utilitarian garden to the side of your property, where it's not in full view, because you'll be cutting most of the flowers.

You are, after all, growing the flowers as a crop intended for harvesting, so this is a practical approach. The second school favors a cottage-garden style planted with enough abundance that the flowers you clip for bouquets won't be missed.

In either case, you'll want to choose flowers—both annuals and perennials—that last when cut or are especially good for pressing or drying.

THE ROW APPROACH

Your cut-flower garden might be as simple as including a row or two of zinnias, snapdragons, and gladiolus in the vegetable garden. Or you might wish to devote several hundred square feet of row space to flowers. Because a utilitarian cut-flower garden is just a bare plot of earth in the winter and may be devoid of beauty during the growing season and because you'll be harvesting the flowers as soon as they open, you may want to put it in an out-of-the-way location.

Choose a sunny spot in the back or side yard, and prepare the soil as you would for any new garden. Create beds or rows about 3 to 4 feet wide (no deeper than you can reach into) and leave 2-foot-wide paths in between. Devote several rows to perennials and hardy bulbs, keeping

Top: Peonies, with their sumptuous beauty and delightful fragrance, put on quite a show both in the garden and in the vase. Here they grow in a permanent cut-flower bed so their long-stemmed flowers can be clipped for bouquets without robbing a display garden of its essential blossoms.

Bottom: A picket fence encloses this combination vegetable and cut-flower garden, giving it structure and keeping out the rabbits. In spring, tulips fill the beds. After their flowers are cut, the bulbs are pulled out and replaced with annual flowers, vegetables, and culinary herbs.

LONG-LASTING FLOWERS FOR CUTTING GARDENS

PERENNIALS FOR CUTTING
SPRING
Dicentra spectabilis (common bleeding heart)
Helleborus spp. (Christmas and Lenten roses)

SUMMER
Achillea filipendulina (fern-leaf yarrow)
Alstroemeria aurantiaca (Peruvian lily)
Asclepias tuberosa (butterfly weed)
Astilbe x *arendsii* (astilbe)
Chrysanthemum parthenium (feverfew, matricaria)
Chrysanthemum x *superbum* (shasta daisy)
Coreopsis grandiflora (coreopsis, tickseed)
Delphinium x *elatum* (delphinium)
Dianthus barbatus (sweet William)
Digitalis purpurea (foxglove)
Echinops ritro (globe-thistle)
Gypsophila paniculata (baby's breath)
Iris hybrida (bearded iris)
Lupinus hybrids (lupine)
Paeonia lactiflora (Chinese peony)
Phlox paniculata (garden phlox, summer phlox)

LATE SUMMER AND FALL
Aconitum carmichaelii (azure monkshood)
Aster novi-belgii x *novae-angliae* (Michaelmas
    daisy, fall aster)
Chrysanthemum x *morifolium* (garden mum)
Echinacea purpurea (purple coneflower)
Limonium latifolium (sea lavender, statice)
Rudbeckia fulgida (orange coneflower)

BULBS FOR CUTTING
SPRING
Allium aflatunense (Persian onion)
Convallaria majalis (lily-of-the-valley)
Narcissus hybrids (trumpet and large-cup daffodils)
Tulipa x *hybrida* (hybrid tulips)
Zantedeschia aethiopica (calla lily)

SUMMER
Freesia hybrids (freesia)
Gladiolus x *hortulanus* (gladiolus)
Lilium hybrids (lilies)
Polianthes tuberosa (tuberose)
Zantedeschia aethiopica (calla lily)

LATE SUMMER AND FALL
Amaryllis belladona (belladona lily, naked lady)
Dahlia x *pinnata* (dahlia)

ANNUALS FOR CUTTING
Antirrhinum majus (snapdragon)
Calendula officinalis (pot marigold)
Callistephus chinensis (China aster, annual aster)
Celosia cristata (cockscomb)
Centaurea cyanus (bachelor's button, cornflower)
Cleome hasslerana (spider flower)
Consolida ambigua (rocket larkspur)
Cosmos bipinnatus (cosmos)
Eustoma grandiflora (prairie gentian, lisianthus)
Gaillardia pulchella (annual blanket-flower)
Gerbera jamesonii (gerbera daisy, transvaal daisy)
Heliotropium arborescens (heliotrope)
Lathyrus odoratus (sweet pea)
Matthiola incana (stock)
Nigella damascena (love-in-a-mist)
Papaver spp. (poppies)
Pelargonium x *hortorum* (zonal geranium)
Petunia x *hybrida* (petunia)
Salvia farinacea (mealy-cup sage)
Schizanthus pinnatus (butterfly flower,
    poor man's orchid)
Tagetes spp. (marigolds)
Viola x *wittrockiana* (pansy)
Zinnia elegans (zinnia)

ROSES FOR CUTTING
HYBRID TEA:
'Bewitched,' 'Color Magic,' 'Duet,' 'Mr. Lincoln,'
'New Day,' 'Olympiad,' 'Paradise,' 'Pascali,' 'Peace,'
'Touch of Class,' 'Tropicana,' 'Voodoo'

GRANDIFLORA:
'Ole,' 'Pink Parfait,' 'Queen Elizabeth,' 'Sonia,' 'Viva'

FLORIBUNDA:
'Cherish,' 'Deep Purple,' 'Iceberg,' 'Intrigue,'
'Playboy'

These flowers last a long time when cut and used in flower arrangements. Choose from this list when designing your cut-flower garden.

Gladiolus x *hortulanus*

them separate from the annuals and tender bulbs, so that your yearly tilling and planting won't disturb the perennial plants.

If you must locate the cut-flower garden in a prominent location, enclose it with an attractive fence or low hedge to hide the flowerless plot. Design a small display garden in front of the fence and plant it with flowers that you do not intend to cut. This scheme transforms the cut-flower garden into a beautiful sight.

CARING FOR YOUR CUT-FLOWER GARDEN

Most of the flowers in a cutting garden should be annuals because they bloom profusely, producing more blossoms as soon as you cut off the newly opened ones. To keep annuals blooming, fertilize them regularly and cut off dead flowers that weren't cut when fresh unless you intend to use the seedpods for crafts projects, in which case you'll want to harvest the pods at the appropriate time.

Annuals need replanting every year and because they feed heavily it's a good idea to annually till compost or aged manure into their garden space at planting time. Regular weeding is another chore, which can be accomplished by hoeing as you would a vegetable garden unless you mulch after planting. In a mulched garden, weeds will be less troublesome and can be pulled easily by hand.

Perennials require a topdressing of compost or manure every spring to keep the soil healthy. You may need to divide them every few years. Staking can be more important in a cut-flower garden than in a display garden to ensure straight stems for your arrangements.

EVERLASTINGS FOR CUTTING GARDENS

These flowers dry well, either left on the plant in the garden or when cut and hung upside down in a cool, airy spot. Grow these flowers to use for everlasting dried-flower arrangements.

Moluccella laevis

PERENNIALS AND BIENNIALS FOR AIR-DRYING

SUMMER
Achillea filipendulina (fern-leaf yarrow)
Achillea millefolium (common yarrow)
Lavandula angustifolia (lavender)

LATE SUMMER AND FALL
Anaphalis cinnamomea (pearly everlasting)
Artemisia ludoviciana 'Silver King'
    (white sage, wormwood)
Echinops ritro (globe-thistle)
Eryngium amethystinum (amethyst sea holly)
Gypsophila paniculata (baby's breath)
Limonium latifolium (sea lavender, statice)
Sedum x *telephium* 'Autumn Joy' (autumn joy
    stonecrop)

ANNUALS FOR AIR-DRYING
Celosia cristata (cockscomb)
Gomphrena globosa (globeflower, globe
    amaranth)
Helichrysum bracteatum (strawflower)
Limonium sinuatum (statice)
Lunaria annua (money-plant, dollar-plant,
    honesty); seedpods
Moluccella laevis (bells-of-Ireland)
Nigella damascena (love-in-a-mist); seedpods
Salvia viridis (painted sage)

BULBS FOR AIR-DRYING
Allium aflatunense (Persian onion); seedpods
Allium schoenoprasum (chive)

ORNAMENTAL GRASSES FOR AIR-DRYING
Briza media (quaking grass, rattlesnake grass)
Chasmanthium latifolium (northern sea oats,
    wild oats)
Miscanthus sinensis (eulalia grass, silver grass)
Pennisetum alopecuroides (fountain grass)

CUTTING GARDEN

Designed for efficiency as well as beauty, this cutting garden features easy-to-tend raised beds of cut flowers surrounded by a decorative picket fence.

Perennials, annuals, and bulbs are planted in separate beds to make caring for them easy.

PERENNIALS

A   *Phlox paniculata* (garden phlox), 5

B   *Rudbeckia fulgida* 'Goldsturm' (orange coneflower), 2

C   *Coreopsis grandiflora* (coreopsis, tickseed), 4

D   *Chrysanthemum* x *superbum* 'Alaska' (shasta daisy), 3

E   *Gypsophila paniculata* (baby's breath), 2

F   *Paeonia lactiflora* (Chinese peony), 2

G   *Iris hybrida* (bearded iris), 3

H   *Delphinium* x *elatum* (delphinium), 3

I   *Chrysanthemum* x *morifolium* (garden mum, rust), 5

J   *Chrysanthemum* x *morifolium* (garden mum, gold), 5

K   *Chrysanthemum* x *morifolium* (garden mum, orange), 5

L   *Chrysanthemum parthenium* (feverfew), 4

M   *Aster novi-belgii* x *novae-angliae* (Michaelmas daisy, fall aster), 3

N   *Echinops ritro* (globe-thistle), 2

O   *Stachys byzantina* (lamb's-ears), 60

BULBS

P   *Lilium* 'Casa Blanca' (Oriental lily), 6

Q   *Gladiolus* x *hortulanus* (gladiolus), 9

R   *Tulipa* x *hybrida* (tulips), 27

S   *Convallaria majalis* (lily-of-the-valley), 10

T   *Lilium* 'Stargazer' (Oriental lily), 5

U   *Allium aflatunense* (Persian onion), 8

V   *Narcissus* hybrids (trumpet, large-cup daffodils), 24

ROSES

W   *Rosa* hybrid (hybrid tea rose), 4

ANNUALS

X   *Viola* x *wittrockiana* (pansy), 24

Y   *Antirrhinum majus* (snapdragon), 8

Z   *Cosmos bipinnatus* (cosmos), 9

AA   *Salvia farinacea* (mealy-cup sage), 15

BB   *Centaurea cyanus* (bachelor's button, cornflower), 6

CC   *Celosia cristata* (cockscomb), 10

VINES

DD   *Clematis* 'Nelly Moser' (clematis), 5

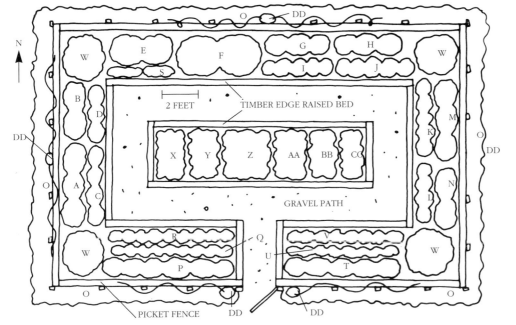

A CUT-FLOWER GARDENER

Louise Mercer grows unusual annuals, perennials, and herbs in her Long Island, New York, garden to cut or dry for the arrangements and bouquets she fashions for her floral design business, The Tender Thicket.

Besides the cottage-style gardens immediately surrounding their house, Louise and her husband, Wayne, cultivate a 3,000-square-foot cut-flower and vegetable garden. The garden is laid out in rows so it's easy to care for by the organic methods they prefer. Wayne tills the garden in spring with a power tiller, churning in composted cow manure and the winter rye they sow in fall as a cover crop. In March they begin sowing flower and vegetable seeds in flats under 10 sets of lights in their basement. Many of the flowers Louise grows are garden flowers or wild types usually unavailable from florists and preferred by her clients for their weddings and parties. These she fashions into naturalistic wreaths, arrangements, nosegays, and bouquets that look as if the flowers were gathered during a walk along a country lane. One flower she declares is a must in any cut-flower garden is the old-fashioned annual called love-in-a-mist (*Nigella damascena*), which she grows along the garage. Louise uses the cut flowers and misty green foliage as fillers in fresh arrangements and also harvests stems after the foliage has dried and the flowers have turned into beautiful inflated seedpods.

Louise cultivates the heat-loving herbs she uses in wreaths in this cottage-style cutting garden along the garage. The garden looks attractive despite its utilitarian purpose because creeping plants tumble about the stone walls and walk, which her husband built, providing decoration after taller flowers are cut.

AN EASY-CARE PATIO GARDEN

A patio or deck provides the perfect viewing spot for your country garden and expands your home's living space to include the outdoors. By trading in some of your lawn for bricks or flagstones, you'll also reduce your yard maintenance chores considerably. Locate the patio directly off the house, with access through the kitchen door or sliding glass doors from the living room or dining room. This physical link to the house makes the patio a convenient extension of your home's living space, but it also visually anchors it

to the landscape. A patio located away from the house may look as though it's floating in space unless a large garden or structure links it to the rest of the yard.

Be sure your patio has enough room for people to move around easily and to hold table and chairs as well as lounge furniture. Keep the patio in scale with the rest of the landscape; the usual rule of thumb is to make the patio no more than one-third the size of the yard. (City gardeners can effectively pave over an entire small yard, leaving perimeter planting borders.)

The narrow brick patio outside the picture window and French doors brings the outdoors just a step away, making a perfect place to sit on a pleasant day. Filling the immediate view from the window with blossoms, flower-filled containers bring the garden indoors when there's no time to step outside.

PLANTING FOR A COUNTRY LOOK

Just because it's made of bricks or stones doesn't mean that your patio must be a sterile place. To give it a country look, bring the flower garden right up to the patio to soften its edges. Use the patio itself as another place to grow flowers. Group clay, wooden, or cement planters brimming with annual flowers into focal points around the edges of the patio, flanking the door to the house, and beside a prominent piece of furniture. You can even plant the spaces between the paving stones with paving plants.

Paving plants are low rock garden plants that can grow happily between the cracks in pavement. Most tolerate being lightly walked on; those that don't will do well and look pretty if planted in an out-of-the way crack at the side of the patio.

Paving plants added to the spaces between the flagstones in your patio (you may wish to design it with extra-large spaces and planting pockets) sprawl delightfully over the stones, softening their appearance and creating a romantic, slightly disheveled look.

CHOOSING MASONRY

Almost any type of paving works in a country garden as long as it is laid in an informal pattern. The more weathered it looks, however, the better it blends with the garden. Flagstones or rubble should be of varying sizes and shapes and placed irregularly, not in rigid patterns. Choose a busy old-fashioned-looking design such as basket weave rather than the more formal straight-lined patterns when laying bricks. Choose used paving bricks, not new bright red ones, if you can.

A patio can be mortared or mortarless, but if you want to grow paving plants, be sure the stones or bricks are unmortared. A mortarless patio is easier and less expensive to install than a mortared patio and better survives the stress of freezing and thawing in cold climates. Mortared bricks, however, look more romantic and old-fashioned than mortarless ones, especially if you use mortar that contrasts with the color of the bricks. For example, used, soft pink paving bricks combined with light gray mortar creates a weathered look that perfectly complements the romance of a cottage garden.

Above: Clove-scented pinks (*Dianthus* spp.) and sweet alyssum (*Lobularia maritima*) sprout between the stones, turning the patio into a sensual garden.

Opposite: Two forms of paving—bricks placed on edge in a diagonal pattern and random stones—create a country atmosphere surrounding this Victorian-style garden house.

PAVING PLANTS FOR PATIO GARDENS

These low-growing, fine-textured plants can tolerate the hot, dry conditions between paving stones, and most will tolerate being walked on lightly. Tuck them between stepping stones, bricks, and patio blocks to soften the look of the masonry.

PERENNIALS FOR PAVING

SPRING
Ajuga reptans (bugleweed, carpet bugle)
Aubrieta deltoidea (rock cress)
Phlox subulata (moss pink)

SUMMER
Achillea tomentosa (woolly milfoil)
Armeria maritima (sea pink, thrift)
Campanula carpatica (Carpathian bellflower)
Cerastium tomentosum (snow-in-summer)
Lysimachia nummulara (moneywort, creeping Jenny, creeping Charley)

Mentha requienii (Corsican mint)
Sedum acre (goldmoss sedum)
Thymus pseudolanuginosus (woolly thyme)
Thymus praecox arcticus (mother of thyme)

ANNUALS FOR PAVING
Brachycome iberidifolia (swan river daisy)
Dyssodia tenuiloba (Dahlberg daisy, golden fleece)
Eschscholzia californica (California poppy)
Lobelia erinus (edging lobelia)
Lobularia maritima (sweet alyssum)
Portulaca grandiflora (moss rose)
Viola tricolor (Johnny-jump-up)

SUCCESSFUL CONTAINER GARDENS

The best-looking containers are designed to be small gardens holding several types of flowers—upright ones to create height, bushy ones for fullness, and cascading types to soften the container's edge. Here a hibiscus, a tropical shrub, is softened with cascading verbena.

Growing flowers in containers is one way to get color where you want it—right beside the front door or as a focal point on the patio. Here are some planting and growing tips to ensure your success with container growing.

• Be sure the container has a drainage hole, and cover it with a piece of window screen to keep the soil in the planter.

• Choose a lightweight, peat-based soil mix as a growing medium, not garden soil.

• Water thoroughly several times a week because containers dry out rapidly. Hooking up containers to an automatic drip irrigation system saves labor and keeps plants healthy.

• Fertilize once a week using a ¼-strength dilution of soluble high-phosphate fertilizer such as 10-20-20, or mix time-release fertilizer pellets designed for bedding plants (such as Osmocote®) into the soil mix for a three-month nutrient supply.

• Closely plant several types of annuals in each container, using trailing plants to tumble over the edges of the containers and upright plants to provide height.

BRICK PATTERNS

Bricks can be arranged in a variety of attractive patterns to create a welcoming walk or spacious patio. Choose a pattern whose texture and mood suits your garden's design. The patterns shown here are popular and well-known to any experienced mason .

TRADITIONAL

JACK-ON-JACK

GEOMETRICAL

HERRINGBONE

PINWHEEL

BASKET WEAVE

HALF-BASKET
WEAVE

WHORLING
SQUARE

PATIO GARDEN

Blooming predominately in shades of orange, peach, blue, and white, the garden creates a bright transition from patio to lawn. Paving plants, planters filled with annuals, and a small shade garden soften the stones and echo the border.

PERENNIALS

A *Anaphalis triplinervis* (pearly everlasting), 3
B *Campanula persicifolia* 'Telham Beauty,' 3
C *Heuchera micrantha* 'Palace Purple' (purple-leaf coralbells), 4
D *Veronica spicata* (spiked speedwell), 8
E *Bergenia cordifolia* (heart-leaf bergenia), 5
F *Hemerocallis* 'Stella de Oro' (daylily), 6
G *Aster* 'Mt. Everest' (fall aster), 1
H *Chrysanthemum* x *rubellum* 'Mary Stoker,' 3
I *Iris siberica* 'Caesar's Brother' (Siberian iris), 2
J *Liatris spicata* 'Floristan White' (spike gayfeather), 3
K *Achillea millefolium* 'Orange Queen' (common yarrow), 5
L *Solidago* hybrid 'Peter Pan' (goldenrod), 1
M *Aquilegia flabellata* (fan columbine), 3
N *Sedum* x *telephium* 'Autumn Joy' (autumn joy stonecrop), 1
O *Geranium pratense* (cranesbill), 5
P *Aquilegia* x *hybrida* 'Crimson Star' (hybrid columbine), 3
Q *Coreopsis verticillata* 'Moonbeam' (threadleaf coreopsis), 5
R *Campanula carpatica* 'Wedgewood Blue' (bellflower), 10
S *Thymus praecox arcticus* (mother of thyme), 3
T *Astilbe taquetii* 'Superba' (fall astilbe), 3
U *Hosta plantaginea* (August lily), 3
V *Polemonium caeruleum* (Jacob's ladder), 6
W *Liriope muscari variegata* (blue lilyturf), 5
X *Iris cristata* (crested iris), 1
Y *Viola cornuta* 'Jersey Gem' (horned violet), 3
Z *Lamium maculatum* 'White Nancy' (spotted dead nettle), 2

ANNUALS

AA *Petunia* x *hybrida* 'Coral Flash' (petunia), 24
BB *Nicotiana alata* 'Nicki White' (flowering tobacco), 36
CC *Centaurea cineraria* 'Silverdust' (dusty miller, silver lace), 6
DD *Verbena* x *hybrida* 'Peaches and Cream' (verbena), 14
EE *Dyssodia tenuiloba* (Dahlberg daisy), 7
FF *Lobularia maritima* 'Carpet of Snow' (sweet alyssum), 12
GG *Lobelia erinus* 'Cambridge Blue' (edging lobelia), 25

ORNAMENTAL GRASSES

HH *Pennisetum alopecuroides* (fountain grass), 1

BULBS

II *Lycoris squamigera* (resurrection lily), 12
JJ *Chionodoxa luciliae* (glory-of-the-snow), 25
KK *Narcissus* x *poeticus* (pheasant's-eye narcissus), 12
LL *Tulipa clusiana* (candystick tulip), 24
MM *Crocus* x *vernus* (Dutch crocus), 25

ROSES

NN *Rosa* 'Fred Loads' (shrub rose), 3

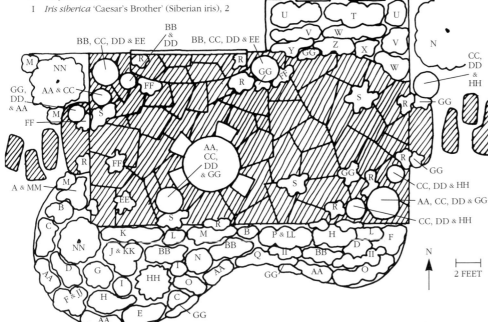

N

2 FEET

Above left: Most Oriental lilies, such as this gold-band lily, emit an intoxicating sweet fragrance that permeates the garden when the weather is warm and sultry.

Above right: Appreciated as much for their wonderful fragrance as for their lovely blossoms, many old-fashioned flowers, such as the dame's rocket (*Hesperis matronalis*) and hybrid musk roses (*Rosa* 'Penelope') shown here, perform beautifully in today's gardens.

GARDENING FOR FRAGRANCE

In past eras, people placed high value on scents and even endowed fragrant flowers and herbs with magical qualities. Perfumes, derived from flowers, fought body odors in the Middle Ages, when bathing was an infrequent occurrence. Herbs strewn on floors inside houses covered up bad odors. Fragrant plants, such as the lovely apothecary rose, were even thought to ward off the plague.

Today, we still value perfume for its sex appeal and ability to ignite romantic feelings. And the sweet, spicy, musky, and fruity fragrances of the flowers and foliage in our gardens provide one of the most delightful—and memorable—experiences of gardening.

A flower's fragrance comes from volatile oils stored in special glands on the petals. Their delicious scent attracts pollinating insects such as bees and butterflies. Floral perfume may be most noticeable on warm, humid days when the air is still, because the volatile oils linger in the air. Many flowers, especially white ones, save their perfume for the evening, because moths serve as their pollinators.

Aromatic leaves usually accumulate oil glands below the leaf surface, releasing their scent only when the leaves are crushed or broken. Some, however, store oils in surface glands, which readily release their aroma when warmed by the sun or gently brushed by a foot or skirt. Scented foliage, often with an astringent or resinous scent, is a defense mechanism that deters insects and animals from munching too much.

Scent appeal is a very personal matter. Some fragrances appeal to some people but not to others—one person's rose may be another person's skunk cabbage. Many people, for instance, dislike the aroma of marigolds or chrysanthemums, while their scent evokes pleasant memories for others.

OLD-FASHIONED FLOWERS FOR FRAGRANCE

Many of today's modern hybrid flowers lack the wonderful perfume of the cherished cottage garden plants. Regrettably, in the search for a larger, more bepetaled rose, its fragrance sometimes got left behind in the compost pile. Many modern roses have no remarkable scent, while the old garden roses of yesteryear were cherished as much for their perfume as for their beauty.

You may need to seek out the simpler old-fashioned flowers to plant in your garden if a heady fragrance is your goal. Heliotrope, for example, is an old-fashioned annual that has for the most part escaped the breeder's attention. To some people's noses, this wild Peruvian plant smells like a fresh-baked cherry pie, and indeed its common name is cherry pie in England. The most popular modern cultivar, however, is a scentless, dark-purple dwarf called 'Marine.' You can get seeds for the unimproved, fragrant species from a specialty catalog.

Right: Designed for strolling and sitting among fragrant plants, this informal garden creates a wonderful sensual experience for anyone who lingers in it. Blooming in July are: fragrant daylily (*Hemerocallis* 'Hyperion'), Oriental lily (*Lilium* 'Casa Blanca'), and the species form of flowering tobacco (*Nicotiana alata*).

Above: Thyme (*Thymus* spp.) sprawls over the treads of a stone stairway, releasing its herbal scent when anyone climbs the stairs.

DESIGNING A FRAGRANCE GARDEN

Although fragrant flowers and plants with aromatic foliage work in any style or type of garden, you'll enjoy them most if you locate them in a frequently visited area of your property. Along the walk to the front door, beside a patio, and under a window are good locations. This is, after all, a garden to be smelled even more than it is to be viewed.

Many public gardens have "gardens for the blind" filled with fragrant plants. These gardens usually feature raised beds, which bring the aromatic plants right up to nose level. You might want to do the same.

It's best to locate plants whose aroma develops when the foliage is crushed along a walkway so that as you brush past them you release their fragrant oils. You can tuck low-growing scented herbs, such as thyme, chamomile, and Corsican mint between the paving stones in a walk or patio. Be sure to position resinous plants such as rosemary and scented geraniums in full-sun locations, where the heat of the day releases their fragrant oils.

A garden designed to be enjoyed in the evening features night-scented plants in white or pastel shades so they can be seen easily in the dim light. For the enjoyment of family and friends, plant such a garden surrounding a patio and place fragrant plants in containers along the house where their heady perfume will float through the night air on sultry summer evenings.

FRAGRANT GARDEN

Take a leisurely stroll through this country garden—the stepping stones are designed to slow down your pace—and find yourself enveloped with heavenly fragrances. Every plant in this garden—from the roses to the violets—is scented.

PERENNIALS

A   *Viola odorata* (sweet violet), 10
B   *Galium odoratum* (sweet woodruff), 25
C   *Stachys byzantina* 'Silver Carpet' (lamb's-ears), 17
D   *Paeonia lactiflora* 'Avalanche' (Chinese peony), 2
E   *Phlox paniculata* 'White Admiral' (garden phlox), 3
F   *Monarda didyma* 'Croftway Pink' (bee-balm), 3
G   *Chrysanthemum* x *morifolium* 'Yellow Bird' (garden mum), 5
H   *Salvia officinalis* 'Tricolor' (garden sage), 1
I   *Astilbe chinensis* 'Pumila' (Chinese astilbe), 3
J   *Lavandula angustifolia* 'Munstead Dwarf' (lavender), 5
K   *Hemerocallis* 'Hyperion' (daylily), 3
L   *Perovskia atriplicifolia* (Russian sage), 1
M   *Hesperis matronalis* (dame's rocket), 6
N   *Alchemilla mollis* (lady's mantle), 4
O   *Hosta plantaginea* (August lily), 3
P   *Monarda didyma* 'Violet Queen' (bee-balm), 2
Q   *Phlox paniculata* 'Progress' (garden phlox), 2
R   *Chrysanthemum* x *morifolium* 'Alert' (garden mum), 5
S   *Saponaria officinalis* (bouncing Bet), 2

ANNUALS

T   *Perilla frutescens* 'Crispa' (beefsteak plant), 12
U   *Dianthus chinensis* 'Raspberry Parfait' (China pink), 15

BULBS

V   *Hyacinthus orientalis* 'City of Haarlem' (hyacinth), 50
W   *Narcissus jonquilla* 'Geranium,' 50
X   *Lilium* 'Black Dragon' (trumpet lily), 3
Y   *Lilium* 'Golden Temple' (trumpet lily), 3
Z   *Polianthes tuberosa* (tuberose), 7

ROSES

AA   *Rosa rugosa* 'Blanc Double de Coubert,' 1
BB   *Rosa* 'Graham Thomas' (English rose), 1
CC   *Rosa* 'Penelope' (hybrid musk rose), 1

90

FRAGRANT PLANTS

These plants boast either scented flowers or scented foliage. Those marked with an * release their aromas primarily at night.

FRAGRANT PERENNIALS

SPRING
Arabis caucasica (wall rock cress)
Galium odoratum (sweet woodruff)
Viola odorata (sweet violet)

SUMMER
Alchemilla mollis (lady's mantle)
Calamintha nepeta (calamint)
Centranthus ruber (red valerian, Jupiter's beard)
Chamaemelum nobile (chamomile)
Dianthus spp. (pinks)
Hemerocallis 'Hyperion' (daylily)
Hesperis matronalis (dame's rocket, sweet rocket)*
Hosta plantaginea (August lily)*
Lavandula angustifolia (lavender)
Mentha spp. (mints)
Monarda didyma (bee-balm, oswego tea)
Nepeta x *faassenii* (catmint)
Origanum vulgare 'Aureum' (golden oregano, golden marjoram)
Paeonia lactiflora (Chinese peony, garden peony)
Phlox paniculata (garden phlox, summer phlox)
Ruta graveolens (rue)
Salvia officinalis (garden sage)
Santolina chamaecyparissus (lavender cotton)
Saponaria officinalis (bouncing Bet)*
Thymus spp. (thymes)

LATE SUMMER AND FALL
Chrysanthemum x *morifolium* (garden mum)
Perovskia atriplicifolia (Russian sage)

FRAGRANT ANNUALS
Anethum graveolens (dill)
Cheiranthus cheiri (wallflower)
Clarkia amonea (godetia, satin flower)
Datura metel (downy thorn apple, horn-of-plenty)*
Dianthus chinensis (China pink)
Lathyrus odoratus (sweet pea)
Matthiola incana (stock)
Nicotiana alata (flowering tobacco)*
Ocimum basilicum (sweet basil)
Pelargonium spp. (scented geraniums)
Perilla frutescens (perilla, beefsteak plant, shiso)
Petunia x *hybrida* (petunia)
Phlox drummondii (annual phlox)

Polianthes tuberosa

FRAGRANT BULBS

SPRING
Convallaria majalis (lily-of-the-valley)
Hyacinthus orientalis (Dutch hyacinth)
Narcissus jonquilla (jonquil)
Narcissus x *tazetta* (paperwhite narcissus)
Tulipa x *hybrida* 'Bellona,' 'Christmas Marvel,' 'General De Wet,' 'Golden Melody,' 'High Society' (hybrid tulips)

SUMMER
Acidanthera murielae (Abyssinian gladiolus)
Lilium spp. and hybrids (lilies)
Freesia hybrids (freesia)
Polianthes tuberosa (tuberose)*

LATE-SUMMER AND FALL
Amaryllis belladona (belladona lily, naked lady)
Lycoris squamigera (resurrection lily, naked ladies)

FRAGRANT ROSES

LARGE-FLOWERED CLIMBERS:
'America,' 'Climbing Crimson Glory,' 'Dan Juan,' 'Elegance,' 'New Dawn,' 'White Dawn'

HYBRID TEA:
'Blue Moon,' 'Broadway,' 'Chrysler Imperial,' 'Crimson Glory,' 'Curly Pink,' 'Fragrant Cloud,' 'Mr. Lincoln,' 'Rosyln Carter,' 'Sheer Bliss,' 'Sunsprite,' 'Sutter's Gold,' 'Sweet Surrender,' 'Tiffany,' 'Voodoo'

FLORIBUNDA:
'Amber Queen,' 'Angel Face,' 'Fashion,' 'Iceberg,' 'Intrigue,' 'Saratoga,' 'Spartan,' 'Sun Flare,' 'Sunsprite'

GRANDIFLORA:
'Arizona,' 'Queen Elizabeth,' 'Sonia,' 'White Lightnin''

OLD GARDEN ROSES:
Moss roses, Musk roses, Hybrid musk roses, Bourbon roses, Centifolia roses, Damask roses

ENGLISH ROSES:
'Graham Thomas,' 'Heritage,' 'Mary Rose,' 'Othello'

SHRUB ROSES:
'Blanc Double de Coubert,' 'Dortmund,' 'Erfurt,' 'Frau Dagmar Hastrup,' 'Kathleen,' 'Penelope'

ROMANTIC OLD GARDEN ROSES

The roses of yesteryear, collectively called old garden roses, are the roses of myth and legend, of poetry and romance—the flower that throughout history has symbolized romantic love, beauty, and youth. These recently rediscovered roses, not their modern counterparts, are the roses cultivated for their perfume, the roses mentioned in Ancient Greek myths, the roses carried back from the Far East as trophies by gallant knights in shining armor. These are the roses that symbolized the warring clansmen in the War of the Roses, that figured in Shakespeare's *A Midsummer Night's Dream,* and that were featured in Dutch Master paintings. Old roses are the luxuriant roses grown in country estates and cottage gardens of the 18th and 19th centuries.

Most old garden roses grow into large shrubs or rampant climbers and bloom lavishly but once a year, although some repeat their bloom. They may have clusters of five-petaled flowers with whorls of showy yellow stamens in their centers (called a "single"), or be so endowed with petals that the open flowers weigh the branches down (called a "double"). Unlike the long petals of the high-centered modern rose, the central petals of a double-flowered old garden rose are short, forming a tightly folded center (described as being "quartered") when fully open and giving the cup-shaped flower a voluptuous appearance. Most emit a rich, sensual perfume. Pastel pink, crimson, and rose-red, often with mauve or lavender overtones, are the most prevalent floral colors, although white and rich purple roses also grace these old-fashioned beauties.

ANCIENT ROOTS

Three roses—the gallica roses (*Rosa gallica*), alba roses (*Rosa* x *alba*), and damask roses (*Rosa* x *damascena*)—are among the oldest plants still cultivated. Grown in the Far and Near East during Biblical times, these roses probably were brought to Western Europe by the Crusaders. The blood of the gallica rose, and perhaps the damask and alba roses as well, flows somewhere in the family tree of every known old garden or modern rose.

The apothecary rose (*Rosa gallica officinalis*)—with beautiful semidouble, crimson-pink flowers on a 4-foot-tall-and-wide shrub—was commercially grown in France for preserves, effusions, and healing potions during the Middle Ages. In England, this highly fragrant rose became the emblem of the House of Lancaster, while a white, semidouble alba rose (*Rosa alba*

Below: The gallica rose 'Charles de Mills' (*Rosa gallica)* features huge, flat, wavy-petaled blossoms that open crimson and slowly age to deep purple.

Left: Most old garden roses form handsome shrubs cloaked with attractive leaves and produce a profusion of flowers once a year. The damask rose 'Isphahan' (*Rosa* x *damascena*), shown here with a soft underplanting of fragrant lady's mantle (*Alchemilla mollis*), produces its fragrant blossoms for as long as two months beginning in early summer.

Damask roses produce sprays of very fragrant blossoms noted for their rich damask scent. The flowers are a source of attar of roses, highly prized in perfume making. This one is the cultivar 'La Ville de Bruxelles,' whose blossoms are among the largest of the old garden roses.

semi-plena) represented the House of York. After these two houses warred (the War of the Roses, as it was coincidentally called), the two houses were joined under the leadership of the Tudors. The Tudors devised an emblem featuring both roses combined into one, which later became the badge of England. The Tudor rose is actually two roses, one inside the other.

Damask roses (*Rosa* x *damascena*), thought to have originated near Damascus during Biblical times, probably descended from a natural hybrid between a local wild rose and a gallica rose. Damask roses possess a sweet perfume coveted throughout history. Ancient Romans grew damask roses in vast quantities, using the fragrant petals for rose water and scented oils and balms. They even strew the petals on their beds and floors to enhance their infamous orgies.

During the Renaissance, roses became prized garden plants, making the move from apothecary cloister gardens to the royalty's ornamental gardens. The gardeners of the British, French, and Dutch aristocracy began collecting and hybridizing roses during the 18th and 19th centuries, developing several dozen groups of old garden roses, many of which can still be found today. Cultivars in each group of old garden roses have the same species in their ancestry and bear a family resemblance to the group.

The centifolia roses, whose origins are shrouded in mystery, feature the most voluptuous flowers, often referred to as cabbage roses because of their rounded, many-petaled blossoms. These are the roses depicted in Victorian paintings, fabrics, and wallpapers. The Dutch introduced more than 200 cultivars of cabbage roses between 1580 and 1710. The moss rose, with its bristly stems and calyxes that release a resinous fragrance, originated as a sport of the centifolia roses in the mid-18th century.

Early in the 18th century, trade with the Orient brought two tender, repeat-flowering roses—the tea and China roses—to Western gardens. These continuous-flowering roses also bloomed in colors yet unseen by English, French, and Dutch gardeners: red, yellow, and orange. Their buds possessed a more elegant, elongated appearance.

Hybrids between China and tea roses and the earlier old garden roses produced astonishing results: the extremely fragrant clustered blossoms of the bourbon and portland roses, which were hybridized extensively at Empress Josephine's palace, the Chateau de Malmaison near Paris.

Noisette roses, first discovered on a plantation in South Carolina in 1760 and later refined in France, enjoyed a brief day in the sun. Featuring lovely clusters of constantly blooming fragrant flowers, this group unfortunately lacked winter hardiness because of its tea rose parentage. While noisette roses perform well in the American South, French gardeners longed for a more cold-hardy rose with similar looks. Portland roses, developed from a red China rose and a bourbon rose, filled this bill for a short time, until hybrid perpetual roses appeared. Featuring even larger, globular, fragrant flowers that bloomed throughout the season, hybrid perpetual roses captivated Victorian gardeners. It became fashionable to exhibit them in flower shows and for ladies to carry a cut flower as a nosegay.

The first hybrid tea rose, introduced in 1867 and bred from a tea rose and a hybrid perpetual rose, put an end to all that, and old garden roses were quickly forgotten in all the excitement. The era of the modern rose had begun. Hybrid teas seemed to be the ultimate in roses: large, elegant, high-centered, fragrant blossoms that bloomed repeatedly from early summer through fall on reasonably cold-hardy plants .

All other groups of roses developed after 1867 are termed modern roses; previous groups and new hybrids made in those groups are termed old garden roses. Modern roses include hybrid teas, grandifloras, floribundas, polyanthas, ramblers, climbers, and the latest group—English roses, which offer considerable old garden rose character.

RESURRECTED FROM THE PAST

Out of fashion for about 100 years after the aristocracy discarded them, old garden roses managed to survive through the years in humble cottage gardens. Now, old cultivars are being propagated and reintroduced from plants found growing in abandoned gardens. They are enjoying a resurgence of popularity, and deservedly so. Old garden roses, according to some enthusiasts, shouldn't even share the same name as modern hybrid tea roses, so different are they in appearance and temperament.

In contrast to modern roses, old roses are usually large, garden-worthy shrubs or climbers rather than the stiff, sparsely branched bushes of the hybrid teas and floribundas. Their flowers usually are highly fragrant and born in luxuriant clusters. Most old roses make handsome specimens even when out of bloom, with a heavy cloak of leaves in summer, bright red berrylike rose hips from fall well into winter, and colorful thorny branches when leafless. Unlike modern roses, these tough, easy-to-care-for plants don't need coddling to get them through the winter or save them from the ravages of pests and diseases.

OLD ROSES IN YOUR GARDEN

Because they grow into handsome, shrubby plants with good root systems, old garden roses combine well with perennials, bulbs, and orna-

Left: The fragrant blossoms of the English rose 'Graham Thomas,' one of the few yellow shrub roses, bloom nonstop on a shapely, garden-worthy plant.

Above: Although their blossoms and plant shapes resemble old garden roses, the new English roses have a distinct advantage—they bloom repeatedly. Shown here in a June garden is 'Kathryn Morley.'

Old garden roses bring beauty of flower and form to this country-style Connecticut garden when they come into full bloom in June. Creating a softening border in complementary colors is an edging of catmint (*Nepeta* x *faassenii*), which blooms repeatedly if cut back after each flush of flowers.

mental grasses. Annuals should be carefully planted beneath them so as to not harm the rose's roots. These roses fit perfectly into mixed borders and need not be segregated into separate beds, as so often is done with finicky modern roses whose root systems and disease-prone foliage can't compete with other plants.

Although you can use them in both formal and informal gardens, old garden roses look best in country and cottage gardens because their exuberant growth gives them a casual, unkempt air. Their wildness and sensuality suits them to the rumble-tumble of a vine-draped cottage. The

more lanky growers among them, such as the cabbage roses, look delightful tied up to cascade from a pillar, arch, fence, or garden gate.

Because they bloom in early summer to mid-summer, you'll want to highlight the rose blossoms with companion plants that bloom at the same time. Blue, lavender, purple, pastel pink, or white flowers suit the rosy colors of any and all old garden roses. Although not actually an old garden rose, rambling roses, which can ascend a tree or low building, share the romantic air of an old garden rose and make good companions.

Bourbon, portland, and hybrid perpetual roses—as well as the modern English roses that belong with old garden roses—repeat their bloom in midsummer and early fall, so be sure to provide blooming companions for them, too. Try using neighboring plants with colored foliage so you'll get spring through fall mileage out of the same plants. Silver-foliaged plants such as artemisia and lamb's-ears and purple-foliaged plants such as 'Burgundy Glow' bugleweed and 'Palace Purple' coralbells as well as smokebush and purple barberry shrubs also complement the color scheme.

While you're thinking about enhancing the old roses with companion plants, be sure to plan the garden to include plenty of flowers that bloom both before and after old roses. You can design a complete garden picture with spring-flowering bulbs and perennials to form skirts of flowers under the rosebushes and then add annuals, late-summer- and fall-blooming perennials, lilies, and ornamental grasses to provide the main garden interest in the months after the majority of the roses wane.

GROWING OLD ROSES

In general, old garden roses are much easier to care for and more disease-resistant than modern roses. Each group differs a little in its pruning needs, and some will even tolerate a bit of shade.

This Northwest cottage garden relies on repeat-blooming, old-fashioned-looking roses for summer-long color and fragrance. Shown in late May are, from left to right: English roses 'Wife of Bath' and 'Mary Rose,' *Rosa rugosa* 'Grootendorst,' and large-flowered climber 'Madame Grégoire Staechelin' on the arbor.

OLD-FASHIONED ROSE GARDEN

The rugged character of this country garden, complete with a rough-hewn fence and fieldstone patio, makes the perfect setting for a collection of romantic roses. Companion plants bloom in shades of pink and blue, with silver and purple foliage plants.

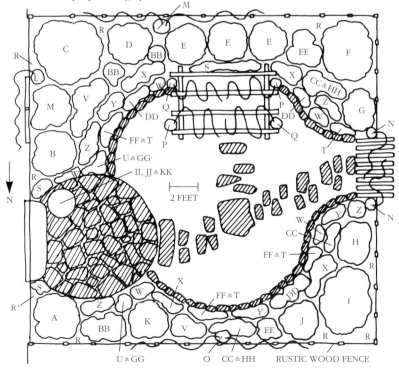

ROSES

A   'Madame Hardy' (damask), 1

B   'Gertrude Jekyll' (English), 1

C   'Semi Plena' (alba), 1

D   'Louise Odier' (bourbon), 1

E   'Reine des Violettes' (hybrid perpetual), 3

F   'Queen of Denmark' (alba), 1

G   'Othello' (English), 1

H   'Rosa Mundi' (gallica), 1

I   'Maréchal daVoust' (moss), 1

J   'Mary Rose' (English), 1

K   'Heritage' (English), 1

L   'Climbing Cécile Brünner' (climbing polyantha), 1

M   'Magna Charta' (hybrid perpetual), 1

N   'Zéphirine Drouhin' (bourbon), 2

O   'Paul Ricault' (centifolia), 1

P   'Lavender Lassie' (hybrid musk), 2

Q   'Sombreuil' (hybrid tea), 2

PERENNIALS

R   *Galium odoratum* (sweet woodruff), 20

S   *Ajuga reptans* 'Burgundy Glow' (bugleweed), 6

T   *Stachys byzantina* (lamb's-ears), 13

U   *Nepeta* x *faassenii* (catmint), 4

V   *Platycodon grandiflorus* 'Shell Pink' (balloon flower), 3

W   *Campanula portenschlagiana* (Dalmation bellflower), 8

X   *Geranium pratense* 'Mrs. Kendall Clarke' (cranesbill), 4

Y   *Lavandula angustifolia* 'Hidcote' (lavender), 6

Z   *Campanula glomerata* 'Superba' (clustered bellflower), 8

AA   *Campanula lactiflora* (milky bellflower), 3

BB   *Phlox carolina* 'Miss Lingard' (Carolina phlox), 4

CC   *Artemisia* x 'Powis Castle' (white sage), 4

DD   *Heuchera micrantha* 'Palace Purple' (purple-leaf coralbells), 8

EE   *Aconitum carmichaelii* (azure monkshood), 3

BULBS

FF   *Tulipa pulchella* (dwarf taurus tulip), 40

GG   *Crocus* x *vernus* (Dutch crocus), 30

HH   *Narcissus triandrus*, (angel's tears), 40

ANNUALS

II   *Salvia farinacea* 'Victoria' (mealy-cup sage), 4

JJ   *Petunia* x *hybrida* 'Appleblossom' (petunia), 2

KK   *Brachycome iberidifolia* (swan river daisy), 3

97

CHAPTER FOUR

DESIGNING TRADITIONAL GARDENS

Create a Backyard Haven with a Formal, Symmetrical Garden

Opposite: A formal English border, such as the one shown here, features straight lines, crisp edges, and repeating masses of flowers. Shown: catmint (*Nepeta* x *faassenii* 'Six Hills Giant'), lady's mantle (*Alchemilla mollis*), sundrops (*Oenothera tetragona*), and astilbe (*Astilbe* x *arendsii* 'Fanal').

Left: Fashioned in the shape of a Celtic knot, this knot garden creates a formal effect and year-round structure in a courtyard garden. Boxwood forms the knot, which is filled with forget-me-nots (*Myosotis sylvatica*) in spring and different flowers in other seasons.

Traditional flower gardens, designed with straight or gently curving lines and well-groomed plantings, create a refuge from the chaos of the outside world. Formal and symmetrical by their very nature, yet brimming with flowers, traditional gardens bring a sense of order and peace that appeals to many people and blends with traditional styles of architecture.

The traditional perennial flower border has its roots in turn-of-the-century England, when the genteel class discovered the humble cottage garden and transformed it into a grand-scale flower garden. The lavish result still symbolizes the epitome in flower gardening the world over, for nothing conjures up a more flower-filled image than the thought of an "English garden."

FROM CHAOS TO GRANDEUR AND BACK AGAIN

During the Renaissance, cottage gardens continued to quietly flourish relatively unchanged along the country lanes of the British Isles, while the pleasure gardens of the aristocracy underwent dramatic changes. Although still patterned after monastery gardens, with parallel walks crossing at right angles in their centers, the gardens of the rich began to feature large numbers of flowers. (The vegetables and herbs were separated into walled kitchen gardens.) Clipped lavender, boxwood, hyssop, lavender cotton, or rosemary hedges made decorative edges along the walks, and perennial flowers filled the beds.

Eventually, the straight lines of these formal gardens began to twist and turn, but still in a methodical fashion. The knot garden was born in England during 16th-century Elizabethan times and dominated garden design during that century. Probably influenced by the Oriental carpets that were being imported into Europe, knot gardens featured clipped plants arranged to form interlocking patterns resembling heralds or coats of arms. Clipped evergreen herbs or shrubs formed the knots, while small herbs and flowers such as violets, daisies, basil, and marjoram filled the spaces between the knots.

During the 17th century, wealthy Europeans began planting elaborate landscapes composed of vast lawns and trees, eschewing colorful blossoms in favor of clipped greenery. The French aristocracy developed grand landscapes, called parterres, featuring lawns and sheared boxwood hedges in elaborate geometrical patterns meant to resemble an embroidery. Colored gravel, not flowers, filled out the patterns.

The English, however, continued to indulge in flowers, and their gardens took a different road from the formal greenery of French and Italian gardens. Enthralled with the tender, exotic plants being discovered and brought back from distant lands, English gardeners indulged in a riot of explosive floral color. Tender annual flowers were propagated in hothouses and then planted in rows and blocks composed of a single type of flower in a style called bedding out. These extravagant summer gardens were patchworks of flamboyant colors—the more outrageous the better. We still see annuals bedded out this way in parks and municipal plantings, although the style has lost favor among most sophisticated garden designers.

Before the turn of the century, several innovative British garden designers, most notably Gertrude Jekyll and William Robinson, rebelled against the bedding out trend, finding it too contrived and costly. They sought inspiration from the English cottage garden, turning back to hardy flowering plants—perennials, herbs, bulbs, roses, and flowering vines—to create an ever-changing display of flowers on a grand scale. It's primarily the garden style created during this time that we think of today when we use the term "English garden."

ENGLISH BORDERS

Gertrude Jekyll studied art as a young woman but later turned her talents to designing gardens, employing the skills and sensitivity of a painter in her English flower borders. She approached garden design as if the gardens were living paintings, carefully arranging plants in juxtaposition with one another for their color and textural effects and using her artist's eye to create balance and proportion.

Although we think of them as formal today, Gertrude Jekyll's designs were much more naturalistic and informal than the garish color patterns popular during Queen Victoria's era. She allowed plants to tumble and spill around each other in free-form drifts rather than relegating them to stiff blocks, but within a formal framework of neatly pruned hedges, grand lawns, and walkways. Flowers and foliage plants exploded in masses of a single type—as if they were bold brush strokes on a canvas—but because she relied on hardy perennials, the floral show was soft and ever changing.

Opposite top: A gently curving herbaceous border, designed in the English tradition, fills the front and side yards of this Oregon landscape with flowers and greenery. A tall evergreen hedge provides a backdrop for the blossoms and creates a necessary privacy screen, while a curving lawn invites visitors to stroll.

Opposite bottom: Elegant, perfectly groomed, and overflowing with billowing flowers, this double border represents the epitome of the formal English garden. The generous drifts of flowers repeat along the length of the borders and from side to side, creating a sense of continuity and harmony. A brick wall encloses the space, providing a backdrop for one border, and a gravel walk leads visitors to the shade of a wisteria-clad arbor.

CREATING AN HERBACEOUS BORDER

You can take inspiration from Gertrude Jekyll and adapt the dramatic herbaceous borders of her beautiful English estate gardens to your own property. Considerably scaled down, but using the same principles of design, your English garden will overflow with glorious flowers from spring through fall. Like the traditional English border, yours can rely on herbaceous perennials as the garden mainstays, and include clumps of spring-blooming bulbs for early color and annuals for summer through fall continuity. Old garden roses might be used in large borders as shrubs or climbers.

Design your herbaceous border along the edge of a lawn or walk with a hedge as a uniform green background—privet, yew, boxwood, or Japanese holly make good choices. For a true traditional effect, the hedge should be sheared into a neat green wall about 4 or 5 feet tall. An-

101

informally pruned hedge works almost as well, however, and requires less work to maintain, as long as you allow enough room for the hedge to grow to its ultimate size.

Athough most American properties don't have walls enclosing them, you're in luck if a tall brick or stone wall borders your garden. Use the wall as a wonderful backdrop to the flowers and train climbing roses and vines to grow up and over it.

Create the border with a straight or gently curving front edge, making its depth in proportion to its length. Jekyll's borders could be as long as 150 feet and as wide as 12 feet, but you can create an effective display with a border 20 to 25 feet long and 4 to 6 feet deep. Include a narrow path at the back of a deep border so you can easily tend the plants in the rear.

RULES OF PROCEDURE

One of Jekyll's ways of using flower color was to begin a border with cool blues, lavenders, and pinks at one end and work her way down the border so that hot yellows and oranges predominated in the center of the border's length. The border then shifted back to cool colors, with masses of purple and lavender flowers at the far end. This arrangement creates a feeling of great distance. White flowers punctuated these borders throughout.

You can follow a similar scheme in your border, or apply the color rules discussed in Chapter 2. Whatever color scheme you choose, don't skimp on plants. The formality of the English garden demands that you closely follow the design rules laid out in Chapter 2. Create large drifts by planting at least three to 10 of each kind of flower together. Arrange plants by height to create a foreground, midground, and background; and repeat plants throughout the length of the border to give it rhythm.

CREATING A DOUBLE BORDER

One of Gertrude Jekyll's most formal styles of garden design is a double border, where two long, straight herbaceous borders run along each side of a wide gravel path. The borders need not be mirror images, but by repeating flowers and flower combinations from one side of the border to the other, the entire garden holds together, resembling a wonderful picture. The borders should be backed up with formally clipped hedges or stone or brick walls, although a fence is a more American solution.

You can create a double border along the side of your property, as a separate garden room, or along the property's main axis, perhaps running straight out from a door or sitting area. You

Opposite: Clipped hedges enclose this double border and create a dark green background to set off the flowers. Tall perennials grow in front of the hedge, with the midground and foreground planted with tulips in spring and annuals in summer.

Above: An ivy-covered stone wall makes a striking backdrop to a garden, giving it a sense of enclosure while setting off the flowers.

might want to edge the entire length of both borders with a uniform plant, such as clipped boxwood, or choose any of Jekyll's other favorite edgers, such as coralbells, edging candytuft, or lamb's ears.

A double border is a dramatic, but formal, garden. Because hedges or walls enclose it, the garden becomes a lovely separate room with an inviting path to lead you among the garden riches. The path allows you to stroll slowly along the border, enclosed within the intimacy of the living walls of greenery and flowers. You might want to place a garden bench—a stone or teak bench is traditional—in an alcove at the end of the border or in a cutout along its length.

Left: A teak garden bench—traditional in English gardens—provides a place to sit and contemplate the rich pageant of flowers. Shown in midsummer are: purple coneflower (*Echinacea purpurea* 'Magnus'), false sunflower (*Heliopsis helianthoides*), shasta daisy (*Chrysanthemum* x *superbum* 'Alaska'), and lamb's-ears (*Stachys byzantina*).

The climate and soil in Memphis, Tennessee, bears no resemblance to the idyllic growing conditions of the British Isles, but that didn't stop Kitty from creating an English-style double border at her home. She and Neil combated the heavy clay soil by first turning it over to a depth of 1 foot, then spreading 4 inches of peat moss and 2 inches of sand on top and turning and turning and turning, until all of the ingredients were well mixed. They top-dress the garden with 2 inches of rotted horse manure every fall. The extensive soil amendments raised the soil level, so they created gently sloped raised beds to facilitate runoff

A DOUBLE BORDER GARDENER

After years of enthusiastic gardening, Kitty Taylor recently made her hobby into her profession and launched a garden design business. As an outcome of Kitty's endeavor, her husband, Neil, launched a second career by starting a nursery. Neil says now she gets up in the morning with a new zest for life.

The double border, shown here in late spring before the warm-season lawn grass has greened up, acquires a gracious, formal feeling from its straight lines and repetition of flowers from side to side. A fence encloses the garden on both sides, creating a separate garden room, and a wooden clematis-clad arbor creates a shady retreat for an English teak bench. The purple iris so prominently featured is Siberian iris (*Iris siberica* 'Caesar's Brother'), and the blue flowers are willow amsonia (*Amsonia tabernaemontana*).

and prevent waterlogging. Kitty chose to border the raised beds with Tennessee hardwood landscape timbers—an economical local product—rather than stones, which are costly because they must be imported into her area. She uses stones in other parts of the garden, however.

Summer's sultry weather is even more difficult to deal with, but Kitty combats it with heat-loving flowers. Her standbys include: Carolina lupine, salvias, veronicas, 'Moonbeam' coreopsis, balloon flower, purple coneflower in both its purple and white forms, boltonia, and ornamental grasses.

Ellen's California garden gets its English style from straight symmetrical lines and lavish brush strokes of repeating flowers. Skillful interplanting of tulips, pansies, and sweet alyssum packs a lot of color into a small space. When the tulips pass and hot weather puts an end to winter and spring annuals, Ellen plants heat defiers such as zinnia and blue salvia. She cuts back and fertilizes pansies and alyssum to encourage rebloom when cooler weather returns.

AN ENGLISH BORDER GARDENER

With a Ph.D. in botany, Ellen Henke certainly studied her science, but she cultivated her talent for garden design on her own. Ellen loves to experiment with new flowers because she knows that mistakes with perennials and annuals are easy to fix.

Eight years ago, Ellen turned a hillside of junipers and ivy into an English garden by the sweat of her brow. Her husband, George, helped remove the junipers, while she painstakingly pulled the ivy roots. Because a power tiller can't dig deeply enough, Ellen turned the clay soil three times with a garden fork, deeply working in loads of mushroom and chicken compost. Every year the soil gets better because she top-dresses the flowers twice a year with homemade compost.

Even though the garden is in a water-rationed area, Ellen has water to spare because she groups plants according to water use and waters with a zoned irrigation system that delivers different amounts to different areas. A postage-stamp-size lawn sets off the garden; high-water-use plants surround the lawn. California natives farther up the hill require less water.

105

PERENNIALS FOR ENGLISH BORDERS

These perennials make excellent additions to an English border or island bed. When designing your garden, arrange the flowers according to height, with the lowest plants (6 inches to 1½ feet tall) in the foreground, intermediate plants (1½ to 3 feet tall) in the midground, and tall plants (3 to 5 feet tall) in the background. For a narrow border, use the tallest of the intermediate plants in the background. Keep in mind that heights vary according to cultivar; selections of some normally tall perennials may be lower growing and more compact.

EDGING AND FOREGROUND, SPRING

Ajuga spp. (bugleweeds)
Alchemilla spp. (lady's mantles)
Aurinia saxatilis (basket-of-gold)
Bellis perennis (English daisy)
Bergenia cordifolia (heart-leaf bergenia)
Chrysogonum virginianum (goldenstar)
Dicentra eximia (fringed bleeding heart)
Epimedium spp. (barrenworts)
Helleborus spp. (Christmas rose and Lenten rose)
Heuchera micrantha 'Palace Purple' (purple-leaf coralbells)
Heuchera sanguinea (coralbells)
Iberis sempervirens (edging candytuft)
Iris cristata (crested iris)
Lamium maculatum (spotted dead nettle)
Nepeta x *faassenii* (catmint)
Phlox subulata (moss pink)
Polemonium caeruleum (Jacob's ladder)
Primula veris (cowslip primrose)
Primula x *polyantha* (polyanthus primrose)
Pulmonaria spp. (lungworts)
Pulsatilla vulgaris (pasque flower)
Ruta graveolens (rue)
Santolina chamaecyparissus (lavender cotton)
Stachys byzantina (lamb's-ears)
Viola cornuta (horned violet, tufted pansy)
Viola labradorica (Labrador violet)
Viola odorata (sweet violet)
Viola tricolor (Johnny-jump-up)

EDGING AND FOREGROUND, SUMMER

Armeria maritima (sea pink, thrift)
Artemisia schmidtiana 'Silvermound' (silvermound mugwort)
Astilbe chinensis 'Pumila' (dwarf Chinese astilbe)
Astilbe simplicifolia (star astilbe)
Brunnera macrophylla (Siberian bugloss)
Campanula carpatica (Carpathian bellflower)
Campanula garganica (Gargano bellflower)
Campanula glomerata (clustered bellflower)
Cerastium tomentosum (snow-in-summer)
Chrysogonum virginianum (goldenstar)
Coreopsis rosea (pink coreopsis)
Dianthus spp. (pinks)
Erigeron x *hybridus* (fleabane)
Heuchera micrantha 'Palace Purple' (purple-leaf coralbells)

Lavandula angustifolia (lavender, English lavender)
Nepeta x *faassenii* (catmint)
Oenothera speciosa (showy evening primrose)
Prunella x *webbiana* (self-heal)
Ruta graveolens (rue)
Salvia x *superba* (hybrid blue salvia, hybrid sage)
Santolina chamaecyparissus (lavender cotton)
Saponaria ocymoides (rock soapwort)
Scabiosa caucasica (pincushion flower, scabious)
Stachys byzantina (lamb's-ears)
Stokesia laevis (Stokes' aster)
Verbena canadensis (clump verbena, rose verbena)
Veronica spicata (spiked speedwell)
Viola cornuta (horned violet)

EDGING AND FOREGROUND, LATE SUMMER AND FALL

Anaphalis cinnamomea (pearly everlasting)
Artemisia schmidtiana 'Silvermound' (silvermound mugwort)
Ceratostigma plumbaginoides (leadwort, plumbago)
Chrysanthemum weyrichii (Miyabe)
Chrysanthemum x *morifolium* (garden mum)
Chrysogonum virginianum (goldenstar)
Geranium spp. (cranesbills)
Heuchera micrantha 'Palace Purple' (purple-leaf coralbells)
Liriope muscari (blue lilyturf)
Ruta graveolens (rue)
Santolina chamaecyparissus (lavender cotton)
Stachys byzantina (lamb's-ears)
Verbena canadensis (clump verbena, rose verbena)

MIDGROUND, SPRING

Aquilegia x *hybrida* (hybrid columbine)
Dicentra spectabilis (common bleeding heart)
Mertensia virginica (Virginia bluebells)

MIDGROUND, SUMMER

Acanthus spp. (bear's breeches)
Achillea spp. (yarrows)
Amsonia tabernaemontana (willow amsonia)
Asclepias tuberosa (butterfly weed)
Asphodeline lutea (Jacob's-rod, king's-spear)
Astilbe x *arendsii* (astilbe)
Baptisia australis (blue wild indigo)
Belamcanda chinensis (blackberry lily)
Calamintha nepeta (calamint)

Campanula lactiflora (milky bellflower)
Campanula persicifolia (peach-leaf bellflower)
Centaurea montana (mountain bluet)
Centranthus ruber (red valerian, Jupiter's beard)
Chrysanthemum parthenium (feverfew, matricaria)
Chrysanthemum x superbum (shasta daisy)
Coreopsis spp. (coreopsis, tickseed)
Crambe cordifolia (colewort)
Delphinium x elatum (delphinium)
Dictamnus albus (gas plant)
Digitalis spp. (foxgloves)
Eryngium amethystinum (amethyst sea holly)
Gypsophila paniculata (baby's breath)
Hemerocallis hybrids (daylilies)
Hesperis matronalis (dame's rocket, sweet rocket)
Hosta spp. (hostas)
Iris ensata (Japanese iris)
Iris hybrida (bearded iris)
Iris siberica (Siberian iris)
Kniphofia uvaria (red-hot poker, torchlily)
Liatris spicata (spike gayfeather, blazing star)
Limonium latifolium (sea lavender, statice)
Linum perenne (blue flax)
Lobelia cardinalis (cardinal flower)
Lobelia siphilitica (big-blue lobelia)
Lupinus hybrids (lupine)
Lychnis chalcedonta (Maltese cross)
Lysimachia clethroides (gooseneck loosestrife)
Malva alcea (hollyhock mallow)
Monarda didyma (bee-balm, oswego tea)
Oenothera tetragona (common sundrops)
Paeonia lactiflora (Chinese peony, garden peony)
Papaver orientale (Oriental poppy)
Phlomis russeliana (sticky Jerusalem sage)
Phlox carolina (Carolina phlox)
Phlox paniculata (garden phlox, summer phlox)
Physostegia virginiana (obedient plant, false
    dragonhead)
Platycodon grandiflorus (balloon flower)
Polygonum bistorta (knotweed, snakeweed)
Rodgersia aesculifolia (fingerleaf rodgersia)
Salvia x superba (hybrid blue salvia, hybrid sage)
Sidalcea malviflora (checkerbloom, prairie mallow)
Sisyrinchium striatum (Argentine blue-eyed grass)
Tradescantia x andersoniana (spiderwort)
Verbascum x hybridum (mullein)
Veronica longifolia (speedwell)
Yucca filamentosa (Adam's needle, needle palm)

MIDGROUND, LATE SUMMER AND FALL

Aconitum spp. (monkshoods)
Anemone x hybrida (Japanese anemone)
Artemisia ludoviciana (white sage, wormwood)
Aster novi-belgii x novae-angliae (Michaelmas daisy,
    fall aster)
Aster x frikartii (Frikart's aster)
Begonia grandis (hardy begonia)
Chelone glabra (turtle-head)
Chrysanthemum x rubellum (hybrid chrysanthemum)
Echinacea purpurea (purple coneflower)
Echinops ritro (globe-thistle)
Gaura lindheimeri (white gaura)
Lythrum virgatum (wand loosestrife)
Rudbeckia fulgida (orange coneflower)
Sedum spectabile (showy stonecrop)
Solidago hybrids (goldenrod)

BACKGROUND, SUMMER

Alcea rosea (hollyhock)
Angelica archangelica (wild parsnip, cow parsnip,
    archangel)
Aruncus dioicus (goat's beard)
Cimicifuga racemosa (snake-root, cohosh)
Filipendula rubra (queen-of-the-prairie)
Hibiscus moscheutos (rose mallow, swamp mallow)
Ligularia stenocephala (golden ray)
Macleaya cordata (plume poppy)
Thalictrum rochebrunianum (Japanese meadow-rue,
    lavender mist)
Thermopsis caroliniana (southern lupine)
Veronicastrum virginicum (culver's root)

BACKGROUND, LATE SUMMER AND FALL

Aster novi-belgii x novae-angliae (Michaelmas daisy,
    fall aster)
Astilbe taquetii 'Superba' (fall astilbe)
Boltonia asteroides (white boltonia)
Cimicifuga ramosa (branched bugbane)
Cimicifuga simplex (Kamchatka bugbane)
Eupatorium fistulosum (Joe-Pye weed)
Helenium autumnale (sneezeweed)
Helianthus angustifolius (fall sunflower)
Heliopsis helianthoides scabra (false sunflower)
Lythrum salicaria (purple loosestrife)
Perovskia atriplicifolia (Russian sage)
Ratibida pinnata (yellow coneflower)
Rudbeckia nitida (shining coneflower)

Alcea rosea

DOUBLE BORDER

With straight edges, a brick edging, and a neatly clipped background hedge, this formal double border shows off its flowers to perfection. Each border is a mirror image of the other, magnifying the impact twofold.

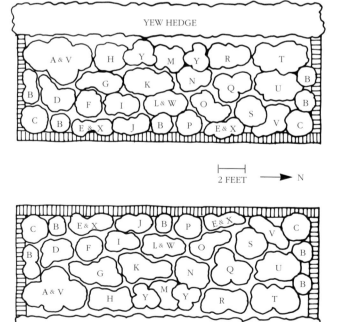

2 FEET ⟶ N

PERENNIALS

A *Hemerocallis* 'Summer Sun' (daylily), 8

B *Heuchera micrantha* 'Palace Purple' (purple-leaf coralbells), 12

C *Artemisia schmidtiana* 'Silvermound' (silvermound mugwort), 4

D *Lupinus* 'Russell Hybrid Blue' (lupine), 6

E *Stachys byzantina* 'Silver Carpet' (lamb's-ears), 12

F *Sedum spectabile* 'Meteor' (showy stonecrop), 2

G *Centranthus ruber* (red valerian), 8

H *Aster novi-belgii* x *novae-angliae* 'September Ruby' (fall aster), 4

I *Veronica spicata* 'Icicle' (spiked speedwell), 10

J *Dianthus plumarius* 'Evangeline' (cottage pink), 17

K *Physostegia virginiana* 'Summer Snow' (obedient plant), 14

L *Coreopsis verticillata* 'Zagreb' (threadleaf coreopsis), 10

M *Boltonia asteroides* (white boltonia), 4

N *Anemone* x *hybrida* 'Honorine Jobert' (Japanese anemone), 6

O *Aquilegia* x *hybrida* (hybrid columbine), 6

P *Aster* x *frikartii* (Frikart's aster), 4

Q *Iris siberica* (Siberian iris), 6

R *Filipendula rubra* 'Venusta' (queen-of-the-prairie), 6

S *Paeonia lactiflora* 'Cinderella' (Chinese peony), 2

T *Delphinium* x *elatum* 'Giant Pacific Hybrid' (delphinium), 6

U *Oenothera tetragona* (common sundrops), 6

V *Salvia* x *superba* 'May Night' (hybrid blue salvia), 5

BULBS

W *Narcissus* hybrid 'Mt Hood' (trumpet daffodil), 30

X *Tulipa* 'Maravilla' (late double peony tulip), 40

Y *Lilium* 'Thunderbolt' (trumpet lily), 12

ANNUALS

Z *Pelargonium peltatum* (ivy geranium), 6

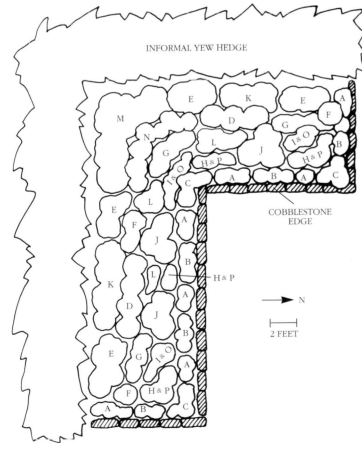

INFORMAL YEW HEDGE

COBBLESTONE
EDGE

N

2 FEET

ENGLISH BORDER

The flowers in this perennial border are arranged in
repeating groups in the traditional style of formal
English gardens. Standing out beautifully against the
dark green hedge and cobblestone edging, the
blossoms put on a changing show of pink, blue,
purple, and white from spring through fall.

PERENNIALS

A   *Iberis sempervirens* (edging candytuft), 14

B   *Campanula carpatica* 'Blue Clips' (Carpathian bellflower), 13

C   *Aurinia saxatilis* 'Citrinum' (basket-of-gold), 9

D   *Iris siberica* 'Silver Edge' (Siberian iris), 7

E   *Phlox paniculata* 'Bright Eyes' (garden phlox), 9

F   *Echinops ritro* 'Taplow Blue' (globe-thistle), 4

G   *Anemone* x *hybrida* 'Queen Charlotte' (Japanese anemone), 6

H   *Hemerocallis* 'Cherry Cheeks' (daylily), 9

I   *Artemisia* x 'Valerie Finnis' (white sage), 4

J   *Sedum spectabile* 'Meteor' (showy stonecrop), 6

K   *Aster novi-belgii* x *novae-angliae* 'Treasure' (fall aster), 5

L   *Platycodon grandiflorus* 'Shell Pink' (balloon flower), 6

M   *Eupatorium fistulosum* 'Atropurpureum' (Joe-Pye weed), 4

BULBS

N   *Lilium* 'Casa Blanca' (Oriental hybrid lily), 7

O   *Tulipa* x *hybrida* 'Angelique' (peony-flowered tulip), 30

P   *Hyacinthus orientalis* 'Pink Pearl' (Dutch hyacinth), 40

MIXED BORDER

William Robinson is credited with creating the mixed border in England around the turn of the century. He advocated more natural-looking landscapes than were currently popular, favoring sweeping lawns edged with mixed borders of perennials, shrubs, and old garden roses and flowering vines spilling over walls and twining up trees. His designs, which were influenced by Gertrude Jekyll, were grand affairs intended to blend the vast rolling lawns of the British country estates with their wooded surroundings. Both native and exotic species carried out his elaborate landscape designs.

Re-created on a small scale, Robinson's ideas make wonderful sense for today's suburban properties. The major disadvantage of a traditional flower border is that it lies lifeless for months in winter. If the garden is visible from the house or front entrance, you'll be getting a full view of a bare strip of ground throughout winter. You

This easy-care garden, shown in mid-September, relies on deciduous and broad-leaved evergreen shrubs for floral beauty and year-round structure. Annuals and perennials provide skirts of flowers in front of and in between the shrubs.

can solve this dilemma and still have flowers by designing a mixed border, a border that includes evergreen and deciduous shrubs, vines, ornamental grasses, and small trees along with perennials, bulbs, and annuals.

By including flowering shrubs and small trees in your border, it can be as colorful as an herbaceous border and much easier to care for. Woody plants, once established, won't need staking, deadheading, or dividing the way herbaceous plants do. And if you space shrubs according to their mature sizes, they should need only occasional pruning.

Deciduous shrubs, which drop their leaves in autumn, offer spring or summer flowers followed by gleaming berries in fall and winter. Their leaves usually turn fiery hues in autumn before dropping. In winter, the outlines of their bare branches and the texture and color of their bark create a pleasing design.

Evergreens, while changing less dramatically than deciduous plants, offer welcome greenery in winter, when much of the landscape appears brown and bare. Needle-leaf evergreens, such as yews, look much the same throughout the year and provide a steady, fine-textured greenery to offset other plants. Broad-leaved evergreens, such as rhododendrons, produce attractive flowers and sometimes colorful berries, and are appreciated for their bold-textured, year-round greenery. Whether deciduous or evergreen, woody plants give the garden year-round structure, adding to the garden picture throughout the year.

DESIGNING A MIXED BORDER

In suburban areas, mixed borders have to be simpler versions of Robinson's turn-of-the-century creations. Design your mixed border to surround the perimeter of the entire lawn, with a fence as a background if you wish. A mixed border also

Top: This garden's form, color, and texture depend heavily on shrubs and trees, with perennials and ornamental grasses filling the spaces in between.

Bottom: Rather than rows of boring unchanging evergreens, the entrance to this home features a colorful and ever-changing mixed border. Composed of a skeleton of trees, shrubs, and vines fleshed out with flowering perennials and annuals, the garden provides bursts of flowers and lovely foliage in all seasons.

111

makes a much more interesting foundation planting than the traditional collection of evergreen shrubs.

Designing a satisfactory mixed border takes some skill. You have to carefully integrate the herbaceous and woody plants into a pleasing combination. Planting a row of flowers in front of shrubs, or mixing flowers and shrubs randomly with each other in the border won't create a pleasing structure. Your goal should be to arrange the woody plants in groups within the mixed border to form an attractive layout, one that looks good especially in winter.

Shrubs and small trees can take up about a half to two-thirds of the space in a border. Group shrubs together in widely spaced drifts, making sure to leave enough growing space for them to mature. Use tall shrubs in the background, medium-size ones in the midground, and low ones in the foreground, combining shapes so that they work well together. For example, nestle a low-spreading shrub under the arching branches of a vase-shaped shrub, and add a single columnar shrub as a punctuation mark among a group of rounded ones.

Plant masses of perennials, bulbs, and annuals in the bays between the shrub groupings. Again, consider shape, size, and vigor when making your choices. Tall lilies look great emerging from behind a group of rounded bumald spireas, and mounds of impatiens fill in prettily beneath the arching boughs of a vase-shaped viburnum.

Because shrubs and trees grow much larger than perennials, be sure the border is deep enough to accommodate layers of plants—12 to 15 feet deep is not too much. Make the garden's outlines curved, taking care that the border carves out an appealing shape around the yard. In-curves look best opposite out-curves. The garden looks balanced if you group shrubs in the

112

widest parts of the border. You also might place a small tree such as a flowering dogwood or crab apple behind the shrubs to give the planting height and dimension. Plant the border's narrow in-curves with herbaceous plants or low spreading shrubs.

Because most shrubs bloom in spring, you might choose spring bulbs to bloom with the shrubs, filling in the rest of the border with summer-blooming perennials and annuals that will take over after the shrubs finish blooming. Select a few star fall-blooming perennials and ornamental grasses to combine with the reds and golds of the fall foliage and berry display.

For summer-flowering shrubs, any of the modern shrub roses make wonderful additions to a mixed border. Give these large growers plenty of space to mature and you'll be rewarded with month after month of bright blossoms and often brilliant fall berries. Ground-cover roses work well in the foreground of a mixed border, but they, too, need plenty of growing room.

Deciduous shrubs, such as this orange-flowered Exbury azalea, bloom in glorious profusion in spring or summer but provide enduring interest from foliage and woody stems. Many also shout again with color when their leaves change in autumn or when berries ripen. The native plants shown in this shade garden with the Exbury azalea are wild blue phlox (*Phlox divaricata*) and sensitive fern (*Onoclea sensibilis*).

EASY-CARE MIXED BORDER

The shrubs and trees in this mixed border give it year-round structure and feature dramatic flowers, colorful foliage, and brilliant berries for long-lasting color Herbaceous plants fill the gaps and provide a crisp edging,

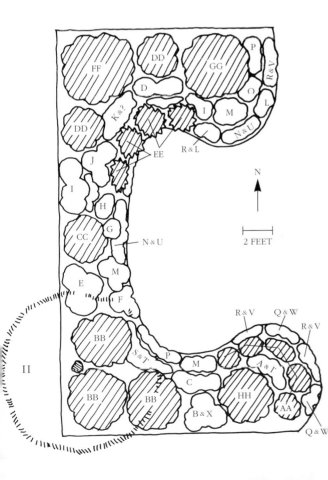

N

2 FEET

PERENNIALS

A *Chrysanthemum* x *rubellum* 'Clara Curtis' (hybrid chrysanthemum), 5

B *Iris siberica* 'Snow Queen' (Siberian iris), 3

C *Aster novi-belgii* x *novae-angliae* 'September Ruby,' 2

D *Hemerocallis* 'Catherine Woodbury' (daylily), 3

E *Anemone* x *hybrida* 'Margarete' (Japanese anemone), 3

F *Geranium sanguineum* (bloody cranesbill), 3

G *Aquilegia* x *hybrida* 'Heavenly Blue,' 1

H *Campanula glomerata* 'Joan Elliott' (clustered bellflower), 2

I *Phlox maculata* 'Miss Lingard' (spotted phlox), 3

J *Iris siberica* 'Blue Moon' (Siberian iris), 3

K *Echinacea purpurea* 'Magnus' (purple coneflower), 3

L *Chrysanthemum parthenium* 'Snowball' (feverfew), 4

M *Coreopsis verticillata* 'Moonbeam' (threadleaf coreopsis), 5

N *Stachys byzantina* 'Silver Carpet' (lamb's-ears), 7

O *Hosta sieboldiana* 'Elegans' (blue-leaf hosta), 1

P *Liriope muscari* 'Variegata' (blue lilyturf), 9

ANNUALS

Q *Torenia fournieri* 'Blue Panda' (wishbone flower), 12

R *Tagetes pumila* 'Lemon Gem' (signet marigold), 48

S *Impatiens wallerana* 'Accent White' (impatiens), 12

BULBS

T *Narcissus* x *cyclamenius* 'February Gold' (cyclamen daffodil), 25

U *Hyacinthus orientalis* (Dutch hyacinth), 25

V *Scilla siberica* (Siberian squill), 75

W *Crocus* x *vernus* (Dutch crocus), 50

X *Lycoris squamigera* (resurrection lily), 5

SHRUBS

AA *Berberis thunbergii* 'Crimson Pygmy' (dwarf purple barberry), 5

BB *Azalea* 'Delaware Valley White' (azalea), 3

CC *Rosa* 'Betty Prior' (floribunda rose), 1

DD *Buddleia alternifolia* 'Nanho Purple' (butterfly bush), 2

EE *Juniperus squamata* 'Blue Star' (dwarf juniper), 1

FF *Rosa glauca* (redleaf rose), 3

GG *Viburnum carlesii* 'Compactum' (spicebush viburnum), 1

HH *Hydrangea quercifolia* (oakleaf hydrangea), 1

TREES

II *Malus floribunda* 'Snowdrift' (crab apple), 1

Created in the Victorian style made popular by Empress Josephine, this formal rose garden gets much of its appeal from the geometrical structure created by the brick walks and low, clipped, evergreen hedges. The floribunda roses blooming freely in the beds are the cultivar 'Summer Fashion.'

FORMAL ROSE GARDENS

The Empress Josephine, Napoleon's wife, is the most famous rose gardener in history. Her passion for flowers, roses in particular, led her to attempt to collect every known type of rose in her gardens at the Chateau de Malmaison near Paris. Her rose garden, which was begun in 1806 and existed until shortly after her death in 1814, boasted between 110 and 200 different kinds of roses.

Josephine's garden was formally designed and geometrically laid out with beds and walkways arranged perhaps in the pattern of a Union Jack. The roses she collected were the shrubby plants that now are called old garden roses. Her garden, however, inspired the rose gardens we plant today with modern rosebushes—hybrid teas, grandifloras, and floribundas.

Rose gardens, especially those featuring modern roses, still follow the formal arrangement Josephine used. Roses are spaced out in rows within the beds and the soil heavily mulched to retain moisture. Often the beds are curved, with walks laid out in concentric circles. This style makes caring for the high-maintenance plants easy, providing access for pruning and allowing

air to circulate freely to discourage fungus diseases. The sterile planting scheme does little to enhance the beauty of the roses or detract from their faults, however.

DESIGNING A ROSE GARDEN

You can make your rose garden far more beautiful than the norm with just a little effort. Plant each bed with only one rose cultivar to avoid the spotty look that results from mixed floral colors and varying plant heights. Feature a different colored rose in each bed, but plan the colors in neighboring beds to look good together. If your goal is to grow perfect rose flowers, choose hybrid tea roses, whose elegant, high-centered flowers bloom individually on tall stems. If you want the most color impact, select floribunda roses, whose smaller flowers bloom in lavish clusters. Grandiflora roses grow quite tall, so use them where their height seems appropriate.

You might want to locate a tree rose (rose standard) in the center of each bed to create a bit of drama and a focal point. The tree rose could be the same or a different rose cultivar from those in the bed. In the garden's center, where the paths meet, install a garden ornament such as a gazing globe, sculpture, sundial, or another tree rose. You also might consider framing the garden's entrance with an arch or pergola planted with large-flowered climbers or rambling roses, or growing them on a latticework fence surrounding or backing up the garden.

Because hybrid tea and floribunda roses are admired solely for their flowers—not for their foliage and form, which is sparse and leggy—you'll want to partially camouflage the bushes. Traditionally, in the manner of a Victorian garden, a low, clipped, boxwood hedge outlines each bed, giving the garden year-round structure and form while hiding the rosebushes' unattractive bottoms. You might want to substitute similar-looking dwarf Japanese holly (*Ilex crenata* 'Compacta') in northern regions where boxwood is not hardy.

Flowering plants and silver-foliaged plants make lovely, though less traditional, edgings. Grown in herb gardens for its fragrant flowers and foliage, lavender's gray, needlelike leaves form neat mounds perfect for edging roses. Topped in early summer with spires of purple flowers, lavender makes a wonderful contrast to the globular rose flowers. Catmint looks similar to lavender, although it is softer and floppier. Its loose wands of lavender-blue flowers repeat throughout the summer if cut back. Lavender cotton has tight whorls of scaly, silvery-gray leaves and responds well to clipping. Use it to form a low, formal edging whose gleaming color shines like polished metal, reflecting the beauty of any color of rose you grow.

ROSE COMPANIONS

Modern roses usually aren't combined with any other plants except their edgings, because their shallow roots need plenty of moisture and nutrients. If other plants crowd around them, roses may suffer from the competition. By choosing carefully, however, you can arrange companion plants to surround the roses and enhance the garden's beauty without harming the rosebushes. Select low-growing plants that won't shade the roses' leaves and ones that thrive with the same watering and fertilizing regime as the roses.

Blue and lavender-blue flowers look beautiful planted as companions to roses because roses bloom in every color but these. Blues and lavenders make happy counterparts to every color of rose—to the red and pink hues so prevalent among them and also to the less typical orange, apricot, yellow, and creamy white ones.

Above: A low hedge of dwarf boxwood creates an attractive edging that also helps hide the leggy stems that are the bane of modern roses.

Left: Companion plants can dramatically enliven rose gardens. In this pretty combination, beach wormwood (*Artemisia stelleriana* 'Silver Brocade') offers a silvery mat of foliage as a lovely foil to the dark green leaves and brilliant flowers of the miniature rose 'New Beauty.'

115

COMPANION PLANTS FOR FORMAL ROSE GARDENS

These plants are low-growing or ground-covering types that look good used as borders, edgings, or skirts of flowers and foliage beneath modern bush roses. They help hide the rose plants' leggy growth without shading the leaves or competing too much for moisture or nutrients.

PERENNIALS AND BIENNIALS

SPRING

Ajuga reptans (bugleweed, carpet bugle)
Alchemilla spp. (lady's mantles)
Galium odoratum (sweet woodruff)
Heuchera spp. (coralbells)
Iberis sempervirens (edging candytuft)
Lamium maculatum (spotted dead nettle)
Myosotis scorpioides (forget-me-not)
Ruta graveolens (rue)
Viola cornuta (horned violet)

SUMMER

Artemisia schmidtiana 'Silvermound' (silvermound mugwort)
Campanula portenschlagiana (Dalmatian bellflower)
Cerastium tomentosum (snow-in-summer)
Coreopsis rosea (pink coreopsis)
Geranium spp. (cranesbills)
Lavandula angustifolia (lavender)
Nepeta x *faassenii* (catmint)
Santolina chamaecyparissus (lavender cotton)
Stachys byzantina (lamb's-ears)

LATE SUMMER AND FALL

Ceratostigma plumbaginoides (leadwort)

ANNUALS

Ageratum houstonianum (flossflower)
Lobelia erinus (edging lobelia)
Lobularia maritima (sweet alyssum)
Nigella damascena (love-in-a-mist)
Torenia fournieri (wishbone flower)

The list above includes many low-growing perennials and self-seeding annuals that make perfect companions for roses. Plant them in large numbers to fill in the beds around and beneath the roses, retaining a formal and symmetrical effect. Try fast-spreading sweet woodruff to blanket the ground with pretty whorls of dainty green leaves and diminutive, white spring flowers. Any of the many species of cranesbills make beautiful companions to roses, their small flowers blooming with the roses and their palmate leaves creating pretty texture contrasts. Silver-foliaged plants, such as artemisias and lamb's-ears, provide months of gleaming contrast to rose flowers and foliage. Clematis vines make tried-and-true companions to climbing roses. The two can share the same space, intertwining without smothering each other, and the satiny blue, lavender, or purple clematis blossoms provide a luscious contrast to the rose blossoms.

Catmint (*Nepeta* x *faassenii* 'Six Hills Giant') creates a camouflaging skirt of beautiful lavender-blue flowers and silvery foliage that sets off these pink roses to perfection. Catmint reblooms if faded flowers are cut back.

TRADITIONAL ROSE GARDEN

Laid out in classical geometrical fashion with silver-foliaged catmint edging the beds, this rose garden is a pleasure to stroll through and easy to tend. A tree rose forms a pivotal focal point, and a bench beneath an arbor of climbing roses provides a spot for sitting and taking in the scents.

PERENNIALS

A   *Nepeta* x *faassenii* (catmint), 196

ROSES

B   'Barbara Bush' (hybrid tea rose), 5
C   'Peace' (hybrid tea rose), 5
D   'Tropicana' (hybrid tea rose), 5
E   'Mr. Lincoln' (hybrid tea rose), 5
F   'Cartwheel' (miniature rose), 3
G   'Small Miracle' (miniature rose), 3
H   'Sargeant Pepper' (miniature rose), 3
I   'Paper Doll' (miniature rose), 3
J   'Lucille Ball' (tree rose), 1
K   'Climbing American Beauty' (climber), 2

ISLANDS OF FLOWERS

Like a tropical island surrounded by a surging sea, an island flower bed stands in isolation enveloped by an expanse of lawn. This positioning departs from the conventional arrangement of flowers and shrubs in plots backed up against a hedge, wall, or fence or along the side of a house. A style developed and popularized by Alan Bloom, one of Britain's most notable 20th-century nurserymen, island bedding solves many problems for present-day gardeners.

An arrangement of both borders and island beds provides a lot of growing space on any size property. On a large property, the usual extensive lawn means that the flower border around the property's edges is far away; an island bed can bring the flowers closer, while echoing border plantings. On a small property, an island bed or two provides additional growing space if the borders along the yard aren't sufficient to indulge a gardening hobby.

You'll find that an island bed is far easier to maintain than a border of the same size because you can reach it from all sides. Weeding, deadheading, staking, and other chores are far simpler when you can reach the plants from the garden's edges. An island bed basks in full sun and gets plenty of air circulation so plants grow stronger and healthier, needing less staking and less pest control.

DESIGNING AN ISLAND BED

Position the island bed off-center in the lawn, shaping it as an oval, egg-shaped, kidney-shaped, or whatever gently curving irregular shape fits the contours and size of the lawn and border plantings. Make sure the island bed is large enough to visually anchor the landscape, balancing the spaces of the open lawn. A small island looks puny and lost if surrounded by a sea of lawn. When designing the bed's dimensions, move back from the garden and look at it from inside the house or at the front door, and gauge the proportions of the garden.

Because an island bed will be viewed from all sides, great care must go into its planning so that the garden appears as beautiful from one angle as from another. Position the tallest plants in the bed's center and scale down the plant heights toward the outer edges and far ends of the island, using one or more types of edging plants around the perimeter. This way no plant hides another. The narrower the bed, the shorter the tallest flowers should be in the center. Usually, the tallest plant should be no more than half the bed's width so the planting won't look off-balance or top-heavy.

You might want to create a sense of balance and rhythm by repeating drifts of flowers and plant combinations throughout the bed. Repeat from one side to the other, perhaps in a

Designed to be viewed from all sides, this island bed stands out from the lawn because it features a border of edging plants whose flowers and foliage colors contrast well with the grass. The terra-cotta birdbath creates an attractive focal point among the perennials.

Two semicircular island beds designed with a lawn path in between create a pleasing sense of symmetry in this large backyard. While trees shade the borders around the property's edges, the island beds bask in full sun, providing excellent growing conditions for the herbs and perennials planted in them.

triangular placement—one grouping on one side and two repetitions on the opposite side—to create an effective rhythm rather than arranging them directly opposite each other.

An island bed has no immediate backdrop; its background may be a distant view or the plantings bordering the property. This borrowed background plays a part in how the island bed looks, however. Stroll around your proposed site and view it from all angles, considering how the distant backdrop will work with the garden. You might consider planting an evergreen screen to give the garden more intimacy and hide a distracting view to the street, for example.

Large island beds can be transformed into mixed borders, with shrubs and small trees in the middle and ground-covering flowers and low plants at the edges. This paints a more interesting winter scene than you'd have if you used only herbaceous plants.

In a tree-studded front or back yard, where lawn struggles to grow in the shade, an island bed makes a perfect solution. You might create a large island bed to flow around and under the trees, turning the site into a lovely shade garden filled with ferns, shade-loving perennials and annuals, and even shrubs and small trees if the site is large enough.

EASY-CARE ISLAND BED

The hot colors of this bed carry across a long distance, creating a brilliant island of blossoms amid a green sea of lawn. Generous splashes of white-flowered annuals and silver and blue-gray foliage tone down the bright red and gold perennial blossoms, while providing months of continual color.

N

2 FEET

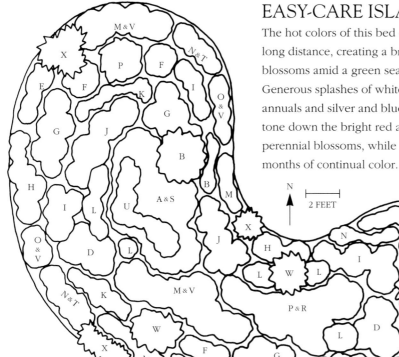

PERENNIALS

A   *Hibiscus moscheutos* 'Lord Baltimore' (rose mallow), 5
B   *Veronica spicata incana* (woolly speedwell), 6
C   *Hemerocallis* 'Hyperion' (daylily), 7
D   *Monarda didyma* 'Mahogany' (bee-balm), 6
E   *Chrysanthemum weyrichii* (Miyabe), 5
F   *Veronica spicata* 'Red Fox' (spiked speedwell), 6
G   *Achillea* x 'Moonshine' (moonshine yarrow), 10
H   *Iberis sempervirens* 'Autumn Beauty' (edging candytuft), 16
I   *Chrysanthemum* x *superbum* 'Alaska' (shasta daisy), 11
J   *Liatris scariosa alba* (tall gayfeather), 12
K   *Artemisia ludoviciana* 'Silver King' (white sage), 6
L   *Papaver orientale* 'Springtime' (Oriental poppy), 6

ANNUALS

M   *Tagetes tenuifolia* 'Lemon Gem' (dwarf signet marigold), 60
N   *Nicotiana alata* 'Nicki Red' (flowering tobacco), 30
O   *Zinnia angustifolia* 'Classic White' (narrow-leaf zinnia), 18
P   *Nicotiana sylvestris* (great-flowering tobacco), 12

BULBS

Q   *Narcissus jonquilla* 'Cheerfulness' (jonquil), 50
R   *Tulipa* x *hybrida* 'Golden Melody' (hybrid tulip), 50
S   *Narcissus* x *hybrida* 'Carlton' (hybrid daffodil), 50
T   *Hyacinthus orientalis* (Dutch hyacinth), 36
U   *Allium aflatunense* (Persian onion), 15
V   *Tulipa batalinii* 'Bright Gem' (bokhara tulip), 100

ORNAMENTAL GRASSES

W   *Helictotrichon sempervirens* (blue oat grass), 3
X   *Festuca ovina* 'Elijah Blue' (blue fescue), 10

EASY-CARE PERENNIALS

These perennials grow larger and sturdier year after year but are not invasive. They rarely need dividing or staking, so they're almost care-free if given proper growing conditions.

SPRING
Amsonia tabernaemontana (willow amsonia)
Chrysogonum virginianum (goldenstar, green and gold)
Corydalis lutea (yellow corydalis)
Dicentra eximia (fringed bleeding heart)
Dicentra spectabilis (common bleeding heart)
Dictamnus albus (gas plant)
Helleborus spp. (Christmas rose and Lenten rose)

SUMMER
Achillea filipendulina (fern-leaf yarrow)
Aruncus dioicus (goat's beard)
Asclepias tuberosa (butterfly weed)
Astilbe spp. (astilbes)
Baptisia australis (blue wild indigo)
Campanula spp. (bellflowers)
Corydalis lutea (yellow corydalis)
Filipendula rubra (queen-of-the-prairie)
Hemerocallis cultivars (daylilies)
Hosta spp. (hostas)
Iris siberica (Siberian iris)
Paeonia lactiflora (garden peony, Chinese peony)
Papaver orientale (Oriental poppy)
Platycodon grandiflorus (balloon flower)
Thermopsis caroliniana (southern lupine, Carolina lupine)

LATE SUMMER AND FALL
Aconitum spp. (monkshoods)
Anemone x *hybrida* (Japanese anemone)
Cimicifuga spp. (bugbanes)
Corydalis lutea (yellow corydalis)
Rudbeckia fulgida 'Goldsturm' (orange coneflower)
Sedum spp. (stonecrops)

HIGH-MAINTENANCE PERENNIALS

These perennials are fussy or short-lived plants that demand more care than most. Some die unless growing conditions are perfect, others need staking or frequent division, and still others are highly susceptible to pests. Grow them only if you have time to pamper them.

Anthemis tinctoria (golden marguerite)
Aster novi-belgii x *novae-angliae* (Michaelmas daisy, fall aster)
Chrysanthemum x *morifolium* (garden mum)
Delphinium x *elatum* (delphinium)
Helenium autumnale (sneezeweed)
Lobelia cardinalis (cardinal flower)
Lupinus hybrids (lupine)
Monarda didyma (bee-balm, oswego tea)
Phlox paniculata (garden phlox)
Primula spp. (primroses)
Rosa hybrids (hybrid tea and floribunda roses)
Stokesia laevis (Stokes' aster)
Tradescantia virginiana (spiderwort)

EASY-CARE ANNUALS

Most annuals require a lot of attention to do well. The ones listed here need less care and don't need to be deadheaded for continuous blooming.

Begonia x *semperflorens* (wax begonia)
Brachycome iberidifolia (swan river daisy)
Browallia speciosa (amethyst flower)
Catharanthus roseus (Madagascar periwinkle)
Celosia cristata (cockscomb)
Cleome hasslerana (spider flower)
Dyssodia tenuiloba (Dahlberg daisy)
Impatiens wallerana (impatiens, busy lizzie)
Lobelia erinus (edging lobelia)
Lobularia maritima (sweet alyssum)
Sanvitalia procumbens (creeping zinnia)
Verbena x *hybrida* (verbena)
Zinnia angustifolia (narrow-leaf zinnia)

HIGH-MAINTENANCE ANNUALS

Although most annuals need regular care to encourage constant flowering, these are especially demanding. They may fail to bloom if conditions aren't just right, need deadheading every few days, or succumb to disease.

Antirrhinum majus (snapdragon)
Callistephus chinensis (China aster, annual aster)
Lathyrus odoratus (sweet pea)
Pelargonium x *hortorum* (zonal geranium)
Petunia x *hybrida* (petunia)
Phlox drummondii (annual phlox)
Tagetes cultivars (marigolds)
Viola x *wittrockiana* (pansy)
Zinnia elegans (common zinnia)

CHAPTER FIVE

DESIGNING NATURALISTIC GARDENS

Bring Home a Small Piece of Nature's Magnificence

Opposite: Shade-loving exotics look at home alongside woodland wildflowers, as long as they are combined in a design that looks as if nature did the arranging. Shown, an exotic hosta (*Hosta sieboldiana*) with natives downy phlox (*Phlox pilosa*) and beech ferns (*Thelypteris hexagonoptera*).

Left: Butterflies prefer flowers that offer a solid landing platform along with a plentiful nectar supply. Here a swallowtail visits an Oriental lily (*Lilium rubrum*), bringing fluttering wings and a burst of moving color to a naturalistic garden.

Mother Nature designs her landscapes with a generous hand, planting the flowers of field and forest, mountaintop and desert in spontaneous patterns of bloom. You can recapture the pleasure and serenity of a wild place in your own yard by artfully arranging wildflowers in a naturalistic setting. Because these pretty flowers require a distinct habitat, flourishing where soil, exposure, and moisture create a growing niche favorable to their particular needs, you'll be most successful by matching plants to sites that closely imitate their native habitats.

Many exotics (plants native to other parts of the world) look right at home planted alongside native wildflowers. The flowers you choose should appear to be wild ones—delicate and free looking—not top-heavy with voluptuous flowers like many popular garden hybrids. A plant, native or not, belongs in your naturalistic landscape if it adapts to your garden's growing conditions and if it looks at home in the design.

FUSS-FREE GARDENS

Gardening naturalistically with well-adapted natives is a low-maintenance alternative to traditional flower gardening. Don't be mislead into thinking that wildflowers are totally care-free and immune to pests and diseases, however; such is not the case. As with any garden plant, wildflowers must be given their preferred growing conditions and at least a minimum of care. Wildflowers get munched on as readily as traditional garden plants, and they, too, suffer the effects of extreme drought or cold. They may, however, be a bit tougher and better adapted to your climate than many popular garden hybrids, which are selected more for their beauty than for their adaptability. And in a naturalistic design, you'll be less likely to notice a chewed leaf or imperfect flower, which might be an eyesore in a formally groomed garden.

WOODLAND GARDENS

The delicate blossoms of wild blue phlox, great white trillium, Virginia bluebells, and scores of other enchanting woodland wildflowers can be yours to enjoy without hiking into the wild. All you need is a wooded site and humus-rich soil where you can copy the forest environment. Forest plants occur in horizontal layers from the sky to the ground, with canopy trees overhead, understory trees and shrubs in between, and wildflowers, ferns, and mosses on the ground.

The forest floor has a 4- to 8-inch-deep layer of loose, humus-rich soil consisting of rotted leaves and twigs above a more solid soil. The humus and the soil underneath are acidic, varying from very acid (pH 4 to 5) to slightly acid (pH 6 to 6.9). This rich, acid soil is the key to growing a successful woodland wildflower garden, but, if you don't have it, you can create it.

CREATING A WOODLAND GARDEN

Site your woodland garden where overhead trees cast dappled shade throughout the day and where the soil is loose and crumbly. This may be in a natural woodland or in a small grove or group of trees, or even under one large, deep-rooted, wide-spreading tree.

Evaluate the soil by feeling it. If you can scrape off the humus with your hands, then it is an excellent site for a woodland garden. If the soil is hard, compacted, and root filled, defying a trowel, you'll have to improve it. Poor soil results when tree leaves have been raked off and carted away year after year instead of being allowed to rot naturally into leaf mold, or when the trees overhead have surface roots that have compacted and dried out the soil.

When given the humus-rich, moist soil and light shade they prefer, woodland wildflowers multiply to create a lavish carpet of springtime color. Shown here are great white trillium (*Trillium grandiflorum*) and Virginia bluebells (*Mertensia virginica*).

You can renew poor soil by spreading chopped up leaves and twigs over the soil in a deep layer. Dust the leaves with compost activator and keep them moist to speed up decomposition. The rotting leaves encourage earthworms, which burrow deeper into the soil, loosening up the lower layers. You may have to repeat this procedure for several years until the humus becomes deep enough to plant in.

Once you've selected a site, clear out undesirable underbrush, invasive vines, and small saplings, but leave behind good-looking shrubs in strategic places beneath the canopy trees. Trim low-hanging branches and open up the canopy so that a dappled light falls below.

Lay out a path to meander among the trees and cover it with wood chips. The path gives structure to the garden, beckons you to explore, and protects the delicate plants from being trampled. You might edge the path with stones or logs, but leave it unedged for the most natural look.

Do not dig deeply or turn over the soil in a woodland site—cultivating the soil destroys the soil's layering and disrupts the trees' root systems. Dig small, individual holes for flowers and ferns. You can dig planting holes for shrubs and small understory trees such as dogwoods and azaleas, but do not excavate wide areas or cut through large tree roots. Plant somewhere else.

Woodland wildflowers are spring-blooming, ephemeral plants. Most do their stuff before the

Wildflower gardens need less care than formal flower gardens—leaving you time to relax on the weekends—because given the proper conditions, woodland plants are almost self-sufficient. Shown here: cinnamon fern (*Osmunda cinnamomea*), wild blue phlox (*Phlox divaricata*), Solomon's-seal (*Polygonatum biflorum*), and golden groundsel (*Senecio aureus*).

overhead canopy of leaves has blocked out significant sunlight then die to the ground by midsummer. If you add a generous number of ferns to your garden, you'll find their lovely foliage sustains the garden into fall after the ephemerals disappear for the year.

Arrange wildflowers and ferns in groups under the trees and along the edges of paths; don't set them out in rows. Take your cues from nature and don't worry about leaving open space between the groups. Plant spreading types so they can roam freely and fill into dramatic swathes. Sprinkle taprooted types here and there, combining them to form pretty pictures with each other or with ground-covering plants.

Woodland plants always have a protective covering of humus over their roots and so should yours. After planting, apply a loose covering of shredded leaves or humus around the wildflowers. Don't leave the soil exposed to drying sun and wind.

SHOPPING FOR WILDFLOWERS

Woodland wildflowers are not easily propagated by seeds, so you'll need to purchase grown plants. Because they mature slowly from seeds, woodland plants are expensive. Beware of bargain wildflowers because, more likely than not, they are wild gathered. Unscrupulous nurserymen may collect wildflowers, then sell them, ravaging their native habitat.

Not only is gathering wildflowers unethical and sometimes illegal, but the resulting plants usually die in your garden because they were mistreated and shocked during gathering. Nursery-propagated wildflowers will be the most likely plants to flourish. Don't gather wildflowers yourself; purchase them from suppliers that assure you their plants are nursery propagated.

Top: Spreading happily into glorious clusters, two native phloxes create an eye-catching color combination in a Long Island, New York, garden. Shown are wild blue phlox (*Phlox divaricata*) and a hot-pink cultivar of creeping phlox (*Phlox stolonifera* 'Home Fires').

Left: When purchasing wildflowers such as dog-tooth violet (*Erythronium americanum*) for your garden, be sure they have been propagated in the nursery, not gathered from the wild. Wild-gathering is unethical and illegal.

NATIVE WILDFLOWERS FOR WOODLAND GARDENS

PERENNIALS

SPRING

Aquilegia canadensis (American columbine)
Dicentra eximia (fringed bleeding heart)
Galium odoratum (sweet woodruff)*
Hedyotis caerulea (bluets, Quaker ladies)
Iris cristata (crested iris)
Mertensia virginica (Virginia bluebells)
Phlox divaricata (wild blue phlox, woodland phlox)
Phlox pilosa (Carolina phlox)
Phlox stolonifera (creeping phlox)
Polemonium caeruleum (Jacob's ladder)
Polygonatum biflorum (small Solomon's seal)
Sanguinaria canadensis (bloodroot)
Tiarella spp. (foamflowers)
Viola spp. (violets)

SUMMER

Aruncus spp. (goat's beards)
Chrysogonum virginianum (goldenstar, green and gold)
Cimicifuga racemosa (snake-root, cohosh)

Dicentra eximia (fringed bleeding heart)
Lysimachia punctata (yellow loosestrife, circle flower)*

LATE SUMMER AND FALL

Aconitum spp. (monkshoods)
Dicentra eximia (fringed bleeding heart)

FERNS

Adiantum pedatum (maidenhair fern)
Athyrium filix-femina (lady fern)
Dryopteris marginalis (marginal shield fern)
Matteuccia struthiopteris (ostrich fern)
Osmunda cinnamomea (cinnamon fern)
Osmunda regalis (royal fern)
Polystichum acrostichoides (Christmas fern)

BULBS

SPRING

Arisaema triphyllum (Jack-in-the-pulpit)
Camassia leichtlinii (camas)
Erythronium americanum (dog-tooth violet)
Trillium spp. (trilliums, wake robins)

These plants grow wild in the woodlands of North America and are easy to obtain from wildflower nurseries. Those marked with an * are European species that have naturalized here. All will thrive in a woodland garden.

WOODLAND HOUSEKEEPING CHORES

Once established, a woodland garden requires very little work. You should keep newly planted wildflowers moist until established, but thereafter they can pretty much care for themselves. Watering your woodland garden during periods of spring or early summer drought prolongs their seasonal display of flowers and foliage but is not a necessity. Rapidly spreading plants, such as creeping foamflower, sweet woodruff, and creeping phlox, may need division or some controlling in a small site, or you may prefer to let them wander. Don't deadhead wildflowers; let them set seed and multiply.

Your toughest chore is optional: raking leaves in autumn. You can let the fallen leaves remain where they drop to decompose on their own, or you can help them along a bit. Many wildflower gardeners like to rake and shred leaves, returning them to the woodland floor. The shredded leaves look attractive and decompose more readily than whole leaves, and the wildflowers seem to do better. Various leaf-chopping machines, or even your lawn mower, can be used for this chore. With an annual dressing of shredded leaves, your wildflower garden will flourish into spectacular bloom without needing fertilizer.

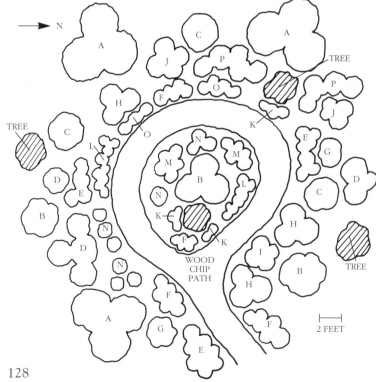

N →

TREE

TREE

WOOD
CHIP
PATH

2 FEET

WOODLAND WILDFLOWER GARDEN

A wood-chip path meanders beneath the canopy created by several large trees, leading you on a tour of this pretty wildflower garden. Dainty flowers carpet the woodland floor in spring, while fine-textured ferns in various shades of green flourish in summer's shade. If the wildflowers are happily situated, they will spread into large clumps and seed themselves throughout the garden, making a prettier show with each passing year.

FERNS

A   *Matteuccia struthiopteris* (ostrich fern), 9

B   *Osmunda cinnamomea* (cinnamon fern), 2

C   *Adiantum pedatum* (maidenhair fern), 3

D   *Polystichum acrostichoides* (Christmas fern), 8

PERENNIALS AND BULBS

E   *Phlox divaricata* (wild blue phlox), 22

F   *Chrysogonum virginianum* (goldenstar), 22

G   *Arisaema triphyllum* (Jack-in-the-pulpit), 2

H   *Trillium grandiflorum* (great white trillium), 9

I   *Polygonatum biflorum* (small Solomon's seal), 5

J   *Phlox pilosa* (Carolina phlox), 7

K   *Erythronium americanum* (dog-tooth violet), 8

L   *Iris cristata* (crested iris), 16

M   *Dicentra eximia* (fringed bleeding heart), 10

N   *Sanguinaria canadensis* (bloodroot), 10

O   *Phlox stolonifera* (creeping phlox), 8

P   *Mertensia virginica* (Virginia bluebells), 9

WOODLAND GARDENER

Paul Moore and his father own a thriving nursery business, but Paul takes the nontraditional route for his own garden. Rather than landscaping his home with the annuals displayed at his garden center, he developed his property into a low-maintenance wild-flower haven.

With two children to raise and two businesses to run, Paul and his wife, Nancy, don't have much time to garden. Working six long days a week at his garden center, Paul needed his own garden to be a retreat from business. Rather than using the traditional plants sold at his nursery, he selected native plants and turned his Nashville property into a naturalistic wildflower haven. His garden echoes—and intensifies—the beauty of the woodland surrounding his home.

Although woodland plants generally can take care of themselves if planted in humus-rich, moist soil, Paul coddles his and has enjoyed amazing results. He fertilizes once a year in late winter with composted chicken manure, and the flowers have spread enthusiastically. He also keeps the woodland neater than Mother Nature would by raking and shredding leaves to reapply as mulch, laying down a wood-chip path, and mulching with pine needles close to the house for a dressier appearance.

Ironically, Paul's garden is now no longer a retreat from business, but a reminder of it. When he innocently displayed a photograph of his garden at the nursery, everyone in town seemed to want a wild garden, too. Now Paul creates wild-flower gardens for his customers.

In late spring, after most of the wildflowers that form a carpet of blossoms begin to fade, the woodland beside Paul's house takes on a quiet beauty. A path winding among the trees to a wooden bench invites a stroll through the garden and gives the space structure and shape. Native ferns and non-native hostas provide summer greenery.

NEW AMERICAN GARDENS

Do away entirely with lawn, foundation plantings, formal flower beds, and property-bordering hedges; then, expand your flower garden to take up most of your property. The result: a "new American garden." This innovative garden style, which was popularized by the landscape design firm Oehme, van Sweden, and Associates, takes its inspiration primarily from the American prairie. It's reminiscent of a modern artist's interpretation of a prairie—bold brush strokes of ornamental grasses and tall, dramatic flowers create a ground-covering tapestry. The garden changes with every season and looks beautiful all year long.

Although the ornamental grasses suggest a prairie, the New American-style garden doesn't look like a real one. The grasses and flowers aren't evenly dispersed, as they would be in a real prairie, but are grouped for effect in a dramatic style similar to an English perennial border. A big difference is that the garden covers most of the landscape rather than being confined to a bed or border. Even though your New American-style garden will be decidedly American in character, the plants in it do not have to be natives. Any plants that thrive under the same growing conditions will do.

CREATING AN AMERICAN GARDEN

When designing a New American-style garden, choose long-blooming perennials with good-looking foliage so the plants always add interest to the scene. The dried foliage and seed heads of most ornamental grasses—and even of many perennials, such as black-eyed Susans and 'Autumn Joy' sedum—look stunning in the fall and winter garden.

Arrange the plants in bold masses so they make an eye-catching splash. Carefully orchestrate the scene so that taller plants don't block shorter ones, and so that something is always in bloom. You can use groups of evergreen trees and shrubs as a backdrop to the ever-changing display of more colorful plants. The evergreens may go unnoticed during the growing season, but they add essential structure and color in winter, when the rest of the garden lies dormant.

In autumn, many of the grasses and flowers set seed and their foliage changes color, creating a lovely seasonal display. Allow this natural cycle to progress without cutting off the seedpods or dried foliage, and the garden will be transformed into a giant dried flower arrangement for your fall and winter enjoyment. The dried foliage and pretty seedpods contribute to the naturalistic character of the garden and provide shelter and food for birds, giving you a pretty scene to enjoy during the dormant season.

No boring lawn here. Instead an assortment of ornamental grasses and flowering perennials puts on a changing display of colors and textures throughout the year in this side yard. A curving path leads visitors from the front of the house to the deck and pool at the back. Photographed in September, the garden has become lush and full as the grasses and late-season perennials begin to flower.

You'll need to cut down the dried foliage and stems in late winter to make way for new growth. This measure temporarily leaves the garden bare. By including masses of spring-flowering bulbs in between the perennials and ornamental grasses, you can keep the garden from looking barren for very long. Arrange drifts of crocus, daffodils, tulips, and alliums throughout the garden to provide an effective sequence of bloom all spring. Soon after you cut the garden back, the crocus sprout and burst into bloom. Ornamental grasses and bulbs work well together because the later bulbs finish blooming about the time the grass blades start filling in enough to camouflage the bulbs' withering foliage.

INSTALLATION AND CARE

Site an ornamental grass garden in full sun, and prepare the soil as you would for any garden, by tilling and working in organic matter and removing roots of perennial weeds. Then lay out your design. Space grasses as far apart as they grow tall—some grow rapidly into huge specimens.

Reminiscent of a natural prairie, the New American-style garden features sweeps of ornamental grasses and big clumps of bold perennials. Making a noble splash of color in July are maiden grass (*Miscanthus*), golden ray (*Ligularia*), daylily (*Hemerocallis*), coneflower (*Rudbeckia*), and gayfeather (*Liatris*).

PLANTS FOR NEW AMERICAN GARDENS

These plants possess beautiful flowers, eye-catching foliage, and perhaps even striking seedpods—making them favorites for the dramatic gardens designed in the New American style.

Stachys byzantina

PERENNIALS AND BIENNIALS
SPRING
Ajuga reptans (bugleweed, carpet bugle)
Alchemilla spp. (lady's mantles)
Bergenia cordifolia (heart-leaf bergenia)
Epimedium x *youngianum* (barrenwort, bishop's hat)
Heuchera micrantha 'Palace Purple' (purple-leaf coralbells)
Stachys byzantina (lamb's-ear)

SUMMER
Acanthus spp. (spiny bear's breeches)
Achillea spp. (yarrows)
Angelica archangelica (wild parsnip, archangel)
Artemisia spp. (white sages, wormwoods)
Aruncus spp. (goat's beards)
Aster x *frikartii* (Frikart's aster)
Astilbe spp. (astilbes)
Baptisia australis (blue wild indigo)
Coreopsis verticillata (threadleaf coreopsis)
Crambe cordifolia (colewort)
Cynara cardunculus (cardoon)
Eryngium amethystinum (amethyst sea holly)
Filipendula rubra (queen-of-the-prairie)
Gaura lindheimeri (white gaura)
Hemerocallis hybrids (daylily)
Heuchera micrantha 'Palace Purple' (purple-leaf coralbells)
Hibiscus moscheutos (rose mallow, swamp mallow)
Hosta species and hybrids (hostas)
Stachys byzantina (lamb's-ears)
Verbena bonariensis (Brazilian verbena)
Yucca filamentosa (Adam's needle, needle palm)

LATE SUMMER AND FALL
Anemone x *hybrida* (Japanese anemone)
Artemisia spp. (white sages, wormwoods)
Aster x *frikartii* (Frikart's aster)

Boltonia asteroides (white boltonia)
Ceratostigma plumbaginoides (leadwort, plumbago)
Cimicifuga simplex (Kamchatka bugbane)
Echinacea purpurea (purple coneflower)
Echinops ritro (globe-thistle)
Eupatorium fistulosum (Joe-Pye weed)
Gaura lindheimeri (white gaura)
Heuchera micrantha 'Palace Purple' (purple-leaf coralbells)
Ligularia stenocephala (golden ray)
Perovskia atriplicifolia (Russian sage)
Rudbeckia fulgida 'Goldsturm' (orange coneflower)
Salvia pratensis (meadow sage, meadow clary)
Sedum x *telephium* 'Autumn Joy' (autumn joy stonecrop)
Sedum x 'Vera Jameson'
Solidago hybrids (goldenrods)
Stachys byzantina (lamb's-ears)

ANNUALS
Centaurea cineraria (dusty miller, silver lace)
Cleome hasslerana (spider flower)
Cosmos spp. (cosmos)
Gomphrena globosa (globeflower, globe amaranth)
Helianthus annuus (sunflower)
Heliotropium arborescens (heliotrope)
Melampodium paludosum (melampodium, black-foot daisy)
Nicotiana sylvestris (great-flowering tobacco)
Nicotiania langsdorfii (green-flowered tobacco)
Nigella damascena (love-in-a-mist)
Ocimum basilicum 'Purple Ruffles' (sweet basil)
Perilla frutescens (beefsteak plant, perilla, shiso)
Ricinus communis (castor oil plant, castor bean)
Sanvitalia procumbens (creeping zinnia)
Tagetes tenuifolia (signet marigold)
Tithonia rotundifolia (Mexican sunflower)
Zinnia angustifolia (narrow-leaf zinnia)

BULBS

SPRING

Crocus chrysanthus (snow crocus)
Crocus x *vernus* (Dutch crocus)
Fritillaria imperalis (crown imperial)
Iris reticulata (reticulated iris)
Narcissus spp. and hybrids (daffodils)
Tulipa x *hybrida* (hybrid tulips)

SUMMER

Allium spp. (ornamental onions)
Crocosmia x *crocosmiiflora* (montbretia)

LATE SUMMER AND FALL

Canna x *generalis* (canna lily)

ORNAMENTAL GRASSES

Calamagrostis acutiflora 'Stricta'
   (feather reed grass)
Carex morrowii (Japanese sedge grass)
Carex stricta 'Bowles Golden' (Bowles
   golden grass)
Chasmanthium latifolium (northern sea oats)
Cortaderia selloana 'Pumila' (dwarf pampas grass)
Deschampsia caespitosa (tufted hair grass)
Elymus arenarius 'Glaucus' (blue wild rye, blue
   lyme grass)
Festuca ovina 'Glauca' (blue fescue)
Helictotrichon sempervirens (blue oat grass)
Imperata cylindrica 'Red Baron' (Japanese
   blood grass)
Miscanthus sinensis (eulalia grass, silver grass)
Molinia caerulea (moor grass, purple moor grass)
Ophiopogon planiscapus 'Nigrescens'
   (black mondo grass)
Panicum virgatum (switch grass)
Pennisetum alopecuroides (fountain grass)
Pennisetum orientale (Oriental fountain grass)
Pennisetum setaceum (purple fountain grass)
Phalaris arundinacea var. *picta* (ribbon grass)

Use a heavy mulch to deter weeds until the garden fills in. In shady locations, only a few ornamental grasses will thrive, but you still can create a naturalistic garden with tall ferns, hostas, and shade-loving flowers.

Locate the garden where you can enjoy it from indoors and out. If you have eliminated lawn altogether in favor of your New American-style garden, be sure to include a deck or terrace where you can sit outdoors and enjoy the garden. Incorporate a path winding through the plants so you can explore and have easy access for maintenance chores.

If you've selected plants well adapted to your soil, exposure, and climate, they will thrive with very little care, needing no fertilizer and requiring water only during drought. Ornamental grasses and prairie wildflowers are deep rooted and can get by on whatever nutrients the soil supplies. Fertilizer makes them grow even larger than their normally massive height.

As with a meadow garden, you have one major annual chore: cutting down the overwintered stems and foliage. Ornamental grasses such as *Miscanthus* can be extremely ornery. You'll need to cut them back with hedge shears, a weed whacker, or a sickle or scythe. Rake away the remains or shred the dried stems and grass blades, and use this haylike material to mulch the soil. Cut the old growth back before new growth begins in spring, or you will damage the new blades and they will look unsightly all summer.

Ten or 20 years down the road, some of the grasses may develop unsightly hollow centers, which can be remedied only by dividing them. Be forewarned: This can be an arduous chore because the grass roots are so tough and massive that you'll need an ax or even a chain saw to cut them apart.

Orange coneflower (*Rudbeckia fulgida*), a sun-loving wildflower, combines effectively with the upright sheaves of feather reed grass (*Calamagrostis acutiflora* 'Stricta'), creating a wild prairie look in a large-scale Ohio garden. The dried seed heads of both plants hold up well through the winter, adding natural drama to the landscape during the off-season.

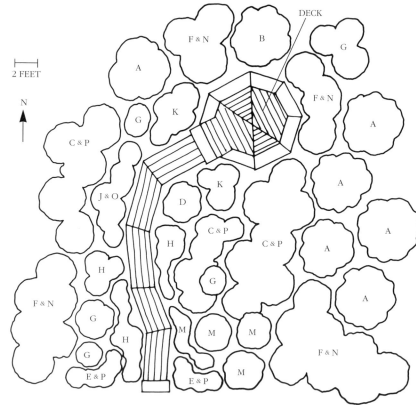

NEW AMERICAN GARDEN

A low boardwalk leads through this garden of ornamental grasses and vibrant flowers to an octagonal deck with benches around the edges. Here you can sit in the sun and enjoy the sights and sounds of the garden.

ORNAMENTAL GRASSES

A   *Miscanthus sinensis* 'Gracillimus' (maiden grass), 6
B   *Miscanthus sinensis* 'Zebrinus' (zebra grass), 1
C   *Calamagrostis acutiflora* 'Stricta' (feather reed grass), 12
D   *Pennisetum alopecuroides* (fountain grass), 2
E   *Imperata cylindrica* 'Red Baron' (Japanese blood grass), 8

PERENNIALS

F   *Hemerocallis* hybrid (daylily), 20
G   *Baptisia australis* (blue wild indigo), 5
H   *Coreopsis verticillata* (threadleaf coreopsis), 10
I   *Aster* x *frikartii* (Frikart's aster), 3
J   *Rudbeckia fulgida* 'Goldsturm' (orange coneflower), 11
K   *Sedum* x *telephium* 'Autumn Joy' (autumn joy stonecrop), 7
L   *Stachys byzantina* 'Silver Carpet' (lamb's-ears), 8
M   *Yucca filamentosa* 'Goldband' (Adam's needle), 3

BULBS

N   *Narcissus* 'Carlton' (daffodil), 200
O   *Allium aflatunense* 'Purple Sensation' (Persian onion), 36
P   *Crocus* x *vernus* (Dutch crocus), 60

Carole's suburban Maryland home doesn't resemble the typical home in her neighborhood, because the landscape looks dramatically different. She planted great curving borders of ornamental grasses and long-blooming perennials in sunny areas and wildflowers, ground covers, and ferns in shady areas. The only lawn forms a path through the yard, leading from the front garden through the side garden, and around to the back garden—the entire property seems like one large flower bouquet.

Carole's garden, which she planned and constructed herself, uses form and shape with an

NEW AMERICAN GARDENER

An expert on native plants, ornamental grasses, and the New American-style garden, Carole Ottesen has written several books and gives lectures on these subjects. She's happiest, however, when dirtying her hands in her garden.

artist's touch. A perfectly round small patio formed from concentric circles of bricks creates an attractive entrance to the front door, which is framed by great sheaves of ornamental grasses. The roundness is echoed by a large pottery urn placed to the side.

Carole particularly enjoys her New American-style landscape because it evokes the natural landscape of her Midwestern childhood. The ornamental grasses—she grows both native and exotic types—tie themselves to what's around them. Calling herself a lazy gardener, Carole appreciates native plants in her garden because, if grown in the appropriate region and sited properly, she says, they can be allowed to do their own thing with practically no care at all.

November, a month when most gardens look cold and bare, brings dramatic warm colors to Carole's Maryland garden. The grasses (*Miscanthus sinensis* 'Purpurascens') take on warm, earthy hues while their feathery seed heads catch the angled rays of the winter sun. *Sedum* x *telephium* 'Autumn Joy' is a favorite for mass planting because it looks good through much of the year.

ROCK GARDENS

If you're lucky enough to have a natural rock outcropping on your property, you can use the site to create a wonderful naturalistic garden. A spot in full sun can be planted with alpine plants (ones native to mountainous regions above the tree line) to imitate a piece of windswept mountaintop or with saxatile plants (those that flourish in stony and rocky soil). These special plants are adapted to harsh growing conditions and usually grow as small tufts, mats, or buns of dainty flowers and foliage. Grow them for their individual beauty rather than for a bold mass of color. If your land is free of rocks, you can haul some in and make your own naturalistic rock garden or build a rock wall to create the perfect environment for growing these charming plants.

STONES AND SOIL

The secret to success with rock garden plants is in supplying the right kind of soil and rocks. Alpine and saxatile plants need moisture-retentive, but extremely fast-draining, soil of low to moderate nutrition. They rot in rich or damp soil. The right soil preparation for most rock garden plants contains one-third coarse sand, fine gravel, or stone chips; one-third peat or leaf mold; and one-third loamy soil. Usually, you'll need to amend your garden soil to meet these specifications before you install rocks and plants, although gravelly soil needs no help.

Porous rocks, such as limestone, sandstone, shale, and tuffa, work best for alpine plants and are preferred over nonporous types such as marble, basalt, and granite. Because porous rocks absorb water, they keep the roots of the alpine plants cool and moist just as they are in their home environment.

CREATING A ROCK GARDEN

You can obtain rocks for a naturalistic rock garden from a stone yard. Locally quarried rocks cost less than imported ones. A rock garden looks best if constructed from one type of rock and if the rocks are arranged to look like a series of natural outcroppings. Choose the largest rocks you can handle alone or with whatever help you can borrow or hire. Some rock gardeners joke about the size of their rocks, nicknaming them one-person, two-person, and three-person rocks according to the number of persons it took to lift them. (If you have the inclination and the funds, a grand rock garden of massive stones can be created with the help of a landscape designer and some heavy machinery.)

If possible, choose an open north- or east-facing sloping site or create a mound or hill from a fast-draining soil mix. Install the largest rocks first, creating the structure of your garden from a few significant boulders. Then add additional rocks, grouping them into a balanced arrangement.

Avoid laying the rocks on top of the soil. Instead, partially bury them in the amended soil as you would find them in nature. Tilt rocks that jut out from a slope a bit backward so they catch water and funnel it back into the soil. Stratified rocks should be aligned all in the same plane,

Fitted neatly into the contours of a small slope, this rock garden offers the perfect drainage and sunny exposure needed by its alpine inhabitants. Notice how the rocks are skillfully "planted" in the ground to look like natural outcrops, giving the garden a beautiful, natural look and year-round structure.

looking as if they were jolted out of the ground together. You can place them projecting out from the side of the hillside or out of a flat or rolling piece of high ground. Rounded rocks might be "planted" in a flat area at the base of a slope to imitate a mountainous boulder field left behind by an ancient glacier.

Once you've arranged the rocks to your satisfaction, position the rock garden plants where they would naturally grow. Many do best nestled up against a rock, where their roots receive extra water from runoff and shade from the rock's small shadow. You might want to artfully add some dwarf conifers to the rock garden, where they will imitate the contorted specimens found on windswept mountain peaks. These evergreens also add to the garden's structure and year-round appeal.

A mulch of fine gravel or pebbles applied to the soil surface keeps the plant crowns high and dry, preventing rotting. It also keeps dirt from splashing on the tiny plants. The stony mulch is attractive as well, giving that final, natural-looking touch to the rock garden.

WALL GARDENS

A rock retaining wall installed along an existing bank can serve a dual purpose, acting to level out a slope and hold the soil behind it and as a place to grow rock garden plants. You can garden in a wall only if it is a dry wall, one built without mortar. Ideally, you should build the wall with the intention of planting a rock garden in it so you can layer soil between the stones and install the plants as you build the wall.

Use the flattest stones you can find to build the wall. A wall more than 2 feet tall requires a foundation, which can be made by excavating 6 inches to 1 foot of soil from the path of the wall and lining it with several inches of gravel before

HOW TO PLACE ROCKS

When constructing a rock garden, be sure to use similar-looking rocks and arrange them as they would be found in nature.

Top right: Construct a stratified look by burying groups of flat rocks so that only their ends peak through the soil. Tilt the rocks with a backward slant so water drains back into the slope rather than running off.

Bottom right: Large, rounded rocks should be partially or almost completely buried and angled to channel water.

you begin laying the stones. Lay the stones with an inch or two of fast-draining soil between each layer and backfill the wall with the mixture as you go. Place plants—seedlings and small cuttings are best—with their crowns just below the surface of the wall. Gently spread and flatten their root balls as you place a stone on top.

Be sure to leave no air pockets or spaces between the soil in the wall and the earth in the slope. Position each successive layer so the stones cover the joints in the layer below. This keeps water from eroding the soil. Slant the wall backward—1 inch for every 1 foot of height—because a slight angle holds the slope best and allows water to seep down to all the plants in the wall, while keeping them basking in the sun.

If you already have an existing dry wall that you wish to garden in, plants may not get established easily if there is no soil between the layers. Use a crow bar to carefully pry the rocks up a bit and gently push a small rock garden plant with its roots wrapped in damp sphagnum moss into the crevice. Pack in some soil if you can. Position the plant so the crown is just below the wall's surface. You also may be able to sow seeds in a cake of soil and push this into a crack where the seedlings will sprout and send their roots deeper into the soil behind the wall.

Once your wall garden is established, many of the plants will tumble across the top and others will cascade down the face in a colorful waterfall of flowers. Some will even self-sow, delighting you by popping up in the tiniest crevices. When planting or thinning self-sown seedlings, avoid positioning plants too close together, for part of the beauty of your wall garden is in the rocks themselves.

CAREFUL ATTENTION

Because many rock garden plants are small and slow growing, they can quickly become overgrown with weeds. Regular hand weeding is a must in caring for your rock garden or wall. Rock garden plants thrive on lean soil, so you won't need to fertilize them and you'll only need to water in times of drought. In cold areas without a continuous winter snow cover, you may want to protect plants with a covering of evergreen boughs to keep the ground frozen in winter.

Each spring when you tidy up the garden, remove dead foliage and cut back invasive plants. At this time you also can work some fresh soil mixture around the bases of the plants and into the dead centers of any clumps or tufts. This helps the centers fill in again.

PLANTS FOR ROCK WALLS AND GARDENS

These are the easiest plants for beginning rock gardeners to grow. If you become hooked on rock gardening as a hobby, you can graduate to an ecclectic assortment of specialty plants.

Crocus x *vernus*

PERENNIALS

SPRING
Aquilegia spp. (columbines)
Arabis spp. (wall rock cresses)
Armeria maritima (sea pink, thrift)
Aubrieta deltoidea (rock cress)
Aurinia saxatilis (basket-of-gold)
Corydalis lutea (yellow corydalis)
Iberis sempervirens (edging candytuft)
Phlox subulata (moss pink)
Potentilla tabernaemontani (spring cinquefoil)
Pulsatilla vulgaris (pasque flower)

SUMMER
Campanula carpatica (Carpathian bellflower)
Campanula portenschlagiana (Dalmatian bellflower)
Cerastium tomentosum (snow-in-summer)
Corydalis lutea (yellow corydalis)
Delosperma cooperi (hardy iceplant)
Dianthus spp. (pinks)
Geranium spp. (cranesbills)
Geum quellyon (geum)
Gypsophila repens (baby's breath)
Heuchera spp. (coralbells)
Leontopodium alpinum (edelweiss)
Petrorhagia saxifraga (coat flower, tunic flower)
Saponaria ocymoides (rock soapwort)
Scabiosa caucasica (pincushion flower, scabious)
Scutellaria baicalensis (skullcap)
Thymus pseudolanuginosus (woolly thyme)

LATE SUMMER AND FALL
Anaphalis cinnamomea (pearly everlasting)
Corydalis lutea (yellow corydalis)
Petrorhagia saxifraga (coat flower)
Sedum cauticolum
Sedum kamtschaticum (golden stonecrop)
Sedum spathulifolium

ANNUALS

Brachycome iberidifolia (swan river daisy)
Cheiranthus cheiri (wallflower)
Dianthus chinensis (China pink)
Eschscholzia californica (California poppy)
Euphorbia marginata (snow-on-the-mountain)
Felicia amelloides (blue daisy, blue marguerite)
Gaillardia pulchella (annual blanket-flower)
Gazania rigens (gazania)
Iberis umbellata (annual candytuft)
Lantana spp. (lantanas)
Lobelia erinus (edging lobelia)
Lobularia maritima (sweet alyssum)
Melampodium paludosum (black-foot daisy)
Nierembergia hippomanica violacea (cupflower)
Nigella damascena (love-in-a-mist)
Sanvitalia procumbens (creeping zinnia)
Verbena x *hybrida* (verbena)
Zinnia angustifolia (narrow-leaf zinnia)

BULBS

SPRING
Bulbocodium vernum (spring meadow saffron)
Crocus chrysanthus (snow crocus)
Crocus x *vernus* (Dutch crocus)
Fritillaria meleagris (checkered lily)
Iris danfordiae (Danford iris)
Iris reticulata (reticulated iris)
Narcissus x *cyclamenius* (cyclamen daffodil)
Scilla siberica (Siberian squill)
Tulipa spp. (tulips)

SUMMER
Allium spp. (ornamental onions)

LATE SUMMER AND FALL
Allium spp. (ornamental onions)
Crocus sativus (saffron crocus)
Crocus speciosus (fall crocus)
Cyclamen coum (winter cyclamen)
Cyclamen hederifolium (hardy cyclamen)
Sternbergia lutea (winter daffodil)

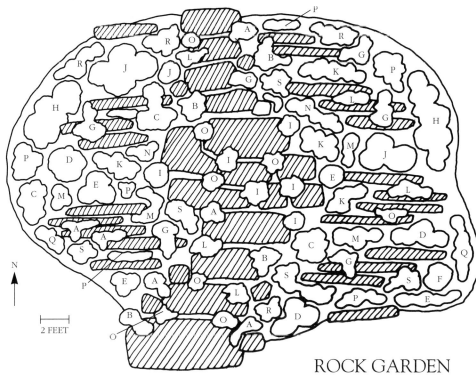

PERENNIALS

A *Thymus pseudolanuginosus* (woolly thyme), 4

B *Phlox subulata* (moss phlox), 3

C *Campanula portenschlagiana* (Dalmatian bellflower), 3

D *Iberis sempervirens* (edging candytuft), 7

E *Dianthus plumarius* (cottage pink), 10

F *Scabiosa caucasica* (pincushion flower), 1

G *Aurinia saxatilis* (basket-of-gold), 4

H *Campanula carpatica* (Carpathian bellflower), 18

I *Corydalis lutea* (yellow corydalis), 5

J *Geranium sanguineum striatum* (cranesbill), 8

K *Delosperma cooperi* (hardy iceplant), 5

ANNUALS

L *Brachycome iberidifolia* (swan river daisy), 6

M *Eschscholzia californica* (California poppy), 9

N *Nierembergia hippomanica violacea* (cupflower), 12

O *Lobularia maritima* (sweet alyssum), 21

BULBS

P *Crocus chrysanthus* (snow crocus), 36

Q *Iris reticulata* (reticulated iris), 50

R *Tulipa kaufmanniana* (water lily tulip), 36

S *Tulipa batalinii* 'Bright Gem' (Bokhara tulip), 72

ROCK GARDEN

Slabs of stones form a gentle stairway leading up and over this mounded rock garden. You can pause at the small patiolike area and enjoy the fragrant plants tucked between the stones. The sides of the mound feature stone outcroppings arranged in stratified layers and draped with cascades of pretty flowers and foliage.

Once a lawn bounded by rock retaining walls bordering the street above, the front yard of this small corner property now features a rock garden packed with rare and unusual plants. The garden wraps around the entire house, and not a blade of grass grows anywhere. Instead, rock outcroppings, gravel paths, stone steps, and a spectacular array of flowers and foliage create a wonderful naturalistic scene that can be viewed and enjoyed both from indoors and out.

A ROCK GARDENER

Before her children were grown, Jan Waltemath had no time for gardening. Now, a dozen years later, she has become a passionate and knowledgeable gardener. Jan starts many of the rare plants in her garden from seeds gleaned from plant society seed exchanges.

About 12 years ago, when her four daughters were grown, Jan turned from nurturing children to nurturing plants. She began transforming the property surrounding her Portland, Oregon, home into a plant lover's haven. Capitalizing on the existing stone walls, which were serving no function other than to retain soil and create level ground, Jan ripped out rhododendrons and azaleas that concealed the rocks and tucked small alpine plants into the crevices. On more level ground she arranged perennials, ornamental grasses, flowering shrubs, and ferns.

To counteract Portland's soggy weather, Jan creates fast-draining soil amended with grit brought back from the Cascade Mountains and top-dresses with gravel. She avoids the jumbled look of a plant collector's garden by planting according to color scheme, giving the garden a cohesive feel yet allowing herself to pack in all the species and rare finds she treasures.

GARDENS TO ATTRACT HUMMINGBIRDS AND BUTTERFLIES

Hummingbirds and butterflies may be surprise visitors to almost any garden, but a garden designed especially to attract them can come alive with their iridescent colors and eye-catching movements. Although hummingbirds and butterflies don't have identical needs, both get much of their nourishment from flower nectar. You can plant a garden to entice one or the other, or both, because they're attracted to many of the same flowers.

A garden designed to attract butterflies and hummingbirds need not conform to any garden style. You can make it naturalistic or formal, although butterflies and hummingbirds have evolved as pollinators to many lovely wildflowers, so you may want to plant the garden with native plants in a naturalistic style. Whatever style of garden you prefer, certain key ingredients must be met: a nectar source, supplemental food sources, a suitable water supply, sunlight, and shelter. Other than that, your garden can be anything you want it to be. One thing any hummingbird and butterfly garden is certain to be, however, is colorful, because it will be filled with cascades of flowers and fluttering wings.

HUMMINGBIRD HABITS

One hummingbird species or another is likely to dart and hover in your garden at some time during the year. Some will just pass through on their migratory route to and from South and Central America; others may arrive in spring and remain until fall. Of the 340 hummingbird species, only 10 are found north of the Mexican border and only one—the ruby-throated hummingbird—settles east of the Mississippi River. Hummers are uncommon in the treeless Plains states and common in Arizona and the Western states. They live year-round in the Sunbelt.

Unique among birds, hummingbirds have a special wing structure that allows them to hover and fly backward. They're fast, too, flying at speeds of 25 to 50 miles per hour and dive-bombing at 60 miles per hour during mating rituals. When hovering above a flower, their wings beat up to 80 times a second, explaining why all you experience is a blur of colorful feathers and the drum of pounding wings.

Hummingbirds live year-round in the Sunbelt, finding a ready nectar supply in the desert wildflowers. The shrubs and flowers in this naturalistic Arizona garden offer a concentration of blossoms preferred by hummingbirds, including the pink and red tubular flowers of beard-tongue (*Penstemon barbatus*).

Red attracts hummingbirds like a magnet. Although they visit flowers of other colors— orange and pink are also favorites—they prefer red flowers over all others and even curiously investigate anything red they encounter, including red clothes hanging on the line. Their long, narrow bills and needlelike tongues allow them to secure nectar from tubular flowers unreachable by bees and butterflies. In return for the nectar, they pollinate the flowers. When a hummingbird buries its head deep inside a tubular flower, pollen brushes off onto its head and receives a free ride to the next blossom. Hummers will visit nectar-laden flat flowers but prefer tubular shapes because they need not compete with bees and butterflies for the nectar.

CREATING A HUMMINGBIRD GARDEN

To create a garden designed to attract hummingbirds, plant plenty of red, tubular flowers. These invite migrating birds to stop in your garden, and they may decide to take up residence for the summer if the garden offers enough other nectar-rich blossoms. Be sure to plant lots of flowers—a single hummingbird needs to visit hundreds of flowers a day to fuel its high metabolism. Choose annuals, such as red salvia and fuchsia, that bloom all-season and perennials that open sequentially, so your resident hummers won't ever find themselves without food.

Arrange the flowers in beds and borders around a large, sunny lawn so the birds can get to them easily. Avoid blocking the flowers with tall foliage or structures that impede the birds' hovering and lightning-fast flight. You may want to plant hummingbird favorites in window boxes or hanging baskets on a porch or near a patio or window so you can enjoy the birds up close. They aren't shy so you can lure them quite near.

One of the easiest hummingbird-attracting flowers you can grow is the annual red salvia (*Salvia splendens*). Plant masses of it and you'll have an almost unending nectar supply that may lure a pair of hummingbirds to settle in your garden for the entire growing season.

Hummingbirds also eat insects, which they catch on the wing in midair or pick off flowers. Be careful with insecticides; indiscriminate spraying may rob your feathered friends of an essential protein source.

Hummingbirds need water but will not drink or bathe in water as deep as that in most birdbaths. They prefer to dart in and out of the spray from a waterfall or fine-spray sprinkler and drink dewdrops and water that settles in a cupped leaf or indentation of a rock. You can cater to their water needs with a shallow basin. Better yet, include an artificial garden pool and fountain or trickling waterfall in your garden design.

PLANTS TO ATTRACT HUMMINGBIRDS

PERENNIALS

SPRING
Aquilegia spp. (columbines)
Dicentra spp. (bleeding hearts)
Pulmonaria spp. (lungworts)

SUMMER
Alcea rosea (hollyhock)
Asclepias tuberosa (butterfly weed)
Dianthus barbatus (sweet William)
Digitalis spp. (foxgloves)
Heuchera spp. (coralbells)
Kniphofia uvaria (red-hot poker, torchlily)
Mimulus guttatus (common monkey flower)
Monarda didyma (bee-balm, oswego tea)
Penstemon spp. (beard-tongues)

LATE SUMMER AND FALL
Hosta spp. and hybrids (hosta)
Lobelia cardinalis (cardinal flower)

ANNUALS
Antirrhinum majus (snapdragon)
Consolida ambigua (rocket larkspur)
Fuchsia x *hybrida* (fuchsia)
Ipomoea purpurea (morning glory)
Lantana spp. (lantanas)
Lobelia erinus (edging lobelia)
Mirabilis jalapa (four-o'clock)
Nicotiana spp. (flowering tobacco)
Pelargonium peltatum (ivy geranium)
Pelargonium x *hortorum* (zonal geranium)
Petunia x *hybrida* (petunia)
Phlox drummondti (annual phlox)
Salvia splendens (red salvia, scarlet sage)

BULBS
SUMMER
Canna x *generalis* (canna lily)
Gladiolus x *hortulanus* (gladiolus)

LATE SUMMER AND FALL
Canna x *generalis* (canna lily)
Dahlia x *pinnata* (dahlia)

Fuchsia x *hybrida*

Hummingbirds favor red, scentless, nectar-laden, tubular flowers, but they like pink and orange blossoms, too. These flowers are sure to lure hummingbirds to your garden.

Most yards with trees and shrubs provide enough shelter for hummingbirds. A hummingbird might build its thimble-size nest on a tree limb, light fixture, or tangle of vines. The nest is camouflaged with spider webs, bits of bark, and leaves, and is so tiny that you'll probably never notice it.

Even though your garden may offer plenty of nectar-laden flowers, experts advise including at least one hummingbird feeder. This supplemental food source helps out with their high-calorie diet needs and supplies emergency food in case of flower failure. Suspend the feeder in the shade of a tree or porch and keep it filled. Small feeders may need replenishing once or twice a day.

You can purchase a commercial mixture, but a home brew is just as good. Make the sugar-water solution by combining 1 part sugar to 5 parts water and boiling it to dissolve the sugar and kill bacteria and mold. You can store it in the refrigerator safely for up to a week. Clean the feeder thoroughly at least once a week, more often if signs of algae or mold appear.

Because hummingbirds can be quite territorial and sometimes aggressive, separate feeders by at least 6 feet to prevent one bird from dominating them all. A better solution is to locate several feeders out of sight of one another. The more feeders you have, the more individual birds your garden can support.

Once you've lured a pair of hummingbirds to your garden, you can be sure they will come back year after year, for they have great memories. These intriguing birds will delight you with their swift flight, bright colors, and keen intelligence. They remember exactly where you hung the feeder the previous year and buzz around it in spring if they find the spot empty. Hummingbirds may sometimes follow the person who fills the feeder, darting and hovering to catch her attention. They have even been known to become tame enough to perch on a finger.

ATTRACTING BUTTERFLIES

Like hummingbirds, butterflies feed on nectar-rich flowers, but they prefer flat heads or narrow spikes of numerous tiny flowers that offer a landing platform or perch to hold onto when feeding. Flowers in the daisy family are butterfly favorites and are certain bets to attract butterflies anywhere in the country. Although hummingbird flowers are rarely fragrant, butterfly flowers often emit a heady perfume. The flowers that attract butterflies are bright and colorful, but butterflies see only the ultraviolet color patterns in the flowers. These patterns are invisible to humans, but they draw a clear road map to the nectar source for butterflies and bees.

When designing your garden to attract butterflies, plant large masses of individual flowers rather than single flowers scattered here and there. This large splash of blossoms beckons butterflies by sight and smell. Butterflies also visit the flowers of many trees, shrubs, and vines; favorites include butterfly bush, azaleas, honeysuckle, lilac, viburnum, wisteria, and spicebush.

Locate your garden in full sun but protected from strong winds by a fence or living wind-break. Butterflies appreciate a naturalistic, meadowlike garden of flowers and grasses. If the right flowers are present, however, they won't turn their feelers up at a formal garden.

Butterflies need water but prefer to drink from mud puddles rather than from deeper water. Often they congregate around a water source. You can easily supply water by filling a shallow basin with clean sand and keeping it flooded. Sink the basin in a sunny spot in the garden. Because butterflies are cold-blooded, they need to bask in the sun to warm up enough to fly. Provide them with flat rocks for sunning, although they also will light on stone or brick walls, paths, patios, and even deck railings.

THE GOOD WITH THE BAD

The butterflies that we so delight in, with their languid flight and fluttering colors, have a less agreeable side. This winged form is just one stage of their life cycle; the other is a caterpillar stage. A butterfly's main mission in life is to mate and lay eggs that hatch into caterpillars. Usually living for about two weeks, the female butterfly lays eggs on the undersides of a host plant—generally a different type of plant than it feeds on for nectar. The eggs hatch in a few days into tiny larvae, which mature into caterpillars. The caterpillars live for several weeks, growing ever larger and eating the foliage or flowers of the host plant.

For better enjoyment, you can lure butterflies up close by planting butterfly-attracting plants in containers on a sunny patio. Butterflies prefer fragrant flowers, so you'll also be creating a delightful sensory experience to enjoy while sitting in the shade of an umbrella. This garden includes: flowering tobacco (*Nicotiana*), catmint (*Nepeta*), daylily (*Hemerocallis*), black-eyed Susan (*Rudbeckia*), and two species of butterfly bush (*Buddleia*).

When the caterpillar stops feeding, it goes through a metamorphosis, forming a saclike chrysalis with a pupae inside. The pupae transforms itself from a caterpillar into a winged butterfly to continue the life cycle.

Depending on the type of butterfly and the climate, some butterflies go through several generations in a single season before hibernating or migrating for the winter. To keep many butterflies in your garden, you also need to supply a food source for the caterpillars because most butterflies fly no more than several hundred yards from where they emerged from their chrysalis.

Fortunately, only two butterfly species admired for their elegant appearance have caterpillar stages that are destructive to garden plants. The other types feed on weeds or trees and shrubs that easily withstand the feeding injury. Eastern black swallowtails, gorgeous butterflies with long, iridescent tails and bright eyelike spots, come from brightly striped green-and-yellow caterpillars that munch on plants in the carrot family, notably parsley, dill, and carrots, but also on the pretty roadside weed Queen-Anne's lace. You can attract and keep this butterfly in your garden by planting plenty of parsley and dill. The caterpillar stage of the European cabbage white butterfly, a delightful little bright white butterfly, feeds on cabbage family plants, zonal geraniums, and a few other garden flowers.

Other good plants for feeding the caterpillar stages of popular butterflies include sassafras, willow, cherry, and locust trees; spicebush; violets; clover; milkweeds; nasturtium; thistles; and hollyhocks. Many of these may be present in nearby wild areas, vacant lots, or undeveloped areas of your property.

Remember that spraying your entire property with insecticides usually destroys the caterpillar stages of the beautiful butterflies you are hoping to enjoy. It's better for your plants, the butterflies, and the environment to use insecticides only when a serious pest occurs and then only on the affected plants. You can hand-pick destructive caterpillars off your flowers and vegetables if you wish to spare the butterflies. You also can plant plenty for both you and the caterpillars, covering your share with fine netting to prevent egg-laying, or selectively spraying only those plants you wish to protect.

If you become serious about butterfly gardening, you can consult a good field guide to determine which species are most likely to frequent your area and then plant the specific host and nectar plants to attract them. Meanwhile, planting masses of the flowers listed in the chart opposite will get you started.

Butterflies flock to spider flowers (*Cleome hasslerana*), finding their nectar-laden blossoms easy to hold on to. Although people don't always find this long-blooming annual's musty scent appealing, butterflies apparently do.

PLANTS TO ATTRACT BUTTERFLIES

PERENNIALS AND BIENNIALS
SPRING
Arabis caucasica (wall rock cress)
Aubrieta deltoidea (rock cress)
Aurinia saxatilis (basket-of-gold)
Corydalis lutea (yellow corydalis)
Iberis sempervirens (edging candytuft)
Primula spp. (primroses)
Viola spp. (violets)*

SUMMER
Achillea spp. (yarrows)
Alcea rosea (hollyhock)*
Armeria maritima (sea pink, thrift)
Asclepias tuberosa (butterfly weed)
Astilbe spp. (astilbes)
Baptisia australis (blue wild indigo)
Coreopsis spp. (coreopsis, tickseed)
Crambe cordifolia (colewort)*
Dianthus spp. (pinks)
Erigeron x *hybridus* (fleabane)
Eryngium spp. (sea hollies)
Gaillardia x *grandiflora* (blanket-flower)
Hemerocallis hybrids (daylilies)
Hesperis matronalis (dame's rocket)
Lysimachia clethroides (gooseneck loosestrife)
Monarda didyma (bee-balm, oswego tea)
Phlox spp. (phloxes)
Saponaria ocymoides (rock soapwort)
Scabiosa caucasica (pincushion flower, scabious)
Sidalcea malviflora (checkerbloom)
Stokesia laevis (Stokes' aster)
Thalictrum rochebrunianum (Japanese meadow-rue, lavender mist)

LATE SUMMER AND FALL
Anemone x *hybrida* (Japanese anemone)
Aster spp. (asters)
Echinacea purpurea (purple coneflower)
Echinops ritro (globe-thistle)
Eupatorium fistulosum (Joe-Pye weed)
Helianthus spp. (sunflowers)
Rudbeckia spp. (coneflowers)
Salvia spp. (sages)
Sedum spp. (stonecrops)
Sidalcea malviflora (checkerbloom)
Solidago hybrids (goldenrod)

ANNUALS
Ageratum houstonianun (flossflower)
Anethum graveolens (dill) *
Antirrhinum majus (snapdragon) *
Borago officinalis (borage)*
Cleome hasslerana (spider flower)
Consolida ambigua (rocket larkspur)
Coreopsis tinctoria (golden coreopsis, calliopsis)
Cosmos bipinnatus (cosmos)
Dahlia x *hybrida* (annual dahlia)
Dianthus chinensis (China pink)
Felicia amelloides (blue daisy, blue marguerite)
Gaillardia pulchella (annual blanket-flower)
Helichrysum bracteatum (strawflower)
Heliotropium arborescens (heliotrope)
Iberis umbellata (annual candytuft)
Ipomoea tricolor (morning glory)
Lantana spp. (lantanas)
Lavatera trimestris (tree mallow, annual mallow)
Lobularia maritima (sweet alyssum)
Petunia x *hybrida* (petunia)
Petroselinum crispum (parsley) *
Phlox drummondii (annual phlox)
Sanvitalia procumbens (creeping zinnia)
Schizanthus pinnatus (butterfly flower)
Tagetes spp. (marigolds)
Tithonia rotundifolia (Mexican sunflower)
Tropaeolum majus (nasturtium) *
Verbena x *hybrida* (verbena)
Zinnia spp. (zinnias)

BULBS
SPRING
Allium spp. (ornamental onions)

SUMMER
Lilium spp. (lilies)

These plants offer fragrant, nectar-rich flowers shaped with a landing platform—the ideal flowers to attract butterflies. Those marked with an * also serve as host plants for caterpillars.

Zinnia

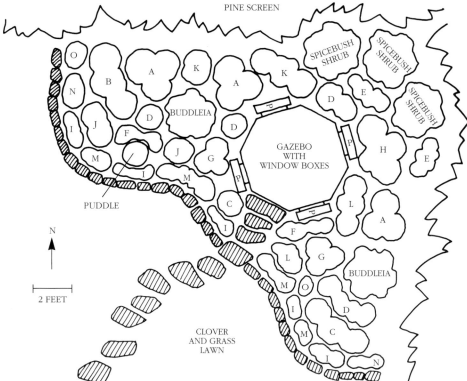

PINE SCREEN

SPICEBUSH SHRUB

SPICEBUSH SHRUB

SPICEBUSH SHRUB

BUDDLEIA

GAZEBO WITH WINDOW BOXES

PUDDLE

BUDDLEIA

N

2 FEET

CLOVER AND GRASS LAWN

BUTTERFLY GARDEN

You can enjoy butterflies up close in this gazebo surrounded by a sea of nectar-laden flowers. Designed to attract butterflies from spring through fall, this garden also contains caterpillar host plants located in inconspicuous places.

PERENNIALS

A *Alcea rosea* (hollyhock), 9

B *Rudbeckia fulgida* 'Goldsturm' (orange coneflower), 3

C *Sedum* 'Autumn Joy' (autumn joy stonecrop), 4

D *Hesperis matronalis* (dame's rocket), 6

E *Viola odorata* (sweet violet), 7

F *Coreopsis verticillata* (threadleaf coreopsis), 3

G *Asclepias tuberosa* (butterfly weed), 6

H *Hemerocallis* hybrid (daylily), 4

I *Aurinia saxatilis* (basket-of-gold), 9

J *Monarda didyma* (bee-balm, oswego tea), 3

K *Rudbeckia nitida* (shining coneflower), 4

L *Anemone* x *hybrida* (Japanese anemone), 4

ANNUALS

M *Phlox drummondii* (annual phlox), 18

N *Petroselinum crispum* (parsley), 12

O *Tropaeolum majus* (nasturtium), 6

P *Petunia* x *hybrida* (petunia), 12

150

HUMMINGBIRD GARDEN

Backed by a vine-covered latticework fence with a decorative arbor framing the entrance, this formal garden provides the appropriate spring-through-fall flowers to attract hummingbirds.

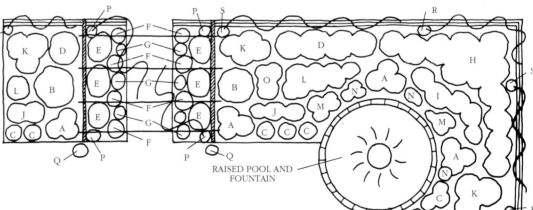

RAISED POOL AND FOUNTAIN

2 FEET

PERENNIALS

A *Aquilegia* 'Star Red' (columbine), 7
B *Dicentra spectabilis* (bleeding heart), 2
C *Heuchera* 'Matin Bells' (coralbells), 14
D *Monarda didyma* 'Cambridge Scarlet' (bee-balm, oswego tea), 9
E *Hosta* 'Honeybells' (August lily), 6
F *Mertensia virginica* (Virginia bluebells), 8
G *Pulmonaria saccharata* 'Mrs. Moon' (Bethlehem sage), 6
H *Digitalis* x *mertonensis* (strawberry foxglove), 12
I *Lobelia cardinalis* (cardinal flower), 5
J *Dianthus barbatus* 'Scarlet Beauty' (sweet William), 6

ANNUALS

K *Nicotiana sylvestris* (great-flowering tobacco), 10
L *Salvia splendens* 'Hotline Red' (red salvia), 18
M *Mimulus* x *hybridus* (monkey flower), 10
N *Lobularia erinus* (edging lobelia), 8
O *Salvia farinacea* 'Victoria' (mealy-cup sage), 8
P *Ipomoea tricolor* 'Heavenly Blue' (morning glory), 4

VINES

Q *Wisteria sinensis* (Chinese wisteria), 1
R *Clematis* x *hybrida* 'Niobe' (red clematis), 3
S *Lonicera* x *brownii* 'Dropmore Scarlet,' 2

CHAPTER SIX

DESIGNING PROBLEM-SITE GARDENS

Transform a Difficult Site into an Easy-Care Garden

Opposite: Shady sites such as this city garden can come alive with color if planted with shade-loving perennials, bulbs, and ground covers. Naturalized beneath the dogwood tree are summer snowflakes (*Leucojum aestivum*) and wood hyacinths (*Hyacinthoides hispanica*).

Left: Orange coneflower (*Rudbeckia fulgida*), baby's breath (*Gypsophila paniculata*), shasta daisy (*Chrysanthemum* x *superbum*), zinnia (*Zinnia elegans*), and African marigold (*Tagetes erecta*) flourish in the hot, baking sun of this Indiana garden located beside a driveway.

Not all of us find ourselves blessed with a garden site basking in life-giving sun or boasting fertile soil. Although most properties have so-called average soil and have their share of sunny and shady spots, some sites daunt even the best gardeners. A combination of sandy soil and unrelenting sun can cook flowers to a cinder, while a constantly wet site that drains poorly or catches runoff from higher ground rots plants into moldy masses. And deep shade drives many flower gardeners to despair.

No matter how hostile your garden's growing conditions may seem, however, take hope.

Almost any site can be turned into a splendid garden with some knowledgeable effort. The easiest way is to take inspiration from the old adage, "If you can't beat 'em, join 'em." Don't insist on growing the flowers so familiar to the English flower border in those imperfect sites—that's a no-win situation. Instead, join forces with the site's growing conditions and cultivate flowers and plants that prefer those difficult conditions. After all, adversity is relative—all plants are not created equal. Some actually crave the hostile environment that others disdain.

TURN SHADE INTO AN ASSET

A shady garden site can become the most beautiful spot on your property, if you are armed with a palette of shade-loving plants and the know-how to properly grow them. Your shady site can offer a cool welcome on a hot summer's day when filled with alluring flowers and soft foliage spread out beneath a high canopy of leafy boughs. Most gardeners err when gardening in the shade by struggling to grow plants that need more sun than the site offers. Shade-loving plants have adapted to low light, often by developing delicate, thin leaves that efficiently absorb whatever sun falls on them. Other shade lovers, especially woodland wildflowers, adapt to shady sites by growing and blooming under deciduous trees during early spring, before the overhead tree foliage blocks out much of the sunlight. Such plants enjoy the bright light of spring and may go dormant and die to the ground during summer after the trees have fully leafed out.

The other challenge posed by shady sites isn't so obvious as the lack of sun. Shaded locations are thought to be cool and damp, but certain shady spots harbor poor, dry soil. This is because surface tree roots suck up all the available moisture and nutrients, robbing shallow-rooted perennials and ground covers of their share. A thick canopy of tree leaves may worsen the problem, serving as an umbrella and deflecting rain from the ground beneath. Lack of moisture, not lack of light, often proves to be the culprit when shade-loving plants fail to thrive in their preferred light conditions.

Dry, root-clogged soil feels and looks hard and compacted; when you try to dig a hole with a trowel or shovel, it can't easily penetrate the ground. If you discover that the soil in your potential shade garden is hard and compacted, try digging in lots of organic matter, such as rotted manure or compost, as long as you don't interfere with major tree roots. If tree roots prevent your digging a planting hole for a shade-loving shrub or perennial, you can sever all interfering roots smaller than 1 inch in diameter without harming the tree.

Where you fear that digging will tamper with tree roots, spread a layer of topsoil no more than 4 inches deep over the ground. Cover this layer with a 2-inch-deep mulch of chopped-up leaves, which will decompose into a rich humus. Anything deeper may smother the roots. Earthworms ought to move into the decomposing leaves, further speeding the decomposition, and the worms also will burrow into the harder subsoil beneath the topsoil, helping to make it more amenable to gardening. Where shallow-rooted trees pose a problem, you'll be waging a continual battle and will need to thickly replenish the mulch each year.

When gardening in the dry shade under a tree, water regularly and deeply during summer. Where you might usually apply an inch of water a week to satisfy your garden's needs, when gardening in the dry soil beneath maples, beeches, and sycamores, you may need to apply 2 inches of water—1 inch for the trees and 1 inch for the flowers.

Opposite: Shade need not be a deterrent to growing a fabulous garden; as long as the soil is loose, fertile, and moist, many types of beautiful plants will flourish. Here, under the shade of a high-pruned pine tree, astilbe (*Astilbe* x *arendsii* 'Appleblossom' and 'Fanal'), August lily (*Hosta plantaginea*), and Japanese painted fern (*Athyrium goeringianum pictum*) create a lovely combination of contrasting foliage textures and flower colors.

Below left: A pine-straw path edged with cowslip primrose (*Primula veris*), Christmas ferns (*Polystichum acrostichoides*), and Lenten roses (*Helleborus orientalis*) leads visitors beneath the trees in this colorful shade garden.

DEFINING YOUR SHADE

In learning to garden in the shade, first consider which type of shade you have, because the type of shade determines which plants will grow best.

Deep shade is usually defined as all-day shade where no direct sun ever reaches the ground; this often occurs under heavily foliaged trees. Deep shade may be dry or moist depending on the particular site. Fewer plants thrive in this type of shade, especially if dry, than in brighter conditions.

Part shade or **half shade** means shade for part of the day with direct sunlight during the other part. Many sun-loving plants bloom well in half shade because they receive from four to six hours of direct sun each day, although they may not perform as well as in all-day sun. Morning shade followed by afternoon sun may be too hot for many shade plants, causing them to wilt in the heat. The cooler morning sun with afternoon shade pleases many flowering shade lovers.

Light shade or **filtered shade** occurs under a canopy of open-branched trees where spots of sunshine filter to the ground in a constantly shifting play of dappled shadows. A wide selection of plants prospers in filtered shade.

Open shade occurs on the north side of a building, where no direct sunlight falls but where light may be reflected to the ground from surrounding walls. You can brighten such spots by painting the walls a light color. Open shade often remains damp, unless the building creates a rain shadow and blocks rainfall from reaching the ground.

You can often turn a densely shaded site into a lightly shaded one, where you can grow a wider choice of plants, by thinning out a few tree branches. Cut branches off right at the trunk, or remove side branches where they fork into a Y. Don't leave behind unsightly stubby branches, which will sprout unnatural-looking new growth. You may have to remove or thin out branches every few years to maintain the light shade conditions.

Shade-loving plants don't usually bloom as abundantly as sun worshipers, perhaps as an energy-conserving measure, but you can enjoy a host of pretty flowers in the shade if you choose the right kinds. Your shade garden will rely on an assortment of beautiful foliage plants for much of its allure. Plants with finely divided fernlike leaves and with gargantuan tropical-looking leaves will combine to create a verdant setting. You will gain a new appreciation for the color green, for it isn't just one color but a rainbow of tints and hues, from emerald green to chartreuse, from blue-green to dusky gray-green.

Plants with white-variegated leaves or white or pastel flowers look especially good in shade gardens, because they brighten up the shadows. Avoid dark red or purple flowers in shady spots because they recede further into the dimness. Golden-leaved plants and yellow flowers create the impression of a beam of sunshine scattered across the garden floor, a pretty sight that will entice any gardener into the yard.

Opposite top: A white wall reflects light into the shade created by trees, brightening the space and allowing a lovely collection of foliage and flowering perennials to flourish. Included are: hosta (*Hosta*), Lenten rose (*Helleborus orientalis*), hybrid columbine (*Aquilegia* x *hybrida*), bugleweed (*Ajuga reptans*), and English ivy.

Opposite bottom: Impatiens are one of the few annuals that bloom lavishly in shade. Be sure to give them and other shade plants plenty of water because they must compete with tree roots for the available moisture.

Above: White flowers and white-variegated foliage brighten the shadows of a shade garden like beacons of light. This pretty spring combination includes variegated hosta (*Hosta* 'Medio-picta') and white-flowered azaleas and daffodils planted in a sea of sweet woodruff (*Galium odoratum*). A brick mowing strip helps keep the ground cover in bounds.

Left: Undaunted by shade cast by trees and a building, this side-yard garden becomes an inviting place to walk when planted with shade-loving hosta (*Hosta*), lungwort (*Pulmonaria*), wild blue phlox (*Phlox divaricata*), green and gold (*Chrysogonum virginianum*), bleeding heart (*Dicentra eximia*), foamflower (*Tiarella*), and Christmas rose (*Helleborus*).

158

SHADE-LOVING FLOWERS AND FOLIAGE

These plants prosper in shady sites where more familiar border plants languish. Those marked with an * do well in difficult dry-shade conditions.

Digitalis purpurea

PERENNIALS AND BIENNIALS
SPRING
Alchemilla mollis (lady's mantle)*
Dicentra eximia (fringed bleeding heart)
Dicentra spectabilis (common bleeding heart)
Epimedium spp. (barrenworts)*
Lamium maculatum (spotted dead nettle)
Lunaria annua (money-plant, honesty)
Myosotis sylvatica (woodland forget-me-not)
Phlox stolonifera (creeping phlox)
Polemonium caeruleum (Jacob's ladder)
Primula spp. (primroses)
Pulmonaria saccharata (Bethlehem sage)
Viola labradorica (Labrador violet)*
Viola odorata (sweet violet)

SUMMER
Astilbe chinensis 'Pumila' (dwarf
   Chinese astilbe)*
Astilbe simplicifolia (star astilbe)*
Astilbe x *arendsii* (astilbe)
Cimicifuga spp. (bugbanes)
Corydalis lutea (yellow corydalis)*
Digitalis purpurea (foxglove)
Helleborus spp. (Christmas rose and Lenten rose)
Hemerocallis fulva (tawny daylily)
Hosta spp. and cultivars (hostas)*

LATE SUMMER AND FALL
Aconitum spp. (monkshoods)
Anemone x *hybrida* (Japanese anemone)
Astilbe taquetii 'Superba' (fall astilbe)
Begonia grandis (hardy begonia)
Cimicifuga simplex (Kamchatka bugbane)
Corydalis lutea (yellow corydalis)*
Dicentra eximia (fringed bleeding heart)
Eupatorium coelestinum (hardy ageratum)
Hosta spp. and cultivars (hostas)*
Ligularia spp. (golden rays)
Liriope muscari (blue lilyturf)

ANNUALS
Begonia x *semperflorens* (wax begonia)
Coleus x *hybridus* (coleus)
Impatiens wallerana (impatiens)
Lobularia maritima (sweet alyssum)
Torenia fournieri (wishbone flower)
Viola x *wittrockiana* (pansy)

ORNAMENTAL GRASSES
Carex morrowii (Japanese sedge grass)
Carex stricta 'Bowles Golden' (Bowles
   golden grass)
Chasmanthium latifolium (northern sea oats)
Hakonechloa macra 'Aureola' (Japanese
   wind grass)

BULBS
SPRING
Convallaria majalis (lily of the-valley)
Galanthus nivalis (snowdrop)
Hyacinthoides hispanica (wood hyacinth)
Leucojum aestivum (summer snowflake)

SUMMER
Agapanthus hybrids (African lilies)
Begonia x *tuberhybrida* (tuberous begonia)
Caladium x *hortulanum* (fancy-leaved caladium)

LATE SUMMER AND FALL
Begonia x *tuberhybrida* (tuberous begonia)
Caladium x *hortulanum* (fancy-leaved caladium)
Lilium martagon (Turk's cap lily)
Lycoris squamigera (resurrection lily)

SHADE GARDEN UNDER A TREE

In this design, the shady ground under a high-branched, deep-rooted tree is transformed from a barren patch of dirt into a beautiful garden. The circular seat ringing the trunk provides a cool, quiet place to sit and relax while enjoying the garden, which blooms from spring through fall. A wood-chip mulch keeps the plants cool and moist and the path mud free.

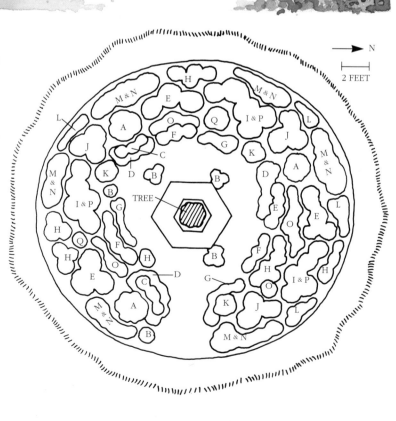

PERENNIALS AND BIENNIALS

A   *Hosta sieboldiana* 'Elegans' (blueleaf hosta), 3

B   *Viola cornuta* (horned violet), 11

C   *Hosta* 'Ginko Craig,' 9

D   *Lamium maculatum* 'White Nancy' (spotted dead nettle), 12

E   *Astilbe taquetii* 'Superba' (fall astilbe), 9

F   *Liriope muscari* (blue lilyturf), 9

G   *Phlox stolonifera* (creeping phlox), 15

H   *Dicentra eximia* (fringed bleeding heart), 15

I   *Digitalis purpurea* (foxglove), 15

J   *Cimicifuga* 'The Pearl' (bugbane), 9

K   *Begonia grandis* (hardy begonia), 3

L   *Ajuga reptans* 'Burgundy Glow' (bugleweed), 16

ANNUALS

M   *Impatiens wallerana* 'Accent Pink' (impatiens), 52

BULBS

N   *Galanthus nivalis* (snowdrop), 120

O   *Narcissus* 'Thalia' (narcissus), 36

P   *Hyacinthoides hispanica* (wood hyacinth), 60

PERENNIALS

A *Hemerocallis* 'Hyperion' (daylily), 10
B *Epimedium* 'Roseum' (barrenwort), 8
C *Alchemilla mollis* (lady's mantle), 6
D *Hosta* 'Sum and Substance,' 1
E *Astilbe* x *arendsii* 'Bridal Veil' (astilbe), 6
F *Primula veris* (cowslip primrose), 8
G *Ligularia* 'The Rocket' (golden ray), 5
H *Liriope muscari* (blue lilyturf), 5
I *Helleborus* spp. (Christmas rose), 3
J *Hosta* 'August Moon,' 8
K *Hosta lancifolia* (lanceleaf hosta), 8

ANNUALS

L *Torenia fournieri* (wishbone flower), 24
M *Impatiens wallerana* 'Accent Lavender' (impatiens), 28

BULBS

N *Narcissus* 'Ice Follies' (daffodil), 55
O *Crocus chrysanthus* (snow crocus), 30

FERNS

P *Osmunda cinnamomea* (cinnamon fern), 3

ORNAMENTAL GRASSES

Q *Hakonechloa macra* 'Aureola'
    (Japanese wind grass), 3

SHADY FOUNDATION

This welcoming side-yard garden flourishes in the bright shade on the north side of the house.

Somewhat formal in design, the brick-edged garden decorates the side entrance and stone patio, which creates a pleasant place for dining amid the flowers and foliage.

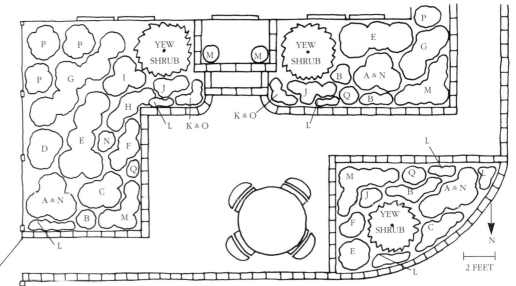

Above: Undaunted by hot sun and poor soil, daylily (*Hemerocallis*), gayfeather (*Liatris*), and balloon flower (*Platycodon*) make prolific bloomers in July.

Right: The annuals, perennials, and grasses used here take the dry, sandy soil of the seashore in stride. Included are: sweet alyssum (*Lobularia*), verbena (*Verbena*), autumn joy stonecrop (*Sedum*), lavender cotton (*Santolina*), fountain grass (*Pennisetum*), and blue fescue (*Festuca*), along with bluebeard shrubs (*Caryopteris*).

HOT, DRY SITES

Sandy soil is usually dry because it lacks organic matter, the essential component that absorbs water like a sponge and slowly releases it to thirsty plants. Rain and irrigation water run right through sandy soil. In addition, sandy soil usually contains few nutrients, so plants may languish for lack of essential elements. Baking hot sun, especially on a slope where water runs off quickly, combined with sandy soil spells disaster for many garden plants. The sun dries them out fast, and lost water cannot be easily replenished from soil that holds little water to begin with.

Although you can dramatically improve poor soil's water-holding capacity by working in copious amounts of organic matter such as rooted manure, leaf mold, or compost, the effort involved is enormous. This is especially difficult on a slope. An easier solution is to design a garden using plants adapted to the tough growing conditions. Many attractive plants, notably ones hailing from the Mediterranean, thrive in sharply draining soil and get by with very few nutrients. These thrifty plants frequently can be recognized by their hairy leaves, often covered with silvery or gray felt or a downy coat. The hairy coating actually shades the leaf surface from scorching rays, reducing water evaporation. Many of these Mediterranean plants are herbs, such as lavender and thyme, prized for their aromatic oils, which are used to flavor food or make perfumes. They'll perfume your garden with delicious scents, too, even if you don't use them for a more practical purpose.

Other drought-tolerant plants, such as the perennial sunflowers native to the prairies of the

162

Great Plains, have extensive root systems that penetrate deeply into the ground in search of moisture. Or, like sedums and stonecrops, they may have fleshy leaves or roots that store water to use in periods of drought.

Choose these sun-loving, drought-tolerant plants to create a garden in hot, poor-soil conditions. Your garden will be a delightful display of low-maintenance flowers and foliage, and you can design it in any style you wish: create a formal border to frame a lawn, or plant a terraced hillside with plants spilling over retaining walls. As long as you choose the right plants for the growing conditions, you'll be rewarded with easy care beauty in an otherwise difficult site.

DROUGHT-PROOFING MEASURES

Although transforming thin, sandy soil into a rich loam may be too much work, or downright impossible—especially on a hillside—any effort you do put into the soil will pay drought-proofing dividends later. Spread an inch or two of organic matter across the soil surface when preparing a new bed, and work it into the top 6 inches of soil. After planting, cover the exposed soil with a 3- to 4-inch-thick organic mulch and renew it every year. The mulch effectively will reduce evaporation from the soil surface and slowly break down into vital organic matter to replenish the soil. These simple measures will help stave off thirst later.

Be sure to water newly installed plants throughout their first growing season—even if they are drought-tolerant types—to help them establish good root systems. Once they become established, drought-tolerant flowers will be able to survive on normal rainfall even in dry-summer areas. They may perform better, however, if you water them during extended dry periods. When you do water them, be sure to let the sprinkler

run slowly and for a long time. This allows water to soak several feet into the ground, encouraging roots to go down after it once surface water is depleted. Deep-rooted plants will be immune from the baking hot weather that can cook surface-rooted plants.

Feverfew (*Chrysanthemum parthenium*), catmint (*Nepeta* x *faassenii*), golden marguerite (*Anthemis tinctoria*), threadleaf coreopsis (*Coreopsis verticillata*), and narrow-leaf zinnia (*Zinnia angustifolia*) all flourish in sandy soil.

163

DROUGHT-TOLERANT FLOWERS

These flowers won't wither in hot, dry locations where poor soil and full sun combine to challenge other plants.

Papaver

PERENNIALS

SPRING
Aurinia saxatilis (basket-of-gold)
Euphorbia polychroma (cushion spurge)
Pulsatilla vulgaris (pasque flower)

SUMMER
Acanthus mollis (spiny bear's breeches)
Achillea spp. (yarrows)
Anthemis tinctoria (golden marguerite)
Armeria maritima (sea pink, thrift)
Asclepias tuberosa (butterfly weed)
Belamcanda chinensis (blackberry lily)
Calamintha nepeta (calamint)
Cerastium tomentosum (snow-in-summer)
Coreopsis verticillata (threadleaf coreopsis)
Delosperma cooperi (hardy iceplant)
Gypsophila spp. (baby's breath)
Iris hybrida (bearded iris)
Lavandula angustifolia (lavender)
Limonium latifolium (sea lavender, statice)
Nepeta spp. (catmints)
Oenothera berlandieri (showy evening primrose)
Santolina chamaecyparissus (lavender cotton)
Saponaria ocymoides (rock soapwort)
Scutellaria baicalensis (skullcap)
Thymus spp. (thymes)
Verbena canadensis (clump verbena)
Yucca filamentosa (Adam's needle)

LATE SUMMER AND FALL
Echinacea purpurea (purple coneflower)
Echinops ritro (globe-thistle)
Eryngium amethystinum (amethyst sea holly)
Gaura lindheimeri (white gaura)
Helianthus angustifolius (fall sunflower)
Heliopsis helianthoides scabra (false sunflower)
Liatris spicata (spike gayfeather)
Perovskia atriplicifolia (Russian sage)

Rudbeckia fulgida (orange coneflower)
Santolina chamaecyparissus (lavender cotton)
Sedum spp. (stonecrops)
Sempervivum tectorum (hens-and-chicks)
Stachys byzantina (lamb's-ears)
Verbena canadensis (clump verbena)

ANNUALS
Brachycome iberidifolia (swan river daisy)
Calendula officinalis (pot marigold)
Cleome hasslerana (spider flower)
Cosmos bipinnatus (cosmos)
Cosmos sulphureus (yellow cosmos)
Eschscholzia californica (California poppy)
Gaillardia pulchella (annual blanket-flower)
Helianthus annuus (sunflower)
Helichrysum bracteatum (strawflower)
Mirabilis jalapa (four-o'clock)
Nigella damascena (love-in-a-mist)
Papaver spp. (poppies)
Portulaca grandiflora (moss rose)
Sanvitalia procumbens (creeping zinnia)
Tagetes spp. (marigolds)
Verbena x *hybrida* (verbena)
Zinnia angustifolia (narrow-leaf zinnia)

BULBS

SPRING
Allium spp. (ornamental onions)
Crocus spp. (crocus)
Tulipa spp. (tulips)

SUMMER
Allium spp. (ornamental onions)

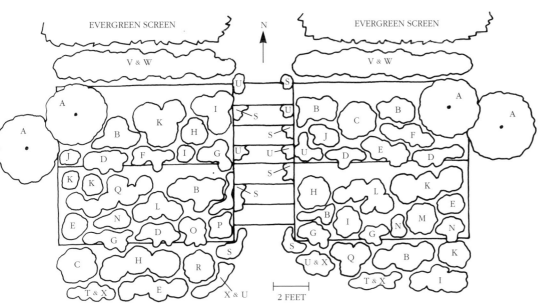

EVERGREEN SCREEN

EVERGREEN SCREEN

V & W

V & W

N

2 FEET

HOT, DRY SLOPE

Where hot sun and a sloping site combine to create difficult dry-soil conditions, terracing with landscape timbers or a stone wall allows you to improve the soil and slow water runoff by creating flat areas to hold plants. The design relies on sun-loving, drought-resistant flowers to cascade over the retaining wall, softening their appearance.

ROSES

A *Rosa rugosa* (rugosa rose), 4

PERENNIALS

B *Coreopsis verticillata* 'Moonbeam,' 15
C *Perovskia atriplicifolia* (Russian sage), 2
D *Cerastium tomentosum* (snow-in-summer), 8
E *Nepeta* x *faassenii* (catmint), 9
F *Oenothera berlandieri* (showy evening primrose), 2
G *Saponaria ocymoides* (rock soapwort), 5
H *Sedum* x *telephium* 'Autumn Joy' (stonecrop), 5
I *Achillea* x 'Moonshine' (yarrow), 3
J *Santolina chamaecyparissus* (lavender cotton), 4
K *Echinacea purpurea* (purple coneflower), 8
L *Liatris spicata* (spike gayfeather), 8
M *Gaura lindheimeri* (white gaura), 1
N *Sedum* x 'Vera Jameson,' 4
O *Aurinia saxatilis* 'Citrinum' (basket-of-gold), 1
P *Stachys byzantina* (lamb's-ears), 1
Q *Iris hybrida* (bearded iris), 5
R *Euphorbia polychroma* (cushion spurge), 1
S *Thymus pseudolanuginosus* (woolly thyme), 7

ANNUALS

T *Zinnia angustifolia* (narrow-leaf zinnia), 12
U *Brachycome iberidifolia* (swan river daisy), 18
V *Cleome hasslerana* (spider flower), 24

BULBS

W *Tulipa* spp. (tulips), 60
X *Crocus* spp. (crocus), 100

POORLY DRAINED SITES

If you're faced with a poorly drained site that looks like a mud flat throughout the year or actually accumulates standing water, take another look and begin to think of this site as an asset instead of a liability. Don't go to the expense and effort of bringing in fill or installing drainage tiles to dry out the area. Instead, let nature guide you. You can create a lovely bog garden in that otherwise ugly spot.

A unique and beautiful assortment of plants prefers soggy soil and even flourishes in standing water. These special plants of the bogs, wet meadows, and pond and stream edges may not grow in an ordinary garden, so look on your challenging garden site as an opportunity to grow some very special plants. You also can use these water-loving flowers to adorn the edges of a natural pond or stream bank. Plant clumps of them in a naturalistic arrangement anywhere the ground is wet to gracefully enhance the site Mother Nature saw fit to give you.

Above: A naturalistic planting of water-loving perennials adorns the pond edge where soil squishes underfoot.

Opposite: During rainy weather, water drains and runs forcefully through this area. A clever landscape solution turned the problem site into a lovely garden.

CREATING A BOG GARDEN

If you don't have a sufficiently wet site, you may want to create an artificial bog garden so you can successfully grow these unique plants. You also can easily expand an already wet site for greater landscape impact. It's fairly easy and inexpensive to create a bog garden in a separate area alongside an artificial garden pool or in a low-lying area of your property.

Using a clothesline or garden hose, lay out the shape of your garden. Excavate the area to a depth of 9 inches and then line the hole with a PVC pool liner, available from a water-garden supply company. Fill the lined hole with soil, keeping the bog garden slightly below the grade of the surrounding garden so that natural water runoff will collect in it. Because most bog plants do best in a mucky, heavy clay type of soil, you may want to amend your garden soil with compost, especially if the soil is light. Now you are ready to plant your bog with elegant blue or yellow irises, golden marsh marigolds, and vivid cardinal flowers.

The plants in your bog garden require little care. During the growing season, flood the garden periodically to keep the soil wet. Because the liner keeps water from draining, this shouldn't be a regular chore, but be vigilant during hot, dry spells. Bog plants can survive periods of drought, but their appearance may suffer.

CONSTRUCTING AN ARTIFICIAL BOG

To construct a bog garden along the edge of an artificial pool, extend the liner out from the pond bottom to create shelves to hold pockets of heavy soil. These planting pockets should be about a foot deep and must be completely separate from the pool itself, or the soil will cloud the water.

Install plants that prefer standing water in the pockets. When you add water to the pond, also add water to the planting pockets, keeping the soil constantly wet and boggy.

PLANTS FOR WET OR BOGGY SITES

The plants listed at right will beautify a wet or boggy site with their flowers and foliage. Plants with an * tolerate boggy soil or standing water, especially in spring. Other plants do best in constantly wet to damp soil.

Top left: Yellow flag iris (*Iris pseudacorus*) grows in moist gardens but blooms most lavishly when grown in a boggy site similar to its native habitat.

Bottom left: Japanese Jack-in-the-pulpit (*Arisaema sikokianum*) is a relative of the American native wildflower; both grow in damp to wet sites, reaching their greatest height where the soil is constantly wet.

PERENNIALS
SPRING
Bergenia spp. (bergenias)
Caltha palustris (marsh marigold)*
Myosotis sylvatica (woodland forget-me-not)
Primula japonica (Japanese primrose)
Trollius europaeus (globeflower)

SUMMER
Aruncus dioicus (goat's beard)
Astilbe spp. (astilbes)
Cimicifuga spp. (bugbanes)
Filipendula rubra (queen-of-the-prairie)
Hibiscus moscheutos (rose mallow)
Iris ensata (Japanese iris)*
Iris pseudacorus (yellow flag iris)*
Iris siberica (Siberian iris)*
Iris versicolor (blue flag iris)*
Mazus reptans (mazus)
Mimulus guttatus (common monkey flower)
Rodgersia spp. (rodgersias)
Tradescantia x *andersoniana* (spiderwort)

LATE SUMMER AND FALL
Chelone spp. (turtle-heads)
Cimicifuga spp. (bugbanes)
Eupatorium fistulosum (Joe-Pye weed)
Lobelia cardinalis (cardinal flower)*

ANNUALS
Mimulus x *hybridus* (monkey flower)

FERNS
Dryopteris spp. (wood ferns)
Matteuccia struthiopteris (ostrich fern)
Osmunda cinnamomea (cinnamon fern)
Osmunda regalis (royal fern)

BULBS
SPRING
Arisaema spp. (Jack-in-the-pulpits)

SUMMER
Lilium canadense (Canada lily)
Zantedeschia aethiopica (calla lily)

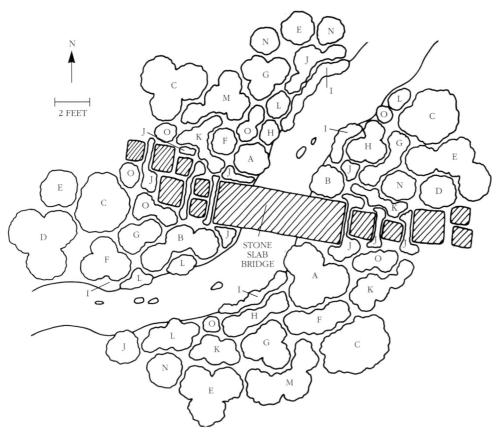

BOG GARDEN

Use this design to beautify a natural stream or wet area created by poor drainage or runoff. Stepping stones through the area and a low bridge provide easy access. The perennials are planned to bloom from early spring until fall.

PERENNIALS
A *Iris pseudacorus* (yellow flag iris), 4
B *Iris ensata* (Japanese iris), 4
C *Rodgersia pinnata superba* (featherleaf rodgersia), 3
D *Aruncus dioicus* 'Kneiffii' (goat's beard), 4
E *Eupatorium fistulosum* (Joe-Pye weed), 8
F *Chelone glabra* (turtle-head), 6
G *Lobelia cardinalis* (cardinal flower), 10
H *Caltha palustris* (marsh marigold), 10
I *Myosotis sylvatica* (woodland forget-me-not), 20
J *Mazus reptans* (mazus), 25
K *Primula japonica* (Japanese primrose), 21

ANNUALS
L *Mimulus* x *hybridus* (monkey flower), 12

BULBS
M *Lilium canadense* (Canada lily), 7

FERNS
N *Osmunda cinnamomea* (cinnamon fern), 4
O *Dryopteris marginalis* (marginal shield fern), 11

A BOG GARDENER

Rubber boots are a mainstay of Sydney Eddison's gardening wardrobe, especially when pulling weeds among the plants in her Connecticut bog garden.

Sydney came by her love of gardening—and her British accent—from her British mother, who married an American and moved to the United States but was never able to have her own garden. Sydney's mother raised her on tales of beautiful English gardens—rather than nursery rhymes—so when Sydney grew up and moved into her own house, her first impulse was to plant flowers. Gardening has been her avocation ever since.

Much of Sydney's property, which she cares for with her husband, Martin, brims with flowers and shrubs in the lavish but informal manner of an English country garden. The wet area behind her barn, separated from the rest of the property by a gated fence, is her favorite garden spot, however. Here she designed a naturalistic garden of wildflowers and bog-loving plants.

Even though the area appears wild, she has tamed it considerably by channeling the water, laying out paths, and planting a mix of native plants and exotics. In early spring, the ground around the vernal pool comes alive with the bright buttercups of the marsh marigold (*Caltha palustris*), followed later in spring by an assortment of primroses (*Primula* spp.) Jack-in-the-pulpits (*Arisaema* spp.), and ferns. In early summer, irises such as the yellow flag (*Iris pseudacorus*) and other bog plants join the abundance of tall ferns. Although the pool dries to a muddy mire in summer, the soil holds enough water to keep the plants content.

Water collects behind the barn in the lowest spot on Sydney's property, forming a pool that often dries up by summer. Sydney forced the runoff feeding the pool into a stream bed by digging a trench and lining it with rocks. A wood-chip path edged with logs marks the high ground. Blooming lavishly in May are Japanese primroses (*Primula japonica*) set off against tall royal ferns (*Osmunda regalis*).

171

CHAPTER SEVEN

DESIGNING COLOR-SCHEME GARDENS

Choose from a Palette of Colorful Flowers to Paint a Garden with Stunning Impact

Opposite: The vibrant annuals in this hot-colored garden sizzle under the July sun, standing out in the strong sunlight against a dark green hedge.

Left: Perennials in cool pink, blue, and lavender hues create a restful combination made all the more alluring by the contrasting flower shapes and a bit of silver foliage.

Color—of flowers and of foliage—evokes a strong emotional impact. Some colors soothe; others excite. Everyone has a favorite color and certain likes and dislikes when it comes to combining colors. Your garden is an excellent place to play with your color preferences. You can literally paint with living color, giving your creativity free reign while designing a garden picture that reflects your personal preferences.

The best gardens have some type of color scheme and are not just a riot of haphazard colors. By following just a few guidelines, you can make a giant step toward using color well. The four garden plans presented here will give you some ideas about designing with color. You can copy them, or use the principles they follow to create your own picture-perfect garden.

COLOR WHEELING

The color wheel can be a wonderful help in learning to create effective color combinations when grouping flowers in your garden design. Think of the flowers you're selecting for your design in terms of where their colors fit among the 12 colors of the basic color wheel. Are they primary, secondary, or intermediate colors? Are they tints, shades, or tones? Then ask yourself what type of statement you want your garden to make. Soft, sophisticated, and soothing? Dramatic and awash in brilliant colors? Will you be sitting beside, walking by, or viewing the flowers from a distance? Answers to these questions will help you choose a successful color scheme for your garden.

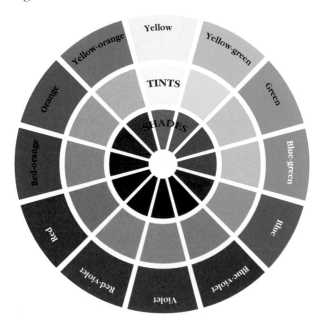

Left: Pastel tints of yellow and violet—two complementary colors—combine to create a wonderful soft effect in this formal garden planted with old-fashioned perennials. Flowers include: dame's rocket (*Hesperis matronalis*), Argentine blue-eyed grass (*Sisyrinchium striatum*), iris (*Iris* x *germanica*), lupine (*Lupinus* hybrid), foxglove (*Digitalis purpurea*), Jacob's-rod (*Asphodeline lutea*), speedwells (*Veronica* spp.), lamb's-ear (*Stachys byzantina*), and horned violet (*Viola cornuta*).

Right: Red and green make a vivid combination of complementary colors. Here, a bright red zinnia (*Zinnia elegans*) seems intensified by the soft effect of the pastel green flowering tobacco (*Nicotiana alata*). The high-contrast color combination is made all the more striking by juxtaposing round zinnia flowers with upright spikes of funnel-form flowering tobacco blossoms.

COMPLEMENTARY COLOR SCHEMES

You can create vibrant, high-contrast combinations by pairing a color with its opposite on the color wheel. Such pairs are termed complementary colors. Complementary color schemes that include a primary color can be dramatically eye-catching: yellow and violet, red and green, and blue and orange. Every autumn Mother Nature displays a wonderful combination of complementary asters and goldenrods along the roadsides in many parts of the country.

By choosing tints and tones of one or both of the complementary pair, you can make a subtler yet still exciting combination. You can create a vibrant blue-and-orange spring combination by pairing deep blue 'Blue Jacket' Dutch hyacinths with 'Melody Orange' pansies, for example. To soften the combination, substitute a pastel orange pansy such as 'Crystal Bowl Orange.' The apricot of the pansy is softer and less demanding than pure, bright orange yet combines well with the richness of the hyacinths. For a more subtle but still vibrant statement, pair the pastel orange pansy with a pastel blue Dutch hyacinth such as 'Wedgewood.'

ANALOGOUS COLOR SCHEMES

Colors that are next-door neighbors on the color wheel are called analogous colors. A color scheme based on analogous colors and their tints and shades reaches a level of sophistication and beauty that primary and complementary color schemes cannot. Combining violet with its neighbors, red-violet and red, along with their tints and shades, creates a color scheme rich in soft, delicate contrasts. When choosing analogous colors for a planting scheme, consider the coolness or warmness of the colors, too. (See page 177.)

You may want to create a garden in pastel versions of analogous colors so that it feels light and airy. To avoid boredom, however, you can jazz it up a bit by including several splashes of dark shades of these colors for a riveting contrast. A pastel violet and red-violet garden comes alive with a few splashes of deep magenta or purple, for instance. You also can add a focal point of a complementary color from across the color wheel, in this case a bold dash of yellow.

Notice the different effects created by combining the blue grape hyacinth (*Muscari* 'Blue Spike') with colors adjacent or opposite on the color wheel.
Left: Analogous violet peony-flowered tulips (*Tulipa* x *hybrida* 'Maravilla') result in a peaceful effect.
Right: Complementary golden yellow tulips (*Tulipa batalinii* 'Bright Gem') add color impact.

COLOR TEMPERATURE

Every primary and secondary color of the color wheel has both warm and cool versions, which make up the six intermediate colors of the color wheel. When yellow is added to a color, it becomes warm; when blue is added, it becomes cool. Yellow-green is a warm, sunny hue reminiscent of sun-struck foliage, and blue-green is a cool hue that calls to mind a cloudy day. Scarlet, an orange-red created by adding yellow to red, screams with heat, but crimson, a color made by adding blue to red, soothes and refreshes. The cool and warm versions of a color rarely look good together. Magenta (a cool red) and scarlet (a warm red), for example, don't look good together even though they are located near each other on the color wheel.

If you consider the coolness or hotness of a flower's color, you can take a lot of the guesswork out of designing with color. Plan a flower garden that will contain mostly warm or cool colors and none of them will clash, no matter how many colors you've included. For example, if you are looking for another flower to bloom alongside an orange-red oriental poppy, a salmon-pink iris would make a better choice than a lavender-pink one because the first iris has a bit of yellow in its makeup and the second has a bit of blue.

You don't have to follow this rule to the letter, however. Hot and cool colors do look good together. Blue and yellow are an excellent combination because they are primary colors. Use this temperature rule when straying from the primary colors and you can't go wrong. Then mix in a couple of bold clumps of the opposite temperature. Include a clump of fiery orange daylilies as a surprise among a cool collection of lavender, purple, and blue blossoms, for example, and your garden will sizzle with excitement.

Top left: These two flowers combine beautifully because each is a warm hue of pink. The darker sweet William (*Dianthus barbatus*) sets off perfectly the lighter astilbe (*Astilbe* x *arendsii* 'Peach Blossom') for a subtle color statement.

Bottom left. Blue goes well with both warm and cool hues. Here it creates a vibrant combination with yellow. Shown are balloon flowers (*Platycodon grandiflorus*) with Asiatic lilies (*Lilium* 'Connecticut Yankee').

177

BLUE-AND-YELLOW GARDEN

This hedge-backed formal border is orchestrated to bloom in blue and yellow—with some softening silver foliage—from spring through fall. For a larger site, create a double border with a path through the middle by echoing the plants used here on the opposite side.

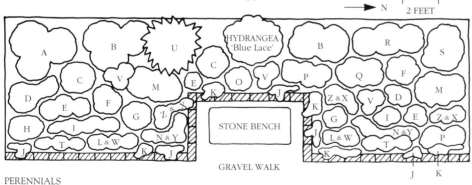

PERENNIALS

A *Baptisia australis* (blue wild indigo), 3

B *Aster novi-belgi* x *novae-angliae* 'Eventide' (Michaelmas daisy, fall aster), 5

C *Perovskia atriplicifolia* (Russian sage), 2

D *Solidaster luteus* (solidaster), 2

E *Aquilegia* x *hybrida* 'Heavenly Blue' (columbine), 5

F *Phlomis russeliana* (sticky Jerusalem sage), 2

G *Artemisia schmidtiana* 'Silvermound' (silvermound mugwort), 2

H *Aster* x *frikartii* 'Monch' (Frikart's aster), 1

I *Veronica latifolia* 'Crater Lake Blue,' 5

J *Aurinia saxatilis* 'Citrinum' (basket-of-gold), 5

K *Phlox subulata* 'Emerald Blue' (moss pink), 5

L *Campanula carpatica* 'Blue Clips' (Carpathian bellflower), 5

M *Platycodon grandiflorus* (balloon flower), 16

N *Coreopsis verticillata* 'Moonbeam' (threadleaf coreopsis), 6

O *Centaurea montana* (mountain bluet), 1

P *Campanula glomerata* 'Joan Elliott' (clustered bellflower), 5

Q *Echinops ritro* 'Taplow Blue' (globe-thistle), 1

R *Iris siberica* 'Blue Moon' (Siberian iris), 3

S *Amsonia tabernaemontana* (willow amsonia), 1

ORNAMENTAL GRASSES

T *Festuca ovina* 'Glauca' (blue fescue), 6

U *Miscanthus sinensis* 'Gracillimus' (maiden grass), 1

BULBS

V *Lilium* 'Connecticut Yankee' (Asiatic lily), 9

W *Chionodoxa luciliae* 'Gigantea' (glory-of-the-snow), 25

X *Tulipa* x *hybrida* 'Sweet Harmony' (hybrid tulip), 36

Y *Tulipa* x *hybrida* 'Blue Aimable' (hybrid tulip), 24

ANNUALS

Z *Salvia farinacea* 'Victoria' (mealy-cup sage), 18

PINK GARDEN

Pastel and rose-pink flowers bloom in this very feminine garden from spring through fall. Splashes of purple-leaved foliage plants create dark contrasts, which make the blossoms seem even pinker.

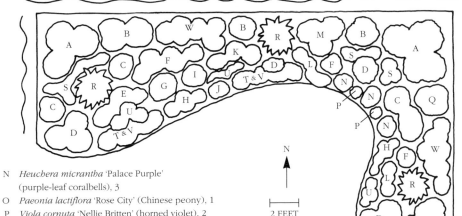

2 FEET

PERENNIALS

A *Phlox paniculata* 'Bright Eyes' (garden phlox), 7
B *Boltonia asteroides* 'Pink Beauty' (boltonia), 3
C *Anemone* x *hybrida* 'September Charm' (Japanese anemone), 3
D *Chrysanthemum* x *rubellum* 'Clara Curtis' (hybrid chrysanthemum), 4
E *Chrysanthemum weyrichii* 'Pink Bomb' (miyabe), 3
F *Physostegia virginiana* 'Bouquet Rose' (obedient plant), 7
G *Sedum spectabile* 'Meteor' (showy stonecrop), 1
H *Bergenia cordifolia* 'Perfecta' (heart-leaf bergenia), 9
I *Platycodon grandiflorus* 'Shell Pink' (balloon flower), 1
J *Sedum* x 'Vera Jameson' (Vera Jameson stonecrop), 3
K *Liatris spicata* 'Kobold' (spike gayfeather), 3
L *Aquilegia* x *hybrida* 'Nora Barlow' (columbine), 5
M *Monarda didyma* 'Croftway Pink' (bee-balm), 3

N *Heuchera micrantha* 'Palace Purple' (purple-leaf coralbells), 3
O *Paeonia lactiflora* 'Rose City' (Chinese peony), 1
P *Viola cornuta* 'Nellie Britten' (horned violet), 2
Q *Dicentra spectabilis* (common bleeding heart), 1

ORNAMENTAL GRASSES

R *Pennisetum setaceum* 'Atrosanguineum' (purple fountain grass), 1

BULBS

S *Lilium longifolium* 'Pink Tiger,' 14
T *Tulipa* x *hybrida* 'Angelique,' 28

ANNUALS

U *Ocimum basilicum* 'Purple Ruffles' (basil), 10
V *Petunia* x *hybrida* 'Supercascade Blush' (petunia), 16
W *Cleome hasslerana* 'Rose Queen' (spider flower), 6

HOT COLOR SCHEMES

Yellow evokes a feeling of sunshine and warmth. It is a cheerful, uplifting color. Hot colors—those with yellow in them, especially orange and scarlet—advance, appearing closer than they are. They're also easy to see from a distance. A garden composed of gold, yellow, orange, and scarlet flowers glows with fire like an exhilarating beam of sunlight breaking through a cloudy sky.

Not everyone likes hot-colored gardens because they can be too strong and dazzling. To subdue a hot-colored garden, add a generous allotment of warm pastel or creamy white flowers. The pale yellow of 'Moonbeam' coreopsis, for example, blends prettily with hotter colors, drawing off some of their heat. Creamy white, with its touch of yellow, creates less contrast than the brilliance of pure white flowers.

Don't overlook the diluting ability of kelly-green foliage. True green looks wonderful with red and orange. If interspersed among dense clusters of bright flowers, green diminishes their intensity.

When designing a hot-colored garden, beware of reds. True scarlet is an orange-red and goes beautifully with other hot-colored blossoms. Many garden catalogs err in describing flower colors, especially reds. What catalogs often call scarlet may actually be crimson, a bluish red, and vice versa. Let your eyes, not catalog descriptions, influence your decisions. You may even want to pluck a flower petal and carry it around your garden or nursery to see which colors go well together and which do not, before making planting decisions.

Left: Hot colors have yellow in them and create a warm, sunny feeling. Here several hot-colored annuals combine for an intense effect. Shown are: black-eyed Susan (*Rudbeckia hirta* 'Rustic Colors'), African marigold (*Tagetes erecta*), pot marigold (*Calendula officinalis* 'Bon Bon'), cockscomb (*Celosia cristata* 'Century Yellow'), and narrow-leaf zinnia (*Zinnia angustifolia*).

Below: Although still warm and sunny, pastel yellow appears less intense and less hot than richer hues of yellow.

HOT COLOR GARDEN

This garden won't give you a sunburn, but it glows with warm, sunny color from early spring through fall. The monochromatic color scheme is relieved by using both pastel and rich hues of yellow with splashes of pure, bright orange included in every season to create daring focal points.

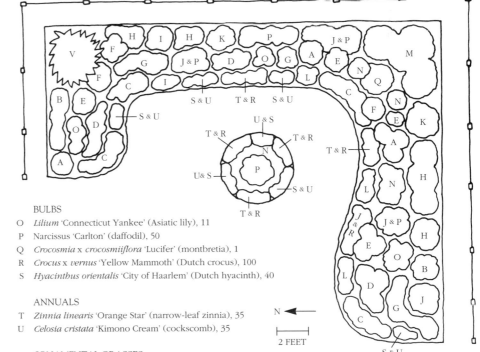

PERENNIALS

A *Iris siberica* 'Butter and Sugar' (Siberian iris), 5
B *Achillea filipendulina* 'Coronation Gold' (fern-leaf yarrow), 7
C *Coreopsis verticillata* 'Moonbeam' (threadleaf coreopsis), 10
D *Oenothera tetragona* (common sundrops), 5
E *Aquilegia* x *hybrida* 'Yellow Music' (columbine), 6
F *Papaver orientale* 'Prince of Orange' (Oriental poppy), 2
G *Rudbeckia fulgida* 'Goldsturm' (orange coneflower), 8
H *Helenium autumnale* 'Red-gold Hybrids' (sneezeweed), 4
I *Ligularia stenocephala* 'The Rocket' (golden ray), 1
J *Hemerocallis* hybrids 'Hyperion' (daylily), 4
K *Thermopsis caroliniana* (southern lupine), 2
L *Chrysogonum virginianum* (goldenstar), 5
M *Rudbeckia nitida* (shining coneflower), 3
N *Achillea* x 'Moonshine' (moonshine yarrow), 10

BULBS

O *Lilium* 'Connecticut Yankee' (Asiatic lily), 11
P Narcissus 'Carlton' (daffodil), 50
Q *Crocosmia* x *crocosmiiflora* 'Lucifer' (montbretia), 1
R *Crocus* x *vernus* 'Yellow Mammoth' (Dutch crocus), 100
S *Hyacinthus orientalis* 'City of Haarlem' (Dutch hyacinth), 40

ANNUALS

T *Zinnia linearis* 'Orange Star' (narrow-leaf zinnia), 35
U *Celosia cristata* 'Kimono Cream' (cockscomb), 35

ORNAMENTAL GRASSES

V *Miscanthus sinensis* 'Strictus' (porcupine grass), 1

N

2 FEET

COOL COLOR SCHEMES

Cool colors—those with a generous allotment of blue—create a romantic, misty feeling in a garden. Blue, lilac, purple, lavender, and violet refresh the spirit with their icy mood. Cool colors are weak colors, however. They seem to recede and appear farther away than they actually are. So don't plant a cool-colored garden in a far-off vista or it will disappear from view.

A word on blue. True blue—the color of sapphires—is hard to come by in flowers, perhaps because most pollinating insects, except for bees, aren't attracted to the color. Most blue flowers have a component of red, making them lean more toward lavender or violet than true blue. True blue flowers look stunning with almost any other flower color. True blue perennials include monkshood, lungwort, Virginia bluebells, Italian bugloss, leadwort, delphinium, borage, veronica, and *Geranium* 'Mrs. Kendall Clarke.' Annuals include lobelia, forget-me-not, cornflower, morning glory 'Heavenly Blue,' and evolvulus. Bulbs include Siberian squill, grape hyacinth, agapanthus, and 'Blue Jacket' Dutch hyacinth.

You can spice up a cool color scheme by adding analogous colors such as pink and magenta or by adding splashes of the complementary yellow and orange. Gertrude Jekyll, the famous British garden designer known for her lavish color schemes, always included yellow flowers or foliage in her blue borders.

Another way to enhance a cool color scheme is by interspersing silver- and gray-leaved plants among the flowers. The silvery leaves of lamb's-ears or artemisia, for example, make blue and lavender flowers more intense. Purple foliage, from such plants as beefsteak plant, 'Burgundy Glow' bugleweed, or 'Palace Purple' coralbells, adds a deep, opulent hue that seems to magnify blue, violet, and lavender flowers tenfold.

Left: Cool floral colors and silver foliage create a romantic, misty effect. Shown here are garden phlox (*Phlox paniculata* 'Bright Eyes'), speedwell (*Veronica longifolia* 'Blue Charm'), lamb's-ears (*Stachys byzantina*), and flowering tobacco (*Nicotiana alata*).

Below: This cool blue border becomes more exciting with the addition of yellow flowers. The naturalistic planting features sundrops (*Oenothera tetragona*) and several types of bellflower (*Campanula*).

Above: Surrounding the lawn and bordering the street, this garden stops traffic with its warm-and-cool color scheme. Redleaf rose (*Rosa glauca*) creates a focal point of dusky purple amid violet-blue and yellow perennials. Included are: cranesbills (*Geranium himalayense* and *pratense*), hybrid sage (*Salvia* x *superba* 'May Night'), yarrow (*Achillea taygetea*), lily leek (*Allium moly*), lady's mantle (*Alchemilla mollis*), and Jerusalem sage (*Phlomis russeliana*).

Left: Annuals and perennials combine to create a long-lasting cool color scheme. Plants with purple leaves— beefsteak plant (*Perilla frutescens*) and *Sedum* x 'Vera Jameson'—help to carry the color scheme while flowers go in and out of bloom. Also shown are: heliotrope (*Heliotropium arborescens* 'Marine') and Frikart's aster (*Aster* x *frikartii*) with later-blooming Japanese anemone (*Anemone* x *hybrida*) and butterfly bush (*Buddleia*).

183

MONOCHROMATIC COLOR SCHEMES

Gardens designed in a single color are difficult to do well. All too often colors don't match or they may even clash because the flowers include warm and cool versions of the desired color. For instance, a pink garden may include peachy pink (a warm hue) and mauve-pink (a cool hue), two pinks that don't blend well together. A monochromatic garden may eventually evolve into a pretty garden of analogous colors, which is not necessarily bad.

AN ALL-WHITE GARDEN

The most dramatic monochromatic garden is an all-white garden. It shines during the day, reflecting sunlight like a mirror. At dusk and at night, however, this elegant garden comes into its own, because the ghostly white flowers glow like lanterns in the moonlight. A low-wattage outdoor light will render the flowers visible on even the darkest nights.

Foliage plays an important role in a white garden: green leaves contrast with the white flowers, setting them apart in the dark. A dark green hedge or painted fence makes the best background to set off the blossoms. Silver, gray, blue-green, and white-and-green variegated plants used as an edging and interspersed among the white flowers enhance the blossoms, making the garden all the more snowy white.

Many of the flowers you might include in your white garden are fragrant, especially at night. Design a fragrant white garden to surround a patio, and you've created a very special place to entertain or relax with a book on a summer's evening. The glowing flowers and sweet fragrance create a romantic and magical setting of unparalleled elegance.

Above: A classic monochromatic color scheme is the all-white garden, which usually relies heavily on silver-leaved foliage plants to heighten the elegant white effect.

Left: Flowers in an all-white garden glow romantically in the moonlight, reflecting any available light. Combined here are: garden phlox (*Phlox paniculata* 'World Peace'), a white-flowered purple coneflower (*Echinacea purpurea* 'White Swan'), and silvery blue globe-thistle (*Echinops ritro* 'Taplow Blue.'

WHITE GARDEN

Designed in a horseshoe shape with a dark green hedge as a background, this all-white garden makes an elegant statement. White flowers combine with silver and white-striped foliage for a long-lasting glow.

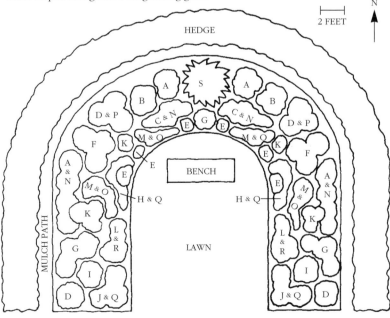

PERENNIALS

A *Phlox maculata* 'Miss Lingard' (Carolina phlox), 10
B *Centranthus ruber albus* (white valerian), 2
C *Physostegia virginiana* 'Summer Snow' (obedient plant), 8
D *Iris siberica* 'Snow Queen' (Siberian iris), 8
E *Viola cornuta* 'White Perfection' (horned violet), 6
F *Platycodon grandiflorus* 'Fuji White' (balloon flower), 6
G *Anemone* x *hybrida* 'Honorine Jobert' (Japanese anemone), 7
H *Stachys byzantina* 'Silver Carpet' (lamb's-ears), 12
I *Paeonia lactiflora* 'Moon of Nippon' (Chinese peony), 2
J *Artemisia schmidtiana* 'Silvermound' (silvermound mugwort), 6
K *Echinacea purpurea* 'White Swan' (purple coneflower), 8

ANNUALS

L *Petunia* x *hybrida* 'Carpet White' (petunia), 24
M *Salvia farinacea* 'Silver White' (mealy-cup sage), 40

BULBS

N *Narcissus* 'Mt. Hood' (daffodil), 30
O *Tulipa* x *hybrida* 'White Triumphator' (hybrid tulip), 44
P *Lilium* 'Casa Blanca' (Oriental lily), 6
Q *Hyacinthus orientalis* 'Mont Blanc' (Dutch hyacinth), 50
R *Crocus* x *vernus* 'Peter Pan' (Dutch crocus), 60

ORNAMENTAL GRASSES

S *Miscanthus sinensis* 'Variegatus' (silver grass), 1

When Moya moved into her present home about six years ago, she was so eager to get gardening that she didn't take time to plan. She just began planting anywhere she could stick a perennial. One would never know the garden's haphazard origins now from looking at the wondrous results—luxurious English-style flower gardens surround the Tudor-style stone house in explosive profusion.

The savvy color schemes in Moya's gardens result more from happenstance than planning, she claims. By buying flowers in colors that appealed to her—pink, lavender, blue, and white—and avoiding orange and red, which she doesn't like, her gardens turned out to be pleas-

A COLOR-SCHEME GARDENER

A speech and hearing professor and a passionate gardener, Moya Andrews cultivates flower gardens throughout the corner property surrounding her Indiana home. One garden is all-white, another multicolored, but most feature predominately cool colors: pink, blue, lavender, and purple.

antly color-coordinated. Moya quips that these unplanned gardens have worked out more successfully than those she carefully planned.

Moya enjoys giving away her flowers as much as she does growing them. Almost everything she grows she chooses for its cutting ability. Wherever she goes, whether to the hairdresser, the doctor, or a friend, she takes bouquets and nosegays with her as gifts. Moya lives by the Chinese proverb, "The fragrance of a flower stays in the hands of those who give them." And in her case, the adage has certainly proven true.

Decorating the walk leading to the front door, and with stepping stones linking walk to driveway, this purple-and-pink garden is Moya's latest addition. Featured are prairie gentians (*Eustoma grandiflora*), Madagascar periwinkle (*Catharanthus roseus*), and crape myrtlettes (a dwarf form of the shrub *Lagerstromea*).

186

PLANTS WITH VARIEGATED GREEN-AND-WHITE FOLIAGE

PERENNIALS

Hosta 'Albo-marginata,' 'Francee,' 'Ginko Craig,' 'Medio-picta,' 'Thomas Hogg' (hosta)
Iris pallida 'Alba-variegata' (sweet iris)
Lamium maculatum (spotted dead nettle)
Liriope muscari 'Silver Dragon' (blue lilyturf)
Mentha suaveolens 'Variegata' (variegated pineapple mint)
Phlox paniculata 'Nora Leigh' (garden phlox)
Physostegia virginiana 'Variegata' (obedient plant)
Polygonatum odoratum 'Variegatum' (fragrant Solomon's seal)
Pulmonaria saccharata 'Mrs. Moon' (Bethlehem sage)

ANNUALS

Coleus x *hybridus* (coleus)
Hypoestes phyllostachya 'Splash Select White' (polka-dot plant)

ORNAMENTAL GRASSES

Carex morrowii 'Variegata' (silver-edged Japanese sedge grass)
Miscanthus sinensis 'Morning Light' (silver grass)
Miscanthus sinensis 'Variegatus' (variegated silver grass)
Phalaris arundinacea var. *picta* (ribbon grass)

PLANTS WITH VARIEGATED GOLD-AND-GREEN LEAVES

PERENNIALS

Hosta 'Aureo-marginata,' 'Francis Williams,' 'Gold Standard,' 'Kabitan' (hosta)
Iris pallida 'Variegata' (variegated sweet iris)
Lamiastrum galeobdolon 'Herman's Pride' (variegated nettle)
Liriope muscari 'Gold Banded' (lilyturf)
Yucca filamentosa 'Bright Edge,' 'Golden Sword' (Adam's needle, needle palm)

ANNUALS

Coleus x *hybridus* (coleus)

ORNAMENTAL GRASSES

Carex morrowii 'Aureo-variegata' (yellow striped Japanese sedge grass)
Hakonechloa macra 'Aureola' (Japanese wind grass)
Miscanthus sinensis 'Strictus' (porcupine grass)
Miscanthus sinensis 'Zebrinus' (zebra grass)

PLANTS WITH GOLDEN FOLIAGE

PERENNIALS

Chrysanthemum parthenium aureum (golden feather)
Filipendula ulmaria 'Aurea' (queen-of-the-meadow)
Hosta 'August Moon,' 'Gold Edger,' 'Piedmont Gold,' 'Sum and Substance' (hosta)
Lamium maculatum aureum (golden spotted nettle)

GRASSES

Carex stricta 'Bowles Golden' (Bowles golden grass)

PLANTS WITH BLUE OR BLUE-GRAY LEAVES

PERENNIALS

Centranthus ruber (red valerian)
Hosta 'Blue Cadet,' 'Hadspen Blue,' 'Krossa Regal' (hosta)
Hosta sieboldiana 'Elegans' (hosta)
Ruta graveolens (rue)
Salvia officinalis (garden sage)

GRASSES

Elymus arenarius glaucus (blue lyme grass, blue wild rye)
Festuca amethystina (sheep's fescue)
Festuca ovina 'Glauca' (blue fescue)
Helictotrichon sempervirens (blue oat grass)

WHITE FLOWERS

PERENNIALS AND BIENNIALS

SPRING

Aquilegia caerulea 'Kristall' (columbine)
Arabis caucasica 'Snow Cap' (wall rock cress)
Bellis perennis 'White Carpet' (English daisy)
Caltha palustris 'Alba' (marsh marigold)
Dicentra eximia 'Snowdrift,' 'Sweetheart' (fringed bleeding heart)
Dicentra spectabilis 'Alba,' 'Pantaloons' (common bleeding heart)
Galium odoratum (sweet woodruff)
Helleborus niger (Christmas rose)
Iberis sempervirens (edging candytuft)
Iris cristata alba (crested iris)
Iris siberica 'Snow Queen,' (Siberian iris)
Lunaria annua alba (money-plant, honesty)
Phlox divaricata 'Fuller's White' (wild blue phlox)
Phlox stolonifera 'Bruce's White' (creeping phlox)
Phlox subulata 'Snowflake' (moss pink)
Primula japonica 'Album' (Japanese primrose)
Pulmonaria officinalis 'Sissinghurst White' (lungwort)
Tiarella cordifolia (Allegheny foamflower)
Viola cornuta 'White Perfection' (tufted pansy)
Viola odorata 'White Czar' (sweet violet)

SUMMER

Achillea millefolium 'Snowtaler' (common yarrow)
Angelica archangelica (wild parsnip)
Armeria maritima 'Alba' (sea pink, thrift)
Aruncus dioicus (goat's beard)
Astilbe x *arendsii* 'Bridal Veil,' 'Deutschland,' 'Diamond' (astilbe)
Baptisia alba pendula (false indigo)
Campanula carpatica 'White Clips,' 'Wedgewood White' (Carpathian bellflower)
Centranthus ruber albus (white valerian)
Cerastium tomentosum (snow-in-summer)
Chrysanthemum maximum (shasta daisy)
Crambe cordifolia (colewort)
Delphinium grandiflorum 'Album' (Chinese delphinium)
Delphinium x *elatum* 'Galahad,' 'Ivory Towers' (delphinium)
Dictamnus albus (gas plant)
Digitalis purpurea 'Alba' (foxglove)
Erigeron x *hybridus* 'Quakeress White' (fleabane)

Gypsophila paniculata (baby's breath)
Hesperis matronalis alba (dame's rocket)
Iris ensata 'Henry's White,' 'Moonlight Wave' (Japanese iris)
Iris hybrida 'Lacy Snowflake,' 'Skating Party' (bearded iris)
Lavandula angustifolia 'Alba' (lavender)
Lychnis coronaria alba (rose campion)
Lysimachia clethroides (gooseneck loosestrife)
Monarda didyma 'Snow White' (bee-balm)
Paeonia lactiflora 'Alesia,' 'Festiva Maxima,' 'Jacob Styer,' 'Jan Van Leeuwen,' 'Moon of Nippon,' 'Mildred May' (Chinese peony)
Papaver orientale 'Perry's White,' 'Snow Queen,' 'White King' (Oriental poppy)
Phlox maculata 'Miss Lingard' (Carolina phlox)
Phlox paniculata 'David,' 'Mt. Fuji,' 'White Admiral,' 'World Peace' (garden phlox)
Platycodon grandiflorus 'Fuji White' (balloon flower)
Veronica spicata 'Icicle' (spiked speedwell)

LATE SUMMER AND FALL

Anaphalis triplinervis (three-veined pearly everlasting)
Anemone x *hybrida* 'Honorine Jobert,' 'Whirlwind' (Japanese anemone)
Aster novi-belgii x *novae-angliae* 'Bennington White,' 'Mt. Everest,' 'Snow Flurry,' 'Wedding Lace,' (Michaelmas daisy, fall aster)
Boltonia asteroides 'Snowbank' (boltonia)
Chrysanthemum nipponicum (Montauk daisy)
Chrysanthemum parthenium 'Snowball' (feverfew)
Chrysanthemum weyrichii 'White Bomb' (Miyabe)
Chrysanthemum x *morifolium* many cultivars (garden mum)
Cimicifuga simplex (Kamchatka bugbane)
Echinacea purpurea 'White Luster,' 'White Swan' (purple coneflower)
Eupatorium coelestinum 'Alba' (mist flower)
Hosta plantaginea (August lily)
Liatris scariosa alba 'White Spire' (tall gayfeather)
Physostegia virginiana 'Summer Snow' (obedient plant)

ANNUALS

Ageratum houstonianum 'Summer Snow' (flossflower)
Antirrhinum majus 'White Wonder' (snapdragon)
Begonia x *semperflorens* 'Viva' (wax begonia)
Browallia speciosa 'White Bells' (amethyst flower)
Catharanthus roseus 'Peppermint Cooler' (Madagascar periwinkle)
Cosmos bipinnatus 'Purity,' 'Sonata' (cosmos)
Euphorbia marginata 'Summer Icicle' (snow-on-the-mountain)
Impatiens wallerana 'Accent White,' 'Dazzler White,' 'Elfin White'
    (impatiens)
Lobelia erinus 'Fountain White,' 'Paper Moon' (edging lobelia)
Lobularia maritima 'Carpet of Snow,' 'Sweet White' (sweet alyssum)
Nicotiana alata 'Dwarf White Bedder' (flowering tobacco)
Nicotiana sylvestris (great-flowering tobacco)
Nierembergia hippomanica violacea 'Mount Blanc' (cupflower)
Pelargonium x *hortorum* 'Dynamo White,' 'Elite White'
    (zonal geranium)
Petunia x *hybrida* 'Carpet White,' 'Merlin White,' 'Sonata' (petunia)
Phlox drummondii 'Palona White,' 'Palona White with Eye'
    (annual phlox)
Salvia farinacea 'Porcelain,' 'Silver White' (mealy-cup sage)
Verbena x *hybrida* 'Romance White' (verbena)
Viola x *wittrockiana* 'Crystal Bowl White,' 'Melody White,'
    'Melody White with Blotch,' 'Paper White,' 'White Maxim' (pansy)
Zinnia linearis 'Classic White' (narrow-leaf zinnia)

BULBS

SPRING

Anemone blanda 'White Splendor' (Grecian windflower)
Convallaria majalis (lily-of-the-valley)
Crocus chrysanthus 'Prinz Claus,' 'Purity' (snow crocus)
Crocus x *vernus* 'Peter Pan' (Dutch crocus)
Hyacinthoides hispanica 'White City' (wood hyacinth)
Hyacinthus orientalis 'L'Innocence,' 'Mont Blanc' (Dutch hyacinth)
Iris reticulata 'Natascha' (reticulated iris)
Iris x *xiphium* 'Casablanca,' 'White Wedgewood' (Dutch iris)
Muscari botryoides 'Album' (grape hyacinth)
Narcissus hybrids 'Mt. Hood,' 'White Ideal' (daffodil)
Narcissus triandrus 'Ice Wings,' 'Thalia' (narcissus)

Trillium grandiflorum (great white trillium)
Tulipa x *hybrida* 'Ivory Floradale,' 'Schoonord,' 'White Dream,'
    'White Triumphator' (hybrid tulips)
Zephranthes atamasco (rain lily)

SUMMER

Agapanthus africanus (African lily)
Begonia x *tuberhybrida* 'Non-stop White' (tuberous begonia)
Galanthus spp. (snowdrops)
Gladiolus x *hybrida* 'St. Mary' (gladiolus)
Lilium 'Bunny Puff,' 'Snowy Owl,' 'White Swallow' (Asiatic lilies)
Lilium 'Casa Blanca,' 'Fine Art' (Oriental lilies)
Polianthes tuberosa (tuberose)

LATE SUMMER AND FALL

Agapanthus africanus (African lily)
Begonia x *tuberhybrida* 'Non-stop White' (tuberous begonia)
Crocus achroleuces (crocus)
Crocus sativus albus (white saffron crocus)
Dahlia x *pinnata* 'Playa Blanca,' 'Sneezy,'
    'Snow Country' (dahlia)

Trillium grandiflorum

BLUE, LAVENDER, OR PURPLE FLOWERS

PERENNIALS AND BIENNIALS

SPRING

Ajuga reptans (bugleweed)

Aubrieta deltoidea 'Purple Gem,' 'Royal Blue' (rock cress)

Brunnera macrophylla (Siberian bugloss)

Iris cristata (crested iris)

Iris siberica 'Blue Brilliant,' 'Blue Moon,' 'Caesar's Brother,' 'Pembina,' 'Perry's Blue,' 'Silver Edge' (Siberian iris)

Lunaria annua alba (money-plant, honesty)

Mertensia virginica (Virginia bluebells)

Myosotis scorpioides (forget-me-not)

Omphaloides verna (blue-eyed Mary)

Phlox divaricata laphamii, 'Dirigo Ice' (woodland phlox)

Phlox stolonifera 'Blue Ridge,' 'Sherwood Purple' (creeping phlox)

Phlox subulata 'Cushion Blue,' 'Emerald Blue' (moss pink)

Polemonium caeruleum 'Blue Pearl' (Jacob's ladder)

Pulmonaria spp. (lungworts)

Pulsatilla vulgaris (pasque flower)

Viola cornuta 'Jersey Gem' (horned violet)

Viola labradorica (Labrador violet)

Viola odorata (sweet violet)

SUMMER

Anchusa azurea (Italian bugloss)

Aquilegia x *hybrida* 'Heavenly Blue' (columbine)

Baptisia australis (blue wild indigo)

Campanula carpatica (Carpathian bellflower)

Centaurea montana (mountain bluet)

Delphinium x *elatum* 'Blue Bird,' 'Blue Jay,' 'Summer Skies' (delphinium)

Delphinium grandiflorum 'Blue Butterfly' (Chinese delphinium)

Dianthus barbatus (sweet William)

Erigeron x *hybridus* (fleabane)

Geranium himalayense 'Johnson's Blue' (Himalayan cranesbill)

Geranium pratense 'Mrs. Kendall Clarke' (wild cranesbill)

Iris ensata 'Activity,' 'Favour,' 'Moriah' (Japanese iris)

Iris hybrida 'Blue Staccato,' 'Midnight Hour,' 'Sapphire Hills' (bearded iris)

Lavandula angustifolia 'Hidcote,' 'Munstead Dwarf' (lavender)

Limonium latifolium (sea lavender)

Linum perenne (blue flax)

Lupinus hybrids 'The Govenor' (lupine)

Mazus reptans (mazus)

Monarda didyma 'Blue Stocking,' 'Purple Crown' (bee-balm)

Nepeta x *faassenii* (catmint)

Penstemon barbatus 'Prairie Dusk' (beard-tongue)

Phlox paniculata 'Blue Boy,' 'Blue Lagoon,' 'The King' (garden phlox)

Platycodon grandiflorus (balloon flower)

Prunella x *webbiana* 'Purple Loveliness' (self-heal)

Salvia x *superba* (hybrid blue salvia)

Scabiosa caucasica 'Blue Butterfly,' 'Blue Danube,' 'Klaus Jelitto' (pincushion flower)

Scutellaria baicalensis (skullcap)

Stokesia laevis 'Blue Danube,' 'Compliment' (Stokes' aster)

Thalictrum aquilegifolium (columbine meadow-rue)

Thalictrum rochebrunianum (Japanese meadow-rue)

Tradescantia x *andersoniana* 'Zwanenburg Blue' (spiderwort)

Verbena bonariensis (Brazilian verbena)

Verbena canadensis 'Homestead Purple' (clump verbena)

Veronica latifolia 'Crater Lake Blue' (Germander speedwell)

Veronica longifolia 'Blue Charm,' 'Foerster's Blue' (speedwell)

Veronica spicata 'Blue Peter,' 'Sunny Border Blue' (spiked speedwell)

LATE SUMMER AND FALL

Aconitum spp. (monkshoods)

Aster azureus (sky blue prairie aster)

Aster novi-belgii x *novae-angliae* 'Blue Gown,' 'Eventide,' 'Hella Lacy,' 'Marie Ballard,' 'Purple Dome,' 'Professor Kippenburg,' (Michaelmas daisy, fall aster)

Aster x *frikartii* 'Monch' (Frikart's aster)

Ceratostigma plumbaginoides (leadwort)

Echinops ritro 'Taplow Blue,' 'Taplow Purple' 'Veitch's Blue,' (globe-thistle)

Eupatorium coelestinum (mist flower)

Gentiana spp. (gentians)

Liriope muscari 'Big Blue,' 'Royal Purple' (blue lilyturf)

Lobelia siphilitica (big-blue lobelia)

Perovskia atriplicifolia (Russian sage)

Salvia pratensis (meadow sage)

Viola x *wittrockiana*

ANNUALS

Ageratum houstonianum 'Blue Blazer,' 'Blue Improved,' 'Blue Ribbon,' 'Capri,' 'Hawaii Hybrid' (flossflower)

Antirrhinum majus 'Floral Showers Purple,' 'Liberty Lavender' (snapdragon)

Borago officinalis (borage)

Brachycome iberidifolia 'Blue Splendor,' 'Blue Star,' 'Purple Splendor' (swan river daisy)

Browallia speciosa 'Blue Bells Improved,' 'Blue Troll,' 'Marine Bells,' 'Powder Blue' (amethyst flower)

Callistephus chinensis 'Matsumoto Blue,' 'Matsumoto Light Blue' (China aster)

Centaurea cyanus 'Blue Boy Double,' 'Blue Diadem,' 'Dwarf Blue Midget,' 'Jubilee Gem' (bachelor's button)

Consolida ambigua 'Blue Spire,' 'Giant Dark Blue,' 'Giant Light Blue,' 'Imperial Blue Bell' (rocket larkspur)

Cynoglossum amabile 'Blue Showers' (Chinese forget-me-not)

Eustoma grandiflora 'Blue Lisa,' 'Blue Picotee,' 'Misty Blue' (prairie gentian)

Felicia amelloides (blue daisy)

Gomphrena globosa 'Purple Buddy' (globeflower)

Impatiens wallerana 'Accent Lavender-blue,' 'Blue Pearl,' 'Tempo Lavender' (impatiens)

Ipomoea tricolor 'Heavenly Blue' (morning glory)

Lantana montevidensis (weeping lantana)

Lobelia erinus 'Blue Cascade,' 'Sapphire,' 'Crystal Palace,' 'Cambridge Blue' (edging lobelia)

Lupinus texensis (Texas blue-bonnet)

Nierembergia hippomanica violacea 'Purple Robe' (cupflower)

Nigella damascena (love-in-a-mist)

Petunia x *hybrida* 'Blue Joy,' 'Blue Lace,' 'Blue Skies,' 'Lacy Sails,' 'Midnight Madness,' 'Plum Blue,' 'Plum Purple,' 'Prime Time Blue,' 'Prime Time Light Blue,' 'Purple Joy,' 'Sky Joy,' 'Ultra Blue,' 'Ultra Blue Star,' (petunia)

Phlox drummondii 'Palona Light Blue' (annual phlox)

Salvia farinacea 'Victoria' (mealy-cup sage)

Salvia viridis 'Oxford Blue' (painted sage)

Torenia fournieri 'Blue Panda,' 'Clown Blue,' 'Clown Violet' (wishbone flower)

Verbena speciosa 'Imagination'

Verbena x *hybrida* 'Armour Purple' (verbena)

Viola x *wittrockiana* 'Accord Blue Blotch,' 'Universal Blue Blotch,' 'Universal Light Blue,' 'Universal Purple,' 'Universal True Blue,' 'Vicking Blue,' 'Vicking Purple' (pansy)

BULBS

SPRING

Allium aflatunense 'Purple Sensation' (Persian onion)

Allium azureum (blue globe onion)

Allium christophii (star-of-Persia)

Allium giganteum (giant onion)

Anemone blanda 'Blue Shades,' 'Blue Star' (Grecian windflower)

Brodiaea coronaria 'Queen Fabiola' (triplet lily)

Chionodoxa luciliae (glory-of-the-snow)

Crocus chrysanthus 'Blue Ribbon' (snow crocus)

Crocus x *vernus* 'Purpurea,' 'Queen of the Blues,' 'Remembrance' (Dutch crocus)

Fritillaria meleagris (checkered lily)

Fritillaria persica (Persian fritillaria)

Hyacinthoides hispanica 'Blue Queen,' 'Excelsior' (wood hyacinth)

Hyacinthus orientalis 'Blue Jacket,' 'Delft Blue,' 'Wedgewood' (Dutch hyacinth)

Iris reticulata (reticulated iris)

Muscari armeniacum 'Blue Spike' (blue grape hyacinth)

Muscari azureum (azure grape hyacinth)

Muscari botryoides (grape hyacinth)

Puschkinia scilloides (striped squill)

Scilla siberica 'Spring Beauty' (Siberian squill)

Tulipa x *hybrida* 'Blue Aimable,' 'Blue Parrot,' 'Boccherini,' 'Cum Laude,' 'Dr. An Wang,' 'Hans Anrud,' 'Purple Star' (hybrid tulip)

SUMMER

Agapanthus africanus nana 'Blue Peter' (African lily)

Camassia leichtlinii (camas)

Iris x *xiphium* 'Ideal,' 'Professor Blaauw,' 'Purple Sensation' (Dutch iris)

LATE SUMMER AND FALL

Agapanthus africanus nana 'Blue Peter' (African lily)

Allium senescens glaucum (fall lily leek)

Allium sphaerocephalum (drumstick chives)

YELLOW AND GOLD FLOWERS

PERENNIALS AND BIENNIALS

SPRING

Aquilegia canadensis 'Corbett' (American columbine)
Aquilegia chrysantha 'Yellow Queen' (golden columbine)
Aquilegia x *hybrida* 'Yellow Music,' 'Maxistar' (columbine)
Aurinia saxatilis (basket-of-gold)
Caltha palustris (marsh marigold)
Chrysogonum virginianum (goldenstar)
Corydalis lutea (yellow corydalis)
Doronicum caucasicum (leopard's bane)
Epimedium x *versicolor* 'Sulphureum' (barrenwort)
Euphorbia polychroma (cushion spurge)
Iris siberica 'Butter and Sugar' (Siberian iris)
Potentilla verna (spring cinquefoil)
Primula veris (cowslip primrose)
Primula x *polyantha* 'Yellow' (polyanthus primrose)
Thermopsis caroliniana (southern lupine)
Trollius europaeus (globeflower)
Viola cornuta 'Lutea Splendens,' 'Scottish Yellow' (horned violet)

SUMMER

Achillea filipendulina 'Coronation Gold' (fern-leaf yarrow)
Achillea millefolium 'Hope' (common yarrow)
Achillea tomentosa (woolly milfoil)
Achillea x 'Moonshine' (moonshine yarrow)
Alcea rosea 'Chater's Yellow' (hollyhock)
Anthemis tinctoria (golden marguerite)
Asclepias tuberosa 'Hello Yellow' (butterfly weed)
Centaurea macrocephala (Armenian basket flower)
Coreopsis grandiflora (coreopsis, tickseed)
Coreopsis verticillata (threadleaf coreopsis)
Corydalis lutea (yellow corydalis)
Delosperma cooperi (hardy iceplant)
Digitalis ambigua (yellow foxglove)
Gaillardia x *grandiflora* 'Aurea Pura,' 'Golden Goblin,' 'The Sun' (blanket-flower)
Geum quellyon 'Lady Strathedon' (geum)
Hemerocallis hybrids 'Happy Returns,' 'Hyperion,' 'Penny's Worth,' 'Stella de Oro,' 'Summer Sun,' many more (daylily)
Iris pseudacorus (yellow flag iris)

Iris hybrida, many cultivars (bearded iris)
Kniphofia uvaria 'Primrose Beauty' (red-hot poker)
Ligularia spp. (golden rays)
Linaria vulgaris (toadflax)
Lupinus hybrids 'Gallery Yellow,' 'Russel Hybrids Yellow' (lupine)
Lysimachia nummulara (moneywort, creeping Jenny)
Lysimachia punctata (yellow loosestrife)
Oenothera tetragona (sundrops)
Phlomis russeliana (sticky Jerusalem sage)
Verbascum x *hybridum* (mullein)

LATE SUMMER AND FALL

Chrysanthemum x *morifolium* many cultivars (garden mum)
Chrysanthemum x *rubellum* 'Mary Stoker' (hybrid chrysanthemum)
Corydalis lutea (yellow corydalis)
Helenium autumnale 'Butterpat' (sneezeweed)
Helianthus angustifolius (fall sunflower)
Heliopsis helianthoides scabra (false sunflower)
Ratibida pinnata (yellow coneflower)
Rudbeckia fulgida 'Goldsturm' (orange coneflower)
Rudbeckia nitida (shining coneflower)
Sedum kamtschaticum (Kamschatka stonecrop)
Senecio aureus (golden groundsel)
Solidago hybrids (goldenrod)

ANNUALS

Antirrhinum majus 'Lemon Rocket,' 'Liberty Yellow,' 'Yellow Bicolor' (snapdragon)
Calendula officinalis 'Kablouna Gold,' 'Sunglow,' 'Yellow Bon Bon' (pot marigold)
Celosia cristata 'Castle Yellow,' 'Century Yellow,' 'Kimono Yellow' (cockscomb)
Cheiranthus cheiri 'Cloth of Gold' (wallflower)
Coreopsis tinctoria (golden coreopsis)
Cosmos sulphureus 'Ladybird Yellow' (yellow cosmos)
Dahlia x *hybrida* 'Sunny Yellow' (annual dahlia)
Dyssodia tenuiloba (Dahlberg daisy)
Eschscholzia californica (California poppy)
Eustoma grandiflora 'Heidi Yellow' (prairie gentian)
Gaillardia pulchella 'Yellow Plume' (annual blanket-flower)
Gazania rigens 'Bright Yellow Daybreak' (gazania)

Gerbera jamesonii 'Golden Yellow Festival,' 'Tempo Yellow' (gerbera daisy)

Helianthus annuus (sunflower)

Helichrysum bracteatum 'Golden Bikini' (strawflower)

Limonium sinuatum 'Sunset,' 'Yellow Soiree' (statice)

Linaria macroccana (toadflax)

Matthiola incana 'Yellow' (stock)

Melampodium paludosum 'Medallion,' 'Showstar' (black-foot daisy)

Nicotiana alata 'Lemon-Lime' (flowering tobacco)

Papaver nudicaule 'Wonderland Yellow Shades' (Iceland poppy)

Petunia x *hybrida* 'Summer Sun' (petunia)

Portulaca grandiflora 'Sundial Gold,' 'Sundial Yellow' (moss rose)

Sanvitalia procumbens 'Gold Braid' (creeping zinnia)

Tagetes spp. many cultivars (marigolds)

Thunbergia alata 'Yellow with Eye' (black-eyed Susan vine)

Tithonia rotundifolia 'Yellow Torch' (Mexican sunflower)

Tropaeolum majus 'Whirlybird Gold' (nasturtium)

Viola x *wittrockiana* 'Crystal Bowl Primrose,' 'Melody Yellow,' 'Sunset Maxim,' 'Yellow Maxim' (pansy)

Zinnia elegans 'Peter Pan Gold,' 'Yellow Dasher,' 'Yellow Ruffles' (common zinnia)

Gazania rigens

BULBS

SPRING

Clivia minata (clivia, Kaffir lily)

Crocus chrysanthus (snow crocus)

Crocus x *vernus* 'Yellow Mammoth' (Dutch crocus)

Eranthis hyemalis (winter aconite)

Erythronium americanum (dog-tooth violet)

Freesia hybrids 'Royal Gold' (freesia)

Fritillaria imperalis 'Lutea Maxima' (crown imperial)

Hyacinthus orientalis 'City of Haarlem,' 'Lemon Queen' (Dutch hyacinth)

Iris danfordiae (Danford iris)

Narcissus spp. many cultivars (daffodils)

Ranunculus asiaticus 'Yellow' (Persian buttercup)

Tulipa batalinii 'Bright Gem,' 'Yellow Jewel' (Bokhara tulip)

Tulipa clusiana (lady tulip)

Tulipa sylvestris (Florentine tulip)

Tulipa tarda (Kuenlun tulip)

Tulipa x *hybrida* 'Georgette,' 'Golden Apeldoorn,' 'Jewel of Spring,' 'Sweet Harmony,' 'West Point' (tulip)

SUMMER

Allium moly (lily leek)

Begonia x *tuberhybrida* 'Diamont Yellow,' 'Non-stop Yellow' (tuberous begonia)

Canna x *generalis* 'Liberty Yellow,' 'Yellow King Humbert,' 'Butterscotch' (canna lily)

Crocosmia x *crocosmiiflora* 'Jenny Bloom,' 'Norwich Canary' (montbretia)

Gladiolus hybrids 'Gold Coin' (gladiolus)

Iris x *xiphium* 'Golden Harvest' (Dutch iris)

Lilium 'Connecticut Yankee,' 'Cream Puff,' 'Dreamland,' 'Impala,' 'Lemon Custard,' 'Sunny Twinkle' (Asiatic hybrid lilies)

Lilium 'Golden Showers,' 'Golden Splendor' (Chinese trumpet lilies, Aurelian lilies)

Lilium longifolium 'Yellow Tiger' (tiger lily)

LATE SUMMER AND FALL

Begonia x *tuberhybrida* 'Diamont Yellow,' 'Non-stop Yellow' (tuberous begonia)

Dahlia x *pinnata* 'Kevin Floodlight,' 'Playboy' (dahlia)

Sternbergia lutea (winter daffodil)

PINK, ROSE, AND MAGENTA-PINK FLOWERS

PERENNIALS AND BIENNIALS

SPRING

Aquilegia x *hybrida* 'Nora Barlow,' 'Heidi' (columbine)

Bergenia cordifolia 'Perfecta' (heart-leaf bergenia)

Dicentra eximia (fringed bleeding heart)

Dicentra spectabilis (common bleeding heart)

Lamium maculatum 'Beacon Silver,' 'Shell Pink' (spotted dead nettle)

Lunaria annua (money-plant, honesty)

Phlox pilosa ozarkana (downy phlox)

Phlox stolonifera 'Home Fires' (creeping phlox)

Phlox subulata 'Emerald Pink,' 'Millstream Daphne' (moss pink)

Primula japonica 'Carmina' (Japanese primrose)

Primula x *polyantha* (polyanthus primrose)

Prunella x *webbiana* 'Loveliness' (self-heal)

Saponaria ocymoides (rock soapwort)

Viola cornuta 'Nellie Britten' (horned violet)

Viola odorata 'Rosina' (sweet violet)

SUMMER

Achillea millefolium 'Appleblossom' (common yarrow)

Alcea rosea 'Newport Pink' (hollyhock)

Armeria maritima (sea pink, thrift)

Astilbe x *arendsii* 'Fanal,' 'Peach Blossom,' 'Rheinland' (astilbe)

Astilbe simplicifolia 'Sprite' (star astilbe)

Centranthus ruber roseus (red valerian)

Chrysanthemum coccineum 'Roseum' (painted daisy)

Chrysanthemum x *rubellum* 'Clara Curtis' (hybrid chrysanthemum)

Coreopsis rosea (pink coreopsis)

Delphinium x *elatum* 'Cameliard' (delphinium)

Dianthus barbatus (sweet William)

Dianthus deltoides 'Zing Rose' (maiden pink)

Dianthus gratianopolitanus 'Bath's Pink' (cheddar pink)

Dianthus plumarius (cottage pink)

Dictamnus albus 'Purpureus' (gas plant)

Digitalis x *mertonensis* (strawberry foxglove)

Geranium endressii 'Wargrave Pink' (Endrew's geranium)

Geranium sanguineum (bloody cranesbill)

Gypsophila paniculata 'Pink Fairy' (baby's breath)

Hemerocallis hybrids 'Catherine Woodbury,' 'Cherry Cheeks,' 'Knob Hill,' 'Pink Lavender Appeal,' 'Theresa Hall' (daylily)

Hesperis matronalis (dame's rocket)

Heuchera sanguinea 'Chatterbox' (coralbells)

x *Heucherella tiarelloides* 'Bridget Bloom' (foamy bells)

Iris hybrida 'Beverly Sills,' 'Vanity' (bearded iris)

Lavandula angustifolia 'Jean Davis' (lavender)

Lupinus hybrids 'Chatelaine' (lupine)

Lychnis coronaria (rose campion)

Malva alcea 'Fastigiata' (hollyhock mallow)

Monarda didyma 'Croftway Pink,' 'Marshall's Delight,' (bee-balm)

Oenothera speciosa 'Rosea' (showy evening primrose)

Paeonia lactiflora 'Auten's Pride,' 'Doris Cooper,' 'Edulus Superba,' 'Gene Wild,' 'Japanese Pink,' 'Rose City' (Chinese peony)

Papaver orientale 'Raspberry Queen,' 'Springtime' (Oriental poppy)

Penstemon barbatus 'Elfin Pink,' 'Rose Elf' (beard-tongue)

Phlox maculata 'Alpha' (wild sweet William)

Phlox paniculata 'Bright Eyes,' 'Eva Cullum,' 'Pinafore Pink' (garden phlox)

Platycodon grandiflorus 'Fuji Pink,' 'Shell Pink' (balloon flower)

Polygonum bistorta (snakeweed, knotweed)

Sidalcea malviflora 'Elsie Heugh,' 'Partygirl' (prairie mallow)

Veronica longifolia 'Rosea' (speedwell)

Veronica spicata 'Minuet' (spiked speedwell)

LATE SUMMER AND FALL

Anemone x *hybrida* 'Margarete,' 'Queen Charlotte,' 'September Charm' (Japanese anemone)

Anemone vitifolia 'Robustissima' (grape-leaf anemone)

Aster novi-belgii x *novae-angliae* 'Alma Potschke,' 'Harrington's Pink,' 'Pink Bouquet' (Michaelmas daisy, fall aster)

Astilbe chinensis var. *pumila* (dwarf Chinese astilbe)

Astilbe taquetii 'Superba' (fall astilbe)

Begonia grandis (hardy begonia)

Boltonia asteroides 'Pink Beauty' (boltonia)

Chelone lyonii (pink turtle-head)

Chrysanthemum x *morifolium* 'Glamour,' 'Pink Daisy,' 'Pink Pagoda' (garden mum)

Chrysanthemum weyrichii 'Pink Bomb' (miyabe)

Digitalis purpurea (foxglove)

Echinacea purpurea 'Bright Star,' 'Magnus' (purple coneflower)

Eupatorium fistulosum (Joe-Pye weed)

Filipendula rubra (queen-of-the-prairie)

Hibiscus moscheutos 'Anne Arundel' (rose mallow)

Liatris spicata (spike gayfeather)

Lythrum salicaria 'Morden Pink' (purple loosestrife)
Physostegia virginiana 'Bouquet Rose,' 'Vivid' (obedient plant)
Sedum cauticolum
Sedum spectabile 'Meteor' (showy stonecrop)
Sedum x 'Vera Jameson' (Vera Jameson stonecrop)

ANNUALS

Antirrhinum majus 'Liberty Light Pink,' 'Rocket Pink,' 'Tahiti Pink'
    (snapdragon)
Begonia x *semperflorens* 'Encore Light Pink,' 'Encore Pink,'
    'Encore Pink 'n Bronze,' 'Prelude Pink' (wax begonia)
Campanula medium rosea (Canterbury bells)
Catharanthus roseus 'Pinkie,' 'Tropicana Bright Eye,'
    'Tropicana Pink' (Madagascar periwinkle)
Celosia cristata 'Castle Pink,' 'Kimono Rose' (cockscomb)
Celosia spicata 'Flamingo Feather,' 'Flamingo Purple' (wheat celosia)
Cleome hasslerana 'Cherry Queen,' 'Rose Queen' (spider flower)
Cosmos bipinnatus 'Imperial Pink' (cosmos)
Dianthus chinensis 'Carmine Rose,' 'Ideal Pink,' 'Pink Charm,'
    'Telstar,' 'Telstar Pink' (China pink)
Eustoma grandiflora 'Echo Pink,' 'Heidi Cherry Blossom,'
    'Mermaid Pink' (prairie gentian)
Gomphrena globosa (globeflower)
Impatiens wallerana 'Accent Deep Pink,' 'Dazzler Pink,'
    'Pink Tempo,' 'Super Elfin Blush,' 'Super Elfin Pink,'
    'Super Elfin Swirl' (impatiens)
Lathyrus odoratus (sweet pea)
Lavatera trimestris (tree mallow)
Lobelia erinus 'Rose Fountain' (edging lobelia)
Matthiola incana 'Cinderella Pink,' 'Midget Rose' (stock)
Nicotiana alata 'Domino Pink with White Eye,' 'Domino Salmon
    Pink,' 'Starship Rose-Pink' (flowering tobacco)
Papaver nudicaule 'Wonderland Pink Shades' (Iceland poppy)
Pelargonium peltatum (ivy geranium)
Pelargonium x *hortorum* 'Elite Pink,' 'Orbit Appleblossom,'
    'Orbit Pink,' 'Orbit Rose' (zonal geranium)
Pentas lanceolata 'Cheers' (Egyptian star-cluster)
Petunia x *hybrida* 'Falcon Blush Pink,' 'Merlin Pink,' 'Pink Carpet,'
    'Pink Dreams,' 'Supercascade Blush,' 'Supermagic Pink' (petunia)
Phlox drummondii 'Palona Deep Rose' (annual phlox)
Portulaca grandiflora 'Sundial Pink,' 'Sundial Pink Peppermint,'
    'Sundial Fuchsia' (moss rose)

Salvia coccinea 'Cherry Blossom'
Torenia fournieri 'Pink Panda' (wishbone flower)
Viola x *wittrockiana* 'Imperial Frosty Rose,' 'Imperial Pink Shades,'
    'Melody Pink Shades' (pansy)
Zinnia elegans 'Dasher Pink,' 'Dreamland Pink,' 'Peter Pan Pink'
    (common zinnia)

BULBS

SPRING

Anemone blanda 'Pink Star' (Grecian windflower)
Chionodoxa luciliae 'Pink Giant' (glory-of-the-snow)
Cyclamen hederifolium (hardy cyclamen)
Hyacinthoides hispanica 'Rosabelle' (wood hyacinth)
Hyacinthus orientalis 'Anna Marie,' 'Pink Pearl' (Dutch hyacinth)
Narcissus hybrids 'Pink Champion,' 'Pink Charm,' 'Rosy Clouds,'
    'Salome' (daffodils)
Tulipa pulchella violaceae (dwarf Taurus tulip)
Tulipa x *hybrida* 'Angelique,' 'Douglas Baader,' 'Dreamland,' 'Pink
    Impression,' 'Menton' (hybrid tulips)

SUMMER

Begonia x *tuberhybrida* 'Non-stop Pink,' 'Non-stop Rose Pink,'
    'Ruffled Pink' (tuberous begonia)
Canna x *generalis* 'Angel Pink,' 'Liberty Pink,' 'Pink President'
    (canna lily)
Gladiolus x *hortulanus* 'China Glow,' 'Dawn Glow,'
    'Rose Garden' (gladiolus)
Lilium 'Pink Perfection' (Aurelian trumpet lilies)
Lilium 'Corsica,' 'Malta' (Asiatic lilies)
Lilium 'Crimson Elegance,' 'Le Reve,' 'Noblese,'
    'Rose Elegance,' 'Stargazer,' 'Treasure'
    (Oriental lilies)
Lilium longifolium 'Pink Tiger' (tiger lily)
Zephranthes grandiflora (zephyr lily)

LATE SUMMER AND FALL

Amaryllis belladona (belladona lily)
Colchicum autumnale (autumn crocus)
Cyclamen coum (winter cyclamen)
Dahlia x *pinnata* 'Lipoma,'
    'Lucky Number,' 'Orion' (dahlia)
Lycoris squamigera (resurrection lily)

Portulaca grandiflora

ORANGE, SCARLET (ORANGE-RED), AND CORAL FLOWERS

PERENNIALS AND BIENNIALS

SPRING

Aquilegia canadensis (American columbine)
Mimulus cardinalis (scarlet monkey flower)
Viola cornuta 'Chantreyland' (horned violet)

SUMMER

Achillea millefolium 'Orange Queen,' 'Paprika' (common yarrow)
Asclepias tuberosa (butterfly weed)
Belamcanda chinensis (blackberry lily)
Dianthus barbatus 'Scarlet Beauty' (sweet William)
Gaillardia x *grandiflora* 'Goblin' (blanket-flower)
Geum quellyon 'Fire Opal,' 'Mrs. Bradshaw' (geum)
Hemerocallis fulva (tawny daylily)
Hemerocallis hybrids 'Bertie Ferris,' 'Buzz Bomb,' 'Hot Embers,' many more (daylily)
Iris hybrida 'Queen of Hearts,' 'Sultan's Palace,' 'Wayside Elegance' (bearded iris)
Kniphofia uvaria 'Pfitzeri,' 'Shining Sceptre' (red-hot poker)
Ligularia dentata 'Desdemona' (big-leaf ligularia)
Lynchnis chalcedonia (Maltese cross)
Paeonia lactiflora 'Coral and Gold,' 'Coral Isle,' 'Crusader' (Chinese peony)
Papaver orientale 'Beauty of Livermore,' 'China Boy,' 'Prince of Orange' (Oriental poppy)
Phlox paniculata 'Orange Perfection,' 'Sandra' (garden phlox)

LATE SUMMER AND FALL

Chrysanthemum x *morifolium* 'Deep Regards,' 'Victory' (garden mum)
Helenium autumnale 'Moerheim Beauty,' 'Red-gold Hybrids' (sneezeweed)

ANNUALS

Antirrhinum majus 'Orange-scarlet Sonnet,' 'Tahiti Orange' (snapdragon)
Calendula officinalis 'Bon Bon Orange' (pot marigold)
Celosia cristata 'Castle Scarlet,' 'Kimono Orange' (cockscomb)
Cheiranthus cheiri 'Fire King,' 'Orange Bedder' (wallflower)
Coreopsis tinctoria (golden coreopsis)

Cosmos sulphureus 'Ladybird Orange,' 'Sunny Red' (yellow cosmos)
Dahlia x *hybrida* 'Sunny Red' (annual dahlia)
Dianthus chinensis 'Scarlet Charms' (China pink)
Eschscholzia californica 'Dalli,' 'Orange King' (California poppy)
Gazania rigens 'Bright Orange Daybreak,' 'Ministar Tangerine' (gazania)
Gerbera jamesonii 'Festival Orange' (gerbera daisy)
Impatiens wallerana 'Accent Orange,' 'Accent Orange Star,' 'Dazzler Orange,' 'Dazzler Scarlet,' 'Super Elfin Orange,' 'Super Elfin Scarlet' (impatiens)
Nemesia strumosa 'Orange Prince' (nemesia)
Papaver nudicaule 'Wonderland Orange Shades' (Iceland poppy)
Papaver rhoeas (corn poppy)
Pelargonium x *hortorum* 'Forever Yours,' 'Orange Appeal,' 'Pinto Salmon Orange,' 'Tango,' 'Tetra Scarlet' (zonal geranium)
Petunia x *hybrida* 'Coral Flash,' 'Flame Carpet,' 'Highlight Coral,' 'Prisom Salmon Halo,' 'Spring Madness,' 'Supermagic Orange' (petunia)
Phlox drummondii 'Deep Salmon,' 'Light Salmon' (annual phlox)
Portulaca grandiflora 'Sundial Orange,' 'Sundial Scarlet' (moss rose)
Salvia splendens 'Flare' (red salvia)
Sanvitalia procumbens (creeping zinnia)

Lilium 'Enchantment'

Tagetes spp. many cultivars (marigolds)
Thunbergia alata 'Orange with Eye' (black-eyed Susan vine)
Tithonia rotundifolia (Mexican sunflower)
Tropaeolum majus 'Jewel Mix,' 'Tip-top Apricot,' 'Tip-top Scarlet'
　(nasturtium)
Verbena x *hybrida* 'Peaches and Cream' (verbena)
Viola x *wittrockiana* 'Crystal Bowl Orange,' 'Orange Maxim,'
　'Orange Prince,' 'Padparadja,' 'Universal Orange' (pansy)
Zinnia angustifolia 'Golden Orange,' 'Orange Star' (narrow-leaf
　zinnia)
Zinnia elegans 'Dasher Orange,' 'Orange King,' 'Peter Pan Orange,'
　'Scarlet Flame,' 'Splendor Scarlet' (common zinnia)

BULBS

SPRING
Clivia minata (clivia, Kaffir lily)
Freesia hybrids 'Pimpernel' (freesia)
Fritillaria imperialis 'Orange Brilliant' (crown imperial)
Gladiolus hybrids 'Fall Classic' (gladiolus)
Hyacinthus orientalis 'Gypsy Queen' (Dutch hyacinth)
Narcissus hybrids 'Bella Vista,' 'Mondragon,' 'Sentinel' (trumpet and
　large-cup daffodils)
Tulipa greigii (greigii tulip) 'Cape Cod,' 'Princess Charmante'
Tulipa kaufmanniana 'Cherry Orchard,' 'Orange Elite'
　(water lily tulip)
Tulipa x *hybrida* 'Apricot Beauty,' 'Ballerina,' 'General DeWet,'
　'Orange Wonder,' 'Orange Sun' (hybrid tulips)

SUMMER
Begonia x *tuberhybrida* 'Buttery Orange,' 'Non-stop Copper,'
　'Orange Cascade,' 'Tahiti' (tuberous begonia)
Canna x *generalis* 'Lucifer,' 'Standt Fellbach,' 'Wyoming' (canna lily)
Crocosmia x *crocosmiiflora* 'Lucifer' (montbretia)
Lilium 'Thunderbolt' (Aurelian trumpet lilies)
Lilium 'Avignon,' 'Enchantment' (Asiatic hybrid lilies)
Lilium longifolium 'Orange Tiger' (tiger lily)

LATE SUMMER AND FALL
Dahlia x *pinnata* 'Brio,' 'Mrs. Eileen' (dahlia)
Lycoris radiata (spider lily)
Tigridia pavonia (tiger flower)

SILVER OR GRAY FOLIAGE

PERENNIALS AND BIENNIALS
Acanthus mollis (bear's breeches)
Achillea tomentosa (woolly milfoil)
Achillea x 'Moonshine' (moonshine yarrow)
Anaphalis triplinervis (three-veined pearly everlasting)
Artemisia ludoviciana var. *albula* 'Silver King,'
　'Valerie Finnis' (white sage)
Artemisia schmidtiana 'Silvermound'
　(silvermound mugwort)
Aurinia saxatilis (basket-of-gold)
Cerastium tomentosum (snow-in-summer)
Crambe cordifolia (colewort)
Cynara cardunculus (cardoon)
Dianthus deltoides (maiden pink)
Dianthus gratianopolitanus (cheddar pink)
Echinops ritro (globe-thistle)
Eryngium amethystinum (amethyst sea holly)
Lamium maculatum 'White Nancy' (spotted dead nettle)
Lavandula angustifolia (lavender)
Leontopodium alpinum (edelweiss)
Nepeta x *faassenii* (catmint)
Perovskia atriplicifolia (Russian sage)
Ruta graveolens (rue)
Salvia argentea (silver sage)
Santolina chamaecyparissus (lavender cotton)
Stachys byzantina (lamb's-ears)
Thymus pseudolanuginosus (woolly thyme)
Veronica spicata incana (woolly speedwell)

ANNUALS
Senecio cineraria 'Silver Dust' (dusty miller)

RED AND CRIMSON (PURPLISH RED) FLOWERS

PERENNIALS AND BIENNIALS

SPRING
Aquilegia x *hybrida* 'Crimson Star,' 'Red and White Music'
    (hybrid columbine)
Primula japonica 'Carmina,' 'Miller's Crimson' (Japanese primrose)
Primula x *polyantha* 'Red' (polyanthus primrose)
Pulsatilla vulgaris rubra (pasque flower)

SUMMER
Achillea millefolium 'Red Beauty' (common yarrow)
Alcea rosea 'Indian Summer' (hollyhock)
Astilbe x *arendsii* 'Etna,' 'Fanal,' 'Glow,' 'Red Light' (astilbe)
Chrysanthemum coccineum 'Dark Crimson' (painted daisy)
Dianthus barbatus 'Blood Red,' 'Dunnet's Dark Crimson'
    (sweet William)
Dianthus deltoides 'Vampire,' 'Zing Red' (maiden pink)
Geum quellyon 'Red Wings' (geum)
Hemerocallis hybrids 'Cranberry Cove,' 'Crimson Shadow,'
    'Illini Red,' 'Reckless,' 'Sir Lancelot' (daylily)
Heuchera sanguinea 'Matin Bells,' 'Mt. St. Helens,' 'Splendens'
    (coralbells)
Hibiscus x *moscheutos* 'Lord Baltimore,' 'Disco Belle Red'
    (rose mallow)
Lupinus hybrids 'My Castle,' 'The Pages' (lupine)
Monarda didyma 'Cambridge Scarlet,' 'Gardenview Red'
    (bee-balm, oswego tea)
Paeonia lactiflora 'Bonanza,' 'Charm,' 'Chief Justice,' 'Kansas,'
    'Karen Gray,' 'President Lincoln,' 'Scarlet O'Hara,'
    'Shawnee Chief' (Chinese peony)
Papaver orientale 'Carmine,' 'Cavalier,' 'Warlord' (Oriental poppy)
Phlox paniculata 'Othello,' 'Starfire,' 'Tenor' (garden phlox)
Veronica spicata 'Red Fox' (spiked speedwell)

LATE SUMMER AND FALL
Aster novi-belgii x *novae-angliae* 'Autumn Glory,' 'Crimson
    Brocade,' 'Jenny,' 'Red Star' (Michaelmas daisy, fall aster)
Chrysanthemum x *morifolium* 'Ruby Mound' (garden mum)
Lobelia cardinalis (cardinal flower)

ANNUALS
Amaranthus caudatus 'Love Lies Bleeding' (love-lies-bleeding)
Antirrhinum majus 'Red Rocket,' 'Tahiti Red Bicolor' (snapdragon)
Begonia x *semperflorens* 'Encore Red,' 'Encore Red/Bronze,' 'Bingo
    Red,' 'Prelude Scarlet' (wax begonia)
Celosia cristata 'Kimono Red,' 'Century Red,' 'Fireglow' (cockscomb)
Dahlia x *hybrida* (annual dahlia)
Dianthus chinensis 'Ideal Crimson,' 'Oriental,'
    'Crimson Charm,' 'Princess Crimson' (China pink)
Eschscholzia californica 'Cherry Ripe' (California poppy)
Gerbera jamesonii 'Rainbow Crimson' (gerbera daisy)
Gomphrena globosa 'Strawberry Fields' (globeflower)
Impatiens wallerana 'Blitz Red,' 'Dazzler Red,' 'Deco Red,'
    'Showstopper Red,' 'Super Elfin Red Velvet' (impatiens)
Matthiola incana 'Dwarf Cinderella Red' (stock)
Nicotiana alata 'Domino Red,' 'Nicki Red,' 'Starship Red Improved'
    (flowering tobacco)
Papaver rhoeas (corn poppy)
Pelargonium x *domesticum* (Martha Washington geranium)

Tulipa greigii

Pelargonium x *hortorum* 'Elite Red,' 'Pinto Red' (zonal geranium)

Petunia x *hybrida* 'Merlin Red,' 'Picotee Red,' 'Red Dreams,'
    'Red Madness,' 'Super Cascade Red,' 'Super Magic Red'
    (petunia)

Phlox drummondii 'Palona Carmine' (annual phlox)

Salvia coccinea 'Lady in Red'

Salvia splendens 'Empire Red,' 'Red Hot Sally' (red salvia)

Tropaeolum majus 'Empress of India' (nasturtium)

Verbena x *hybrida* 'Blaze' (verbena)

Viola x *wittrockiana* 'Universal Red' (pansy)

Zinnia elegans 'Big Red,' 'Peter Pan Flame' (common zinnia)

BULBS

SPRING

Ranunculus asiaticus 'Red Shades,' 'Tecalote Red'
    (Persian buttercup)

Tulipa batalinii (Bokhara tulip)

Tulipa linifolia (tulip)

Tulipa greigii 'Red Riding Hood' (greigii tulip)

Tulipa kaufmanniana (water lily tulip)

Tulipa x *hybrida* 'Bastogne,' 'Couleur Cardinal,'
    'General Eisenhower,' 'Red Emperor' (hybrid tulips)

SUMMER

Begonia x *tuberhybrida* 'Deep Red,' 'Non-stop Red'
    (tuberous begonia)

Canna x *generalis* 'Ambassador,' 'Pfitzer's Crimson Beauty,'
    'Red King Humbert' (canna lily)

Gladiolus hybrids 'Red Bird,' 'Red Splendor' (gladiolus)

Lilium 'Red Night,' 'Scarlet Emperor' (Asiatic hybrid lily)

LATE SUMMER AND FALL

Dahlia x *pinnata* 'Babylon,' 'Rote Funten' (dahlia)

PLANTS WITH PURPLE OR BRONZE FOLIAGE

PERENNIALS

Cimicifuga ramosa var. *atropurpurea* 'Brunette' (purple-leaf
    bugbane)

Eupatorium fistulosum 'Atropurpureum' (Joe-Pye weed)

Heuchera micrantha 'Palace Purple' (purple-leaf coralbells)

Lobelia x *speciosa* 'Bee's Flame,' 'Queen Victoria'
    (bronze-leaf cardinal flower)

Penstemon digitalis 'Husker's Red' (beard-tongue)

Rodgersia pinnata superba (rodgersia)

Salvia officinalis 'Purpurea' (purple-leaf sage)

Salvia officinalis 'Tricolor' (tricolor garden sage)

Sedum x 'Vera Jameson' (Vera Jameson stonecrop)

Sedum spurium 'Dragon's Blood' (stonecrop)

Viola labradorica var. *purpurea* (purple-leaf
    Labrador violet)

ANNUALS

Coleus x *hybridus* 'Red Velvet' (red velvet coleus)

Hypoestes phyllostachya 'Confetti Burgundy'
    (polka-dot plant)

Ocimum basilicum 'Dark Opal,' 'Fluffy Ruffles'
    (sweet basil)

Perilla frutescens 'Atropurpurea,' 'Crispa' (beefsteak plant)

Ricinus communis 'Gibbsoni' (castor oil plant)

GRASSES

Imperata cylindrica 'Red Baron' (Japanese blood grass)

Ophiopogon planiscapus 'Nigrescens' (black mondo grass)

Pennisetum setaceum atrosanguineum
    (purple fountain grass)

THE FLORAL PALETTE

ENCYCLOPEDIA OF FLOWERS AND FOLIAGE

In this section you'll find photographs, detailed descriptions, and growing instructions for more than 450 flowering and foliage plants. The plants are arranged by categories: Perennials and Biennials, Annuals, Bulbs, Roses, Ornamental Grasses, and Ferns. Within each category, plants are listed alphabetically by botanical name. If you know only a plant's common name, you can find the botanical name by looking for the common name in the index. The climate heading identifies the hardiness zones where each plant performs best. Although many plants may survive in colder or warmer zones than those listed here, they may not thrive there, so those zones are not listed. See the map on page 394 to determine the hardiness zone for your area.

PERENNIALS AND BIENNIALS

Perennials and self-sowing biennials beautify your garden year after year, flourishing with minimal care.

Acanthus spinosus var. *spinosissimus*

Acanthus spinosus var. spinosissimus
SPINY BEAR'S BREECHES

Grown as much for its bold-textured evergreen leaves as for its flowers, bear's breeches brings sculptural beauty to the garden throughout the year. The 2-foot-long evergreen leaves are lustrous green and deeply divided with lethal-looking white spines along the edges. These spines are actually less sharp than the truly vicious ones tipping the less conspicuous bracts that surround the flowers. The mauve-and-white tubular flowers bloom on tall, dramatic stalks for a month in early summer.

Size: 3 to 4 feet tall in bloom; 3 feet wide.
Light: Full to half sun.
Soil and Moisture: Average to sandy soil. Drought tolerant; avoid winter wetness.
Planting and Propagation: Plant container-grown plants anytime, spacing 3 feet apart. Divide in spring; keep well-watered until established.
Special Care: Handle with leather gloves. Remove winter-tattered leaves in early spring. Very invasive; dig out unwanted plants, taking care to get all root pieces.
Pests and Diseases: Snails and slugs.
Climate: Zones 7–10. Best where summers are hot and dry, but tolerates humidity.
Similar Species: *A. mollis,* spineless leaves, white-and-purple flowers, Zones 8–10; does poorly in humid South.
Garden Use: Dramatic in midground, surrounded by beds and borders where foliage clumps can be admired but tall flower stalks won't block other plants. Locate where a large stand is desired because plant spreads.

Achillea filipendulina
FERN-LEAF YARROW

The flat heads of the saucer-size, bright yellow flowers of fern-leaf yarrow bloom above its dark green, fine-textured foliage all summer if spent flowers are cut regularly. Flowers and foliage have a spicy herbal scent. The popular cultivars listed below bloom longer and need less staking than the species.

Size: 3 to 5 feet tall; 2 feet wide.
Light: Full sun.

Achillea filipendulina 'Coronation Gold'

Soil and Moisture: Average to sandy soil. Very drought tolerant; does poorly in wet, heavy soil.

Planting and Propagation: Plant container-grown plants in spring, spacing 2 feet apart. Divide mature clumps every three or four years in spring or fall. Take stem cuttings in midsummer.

Special Care: Needs staking, especially if grown in rich soil. Remove faded flowers to encourage long blooming.

Pests and Diseases: Root rot in wet soil.

Climate: Zones 3–9.

Cultivars and Similar Species: 'Gold Plate,' 6-inch golden yellow flowers, sturdy 4- to 5-foot-tall stems; 'Parker's Variety,' 4-inch bright yellow flowers, sturdy 3½-foot stems; 'Coronation Gold,' hybrid with numerous 3-inch golden yellow flowers, gray-green leaves, sturdy 3-foot stems, no staking.

Garden Use: Use in middle or back of flower border or herb garden. Excellent cut or dried flower; cut flowers after pollen is visible or flowers will wilt.

Achillea millefolium
COMMON YARROW

This native European wildflower has naturalized in North America where it decorates the roadsides with its pretty flat heads of tiny white flowers from mid- to late summer. The lacy, dark green, silky-haired foliage forms a mat and is said to have medicinal qualities (it has a reputation for healing wounds). The species is very invasive and is best used in a meadow or herb garden, but the cultivars with brightly colored flowers are better behaved and make beautiful additions to borders or cut-flower gardens.

Size: 1 to 3 feet tall; spreads vigorously.

Light: Full sun.

Soil and Moisture: Average to poor soil. Very drought tolerant. Does poorly in wet, heavy soil; may rot in winter-wet soil.

Planting and Propagation: Plant container-grown plants in spring, spacing 2 feet apart.

Achillea millefolium 'Summer Pastels'

Divide mature clumps every two or three years in spring. Take stem cuttings in midsummer.

Special Care: Seed-grown plants may vary in flower color. Cultivars may need staking.

Pests and Diseases: Powdery mildew sometimes troublesome. May rot in damp or wet site.

Climate: Zones 3–9; may get lanky in the South.

Cultivars: 'Rosea,' pale pink; 'Cerise Queen,' bright rose-pink, 1½ feet tall; 'Fire King,' dark red, 2 feet tall; 'Lilac Queen,' lilac; 'Snowtaler,' white. Galaxy hybrids (*A. millefolium* x *A. taygetea*), larger flowers fading from bright

Achillea x 'Moonshine'

to soft shades: 'Salmon Beauty,' light salmon-pink; 'Appleblossom,' medium pink; 'Beacon,' crimson with yellow eyes; 'Paprika,' red with yellow eyes; 'Summer Pastels,' seed-grown, color-coordinated mix of cream, apricot, and scarlet.

Garden Use: Naturalize in meadow garden; use in informal, drought-resistant cottage or herb gardens. Prized for fresh or dried flower arrangements; cut blossoms after pollen is visible.

Achillea x 'Moonshine'
MOONSHINE YARROW

Throughout the summer, this recently developed hybrid produces 2- to 3-inch flower heads in soft primrose yellow fading to creamy yellow. Leaves are deeply dissected and gray-green, creating an overall shimmery effect. Compact and floriferous, this plant can be finicky unless given the correct growing conditions.

Size: 2 feet tall when in bloom; 1½ feet wide.

Light: Full sun.

Soil and Moisture: Average to sandy soil. Drought tolerant; needs excellent drainage.

Planting and Propagation: Plant container-grown plants anytime, spacing 1 foot apart. Divide in early spring every two or three years.

Special Care: Spray for fungus disease in the Southeast. Remove faded flowers.

Pests and Diseases: Susceptible to fungus diseases in areas with high humidity and afternoon rainstorms.

Climate: Zones 3–8; performs poorly in hot, humid areas.

Similar Species: *A. tomentosa* (woolly milfoil), similar but smaller flowers above mat of woolly light green foliage, Zones 3–7; susceptible to fungus in humid areas. Use in rock garden.

Garden Use: Use in informal borders.

Aconitum carmichaelii (*A. fischeri*)
AZURE MONKSHOOD

Resembling a monk's hood pulled down over his face, this blue-flowered perennial produces valuable color for the fall flower garden. The attractive dark green leaves are palmately lobed, resembling those of a delphinium. All plant parts, especially the leaves and roots, are deadly poisonous if eaten, so exercise extreme caution when growing any species of *Aconitum*.

Size: 2 to 3 feet tall; 3 feet wide.

Light: Full to half shade.

Soil and Moisture: Humus-rich, moist, fertile soil; plentiful moisture.

Planting and Propagation: Plant container-grown plants in spring or bare tuberous roots in fall, spacing 3 feet apart. Needs no division and resents disturbance.

Special Care: Best where nights are cool. Needs abundant moisture in full sun locations. May need staking.

Pests and Diseases: Crown rot or mildew sometimes troublesome.

Aconitum carmichaelii

Climate: Zones 3–7; does poorly in the Southeast because summer nights are warm.

Cultivars and Similar Species: 'Arendsii,' 4 feet tall, amethyst blue; *A. c. wilsonii,* 6 feet tall, lavender-blue; *A. napellus* (common monkshood), 3 to 4 feet tall, deeply divided leaves, dark blue flowers in late summer. *A.* x *cammarum* (bicolor monkshood), late summer: 'Bicolor,' blue-and-white, 3 feet tall; 'Bressingham Spire,' violet-blue, 3 feet tall.

Garden Use: Vertical spires of flowers make pretty contrast with daisylike fall flowers. Use in borders and shade gardens.

Ajuga reptans
BUGLEWEED, CARPET BUGLE

Gardeners love this ground-hugging, rapidly spreading perennial for its beautifully textured foliage and short spikes of lavender-blue, late-spring flowers. Prominent veins give the shiny, dark green, semi-evergreen leaves a quilted appearance. Several outstanding cultivars with variegated or colored leaves and purple, pink, or white flowers bring months of color to shady spots.

Size: Leaf mats 3 inches tall; flower spikes 4 inches to 1 foot tall.

Light: Light to full shade; tolerates full sun if kept moist. Bronze types need sun.

Soil and Moisture: Fertile, well-drained, moist soil; moderate to plentiful, even moisture.

Planting and Propagation: Plant container-grown plants anytime, spacing 1 to 1½ feet apart. Seeds don't come true to type. Divide anytime during growing season, as needed.

Special Care: Spreads rapidly; may invade lawn if planted as edging. Remove spent flowers to prevent seeding and improve appearance. Weed out all-green plants that appear among variegated ones. Leaves brown if soil dries.

Pests and Diseases: Crown rot troublesome, particularly in the South. Provide air circulation; apply fungicide.

Climate: Zones 3–9.

Ajuga reptans 'Burgundy Glow'

Cultivars and Similar Species: 'Pink Beauty,' green leaves, pink flowers; *A. r. alba,* green leaves, white flowers; 'Atropurpurea,' dark bronze-purple leaves, blue flowers; 'Burgundy Glow,' variegated white, pink, rose, and green foliage, blue flowers; 'Bronze Beauty,' bronze leaves, blue flowers; 'Gaiety,' bronze-purple leaves, lilac flowers; 'Silver Beauty,' gray-green leaves edged in white, blue flowers. *A. pyramidalis:* more upright, spreads slowly. *A. genevensis:* hairy dark green leaves, upright to 1 foot, blue, pink, or white flowers; spreads slowly.

Garden Use: Excellent carpeting ground cover beneath shrubs or trees in mixed border or combined with taller perennials in shaded border or naturalistic garden.

Alcea rosea
HOLLYHOCK

This beloved flower of European and American cottage gardens is a biennial, producing clumps of heart-shaped, rough-textured leaves the first year from seed and tall flower stalks the next year. The 5-inch flowers unfurl from tightly wrapped buds beginning at the bottoms of the stalks and progressing

Alcea rosea

toward the tops, producing a summer-long display. Hollyhocks sometimes behave as short-lived perennials and also self-sow. Self-sown plants often differ from the parent. Flowers may be single, double, or semidouble and come in yellow, white, rose, pink, red, lavender, and almost-black. They may be ruffled or fringed.

Size: Old-fashioned type can reach 10 feet tall; modern hybrids 2 to 8 feet tall, 1½ feet wide.

Light: Full sun.

Soil and Moisture: Fertile, well-drained soil; water and fertilize regularly.

Planting and Propagation: Sow seeds in early summer and transplant to permanent location early the following spring; start seed of annual types indoors in winter for summer bloom. When flowering ceases, cut off stalks and separate daughter plants near plant base, replanting to perpetuate fancy hybrids.

Special Care: Staking usually needed.

Pests and Diseases: Rust fungus, Japanese beetles, and spider mites disfigure foliage but not flowers; pest control needed.

Climate: Zones 3–8; set out nursery-grown plants each fall in Zones 9–10.

Cultivars: 'Chater's' series, 6 to 8 feet tall, doubles in yellow, white, pink, scarlet, or mixed; 'Indian Spring,' mixed, single, 6 feet tall; 'Powderpuff Mix,' double, white, red, yellow, copper, maroon, and pink ruffles.

Garden Use: Use for vertical effect in background of cottage or informal garden.

Alchemilla mollis
LADY'S MANTLE

This old-fashioned medicinal herb is one of the most beautiful foliage plants you can add to your garden. The gray-green leaves are rounded and somewhat wavy, with tiny scallops decorating the edges. A velvety covering of fine hairs makes the leaves soft to the touch. The hairs also hold shimmering beads of water on dewy mornings. Fluffy sprays of lime-green flowers bloom in early summer.

Size: 1 to 2 feet tall; 1½ feet wide.

Light: Full sun in cool climates; half to light shade elsewhere.

Soil and Moisture: Best in fertile, moist soil; tolerates dry, full shade.

Planting and Propagation: Plant container-grown plants in spring, spacing 1½ feet apart. Division needed infrequently in early spring before flowering. Readily self-sows.

Special Care: Deadhead to avoid reseeding. Cut back in midsummer to renew if foliage looks tired from too much heat or sun.

Pests and Diseases: Fungus diseases troublesome in the Southeast because afternoon showers leave foliage wet overnight.

Climate: Zones 4–8; needs more shade and moisture in hot areas.

Similar Species: *A. vulgaris*, greener flowers, leaves less hairy. *A. alpina* (mountain mantle): smaller plant, deeply lobed leaves with silvery white margins, green flowers, Zones 3–7.

Garden Use: Excellent ground cover or edging. Use in herb, cottage, or informal garden where it can sprawl along walkway. Flowers can be cut for fresh or dried use.

Alchemilla mollis

Alstroemeria aurantiaca
PERUVIAN LILY

Actually native to Chile and not a lily at all, this misnamed plant nevertheless makes a stunning stand of color when in bloom. Sprays of 2-inch trumpet-shaped flowers with speckled throats bloom in early summer and make excellent, long-lasting cut flowers. Colors include yellow, orange, rose, and red. The gray-green leaves are narrow and twisted, cloaking strong, wiry stems.

Alstroemeria aurantiaca 'Margaret'

Size: 3 feet tall; spreads aggressively.

Light: Full sun in cool areas; part shade in hot areas.

Soil and Moisture: Deep, well-drained soil enriched yearly with topdressing of manure or compost. Keep moist in spring and summer, drier in late summer and fall.

Planting and Propagation: Plant fleshy roots 6 inches deep in spring or early fall, spacing 1 to 2 feet apart. Roots produce no top growth the first year. Plant container-grown plants anytime. Sow seeds in place in spring or fall. Do not divide for many years; reestablishes poorly after division.

Special Care: Apply protective winter mulch in cold areas.

Pests and Diseases: Generally trouble free.

Climate: Zones 7–10.

Cultivars: 'Aurea,' golden; 'Dover Orange,' orange-red; 'Lutea,' bright yellow. Ligtu hybrids: similar, with wider range of colors.

Garden Use: Invasive once established, so locate where its wandering ways are welcome, such as in meadow or informal landscape. Dies back in late summer, leaving bare spot; fill in with annuals if desired.

Amsonia tabernaemontana
WILLOW AMSONIA

This Southeastern wildflower deserves to be used more because it's an easy-care plant that adds to the garden scene from spring through fall. It forms stately, almost shrublike clumps of upright stems covered with willowlike dark green leaves that have gray-green undersides. The foliage turns soft gold in autumn. Large sprays of tiny, blue, starlike flowers decorate the stem tips in late spring and early summer, and seedpods that resemble milkweed may develop in late summer.

Size: 3 to 4 feet tall; 2 to 3 feet wide.

Light: Full sun to half shade; blossoms remain most compact in full sun.

Soil and Moisture: Deep, fertile soil; keep moist, especially in sun. Deep roots can tolerate drought.

Amsonia tabernaemontana

Planting and Propagation: Plant container-grown plants in spring, spacing 3 feet apart. Take tip cuttings from side branches in spring. Division not needed but easily done in fall by cutting clump into sections.

Special Care: Cut back to 6 inches after flowering and again later in summer to prevent floppiness in shaded sites.

Pests and Diseases: Generally trouble free.

Climate: Zones 3–10.

Similar Species: *A. montana,* darker flowers, 1¼ feet tall; *A. salicifolia,* more willow-like leaves. *A. angustifolia* (downy amsonia): Zones 7–10.

Garden Use: Use in formal or informal borders, naturalize under high-branched trees, or combine with grasses in New American-style garden.

Anaphalis triplinervis
THREE-VEINED PEARLY EVERLASTING

Masses of furry-looking, buttonlike white flowers with brown centers decorate this perennial in late summer and fall, but the gray-white foliage makes a pretty contrast to green leaves throughout the growing season.

Unlike most gray-leaved plants, this one performs well in moist soil, making it useful in herbaceous borders.

Size: 1½ feet tall; 2 feet wide.

Light: Full sun to part shade.

Soil and Moisture: Tolerant of various soil types, but looks best in moist soil.

Planting and Propagation: Plant container-grown plants in spring or fall, spacing 1½ feet apart. Divide in spring every three to five years. Take tip cuttings in late spring. Sow seeds in place in fall.

Special Care: No special care required.

Pests and Diseases: Stem rot or leaf fungus troublesome in hot, humid areas.

Climate: Zones 3–8.

Similar Species: 'Summer Snow,' dwarf to 8 inches tall, bright white flowers. *A. margaritacea* (pearly everlasting): 2 to 3 feet tall, more drought tolerant. *A. cinnamomea:* 2 feet tall, invasive.

Garden Use: Use as edging to contrast with lawn or to soften wall or walk. Flowers can be dried to use as everlastings.

Anaphalis triplinervis

Anchusa azurea

Anchusa azurea
ITALIAN BUGLOSS, ITALIAN ALKANET

Admired for its sprays of true-blue forget-me-not flowers that appear from late spring into midsummer, Italian bugloss makes a beautiful background plant. Plants are bushy and somewhat ungainly with rough, coarse leaves. They usually need staking.

Size: 3 to 5 feet tall; 2 feet wide.

Light: Full sun

Soil and Moisture: Deep, loose, lean soil. Keep moist but not soggy.

Planting and Propagation Plant container-grown plants in spring, spacing 2 feet apart. Take root cuttings or divide every two years in spring.

Special Care: Cut spent flowers repeatedly to prolong bloom into fall and prevent seeding. Staking recommended. Becomes extra floppy if soil is too fertile. Short lived.

Pests and Diseases: Trouble free except may rot if waterlogged in winter.

Climate: Zones 3–8.

Cultivars: 'Dropmore,' brilliant blue, 4 feet tall, needs staking; 'Loddon Royalist' and 'Royal Blue,' royal blue, 3 feet tall; 'Little John,' deep blue, compact, 1½ feet tall.

Garden Use: Use in back of border where flowers can be enjoyed but coarse foliage and stakes are concealed.

Anemone x *hybrida* (*A. japonica*)
JAPANESE ANEMONE

Hybrids of several wild species, Japanese anemones are one of the most elegant flowers of late summer and fall. Clusters of single or semidouble, shallow-cupped white, rose, or pink flowers feature green buttonlike centers surrounded by a ring of yellow stamens. Silver-furred buds are held on strong, wiry stems. Foliage is bold and palmately lobed, forming handsome dark green clumps.

Size: 3 to 5 feet tall in bloom; 3 feet wide.

Light: Full sun to half or light shade.

Soil and Moisture: Best in moist, deep, fertile soil; performs well in heavy and alkaline soils.

Planting and Propagation: Plant container-grown plants anytime, spacing 2 feet apart. Divide in spring; take root cuttings in fall.

Special Care: Forms large, somewhat invasive clumps. Tall stems occasionally need light staking.

Pests and Diseases: Trouble free.

Climate: Zones 4–8.

Cultivars and Similar Species: 'Honorine Jobert,' white, single; 'Queen Charlotte,' pink, semidouble, 3 feet tall; 'Margarete,' pink, double, 3 feet tall; 'Whirlwind,' white, semidouble, 2 to 3 feet tall; 'September Charm,' silvery mauve, single, 3 feet tall. *A. tomentosa* 'Robustissima': pale pink with darker reverse, mid- to late summer, 2 to 3 feet tall.

Garden Use: Beautiful with asters and ornamental grasses in formal or informal gardens. Excellent cut flowers.

Angelica archangelica
WILD PARSNIP, COW PARSNIP, ARCHANGEL

Reaching a height of 6 feet in early summer, angelica produces thick, hollow stems topped with saucer-size umbels of lacy greenish white flowers. This herb supposedly blooms on the Feast Day of St. Michael the Archangel—hence its botanical name. The huge celerylike leaves of this Syrian native are coarsely cut and bright green with a licorice aroma. A necklace of the leaves is said to ward off evil spirits and witches. The stems are used as an anise flavoring and confectionery.

Size: 5 to 6 feet tall; 3 feet wide.

Light: Full sun to half shade.

*Anemone x *hybrida* 'September Charm'

Angelica archangelica

Soil and Moisture: Moist to wet, fertile soil; do not allow to dry out.

Planting and Propagation: Plant container-grown plants in spring, spacing 3 feet apart, or sow fresh seeds in place and do not cover with soil.

Special Care: Dies after flowering in its second or third year, but removing spent flowers prevents seed formation and death.

Pests and Diseases: Usually trouble free.

Climate: Zones 3–9.

Similar Species: Resembles water parsnip (*Cicuta maculata*), a highly poisonous wildflower. *A. atropurpurea:* North American swampland native, more purplish stems, grows to 6 feet tall.

Garden Use: Use in large border as single specimen or in cluster for architectural effect. Plant by stream or in wet meadow garden.

Anthemis tinctoria
GOLDEN MARGUERITE

Golden marguerite's yellow-petaled, yellow-centered daisies bloom abundantly throughout summer on long stems that are perfect for cutting. The bushy plants have lacy green leaves with woolly white undersides and a chrysanthemumlike scent.

Size: 2 to 3 feet tall; 2 feet wide.

Light: Full sun.

Soil and Moisture: Average to poor soil; drought tolerant.

Planting and Propagation: Plant bare-root or container-grown plants in spring, spacing 1½ feet apart. Divide every two years in spring to keep clumps from dying in the centers. Take stem cuttings in summer.

Special Care: Needs staking if grown in rich soil. Cut stems after flowers fade to promote continual bloom; cut down after flowering ceases to promote dense branching. Short-lived in heavy soil.

Pests and Diseases: Usually trouble free.

Climate: Zones 3–7; tolerates hot, dry conditions but performs poorly in heat and humidity of the South.

Anthemis tinctoria

Cultivars: 'Beauty of Grallagh,' larger, deeper colored flowers; 'E. C. Buxton,' white flowers with yellow centers; 'Moonlight,' large, soft yellow flowers; 'Pale Moon,' large, pale yellow flowers; 'Wargrave,' creamy white flowers with yellow centers; 'Perry's Variety,' golden orange flowers.

Garden Use: Excellent for borders and informal gardens with poor soil. Use in cut-flower garden.

Aquilegia x *hybrida*
HYBRID COLUMBINE

This charming late-spring to early summer bloomer displays clusters of intricate 3- to 4-inch flowers on wiry stems. The plant's rounded petals form a shallow cup set against showy pointed sepals. Decorative, straight spurs with hooked tips shoot back 2 to 6 inches from the bases of the sepals, and resemble a bird's claw, explaining the plant's botanical name, which means eagle. The flowers are usually bicolored and come in all of the colors of the rainbow. Bright green to gray-green fernlike leaves create lovely mounds.

Size: 2 to 3 feet tall; half as wide.

Light: Full sun to part shade in mild climates; part to light shade in hot ones.

Soil and Moisture: Humus-rich to average, well-drained, moist soil. Moderate moisture.

Planting and Propagation: Space container-grown plants 1½ feet apart. Plants usually live only three or four years; they require no division.

Special Care: Remove faded flowers to discourage self-sowing, which produces offspring of different and sometimes inferior colors and forms. Apply winter mulch in coldest regions. May rot in damp soil.

Pests and Diseases: Leaf miners can disfigure foliage in midsummer and are worse on hybrids than species; cut off and destroy infested leaves and fertilize to stimulate attractive new foliage growth.

Climate: Best in Zones 3–8; also does well in Zones 9–10 on the Pacific Coast.

Cultivars and Similar Species: Long-spurred hybrids include: 'McKana Giant' and 'Dragonfly' in pastel shades; 'Star Hybrids,' long-spurred bicolors. 'Beidermeier Hybrids': short-spurred and compact. 'Hensol Harebell': nodding, purple, short-spurred flowers; does well in full shade. *A. canadensis* (American columbine): wildflower native to East Coast, small red-and-yellow flowers on tall stems, attracts hummingbirds; 'Corbett,' pale yellow. *A. caerulea* (Rocky Mountain columbine): Rocky Mountain native, lovely

Aquilegia x *hybrida* 'McKana Hybrid'

blue-and-white flowers; 'Kristall,' white. *A. chrysantha* (golden columbine): yellow, long-spurred Rocky Mountain wildflower; 'Yellow Queen,' lemon-and-gold. *A. flabellata:* low with fan-shaped leaves, clusters of nodding, short-spurred blue-and-white flowers. *A. vulgaris* (granny's bonnet): short-spurred biennial or short-lived perennial: 'Heidi,' pink; 'Nora Barlow,' double, pink-and-mauve.

Garden Use: Despite height, plant in front of border for best effect. Mass-plant in naturalistic settings.

Arabis caucasica (A. albida)
WALL ROCK CRESS

This alpine plant forms a silvery mat of spoon-shaped, toothed leaves that looks attractive throughout the year. Fragrant white or rose-pink four-petaled flowers blanket the plant in early spring, making a pretty combination with small bulb plants.

Size: 10 inches tall; 1½ feet wide.

Light: Full sun.

Soil and Moisture: Fast-draining, lean alkaline soil; moderate moisture.

Planting and Propagation: Plant container-grown plants anytime, spacing 1 foot apart. Divide every two or three years in early fall.

Arabis caucasica

Take stem cuttings in summer.

Special Care: Cut back flower stems after flowering to prevent straggliness.

Pests and Diseases: Root or crown rot in damp location or hot, humid climate.

Climate: Zones 4–7; best in cool climate.

Cultivars and Similar Species: *A. c. variegata,* white flowers, white-edged leaves; *A. c. flore-plena,* double white; 'Snow Cap,' white; 'Spring Charm,' soft rose; 'Rosabella,' rose-pink. *A. procurrens:* green leaves, white flowers, tolerates light shade. *A. aubrietioides:* green leaves, purple flowers.

Garden Use: Plant to creep from crevices in rock garden or dry wall.

Armeria maritima
SEA PINK, THRIFT

This dainty little plant is tough, tolerating drought and even salty sea spray. Thrift forms tufted mounds of grassy green evergreen leaves topped for several weeks in early summer with balls of pink or white flowers bobbing on leafless stems.

Size: 6 inches to 1 foot tall; 1 foot wide.

Light: Full to half sun in the North; light shade in the South.

Soil and Moisture: Well-drained, sandy soil; moderate moisture.

Planting and Propagation: Plant container-grown plants anytime, spacing 1 foot apart. Divide in spring. Sow seeds in fall.

Special Care: Encourage lengthy bloom period by removing flowers as they fade.

Pests and Diseases: May die in center in damp soil or hot, humid climates; cut back to ground to stimulate new growth.

Climate: Zones 4–8.

Cultivars: 'Alba,' white; 'Pride of Dusseldorf,' nearly red; 'Vindictive,' dark pink; *A. m. laucheana,* bright pink.

Garden Use: Mass as ground cover, or use as edging or foreground plant in flower border; tuck around rocks in rock garden or seaside garden.

Armeria maritima

Artemisia ludoviciana var. *albula*
WHITE SAGE, WORMWOOD

Forming ribbons of silver through a garden, this Southwest native provides months of gleaming color. Unlike most artemisia, the aromatic leaves of this species are lance-shaped, not finely cut; stems are upright and covered with woolly white hairs. Inconspicuous white flowers bloom in fall.

Size: 3 feet tall; spreads as wide.

Light: Full sun.

Soil and Moisture: Average to poor, sandy soil. Allow soil to dry between waterings; drought tolerant.

Planting and Propagation: Plant container-grown plants anytime, spacing 2 to 3 feet apart. Divide every year in spring or fall to control aggressive spreading.

Special Care: Can run rampant in garden, spreading by 4-foot-long underground runners. Pull out unwanted sprouts and attached runners in spring, or contain plants by planting in old buckets with the bottoms removed and sunk in garden. Cut back in midsummer if weather causes floppiness.

Pests and Diseases: Root rot in damp site.

Climate: Zones 4–9; best artemisia for the South.

209

Artemisia ludoviciana var. *albula*
'Silver Queen'

Cultivars: Usually sold as the almost identical 'Silver King' (3 feet tall, deep silver) or 'Silver Queen' (2½ feet tall, silver-gray, jagged-edged leaves), but often mixed up and mislabeled. *A.* x 'Powis Castle': deeply cut silver leaves, compact, 2 to 3 feet tall, Zones 5–8. *A.* x 'Valerie Finnis': broadly cut silver leaves, 2 feet tall. *A. absinthium* 'Lambrook Silver': silvery filigreed leaves, Zones 6–9.

Garden Use: Excellent contrast to white, pink, blue, and lavender flowers in informal flower gardens.

Artemisia schmidtiana 'Silvermound'
SILVERMOUND MUGWORT

Forming a silky mound of finely cut silvery leaves, this popular artemisia makes a beautiful addition to northern gardens. The plant doesn't spread aggressively, but where summers are hot and humid the mound may flop

210

open unattractively in mid- or late summer.
Size: 1 to 2 feet tall and wide.
Light: Full sun.
Soil and Moisture: Average to poor soil; moderate moisture. Drought tolerant.
Planting and Propagation: Plant container-grown plants in spring. Take stem cuttings in summer. Divide every few years to retain best shape.
Special Care: Cut woody stems back to several inches in late winter. If mound falls open in midsummer, cut to ground when new growth appears in center.
Pests and Diseases: Root rot in wet-winter site.
Climate: Zones 3–7; performs poorly in the Midwest and South.
Cultivars and Similar Species: May be sold as 'Nana.' *A.* x 'Powis Castle': 4 feet tall, feathery, gray-green mound; withstands hot summers. *A. stelleriana* (beach wormwood): ground-hugging, white-silver leaves.
Garden Use: Effective as edging or combined with bolder-textured plants in foreground.

Aruncus dioicus (A. sylvester)
GOAT'S BEARD

Big but graceful, this native American wildflower sends up foot-long, feathery plumes of creamy white flowers on tall stalks in early summer. Plants are male or female and equally attractive in flower, but males produce showy stamens that last through summer. Leaves are light green and finely dissected, forming handsome clumps beneath the flowers.
Size: Foliage mounds to 3 feet tall, 3 to 5 feet wide; flower stalks to 6 feet tall.
Light: Half to light shade in Zones 5–7; full sun in Zones 3–4 if constantly moist.
Soil and Moisture: Rich, moist, deep soil high in organic matter; abundant water.
Planting and Propagation: Plant container-grown or bare-root plants in spring, spacing 4 to 5 feet apart. Division not necessary but

Artemisia schmidtiana 'Silvermound'

can be done with difficulty in spring by lifting roots and cutting into divisions with one bud eye.
Special Care: If too dry or in too much sun, leaf edges turn brown.
Pests and Diseases: Generally pest free.
Climate: Zones 3–8; difficult in Zones 7–8.
Cultivars and Similar Species: 'Kneiffii,' 3 feet tall, more finely cut leaves. *A. aethusi-*

Aruncus dioicus

folius (dwarf goat's beard): flowers 3 to 4 inches tall, mounds of finely cut leaves attain height of 8 inches to 1 foot. Hybrids of the two species are intermediate in size.

Garden Use: Plant in clusters along woodland edge, along streams, or in other naturalistic settings; also works well in borders if kept moist.

Asclepias tuberosa
BUTTERFLY WEED

Native to prairies and dry fields across much of North America, butterfly weed blooms for a month in midsummer, attracting monarch and swallowtail butterflies to its orange, red, or gold flowers. The showy flat heads of small urn-shaped flowers ripen into 3-inch-long greenish purple seedpods that split open to reveal silky-haired seeds in late fall. The upright stems hold their linear leaves in horizontal rungs, giving the plant a somewhat stiff appearance.

Size: 2 to 3 feet tall; clumps spread 1 to 2 feet.

Light: Full sun.

Asclepias tuberosa

Soil and Moisture: Average to infertile, sandy soil; moderate water. Drought tolerant.

Planting and Propagation: Plant small container-grown plants in spring, spacing 8 inches apart. Do not divide. Sow fresh seeds in fall; may bloom the following summer.

Special Care: Difficult to transplant because of brittle taproot. Emerges in late spring; take care not to damage hidden crowns. Cutting flowers encourages reblooming a month later.

Pests and Diseases: Yellow aphids sometimes disfigure plants in summer.

Climate: Zones 4–9.

Cultivars and Similar Species: 'Gay Butterflies,' seed-grown mix of several colors; 'Hello Yellow,' yellow flowers.

Garden Use: Effective in informal, butterfly, meadow, and cut-flower gardens.

Asphodeline lutea
JACOB'S-ROD, KING'S-SPEAR

This Mediterranean lily makes a strong vertical statement in the early summer garden. Whorls of gray-green, linear leaves cloak the bottoms of the unbranched stems, while fragrant, clear yellow, starlike flowers stud the top foot or two, opening randomly along the spike. Shiny round seedpods form where individual flowers fade. A slow-growing plant, Jacob's-rod eventually forms a nice-size clump in a suitable site.

Size: 3 feet tall; 1 to 2 feet wide.

Light: Full sun.

Soil and Moisture: Average to lean, well-drained soil; moderate water. Drought tolerant.

Planting and Propagation: Plant rhizomatous roots in fall, spacing 1 to 2 feet apart. Divide in fall when crowded.

Special Care: Becomes lanky and floppy in fertile, moist soil.

Pests and Diseases: Usually pest free.

Climate: Zones 5–8. Where winters are cold, goes dormant in winter; where winters are

Asphodeline lutea

warm, may go dormant in hot, dry summers, reappearing in cool weather and remaining green through winter.

Cultivars: 'Florepleno,' double flowers.

Garden Use: Excellent in large-scale rock gardens and formal borders.

Aster novi-belgii x novae-angliae
MICHAELMAS DAISY, FALL ASTER

Most of the graceful late bloomers called Michaelmas daisies or fall asters are hybrids of New England and New York asters and several other species. Billowy masses of tiny, yellow-centered lavender, purple, blue, pink, or white blossoms form clouds of color for a month or two in late summer and fall, beginning between mid-August and mid-September depending on the cultivar. The small, linear leaves covering the upright stems are fine textured but otherwise unremarkable.

Size: Height varies by cultivar, from 8-inch spreading dwarfs to 4- to 5-foot-tall types.

Light: Full sun best; tolerates part or light shade.

Soil and Moisture: Fertile, well-drained, moist soil; plentiful moisture.

Planting and Propagation: Plant container-grown plants in spring or fall, spacing 1¼ to 3 feet apart. Divide by removing and replanting exterior portions of clumps every two years in spring to keep vigorous.

Special Care: Pinch tall types when 6 inches

Aster novi-belgii x *novae-angliae* 'Alma Potschke'

tall and again in early summer to encourage compactness and flowering. Stake tall and medium-tall types. Winter-mulch in Zones 3–5. Spray for mildew.

Pests and Diseases: Mildew and rust often troublesome; avoid wetting foliage, but do not let soil dry out. Water with drip or soaker hose. Choose disease-resistant cultivars.

Climate: Zones 4–8; best where cool and moist.

Cultivars and Similar Species: Dozens of cultivars; tall ones often incorrectly called New England asters and short ones called New York asters. 'Alma Potschke,' magenta-pink, 3½ feet tall, mildew resistant; 'Mt. Everest,' white, 3 feet tall; 'Harrington's Pink,' clear pink, 3 to 5 feet tall, late-blooming; 'Treasurer,' violet-blue, 4 feet tall; 'Crimson Brocade,' crimson-red, 3 feet tall; 'Eventide,' semidouble, purple, 3 feet tall; 'September Ruby,' cerise, disease resistant, 3½ feet tall; 'Professor Kippenburg,' lavender-blue, 1 foot tall; 'Marie Ballard,' powder blue, 4 feet tall; 'Hella Lacy,' large violet-blue, 4 to 5 feet tall; 'Purple Dome,' purple, mildew resistant, 1½ feet tall.

Garden Use: Excellent late-summer and fall color in back of border or in meadow. Fine texture combines with other fall bloomers.

Good cut flower.

Aster x *frikartii*
FRIKART'S ASTER

This lovely but little-known aster is probably the finest of all asters. Resulting from a cross between an Italian and a Himalayan species at a Swiss nursery, this fine perennial has been popular in England for many years. Lavender-blue with yellow centers, the 3-inch-diameter daisies begin blooming in July and continue into October. Plants have a delicate, airy look and are not marred by mildew as are other asters.

Size: 3 feet tall and wide.

Light: Full sun.

Soil and Moisture: Well-drained, moist, fertile soil; plentiful, even moisture.

Planting and Propagation: Plant container-grown plants in spring, spacing 3 feet apart. Divide every three or four years.

Special Care: Winter-mulch in colder zones. Fertilize sparingly.

Pests and Diseases: May rot over winter if soil remains wet.

Climate: Zone 5–8.

Cultivars: Almost indistinguishable are 'Monch,' lavender-blue, sturdy plant; 'Wonder of Staffa,' lighter lavender-blue, prone to flopping.

Garden Use: Excellent combined with yellow flowers in beds and borders.

Aster x *frikartii* 'Monch'

Astilbe chinensis var. *pumila*

Astilbe chinensis var. *pumila*
DWARF CHINESE ASTILBE

This fast-spreading dwarf astilbe forms dense stands of bronze-green toothed leaves and makes an attractive ground cover. Stiff, narrow plumes, densely packed with mauve-pink flowers, appear in late summer, blooming for more than a month.

Size: Foliage 6 to 8 inches high; flower stalks to 1¼ feet tall. Spreads widely by rhizomes.

Light: Light to full shade.

Soil and Moisture: Fertile, moist, well-drained soil best; tolerates dry soil in shade.

Planting and Propagation: Plant bare-root or container plants ½ inch deep in spring, spacing 2 feet apart. Divide in spring or fall when crowded.

Special Care: Remove spent flower stalks.

Pests and Diseases: Same as *A*. x *arendsii*.

Climate: Zones 3–8.

Cultivars: Plants labeled 'Pumila' may vary in height. 'Davidii,' white, 3 to 4 feet tall; 'Finale,' pale pink, 1¼ feet tall.

Garden Use: Use as ground cover beneath shrubs and as edging in mixed borders.

Astilbe simplicifolia
STAR ASTILBE

Unlike other astilbes, star astilbe has undivided leaves, although they are deeply lobed, dark, and glossy. Loose, nodding spires of white or pink flowers cover the compact leafy mounds in mid- to late summer. The seed heads that follow the flowers decorate the plants through fall.

Size: Flower spires to 1½ feet tall.

Light: Light to full shade.

Soil and Moisture: Deep, humus-rich, moist, well-drained soil; best kept moist during growing season. Tolerates some dryness.

Planting and Propagation: Plant bare-root or container plants ½ inch deep in spring, spacing 1 foot apart; divide every four years in spring.

Special Care: Slow to establish. Three years to maturity.

Pests and Diseases: Same as *A.* x *arendsii*.

Climate: Zones 4–8.

Cultivars: 'Sprite,' shell-pink flowers, bronze foliage, 1¼ to 1½ feet tall; 'Bronze Elegance,' rose-pink flowers, bronze foliage, 1½ feet tall; 'William Buchanon,' creamy white, 9 inches tall; 'Hennie Graafland,' delicate pink, 1½ feet tall; 'Aphrodite,' rosy red, 14 inches tall.

Garden Use: Lovely for summer color in naturalistic shade garden combined with wildflowers, hostas, and ferns.

Astilbe simplicifolia

Astilbe taquetii 'Superba'

Astilbe taquetii 'Superba'
FALL ASTILBE

This dramatic astilbe brings color to the back of the border or naturalistic garden in late summer. Tall spires of mauve-pink blossoms tower above clumps of handsome, deeply cut, dark green foliage.

Size: Flowers to 4 feet tall; clumps spread 2½ to 3 feet

Light: Light to part shade.

Soil and Moisture: Deep, humus-rich, moist, well-drained soil; keep moist to wet during growing season.

Planting and Propagation: Plant bare-root plants 2 inches deep in spring, spacing 3 feet apart, or plant container plants. Divide every three or four years in spring or fall.

Special Care: Does not need staking despite height.

Pests and Diseases: Same as *A.* x *arendsii*.

Climate: Zones 4–8.

Cultivars: 'Purple Lance,' dark rose-purple, 3 to 4 feet tall; 'Purpurkerze,' red-purple flowers, purplish stems and leaves, 3 feet tall.

Garden Use: Excellent late color in shaded borders and naturalistic settings.

Astilbe x *arendsii*
ASTILBE

Thriving in shady spots, this long-lived perennial brings both foliage and floral beau-

Astilbe x *arendsii* 'Fanal'

ty to the garden. The foot-long feathery plumes of tiny flowers stand above the foliage and come in a range of colors, including white, pink, rose, lavender, peach, and red. Flowers bloom for about a month beginning in early summer to midsummer, depending on the cultivar. Leaves are divided into pointed leaflets with toothed edges and are glossy dark green or bronze.

Size: Flowers 2 to 3 feet tall; foliage clumps 1 to 2 feet tall and twice as wide.

Light: Light to part shade; tolerates sun in cool regions and if constantly moist.

Soil and Moisture: Deep, humus-rich, moist, well-drained soil; keep moist to wet during growing season.

Planting and Propagation: Plant bare-root plants or container-grown plants ½ inch deep in spring, spacing 1½ to 3 feet apart. Divide every three years in spring or fall.

Special Care: Cut off faded flower stalks if desired; leave for naturalistic appearance. Feed heavily. Leaves scorch and shrivel if soil dries.

Pests and Diseases: Rots in winter-wet soil. Japanese beetles, spider mites troublesome.

Climate: Zones 4–8, but performs poorly in arid and hot, humid regions.

Cultivars and Similar Species: Early: 'Bonn,' medium pink, 2 feet tall; 'Rheinland,' bright pink, 2½ feet tall; 'Red Sentinel,' red, bronze leaves, 2½ feet tall; 'Europa,' pale pink, 1½ feet tall; 'Deutschland,' bright white, 1⅔ feet tall. Mid-Season: 'Amethyst,' lilac-violet, 2 feet tall; 'Bridal Veil,' creamy white, 2½ feet tall; 'Diamond,' dense white, 3 feet tall; 'Etna,' deep red, 2½ feet tall; 'Fanal,' dark crimson, bronze leaf, 2½ feet tall; 'Peach Blossom,' light pink, 3 feet tall; 'Venus,' pale pink, 3 feet tall; 'Hyacinth,' lilac-pink, 2 feet tall. Late: 'Avalanche,' white, 3 feet tall; 'Cattleya,' rose-pink, 1⅓ feet tall; 'Fire,' salmon-red, 3 feet tall; 'Glow,' ruby-red, 1½ feet tall.

Garden Use: Elegant planted in groups in formal or informal gardens; graceful along stream or pond or in woodland garden.

Aubrieta deltoidea
ROCK CRESS

This ground-hugger creates sheets of color in spring about tulip time. The ¾-inch-wide, four-petaled flowers bloom in small clusters on short stems in such profusion that they almost hide the foliage. Flowers may be shades of purple, rose, or blue. The 1-inch-long, gray-green, evergreen leaves are wedge-shaped, toothed, and hairy, cloaking creeping stems with soft color year-round.

Size: Foliage forms 3- to 5-inch-high wide-spreading mat; flowers 6 to 8 inches tall.
Light: Full sun.
Soil and Moisture: Average to sandy, neutral to alkaline soil and perfect drainage; moderate moisture.

Aubrieta deltoidea

Planting and Propagation: Plant container-grown plants in spring, spacing 2 feet apart. Divide in fall. Take cuttings in summer after flowering.
Special Care: Shear off spent flowers to encourage reblooming; shear again in summer if leggy.
Pests and Diseases: Root rot if not well drained.
Climate: Zones 4–8; best with low humidity and cool nights. Does poorly in the South.
Cultivars and Similar Species: 'Purple Gem,' purple, 6 inches tall; 'Cascade,' shades of purple, 4 to 6 inches tall; 'Royal Blue,' shades of blue, lavender, and violet; 'Royal Red,' shades of red, purple, and magenta; 'Red Cascade,' red; 'Variegata,' gold-edged green leaves, blue flowers.
Garden Use: Arrange to spill over rocks and out of crevices in rock gardens and walls. Treat as biennial in spring bulb bedding.

Aurinia saxatilis (Alyssum saxatile)
BASKET-OF-GOLD

This well-known spring flower blooms from early to mid-spring, making a wonderful bulb companion. The tight, rounded clusters of golden yellow, four-petaled flowers are held just above the foliage, completely blanketing its mat-forming, gray, 2- to 5-inch-long, spoon-shaped leaves. Basket-of-gold spreads rapidly into cascading evergreen clumps.

Size: 8 inches to 1 foot high; 1 foot wide.
Light: Full sun.
Soil and Moisture: Average to sandy, well-drained soil; drought tolerant.
Planting and Propagation: Plant container-grown plants in spring, spacing 1 to 1½ feet apart. Take stem cuttings in summer.
Special Care: Cut back after flowering for compactness and for possible reblooming. Resents transplanting.
Pests and Diseases: May rot in winter-wet soil. Flops in rich soil.

Climate: Zones 3–7; poor performer in heat and humidity. Use as biennial in the South, planting in fall and discarding after spring blooming.
Cultivars: 'Citrinum,' pale lemon-yellow, 10 inches tall; 'Compactum,' golden yellow, 6 inches tall, compact; 'Sunny Border Apricot,' apricot, 10 inches tall; 'Dudley Neville Variegated,' apricot-buff flowers, white-variegated leaves; 'Variegatum,' gold-edged leaves.
Garden Use: Best arranged so plants can spill over wall. Compact forms work well as border edging.

Aurinia saxatilis

Baptisia australis
BLUE WILD INDIGO

This easy-to-grow native wildflower slowly forms an impressive shrublike clump of upright stems cloaked with handsome blue-green leaves, which are divided into three smooth-edged leaflets. Spires of light to deep blue, two-lipped flowers appear for several weeks in early summer and attract butterflies. Flowers ripen into attractive, dark brown, inflated seedpods that rustle in the wind.

Size: Upright; 3 to 4 feet tall and as wide.

Baptisia australis

Begonia grandis

Light: Full sun in the North; part shade in the South.

Soil and Moisture: Best in fertile, humus-rich, deep, well-drained soil, but tolerates wide range of soil types; drought tolerant.

Planting and Propagation: Plant container-grown plants in spring, spacing 3 feet apart. Rarely needs division. Sow fresh seeds.

Special Care: Plant in permanent location; taproots make transplanting difficult. May need light staking. Deadhead faded flowers before seeds set to encourage another flush of blossoms.

Pests and Diseases: Generally problem free.

Climate: Zones 3–9.

Similar Species: *B. alba,* white flowers, nodding seedpods, 2 to 3 feet tall; best in rich soil.

Garden Use: Elegant vertical contrast with peony, iris, and shasta daisy in early summer border. Seedpods excellent in dried arrangements; cut in midsummer when brown.

Begonia grandis (B. evansiana)
HARDY BEGONIA

Looking somewhat like a houseplant begonia, this succulent-stemmed plant's most outstanding feature is the brilliant ruby-red veins and undersides of its olive-green leaves. In early September, the loose clusters of satiny translucent pink flowers open and continue until hard frost. The plant has the unusual habit of forming small bulblets in its leaf axils, these drop to the ground in fall and overwinter, growing into small plants the next year.

Size: 1½ to 3 feet tall; 1¼ feet wide.

Light: Full to part shade.

Soil and Moisture: Fertile, humus-rich, moist, well-drained soil; plentiful moisture.

Planting and Propagation: Plant tuberous roots 2 inches deep, spacing 10 inches apart. Division not necessary.

Special Care: Emerges in late spring; take

Belamcanda chinensis

care not to injure buried crowns. Thin out unwanted seedlings.

Pests and Diseases: May rot in soggy soil.

Climate: Zones 7–10; Zone 6 with winter mulch.

Cultivars: 'Alba,' white flowers, red leaf veins and undersides.

Garden Use: Excellent for naturalistic shady gardens; combines well with wildflowers and bulbs, which begin to die to ground when it begins growing. Best planted where light shines from behind, illuminating leaves.

Belamcanda chinensis
BLACKBERRY LILY

This mid- through late-summer bloomer produces loose, see-through sprays of 2-inch orange flowers that resemble six-pointed stars spotted with yellow and crimson. The fans of sword-shaped leaves resemble iris, adding a nice vertical accent to a garden. The flowers of this old-fashioned favorite ripen into seed capsules that split open to reveal clusters of shiny black seeds.

Size: Leaves 2 to 3 feet tall; flower stalks 3 to 4 feet tall. Clumps 1 foot wide.

Light: Full sun to light shade.

Soil and Moisture: Fertile, sandy soil; even moisture. Tallest with good soil and water.

Planting and Propagation: Divide tuberous roots in spring or fall, spacing 1 foot apart. Divide in spring when crowded.

Special Care: Winter-mulch in cold zones.

Pests and Diseases: Iris borer may attack fleshy roots.

Climate: Zones 5–10.

Cultivars: 'Halo Yellow,' unspotted pure yellow in tight clusters; 'Freckle Face,' pale orange, spotted dark orange, shorter.

Garden Use: Use in informal and cottage gardens. Best displayed against dark background. Cut seedpods for dried arrangements.

Bellis perennis
ENGLISH DAISY

Blooming profusely around tulip time and sporadically through summer, this plant makes a perfect edging and bulb companion for a spring flower border. The basal rosette of tidy, spoon-shaped green leaves sends up short stalks of 2-inch yellow-centered daisies that open during the day and close at night. Flowers come in shades of pink or red and white and may be semidouble or double. Although a perennial, English daisy is often treated as a biennial that is set out in fall and replaced with annuals after blooming finishes in spring.

Size: Clumps 6 inches tall, 8 inches wide.

Light: Full sun to half shade.

Soil and Moisture: Fertile, moist soil; do not allow to dry out, especially in sun.

Planting and Propagation: Sow seeds in cold frame in summer and transplant to garden in fall or spring, or plant container-grown plants. Divide in spring after blooming ceases.

Special Care: Winter-mulch in cold climates. Self-sown seedlings do not come true to type. May become lawn weed if allowed to set seed; snip off faded flowers.

Bellis perennis

Pests and Diseases: Powdery mildew sometimes troublesome.

Climate: Zones 4–9. Best in cool climates; performs poorly where hot and humid.

Cultivars: 'Dresden China,' light pink, double; 'Monstrosa,' dark red, double; 'Morning Blush,' pink, 1½ feet tall, reblooms; 'Rosea,' rose-pink; 'White Carpet,' white, single; 'Kito,' cherry, double, 6 inches tall.

Garden Use: Mass as edging for formal gardens, scatter along cottage garden path, or let peak from beneath stones in rock garden.

Bergenia cordifolia
HEART-LEAF BERGENIA

Admired more for its bold-textured clumps of cabbagelike leaves than for its pink flowers, bergenia brings architectural beauty to a flower garden. The 1-foot-long, rounded to heart-shaped green leaves have a leathery texture and gleam like polished wood. Evergreen in most climates and semi-evergreen in the coldest ones, the leaves often take on beautiful reddish hues in fall and winter. Stalks of dark-centered pink or white waxy flowers bloom just above the foliage in late winter and early spring.

Size: 1 foot tall; 1½ feet wide. Spreads into large clumps by rhizomes.

Light: Full sun to part shade; afternoon shade in the South.

Soil and Moisture: Tolerates various soil types, even alkaline, but best in humus-rich, moist soil. Moderate moisture best, but tolerates dry shade.

Planting and Propagation: Plant container-grown plants in spring, spacing 2 feet apart. Divide rhizomes every four years, replanting fairly deep.

Special Care: Remove spent flower stalks. Cut off winter-tattered foliage.

Pests and Diseases: Slugs troublesome.

Climate: Zones 3–8; foliage may be damaged by harsh winters if not snow covered.

Cultivars and Similar Species: 'Perfecta,' rose-red flowers on tall stems. *B. crassifolia*

Bergenia cordifolia

(leather bergenia): smaller oval leaves, light lavender-pink flowers, Zones 4–8. *B. purpurascens:* oval leaves with deep red undersides, magenta flowers, Zones 4–9. Hybrids: 'Bressingham White,' white, 1½ feet tall, late bloomer; 'Purpurea,' dark pink flowers, purple-flushed leaves; 'Evening Glow,' reddish purple flowers, maroon leaves in winter; 'Silver Light,' white flowers flushed pink; 'Bressingham Ruby,' rose-pink flowers, leaves with maroon undersides, deep ruby winter color.

Garden Use: Excellent year-round effect as border or path edging in rock or New American-style garden.

Boltonia asteroides
BOLTONIA

Forming a frothy stand of yellow-centered white, lilac, or purple asterlike flowers for four to six weeks in late summer and fall, compact cultivars of this lanky North American wildflower can be an asset to any flower garden. Leaves are blue-green and willowlike on tall, sparsely branched stems that form a loose, rounded clump.

Size: 3 to 6 feet tall; 3 to 4 feet wide.

Light: Full sun to light shade.

Soil and Moisture: Fertile, moist, well-

Boltonia asteroides

drained soil; drought tolerant once established, but size is reduced.

Planting and Propagation: Plant container-grown plants in spring, spacing 3 feet apart. Divide in spring every three or four years, separating rosettes. Take stem cuttings in summer.

Special Care: Stake in part shade.

Pests and Diseases: Not susceptible to mildew as are asters.

Climate: Zones 4–9; better in hot-summer areas than asters.

Cultivars: Preferred over the species are 'Snowbank,' white, compact to 4 feet tall; 'Pink Beauty,' pale lilac-pink, 3 to 4 feet tall.

Garden Use: Use in back of border to contrast with bolder-textured fall bloomers such as stonecrop, Japanese anemone, chrysanthemums, and ornamental grasses. Hide bare bottoms of stems with other plants.

Brunnera macrophylla
SIBERIAN BUGLOSS

Sprays of dainty, blue, yellow-centered flowers reminiscent of forget-me-nots grace this plant from early spring to early summer, blooming freely at daffodil and tulip time. The 8-inch-wide heart-shaped leaves have a rough, dull green surface with prominent veins. They make attractive, boldly textured clumps that reach their full size only after flowers fade. The leaves look good all summer, contrasting with fine-textured ferns and astilbes in the shady spots where they all thrive.

Size: 1 to 1½ feet tall; twice as wide.

Light: Best in light shade. Tolerates full sun to full shade; needs shade in the South.

Soil and Moisture: Fertile, humus-rich, moist soil. Best if evenly moist. Tolerates some dryness in full shade; needs copious moisture in sun.

Planting and Propagation: Plant bare-root or container-grown plants in spring, spacing 1½ feet apart. Rarely needs division; propagate by root cuttings in fall.

Special Care: Self seeds freely; pull out or transplant self sown seedlings.

Pests and Diseases: Slugs may be troublesome.

Climate: Zones 3–8.

Cultivars: 'Variegata,' creamy white irregularly variegated leaves; needs shade and wind protection.

Garden Use: Mass-plant or allow to self-seed into spacious stands in shade or woodland gardens and waterside plantings.

Calamintha nepeta
CALAMINT

This long-blooming perennial creates a frothy cloud of tiny, blue-tinged white blossoms from midsummer until frost. The petite, gray-green, toothed leaves that stud the upright stems have a minty aroma when crushed and contribute to the plant's weightless appearance. Calamint spreads by creeping rhizomes to form hearty clumps.

Size: 1½ feet tall and wide.

Light: Full sun to light shade.

Soil and Moisture: Well-drained, humus-rich soil; moderate moisture.

Planting and Propagation: Plant container-

Brunnera macrophylla

grown plants in spring, spacing 1½ feet apart. Divide in spring or take cuttings in summer.

Special Care: Cut back to woody base in late winter.

Pests and Diseases: Usually problem free.

Climate: Zones 5–9; heat tolerant.

Similar Species: *C. n. nepeta* (*C. nepetoides*), darker blue flowers; *C. grandiflora,* pink flowers.

Garden Use: Use to create translucent veil of frothy flowers at front of border.

Calamintha nepeta

Caltha palustris
MARSH MARIGOLD

Blooming in early spring before the tree leaves have opened, this marshland wildflower displays its buttercuplike flowers on long stems held above the foliage. The golden yellow flowers have a prominent tuft of stamens in their centers and bring a ray of spring sunshine to any wet site. The rounded leaves are glossy dark green and form handsome clumps until plants go dormant in midsummer.

Caltha palustris

Size: 1 to 1½ feet tall and wide.
Light: Full sun to part shade.
Soil and Moisture: Humus-rich, moist to wet soil; constant moisture, even standing water to 6 inches deep. Tolerates some dryness once dormant.
Planting and Propagation: Plant bare-root plants or container-grown plants 6 inches deep in spring. Divide immediately after flowering every three to five years.
Special Care: Plant goes dormant, dying to ground by midsummer.
Pests and Diseases: Usually trouble free.
Climate: Zones 2–8.

Cultivars and Similar Species: 'Flore-Pleno' and 'Multiplex,' double flowers; 'Alba,' white flowers with yellow stamens.
Garden Use: Plant in naturalistic or wildflower gardens, along stream or pond, in bog garden, or in wet spot in garden.

Campanula carpatica
CARPATHIAN BELLFLOWER

This very popular, long-blooming bellflower features triangular, 2-inch-long, bright green, toothed leaves that form tidy, low mounds from spring through fall. From early summer to midsummer, and sporadically through fall, the plant sends up stem after stem topped with solitary, 2-inch-wide, bowl-shaped flowers. Like most bellflowers, this one has blue or white blossoms and spreads readily into lovely clumps.
Size: 9 inches to 1 foot tall; 1 foot wide.
Light: Full sun to part shade.
Soil and Moisture: Well-drained, average to sandy soil kept moist but never wet.
Planting and Propagation: Plant container-grown plants in spring, spacing 1 foot apart. Divide in spring, every three years.
Special Care: Must deadhead to prolong blooming. Keep roots cool with summer mulch. May self-sow, but rarely weedy.

Campanula carpatica

Pests and Diseases: Short-lived in poorly drained soil or drought conditions. Snails and slugs may be troublesome.
Climate: Zones 3–8.
Cultivars: 'Alba,' white; 'Blue Clips,' blue, 6 to 8 inches tall; 'White Clips,' white, 6 to 8 inches tall; 'Wedgewood Blue,' sky-blue, 6 inches tall; 'Wedgewood White,' white, 6 inches tall; 'China Doll,' plate-shaped, pale blue flowers.
Garden Use: Excellent in foreground of border, as edging along walk, or in rock garden.

Campanula garganica
GARGANO BELLFLOWER

This ground-covering bellflower features bright green, kidney-shaped, 1-inch-long basal leaves and ivy-shaped stem leaves on a trailing plant that spreads aggressively to form mats of evergreen foliage. For several weeks in late spring and early summer, and sporadically through fall, clusters of pale blue to violet, star-shaped, upward-facing flowers with white centers decorate the trailing stems, all but obscuring the leaves.
Size: 5 to 6 inches tall; spreads into 10-inch- to 1-foot-wide clumps.
Light: Full sun to light shade.
Soil and Moisture: Average to fertile, well-

Campanula garganica

drained, neutral to alkaline soil; keep moist but not soggy.

Planting and Propagation: Plant container-grown plants in spring, spacing 1 foot apart. Divide every few years in fall.

Special Care: May be aggressive; divide frequently to control spread.

Pests and Diseases: Snails and slugs may be troublesome.

Climate: Zones 6–8.

Cultivars and Similar Species: Sometimes listed as *C. elatines* var. *garganica*. *C. g. hirsuta:* covered with fine hairs, dusky blue flowers, gray-green leaves.

Garden Use: Makes good ground cover in rock garden or mixed border.

Campanula glomerata
CLUSTERED BELLFLOWER

Blooming profusely from early summer to midsummer, the tall, stiff stems of this upright bellflower hold dense clusters of 1-inch, purple or violet, bell-shaped flowers with pointed petals in the leaf nodes and at the stem tips. Leaves are spear-shaped and hairy. Plants spread rapidly to form open clumps.

Size: 1 to 3 feet tall; 1½ feet wide.

Light: Full sun in the North; part shade in the South.

Soil and Moisture: Humus-rich, well-drained neutral to alkaline soil; keep moist but not soggy.

Planting and Propagation: Plant bare-root or container-grown plants in spring, spacing 1½ feet apart. Divide every three years.

Special Care: Can be invasive; divide every few years to control. Cut back flower stalks after flowering for possible repeat performance. Needs no staking.

Pests and Diseases: Snails and slugs may be troublesome.

Climate: Zones 3–8.

Cultivars: 'Joan Elliott,' dark violet, early flowering, 1½ feet tall; 'Superba,' violet-blue, 2 to 2½ feet tall, invasive, heat tolerant; 'Alba,'

white, 2 feet tall; *C. g. acaulis*, light violet-blue, 3 to 5 inches tall, dwarf variety.

Garden Use: Plant in groups in informal gardens for beautiful early summer blue flowers. Combines well with pink and rose.

Campanula lactiflora
MILKY BELLFLOWER

This tall bellflower forms a loose bush of slender gray-green leaves topped with large, flirtatious panicles of numerous, 1-inch-long, bell-shaped, milky blue to deep blue flowers with white centers. Blossoms appear in midsummer and carry on for several weeks, reblooming readily if stems are cut back after the first flush. Their pale color looks especially lovely when backlit by the sun or viewed in the moonlight.

Size: 3 to 5 feet tall; 3 feet wide.

Light: Full sun to part shade.

Soil and Moisture: Humus-rich, well-drained soil; even moisture.

Planting and Propagation: Plant container-grown plants in spring, spacing 3 feet apart. Take cuttings in spring. Resents division and transplanting.

Campanula glomerata

Campanula lactiflora

Special Care: After flowers fade, cut back stems to just below lowest flowers to encourage reblooming. Self-sows to point of weediness if not deadheaded. Pinch back stems when 6 inches tall to increase bushiness and stem strength. Requires staking to prevent leaning toward the sun and flopping on nearby plants.

Pests and Diseases: Snails and slugs may be troublesome.

Climate: Zones 5–7.

Cultivars: *C. l. alba*, white, 3 to 4 feet tall; 'Loddon Anna,' pale pink, 4 feet tall; 'Pouffe,' pale blue, 1½ feet tall, no staking.

Garden Use: Graceful, long-blooming plant for informal and naturalistic gardens.

Campanula persicifolia
PEACH-LEAF BELLFLOWER

Spires of bell- to saucer-shaped, 1½-inch flowers on tall, straight stems make this bellflower a valuable addition to any flower garden. Blossoms open from the top of the stalk downward, beginning in July and continuing through August if cut back. The clumps of evergreen, rounded basal leaves grow larger every year but are not invasive. Narrow with rounded teeth, the leathery leaves lining the flower stems don't look like peach leaves despite its name.

Size: 1 to 3 feet tall; 2 feet wide.

Light: Full sun to light shade.

Soil and Moisture: Humus-rich, well-drained soil; even moisture.

Planting and Propagation: Plant container-grown plants in spring, spacing 2 feet apart. Divide after flowering every three years.

Special Care: Self-sows. Reblooms if faded flowering stalks are cut back to several inches above the basal mat of foliage.

Pests and Diseases: Snails and slugs may be troublesome.

Climate: Best in Zones 3–6; short-lived in Zones 7–8.

Cultivars: 'Telham Beauty,' pale china blue, 3 to 4 feet tall; 'Alba,' white, 2½ feet tall; 'Grandiflora Blue,' large sky-blue flowers, 2½ feet tall; 'Blue Gardenia,' double, deep silvery blue, 3 feet tall; 'Coerulea,' bright blue, 3 feet tall.

Garden Use: Plant in large groups for excellent vertical effect in formal and informal borders. Long-lasting cut flower.

Campanula portenschlagiana
DALMATIAN BELLFLOWER

This exuberant, mat-forming, blue-flowered beauty looks especially alluring cascading from a wall or spilling around boulders in a rock garden, but it's equally at home beneath shrubs and taller perennials. The 1-inch-wide, upward-facing, bell-shaped flowers form an intense lavender-blue blanket that conceals the evergreen foliage for three or four weeks in late spring and early summer. Flowers may rebloom sporadically through summer. Long-stalked, 2-inch-long, heart-shaped to triangular leaves with jagged teeth form a central rosette from which long trailing stems with smaller leaves reach out in all directions. Flowering branches form along these runners.

Size: 4 to 6 inches tall; spreads to 2 feet or more.

Campanula persicifolia

Campanula portenschlagiana

Light: Full sun to light shade.

Soil and Moisture: Average to humus-rich, moist, well-drained soil; keep moist but never wet or soggy.

Planting and Propagation: Plant container-grown plants in spring, spacing 1 foot apart. Take cuttings in summer. Divide every three years.

Special Care: Must have excellent drainage.

Pests and Diseases: Snails and slugs sometimes troublesome.

Climate: Zones 4–8; performs better in the South than other bellflowers.

Cultivars and Similar Species: 'Resholt,' dark violet. *C. poscharskyana* (Serbian bellflower): similar spreading habit but less invasive, blooms in mid-spring and sporadically through fall, flowers upward-facing flat stars, leaves smaller on shorter stems and with more pointed tips, drought tolerant; *C. p. alba*, white flowers, Zones 3–7.

Garden Use: Best in rock garden, wall, naturalistic garden, and mixed border. Use as edging along walk or in informal border.

Centaurea montana
MOUNTAIN BLUET

The unusual cobalt-blue flowers of mountain bluet are rounded with ragged-edged petals radiating from a reddish purple center, creating a charming spidery effect. Overlapping scales beneath the flowers have a shingled appearance, enhancing the individual flowers. Blossoms first appear at the stem tips, usually blooming from June into July, but will continue for months if deadheaded. The lance-shaped foliage is covered with whitish hairs when young but matures to bright green.

Size: 1½ to 2 feet tall; spreads to form large colonies.

Light: Full sun.

Soil and Moisture: Average to sandy, infertile, well-drained soil. Moderate moisture; drought tolerant.

Planting and Propagation: Plant container-grown plants in spring, spacing 1 foot apart. Divide every three years in fall.

Special Care: Deadhead regularly to extend blooming and prevent weedy self-seeding. Cut back stems to ground when new growth appears at base for late-summer and fall reblooming. May need staking to control floppiness. Spreads aggressively in fertile soil;

Centaurea montana

divide regularly to control.

Pests and Diseases: Root rot in heavy, moist soil.

Climate: Zones 3–8; best where cool.

Similar Species and Cultivars: 'Alba,' white flowers; 'Rosea,' pink flowers; 'Violetta,' violet flowers. *C. macrocephala* (Armenian basket flower): golden yellow, thistlelike blossoms in early summer, 3 to 4 feet tall, Zones 3–7.

Garden Use: Best in informal or naturalistic gardens where neatness not important. Blue flowers combine wonderfully with yellow, orange, and pink flowers.

Centranthus ruber
RED VALERIAN, JUPITER'S BEARD

A Mediterranean native, this cottage garden favorite has naturalized in England and Ireland, where it decorates cliffs and roadsides. Large, domed sprays of tiny, fragrant flowers top the stems in late spring and summer, blooming longest where summers are cool. Flower colors are muted tones of deep coral-pink, soft rose-red, and bright white. The

Centranthus ruber albus

bushy clumps of upright stems bear attractive, waxy, pointed, 4-inch, blue-green leaves that make a soft-toned companion to the flowers.

Size: 2 to 3 feet tall; 1½ feet wide.

Light: Full sun.

Soil and Moisture: Infertile, well-drained, neutral to alkaline soil; moderate moisture. Drought tolerant.

Planting and Propagation: Sow seeds in spring or plant container-grown plants, spacing 1 foot apart. Divide deep, fleshy roots in spring or fall. Flowers first year from seeds.

Special Care: Self-seeds if not deadheaded and can become weedy; seedlings vary in color. Cut back after first bloom to promote more blossoms.

Pests and Diseases: Usually trouble free.

Climate: Zones 5–8.

Cultivars: *C. r. albus*, white; *C. r. coccineus*, deep red; *C. r. roseus*, rose.

Garden Use: Enticing, upright plant for arranging and self-seeding in cracks and crevices of rock garden walls and cottage gardens. Effective border plant, but difficult to combine with most pinks and reds; best with blue, white, and yellow.

Cerastium tomentosum
SNOW-IN-SUMMER

When in full bloom, this carpetlike plant creates quite a sight in late spring and early summer. The dainty, 1-inch-wide, snow-white flowers have five notched petals and bloom in such profusion that they literally obscure the leaves for three or four weeks. When not in bloom, snow-in-summer creates a beautiful effect with its ground-hugging, tiny, woolly white leaves.

Size: 6 inches tall in bloom; spreads to form 2-foot-wide mats.

Light: Full sun.

Soil and Moisture: Average to sandy, infertile soil; moderate water. Drought tolerant.

Planting and Propagation: Plant container grown plants in spring; divide in spring or fall every two years.

Special Care: Shear back hard after flowering. Spreads by underground runners and can become invasive, especially in fertile soil; plant away from less vigorous low plants.

Pests and Diseases: Usually pest free; root rot in moist site.

Climate: Zones 2–7; performs poorly where hot and humid.

Cerastium tomentosum

Cultivars and Similar Species: 'Yo-Yo,' compact and less invasive. *C. biebersteinii:* larger leaves, taller flowers.

Garden Use: Plant as ground cover beneath taller perennials in well-drained, sunny border, or arrange to spill from cracks and crevices in rock wall or garden.

Ceratostigma plumbaginoides
LEADWORT, PLUMBAGO

Slow to get started in spring, this wonderful ground-covering perennial makes its statement late in the growing season. Vivid blue flowers begin to open in late summer and continue well into fall. As petals fall, they leave behind red calyxes, which add a pretty contrast to the continuing show of blue flowers. As the weather cools, the olive-green, egg-shaped leaves turn rich bronze-red.

Size: 8 inches to 1 foot tall; spreads to 1 to 2 feet wide.

Light: Full sun to part or light shade; afternoon shade in the South.

Soil and Moisture: Average, well-drained soil; moderate moisture.

Planting and Propagation: Plant bare-root or container-grown plants in spring, spacing

Ceratostigma plumbaginoides

1 foot apart. Take cuttings in early summer; divide in spring if centers become bare.

Special Care: Cut back woody stems in late winter to stimulate new growth. Doesn't compete well with shallow tree roots.

Pests and Diseases: Root rot in wet soil.

Climate: Zones 5–9; winter-mulch in Zone 5.

Similar Species: *C. willmottianum,* similar flowers and foliage but grows as open subshrub, 2 to 3 feet tall, lacks fall color, Zones 8–10.

Garden Use: Excellent ground cover in combination with spring and fall bulbs, tall perennials, or shrubs in mixed border or shade garden.

Chamaemelum nobile
CHAMOMILE, ROMAN CHAMOMILE

This apple-scented herb is valued for its medicinal properties—tea brewed from its flowers is said to cure skin afflictions and digestive problems. Its healing qualities aside, the plant decorates herb and cottage gardens with its mat of finely divided downy leaves and tiny white summer daisies. If planted closely together and mown high to prevent flowering, chamomile forms a thick mat that can be walked on as a fragrant lawn substitute.

Size: 9 inches tall; spreads to 2 feet.

Light: Full sun.

Soil and Moisture: Fertile to average, well-drained soil; keep moist but not wet.

Planting and Propagation: Plant container-grown plants in spring, spacing 6 inches apart as paving or lawn substitute and 1 foot apart in gardens. Take cuttings in spring; divide in early spring.

Special Care: Harvest flowers for tea when petals begin to curl inward.

Pests and Diseases: Usually trouble free.

Climate: Zones 6–9.

Cultivars and Similar Species: 'Flore-Pleno,' showier double flowers, needs richer soil; 'Treneague,' nonflowering mat-former, best choice for paving. *Matricaria*

Chamaemelum nobile

chamomilla (German chamomile): 2 to 3 feet tall, similar-looking annual, less fragrant.

Garden Use: Paving plant or lawn substitute; attractive massed in herb and cottage gardens.

Chelone lyonii
PINK TURTLE-HEAD

This native wildflower, which makes its home in wet meadows, flourishes in gardens, forming impressive clumps when its growing conditions are met. A late-summer bloomer, turtle-head produces tight clusters of rose-purple snapdragonlike flowers at the tips of its sturdy stems for about a month. The tubular flowers resemble the head of a turtle with its mouth open. The 6-inch-long pointed leaves have small teeth along the edges and are dark green.

Size: 2 to 3 feet tall; 1½ feet wide.

Light: Full sun in boggy site; part shade in moist site.

Soil and Moisture: Fertile, acid, moist or boggy soil; do not allow to dry out.

Planting and Propagation: Plant container-grown plants or dormant roots in spring, spacing 2 feet apart. Divide in early spring.

Chelone lyonii

Take cuttings in spring or early summer.

Special Care: Needs staking only if too shady. Pinch in early summer to make bushier and produce more flowers.

Pests and Diseases: Usually problem free if given sufficient moisture.

Climate: Zones 3–8.

Cultivars and Similar Species: *C. glabra*, pink-tinged white flowers, 3 to 4 feet tall, half as wide, Zones 3–8. *C. obliqua:* deep pink, late summer to fall, 2 to 3 feet tall, half as wide, Zones 4–9; 'Alba,' white flowers.

Garden Use: Late-summer bloomer for moist borders. Naturalize in bog garden or along stream or pond.

Chrysanthemum coccineum (Tanacetum coccineum)
PAINTED DAISY, PYRETHRUM

The first daisy-type flower to bloom in summer, painted daisy makes a bright statement with its 3-inch, yellow-centered, pink, rose, magenta, red, or, occasionally, white flowers. Blossoms appear in June and early July on unbranched stems above clumps of feathery dark green leaves that resemble carrot leaves.

This plant is the source of the natural insecticide pyrethrum.

Size: 1 to 2 feet tall; 1 foot wide.

Light: Full sun.

Soil and Moisture: Average, well-drained, moist soil; water during drought.

Planting and Propagation: Plant bare-root or container-grown plants in spring, spacing 1 foot apart. Divides easily in spring or late summer.

Special Care: Deadhead to prolong bloom. Often needs staking with ring support.

Pests and Diseases: Mildew and rust occasionally troublesome.

Climate: Zones 3–7; performs well where cool and poorly where hot.

Cultivars: 'James Kelway,' deep scarlet; 'Robinson's Hybrids,' mixed colors, large flowers; 'Roseum,' rose-pink; 'Giant Hybrids,' mixed pinks and magenta, white singles and doubles, 1 to 2 feet tall; 'Atrosanguineum,' large single, dark red; 'Duro,' very large magenta, 2⅔ feet tall; 'Sensation,' double, red; 'Evenglow,' salmon-red.

Garden Use: Pretty plant for informal plantings and cottage gardens.

Chrysanthemum coccineum

Chrysanthemum nipponicum

Chrysanthemum nipponicum (Nipponanthemum nipponicum)
NIPPON DAISY, MONTAUK DAISY

A shrubby perennial, this late bloomer makes a lavish display of 3-inch, white, daisy-type flowers with greenish yellow centers in fall. Blossoming usually begins in mid-September and continues until a hard freeze puts a stop to the flowers, often in November. The stems are woody with succulent, toothed, gray-green leaves. Plants form large, attractive mounds

Size: 2 to 4 feet tall and wide.

Light: Full sun.

Soil and Moisture: Sandy to fertile soil; even moisture best, but tolerates drought.

Planting and Propagation: Plant dormant roots or container-grown plants in spring, spacing 2 to 3 feet apart. Take cuttings in early summer; cannot be divided easily.

Special Care: Cut back woody stems in late winter to keep plant compact. Pinch stems every few weeks until midsummer to encourage dense branching and profuse bloom. Dig up and discard overly woody plants and replace with rooted cuttings.

Pests and Diseases: Usually pest free.

Climate: Zones 5–8; responds well to seashore conditions.

Cultivars: Only species is sold.

Garden Use: Excellent plant for bringing late color to beds and borders; use in informal plantings and seashore gardens. Because lower foliage often drops by bloom time, plant in midground to conceal bases of stems.

Chrysanthemum parthenium (Tanacetum parthenium)
FEVERFEW, MATRICARIA

This cottage garden herb, respected as a headache remedy, is beloved for its charming flowers and pretty foliage. From midsummer to fall, daisylike flowers with prominent golden centers ringed with small, bright white petals form tight, flat clusters atop the branched plants. The showiest flowers are double forms with numerous snowy petals and tiny gold centers. Strongly scented with a pungent, peppery aroma, the foliage creates pretty clumps of bright green, deeply divided leaves to offset the dainty flowers.

Size: 2 to 3 feet tall; half as wide.

Light: Full sun.

Soil and Moisture: Average to sandy, well-drained soil; plentiful moisture.

Chrysanthemum parthenium

Planting and Propagation: Plant container-grown plants in spring, spacing 1 foot apart, or sow seeds in spring or fall. Divide annually or take cuttings in spring to perpetuate this short-lived perennial.

Special Care: Pinch in mid-spring to induce bushiness, or may need staking. Individual plants short-lived but self-sows readily; may become weedy in neat gardens.

Pests and Diseases: Aromatic foliage is pest resistant.

Climate: Zones 4–8; winter mulch in Zones 4–6.

Cultivars: *C. p. aureum* (golden feather), golden evergreen foliage, 1 foot tall, white daisies; 'Golden Ball,' yellow, ball-like flowers; 'Silver Ball,' double white flowers with golden centers; 'White Stars,' white buttons; 'White Wonder' ('Ultra Double White'), double daisies; 'Snowball,' double, 8 to 10 inches tall.

Garden Use: Best in informal and cottage gardens because of tendency to self-sow and pop up here and there. Excellent in herb or cut-flower garden; dries well.

Chrysanthemum weyrichii (Dendranthema weyrichii)
MIYABE

This late bloomer, whose 2-inch-wide, daisy-like, white or pink flowers decorate gardens in September and October, harks from the Japanese seashores. One of the latest-blooming perennials in fall, miyabe continues blooming through light frosts, providing a long season of blossoms in any flower garden. Leaves are deep green, lobed, thick, and fleshy, decorating purple-stemmed plants that spread gracefully to make a good ground cover.

Size: 8 inches to 1 foot tall; wide spreading by stolons.

Light: Full sun.

Soil and Moisture: Average to sandy, well-drained soil; moderate moisture.

Planting and Propagation: Plant bare-root

Chrysanthemum weyrichii

or container-grown plants in spring or fall, spacing 1 foot apart. Divide in spring every three or four years.

Special Care: Spreads by stolons, but is not invasive. Do not overwater.

Pests and Diseases: Root rot in wet or damp site.

Climate: Zones 3–9.

Cultivars and Similar Species: 'White Bomb,' 10 inches to 1 foot tall, short-stemmed creamy white flowers age to pale rose; 'Pink Bomb,' pale mauve-pink flowers, 1 foot tall. *C. pacifcum:* lobed green leaves with silver edge and undersides, very late buttonlike gold flowers, spreads rapidly to make an excellent 2-foot-tall ground cover noted for its striking foliage, Zones 6–9.

Garden Use: Works well as edging for path or well-drained border or to create lovely low mounds in rock garden.

Chrysanthemum x *morifolium (Dendranthema grandiflorum)*
CHRYSANTHEMUM, GARDEN MUM

These late-blooming, long-blooming flowers are the mainstay of many fall gardens—the blossoms even withstand a light frost. Flow-

Chrysanthemum x *morifolium* 'Carousel'

er types vary, including tight buttons, single daisies, doubles, and pompons. Colors include rust-reds and copper-oranges as well as bright yellow, gold, lavender-pink, and white. Shapes range from low mounds to tall, loose types, but the garden favorites are cushion mums, which form a neat mound less than 2 feet tall. Some gardeners plant potted blooming mums in fall and treat them as annuals, but the display is softer and more natural when mums grow as perennials.

Size: 8 inches to 3 feet tall and wide.

Light: Full sun.

Soil and Moisture: Fertile, humus-rich, moist, well-drained, acid soil; plentiful moisture.

Planting and Propagation: Plant bare-root or small container-grown plants in spring, spacing 1 foot apart. Divide every two or three years in spring to keep vigorous.

Special Care: Fertilize monthly during summer. Pinch stem tips every two weeks from spring through midsummer (July 15 in the North; August 1 to August 15 in the South) to promote bushiness and delay bloom until fall. Mulch in summer to keep soil cool and

moist. Mulch loosely in winter after soil freezes to prevent alternate freezing and thawing. Cut back old stems in early spring.

Pests and Diseases: Root rot in wet sites. Aphids and spider mites often serious.

Climate: Zones 5–9.

Cultivars: Numerous cultivars available. Choose cold-hardy mums, not tender florist types, as garden perennials. (Hardy types produce an overwintering rosette of foliage.) In northern areas, select early blooming types; in southern areas, select late-blooming types.

Garden Use: Arrange mums in drifts in foreground or middle of formal and informal beds and borders.

Chrysanthemum x *rubellum* (*Dendranthema* x *rubella*)
HYBRID CHRYSANTHEMUM

This cold-hardy, daisy-type chrysanthemum is a hybrid discovered in 1929; its exact parentage is unknown. The compact plants branch nicely to form loose mounds of deeply lobed, tooth-edged leaves with hairy undersides. These are topped with charming, lightly fragrant, bright pink or yellow daisies with raised yellow centers from midsummer into fall.

Size: 1 to 3 feet tall; to 3 feet wide.

Light: Full sun in the North; light shade in hot areas.

Soil and Moisture: Average, well-drained soil; moderate moisture.

Planting and Propagation: Plant container-grown plants in spring, spacing 3 feet apart. Divide in spring every four or five years.

Special Care: Spreads rapidly in light soil; avoid overfertilizing. Pinch in early summer to promote compactness and later blooming. Shear after summer flush of blossoms wanes to promote fall bloom.

Pests and Diseases: Usually trouble free.

Climate: Zones 4–9.

Cultivars: 'Clara Curtis,' the usual form sold, bright pink with yellow centers, 2 feet tall;

Chrysanthemum x *rubellum* 'Clara Curtis'

'Mary Stoker,' straw-yellow turning buttery apricot with age, yellow centers, a bit leggy.

Garden Use: Easy-care perennial for long season of color in informal borders and cottage gardens. Combines well with blue and purple flowers.

Chrysanthemum x *superbum* (*C. maximum* and *Leucanthemum* x *superbum*)
SHASTA DAISY

This hybrid of two European daisies was created by the American plantsman Luther Burbank during the late 19th century. He sought to create a large-flowered daisy with long, strong stems perfect for cutting. The result is the beloved Shasta daisy, a perennial noted for its floriferous nature. Blossoms appear lavishly in June and July and continue into fall if plants are deadheaded. The 2- to 3-inch, white, yellow-centered flowers may be single, double, or semidouble and make excellent cut flowers. Unlike leaves of most chrysanthemums, these are coarsely toothed,

Chrysanthemum x *superbum* 'Alaska'

not lobed, and dark green. The leaves, which are larger near the ground, form a dense clump beneath the sparsely foliaged flowering stems; a rosette of evergreen basal leaves overwinters.

Size: 6 inches to 3 feet tall; 1½ feet wide.

Light: Full sun in most areas; part shade where summers are hot and dry. Doubles do best in part shade.

Soil and Moisture: Deep, fertile, well-drained, neutral to alkaline soil; moderate moisture.

Planting and Propagation: Plant container-grown plants in spring, spacing 2 feet apart. Divide every other year in early spring.

Special Care: Deadhead regularly or cut back after first flush to promote reblooming. Winter-mulch in the North. Stake tall cultivars with rings. Short-lived, especially in wet winter soil.

Pests and Diseases: Aphids and verticillium wilt sometimes troublesome.

Climate: Zones 4–9.

Cultivars and Similar Species: Singles: 'Alaska,' large white, 20 inches tall; 'Snow Lady,' 2½-inch pure-white early blossoms, 6 to 8 inches tall; 'Star Burst,' 6-inch early blossoms, 3 feet tall; 'Little Princess,' large flowers, compact to 1 foot tall; 'Snowcap,' pure

white, 10 inches to 1 foot tall; 'Polaris,' white, 3 feet tall. Doubles: 'Aglaya,' frilly fully double, 2⅓ feet tall; 'Marconi,' fully double, 4-inch early blooms, 3 feet tall; 'Thomas Killen,' large flowers with double row of petals, crested gold centers, sturdy, to 2½ feet tall; 'Cobham Gold,' double row of creamy yellow petals with gold centers, 1¼ to 1½ feet tall.

Garden Use: Plant in masses in formal border, as edging or middle-of-border plant, depending on height. Scatter about cottage garden or informal planting. Favorite cut flower; choose tall types.

Chrysogonum virginianum
GOLDENSTAR, GREEN AND GOLD

This wildflower is native to woodland clearings from Pennsylvania south to Louisiana. The 1-inch, golden yellow flowers are star-like, with five petals and long stalks. They smother the ground-hugging plants in spring and bloom less profusely through summer and fall, if the weather isn't too hot. The tidy green triangular leaves are hairy with scalloped edges and form a thick mat that remains evergreen in the mildest areas. Goldenstar makes a beautiful and unusual ground cover for a semishady spot.

Size: 6 to 10 inches tall; spreads 1 to 2 feet.

Light: Full sun to full shade; shade needed in southern zones.

Soil and Moisture: Fertile, well-drained, moist soil; plentiful moisture, especially in sunny site.

Planting and Propagation: Plant bare-root or container-grown plants in spring, spacing 1 foot apart. Divide in spring or fall every two or three years.

Special Care: Self-sows but rarely becomes weedy.

Pests and Diseases: Sometimes suffers from mildew if too shady.

Climate: Zones 5–9.

Cultivars: *C. v. australe*, compact to 6 inches tall, spreads rapidly but flowers are smaller.

Chrysogonum virginianum

'Springbrook,' 3 to 5 inches tall, small flowers; 'Allen Bush,' long blooming, 8 inches tall; 'Pierre,' clump forming, long blooming.

Garden Use: Excellent ground cover for wildflower garden, bordering shady walk, or as ground cover in mixed border or under taller perennials. Flower color a bit brassy; combines well with hot colors and green foliage plants such as hosta.

Cimicifuga simplex
KAMCHATKA BUGBANE

This Russian woodland wildflower captivates gardeners in late fall, blooming for several weeks in September and October, when most flowers are long gone. The arching wandlike inflorescences rise above the foliage and are densely packed with tiny white flowers made up of minuscule petals and long, decorative stamens, creating the feathery appearance of bottlebrushes. The flowers look especially engaging when back-lit by the low rays of the autumn sun. The compound toothed leaves are handsome all season, making bold, dark green clumps. The plants spread each year but are never invasive. The several available cultivars are showier than the species and are preferred for most gardens.

Cimicifuga simplex

Size: 3 to 4 feet tall when in bloom; 3 feet wide.

Light: Full sun only if constantly moist; light to full shade best, especially in the South.

Soil and Moisture: Humus-rich, deep, moist, acid soil; abundant water.

Planting and Propagation: Plant bare-root or container-grown plants in spring, spacing 4 feet apart. Rarely needs division.

Special Care: Keep constantly moist or leaf margins will brown and plants will become stunted. Usually needs no staking.

Pests and Diseases: Usually pest free.

Climate: Zones 3–8.

Cultivars and Similar Species: 'White Pearl,' 2-foot-long, very dense, white flower spikes. *C. racemosa* (snake-root, cohosh): midsummer to late-summer bloomer, foliage clumps 4 to 6 feet tall, flower wands 2 feet long and upright to 6 feet, may need staking, native wildflower, Zones 3–8. *C. ramosa* (branched bugbane): many dense, upright flower wands, very ornamental, fall bloomer, 7 feet tall, native wildflower, Zones 3–8. *C. r. atropurpurea:* dark purple foliage; 'Brunette,' bronze foliage.

Garden Use: Plant in large stands in flower borders and woodland settings. Combines well with Japanese anemones, late asters, monkshood, and late chrysanthemums.

Coreopsis grandiflora
COREOPSIS, TICKSEED

Native to the grasslands and roadsides of the Midwest, coreopsis has long been a popular garden flower because of its extended blooming season. Daisylike flowers, 2 inches across, with golden yellow petals and orange-yellow centers bring hot color to the garden from early to late summer if faded flowers are removed. Flowers open from knoblike buds on long, wiry stems that stand well above the clump of basal foliage. Leaves are deeply cut into oblong or lanceolate segments, form tufts near the base of the plant, and are scattered partway up the flowering stems. Plants are unfortunately short-lived, surviving usually for two to four years; self-sown seedlings do not come true to type.

Size: 2 to 3 feet tall; 1½ to 2 feet wide.

Light: Full sun.

Soil and Moisture: Average to sandy, well-drained, infertile soil; moderate moisture. Drought tolerant.

Planting and Propagation: Plant container-grown plants in spring, spacing 1 foot apart. Divide each year in spring for best longevity.

Special Care: May flop and sprawl if soil is

Coreopsis grandiflora

rich and fertile; stake with ring support to hold flower stems. Deadhead regularly for long bloom and to prevent self-seeding, cutting back flower stalks for best appearance. Do not fertilize.

Pests and Diseases: Mildew frequently troublesome; occasionally bothered by leafspot, aphids, or cucumber beetles. Root rot in winter-wet soil.

Climate: Zones 5–9; blooms longest when cool.

Cultivars and Similar Species: *C. lanceolata*, similar, bright yellow daisies with brownish centers, 8 to 10 inches tall. The following cultivars may be randomly attributed to either species: 'Early Sunrise,' 1½ to 2 feet tall, early flowering, double; 'Sunray,' double 2-inch flowers, 2 feet tall; 'Goldfink,' deep yellow, very floriferous, 9 inches tall, dense ground-covering foliage; 'Sunburst,' semidouble flowers, 2 feet tall; 'Baby Sun,' single, bright yellow, 20 inches tall.

Garden Use: Charming plant in informal and formal gardens; allow to self-seed in meadow plantings and cottage gardens. Excellent cut flower.

Coreopsis rosea
PINK COREOPSIS

With its fine-textured flower and foliage, this recently introduced plant resembles a pink-flowered version of the popular yellow-flowered threadleaf coreopsis. Flowers are ¾ inch across with rose-pink petals surrounding a central yellow disk and are held on short stems just above the leaves from midsummer to late summer. The leaves are tiny and linear, cloaking the sprawling stems. Unlike other species of coreopsis, this one is not drought tolerant.

Size: 1 to 1¼ feet tall; 1½ feet wide. Spreads rapidly by rhizomes

Light: Full sun.

Soil and Moisture: Fertile, heavy, moist soil best; provide abundant water.

Planting and Propagation: Plant container-

Coreopsis rosea

Coreopsis verticillata 'Moonbeam'

Corydalis lutea
YELLOW CORYDALIS

A delightful plant for rock gardens and naturalistic plantings, yellow corydalis is a carefree plant that blooms from spring until hard frost. Loose sprays of lacelike, blue-green leaves divided into rounded lobes form low leafy mounds that remain evergreen through winter. Sprays of ½-inch-long, tubular, spurred, pastel yellow blossoms are produced continously without any deadheading.
Size: 1¼ feet tall; spreads to 1½ feet.
Light: Light to full shade.
Soil and Moisture: Gravelly to fertile, well-drained soil; tolerates alkaline sites. Best if kept moist, but tolerates drought.
Planting and Propagation: Plant container-grown plants in spring, spacing 1 foot apart. Divide or transplant seedlings in fall.
Special Care: Needs no deadheading. Reseeds vigorously, but easy to transplant when small. Pull out and discard if it pops up where it's not wanted.
Pests and Diseases: Usually pest free.
Climate: Zones 5–7.
Similar Species: *C. cheilanthifolia*, fernlike, bronze-tinged leaves, bright yellow spurred flowers in spring, 1 foot tall, Zones 5–8.

Corydalis lutea

grown or bare-root plants in spring, spacing 1 foot apart. Divide every other year in spring or fall.
Special Care: Performs poorly if allowed to dry out. Shear off faded flowers to encourage reblooming.
Pests and Diseases: Mildew in shade.
Climate: Zones 4–8.
Cultivars: 'Nana,' 6 inches tall; 'Alba,' very pale pink (not white) petals, yellow centers.
Garden Use: Lovely as foreground planting or path edging. Combines well with blue flowers.

Coreopsis verticillata
THREADLEAF COREOPSIS

One of the easiest and longest blooming perennials for sunny gardens, threadleaf coreopsis blooms from midsummer into fall. Leaves are indeed divided into threadlike segments, cloaking upright stems that form wide-spreading, bushy plants. The 2-inch-wide daisylike flowers have narrow, bright yellow petals and small, dark yellow centers, covering plants with sunny stars for an engaging, fine-textured effect.

Size: 2 to 3 feet tall; spreads rapidly by rhizomes to 3 or more feet wide.
Light: Full sun best; tolerates light shade.
Soil and Moisture: Average to sandy, infertile soil; moderate moisture. Drought tolerant.
Planting and Propagation: Plant container-grown or bare-root plants in spring, spacing 1½ feet apart. Divide every few years in spring or fall.
Special Care: Shear off faded flowers when blooms become sparse to encourage another flush of flowers. May be invasive in fertile, moist soil. Late to emerge in spring.
Pests and Diseases: May be nibbled on by rabbits; otherwise pest free.
Climate: Zones 3–9.
Cultivars: 'Zagreb,' golden yellow flowers, 1¼-foot-tall dwarf; 'Golden Showers,' 2½-inch bright golden yellow flowers, 2 to 3 feet tall, long blooming; 'Moonbeam,' very popular hybrid with pastel yellow flowers, long blooming, 1½ feet tall.
Garden Use: Wonderful for providing fine texture contrast to bolder flowers and foliage. 'Moonbeam' combines well with almost any other flower color. Dried stems look pretty in winter garden.

Garden Use: Tuck into crevices of rock walls, peaking from stones in rock garden, or between pavers in patio or walkway. Also performs well in informal gardens and naturalistic woodland gardens.

Crambe cordifolia
COLEWORT

A giant among perennials, this cabbage-family ornamental brings drama to the garden when it blooms in early summer. The heart-shaped, blue-green leaves, which measure up to 2 feet long, have wavy edges and are covered with stiff hairs. Leaves form a dramatic basal rosette and climb sparsely up the flowering stems. Reaching up to 6 feet tall, the many-branched, pale green flowering stem forms a huge, lacy cloud of tiny white flowers reminiscent of a jumbo baby's breath. Flowers have a bad odor when smelled up close.

Size: 6 feet tall and 4 feet wide when in bloom; foliage clumps to 3 feet tall.

Crambe cordifolia

Light: Full sun.

Soil and Moisture: Average to fertile, deep, well-drained, alkaline soil; keep moist.

Planting and Propagation: Plant container-grown plants or seedlings in spring, spacing 3 feet apart. This long-lived perennial forms a woody rootstock and a single clump that doesn't need dividing.

Special Care: Stake flowering stalk to keep it upright. Cut off faded flower stalks to prevent seeding.

Pests and Diseases: Leaves often marred by caterpillars, aphids, and other cabbage-family pests; pesticide program helpful.

Climate: Zones 6–9.

Similar Species: *C. maritima* (sea kale), white flowers on 2-foot stems in early summer, silvery green, waxy, edible leaves. Sandy soil best; tolerates seashore conditions.

Garden Use: Allow plenty of growing space. Flowers form a fine-textured veil through which bolder plants can be seen.

Cynara cardunculus
CARDOON

Resembling a beautiful thistle, cardoon features deeply dissected, silvery gray-green, prickly leaves with woolly white hairs on the undersides. Lower leaves may be 3 feet long and form an attractive, fountainlike, basal clump. Smaller leaves climb up the flower stalks. Flowering stems arise in summer, featuring solitary purple thistlelike flowers on branched stems that open from artichokelike buds.

Size: 6 feet tall in bloom; 3 feet wide.

Light: Full sun in most areas; afternoon shade in hottest areas.

Soil and Moisture: Fertile, deep, well-drained soil; drought tolerant, but benefits from occasional deep watering.

Planting and Propagation: Plant container-grown plants in spring, spacing 3 feet apart. Divide in spring.

Special Care: Provide winter mulch in coldest zones.

Cynara cardunculus

Pests and Diseases: Slugs, snails, and aphids troublesome.

Climate: Zones 6–8; thrives on heat.

Cultivars: Only species is usually sold.

Garden Use: A dramatic plant for architectural contrast it makes with fine-textured and darker-foliage plants.

Delosperma cooperi
HARDY ICEPLANT

Of the many species of iceplants that hail from the Mediterranean, only two are cold-hardy enough to be widely useful in North American gardens. This rapidly spreading ground-covering perennial has low, creeping stems that root as they go, making them excellent erosion-control plants on a slope. Fleshy and succulent, the bright green leaves store so much water that the plants make an excellent fire-retardant planting, but the main attraction is the spectacular flowers. The 4-inch-wide, many-petaled blossoms appear in plant-smothering numbers from mid- to late summer. The satiny, rosy-purple petals surround prominent creamy yellow centers and literally glisten in the sun.

Delosperma congestum nubigenum

Size: 5 inches tall; spreads to 2 feet wide.

Light: Full sun in most areas; afternoon shade in desert climates.

Soil and Moisture: Average to sandy, well-drained soil. Allow to dry between waterings; very drought tolerant once established.

Planting and Propagation: Plant container-grown plants or rooted cuttings in spring, spacing 1½ feet apart. Take cuttings in spring, summer, or fall.

Special Care: Care free.

Pests and Diseases: Fungus diseases if given too much water.

Climate: Zones 6–10.

Similar Species: *D. congestum nubigenum*, similar with yellow flowers; 'Alba,' white flowers, Zones 4–10.

Garden Use: Excellent in rock gardens, in seashore gardens, and as small-scale ground cover or erosion control for low-water-use landscapes.

Delphinium x *elatum*
DELPHINIUM

One of the most glamorous—and finicky—perennials to grace English gardens, delphiniums bring striking tall spires of flowers to summer borders where the climate suits and gardeners are willing to fuss with them. The rewards are worth it when the dramatic blossoms begin to unfold at the bottoms of the spires. Flowers are rounded in outline and spurred; often a central small ring of petals rests among the outer petals, creating a so-called "bee" in a contrasting color. The boldly cut, maplelike leaves form handsome dark green clumps that send up several spikes so densely crowded with blossoms that they may topple from their own weight if not staked. Classic delphiniums grow as high as 7 feet, but shorter strains are easier to grow and more durable during foul weather. Colors are cool: alluring shades of true blue, lavender, purple, pink, white, and bicolored, including pastels and intensely saturated hues. Plants are usually short-lived, surviving five years in the Pacific Northwest and Northeast and only two or three years elsewhere.

Size: 3 to 7 feet tall; 1 to 3 feet wide, depending on cultivar.

Light: Full sun in most climates; light shade in hottest areas, where adapted.

Soil and Moisture: Fertile, deep, alkaline soil rich in organic matter; keep evenly moist with ample water.

Planting and Propagation: Plant container-grown plants in spring, taking care to place crown at soil level because planting too deeply causes crown rot. Space tall types 3 feet apart. Divide every other year for best longevity, or take cuttings from basal growth in spring. Easily grown from commercial seed. In areas with hot summers or mild winters, plant in fall and remove after flowering finishes in summer.

Special Care: Thin young plants to three shoots when 6 inches tall, mature plants to four or five shoots. Tall types must be individually staked, beginning when 1 foot tall, to prevent brittle stems from breaking. Plant in location sheltered from wind. Fertilize monthly during bloom season. Mulch heavily to keep soil cool. For repeat blooms, cut spent flower spikes just below lowest blossom; when new growth is 6 inches tall, remove spent flower stalk at ground.

Pests and Diseases: Slugs, snails, mites, and mildew very troublesome; regular pest control program advisable.

Climate: Zones 2–7. Best where summers are moist and cool to warm—not hot—and winters are cold.

Cultivars and Similar Species: Mid-Century Hybrids, mildew resistant, 4 to 5 feet tall: 'Ivory Towers,' white; 'Moody Blues,' light blue; 'Rose Future,' pink; 'Ultra Violet,' dark blue-violet; 'Magic Fountains,' mixed colors, dwarf to 3 feet tall. Pacific Hybrids, 4 to 5 feet tall, huge single to semidouble flowers: 'Black Knight,' deep violet with black eye; 'Astolat,' lavender to pink with dark eye; 'Blue Bird,' mid-blue with white eye; 'Galahad,' all white; 'Summer Skies,' sky blue with white eye. Blackmore and Langdon hybrids, mixed colors with extremely large flower spikes. Connecticut Yankee strain, heavily branched, 2½ to 3½ feet tall, similar to *D.* x *belladonna*; 'Blue Fountains,' blue, white, or mauve, Zones 3–8. *D.* x *belladonna* (belladonna delphinium): 2 to 3 feet tall,

Delphinium x *elatum* 'Blue Springs'

branched stems with central branch blooming first, many cultivars. *D. grandiflorum* (Chinese delphinium): finely divided leaves, 1 to 2 feet tall, loose spires of blue, violet, or white single spurred flowers, Zones 3–7; 'Blue Butterfly,' vivid deep blue, 1 foot tall, long blooming; 'Album,' white.

Garden Use: Elegant and almost essential in back of formal gardens. Also traditional along fences in cottage gardens. Combines well with iris, peonies, daylilies, Shasta daisies, and lilies.

Dianthus barbatus
SWEET WILLIAM

This old-fashioned cottage garden flower is a biennial or short-lived perennial, sometimes treated as an annual because it blooms so quickly from seed. Like other members of the pinks family, sweet William bears flowers with fringed petals and contrasting eyes. Unlike other members, however, the flowers are only lightly scented. They are borne in large, flat-topped clusters atop bushy plants with 3-inch-long, lance-shaped, glossy dark green leaves. The bloom season lasts from early summer to midsummer. Flower colors include shades of pink, red, purple, white, and multicolors. Sweet William self-sows prolifically, but it may not come true to type.

Size: 1 to 1½ feet tall; 1 foot wide.

Light: Full sun in most areas; some afternoon shade helpful in the South.

Soil and Moisture: Rich, well-drained, alkaline soil; plentiful moisture.

Planting and Propagation: Plant container-grown plants in spring, spacing 1 foot apart. Divide every two or three years, or take cuttings in spring to maintain a selected cultivar.

Special Care: Add lime to the soil where soil is neutral or acid. Remove flowering stems at ground level after flowers fade to reduce self-seeding and promote possible repeat bloom. Short-lived in the North; long-lived in the South.

Pests and Diseases: Usually pest free.

Dianthus barbatus

Climate: Zones 3–9; longest-lived with cool summers and mild winters.

Cultivars: 'Newport Pink,' rich coral-pink; 'Blood Red,' darkest red, 1¼ feet tall; 'Homeland,' deep red; 'Scarlet Beauty,' scarlet; 'Pink Beauty,' soft pink; 'White Beauty,' white; 'Indian Carpet,' mixed colors, 10 inches tall, often grown as annual.

Garden Use: Mass-plant in formal gardens. Scatter about cottage garden and allow to self-sow. Long-lasting cut flower.

Dianthus deltoides
MAIDEN PINK

These charming plants produce a blanket of lightly scented ¾-inch flowers with sharp-tooth ("pinked") petals in such profusion that they totally obscure the foliage. The flowers bloom on branched stems for two months in spring and early summer, reblooming if sheared. Cultivars are available as named selections or mixed seed strains in shades of pink, magenta-red, and white, all marked with a crimson ring in the flower's center. The grasslike 4- to 6-inch-long green leaves grow on creeping stems that form a thick evergreen mat. Leaves take on a rosy flush during cool weather.

Size: Foliage 6 inches tall; spreads to 2-foot-wide mats. Flower stalks 8 inches to 1 foot in height.

Dianthus deltoides

Light: Full sun to light or half shade.

Soil and Moisture: Average to sandy, alkaline soil; moderate moisture.

Planting and Propagation: Plant container-grown plants in spring, spacing 1½ feet apart. Divide in early spring if plants aren't too woody; better to propagate by stem cuttings broken at a node after blooming ceases.

Special Care: Self-sows and may be a bit weedy in tidy gardens. Shear back drastically in early spring before growth starts. Shear after flowering to prevent seeding, for neatness, and to promote rebloom. To keep center of mat from dying out, sift sand into middle of plant in spring and fall. Cover with evergreen boughs in winter in coldest areas. Apply lime in spring if soil is not alkaline.

Pests and Diseases: Red spider mites sometimes troublesome during hot, dry summers. Crown rot or root rot common if grown too wet. Rabbits may eat plants.

Climate: Zones 3–9; performs well in the South.

Cultivars and Similar Species: 'Zing,' bright scarlet; 'Zing Rose,' rose-red, 6 inches tall; 'Albus,' white, 6 inches tall; 'Brilliant,' bright rose-pink, single, 4 inches tall.

Garden Use: Excellent ground cover in rock garden, along path, or between pavers in patio. Plant in wall crevices or as garden edging. Combine with old garden roses.

Dianthus gratianopolitanus
CHEDDAR PINK

Named after the Cheddar Gorge in England, where the plant is native, this delightfully fragrant pink forms a tussock of stiff, linear, gray-green, evergreen leaves. The single, 1-inch-wide, pink to rose flowers have enchanting fringed petals and bearded throats and are richly scented with a sweet, spicy, clove fragrance. Blossoms appear in profusion from spring to late summer if they are regularly deadheaded, but do not rebloom later in the summer even if sheared.

Size: Flower stems 6 to 10 inches tall above mat of foliage that spreads to 1 foot.

Light: Full sun in most areas; light shade in hottest regions.

Soil and Moisture: Average to sandy, well-drained, alkaline soil; moderate moisture.

Planting and Propagation: Plant container-grown plants in spring, spacing 1½ feet apart. Rejuvenate plantings that begin to lose vigor by taking stem cuttings in spring. Division not recommended.

Special Care: May rot in winter-wet soil; top-dress with pea gravel. Remove flowers as they fade, snapping off stems or shearing at nodes to promote reblooming. Cover with

Dianthus gratianopolitanus

evergreen boughs in winter in coldest areas. Apply lime in spring if soil is not alkaline.

Pests and Diseases: Red spider mites sometimes troublesome during hot, dry summers. Crown rot or root rot common if grown too wet. Rabbits may eat plants.

Climate: Zones 3–9; best with cool to mild summers.

Cultivars: 'Bath's Pink,' soft pink with red eye; 'Flore-plena,' double, light pink; 'Tiny Rubies,' double, light crimson-pink, 4 inches tall; 'Rose Queen,' double, bright rose, 6 inches tall; 'Petite,' single, light-pink, 4 inches tall; 'Little Boy Blue,' frilled white flower with rose specks, intense blue foliage.

Garden Use: Perfect rock garden plant where it forms tussocks of flowers and foliage nestled against side of large rock. Plant in foreground of well-drained formal border or edge path where growing conditions are right.

Dianthus plumarius
COTTAGE PINK

The petals of the cottage pinks are deeply fringed or plumed—rather than "pinked"—inspiring their botanical name. A beloved cottage garden flower, this pink is extremely fragrant, possessing an intense, spicy, clove perfume. Flowers are borne in pairs or clusters on wiry stems and may be single, semidouble, or double, in pink, rose, magenta, or white, often with a contrasting eye. Blooming is in late spring and early summer, and sporadically until frost if deadheaded. The extremely narrow, 1- to 4-inch-long, gray-green leaves have conspicuous veins. Plants form a mat that grows into a wide, loose hummock.

Size: Foliage 6 inches tall; flower stalks to 2 feet tall. Spreads to form 1-foot-wide mat.

Light: Full sun.

Soil and Moisture: Humus-rich, well-drained, alkaline soil; moderate moisture.

Planting and Propagation: Plant container-

Dianthus plumarius

grown plants in spring, spacing 10 inches apart. Divide every two or three years in late summer by cutting back plants, separating into sections, and replanting deeply. May also take cuttings in summer.

Special Care: Shear back drastically in early spring before growth starts and again after flowering to prevent seeding, for neatness, and to promote rebloom. Apply lime in spring if soil is not alkaline.

Pests and Diseases: Red spider mites sometimes troublesome during hot, dry summers. Crown rot or root rot common if grown too wet; may rot in winter-wet soil. Rabbits may eat plants.

Climate: Zones 3–9.

Cultivars and Similar Species: 'Essex Witch,' semidouble, range of pink, white, or salmon; 'Spring Beauty,' double, mixed pink, rose, salmon, white. *D.* x *allwoodii* (hybrid of *D. plumarius* and *D. caryophyllus*), looser and taller blue-gray mat, bears flowers in pairs, scented, flowers less deeply fringed, reblooms if sheared.

Garden Use: Rock and cottage garden favorite; also lovely as edging in informal border.

Dicentra eximia
FRINGED BLEEDING HEART

Native to forest floors from New York to Georgia, this beguiling wildflower decorates shady gardens from early spring through fall with pink flowers and gray-green foliage. The fernlike leaves form a vase-shaped clump from which arise graceful upright stems with dangling 1-inch-long heart-shaped blossoms. Unlike many spring-blooming woodland flowers, fringed bleeding heart does not die to the ground by summer but remains attractive until frost. As long as conditions are cool and soil is moist, flower stalks appear sporadically throughout summer and more profusely in fall, especially so with the hybrids.

Size: 9 inches to 1½ feet tall; 1¼ feet wide.
Light: Light to full shade.
Soil and Moisture: Humus-rich, well-drained, moist soil; even moisture.
Planting and Propagation: Plant container-grown plants in spring, spacing 1 foot apart. Divide clumps every three years in fall.
Special Care: Self-sows prolifically, but flower colors may not come true to type; easy to weed out or transplant as desired.
Pests and Diseases: May rot in winter-wet soil.

Dicentra x 'Luxuriant'

Climate: Zones 3–9.
Cultivars and Similar Species: 'Alba,' milky white flowers, light green leaves, less vigorous, to 1 foot tall. *D. formosa* (western bleeding heart): similar appearance but spreads by rhizomes, blooming begins in mid-spring, more drought tolerant, less tolerant of heat and humidity. Sometimes attributed to *D. eximia*: 'Zestful,' deep rose; 'Sweetheart,' snow-white; 'Bountiful,' soft rosy-red flowers, fine-cut blue-green leaves; 'Adrian Bloom,' ruby-red. Hybrids: 'Luxuriant,' deep rose-pink flowers (not red as advertised), 1¼ feet tall, blue-green leaves, very floriferous, Zones 3–7; 'Snowdrift,' pure white, 1¼ feet tall. *D. cucullaria* (Dutchman's Breeches): white flowers and blue-green foliage, dies to ground by summer.
Garden Use: Beautiful in shade gardens and woodland gardens combined with ferns, hostas, and wildflowers such as creeping phlox, sweet woodruff, and violets.

Dicentra spectabilis
COMMON BLEEDING HEART

Often called old-fashioned bleeding heart, this plant was collected in China and introduced in 1842 to gardeners in England, where it immediately became popular. One of the earliest perennials to bloom, bleeding heart blossoms begin in mid-spring and continue for four or more weeks into early summer, accompanying tulips and spring-flowering trees and shrubs. Its arching sprays are strung with dancing white-tipped pink hearts laced through the large clumps of boldly cut, ferny green foliage. Practically foolproof to grow—as long as it has light shade and moist soil—this long-lived perennial from grandmother's garden returns year after year to create a magnificent spring show. Plants usually go dormant during summer after hot weather arrives but may remain green all summer in cool, moist climates.
Size: 2 to 3 feet tall; 3½ feet wide.

Dicentra spectabilis

Light: Light shade best; tolerates full sun if kept moist.
Soil and Moisture: Humus-rich, fertile, well-drained, moist soil; plentiful water.
Planting and Propagation: Plant dormant roots or container-grown plants in spring, spacing 2 to 3 feet apart. Division not necessary. Propagate from cuttings.
Special Care: Drought encourages dormancy; mulch soil to keep cool and moist to prolong summer foliage.
Pests and Diseases: Sometimes aphids.
Climate: Zones 2–9.
Cultivars: 'Alba,' pure white, less vigorous, pale green leaves; 'Pantaloons,' pure white, more vigorous than 'Alba.'
Garden Use: Magnificent in cottage gardens and formal borders. Combine with low ferns or hostas, which will fill in bare spots left when plants go dormant. Charming cut flower.

Dictamnus albus
GAS PLANT

Said to give off an ignitable gas when its roots are dug up, gas plant also has volatile oils in its foliage, flowers, and seeds. The lemon-scented oil is most noticeable when the leaves are crushed. This stately, long-lived perennial slowly grows to form an impressive clump of handsome divided foliage and elegant spires of snowy white, pink, or mauve-purple flowers. Glossy dark green leaves are divided into 2-inch-long, toothed leaflets covered with pretty translucent dots. The irregular-shaped flowers are 1 inch long with long, decorative stamens and appear in dense racemes for two weeks in early summer. The star-shaped seedpods that follow are attractive, but they burst open to fling seeds all over the garden; they are perhaps best cut for dried arrangements.

Size: 3 to 4 feet tall; 3 feet wide.

Light: Full sun to light shade.

Soil and Moisture: Fertile, heavy, moist soil best; moderate moisture. Somewhat drought tolerant once established.

Planting and Propagation: Plant bare-root or container-grown plants in spring, spacing 3 feet apart. Division unnecessary and usually unsuccessful. Propagate by gathering seeds and sowing immediately outdoors in nursery bed for erratic germination the next spring and summer.

Dictamnus albus 'Purpureus'

Special Care: Needs no staking because stem bases are woody and strong. Do not disturb roots. Slow to establish and bloom; gets better every year. Foliage may cause rash.

Pests and Diseases: Usually pest free.

Climate: Zones 3–8; best where cool.

Cultivars: *D. albus* 'Purpureus,' mauve-purple flowers with dark-veined petals. 'Rubra': lavender-pink flowers with dark veins.

Garden Use: Plant as specimen plant in border or cottage garden.

Digitalis grandiflora
YELLOW FOXGLOVE

A woodland plant from Greece, yellow foxglove brings soft pastel blossoms to the late spring and early summer garden. Flower spikes are 1 foot long and studded along one

Digitalis grandiflora

side with pendant, brown-speckled, tubular yellow flowers. Leaves are hairy and form basal clumps beneath flower stems.

Size: 2 to 3 feet tall; 2-foot-wide clumps.

Light: Part to light shade.

Soil and Moisture: Fertile, humus rich, acid soil; plentiful moisture.

Planting and Propagation: Plant container-grown plants in spring, spacing 2 to 3 feet apart. Divide every two or three years, in early spring.

Special Care: May rebloom if faded spikes are cut back before seeds set. Division improves longevity.

Pests and Diseases: Mildew and leaf spot may be troublesome in hot, humid areas.

Climate: Zones 3–8.

Similar Species: *D. lutea,* small creamy yellow flowers in narrow spikes, glossy leaves, 2 feet tall, self-sows readily.

Garden Use: Makes an attractive soft yellow accent in woodland and shade gardens. Combines well with blue flowers of Siberian bugloss and blue-eyed Mary.

Digitalis purpurea
FOXGLOVE

A tall biennial or short-lived perennial from grandmother's garden, foxglove self-sows to perpetuate itself year after year. Pendulous, 1- to 2-inch-long, trumpet-shaped blossoms borne on spectacular one-sided spikes begin opening from the bottom of the spike upward in late spring to early summer, lasting for about four weeks. Flowers are lavender with spotted throats in the species, but white or shades of pink, lavender, purple, or yellow in the cultivars. Leaves are downy, forming large basal rosettes and climbing partway up the flower stalks.

Size: 2 to 5 feet tall when in bloom.

Light: Part shade best.

Soil and Moisture: Fertile, humus-rich, moist, acid soil; plentiful moisture.

Planting and Propagation: Plant container-grown plants in spring, spacing 1 foot apart.

Sow seeds in summer for next year's bloom.

Special Care: Do not allow to dry out. Cut off stalks of ripened seedpods and shake out seeds where new plants are desired, or allow to self-sow. May need individual stakes.

Pests and Diseases: Sometimes troubled by powdery mildew, aphids, mealy bugs, and Japanese beetles.

Climate: Zones 4–9.

Cultivars and Similar Species: 'Alba,' ivory-white; 'Apricot Beauty,' apricot-orange; 'Excelsior Hybrids,' flowers borne all around spike in pastel shades of pink, mauve, yellow, and white, 4 to 5 feet tall. 'Foxy,' mixed colors, 2½ feet tall, flowers first year from seed. *D.* x *mertonensis* (strawberry foxglove), rose-pink flowers, 3 to 4 feet tall, short-lived, Zones 3–8.

Garden Use: Lovely massed for vertical effect in borders and in cottage and shade gardens.

Digitalis purpurea

Doronicum caucasicum

Doronicum caucasicum (D. orientale)
LEOPARD'S BANE

There are few yellow flowers that bloom in spring, but this one makes a stunning show when tulips and dogwoods bloom in early to mid-spring. The bright green, heart-shaped, toothed leaves emerge in early spring, forming a clumplike mat from which arise stems of bright yellow daisies. Numerous narrow petals surround a central, golden yellow disk. The plants die back in summer when hot weather arrives but may resprout and rebloom in fall in areas with long, mild autumns.

Size: 1 to 2 feet tall; creeps by underground rhizomes to form wide mats.

Light: Full sun to light shade in cool climates; light to part shade in hot climates.

Soil and Moisture: Humus-rich, well-drained, moist soil; plentiful moisture.

Planting and Propagation: Plant container-grown plants in spring, spacing 1½ feet apart. Divide plants every three years during dormancy in early spring or late summer to prevent dead centers.

Special Care: Keep mulched to protect shallow roots. Do not allow to dry out, even dur-

ing dormancy. Deadheading prolongs bloom. Clean up dead leaves in midsummer.

Pests and Diseases: Usually trouble free.

Climate: Zones 4–7; short lived in warm zones.

Cultivars and Similar Species: 'Magnificum,' 2-inch flowers, 2½ feet tall; 'Spring Beauty,' double flowers, 1 foot tall.

Garden Use: Naturalize in shade garden combined with bluebells and trillium; include ferns, hostas, and astilbes to fill in after plants go dormant. Do not plant annuals, which disturb the shallow roots. Good cut flower.

Echinacea purpurea
PURPLE CONEFLOWER

This long blooming prairie wildflower is closely related to rudbeckia, the orange coneflower, which it resembles in shape but not color. Its big daisylike flowers consist of broad purplish pink, mauve, or white somewhat reflexed petals that can grow to 4 inches long, surrounding a raised rusty-orange center for a startling color combination. Flowers bloom profusely on branched stems in midsummer and sporadically until frost. The rough-textured, arrow-shaped, dark green leaves measure 4 to 8 inches long and cloak upright stems.

Size: 2 to 4 feet tall; 2 feet wide.

Light: Full sun best; tolerates part to light shade.

Soil and Moisture: Average to infertile, well-drained soil; moderate moisture. Drought tolerant.

Planting and Propagation: Plant dormant roots or container-grown plants in spring, spacing 2 feet apart. Divide in spring or fall every four years if needed.

Special Care: Allow flowers to dry into seed heads, which look attractive standing through winter. Do not fertilize. Needs staking only in rich, moist soil.

Pests and Diseases: Japanese beetles and caterpillars sometimes troublesome.

Echinacea purpurea

Climate: Zones 3–8.

Cultivars and Similar Species: 'Magnus,' deep rose-mauve, broad, horizontal petals, 3 feet tall; 'Bright Star,' large old-rose-color petals, maroon centers, 3 to 4 feet tall; 'Bravado,' extra-large mauve-pink flowers, horizontal petals, 2 feet tall; 'Crimson Star,' crimson, 2 feet tall; 'White Swan,' creamy white, 2½ feet tall; 'White Luster,' large pure white, orange centers, 3 feet tall. *E. pallida* (pale coneflower): 4- to 6-inch flowers with spidery pale mauve drooping petals. *E. tennesseensis* (Tennessee coneflower): endangered species, linear leaves, upturned dark mauve petals, greenish pink centers.

Garden Use: Its orange center allows this cool-colored flower to combine well with yellow and orange flowers, with which it otherwise might clash. Use in midground of formal and informal plantings. Naturalize in meadow and butterfly gardens. Combine with ornamental grasses in New American-style landscapes.

Echinops ritro
GLOBE-THISTLE

Unusual both in color and shape, globe-thistle makes quite a statement in mid- and late summer when its perfectly round metallic blue flowers bloom. Bees visit the flowers on sunny days and moths flock to them at night because they contain a sweet nectar. The leaves are attractive, too—thistlelike: dull green on top, spiny, and with silvery white undersides. Globe-thistle looks especially striking combined with white flowers such as garden phlox, boltonia, aster, and white coneflower.

Size: 2 to 4 feet tall; 2½ feet wide.

Light: Full sun best; tolerates part shade.

Soil and Moisture: Average to poor, well-drained soil; best with moderate water, but tolerates drought.

Planting and Propagation: Plant container-grown plants in spring, spacing 2 feet apart. Division not needed for at least three years.

Special Care: May need staking in rich soil. Cut back hard after first flowering for second flush. To dry flower heads, cut before individual flowers open and hang upside down.

Pests and Diseases: Usually pest free.

Climate: Zones 3–8; tolerates heat.

Cultivars: 'Taplow Blue,' soft silvery blue;

Echinops ritro 'Taplow Blue'

'Veitch's Blue,' numerous small darker violet-blue globes, 2 to 3 feet tall; 'Taplow Purple,' rich violet-blue, 3 feet tall.

Garden Use: Plant in groups in formal garden. Excellent dried flower.

Epimedium x *youngianum*
BARRENWORT, BISHOP'S HATS

Grown more for its striking foliage than for its dainty flowers, this ground-covering plant thrives in conditions that daunt many other perennials. The arrow-shaped, toothed, olive-green leaves grow on wiry stems that emerge directly from the ground. Foliage is red-tinged when young, turning deep crimson in fall. Evergreen in warm climates and semi-evergreen in colder areas, the leaves look attractive in winter even if they turn brown. Sprays of nodding ¾-inch pale lavender or white flowers create a delicate effect in early to mid-spring. Some species have spurred flowers resembling tiny columbines; the flowers on this species are not spurred.

Size: 6 to 8 inches tall; 8 inches wide.

Light: Light to full shade.

Soil and Moisture: Best in fertile, humus-rich, moist soil, but established plants tolerate poor, dry soil in full shade.

Planting and Propagation: Plant bare-root

Epimedium x *youngianum* 'Roseum'

or container-grown plants in spring, spacing 1 foot apart. Divide in spring or fall.

Special Care: Cut back foliage in very early spring, especially if winter-tattered, to encourage new growth and reveal flowers.

Pests and Diseases: Usually problem free.

Climate: Zones 5–8.

Cultivars and Similar Species: 'Niveum,' white; 'Roseum,' lavender-pink. *E. grandiflorum:* 1-inch oval leaves, pink-and-white flowers with long spurs; 'Rose Queen,' large, bright pink. *E. pinnatum:* hairy leaves, yellow flowers with brown spurs. *E.* x *versicolor* 'Sulphureum': red-mottled young leaves turning green, yellow spurred flowers, very drought tolerant. *E.* x *rubrum:* red-tinged, heart-shaped new leaves turning green, crimson spurred flowers

Garden Use: Effective edging for beds and borders or along walk or path. Use in shade or woodland garden combined with ferns and flowering perennials. Use as ground cover beneath trees and shrubs.

Erigeron x *hybridus* (*E. speciosus*)
FLEABANE

This roadside wildflower has been gussied up for the garden, where it produces upright, well-branched plants with 6-inch-long basal leaves and small stem-clasping leaves that climb up the flowering stalks. Held in clusters above the foliage, the lavender-blue, pink, or white asterlike flowers feature a multitude of threadlike petals surrounding greenish yellow centers in midsummer.

Size: 2½ feet tall; 2 feet wide.

Light: Full sun.

Soil and Moisture: Average to poor, well-drained soil; moderate moisture.

Planting and Propagation: Plant container-grown plants in spring, spacing 2 feet apart. Divide in fall every two or three years.

Special Care: Do not fertilize; becomes weedy in rich soil. Deadhead to prolong bloom. May need twiggy support. Cut back

Erigeron x *hybridus* 'Darkest of All'

after flowering to rejuvenate foliage and prevent weedy self-sowing.

Pests and Diseases: Powdery mildew and aphids sometimes troublesome.

Climate: Zones 2–8; flowers longest with cool to mild summers.

Cultivars and Similar Species: 'Azure Blue,' light blue; 'Azure Fairy,' lavender; 'Darkest of All,' violet-blue; 'Quakeress,' light mauve-pink; 'Quakeress White,' off-white; 'Pink Jewel,' pink; 'Prosperity,' almost double, mauve-blue.

Garden Use: Best in naturalistic or cottage gardens.

Eryngium amethystinum
AMETHYST SEA HOLLY

Stiff and prickly with spiny blue flower heads, sea hollies add architectural interest and color contrast to a garden. Several species are popular, but the amethyst sea holly is the most cold hardy and very showy. Tall-branched flowering stems, which may be blue, arise from a cluster of basal foliage. This is the only sea holly with spiny, pinnately compound leaves. The flowers are showy

Eryngium amethystinum

from midsummer to frost and look rather like thimbles framed by a starlike ring of steely blue bracts.

Size: 1½ to 2 feet tall; 2 feet wide.

Light: Full sun.

Soil and Moisture: Poor, dry, sandy soil; tolerates drought and seashore conditions.

Planting and Propagation: Plant container-grown plants in spring, spacing 2 feet apart. Separate plantlets from plant base in fall.

Special Care: Resents transplanting. May flop in fertile soil. Pick flowers for drying when fully open for best color retention.

Pests and Diseases: May rot in winter-wet site. Sooty mold may disfigure flowers if humidity is high; improve air circulation.

Climate: Zones 2–8.

Cultivars and Similar Species: *E. giganteum,* 4 to 6 feet tall, silvery all over, a biennial that dies after flowering but self-seeds; 'Miss Willmott's Ghost,' nearly white bracts. *E. alpinum:* very blue pineapple-shaped flowers with finely divided soft bracts, heart-shaped lower leaves, palmately lobed upper leaves, Zones 4–8; 'Amethyst,' metallic blue, 3 feet tall; 'Opal,' metallic blue, 2 feet tall; 'Superbum,' dark blue flowers, 2 to 3 feet tall. *E. bourgatii:* compact, white-veined,

237

spiny palmate silvery foliage, blue-green flowers with long, spiny bracts, Zones 4–8.

Garden Use: Striking plant in beds and borders where adapted. Beautiful against dark background and when backlit. Good fresh-cut or dried flower.

Eupatorium coelestinum
MIST FLOWER, HARDY AGERATUM

A welcome sight in autumn when it produces its lavender-blue flowers, mist flower provides a cooling note to autumn's otherwise hot color scheme. The dense 4-inch heads of misty flowers resemble a looser, taller version of the popular annual ageratum. Leaves are triangular and coarsely toothed on leggy, upright, mahogany-color stems.

Size: 2 to 3 feet tall; spreads by stolons into large stands.

Light: Full sun to light shade.

Soil and Moisture: Average to fertile, moist soil; moderate moisture.

Planting and Propagation: Plant container-grown plants in spring or fall, spacing 1½ feet apart. Divide every two to four years.

Special Care: Emerges in late spring; be cautious not to uproot. Spreads aggressively in

Eupatorium coelestinum

fertile, moist site; may need yearly weeding to contain. Cut back once or twice in summer to promote compactness and tidier nature. May need staking. Mulch well.

Pests and Diseases: Powdery mildew and aphids sometimes troublesome.

Climate: Zones 6–10.

Cultivars: 'Alba,' white; 'Cori,' bright clear blue; 'Wayside Variety,' dwarf to 1¼ feet tall, crinkled leaves.

Garden Use: Best in informal or naturalistic gardens because of tendency to roam and flop.

Eupatorium fistulosum
JOE-PYE WEED

Stunning in size, form, and color, this architectural beauty is a late-summer to fall-blooming wildflower native to moist meadows. Better known as a garden plant in England than here in its homeland, Joe-Pye weed deserves wider planting in large-scale gardens. The handsome, coarsely serrated, foot-long leaves are glossy dark green and arranged in whorls. The stout, upright stems are hollow with purple nodes. Numerous tiny reddish purple flowers make up dramatic rounded compound inflorescences that measure 1½ feet across. The cultivar makes an arresting sight from spring through fall.

Size: 4 to 7 feet tall; 3 feet wide.

Light: Full sun.

Soil and Moisture: Fertile, deep soil; plentiful moisture. Tolerates boggy site.

Planting and Propagation: Plant container-grown plants in spring, spacing 3 feet apart. Division not necessary for years.

Special Care: Pinching in early summer controls height but reduces flower size.

Pests and Diseases: Usually pest free.

Climate: Zones 4–8; may perform poorly in the South.

Cultivars and Similar Species: 'Atropurpureum,' purple flowers, leaves, and stems; 'Gateway,' 5 feet tall, large, rounded, dark mauve flower heads; 'Bartered Bride,' pure

Eupatorium fistulosum 'Gateway'

white. *E. maculatum* (spotted Joe-Pye weed): almost identical but with flatter, denser flower heads. *E. purpureum* (name often erroneously used for plants that actually are *E. fistulosum*): light purple flowers, unspotted blue-green stems, shade loving, Zones 4–8.

Garden Use: Use in large-scale borders, bog and butterfly gardens, and naturalistic and New American-style landscapes.

Euphorbia epithymoides (E. polychroma)
CUSHION SPURGE

Creating symmetrical dense mounds of pale green leaves topped with an electrifying display of chartreuse flowerlike bracts, cushion spurge brings sunshine to the spring garden. Because the bracts hold their color, the show lasts from spring well into summer with an encore of deep red foliage in autumn. Cushion spurge rates as one of the longest-lived and easiest-to-care-for perennials.

Size: 1 to 1½ feet tall and wide.

Light: Full sun in the North; afternoon shade in the South.

Soil and Moisture: Average to sandy, well-drained soil. Even moisture best, but tolerates drought.

Euphorbia epithymoides

Planting and Propagation: Plant container-grown plants in spring, spacing 2 feet apart. Take cuttings after flowering, removing flowering tips. Divide only when mature plants become leggy or floppy.

Special Care: Plant sap may cause rash. May be invasive in moist soil.

Pests and Diseases: Usually pest free.

Climate: Zones 4–8.

Similar Species: *E. palustris*, 3 feet tall, yellow-green bracts. *E. myrsinites:* resembles a succulent with silvery gray leaves arranged spirally around creeping stems, yellow bracts, Zones 5–9.

Garden Use: Use in foreground of formal beds and borders.

Filipendula rubra
QUEEN-OF-THE-PRAIRIE

This magnificent plant produces fluffy foot-tall panicles of tiny, rich pink to peach flowers from early summer to midsummer. Cut into jagged dark green leaflets, the handsome foliage resembles astilbe, to which it is related. A tall, strong-stemmed plant, queen-of-the-prairie is a North American wildflower native to moist meadows and prairies.

Size: 6 to 8 feet tall; 4 feet wide.

Light: Full sun, if kept wet, to part shade.

Soil and Moisture: Deep, fertile, moist soil; plentiful moisture. Tolerates boggy conditions.

Planting and Propagation: Plant container-grown plants in spring, spacing 3 feet apart. Divide tough rootstocks in spring.

Special Care: Rarely needs staking. Cut off faded flowers.

Pests and Diseases: Spider mites and mildew troublesome if soil is too dry.

Climate: Zones 3 to 9; best in areas with cool, moist summers.

Cultivars and Similar Species: 'Venusta,' deep carmine-pink flowers, 4 feet tall; 'Venusta Alba,' white. *F. palmata:* pale pink flattened flower heads, palmately lobed leaves with white hairy undersides, Zones 3–8. *F. hexapetala* (*F. vulgaris*): creamy white flattened inflorescences, carrotlike leaves, 2 to 3 feet tall, tolerates drier soil, Zones 3–8; 'Flore-pleno,' double flowered and showier. *F. ulmaria* (queen-of-the-meadow): creamy white, leaves with white, hairy undersides, 3 to 6 feet tall, Zones 3–9.

Garden Use: Back-of-border plant for large-scale gardens; naturalize in moist meadow or along stream.

Filipendula rubra

Gaillardia x *grandiflora*

Gaillardia x grandiflora
BLANKET-FLOWER

From early summer to mid-fall, blanket-flower brightens gardens with its 3-inch-wide, single or semidouble, daisylike flowers, which are banded with bright colors like an Indian blanket. Rounded, dark burgundy or russet centers surrounded by two-toned, gold-and-maroon petals with jagged notches at their tips provide eye-catching, hot color impact. Leaves are 6 inches long, gray-green, and toothed, somewhat resembling dandelion foliage. A hybrid between an annual and a perennial species, blanket-flower compensates for its long blooming season by living for only two or three years.

Size: 2 to 3 feet tall; 2 feet wide.

Light: Full sun.

Soil and Moisture: Fertile, sandy, well-drained soil. Tolerates seashore conditions. Allow to dry between waterings; drought tolerant.

Planting and Propagation: Plant container-grown plants in spring, spacing 1½ feet apart. Divide in spring, replanting root sections that show new growth. Self-sown seeds may not come true. Take stem cuttings in summer.

Special Care: Deadhead plants to prolong blooming.

Pests and Diseases: Sometimes powdery mildew and leaf hoppers. Crown rot if too wet. Root rot in winter in heavy soil.

Climate: Zones 2–10; heat tolerant.

Cultivars and Similar Species: 'Goblin,' 4-inch flowers with yellow-edged red petals, dwarf to 1 foot tall; 'Golden Goblin,' pale yellow, 1 foot tall; 'Baby Cole,' 3-inch flowers with yellow petals banded with red, dwarf to 8 inches tall; 'Burgundy,' solid wine-red; 'Aurea Pura' and 'The Sun,' solid golden yellow; 'Monarch Mix,' seed-grown, variable mix of solids and bicolors. *G. aristata:* one of its parents, less showy but longer lived; use in naturalistic gardens and meadow plantings.

Garden Use: Cottage and informal gardens. Gaillardia's bicolored blossoms are difficult to combine with other flowers. Best coupled with other hot color flowers or their pastel versions.

Galium odoratum
SWEET WOODRUFF

This rapidly spreading ground-covering herb makes a lovely carpet of fine-textured, bright green foliage and tiny, starlike white flowers. Blossoms appear for about a month in spring, making a perfect backdrop for bulbs and woodland wildflowers, which will grow right through it. The narrow leaves are arranged in whorls around the low, upright stems, for a pretty swirled effect that contrasts perfectly with bolder foliage. Deciduous in cold climates, sweet woodruff hangs onto its hay-scented leaves through winter in the warmest parts of its range.

Size: 4 to 9 inches tall; spreads to cover large areas by underground runners.

Light: Light to dense shade.

Soil and Moisture: Fertile, humus-rich, moist soil best; less rapid spreading in poor or heavy soil. Keep moist.

Planting and Propagation: Plant roots or container-grown plants in spring, spacing 1½ or more feet apart. Divide by cutting mat into sections in spring or fall.

Galium odoratum

Special Care: Prevent from invading lawn with an edging or lawn border.

Pests and Diseases: Usually pest free.

Climate: Zones 4–8.

Cultivars: Only species is sold.

Garden Use: Excellent ground cover for shade and woodland gardens and mixed borders; plant beneath shrubs and taller shade-loving perennials such as hostas, ferns, and astilbes.

Gaura lindheimeri
WHITE GAURA

An airy plant for creating a veil of flowers to soften a bold design, gaura is only recently gaining recognition in American gardens. Native to Louisiana, Texas, and Mexico, gaura has long been loved in British gardens for its loose, open wands of flowers, which bloom well above the foliage. Individual blossoms, which are 1 inch wide and made up of four clawed petals, open a few at a time from the bottom of the wiry stems upward. The stems elongate all season—each plant produces 10 to 12 stalks—and produces a continual crop of flowers from late

spring until a hard freeze. Flowers open white but fade to pink. Willowlike gray-green leaves are held close to the stems and may turn dramatically red in late autumn.

Size: 3 to 4 feet tall; 3 feet wide.

Light: Full sun to part shade.

Soil and Moisture: Deep, sandy, well-drained soil; tolerates clay if well-drained. Even moisture best, but plants are very drought tolerant.

Planting and Propagation: Plant container-grown plants in spring, spacing 2½ feet apart. Forms deep taproot; division difficult and rarely needed.

Special Care: May sprawl in fertile, moist soil. Self-seeds to point of weediness. Cut back, if desired, in midsummer to control size and promote new flowering.

Pests and Diseases: Usually pest free.

Climate: Zones 5–9; tolerates heat of the South and Southwest. In cool areas may not begin blooming until late summer.

Cultivars: 'Whirling Butterflies,' to 3 feet tall; does not set seed.

Garden Use: Despite its height, use near front of border to create soft see-through effect. Wonderful in informal and naturalistic gardens.

Gaura lindheimeri

Gentiana asclepiadea
WILLOW GENTIAN

This graceful European wildflower from the Caucasus Mountains brings lovely true blue flowers to shady gardens in summer and autumn. Slender arching stems feature pairs of willowlike leaves with prominent veins. Flowering begins in late summer in the leaf axils near the middle of the plant and progresses upward, blooming into fall. The 2-inch-long electric blue flowers are bell-shaped with purple-spotted throats.

Size: 1 to 3 feet tall; 1 to 2 feet wide.
Light: Light to full shade.
Soil and Moisture: Fertile, humus-rich, moist, acid soil; constant plentiful moisture.
Planting and Propagation: Plant container-grown plants in spring, spacing 1½ feet apart. Resents division; best done in early spring. Take stem cuttings from nonflowering stems.
Special Care: Mulch heavily.
Pests and Diseases: Rust can sometimes be a problem.
Climate: Zones 5–7; best with cool summers.
Cultivars and Similar Species: 'Alba,' pure white. *G. septemfida lagodechiana:* Asian wildflower, low-growing, 2-inch, lacy-edged, deep blue flowers with white throats in clusters, for rock gardens, sun tolerant, Zones 3–8. *G. andrewsii* (bottle gentian): flask-shaped blue flowers in late summer and fall, native to moist North American meadows, Zones 3–8.
Garden Use: Plant in groups in shade gardens and woodland settings. Combines well with ferns and hostas.

Geranium sanguineum
BLOODY CRANESBILL,
HARDY GERANIUM

Modest looking but useful hardy geraniums are foolproof to grow. With handsome leaves and pretty flowers, this diverse group—they are relatives of the bedding geranium—can solve many problems by weaving between

Gentiana asclepiadea

more flamboyant plants. Bloody cranesbill, with its dark-veined, magenta flowers, is perhaps the brightest of the cranesbills, but its softer-colored cultivars are easier to combine with other flowers. It forms low mounds of deeply divided, hairy leaves, which turn red in fall, and its 2-inch-wide, open-faced, five-petaled flowers bloom all summer.

Size: 1 foot tall in bloom; spreads aggressively as ground cover.
Light: Full sun to light shade; afternoon shade in the South.
Soil and Moisture: Average to fertile, moist soil; tolerates dry shade.
Planting and Propagation: Plant bare-root or container-grown plants in spring, spacing 2 to 3 feet apart for ground cover. Divide in spring or fall when desired.
Special Care: Invasive; locate thoughtfully. Cut back foliage in midsummer if floppy; fresh leaves will grow.
Pests and Diseases: Usually pest free.
Climate: Zones 3–8.

Geranium sanguineum

Cultivars and Similar Species: 'Album,' pure white; 'Purple Flame,' purple; *G. s. striatum* (*G. s. lancastriense*) prostrate, pale pink, dark-veined flowers, blooms summer and fall. *G. endressii* 'Wargrave Pink': salmon-pink notched petals, flowers all summer, shiny divided leaves, 1½ feet tall. *G. himalayense:* large violet-blue flowers with red-purple veins and centers, foliage deeply divided, turns red in fall, 1¼ feet tall; 'Johnson's Blue,' hybrid with clear blue flowers. *G. pratense:* dark violet-blue flowers with reddish veins, 3 feet tall; 'Mrs. Kendall Clarke,' pale blue flowers with rosy veins; 'Silver Queen,' silvery blue flowers. *G. platypetalum:* purple-blue flowers, velvety leaves, 2 feet tall.
Garden Use: Use clump-forming cranesbills in flower borders, spreading types as ground covers. Bloody cranesbill too invasive for formal borders but lovely as companion to old roses, shrubs, or perennials in mixed border. Mass-plant as ground cover under high-branched trees.

241

Geum quellyon

Geum quellyon (G. chiloense)
GEUM, CHILEAN AVENS

For hot colors in early summer, nothing puts on a better show than geum's red, scarlet, orange, or yellow flowers. The ruffly, 1-inch-wide flowers, which may be single, double, or semidouble, are carried in open clusters on wiry stems above a dense rosette of deeply cut, hairy, evergreen leaves, creating an airy effect.

Size: 2 feet tall in bloom; 1½ feet wide.
Light: Full sun where summers are cool; afternoon shade where hot.
Soil and Moisture: Fertile, humus-rich, well-drained, moist soil; moderate moisture.
Planting and Propagation: Plant container-grown plants in spring, spacing 1 foot apart. Divide annually in fall to extend longevity.
Special Care: Rots in winter-wet or poorly drained soil. Usually short-lived. Self-sown seedlings may or may not come true, depending on cultivar.
Pests and Diseases: Occasionally spider mites troublesome.
Climate: Zones 5–7; does poorly in heat and humidity of the South.
Cultivars: 'Lady Strathedon,' double yellow; 'Mrs. Bradshaw,' double red; 'Borisii,' bright orange; 'Fire Opal,' semidouble orange-red; 'Red Wings,' semidouble, dark red; 'Starker's Magnificent,' double, apricot-orange.
Garden Use: Plant in foreground despite height because of airy, see-through nature. Combines well with blue and purple flowers.

Gypsophila paniculata
BABY'S BREATH

Just as baby's breath makes an invaluable lacy filler between large flowers in floral arrangements, it can be used to create a delicate cloudlike effect in flower gardens. Blooming from early summer to midsummer, the huge branched panicles contain about a thousand minuscule white flowers. The narrow, gray-green leaves that decorate the stems beneath the flowers further add to the softened effect.

Size: 3 to 4 feet tall and wide.
Light: Full sun.
Soil and Moisture: Fertile, well-drained, alkaline soil. Best kept moist; tolerates drought.
Planting and Propagation: Plant container-grown plants in spring, spacing 3 feet apart, and setting graft union 1 inch below soil level. Take cuttings after flowering; large, fleshy root resents disturbance.
Special Care: Cut back immediately after

Gypsophila paniculata 'Compacta Plena'

blooming to encourage fall bloom. Staking needed to hold up flower-laden stems. Apply lime annually to acid soils.
Pests and Diseases: Usually pest free.
Climate: Zones 3–9.
Cultivars and Similar Species: 'Bristol Fairy,' white, 2½ feet tall; 'Pink Fairy,' double pink, 1½ feet tall; 'Pink Star,' large double pink, 1½ feet tall; 'Perfecta,' white, individual flowers twice as large, 4 feet tall; 'Compacta Plena,' double flowers, dwarf to 1½ feet tall. *G. repens:* trailing plant, pink or white spring and summer flowers, for rock gardens; 'Alba,' white; 'Rosea,' pale pink.
Garden Use: Use in midground of border to create veil around bolder plants. Essential in cutting garden.

Hedyotis caerulea (Houstonia caerulea)
BLUETS, QUAKER LADIES

This delightful little wildflower forms delicate-looking tufts of foliage topped with masses of small, cross-shaped flowers that turn their pretty faces toward the sky. The ½-inch, four-petaled blossoms are pale blue, violet, or white with yellow centers and are held on slender stems adorned with pairs of tiny, narrow, dark green leaves. Blossoming begins in mid-spring and often continues on through summer. Bluets tend to form clumps created from self-seeding and spreading roots.

Size: 6 to 8 inches tall; 10 inches wide.
Light: Part to light shade.
Soil and Moisture: Average to fertile, well-drained, moist, acid soil; moderate moisture.
Planting and Propagation: Plant container-grown plants in spring, spacing 8 inches apart, or sow seed in fall for spring bloom. Divide in early spring when crowded.
Special Care: Self-seeds and easily invades lawns and tidy gardens.
Pests and Diseases: Pest free.
Climate: Zones 4–8.
Cultivars: Only species is sold.

Hedyotis caerulea

Garden Use: Suited only for naturalistic areas where self-sowing is welcome; plant in meadow garden or wildflower lawn, in woodland under high-branched trees, or along stream or pond.

Helenium autumnale
SNEEZEWEED

A native of moist meadows, this American wildflower got its common name because it was used as a snuff substitute. The abundant 2-inch, hot color flowers bloom on tall, bushy plants, beginning in midsummer and continuing for two months. Petals are wedge-shaped with notched ends that curve down and away from the domed central disk. Colors include clear yellow petals with matching centers, or shades of orange, red, and mahogany with contrasting dark centers. The lance-shaped leaves have winged bases and clasp sturdy, winged stems.

Size: 5 feet tall; 3 feet wide.

Light: Full sun.

Soil and Moisture: Average to heavy, infertile, moist to wet soil; best with plentiful moisture, but tolerates some drought.

Planting and Propagation: Plant container-grown plants in spring, spacing 3 feet apart. Divide every year or two in early spring.

Special Care: Pinch in late spring to reduce height and delay flowering. Keep moist or may lose lower leaves. Needs staking only if grown in fertile soil. Cut back after flowering. Do not overfertilize.

Pests and Diseases: Occasionally troubled by rust or leaf spots.

Climate: Zones 3–8; grows weak and lanky in heat and humidity.

Cultivars: 'Moerheim Beauty,' rusty orange-red petals, brown centers, 3 to 4 feet tall; 'Butterpat,' yellow; 'Rubrum,' mahogany brown; 'Wyndley,' coppery brown, 3 feet tall; 'Brilliant,' deep rusty-scarlet, 3 feet tall; 'Sunball,' yellow with green centers, heavy flowering, 4 feet tall; 'Red-gold Hybrids,' mixed copper, red, gold, and yellow.

Garden Use: Plant in groups in middle to back of beds and borders; naturalize in moist meadow plantings.

Helianthus angustifolius
FALL SUNFLOWER, SWAMP SUNFLOWER

Tall, loose, and a bit rangy, this perennial sunflower brings bold splashes of bright yellow to the late-fall garden, blooming even through a light frost. Fall sunflower produces spectacular clusters of 3-inch, single yellow daisies with brown or purple centers at the tops of tall, many-branched stems. Cultivars offer showy semidouble or double blossoms. Leaves of this species are less coarse looking than most, being narrower and 8 inches to 1 foot long.

Size: 4 to 8 feet tall; 3 to 4 feet wide.

Light: Full sun best; tolerates part shade.

Soil and Moisture: Fertile, moist, well-drained soil; even moisture.

Planting and Propagation: Plant divisions or container-grown plants in spring, spacing 4 feet apart. Divide every two or three years.

Special Care: Fertilize lightly to encourage flowering but not enough to stimulate invasive tendencies. Tall types may need staking, especially in part shade where they will grow even taller. Invasive if not divided often.

Helenium autumnale

Helianthus x *multiflorus* 'Loddon Gold'

Pests and Diseases: Mildew sometimes troublesome.

Climate: Zones 6–9; performs well in the South.

Cultivars and Similar Species: *H.* x *multiflorus*, toothed coarse leaves, yellow-centered blossoms in late summer, 4 to 7 feet tall, Zones 4–8; 'Loddon Gold,' 4-inch deep gold pompon flowers, 4 to 5 feet tall; 'Flore-Plena,' double, bright yellow, resembles chrysanthemum flowers.

Garden Use: Back-of-border plant for cottage gardens and formal borders. Naturalize in meadow plantings and with ornamental grasses in New American-style gardens.

243

Heliopsis helianthoides scabra
FALSE SUNFLOWER

Closely resembling sunflowers, *Heliopsis* bears daisylike flowers with yellow-orange ray petals surrounding greenish yellow or brownish yellow disks throughout summer. The sandpapery, dark green leaves are arrow- to heart-shaped with serrated edges on shrublike plants that are much bushier than *Helianthus*. Plants spread to form extensive clumps.

Size: 2 to 4 feet tall; 2 feet wide.

Light: Full sun to part shade.

Soil and Moisture: Average to fertile, well-drained soil; somewhat drought tolerant but best if watered during dry spells.

Planting and Propagation: Plant container-grown plants in spring, spacing 3 feet apart. Divide every two to three years. Take cuttings in spring or summer.

Special Care: Needs staking. Cut back after flowering.

Pests and Diseases: Usually trouble free.

Climate: Zones 3–9; performs well in the South.

Heliopsis helianthoides scabra 'Summer Sun'

Helleborus orientalis

Cultivars: 'Golden Plume,' fully double, deep yellow flowers, 3½ feet tall; 'Gold Green-heart,' double row of yellow petals and emerald green centers, 3 feet tall; 'Summer Sun,' semidouble, bright gold, 3 feet tall; 'Light of Loddon,' double, bright golden yellow, 3 feet tall; 'Karat,' single, golden orange, 4 to 5 feet tall.

Garden Use: Bright summer color in beds and borders; combines well with ornamental grasses in New American-style gardens.

Helleborus orientalis
LENTEN ROSE

This delightful plant is a must-have because it blooms in late winter, seeming to push up through the melting snow. A tuft of showy yellow-tipped stamens decorates the nodding, buttercuplike, pure-white, rose, or maroon flowers. Blossoms, which are sometimes spotted, stay good-looking into late spring because the petals are actually bracts that remain colorful as seeds ripen. The foot-wide, deeply divided, leathery leaves are evergreen and make attractive stands throughout the year.

Size: Foliage clumps 1½ feet tall; 2 feet wide.

Light: Light to full shade during growing season and in winter.

Soil and Moisture: Fertile, humus-rich, moist, well-drained soil; plentiful moisture.

Planting and Propagation: Plant container-

Hemerocallis 'Chicago Braves'

grown plants in spring, spacing 2 feet apart. Self-sows readily.

Special Care: Cut off winter-tattered foliage to show off flowers better. Easy to grow if soil and light are right.

Pests and Diseases: Usually problem free.

Climate: Zones 4–9.

Cultivars and Similar Species: *H. niger* (Christmas rose), winter-blooming, pure-white flowers age to rose, Zones 3–8. *H. foetidus* (stinking hellebore): apple-green flowers, only roots smell bad, Zones 5–9.

Garden Use: Excellent year-round plant for shade gardens.

Hemerocallis hybrids
DAYLILY

These indispensable, easy-to-grow perennials are the mainstay of many gardens. Extensive breeding has brought about hundreds of cultivars in a range of sizes, colors, and flower shapes, as well as four- to six-week blooming seasons beginning anytime from early summer to fall. Some cultivars even re-bloom. Daylily's strap-shaped, bright green leaves emerge in early spring. The flowers are truly amazing—huge trumpet-shaped affairs in every color except blue and true white and sporting long, curving stamens. Throats are often a contrasting color such as light green or creamy yellow, and petals may be prettily ruffled. Individual flowers last only a day, but each flower scape produces numerous blossoms.

Size: Foliage clumps 1 to 3 feet tall; flower stalks 1 to 5 feet tall, depending on cultivar.
Light: Full sun to half shade.
Soil and Moisture: Tolerates almost any soil, but best in fertile site. Drought tolerant once established, but best with plentiful moisture.
Planting and Propagation: Plant tuberous roots or container-grown plants in spring, spacing 2 feet apart. Divide in spring every three to five years.
Special Care: Remove faded flowers daily if not self-cleaning for best appearance. Cut off flower stalks after flowering ceases.
Pests and Diseases: Usually trouble free
Climate: Zones 3–9.
Cultivars and Similar Species: Cultivars are too numerous to list. Rebloomers include: 'Stella de Oro,' orange-yellow, 1½ feet tall; 'Happy Returns,' pastel lemon-yellow, 1½ feet tall; 'Country Club,' pink with green throat, 1½ feet tall; 'Diamond Anniversary,' peach-pink, 3 feet tall; 'Haunting Melody,' fuchsia-rose, ruffled, 3 feet tall; 'Jenny Sue,' pale peach, ruffled, 2 feet tall; 'Paul Bunyan,' light gold, 3½ feet tall. *H. fulva* (tawny daylily): orange flowers, European wildflower naturalized in North America.
Garden Use: Plant in groups in beds and borders, and for erosion control on banks.

Hesperis matronalis
DAME'S ROCKET, SWEET ROCKET

This fragrant, old-fashioned biennial or short-lived perennial reseeds itself delightfully around the garden. Four-petaled, rose-pink, pink, or white flowers form large, phloxlike heads beginning in late spring or early summer and continuing for a month or more. Their damask-rose scent is most noticeable in the early evening. Leaves are broadly lance-shaped and borne on stout stems.
Size: 2 to 3 feet tall; 1½ feet wide.

Hesperis matronalis

Light: Sun to light shade; shade needed in the South.
Soil and Moisture: Humus-rich, fertile, well-drained, moist soil; moderate moisture.
Planting and Propagation: Sow seeds in spring for flowers the next year, or plant nursery starts, spacing 2 feet apart. Take stem cuttings to increase favorite colors.
Special Care: Remove faded flowers before seeds set to encourage more flowers. Plants decline after flowering; allow some to set seeds, then cut back.
Pests and Diseases: Aphids sometimes troublesome.
Climate: Zones 3–8.
Cultivars: 'Alba,' white.
Garden Use: Excellent in cottage gardens and naturalistic plantings; combine with annuals to fill in midsummer gaps. Naturalize under high-branched trees where soil is moist.

Heuchera micrantha 'Palace Purple'
PURPLE-LEAF CORALBELLS

An evergreen foliage plant par excellence, 'Palace Purple' produces magnificent clumps of heavily veined, maplelike, bronze-purple leaves with purplish rose undersides. When backlit or struck by the low rays of the sun, the foliage glimmers like sparkling garnets. Even when lit from the front, this plant makes a spectacular color statement. Flowers

are tiny white affairs held in airy clusters on wiry stems and are of little consequence.
Size: Foliage clumps 1 foot tall and 1½ feet wide; flower stalks to 1½ feet high.
Light: Full sun to light or part shade; afternoon shade needed in hot areas.
Soil and Moisture: Fertile, humus-rich, acid, well-drained soil; even moisture. Somewhat drought tolerant once established. Performs poorly in clay.
Planting and Propagation: Plant container-grown plants in spring, spacing 1 foot apart. Divide every three or four years in spring or fall. Take stem cuttings in summer. Remove winter-tattered foliage in early spring.
Special Care: Leaves may bleach if sun is too strong. Most purple in spring and fall.
Pests and Diseases: Usually pest free.
Climate: Zones 4–8.
Cultivars and Similar Species: Seed-grown plants vary in color; select cutting-propagated plants or individual plants for best color. *H. americana* 'Garnet': bright red foliage in spring, soft green in summer, dull red in winter, ground cover, heat tolerant.
Garden Use: Edging in formal and informal gardens; excellent texture and color contrasts with gray leaves and gravel paths. Combines well with pink, blue, and lavender flowers for cool effect; shocking used with hot colors such as yellow and orange.

Heuchera micrantha 'Palace Purple'

Heuchera sanguinea
CORALBELLS

Grown for its charming flowers and neat clumps of evergreen foliage, coralbells deserves a spot in most gardens. The loose, airy clusters of ½-inch-long, bell-shaped blossoms rise on wiry stems held above clumps of rounded, gray-mottled leaves with scalloped lobes. Blossoms appear for one to two months beginning in early spring.

Size: Foliage clumps 8 inches high and 1 foot wide; flower stalks 10 inches to 1 foot tall.

Light: Full sun in the North; partial shade in the South.

Soil and Moisture: Humus-rich, very well-drained, neutral to slightly alkaline soil; moderate moisture.

Planting and Propagation: Plant bare-root or container-grown plants in spring, spacing 1 foot apart. Divide in early spring every three years or take stem cuttings in late fall.

Special Care: Remove flower stalks as they fade to encourage further blooming. Apply lime annually where soil is acid. Dig up and reset plants with leggy, woody bases protruding from the ground.

Heuchera sanguinea 'Bressingham Hybrids'

246

Pests and Diseases: Usually pest free.

Climate: Zones 3–8.

Cultivars and Similar Species: Named varieties are usually hybrids attributed indiscriminately to *H. sanguinea* or *H.* x *brizoides,* which has profuse ⅛-inch flowers, rounded lobed foliage, flower stems to 2 feet tall; 'Pretty Polly,' pale pink; 'Freedom,' rose-pink; 'Coral Cloud,' coral-pink; 'June Bride,' pure white, profuse; 'Matin Bells,' red; 'Chatterbox,' deep rose-pink. 'Bressingham Hybrids,' seed-grown large-flowered mix; 'Cherry Splash,' cherry red flowers, white-and-gold-splashed leaves. x *Heucherella tiarelloides* (foamy bells): excellent ground cover with mottled, heart-shaped, shallow-lobed leaves, wiry stems of pinkish flowers in spring and fall, Zones 3–8, needs shade; 'Bridget Bloom,' shell-pink, long blooming.

Garden Use: Elegant edging for formal gardens; lovely in clusters in shade garden.

Hibiscus moscheutos (*H. palustris*)
ROSE MALLOW, SWAMP MALLOW

Rose mallow's startlingly large saucer-shaped flowers measure 6 inches to 1 foot across

Hibiscus moscheutos 'Disco Belle'

and are made up of red, pink, or white petals that are crinkled like tissue paper. Blossoms form in clusters at the tops of tall plants beginning in late summer and continuing until frost. The 8-inch, broadly oval leaves are dark green on top with downy white undersides. Native to marshy areas in eastern North America, rose mallow adapts to moist gardens, forming long-lived clumps that do not spread.

Size: 5 to 8 feet tall.

Light: Full sun to light shade.

Soil and Moisture: Fertile, humus-rich, moist to wet soil; constant moisture.

Planting and Propagation: Plant container-grown plants in spring, spacing 3 feet apart, or sow seed in spring. Division not necessary, but divide in spring if desired.

Special Care: Moisture availability influences height. Needs no staking. Emerges late in spring; avoid digging up.

Pests and Diseases: Japanese beetle and aphid often troublesome.

Climate: Zones 5–9.

Cultivars: 'Southern Belle' series, 10-inch-wide pink, red, or white blossoms, 4 to 6 feet tall; 'Anne Arundel,' 9-inch pink flowers. 'Lady Baltimore,' pink with red centers, 4 feet tall; 'Lord Baltimore,' 10-inch red flowers, 4 to 6 feet tall.

Garden Use: Excellent for damp or wet spots in borders or naturalized in bog garden or along stream. Plant in groups.

Hosta species and hybrids
HOSTA

These spectacular foliage plants feature leaves that are often heavily veined or puckered, ranging in color from emerald-green to frosty blue-gray to golden yellow and may be variegated in all kinds of patterns. The leaves arise directly from the ground, forming lush clumps that vary in size from diminutive dwarfs to knee-high giants. Although many types produce lovely spikes of lilylike lavender, purple, or white flowers in mid- or late

Hosta 'Gold Edger'

summer, their foliage alone is enough to satisfy discerning gardeners—hostas with bright variegations or yellow-green foliage are as eye-catching as flowers and their effect lasts the entire growing season.

Size: 6 inches to 3 feet tall and wide, depending on cultivar.

Light: Light to full shade best. In general, green hostas prefer light to half shade; gold and variegated types, light to three-quarters shade; and blues, light to half or full shade.

Soil and Moisture: Deep, fertile, humus-rich, moist soil and plentiful moisture best, but tolerates average conditions. Some types tolerate dry shade.

Planting and Propagation: Plant bare-root or container-grown plants in spring, spacing 1 to 3 feet apart, depending on cultivar. Needs no division, but mature clumps may be divided in spring.

Special Care: Cut off faded flower spikes.

Pests and Diseases: Slugs and snails very troublesome; monthly control program usually recommended. Some types slug resistant.

Climate: Zones 3–9.

Cultivars and Similar Species: Hundreds of wonderful cultivars available; too numerous to list.

Garden Use: Plant in groups and as speci-

Iberis sempervirens

mens in shade and woodland gardens. Combines well with fine-textured plants such as ferns and astilbes. Use dwarf types as edging or border plantings in formal and informal gardens and large types as specimens.

Iberis sempervirens
EDGING CANDYTUFT

For two months beginning in early spring, rounded, 1-inch-wide clusters of bright white flowers cover the entire plant, transforming it into a snowy mound. Even out of bloom, edging candytuft is a winner—its evergreen leaves, which are arranged in whorls around procumbent stems, make attractive hills of dark green foliage.

Size: 9 inches to 1 foot tall; 1½ feet wide.

Light: Full to half sun.

Soil and Moisture: Average, well-drained, neutral to alkaline soil; moderate moisture.

Planting and Propagation: Plant container-grown plants in spring, spacing 6 inches to 1 foot apart. Needs no division. Take stem cuttings in summer.

Special Care: Cut back by one-third after flowering to keep plants compact and tidy; cut back by two-thirds every few years to reduce woodiness and promote new growth.

Pests and Diseases: Clubroot may be trou-

blesome.

Climate: Zones 3–9.

Cultivars: 'Autumn Snow,' blooms in spring and again in autumn, 9 inches tall; 'Snowflake,' large leaves and flowers, 7 to 8 inches tall, later blooming; 'Purity,' white, 8 inches tall; 'Little Gem,' 6 inches tall; 'Alexander's White,' early blooming, 10 inches tall.

Garden Use: Forms attractive mounds in rock gardens and walls. Use compact forms as edging for formal borders. Combines well with tulips.

Iris cristata
CRESTED IRIS

This native wildflower makes a graceful sight when its small, sweetly fragrant, blue, lavender, or white irises with yellow crests bloom in mid-spring. Low sword-shaped leaves provide a subtle vertical accent the rest of the growing season. Crested iris spreads by creeping rhizomes to form a dense ground cover.

Size: 4 to 8 inches tall; spreads to 1¼ feet.

Light: Part to heavy shade; full sun in constantly moist soil.

Iris cristata

Soil and Moisture: Neutral, humus-rich soil; even moisture.

Planting and Propagation: Plant rhizomes or container-grown plants in spring, spacing 1¼ feet apart. Divide in early fall if desired.

Special Care: Division not needed if given plenty of room to spread.

Pests and Diseases: Slugs often troublesome.

Climate: Zones 3–9.

Cultivars: *I. c. alba*, white flowers; 'Shenandoah Sky,' light blue; 'Abbey's Violet,' deep violet-blue with prominent white and yellow crests.

Garden Use: Plant in large drifts in woodland or shade garden.

Iris ensata (Iris kaempferi)
JAPANESE IRIS

This elegant iris features blossoms that resemble flying birds and blooms later than other iris, usually displaying its huge, flat flowers in midsummer. Blossoms may be white, blue, purple, reddish purple, or lavender pink with yellow crests and often are beautifully marbled or veined with a contrasting color. Leaves grow broad and sword-shaped to 2 feet long with a prominent midrib.

Size: 2½ to 4 feet tall; 2 feet wide.

Light: Full sun to part shade.

Soil and Moisture: Humus-rich, acid, moist to wet soil; plentiful water. Enjoys standing water and boggy conditions.

Planting and Propagation: Plant rhizomes 1 inch deep, or plant container-grown plants in spring, spacing 6 inches apart. Divide in fall every three or four years.

Special Care: Do not allow soil to dry. Will not tolerate alkaline soil. Remove individual flowers as they fade.

Pests and Diseases: Thrips may infest flowers; otherwise pest free.

Climate: Zones 4–9; performs poorly where hot and dry.

Iris ensata

Cultivars and Similar Species: Numerous cultivars. 'Eleanor Parry,' reddish purple; 'Gold Bound,' pure white with gold bands; 'Ise,' palest blue with deep purple-blue veins; 'Nikko,' pale purple with purple veins, 2½ feet tall; 'Pink Frost,' light pink; 'Kagari Bi,' rose-pink with silver veins; 'Moriah,' deep blue veined white; 'Royal Banner,' burgundy; 'Emotion,' white with blue edge. Same growing conditions: *I. versicolor* (blue flag): blue iris-shaped blossoms on similar plants, native plant. *I. pseudacorus* (yellow flag): yellow iris-shaped blossoms with brown veins.

Garden Use: Magnificent in naturalistic gardens along streams and ponds; also works well in formal situations.

Iris hybrida
BEARDED IRIS

Stalks of sumptuous iris flowers brighten borders from spring to midsummer with their lightly fragrant, showy blossoms, which come in every color of the rainbow. New reblooming types produce flowers again in fall. The elegant flowers consist of three, upright, arching petals, called standards, rising above three reflexed petals, called falls. A stripe of dense, yellow hairs creates a beard down the centers of the falls. The broad, sword-shaped, gray-green or bright green leaves grow in flat fans and make a bold contrast to the usual forms of foliage found in the garden. Bearded iris are classified as miniature, dwarf, intermediate, and tall.

Size: 6 inches to 4 feet tall; 10 inches to 2 feet wide.

Light: Full sun.

Soil and Moisture: Fertile, well-drained, alkaline soil; moderate moisture. Drought tolerant once established.

Planting and Propagation: Plant bare-root rhizomes half buried in soil in spring, or plant container-grown plants, spacing 10 inches to 2 feet apart depending on cultivar. Divide every four years in mid- to late summer (fall in mild climates) by pulling apart and cutting rhizome clumps into healthy segments with one leaf fan apiece and cutting back leaves to one-third.

Special Care: Carefully remove individual flowers as they fade; cut back flower scapes after flowering finishes. Tall types may need

Iris hybrida

individual staking. Do not cover rhizomes with mulch; keep free of debris.

Pests and Diseases: Soft rot troublesome in heavy soil; remove yellowing leaves as soon as noticed to prevent spread. Iris borers can be serious; do not leave old leaves to over-winter.

Climate: Zones 3–10.

Cultivars: Thousands of cultivars are available. Bearded irises usually are classified as miniature (4 to 10 inches tall), dwarf (10 inches to 1¼ feet tall), intermediate (1¼ to 2⅓ feet tall), and tall (more than 2⅓ feet tall). Dwarf types bloom in mid- and late spring, intermediate types in late spring and early summer, and tall types in early summer and midsummer. *I. pumila* sometimes used as name for dwarf types.

Garden Use: Use dwarf types in foreground of beds and borders, taller types in mid-ground. Best planted in clusters of a single color.

Iris siberica
SIBERIAN IRIS

More delicate looking than the bearded iris, Siberian iris blooms in late spring or early summer, opening its graceful, beardless, yellow-crested blossoms in succession over several weeks. Flowers may be purple, blue, lilac, or white. The narrow, lancelike leaves form graceful, vase-shaped clumps that make a soft, vertical statement among other plants.

Size: 2 feet tall and wide.

Light: Full sun to light shade.

Soil and Moisture: Humus-rich, slightly acid, moist to wet or boggy soil; plentiful moisture.

Planting and Propagation: Plant rhizomes 1 inch deep, or plant container-grown plants in spring, spacing 2 feet apart. Rarely needs division.

Special Care: Needs no staking. Remove flower stalks before seeds set.

Pests and Diseases: Long lived and usually pest free.

Climate: Zones 3–9; best iris for the South.

Cultivars: Numerous cultivars. 'Caesar,' deep blue-purple; 'Caesar's Brother,' deep purple; 'Cambridge,' pale blue; 'Pembina,' deep blue; 'Snow Queen,' pure white; 'Papillon,' light blue; 'Perry's Blue,' medium blue; 'Sparkling Rose,' rose-wine; 'Illini-charm,' light wine-lilac; 'Silver Edge,' sky blue with silver edge; 'Blue Moon,' violet-blue; 'Butter and Sugar,' hybrid, yellow-and-white flowers.

Garden Use: Excellent in borders, informal settings, and bog gardens.

Kniphofia uvaria
RED-HOT POKER, TORCHLILY

For creating an exotic tropical look and vertical accent in a hot color border, nothing beats red-hot poker. The gray green evergreen leaves are 2 to 3 feet long, sharp-pointed, and form thick, fountainlike clumps. Bottlebrush spikes of flowers rise above the clumps, blooming over a long period from late spring through late summer, depending on the cultivar. The red buds open from the bottom up into yellow, orange, or bicolored

Iris siberica

Kniphofia uvaria

tubular flowers.

Size: 3 to 5 feet tall; 4 feet wide.

Light: Full sun in most areas; afternoon shade in hot, dry climates.

Soil and Moisture: Fertile to average, well-drained soil; moderate moisture. Drought tolerant.

Planting and Propagation: Rarely needs division, but small plants may be removed from edges of main clump.

Special Care: May become unsightly after flowers pass; cut foliage back by half to improve appearance.

Pests and Diseases: May rot in winter if crown becomes waterlogged; tie leaves over crown in winter to exclude water in coldest climates.

Climate: Zones 5–9; tolerates heat and drought.

Cultivars and Similar Species: Late summer to fall: 'Corallina,' coral-red; 'Pfitzeri,' deep orange; 'Primrose Beauty,' bright yellow; 'Springtime,' red flowers at top, white below. All summer: 'Little Maid,' creamy white, 20 inches tall; 'Citrina,' lemon-yellow; 'Royal Castle,' yellow and orange.

Garden Use: Looks best in borders or naturalistic large-scale rock gardens.

Lamium maculatum 'Beacon Silver'

Lamium maculatum
SPOTTED DEAD NETTLE

The foliage of this vigorous, sprawling ground cover provides months of shade-brightening color. The species features green, heart-shaped, scallop-edged leaves striped with white down their centers. Cultivars are showier, displaying large silver blotches or an overall golden color. From mid-spring through summer, whorls of rosy lavender or white hooded flowers bloom above the leaves on short spikes.

Size: 8 inches to 1 foot tall; spreads to 1½ feet.

Light: Full to part shade.

Soil and Moisture: Average to humus-rich, moist soil; plentiful moisture best, especially in sunny spots. Tolerates dry shade.

Planting and Propagation: Plant bare-root or container-grown plants in spring, spacing 1 to 2 feet apart. Divide in fall. Take stem cuttings in summer.

Special Care: Cut back in midsummer if plants become straggly. May smother small woodland flowers.

Pests and Diseases: Slugs and leaf spot or root rot sometimes troublesome. Bare spots result if plants repeatedly dry out.

250

Climate: Zones 3–8.

Cultivars and Similar Species: 'Chequers,' resembles the species with white-striped leaves; 'White Nancy,' white flowers, silver leaves edged green; 'Beacon Silver,' rose-lavender flowers, silver leaves edged green; 'Pink Pewter,' pale pink flowers, silvery leaves; 'Shell Pink,' pale pink flowers, green-and-white leaves; 'Beedham's White,' white flowers, soft yellow white-veined leaves; *L. m. aureum,* pink flowers, soft yellow leaves with white veins; *Lamiastrum galeobdolon:* yellow flowers, invasive, Zones 4–9, evergreen in Zones 7–9; 'Herman's Pride,' narrow, silver-marked leaves, less aggressive.

Garden Use: Wonderful ground cover for shade gardens. Combines well with tulips, hostas, ferns, and other tall shade perennials.

Lavandula angustifolia (*L. officinalis, L. verna,* and *L. spica*)
LAVENDER, ENGLISH LAVENDER

This fragrant herb grows into a compact, rounded woody-based plant consisting of many upright, woolly white stems clad in narrow, aromatic, gray-green to gray, ever-

Lavandula stoechas

green leaves. Tight spikes of scented lavender or purple flowers top the plants for a month in early summer. The flowers are a source of oil of lavender used in perfumes and soaps, and should be harvested when the flower buds show color.

Size: 1 to 3 feet tall and wide.

Light: Full sun.

Soil and Moisture: Average to poor, well-drained, neutral to alkaline soil; highly drought tolerant.

Planting and Propagation: Plant container-grown plants in spring, spacing 1½ feet apart. Divide in fall. Take side-shoot cuttings in summer.

Special Care: Cut back in early spring to just above previous year's growth. Harvest flowers when showing color but not fully open. Shear flowers after they fade to promote rebloom.

Pests and Diseases: May rot in winter-wet soil. Fungus and caterpillars troublesome.

Climate: Zones 5–9; less hardy in heavy, wet soil. Performs poorly in heat and humidity.

Cultivars and Similar Species: 'Hidcote,' silvery leaves, deep purple-blue flowers, 1⅓ feet tall; 'Jean Davis,' pale pink flowers, blue-green leaves, 1¼ feet tall; 'Munstead Dwarf,' very fragrant early violet-blue flowers, 1 foot tall; 'Baby White,' white flowers, 1 foot tall; 'Alba,' white, 3 feet tall, not as cold hardy; 'Lavender Lady,' 10 inches tall, flowers first year from seed, may be sold as bedding plants. *L. stoechas* (Spanish lavender): showy pineconelike spikes of flowers with purple bracts, Zones 7–11.

Garden Use: Excellent for foliage contrast. Plant close together to form low hedge in herb or rose garden. Use as specimens in rock and border plantings.

Leontopodium alpinum
EDELWEISS

This famous plant of the Swiss Alps creates an unusual sight when it blooms in late spring and early summer, because the ivory-white flowers look as if they were constructed from thick felt. The 1- to 2-inch-wide, star-shaped flowers are actually composed of a cluster of tiny yellow flowers surrounded by furry bracts. These bloom above low-spreading mats of narrow silvery leaves.

Size: 8 to 10 inches tall; 1½ feet wide.
Light: Full sun.
Soil and Moisture: Average to poor, well-drained, alkaline soil; moderate water.
Planting and Propagation: Plant container-grown plants in spring, spacing 1 foot apart.

Leontopodium alpinum

Liatris spicata 'Kobold'

Divide in spring if desired, but not necessary for years.
Special Care: Must have well-drained soil; may rot in winter-wet site. Apply gravel mulch to keep crown dry.
Pests and Diseases: Crown rot in heavy soil.
Climate: Zones 4–9.
Similar Species: Several almost identical species sometimes sold.
Garden Use: Delightful rock garden plant; use for color contrast with green plants.

Liatris spicata (L. callilepis)
SPIKE GAYFEATHER, BLAZING STAR

Once an obscure wildflower native to moist meadows, gayfeather now glows in many gardens. Its slender bottlebrushes of rose, purple, or white flowers bloom from mid-summer to fall, attracting bees and butterflies. Unlike many spiked flowers, gayfeather's blossoms open from the top of the spike downward. Leaves are very narrow and arranged in whorls around the tall stems, emphasizing the vertical, feathery effect.

Size: 3 feet tall; 2 feet wide.
Light: Full sun.
Soil and Moisture: Average to sandy, humus-rich soil; keep moist during growing season.
Planting and Propagation: Plant bare-root or container-grown plants in spring, spacing 2 feet apart. Divide clumps of fleshy roots every three or four years in fall, if crowded.
Special Care: May need staking to maintain straight spikes. Cut off faded spikes to promote rebloom. Easy to care for and long lived.
Pests and Diseases: Rootknot nematodes may be troublesome in the South.
Climate: Zones 3–9.
Cultivars and Similar Species: 'Kobold' ('Gnome'), 2½ feet tall, early blooming, stiff spikes of dark violet-purple; 'Floristan White,' creamy white, 3 feet tall; 'August Glory,' purple-blue, 3 to 4 feet tall. *L. scariosa/L. aspera* (tall gayfeather): flowers open almost simultaneously in conical spikes, 3 feet tall, drought resistant; 'White Spire,' white; 'September Glory,' rose-purple. *L. pycnostachya* (Kansas gayfeather), 4 to 5 feet tall, needs staking in gardens, best in meadow.
Garden Use: Makes a striking vertical effect in formal borders and naturalistic plantings. Combines well with ornamental grasses. Good cut flower; remove tops of spikes as flowers fade.

Ligularia stenocephala
GOLDEN RAY

Most species of ligularia are admired more for their mounds of handsome, dramatic foliage than for their flowers. This species, especially the cultivar 'The Rocket,' draws acclaim for both striking flowers and foliage. Light green and triangular shaped with coarse, toothed margins, the leaves may reach a foot long and wide. The tall, unbranched purplish flower stems produce slender, 2-foot-long spikes of deep yellow flowers from mid- to late summer.

Size: 3 to 4 feet tall; 5 feet wide.
Light: Half sun or light shade; afternoon shade a must in hot areas.

Ligularia stenocephala 'The Rocket'

Soil and Moisture: Fertile, humus-rich soil; keep moist to wet during growing season.

Planting and Propagation: Plant bare-root or container-grown plants in spring. Rarely needs division, but may be divided in late fall; keep divisions wet.

Special Care: Difficult to provide enough sun and moisture at the same time. Needs afternoon shade and moist to wet soil to prevent wilting during hot summer days.

Pests and Diseases: Slugs often troublesome.

Climate: Zones 5–8; best in Zones 5–6 and where cool and moist.

Cultivars and Similar Species: 'The Rocket,' compact 3- to 5-foot-tall spikes of lemon-yellow flowers; sometimes listed as *L. przewalskii. L. dentata* (big-leaf ligularia): branched spikes of orange flowers, dramatic kidney-shaped leaves; remove flowers as they form, if they do not appeal to you. 'Desdemona,' beet-red spring leaves become green with dark purple undersides, compact; 'Othello,' similar but later blooming and less compact; 'Greynog Gold,' hybrid, large heart-shaped veined leaves, conical orange-yellow unkempt flower spike.

Garden Use: Excellent foliage and flower effect in naturalistic, shady, wet to boggy site along pond or stream.

Limonium latifolium
SEA LAVENDER, STATICE

This useful perennial thrives under coastal conditions, producing a large, misty cloud of lavender-blue flowers on wiry stems. Flower stalks appear all summer above a basal clump of 10-inch-long leathery green leaves with long petioles.

Size: 2 feet tall; 3 feet wide.

Light: Full sun to light shade.

Soil and Moisture: Average to sandy, well-drained soil; even moisture best, but tolerates drought.

Planting and Propagation: Plant bare-root or container-grown plants in spring, spacing

Limonium perezii

1½ feet apart. Needs no division; propagate by removing side rosettes without disturbing main clump.

Special Care: Established plants resent disturbance. May need staking in rich soil.

Pests and Diseases: Crown rot and root rot if grown too wet and crowded.

Climate: Zones 3–9; tolerates salt spray and seaside conditions.

Cultivars and Similar Species: 'Blue Diamond,' blue flowers; 'Violetta,' deep violet-blue. *L. perezii:* gray-green leaves, flowers dark purple-blue with white centers in airy clouds, Zones 8–11.

Garden Use: Plant in foreground as lacy veil in front of bolder flowers. Papery flowers can be cut fresh or dried if cut before flowers are fully open.

Linum perenne
BLUE FLAX

This delicate-looking plant forms clumps of slender, upright stems decorated with narrow, blue-green leaves and an abundant scattering of pale blue, five-petaled flowers. Each blossom lives but a day, opening on a sunny

Linum perenne

morning and closing up by afternoon, but a seemingly endless supply keeps the plants in bloom for 10 to 12 weeks in late spring and summer.

Size: 1 to 1½ feet tall; 1 foot wide.

Light: Full to half sun.

Soil and Moisture: Average to sandy, well-drained soil; moderate moisture. Drought resistant.

Planting and Propagation: Plant container-grown plants in spring, spacing 1 foot apart. Do not divide; take cuttings in midsummer to propagate.

Special Care: Usually short-lived in winter-wet sites. Self-sows but is not weedy. Cut back after flowering to prevent floppiness.

Pests and Diseases: Grasshoppers sometimes troublesome.

Climate: Zones 4–9; performs well in the South.

Cultivars and Similar Species: 'Saphyr,' dwarf to 8 to 10 inches tall, sapphire-blue flowers; 'Diamond,' dwarf to 10 inches to 1 foot tall, white flowers; *L. p. album,* white flowers, 1½ feet tall.

Garden Use: Arrange in drifts among bolder flowers.

Liriope muscari
BLUE LILYTURF

Plants that tolerate dry shade are rare; this one takes those adverse conditions in stride, forming fountainlike clumps of glossy dark green or variegated evergreen leaves. Leaves are 2 inches wide and 1 to 2 feet long. Plants striped with silver or gold make beautiful color and textural contrasts in shady spots. Although the foliage is its selling point, dense spikes of purplish blue flowers that resemble grape hyacinth and arise from the middle of the clumps in late summer, are a pretty sight.

Size: Clumps to 1 to 1½ feet tall; 2 feet wide.
Light: Half to full shade.
Soil and Moisture: Humus-rich to average, well-drained soil; regular water best, although plants are drought tolerant.
Planting and Propagation: Plant bare-root or container-grown plants in spring, spacing 8 inches to 1 foot apart for ground cover. Division not needed for years, but clumps may be divided in spring if desired.
Special Care: Cut back foliage to 2 inches in late winter to remove winter-tattered leaves and promote lush new growth.
Pests and Diseases: Slugs and snails often troublesome.

Liriope muscari variegata

Climate: Zones 6–9; performs well in both humid and dry climates.
Cultivars: 'Majestic,' violet flowers; 'Munroe's White,' showy bright white flowers; 'Royal Purple,' deep purple; *L. m. variegata,* showy green leaves with creamy white margins, bright lavender flowers; 'Gold Banded,' wide gold marginal stripes may disappear in full sun or deep shade, lavender flowers; 'John Burch,' yellow stripes mostly on margins, dense lilac flowers; 'Silvery Sunproof,' leaves almost white in sun, yellow-green in shade, lavender flowers.
Garden Use: Use as small-scale ground cover or edging; effective as specimen or in drifts in shade garden. Combines well with ferns and hostas.

Lobelia cardinalis
CARDINAL FLOWER

This native wildflower forms colonies of spikey, 1½-inch-long, cardinal-red flowers in moist meadows throughout the eastern half of North America. The blossoms, which bloom for several weeks in late summer, attract hummingbirds. Unusual in both color and form, the tubular flowers flare open into two unequal, deeply cut lips, creating a fring-

Lobelia cardinalis

ed effect. Lance-shaped leaves form a dark green, basal rosette with smaller leaves climbing the tall flower stems.

Size: 2 to 4 feet tall; 1 to 2 feet wide.
Light: Half to light shade. Afternoon shade where hot; full sun in cool-summer areas.
Soil and Moisture: Humus-rich, fertile, moist soil; plentiful moisture or boggy site.
Planting and Propagation: Plant container-grown plants in spring, spacing 1½ feet apart. Divide in fall if desired.
Special Care: Mulch to keep soil moist. Usually short lived in gardens; longer lived and may self-sow in naturally moist areas.
Pests and Diseases: Usually pest free.
Climate: Zones 2–9.
Cultivars and Similar Species: 'Compliment Scarlet,' extra-large flowers. *L. splendens/ L. fulgens* (Mexican lobelia): bronze stems and leaves, short-lived, Zones 7–9. *L.* x *speciosa* (a complex hybrid): longer lived, needs winter mulch; 'Bee's Flame,' vermilion-red flowers, beet-red leaves; 'Queen Victoria,' scarlet flowers, bronze foliage; 'Pink Flamingo,' bright pink.
Garden Use: Looks and performs best if planted near pond or stream.

Lobelia siphilitica
BIG-BLUE LOBELIA

Similar in appearance to cardinal flower, blue lobelia blooms later, producing tighter spikes of 1-inch-long, vivid blue to blue-purple and sometimes white, tubular flowers on tall, unbranched stems. Flowers bloom for about a month in late summer and early fall. This native wildflower may look a bit unkempt but is prized for its blue spikes at a time of year when the gardener's palette is slim.

Size: 2 to 3 feet tall; 1 foot wide.
Light: Morning sun and afternoon shade best; full sun in cool-summer areas.
Soil and Moisture: Humus-rich, moist soil; plentiful moisture.
Planting and Propagation: Plant container-

253

Lobelia siphilitica

grown plants in spring, spacing 1½ feet apart. Divide in spring.

Special Care: Tolerates normal garden conditions better than cardinal flower. Usually short lived. Divide every two or three years to improve longevity. Deadhead to prevent self-sowing. Mulch in winter.

Pests and Diseases: Usually pest free.

Climate: Zones 4–8.

Cultivars and Similar Species: 'Alba,' white flowers; 'Blue Peter,' showier flowers. *L.* x *gerardii/L. vedraiensis* (hybrid of cardinal flower and big-blue lobelia): 3 feet tall, bronze stems, purple flowers.

Garden Use: Use in naturalistic moist or wet gardens; plant in drifts in informal gardens.

Lunaria annua
MONEY-PLANT, DOLLAR-PLANT, HONESTY

This fragrant, spring-blooming biennial transforms its eye-catching flower stalks into stems of silvery, disk-shaped seedpods by midsummer. The showy sprays of magenta,

254

white, or magenta-and-white bicolored blossoms top the oval-leaf plant beginning at tulip time and last into early summer. Then the quarter-size pods decorating the stems begin to change from green to silver. Seedpods look nice in arrangements.

Size: 1½ to 3 feet tall; half as wide.

Light: Partial shade best; tolerates sun.

Soil and Moisture: Average to poor soil; moderate water.

Planting and Propagation: Sow seeds in garden in early spring or fall.

Special Care: Plants will resow to perpetuate themselves but can become weedy. Harvest seedpods in late summer when dry.

Pests and Diseases: Occasionally attacked by cabbage family pests.

Climate: Biennial in Zones 4–8.

Cultivars: 'Munstead Purple Giant,' darker magenta-purple; *L. a. alba*, white. Mixes of magenta, purple, and variegated blossoms available.

Garden Use: Use in informal or naturalistic gardens, in cutting garden, or as cover for spring bulbs. White-flowered forms are easiest to integrate with other flowers.

Lunaria annua

Lupinus hybrids
LUPINE

Hybrid lupines form stately clumps of mat green, silky-haired leaves. The leaves may be a foot across and are rounded in outline but cut into many fingerlike lobes. Dense spikes of pealike flowers rise above the foliage for a month or more in early summer. Flowers come in a variety of colors and may be bicolored. The best-known lupines are the 'Russell Hybrids,' which were bred in England during the first half of this century and created a sensation when first exhibited. They offer a wide color range and dense flower spikes on tall plants. Newer hybrids grow more compactly with shorter, denser spikes. Unfortunately, all hybrid lupines are finicky and short lived in most areas of North America.

Size: 3 feet tall and wide.

Light: Full sun best; tolerates some shade.

Soil and Moisture: Humus-rich, acid, well-drained soil; plentiful moisture.

Planting and Propagation: Plant container-grown plants in spring or fall, spacing 2½ feet apart. Avoid plants with encircling distorted taproots. Take stem cuttings in fall and overwinter in cold frame.

Special Care: Taproot resents disturbance. Mulch to keep soil cool. Deadhead spent spikes to ensure strong plants and promote a possible second bloom. Stake tall types.

Pests and Diseases: Aphids, powdery mildew, slugs, and crown rot sometimes troublesome.

Climate: Zones 4–9. Performs poorly in hot-summer areas; grow as fall-planted, cool-season annual in Zone 6 and southward.

Cultivars: 'Russell Hybrids,' 3 feet tall in solids and bicolors, in shades of white, cream, pink, red, blue, yellow, orange, and purple; usually sold unnamed. Named varieties include: 'Chandelier,' creamy white and yellow; 'Chatelaine,' pink-and-white; 'My Castle,' brick-red; 'Noble Maiden,' pure white; 'The Governor,' purple-blue; 'The

Lupinus hybrids

Pages,' carmine-red. 'Gallery Hybrids,' 1¼ to 1½ feet tall in blue, pink, red, yellow, and white; 'Minarette,' 1½ to 2 feet tall, comes in mixed colors.

Garden Use: Elegant flowers and foliage for massing in formal borders or planting as specimens in informal gardens.

Lychnis chalcedonia
MALTESE CROSS

Few summer bloomers can match the vivid scarlet flowers of maltese cross. Flowers bloom in midsummer, forming dense rounded clusters of orange-red, four-petaled flowers. Hairy, dark green, lance-shaped leaves clasp the upright, unbranched stems beneath the flowers, creating the perfect dark foil. Maltese cross lives longer than other members of its genus.

Size: 2 to 3 feet tall; 1½ feet wide.

Light: Full sun.

Soil and Moisture: Average to sandy, well-drained soil; consistent moisture.

Planting and Propagation: Plant container-grown plants in spring, spacing 1½ feet apart. Divide in spring or fall every three years.

Special Care: Deadhead to prolong bloom. Lower leaves brown if soil dries out.

Pests and Diseases: Whitefly, rust, and root rot sometimes troublesome.

Climate: Zones 3–9.

Cultivars and Similar Species: 'Rauhreif,' white, 2 feet tall; *L. c. alba-plena*, double white. *L.* x *haageana*: scarlet-orange, toothed flowers in loose clusters, 10 inches tall. *L. viscaria* (German catchfly), grasslike tufts, clusters of 1-inch, notch-petaled magenta flowers with sticky stems; *L.* var. *splendens flore-plena*, double magenta; *L. v.* var. *flore-plena* 'Alba,' double white. *L. splendens flore-plena*, double magenta; 'Fire,' magenta; 'Snow,' white.

Garden Use: Plant in drifts in hot color borders or add for drama among cool colors.

Lychnis coronaria
ROSE CAMPION

This old-fashioned, cottage-garden flower makes a simple statement with its gray leaves and small but brilliant flowers. Gray-green, 4-inch-long, oblong leaves form leafy, ground-hugging rosettes from which emerge many slender, felt-covered, gray-white stems. The stems are branched and topped with open clusters of 1-inch-wide, rounded, eye-catching magenta flowers in late spring and early summer. Rose campion is a biennial or short-lived perennial but self-sows readily to perpetuate itself.

Size: Flower stalks to 3 feet tall; leafy rosettes 6 inches tall, 1½ feet wide.

Light: Full to part sun; afternoon shade in hottest areas.

Soil and Moisture: Average to sandy, well-drained soil; moderate moisture. Drought tolerant.

Planting and Propagation: Plant bare-root or container-grown plants in spring, spacing 10 inches apart. Shake out seedpods where new plants are desired.

Special Care: Reseeds and may become weedy; rogue out or transplant seedlings in

Lychnis viscaria

early spring as desired. Cut off flower stalks after seeds are shed to tidy up plants.

Pests and Diseases: Usually pest free.

Climate: Zones 4–8; performs poorly in heat and humidity.

Cultivars and Similar Species: 'Abbotswood Rose,' pink flowers; 'Angel's Blush,' white flowers with rose centers; *L. c. alba*, white flowers. *L. flos-jovis* (flower-of-Jove): gray woolly leaves, loose balls of rose or pink flowers. *L. flos-cuculi* (ragged robin): gray-green, grassy leaves, feathery rose or pink flowers.

Garden Use: Plant in foreground of cottage gardens and informal borders.

Lychnis coronaria

Lysimachia clethroides

Lysimachia clethroides
GOOSENECK LOOSESTRIFE

This rapidly spreading plant develops dense, 10-inch-long, gracefully arching spires of tiny white flowers at the tips of its stems in mid- to late summer. All the inflorescences bend in the same direction, creating a gentle, wavy effect. Stems are unbranched and upright, forming bushy clumps clad in slightly hairy, pointed leaves, which turn attractive bronze-yellow in fall.

Size: 3 feet tall; spreads to large clumps by stoloniferous roots.
Light: Full sun to half shade; tolerates full shade with dry soil.
Soil and Moisture: Fertile to average, well-drained soil; plentiful moisture.
Planting and Propagation: Plant bare-root or container-grown plants in spring, spacing 2 to 3 feet apart. Divide every few years in spring to control spreading.
Special Care: Can become extremely invasive; install barrier to keep in place.
Pests and Diseases: Crown rot and whitefly sometimes troublesome.

256

Climate: Zones 3–8.
Cultivars: Only species is sold.
Garden Use: Best in naturalistic gardens near water where invasiveness is not a problem. Long-lasting cut flower.

Lysimachia nummulara
MONEYWORT, CREEPING JENNY, CREEPING CHARLEY

Named after its dime-size leaves that clasp the low creeping stems, moneywort roots at the nodes, forming an effective ground cover. Yellow, cup-shaped flowers dot the stems between the leaves in late spring and sporadically throughout summer.

Size: 4 to 8 inches tall; 2 feet wide.
Light: Full sun to part shade.
Soil and Moisture: Humus-rich, moist to wet or boggy soil; tolerates dry site in shade.
Planting and Propagation: Plant bare-root or container-grown plants in spring. Divide in spring or fall; take cuttings in summer.
Special Care: Invasive and may colonize lawns. Perishes in dry site.
Pests and Diseases: Usually pest free.
Climate: Zones 3–8.
Cultivars: 'Aurea,' chartreuse spring leaves darken to lime-green.

Lysimachia nummulara 'Aurea'

Garden Use: Naturalize along stream banks and ponds or in shade gardens under taller, sturdy perennials such as Siberian iris, ferns, and hostas. 'Aurea' looks lovely combined with gold-variegated hosta and lilyturf.

Lysimachia punctata
YELLOW LOOSESTRIFE, CIRCLE FLOWER

The upright stems of yellow loosestrife produce whorls of bright yellow flowers in their leaf axils from early through midsummer. The stiff stems form bushy stands, however, so the vertical effect is softened. Also whorled, the lance-shaped, mat-green, slightly hairy leaves set off the yellow blossoms.

Size: 1 to 3 feet tall; 2 to 3 feet wide.
Light: Full sun to part shade.
Soil and Moisture: Average to fertile, moist soil; even moisture best, but tolerates drier soil than other members of genus.
Planting and Propagation: Plant bare-root or container-grown plants in spring, spacing 2 feet apart. Divide every few years in spring.
Special Care: May be invasive; plant where this is not a problem.
Pests and Diseases: Whitefly sometimes troublesome.
Climate: Zones 4–8; best in northern areas.

Lysimachia punctata

Similar Species: *L. ciliata* (fringed loose-strife), native wildflower, light yellow flowers in loose clusters, purplish willowlike leaves.
Garden Use: Allow to roam in informal or cottage gardens; naturalize along streams or woodland edges.

Lythrum salicaria
PURPLE LOOSESTRIFE

This striking European flower is a frequent roadside sight in northern parts of North America where it has naturalized to form dramatic stands of rose-purple spikes in marshes and wet meadows from mid- to late summer. Unfortunately, this pretty roadside weed is actually a wildlife menace. It is now banned in many northern states where wetlands abound because it crowds out native plants that provide food and shelter for wildlife. Although nurserymen claim that sterile cultivars pose no danger, these cultivars are actually only self-sterile and hybridize with other cultivars or species to sow seeds of potential danger. Only use purple loosestrife in gardens well away from natural wetlands, even if not banned in your state. Where it can be safely planted, its vertical flower spikes and heart-shaped, mat-green leaves provide rich

Lythrum salicaria 'Morden Pink'

color and noble height, welcome in the summer garden.
Size: 3 to 5 feet tall and wide; spreads by stoloniferus roots.
Light: Full sun to part shade.
Soil and Moisture: Humus-rich, moist to boggy soil; plentiful moisture.
Planting and Propagation: Plant container-grown plants in spring, spacing 2 to 3 feet apart. Divide in spring as needed to control spread.
Special Care: May need staking in shade. Deadhead to prevent seeding.
Pests and Diseases: Japanese beetles can be serious.
Climate: Zones 3–9; tolerates heat and humidity.
Cultivars and Similar Species: *L. virgatum* (wand loosestrife) almost identical. The following cultivars are erratically attributed to either species and are probably hybrids: 'Fire-candle,' intense magenta, 4 to 5 feet tall; 'Flash Fire,' hot pink; 'The Beacon,' bright magenta, 3½ feet tall; 'Dropmore Purple,' rose-purple, 3 to 4 feet tall; 'Morden's Gleam,' rose, 3 to 4 feet tall; 'Morden Pink,' bright pink, 3 to 4 feet tall; 'Robert,' deep pink, 2 to 3 feet tall; 'Roseum Superbum,' vivid magenta, large flowers; 'Happy,' pink, 1-foot-tall dwarf.
Garden Use: Use tall types in back of border in formal and informal gardens; use shorter types in midground. Lovely in naturalistic settings beside man-made stream or pond. Avoid natural sites because seeds float.

Macleaya cordata (Bocconia cordata)
PLUME POPPY

This plant commands attention with its great height, figlike foliage, and misty flowers. Foot-tall plumes of creamy flowers on chalk-white stems top the bushy stands of upright, unbranched stalks in midsummer. Measuring 8 inches to 1 foot across, the heart-shaped leaves are irregularly lobed and have hairy

Maclaya cordata

white undersides, which flash silver in the breeze.
Size: 5 to 8 feet tall; 5 to 6 feet wide.
Light: Full sun; half shade where hot.
Soil and Moisture: Deep, fertile to average, moist soil; plentiful moisture.
Planting and Propagation: Plant container-grown plants in spring, spacing 3 to 4 feet apart. Divide in spring as needed to control spread.
Special Care: Spreads aggressively; allow plenty of space. Control size by slicing around edge of stand with shovel. Rarely needs staking. Self-sows to point of weediness if not deadheaded. Most invasive in fertile sites. Cut to ground in late winter.
Pests and Diseases: Leaf spots during warm, wet weather.
Climate: Zones 3–8.
Cultivars and Similar Species: *M. microcarpa,* similar appearing but more invasive; 'Coral Plume,' pale coral plumes.
Garden Use: Dramatic plant for informal or naturalistic gardens; plant in rear, but do not obscure beautiful foliage with tall plants. Use as shrublike specimen.

Malva alcea
HOLLYHOCK MALLOW

Resembling a scaled-down hollyhock, this long-bloomer is a true perennial, although it tends to be short-lived. Satiny, 2- to 3-inch-wide light pink to rose-purple or white flowers, made up of five notched petals with darker veins, bloom up and down the upright stems from midsummer to late fall. The downy, rounded leaves have shallow lobes and grow about 6 inches long.

Size: 2 to 4 feet tall; 1½ feet wide.

Light: Full to part sun; light shade best where hot.

Soil and Moisture: Fertile to average, neutral to alkaline, well-drained soil. Drought tolerant where cool; needs moist, humus-rich soil in hot areas.

Planting and Propagation: Plant bare-root or container-grown plants in spring, spacing 1½ feet apart. Does not need division. Take tip cuttings in early summer.

Special Care: Usually needs staking. May self-sow to point of weediness.

Pests and Diseases: Japanese beetles troublesome; thrips and spider mites common where heat stressed.

Climate: Zones 4–8; best where summer nights are cool.

Cultivars and Similar Species: 'Fastigiata,' stronger stems, dark pink flowers, superior cultivar. *M. moschata* (musk mallow): bushier plant with deeply divided, glossy, thread-like stem leaves and three-lobed basal leaves, rose-pink flowers with two-lobed petals, rust disease a problem, Zones 3–5. *M. a. alba*, white; *M. a. rosea*, pink. Naturalized in the Northeast.

Garden Use: Use for vertical effect in informal borders and cottage gardens.

Mazus reptans
MAZUS

This valuable ground cover thrives in moist, shady sites, producing carpets of early flowers and evergreen foliage to beautify the garden throughout the year. Flowers measure almost an inch long—rather large for a plant that hugs the ground as it does—and are tubular with showy, spotted lower lips. Most commonly lavender, a lovely white form also is available. Flowers appear for almost two months from mid-spring through early summer. The lance-shaped, 1-inch-long, toothed, bright green leaves look attractive after flowers pass.

Size: 2 inches tall; spreads 2 feet or more.

Light: Light to full shade.

Soil and Moisture: Humus-rich, moist to wet or boggy soil; plentiful moisture.

Planting and Propagation: Plant bare-root or container-grown plants in spring. Divide in early spring every three or four years to rejuvenate.

Special Care: Plant away from lawn because it can be invasive. May not survive snowless winters in the North; provide winter protection if needed.

Pests and Diseases: Usually pest free.

Climate: Zones 5–8.

Cultivars: *M. r. alba*, white flowers.

Garden Use: Wonderful ground cover in naturalistic gardens, along streams and ponds, or in woodlands beneath taller plants. Withstands foot traffic; plant between pavers in shady, moist site or as lawn substitute.

Mentha suaveolens 'Variegata'
VARIEGATED PINEAPPLE MINT

This pretty and useful herb adds a decorative note with its scallop-edged, rounded, woolly, light green leaves, which feature showy, irregular, creamy white variegations on their edges. White flowers bloom in midsummer

Malva alcea

Mazus reptans

Mentha suaveolens 'Variegata'

near the stem tips. The fruit-scented leaves possess a pineapple fragrance when young, becoming more apple-scented as they mature, and make an enticing addition to drinks and fruit salads.

Size: 1 foot tall; spreads to cover several square feet.

Light: Full sun to light shade.

Soil and Moisture: Humus-rich, fertile, moist soil; plentiful moisture.

Planting and Propagation: Plant bare-root or container-grown plants in spring, spacing 2 feet apart. Divide in spring as desired.

Special Care: Best to confine roots in tidy gardens, or it will take over.

Pests and Diseases: Rust can sometimes be a problem.

Climate: Zones 5–8.

Cultivars and Similar Species: *M. suaveolens* (apple mint), nonvariegated with fruity apple scent, 3 feet tall.

Garden Use: Pretty foreground foliage plant in beds and borders and cottage and herb gardens.

Mentha x *piperita*
PEPPERMINT

An attractive upright and sparsely branched mint, this plant possesses a strong peppermint flavor, while its many cultivars offer scents in a range of gourmet aromas. Peppermint's long-stalked leaves are somewhat downy, dark green, and pointed with toothed edges. The leaf undersides and square stems are purplish green. Dense clusters of pale violet flowers tip the stems in midsummer.

Size: 2 to 3 feet tall; spreads to cover several square feet.

Light: Full sun to part shade.

Soil and Moisture: Humus-rich, fertile, moist soil; moderate water.

Planting and Propagation: Plant bare-root or container-grown plants in spring, spacing 2 feet apart. Divide in spring as desired.

Special Care: Spreads quickly by runners;

Mentha x *piperita*

confine in sunken pots to prevent enthusiastic spread.

Pests and Diseases: Rust can sometimes be a problem.

Climate: Zones 5–8.

Similar Species: Purchase vegetatively propagated plants for best aroma. 'Ginger,' variegated with gold, minty ginger scent; 'Chocolate,' minty chocolate aroma; 'Blue Balsam,' blue-green; 'Lime,' lime scented; 'Lavandula,' mint and lavender aroma; 'Orange,' leaves edged purple, citrus aroma. *M. spicata* (spearmint): smooth oval leaves, milder mint aroma. *M. requienii* (Corsican mint): tiny semi-evergreen leaves with strong crème de menthe aroma, ground cover for moist shade; Zones 7–8.

Garden Use: Plant in herb and cottage gardens where spreading is not a problem.

Mertensia virginica
VIRGINIA BLUEBELLS

This native wildflower pushes through the ground in early spring, showing first a cluster of blue-green leaves enclosing a tightly coiled purple bundle of flower buds. A few weeks later, nodding clusters of sky-blue, bell-shaped flowers and pink buds decorate the coiled ends of the branched stems.

Bluebells bloom with the early spring wildflowers and flowering trees and go dormant in early summer.

Size: 1 to 2 feet tall.

Light: Full spring sun to light shade cast by deciduous trees; shade in the South.

Soil and Moisture: Sandy to heavy, neutral to slightly acid, moist soil; plentiful water during growth and bloom.

Planting and Propagation: Plant container-grown plants in spring or dormant roots in fall, spacing 1 to 1½ feet apart. May be difficult to divide; dig deeply when dormant and separate roots only when overcrowded.

Special Care: Self-seeds where happily situated; do not cut off seed heads. To transplant, dig very deeply and try not to disturb root ball.

Pests and Diseases: Usually pest free.

Climate: Zones 3–8.

Cultivars: 'Alba' white'; 'Rubra,' pink, rare.

Garden Use: Naturalize in moist shade gardens, in woodlands, and along streams and ponds. Looks lovely with trillium, creeping phlox, and other wildflowers; also combines well with daffodils. Interplant with ferns to cover bare spots left in midsummer.

Mertensia virginica

Mimulus cardinalis
SCARLET MONKEY FLOWER

Native to wet areas of the western and south-western United States and Mexico, scarlet monkey flower displays its orange-red flowers throughout summer. Showy yellow stamens peak out between the lips of the tubular flowers, which bloom on long stems near the top of the plant. Plants form sprawling clumps of branched stems cloaked with downy, oval-toothed leaves.

Size: 4 feet tall; 2½ feet wide.

Light: Full to half sun; afternoon shade where hot.

Soil and Moisture: Humus-rich, fertile soil; wet to boggy conditions. Do not allow soil to dry out in summer.

Planting and Propagation: Plant container-grown plants in spring, spacing 2 to 3 feet apart. Divide in spring.

Special Care: Cut back plants when blooming ceases to encourage reblooming in fall.

Pests and Diseases: Usually pest free.

Climate: Zones 7–9.

Similar Species: *M. guttatus* (common monkey flower), fleshy, toothed, oval leaves, upright and sprawling to 2 feet, bright yellow, trumpet-shaped, two-lipped flowers

Mimulus cardinalis

with red-speckled throats in short clusters all summer; used in breeding *M.* x *hybridus* (annual monkey flower).

Garden Use: Long-blooming plant for naturalizing in moist sites, such as along stream banks and in bog gardens.

Monarda didyma
BEE-BALM, OSWEGO TEA

Once used to make tea, this native plant's showy 3- to 4-inch-wide flowers make it as welcome in the flower garden as it is in the herb garden. The fluffy pinwheel-shaped flowers are red in the species, but cultivars come in shades of red, pink, purple, lavender, and white. Blossoms appear from mid- to late summer and attract butterflies and hummingbirds. Bee-balm's upright stems are cloaked with fuzzy, toothed, mint-scented leaves and spread to form large clumps.

Size: 2 to 4 feet tall; spreads to 3 feet wide.

Light: Full sun to partial shade.

Soil and Moisture: Humus-rich, fertile, moist soil; plentiful moisture.

Planting and Propagation: Plant bare-root or container-grown plants in spring, spacing 2 to 3 feet apart. Divide in spring every two or three years.

Special Care: Most susceptible to mildew if soil dries; fungicide program usually needed. Deadhead flowers as they fade to prolong flowering up to two months. Can be invasive; divide regularly.

Pests and Diseases: Mildew often troublesome after flowering; cut plants to the ground and disease-free foliage usually appears. Some cultivars are less susceptible.

Climate: Zones 4–9, but best in the North.

Cultivars and Similar Species: 'Adam,' deep red; 'Cambridge Scarlet,' vivid red; 'Gardenview Red,' rose-red, mildew resistant; 'Croftway Pink,' rose-pink; 'Souris,' bright pink; 'Beauty of Cobham,' pale pink-and-purple; 'Ohio Glow,' bright pink'; 'Mahogany,' maroon-purple; 'Marshall's Delight,' pink, mildew resistant; 'Stone's

Monarda didyma

Throw Pink,' bright pink, mildew resistant; 'Prairie Night,' violet-purple; 'Violet Queen,' magenta-violet, mildew resistant; 'Blue Stocking,' purple; 'Purple Crown,' dark and light purple; 'Snow White,' pure white. *M. fistulosa* (wild bergamot): lavender flowers, less showy but more tolerant of dry soil and mildew. *M. punctata* (horsemint): tiered clusters of yellow-green flowers and showy pink bracts, no mildew, 2 feet tall.

Garden Use: Showy plant for herb gardens and borders. Naturalize in moist site.

Myosotis scorpioides (*M. palustris*)
FORGET-ME-NOT

Forget-me-not produces coiled clusters of tiny pale blue flowers with paler centers and yellow eyes from spring though late summer. Stems are a bit floppy, and roots are stoloniferous, creating a loose, spreading plant with fuzzy leaves.

Size: 6 to 8 inches tall; spreads to 8 inches wide.

Light: Light to part shade best; full sun if soil stays constantly moist.

Soil and Moisture: Humus-rich, fertile, moist to wet soil. Provide plentiful moisture;

Myosotis sylvatica

Nepeta x *faassenii*
CATMINT

This outstanding aromatic plant in the mint family is surely one of the showiest of the family. It produces billowing masses of small, intense lavender-blue blossoms for several weeks in early summer—at the peak of rose season—and again in fall if cut back. When out of bloom, the narrow, silvery, wedge-shaped 1½-inch-long leaves and gently cascading stems make a striking contrast with neighboring green leaves and colorful flowers. Be sure you're getting the real thing when you purchase this catmint; *N. mussinii*, one of its parents and a much less showy plant, is often mislabeled as *N. x faassenii*.

Size: 1 to 1½ feet tall; 2 feet wide.

Light: Full sun best; tolerates half shade.

Soil and Moisture: Average to sandy, very well-drained soil; moderate moisture.

Planting and Propagation: Plant container-grown plants in spring, spacing 1½ feet apart. Divide in spring or fall every three years. Sterile; will not self-sow.

Special Care: In spring, cut new growth back by half when 6 inches tall to encourage branching. Shear halfway after spring bloom to discourage floppiness and encourage rebloom. Performs poorly in heavy soil. Rots in damp soil; *N. x faassenii* more tolerant of moisture and part shade than *N. mussinii*.

Pests and Diseases: Usually pest free, although cats may roll on plants.

Climate: Zones 4–8.

Cultivars and Similar Species: 'Six Hills Giant' (*N. gigantea*), covered with soft violet-blue flowers, 3 feet tall; 'Dropmore Hybrid,' smaller, more linear, much grayer leaves and prettier lavender flowers than species, to 2½ feet tall, needs ringed support. *N. mussinii* (Persian catmint): 1 to 1½ feet tall, spreading and floppy, gray-green rounded leaves, short flower spikes, blooms in spring and fall if cut back. Cultivars: 'Blue Wonder,' 6-inch spikes of lavender-blue flowers, compact mound, 10 inches to 1¼ feet tall; 'White Wonder,' white;

Nepeta x *faassenii*

'Snowflake,' white, compact and low spreading. *N. cataria* (catnip): weedy, pink flowers with gray-green leaves; attracts cats.

Garden Use: Classic edging plant for rose gardens; use in formal flower borders and herb gardens. Combines well with red, purple, pink, pale yellow, and white.

Oenothera speciosa (O. berlandieri)
SHOWY EVENING PRIMROSE, MEXICAN EVENING PRIMROSE

This gorgeous wildflower, which is native to the South-Central U.S., produces 2-inch, bowl-shaped, pale pink translucent flowers with white centers and showy yellow stamens. Flowers open at sunrise and close up into furled blossoms at sunset. Blooming begins in late spring or early summer and lasts into fall. White-flower forms open at night and may age to pink after pollination. Plants are low and a bit sprawling, covered with hairy, 1- to 3-inch-long, gray-green, lobed leaves.

Size: 1 to 2 feet tall; 1½ feet wide.

Light: Full sun.

Soil and Moisture: Average soil; moderate moisture. Drought tolerant.

thrives in boggy site or shallow water.

Planting and Propagation: Plant container-grown plants in spring, spacing 1 foot apart. Divide in spring or fall.

Special Care: Individual plants may be short lived, but abundantly self-sows.

Pests and Diseases: Mildew and spider mites if grown too dry. Leaf rot in the South.

Climate: Zones 3–8.

Cultivars and Similar Species: *M. s. semperflorens*, compact to 8 inches tall, very floriferous medium blue flowers. *M. sylvatica* (woodland forget-me-not), erroneously called *M. alpestris*; biennial or short-lived perennial often treated as cool-season annual, azure blue flowers with yellow eyes in spring and sporadically through summer, upright to 2 feet tall, cultivars often globular 8-inch mounds: 'Royal Blue Compact,' deep blue, compact; 'Indigo Blue,' blue; 'Victoria,' intense indigo blue, compact; 'Victoria Alba,' white, compact; 'Victoria Rosea,' pink, compact; 'Rosea,' pink; 'Sapphire,' bright blue, compact.

Garden Use: Naturalize in woodland, along stream, or in bog garden. Sow seeds of woodland forget-me-not in fall over bulb beds for spring blooms.

Oenothera speciosa 'Rosea'

Oenothera tetragona

Omphaloides verna
BLUE-EYED MARY, NAVEL SEED

Sometimes confused with forget-me-not because its blue flowers and foliage look similar, blue-eyed Mary differs by being a creeping plant with larger flowers—½ inch across—that lack yellow eyes, although they have white throats. The plant blooms lavishly in spring. Long-petioled, oval green leaves look attractive all summer. It's an evergreen in the South.

Size: 8 inches tall; 1 foot wide.

Light: Light to part shade.

Soil and Moisture: Humus-rich, well-drained, moist soil best; tolerates dry shade.

Planting and Propagation: Plant container-grown plants or sow seed in spring, spacing 1 foot apart. Divide in spring or fall if plants become crowded.

Special Care: Spreads rapidly by underground stems. Deadhead to prolong bloom.

Pests and Diseases: Slugs can often be troublesome.

Climate: Zones 6–9.

Cultivars: *O. v. alba*, white flowers.

Garden Use: Charming ground cover for shade and woodland gardens or under shrubs.

Planting and Propagation: Plant bare-root or container-grown plants in spring, spacing 2 to 3 feet apart. Divide as needed in spring.

Special Care: Spreads by stoloniferous roots and can be rampant in rich or fertilized soil.

Pests and Diseases: Usually pest free.

Climate: Zones 5–8; tolerates arid conditions, heat, and humidity.

Cultivars and Similar Species: 'Rosea' (*O. berlandierii*),' slender prostrate grower, light rose-pink flowers; 'Alba,' white day-blooming flowers; 'Siskiyou,' more floriferous and compact, to 3 inches tall, spreads less. *O. rosea:* upright flower buds open pink and age to deep rose.

Garden Use: Plant in informal and naturalistic gardens where aggressive tendencies are welcome.

Oenothera tetragona (*O. fruticosa*)
COMMON SUNDROPS

Common sundrops, a popular species native to eastern North America, is a day bloomer, opening clusters of canary-yellow, saucer-shaped, silky flowers every morning from early summer to midsummer. Lance-shaped green leaves cloak hairy, reddish stems and turn dark red in fall. Plants form overwintering evergreen rosettes.

Size: 1½ inches to 3 feet tall; spreads by underground roots to form large stands.

Light: Full sun.

Soil and Moisture: Average to poor soil; moderate moisture. Drought tolerant.

Planting and Propagation: Plant bare-root or container-grown plants in spring, spacing 2 to 3 feet apart. Divide in spring or fall.

Special Care: In late fall, cut back frost-killed stems and weed undesired plants to keep rampant plant in bounds.

Pests and Diseases: Spittlebugs may be troublesome.

Climate: Zones 3–8.

Cultivars and Similar Species: 'Fireworks,' 1½ feet tall, red stems, red flower buds, bright yellow flowers; 'Highlights,' bright pure-yellow fragrant flowers all summer, 1¼ feet tall; 'Lapsley,' large yellow flowers, 1½ feet tall; 'Sonnewende' ('Summer Solstice'), bright pure-yellow flowers all summer into fall, 2 feet tall; 'Youngii,' bright yellow, fragrant dense flowers mid- to late summer, may rebloom in fall, 1½ feet tall; 'Yellow River,' large yellow flowers, green stems, 1½ feet tall. *O. missouriensis* (Ozark sundrops, Missouri primrose): 4-inch yellow flowers open late afternoon, prostrate and spreading, shiny green leaves, dry sites.

Garden Use: Looks stunning combined with blue flowers in informal gardens.

Omphaloides verna

Origanum vulgare 'Aureum'
GOLDEN OREGANO, GOLDEN MARJORAM

Use this dainty foliage plant—a golden leaved version of the culinary herb—to create a ribbon of long-lasting color in herb or flower gardens. The creeping stems are covered with 1-inch-wide, lime-green, sweetly aromatic, round leaves that keep their color from spring through fall. Small lavender flowers appear in midsummer.

Size: 6 inches tall; wide spreading.
Light: Light shade.
Soil and Moisture: Average, well-drained soil; moderate moisture.
Planting and Propagation: Plant container-grown plants in spring, spacing 1 foot apart. Divide in spring or fall if needed.
Special Care: Shear off dead top growth in early spring. Leaves burn in full sun.
Pests and Diseases: Root rot if too wet.
Climate: Zones 5–9.
Similar Species: *O. dictamnus* (Dittany of Crete), 1-inch, gray-white, fuzzy round leaves on creeping plants, purplish pink flowers in

Origanum vulgare 'Aureum'

midsummer, excellent foliage plant, Zones 7–9, full sun, well-drained soil.
Garden Use: Charming ground cover or edging for herb or flower gardens when combined to echo yellow and chartreuse of larger variegated plants such as hosta, liriope, and ornamental grasses. Use as ground cover beneath tulips; lovely combined with orange, red, purple, and blue flowers.

Paeonia lactiflora
CHINESE PEONY, GARDEN PEONY

Cultivated in China more than 1,400 years ago, this sacred fragrant flower has been a beloved perennial in North American and European gardens for about 150 years. Breeding has brought us hundreds of cultivars in a range of colors, forms, and bloom times. The stunning long-stemmed flowers, which can be shades of white, red, pink, purple, or yellow, are 4 to 8 inches across. Single types have five large petals surrounding a showy center of yellow stamens. Semidouble types have four to eight rings of petals with showy stamens visible. Double types form huge balls of petals. Japanese types are similar to singles but with fringe-like, yellow, pollenless staminoids in the center. These four types can be further separated into early, mid-season, and late bloomers. Peonies form bushy bundles of gorgeous, glossy, dark green leaves cut into bold leaflets and grow slowly into large, long-lived clumps. The plants make an outstanding garden contribution even after the short bloom period, because attractive leaves remain green well into fall, when they may turn gleaming maroon.
Size: 14 inches to 3 feet tall and as wide.
Light: Full sun; afternoon shade in the South.
Soil and Moisture: Deep, humus-rich, fertile, moist soil; plentiful moisture best.
Planting and Propagation: Plant dormant roots with two or three eyes in fall, position-

Paeonia lactiflora

ing eyes 1 to 2 inches below soil surface. Plant well-rooted container-grown plants in spring. Division not necessary, but may be done on mature plants in fall.
Special Care: Slow to establish; new plants may need two or three years to bloom well. May not bloom if planted too deep. Double types need staking. Best to stake individual flower stems inconspicuously rather than using ring support, which may cut stems. Avoid overhead watering when in bloom. Cut blossoms when buds are just beginning to open, leaving two sets of leaves.
Pests and Diseases: Gray mold fungus can be serious. Practice good sanitation; apply fungicide if necessary. Ants on buds are common and harmless.
Climate: Zones 2–8; in the South grow early season, single, and Japanese types for best performance and to avoid disease.
Cultivars and Similar Species: More than 500 cultivars available; too numerous to list. *P. tenuifolia* (fernleaf peony): early red blossoms, finely divided leaves.
Garden Use: Spectacular used as specimen plants in formal or informal gardens, or plant in drifts in large gardens. Excellent cut flower.

Papaver nudicaule 'Champagne Bubbles'

Papaver nudicaule
ICELAND POPPY

The translucent overlapping petals of the Iceland poppy surround a green buttonlike center and a fringe of stamens, scattering sunlight like a silk scarf. The 3- to 6-inch-wide flowers bloom from spring to early summer and may be white, cream, yellow, pink, salmon, or red. Wiry leafless flower stems arise from a rosette of lobed gray-green leaves. Native to the Arctic, Iceland poppy needs cool, sunny weather to flourish and is sometimes treated as an annual.

Size: 1½ feet tall; 6 inches wide.

Light: Full sun; partial shade in the South.

Soil and Moisture: Average, well-drained soil; moderate moisture.

Planting and Propagation: Seedlings resent transplanting. Sow outdoors in fall in mild-winter areas for winter and spring bloom, or indoors in late winter in peat pots, for summer bloom in cool, northern areas. Thin to 8 inches apart. Nursery transplants available in late winter in the South. Where perennial, divide every three years.

Special Care: Fertilize with high-phosphorous, high-potassium fertilizer once danger of frost has passed.

Pests and Diseases: Usually pest free.

Climate: Perennial or biennial in Zones 2–7; may be grown as hardy, cool-season annual in Zones 3–11.

Cultivars: 'Champagne Bubbles,' 3-inch flowers in mix of pastel red, yellow, cream, orange, pink; 'Sparkling Bubbles Mix,' vivid colors; 'Oregon Rainbows,' 6-inch flowers, apricot, peach, pink, cream, picotees, doubles, and singles.

Garden Use: Charming flower for informal gardens, meadows, and containers.

Papaver orientale
ORIENTAL POPPY

This poppy's 6- to 10-inch crepe-paperlike blossoms sway atop tall, prickly stems, creating a spectacular display for about 10 days in early summer. Flowers of the species are flaming-red, but cultivars come in shades of pink, orange, red, salmon, raspberry-purple, or white, with showy dark velvety stamens filling their centers. Black splotches sometimes decorate the petal bases, and fancier hybrids may be bicolored or double. Plants have deep taproots and a basal rosette of coarse thistlelike foliage, which goes dormant by midsummer but produces an overwintering rosette in fall.

Size: Foliage clumps 2 to 3 feet tall and wide; flower stalks 3 to 4 feet tall.

Light: Full sun; part shade in hot areas.

Soil and Moisture: Deep, fertile to average, well-drained soil; moderate moisture.

Planting and Propagation: Plant bare-root plants 1 to 3 inches below soil surface in late summer or early fall, or plant container-grown plants in spring, spacing 2 feet apart. Needs no division for years, but plants can be divided, if desired, in fall.

Special Care: May rot in winter-wet soil. May need staking. Remove faded flower

Papaver orientale

stalks unless seedpods will be harvested.

Pests and Diseases: Usually pest free.

Climate: Zones 2–7; performs best with cool summers.

Cultivars: Early: 'Dubloon,' orange with rosy spots; 'China Boy,' white with orange edges; 'Helen Elizabeth,' crinkled light salmon-pink; 'Red Flame,' fiery red; 'Glowing Rose,' watermelon pink; 'White King,' white with purple splotches. Mid: 'Harvest Moon,' orange-yellow, double; 'Cheerio,' shell pink with rose splotches; 'Carnival,' white with orange edges and black splotches; 'Snow Queen,' bright white with purple splotches; 'Raspberry Queen,' raspberry-pink with black splotches; 'Warlord,' deep red; 'Beauty of Livermore,' fire-engine red. Late: 'Bonfire,' intense red, double, black splotches; 'Golden Promise,' golden orange, purple splotches; 'Spring-time,' white with pink edges.

Garden Use: Striking in cottage gardens and informal plantings; plant in groups of no more than three to avoid large midsummer gap. Combine with later-blooming or leafy plants, such as baby's breath, which fills in bare spots.

Penstemon barbatus 'Elfin Pink'

Penstemon barbatus
BEARD-TONGUE

Related to the snapdragon, beard-tongue produces one-sided spikes of tubular red or pink flowers with flared lips and furry throats. Spikes bloom for about two weeks in early summer above low clumps of narrow leaves, which are nondescript after flowering.

Size: 3 feet tall; 1 foot wide.
Light: Full sun.
Soil and Moisture: Average to gravelly, very well-drained soil; moderate water. Drought tolerant.
Planting and Propagation: Plant container-grown plants in spring, spacing 1 foot apart. Short-lived; propagate by stem cuttings in fall.
Special Care: Do not overwater. Cut back faded flower stalks for possible rebloom.
Pests and Diseases: Black spot fungus sometimes troublesome.
Climate: Zones 2–8; tolerates heat and humidity of the South.
Cultivars and Similar Species: 'Schooley's Yellow,' yellow. Dwarf strains 1 to 2 feet tall: 'Elfin Pink,' clear pink, long blooming; 'Rose Elf,' coral-pink, prolific flowers; 'Prairie Fire,' deep orange-red; 'Prairie Dawn,' pale pink; 'Prairie Dusk,' purple. *P. digitalis:* 'Husker Red,' purple foliage, white flowers, 3 feet tall.
Garden Use: Useful planted in drifts in rock gardens and low-water-use gardens.

Perovskia atriplicifolia
RUSSIAN SAGE

This long-blooming perennial begins its show of lavender-blue, two-lipped flowers in midsummer and carries on into fall. The tiny flowers decorate 1- to 1½-foot-tall, loosely branched panicles that create a delicate, vertical effect above the bushy plants. White, woolly hairs cover the flower stems above gray-green leaves with coarsely toothed edges for an overall misty, fine-textured result. The foliage of this mint family member releases a sagelike pungence when crushed.

Size: 3 to 5 feet tall; 3 feet wide.
Light: Full sun.
Soil and Moisture: Average to sandy or gravelly, well-drained soil; moderate moisture. Drought tolerant.

Perovskia atriplicifolia

Planting and Propagation: Plant container-grown plants in spring, spacing 3 feet apart. Take cuttings in summer. Needs no division.
Special Care: Tends to lean toward the sun; loose staking may be needed; cultivars are stronger stemmed. Cut back woody stems to 1 foot tall in fall or late winter.
Pests and Diseases: Usually pest free.
Climate: Zones 5–9; heat tolerant.
Cultivars: 'Blue Spire,' deep blue flowers, finely dissected leaves, upright growth; 'Longin,' narrow and strongly upright.
Garden Use: Excellent for silvery effect combined with grasses and other large-scale perennials in New American-style gardens and other naturalistic sites.

Petrorhagia saxifraga
(Tunica saxifraga)
TUNIC FLOWER, COAT FLOWER

The wiry stems and needlelike leaves of this lovely rock garden plant form dense cascading mounds with a delicate texture. Tiny pink or white flowers about ⅛ inch across create a mist of blossoms floating above the plant from midsummer into fall.

Petrorhagia saxifraga 'Rosette'

Size: 8 to 10 inches tall; sprawling mound to 1½ feet wide.

Light: Full sun.

Soil and Moisture: Average to moist, well-drained, alkaline soil; moderate moisture.

Planting and Propagation: Plant container-grown plants in spring, spacing 2 feet apart.

Special Care: Cut back woody stems to several inches in late winter.

Pests and Diseases: Usually pest free.

Climate: Zones 5–7.

Cultivars: 'Alba,' white; 'Alba Plena,' double white; 'Rosette,' double rose-pink; 'Lady Mary,' double pink, early to late summer.

Garden Use: Best in rock garden or rock wall where soil is well drained and where stems can cascade.

Phlomis russeliana (P. viscosa)
STICKY JERUSALEM SAGE

One of the showiest members of the mint family, sticky Jerusalem sage gets its name from sagelike, fuzzy, heart-shaped leaves, which are evergreen in Zone 8. The plant possesses the unusual habit of producing flowers in 40 to 50 tight whorls up and down the tall stems, creating a candelabra effect.

Phlomis russeliana

Butter-yellow, the hooded flowers make an arresting show throughout late spring and early summer.

Size: 3 to 5 feet tall.

Light: Full sun in the North; part shade in the South.

Soil and Moisture: Average to sandy, infertile, well-drained soil; moderate moisture. Drought tolerant.

Planting and Propagation: Plant bare-root or container-grown plants in spring, spacing 3 feet apart. Divide in spring or fall.

Special Care: Weak stems may develop in rich soil. May rot in winter-wet site.

Pests and Diseases: Usually pest free.

Climate: Zones 4–8; tolerates seashore conditions.

Similar Species: *P. cashmeriana,* similar with lilac flowers.

Garden Use: Pleasing yellow color that combines well with most other flowers.

Phlox divaricata
WILD BLUE PHLOX, WOODLAND PHLOX

This graceful native wildflower puts on a showy display of long-stemmed clusters of pastel blue, lavender, or white flowers in mid- to late spring. Each five-petaled, 1½-inch-wide flower has a contrasting eye and a light fragrance. The petals are usually slightly lobed, although some cultivars have notched petals. Narrow, dark green leaves decorate the upright flower stems and the creeping, nonflowering stems, which spread out on the soil surface, rooting as they grow.

Size: 1 to 1¼ feet tall in bloom; spreads to form 2-foot-wide clumps.

Light: Light shade.

Soil and Moisture: Humus-rich, fertile, moist soil; plentiful moisture.

Planting and Propagation: Plant bare-root or container-grown plants in spring, spacing 1¼ feet apart. Divide immediately after blooming or in fall.

Special Care: Spreads slowly by creeping rhizomes. Shear back after flowers fade to

Phlox divaricata

neaten appearance and rejuvenate foliage if attacked by mildew.

Pests and Diseases: Somewhat susceptible to mildew and slug damage.

Climate: Zones 3–9.

Cultivars and Similar Species: 'Fuller's White,' pure white, notched petals, extremely floriferous, 10 inches tall; 'Dirigo Ice,' pale blue, 8 inches to 1 foot tall; *P. d. laphamii*, deep blue, rose eye, 1½ feet tall; 'Lodon Grove Blue,' blue, more compact; *P. x chattahoochee,* deep violet-blue with purple eye, long-blooming; *P. pilosa ozarkana* (downy phlox), pale pink, highly mildew resistant, 1¼ feet tall, blooms a bit later, sun tolerant.

Garden Use: Lovely allowed to spread in wildflower or shade garden. Combine with ferns and hostas to provide interest after bloom period.

Phlox maculata
WILD SWEET WILLIAM, SPOTTED PHLOX

Resembling garden phlox, this native species blooms a month earlier and the flower clusters form more conical clusters. Best of all, the darker green leaves resist mildew. The lightly fragrant, ½-inch flowers pack themselves tightly together into showy clusters that top the tall stems in early summer and again later in the year if cut back. Light magenta-pink in the species, garden varieties boast more attractive colors, including snow-white and purer pinks. The upright, hairy stems are usually mottled red.

Size: 2 to 3 feet tall; 2 feet wide.

Light: Full sun to light shade.

Soil and Moisture: Fertile, humus-rich, moist, well-drained soil; plentiful moisture.

Planting and Propagation: Plant bare-root or container-grown plants in spring, spacing 2½ feet apart. Divide every three or four years in spring.

Special Care: Cut back after blossoms fade to encourage rebloom.

Pests and Diseases: More resistant to mildew than garden phlox but affected some. Provide good air circulation, avoid overhead watering.

Climate: Zones 3–9.

Cultivars: 'Miss Lingard,' snow-white, sometimes listed as *P. carolina;* 'Omega,' white with lilac eye; 'Alpha,' rose-pink with dark eye; 'Rosalinde,' dark pink.

Garden Use: Spectacular massed in borders.

Phlox maculata

Phlox paniculata 'Bright Eyes'

Phlox paniculata (P. decussata)

GARDEN PHLOX, SUMMER PHLOX

Today's garden phlox is a far cry from the muddy magenta wild plant found growing along woodland edges in eastern North America. European hybridizers have brought us spectacular flower heads in vivid colors, including crimson, rose, purple, lilac, lavender, red, pink, and white, and a rare pure orange. Blooming usually for a month in July, August, or September, depending on the cultivar, garden phlox often reblooms if immediately cut back. Flower domes are up to 8 inches to 1 foot in diameter and have 1-inch-wide, five-petaled, honey-scented flowers often accented by contrasting eyes. The upright stems are unbranched, with smooth 2- to 5-inch-long lance-shaped leaves.

Size: 3 to 5 feet tall; 2 feet wide.

Light: Full to half sun.

Soil and Moisture: Deep, humus-rich, fertile, moist soil; plentiful moisture.

Planting and Propagation: Plant bare-root or container-grown plants in spring, spacing 3 feet apart. Divide every four years in spring or fall.

Special Care: Difficult to grow well. Remove every second or third new stalk in early spring to encourage strong growth, large flowers, and good air circulation. For a fuller look, pinch tips of foreground stems in early summer so flowers will be lower than on the stems behind. Loose staking may be necessary. Cut off flower heads after flowering to prevent seed formation (seedlings do not come true) and encourage rebloom.

Pests and Diseases: Highly susceptible to mildew; provide good air circulation, avoid wetting foliage, and use fungicide if needed. Choose mildew-resistant cultivars. Mites troublesome in full sun if soil dries out.

Climate: Zones 4–8; best with cool summers.

Cultivars: 'Blue Boy,' near-blue; 'Mt. Fuji,' white, long blooming, mildew resistant; 'The King,' deep purple, long blooming; 'Sir John Falstaff,' salmon-pink, deeper eye, long blooming; 'Starfire,' true red with maroon foliage; 'World Peace,' white, late blooming; 'Sandra,' cherry-red; 'Bright Eyes,' soft pink, rose eye; 'Tenor,' bright red; 'Pinafore Pink,' pink, 1½ feet tall; 'Eva Cullum,' disease resistant, bright pink with red eye; 'Orange Perfection,' clear orange; 'Franz Schubert,' lilac; 'Nora Leigh,' white-edged foliage, lavender flowers.

Garden Use: Beautiful if well grown and scattered in cottage gardens or massed in midground of formal borders.

Phlox stolonifera

CREEPING PHLOX

This beautiful woodland wildflower blooms lavishly in shady gardens from early to mid-spring. Clusters of five-petaled flowers with rounded, unnotched petals and contrasting eyes bloom on leafless stems held 6 to 8 inches above the leaves. The flowers are the most fragrant of the phloxes and may be pink, lavender, blue, or white with yellow eyes. The shiny, oval, 1½-inch leaves are evergreen and form a dense ground cover from trailing runners.

Phlox stolonifera 'Bruce's White'

Phlox subulata

Size: 6 to 8 inches tall in bloom; spreads to form 2-foot-wide mats.

Light: Light to full shade.

Soil and Moisture: Humus-rich, fertile, moist, neutral to acid soil; plentiful moisture.

Planting and Propagation: Plant bare-root or container-grown plants in spring, spacing 1 to 2 feet apart. Divide immediately after blooming or in fall as needed.

Special Care: Mulch lightly to protect shallow roots, but avoid smothering evergreen leaves. Allow to set seeds, if desired, then shear off dried stems.

268

Pests and Diseases: Not as troubled by mildew as are most phloxes.

Climate: Zones 2–8.

Cultivars: 'Blue Ridge,' large, lavender-blue; 'Bruce's White,' large, white with yellow eye; 'Home Fires,' bright rose-pink; 'Pink Ridge,' medium pink, fragrant; 'Sherwood Purple,' rich pastel purple, very fragrant.

Garden Use: Use as ground cover in shade and wildflower gardens and under shrubs. Makes pretty edging along path or in front of shaded border.

Phlox subulata
MOSS PINK

This commonly seen spring bloomer is the easiest of the phloxes to grow. For a month or more beginning in early spring, dense mats of spiky evergreen foliage are obliterated by 1-inch-wide, pink, white, blue, or purple flowers made up of five notched petals. Most often seen in garish pink, cultivars also come in colors that are a bit easier on the eye.

Size: 4 to 6 inches tall; forms wide-spreading mats.

Light: Full to half sun.

Soil and Moisture: Average or sandy, well-drained, neutral to alkaline soil; moderate moisture.

Planting and Propagation: Plant bare-root or container-grown plants in spring, spacing 2 feet apart. Divide immediately after flowering or in fall as desired.

Special Care: Easy to grow. Shear after flowering to neaten.

Pests and Diseases: Spider mites if grown too hot and dry. Root rot in winter-wet site.

Climate: Zones 2–9.

Cultivars and Similar Species: 'Emerald Blue,' medium blue-lavender; 'Emerald Pink,' rose-pink; 'Scarlet Flame,' rose-red; 'White Delight,' large white; 'Amazing Grace,' white with rose centers; 'Atropurpurea,' wine-red; 'Candy Stripe,' pink-and-white, long blooming; 'Appleblossom,' pale pink; 'Coral Eye,'

white with coral eyes, reblooms; 'Snowflake,' compact, white, star-shaped. *P. nivalis* (trailing phlox): unnotched petals, Zones 6–9. *P. mesoleuca* (Mexican phlox): flourishes in Southwest, elsewhere in well-drained rock walls and crevices; new hybrids available in hot colors, blooms all summer.

Garden Use: Makes nice evergreen-edging plant and bulb companion for beds and borders. Excellent in rock gardens and walls.

Physostegia virginiana
OBEDIENT PLANT, FALSE DRAGONHEAD

So named because its snapdragonlike flowers obediently remain facing whichever way they are pushed, this native plant makes a bold addition to any garden. The lance-shaped, shiny dark green leaves with toothed edges are arranged in two ranks, like a cross, around the upright stems. Tightly clustered, 1½-inch-long tubular, two-lipped, pink, magenta-pink, or white flowers are also arranged in ranks, forming striking spires above the leaves from late summer into fall.

Size: 3 to 4 feet tall; forms clumps up to 3 feet wide.

Light: Full to half sun.

Physostegia virginiana 'Vivid'

Soil and Moisture: Average, well-drained, acid soil; moderate to plentiful moisture.

Planting and Propagation: Plant bare-root or container-grown plants in spring, spacing 2 feet apart. Divide in spring every two or three years.

Special Care: Spreads aggressively. Needs staking in fertile soil or shade. Cut back after blooming to encourage rebloom.

Pests and Diseases: Rust fungus sometimes troublesome.

Climate: Zones 2–9; tolerates heat and humidity.

Cultivars: 'Vivid,' compact to 1⅔ feet tall, bright orchid-pink; 'Pink Bouquet,' rose-pink, 3 feet tall; 'Bouquet Rose,' rose-pink, 3 feet tall; 'Summer Snow,' white, earlier blooming, 2½ feet tall, less invasive; 'Variegata,' pink, 3½ feet tall, white-edged leaves.

Garden Use: Excellent for late-summer color in borders and naturalistic gardens.

Platycodon grandiflorus
BALLOON FLOWER

Balloon flower's 3-inch-wide cup-shaped flowers open from beautiful inflated flower buds, which accounts for the common name. Somewhat resembling bellflowers, balloon flower features petals with an intricate netting of dark veins surrounding white stamens and style. Usually rich purplish blue, the long-blooming midsummer flowers also may be pink or white and occasionally double. The upright, succulent stems emit a milky sap if broken and bear oval, blue-green leaves that turn showy golden yellow in fall.

Size: 2 to 3 feet tall; 1⅔ feet wide.

Light: Full sun in the North; part shade in the South.

Soil and Moisture: Deep, fertile to average, well-drained soil; plentiful moisture.

Planting and Propagation: Plant bare-root or container-grown plants in spring, spacing 2 feet apart. Needs no division, but fleshy roots may be carefully divided in spring.

Special Care: Tall forms need staking to pre-

Platycodon grandiflorus

vent floppiness. Emerges late in spring; avoid disturbing. Transplant deep taproots with care. Deadhead individual flowers every few days to promote long flowering; cut back to encourage second bloom flush after flowering ceases.

Pests and Diseases: Usually pest free.

Climate: Zones 3–8.

Cultivars: *P. g. mariesii*, deep blue-lavender, 2½ feet tall, no staking; 'Shell Pink,' pastel pink, 2 feet tall; 'Double Blue,' double violet-blue, 3 feet tall; 'Fuji White,' pure white, 1⅔ feet tall; 'Misato Purple,' purple, 1¼ feet tall, early; 'Hime Murasaki,' lavender-blue, 1 foot tall; 'Fuji Pink,' pink, 1⅔ feet tall; 'Hakone Blue,' double violet-blue, 1⅔ feet tall; *P. g. alba*, white, 3 feet tall.

Garden Use: Excellent in midsummer border; combines well with daylilies, lilies, and Japanese anemones.

Polemonium caeruleum
JACOB'S LADDER

Valued for its dense tufts of delicate-looking leaves and lovely flowers, Jacob's ladder makes a fine choice for a shade garden. This European wildflower's narrowly oval, point-

Polemonium reptans 'Blue Pearl'

ed green leaves are arranged directly across from each other in horizontal pairs like the rungs on a ladder, accounting for the common name. Drooping clusters of blue flowers with prominent yellow stamens bloom above the foliage in late spring and early summer.

Size: 1½ to 2 feet tall and wide.

Light: Tolerates full sun where cool and moist; light to part shade best.

Soil and Moisture: Fertile, humus-rich, well-drained soil; plentiful moisture.

Planting and Propagation: Plant container-grown plants in spring, spacing 1 foot apart. Divide in fall every three or four years. Take cuttings in summer.

Special Care: Browns if too hot and sunny.

Pests and Diseases: Powdery mildew and wilt sometimes cause problems.

Climate: Zones 2–7; best where cool.

Cultivars and Similar Species: *P. c. album*, pure white. *P. reptans* (creeping Jacob's Ladder): light blue, bell-shaped flowers with white stamens and yellow anthers, floppy to 1 foot tall, finer textured, native plant, 'Blue Pearl,' bright blue; 'Firmament,' bright blue, 1⅔ feet tall.

Garden Use: Excellent foliage and flowers for borders and naturalistic shade gardens.

Polygonatum biflorum

Polygonatum biflorum
SMALL SOLOMON'S SEAL

This native American wildflower forms architectural clumps of arching stems decorated with alternately arranged 4-inch-long, egg-shaped blue-green leaves that turn rusty-gold in fall. Bell-shaped, greenish white flowers borne in pairs or triplets dangle from the undersides of the graceful stems in early spring. These turn into round, bright green seedpods resembling peas by midsummer and may ripen to black if they aren't first eaten by birds.

Size: 1 to 3 feet tall; spreads to form equal-size clumps.

Light: Light to full shade.

Soil and Moisture: Best in humus-rich, fertile, acid, moist soil with plentiful moisture; tolerates dry shade once established.

Planting and Propagation: Plant bare-root or container-grown plants in spring, spacing 2 feet apart. Divide in fall if desired.

Special Care: Do not dig from the wild.

Pests and Diseases: Usually pest free.

Climate: Zones 3–9.

Similar Species: *P. commutatum* (great Solomon's), 3 to 7 feet tall, yellow-green flowers in groups of three to eight.

Garden Use: Lovely foliage plant in shade and woodland gardens.

270

Polygonatum odoratum 'Variegatum'
VARIEGATED FRAGRANT SOLOMON'S SEAL

This lovely foliage plant from Eurasia resembles our native common Solomon's seal but grows larger and features creamy white irregular variegations along the leaf margins. Showy, bell-shaped, white flowers with green tips are born in pairs along the undersides of the arching stems and emit a sweet, lilylike fragrance.

Size: 2½ feet tall; forms clumps 3 to 4 feet wide.

Light: Light to full shade.

Soil and Moisture: Best in humus-rich, fertile, acidic, moist soil with plentiful moisture; tolerates dry shade once established.

Planting and Propagation: Plant bare-root or container-grown plants in spring, spacing 2 feet apart. Divide in fall if desired.

Special Care: Easy to grow.

Pests and Diseases: Slugs can sometimes be troublesome.

Climate: Zones 3–9.

Similar Species: The green-leaf species is not as dramatic.

Garden Use: Eye-catching foliage plant for shady locations.

Polygonatum odoratum 'Variegatum'

Polygonum bistorta 'Superbum'

Polygonum bistorta
KNOTWEED, SNAKEWEED, EUROPEAN BISTORT

More commonly grown in Europe than here, knotweed produces 4- to 6-inch-long, arrow-shaped, dark green leaves featuring a prominent white midrib. Leaves create dense clumps that look good all season. From late spring to midsummer, bottlebrush spikes of soft pink flowers bloom on leafless stalks held high above the leaves.

Size: 1½ to 2½ feet tall in bloom; forms 3-foot-wide clumps.

Light: Full sun in the North; part shade in the South.

Soil and Moisture: Fertile, well-drained soil; plentiful moisture. Tolerates wet soil.

Planting and Propagation: Plant bare-root or container-grown plants in spring, spacing 2½ feet apart. Divide in spring, if desired.

Special Care: Performs poorly if soil dries out. Cut off faded spikes for possible rebloom in late summer.

Pests and Diseases: Usually pest free.

Climate: Zones 3–8; best where cool.

Cultivars and Similar Species: 'Superbum,' large rose-pink flowers, better than species.

Garden Use: Unusual plant for moist borders; naturalize in wet sites such as pond borders and stream banks.

Potentilla tabernaemontani (P. verna)
SPRING CINQUEFOIL

One of the showiest of the cinquefoils, spring cinquefoil produces clusters of ½-inch-wide golden yellow flowers in late spring. Leaves are hairy and dull green, divided into five 1-inch-long, wedge-shaped, toothed, palmately lobed leaflets. The plants send out runners that root as they grow and form thick, ground-covering evergreen mats.

Size: 6 to 9 inches tall; forms wide-spreading mats.

Light: Full sun; part shade where hot.

Soil and Moisture: Average to sandy, well-drained soil; moderate water.

Planting and Propagation: Plant bare-root or container-grown plants in spring, spacing 1 to 2 feet apart. Divide in spring or fall as needed.

Special Care: Spreads vigorously; divide regularly to control, or plant where invasiveness is not a problem.

Pests and Diseases: Usually pest free.

Climate: Zones 4–8; best where cool.

Cultivars and Similar Species: 'Nana,' dwarf to 4 inches tall.

Garden Use: Handsome ground cover in naturalistic gardens, rock gardens, and crevices of rock walls.

Primula japonica
JAPANESE PRIMROSE

A candelabra of 1-inch flowers arranged in five or six tiers characterizes this elegant, moisture-loving primrose. Flowers may be purple, magenta, rose, pink, or white with light or dark eyes and bloom from mid-spring to early summer. Plants self-sow where happily situated to create thick stands in a delightful assortment of color patterns.

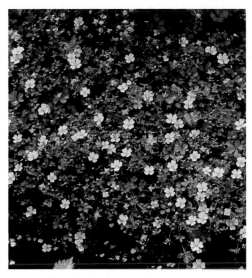

Potentilla tabernaemontani

The rough-textured leaves form basal clumps reminiscent of romaine lettuce.

Size: Flower stalks to 2 feet tall; leafy clumps 8 to 10 inches tall and to 2 feet wide.

Light: Light shade in moist site; part to full sun in wet or boggy site.

Soil and Moisture: Humus-rich to heavy, fertile, acid soil. Needs constantly moist, wet, or boggy site.

Primula japonica

Planting and Propagation: Plant container-grown plants in spring, spacing 3 feet apart. Divide in fall as desired.

Special Care: Mulch heavily to keep soil cool. Water during dry spells.

Pests and Diseases: Slugs and snails.

Climate: Zone 5–7.

Cultivars and Similar Species: 'Potsford White,' white, 1½ feet tall; 'Album,' white, 1⅓ feet tall; 'Carmina,' rose-red; 'Miller's Crimson,' crimson; 'Redfield Hybrids,' cold-hardy mix.

Garden Use: Best grown in naturalistic setting along stream or in bog.

Primula veris
COWSLIP PRIMROSE

This delightful wildflower graces the British countryside in early spring and is a mainstay of cottage gardens. Slender, flowering stems rise above clumps of rough-textured, oblong leaves with hairy white undersides, bearing bright yellow, tubular flowers in dangling bunches that are often one-sided. Although they vary, most cowslips give off a pleasant, light fragrance.

Size: 6 to 8 inches tall; 8 inches wide.

Primula veris

Light: Light shade.

Soil and Moisture: Humus-rich, fertile, well-drained, moist soil; plentiful moisture during growth and blooming. Tolerates dry soil after blooming, unlike most primroses.

Planting and Propagation: Plant bare-root or container-grown plants in early spring, spacing 1 foot apart. Divide every few years in fall if desired.

Special Care: Mulch heavily to keep soil cool in summer. Protect shallow roots from heaving in winter with evergreen boughs.

Pests and Diseases: Slugs and snails can be troublesome.

Climate: Zones 3–8.

Cultivars and Similar Species: *P. veris hortensis,* bright red with yellow centers. *P. elatior* (oxlip): taller stems, upward-facing, sulphur yellow, scentless flowers in one-sided clusters.

Garden Use: Plant in drifts in cottage gardens and along woodland walks.

Primula x *polyantha*
POLYANTHUS PRIMROSE

A favorite springtime florist plant, this primrose's roots are ancient. It was first cultivated and hybridized from several English wildflowers during Elizabethan times. Modern hybrids feature bunches of short-stemmed, 2-inch flowers in electric colors, including blue, purple, yellow, pink, and red with yellow eyes. Blooming throughout spring, polyanthus primrose forms rosettes of small, heavily crinkled, oblong leaves that grow larger after flowering ceases.

Size: Flower stalks to 1 foot tall; leaf clusters 6 to 7 inches tall and wide.

Light: Light shade.

Soil and Moisture: Humus-rich, fertile, moist, well-drained soil; plentiful moisture.

Planting and Propagation: Plant container-grown plants in early spring, spacing 1 foot apart; plant in fall for winter bloom in mild-winter areas. Divide every few years.

Primula x *polyantha*

Special Care: Mulch heavily to keep soil cool in summer. Protect shallow roots from heaving in winter with evergreen boughs. Water during dry spells. Potted florist plants can be transferred to garden when soil warms.

Pests and Diseases: Slugs and snails troublesome; spider mites cause problems if too hot and dry.

Climate: Zones 3–8; performs best with cool summers.

Cultivars and Similar Species: 'Pacific Giants,' seed-grown large-flower hybrids; 'Cresendo Hybrids,' cold hardy, large flowered, tall stemmed, seed grown, may rebloom in fall. *P. vulgaris/P. acaulis* (wild English primrose): long lived and tolerant of drier, hotter sites in Zones 6–9, greenish yellow flowers with starlike gold central marks, borne singly, vivid and pastel hybrids in blue, yellow, red, white. Tender primroses to treat as perennials in Zones 8–11 or as cool-season annuals: *P. malacoides* (fairy primrose), ruffled light green leaves, slender foot-tall stalks of delicate pastel flowers; *P. obconica* (top primrose), rounded leaves, 1¼-foot stalks with ball-like clusters of showy pastel flowers.

Garden Use: Plant in drifts in shade garden or along woodland path.

Prunella x *webbiana*
SELF-HEAL

This mat-forming, evergreen perennial bears wedge-shaped, hairy, dark green leaves topped from early summer to midsummer with showy short whorls of tightly clustered, tubular flowers. Most commonly purple, the two-lipped flowers also may be pink, rose, or white. Plants were once valued for their supposed ability to cure throat ailments and speed wound healing.

Size: 6 inches to 1 foot tall in bloom; spreads to form wide mats.

Light: Full sun to part shade.

Soil and Moisture: Average to fertile, well-drained, moist soil; plentiful moisture.

Planting and Propagation: Plant bare-root or container-grown plants in spring, spacing 1½ feet apart. Divide in spring or fall every few years.

Special Care: Shear off flower heads to prevent self-seeding and to promote rebloom. Can be invasive; plant away from lawns. Do not allow to dry out in sun.

Pests and Diseases: Usually pest free.

Climate: Zones 5–8; best where cool.

Cultivars and Similar Species: 'Loveliness,' lilac, 9 inches tall; 'Purple Loveliness,' deep purple, 1 foot tall; 'Pink Loveliness,' medium

Prunella grandiflora

Pulmonaria angustifolia

pink, 1 foot tall; 'White Loveliness,' white, 8 inches tall. *P. grandiflora:* very similar, but a bit shorter with looser flower clusters.

Garden Use: Use as edging to border, path, or walk, or plant under shrubs and in rock gardens.

Pulmonaria angustifolia
BLUE LUNGWORT

The plainest of the lungworts, this species offers bristly, foot-long, mat-forming, dull green deciduous leaves without any ornamental spotting. Coiled clusters of early spring flowers start out pink in bud and open to intense blue, blooming lavishly when well sited. The cultivars listed below are more garden worthy than the species.

Size: 9 inches to 1 foot tall; 2 feet wide.
Light: Light to full shade.
Soil and Moisture: Humus-rich, fertile, well-drained, moist soil; plentiful moisture.
Planting and Propagation: Plant bare-root or container-grown plants in spring, spacing 1½ to 2 feet apart.
Special Care: Can become invasive; plant where this is not a problem. Remove faded flower stalks.
Pests and Diseases: Powdery mildew occasionally troublesome.

Climate: Zones 2–8; best in the North.
Cultivars: 'Azurea,' deep true blue; 'Munstead Variety,' dainty leaves and deep violet-blue flowers; 'Mawson's Variety,' heart-shaped leaves, deep violet-blue flowers. *P. a. alba:* white flowers. *P. rubra:* late-winter, coral-red flowers, unspotted leaves.
Garden Use: Good bulb companion; also use under shrubs and in mixed borders. The foliage is not especially attractive from midsummer on.

Pulmonaria officinalis
COMMON LUNGWORT

Valued by early herbalists as a cure for lung ailments, this is one of the earliest lungworts to bloom. Bright pink, funnel-shaped flowers, which fade to bluish lilac, open with the earliest bulbs. The bristly, heart-shaped, white-spotted leaves are evergreen, except during the harshest winters.

Size: 1 foot tall; 1½ feet wide.
Light: Light to full shade.
Soil and Moisture: Humus-rich, fertile, well-drained, moist soil; plentiful moisture.
Planting and Propagation: Plant bare-root or container-grown plants in spring, spacing

Pulmonaria officinalis

1 foot apart. Divide after flowering, when needed.
Special Care: Remove faded flower stalks. Remove older leaves, wearing gloves to protect hands from bristles, when they fade in early summer to make room for new fresh growth. Keep soil moist.
Pests and Diseases: Powdery mildew if soil is too dry.
Climate: Zones 3–8.
Similar Species: *P. longifolia,* nonaggressive, clump-forming, long, narrow, pointed leaves dappled with silver, purple-blue flowers; 'Roy Davidson,' very bright spots, Zones 3–8.
Garden Use: Eye-catching ground cover in shade gardens; combine with early bulbs, hostas, ferns, and other tall perennials.

Pulmonaria saccharata
BETHLEHEM SAGE

The most ornamental of the lungworts, Bethlehem sage's rough-haired, elliptical leaves are evergreen with variable spotting—in some types silver spots are distinct, in others spots coalesce into all-over silver. In early spring, coiled clusters of pink flower buds

Pulmonaria saccharata 'Mrs. Moon'

open to pink, funnel-shaped flowers, which age to blue.

Size: 1 to ½ feet tall; 2 feet wide.

Light: Light to full shade.

Soil and Moisture: Humus-rich, fertile, well-drained, moist soil; plentiful moisture.

Planting and Propagation: Plant bare-root or container-grown plants in spring, spacing 1 to 2 feet apart. Divide in spring after flowering ceases.

Special Care: Remove faded flower stalks. Remove older leaves, wearing gloves to protect hands from bristles, when they fade in early summer to allow for fresh growth.

Pests and Diseases: Powdery mildew troublesome if soil is too dry.

Climate: Zones 3–8.

Cultivars and Similar Species: 'Mrs. Moon,' silver spotted leaves, pink flowers turn blue, hybrid with *P. officinalis.* 'Margery Fish,' vigorous; 'Sissinghurst White,' white flowers, silver-spotted leaves; 'Pink Dawn,' pink flowers don't change color, silver spotted leaves; 'Janet Fish,' white-marbled leaves.

Garden Use: Combine with bulbs in early spring shade garden; makes bright ground cover under taller, shade-loving perennials.

Pulsatilla vulgaris (Anemone pulsatilla)
PASQUE FLOWER

Pasque flower blooms in very early spring before its silky-haired, finely dissected, gray-green leaves are fully grown. The 3-inch, satiny flowers are composed of six pointed, wine-red, blue, or purple petals surrounding a center of prominent yellow stamens. Blossoms appear near the ground on fur-covered stems that elongate as flowers fade, eventually holding aloft feathery seed heads, which are as beautiful as the flowers.

Size: Seed-head stalks 9 inches to 1 foot tall above 6-inch-tall, 1-foot-wide foliage clumps.

Light: Full sun in the North; afternoon shade in the South.

Pulsatilla vulgaris

Soil and Moisture: Average, well-drained soil; moderate water. Drought tolerant in cool sites.

Planting and Propagation: Plant container-grown plants in spring, spacing 1 foot apart. Division is not necessary.

Special Care: Resents disturbance. May self-sow, but is not weedy. Foliage dies to ground in midsummer. Provide shade and extra moisture in hotter areas.

Pests and Diseases: Rots in winter-wet soil.

Climate: Zones 5–8.

Cultivars: *P. v. alba,* white; *P. v. rubra,* magenta to wine-red; 'Red Bells,' red; 'Violet Bells,' light violet-blue; 'White Bells,' creamy white; 'Mazur,' semidouble violet; 'Polka,' semidouble white.

Garden Use: Makes lovely specimen in rock gardens; good companion for early bulbs.

Ratibida pinnata
YELLOW CONEFLOWER

This native prairie plant blooms from late spring to midsummer, offering its stunning flowers in branched clusters well above the hairy leaves, which are divided into three to five lance-shaped leaflets with serrated edges. Bright yellow petals droop like swept-back wings from the columnar-shaped raised

Ratibida pinnata

tan disk. Leaves are dark green and finely cut.

Size: 3 to 6 feet tall; 1½ feet wide.

Light: Full sun.

Soil and Moisture: Average, well-drained soil; moderate moisture. Drought tolerant.

Planting and Propagation: Plant bare-root or container-grown plants in spring, spacing 2 feet apart. Divide in spring when crowded.

Special Care: May need staking. Deadhead to prolong blooming.

Pests and Diseases: Usually pest free.

Climate: Zones 3–8.

Similar Species: *Rudbeckia maxima* (giant coneflower), prairie native, similar 5-inch flowers, basal rosette of 2-foot-long, rounded, blue-green leaves, 8 feet tall, Zones 5–9.

Garden Use: Dramatic plant for naturalistic landscapes and New American-style gardens.

Rodgersia aesculifolia
FINGERLEAF RODGERSIA

A foliage plant par excellence, fingerleaf rodgersia bears huge, bronze-tinged, compound leaves resembling horse chestnut leaves. The long-stalked leaves are divided into 7-inch-long leaflets like fingers on a hand. These form a large basal rosette of foliage, above which rises a flat, pyramidal

Rodgersia spp.

Rudbeckia fulgida 'Goldsturm'

cluster of feathery creamy white or pinkish flowers in early summer. Coarse brown hairs cover the leaf veins, stems, and flower stalks.

Size: Foliage clumps 2 to 3 feet high, 3 to 6 feet wide; flower stalks 3 to 6 feet tall.

Light: Light to part shade best; full sun in constantly wet site.

Soil and Moisture: Fertile, humus-rich, moist to boggy soil; plentiful moisture.

Planting and Propagation: Plant container-grown plants in spring, spacing 4 to 5 feet apart. Divide in early spring after four or five years, if desired.

Special Care: Provide plenty of moisture; leaves scorch in too much sun or if too dry.

Pests and Diseases: Usually pest free.

Climate: Zones 5 and 6; performs poorly where hot and humid.

Cultivars and Similar Species: *R. podophylla,* similar with lobed leaf tips, foliage often bronze in spring and fall, Zones 5–7. *R. pinnata* (featherleaf rodgersia): leaves divided into five to nine 8-inch-long leaflets, rose-red flowers in late spring, Zones 5–7. *R. p. superba:* bronze-purple leaves in summer.

Garden Use: Use single specimens in shade or bog gardens, along streams and ponds for dramatic contrasting size and texture. Allow plenty of growing space.

Rudbeckia fulgida
ORANGE CONEFLOWER

Flowers of this prolific bloomer consist of golden orange ray petals surrounding a raised dark brown cone. The 2- to 3-inch-wide daisy-type flowers bloom in branched clusters above coarse foliage from midsummer until frost. The broad, pointed leaves are dark green with a rough texture. Orange coneflower spreads rapidly to form good-sized clumps.

Size: 2 to 3 feet tall; spreads to form 2- to 3-foot-wide clumps.

Light: Full sun best; tolerates half sun.

Soil and Moisture: Fertile to average, humus-rich to clay soil; plentiful moisture best. Drought tolerant once established.

Planting and Propagation: Divide in spring or fall every three or four years.

Special Care: Allow attractive dried seed heads to remain all winter; cut back in early spring. Somewhat invasive.

Pests and Diseases: Usually pest free; mildew sometimes troublesome at end of summer.

Climate: Zones 3–9.

Cultivars and Similar Species: Most garden worthy is 'Goldsturm,' compact and floriferous with 3- to 4-inch-wide flowers; cutting-grown plants superior and more uniform than seed-grown plants. *R. hirta* (black-eyed Susan, gloriosa daisy): short-lived perennial, 1 to 3 feet tall, best treated as an annual, reseeds in meadow gardens, mildew prone; 'Goldilocks,' semidouble, gold; 'Rustic Colors,' mix, golden yellow petals banded with gold, mahogany, rust, or orange; 'Irish Eyes,' green centers, yellow-orange petals.

Garden Use: Popular massed in New American-style landscapes; excellent for late color in informal and cottage gardens or in cut-flower garden.

Rudbeckia nitida
SHINING CONEFLOWER

This tall, dramatic plant provides late-season color with its 5-inch, daisylike flowers, which consist of drooping, bright yellow petals surrounding a greenish, columnar, raised disk. Dark green leaves are rounded with a few coarse teeth, forming a bushy base above which rise the branched and sparsely leafed flowering stems.

Size: 3 to 4 feet tall; 3 feet wide.

Light: Full sun.

Soil and Moisture: Fertile, well-drained soil; plentiful to moderate moisture.

Rudbeckia laciniata 'Autumn Glory'

Planting and Propagation: Plant container-grown plants in spring, spacing 3 feet apart. Divide in spring every four years.

Special Care: Individual stems may need staking, especially in the South or in part shade. Deadheading encourages longer bloom.

Pests and Diseases: Usually pest free.

Climate: Zones 4–10; thrives in heat and humidity of the South.

Cultivars and Similar Species: Very similar *R. laciniata* (green-eyed coneflower, cut-leaf coneflower), drooping lemon-yellow petals surrounding raised olive-green cones in late summer and fall, deeply cut leaves, to 6 feet tall, Zones 3–9. Cultivars of *R. laciniata* but often attributed to *R. nitida*: 'Golden Glow,' double lemon-yellow, 3 to 5 feet tall; 'Herbstsonne' ('Autumn Sun'), 3 to 5 feet tall, needs no staking; 'Autumn Glory,' 5 feet tall; 'Goldquelle' ('Gold Drop'), shaggy double yellow, 2 to 3 feet tall.

Garden Use: Excellent back-of-border plant for informal gardens; naturalize in meadows and mass-plant in New American-style gardens. Long-lasting cut flower.

Ruta graveolens
RUE

Once grown in monastery gardens as a medicinal herb and an antidote to witchcraft, rue adorns today's herb gardens as an aromatic edging or specimen plant. Its bitter leaves should not be ingested but may be dried in bunches and hung up or strewn as an insect repellent. The beautiful, finely cut blue-gray leaves have blunt lobes and form ornamental clumps that are evergreen in warm climates. In midsummer, airy bunches of tiny yellow-green flowers peak above the leaves.

Size: 3 feet tall; 2 feet wide.

Light: Full sun.

Soil and Moisture: Average, well-drained, neutral soil; moderate moisture.

Ruta graveolens

Planting and Propagation: Plant container-grown plants in spring, spacing 2 feet apart. Take cuttings in late summer or early fall.

Special Care: Prune or cut back to woody base in late winter to rejuvenate if desired. Oils from the leaves may cause rash in some people.

Pests and Diseases: Root rot in damp sites.

Climate: Zones 4–9.

Cultivars: 'Blue Mound,' very blue leaves; 'Curly Girl,' very lacy compact plant to 1 foot tall, good blue leaves.

Garden Use: Makes excellent low hedge for edging herb garden; plant for contrasting foliage effect in flower gardens.

Salvia argentea
SILVER SAGE

Grown for its foliage rather than its flowers, silver sage produces a rosette of 6- to 8-inch-long scallop-edged, furry, silvery white leaves that look like velvet. Some gardeners cut off the tall spikes of 1- to 2-inch-long, chalky white, yellow-centered flowers as they develop in late spring or early summer, but others like their ghostly look. Silver sage is a biennial or short-lived perennial; removing the flowers prolongs its garden life.

Salvia argentea

Size: Flower stalks 2 to 3 feet tall; basal foliage rosette 8 inches high and 2 feet wide.

Light: Full sun.

Soil and Moisture: Fertile, humus-rich, well-drained soil; moderate moisture.

Planting and Propagation: Plant container-grown plants in spring, spacing 2 feet apart. Needs no division. Renew by allowing to self-sow.

Special Care: Cut off developing flower stalks if desired.

Pests and Diseases: Slugs sometimes troublesome; rots in winter-wet site.

Climate: Zones 5–9; heat tolerant.

Cultivars: Only species is offered.

Garden Use: Plant near front of border to enjoy leaves; good silvery foliage contrast.

Salvia officinalis
GARDEN SAGE

Grown primarily for the culinary uses of its aromatic evergreen leaves, sage also has a long history of medicinal applications and is highly ornamental. A network of prominent veins runs through the velvety, silvery green, blunt leaves, giving them a pebbly appearance. Some cultivars offer foliage variegated in an array of colors—all retain the lemon-camphor aroma. Spikes of tiny, violet-blue, two-lipped, tubular flowers on tall, whoolly white stalks bloom above the foliage in late spring and early summer.

Size: Foliage clumps 1 to 2 feet tall; flower stalks to 3 feet tall.

Light: Full sun.

Soil and Moisture: Fertile to average, very well-drained soil; moderate moisture. Drought tolerant once established.

Planting and Propagation: Plant container-grown plants in spring, spacing 2 feet apart. Take cuttings in summer.

Special Care: Prune or cut back to near woody base in early spring to renew.

Pests and Diseases: Slugs and spittle bugs sometimes troublesome. May rot in winter-wet site.

Climate: Zones 4–9.

Cultivars: 'Berggarten,' very silvery round leaves; 'Compacta,' 1¼ feet tall; 'Tricolor,' gray-green leaves variegated on edges with creamy white and purple; 'Aurea,' gray-green leaves variegated on edges with golden green, 1½ feet tall; 'Purpurea,' steely purplish gray leaves, 1½ feet tall.

Garden Use: Indispensable in herb gardens; use in cottage and formal gardens for foliage accent among green-leaved plants.

Salvia officinalis 'Purpurea'

Salvia pratensis

Salvia pratensis (S. haematodes)

MEADOW SAGE, MEADOW CLARY

This showy, cold hardy sage arranges its foliage in a large basal rosette. The attractive, 6-inch-long, oblong leaves are wrinkled and hairy with toothed edges. Branched spikes of fragrant, 1-inch, lavender-blue flowers shaped like a parrot's beak bloom above the foliage clumps from late spring into midsummer with repeat bloom possible.

Size: 2 to 3 feet tall; 3 feet wide.

Light: Full sun to light shade.

Soil and Moisture: Fertile to average, well-drained soil; moderate moisture.

Planting and Propagation: Plant container-grown plants in spring, spacing 2 to 3 feet apart. Divide in spring if desired.

Special Care: Individual plants are usually short lived but self-sow to perpetuate themselves in the garden. Leaves get ragged if soil dries out.

Pests and Diseases: Usually pest free.

Climate: Zones 3–9; heat tolerant.

Cultivars and Similar Species: *S. azurea* var. *grandiflora/S. pitcheri* (azure sage), 4 to 6 feet tall, stake with tall brush or allow to lean on nearby plants, Zones 5–9. *Salvia greigii* (autumn sage): crimson or white flowers all summer on bushy 2- to 3-foot-tall plants, Zones 7–9. *Salvia leucantha* (Mexican bush sage): white-and-violet flowers in late summer on shrubby plants 3 to 4 feet tall, green leaves with white, woolly undersides, Zones 8–9.

Garden Use: Attractive vertical effect in beds and borders; cool color combines well with most other flowers.

Salvia x superba (S. nemorosa)

HYBRID BLUE SALVIA, HYBRID SAGE

This hybrid sage is one of the showiest and longest blooming of the cold-hardy salvias. Dense spikes of tubular, purple-violet flowers with showy wine-red bracts bloom above woody-based mounds of pungent foliage in early summer. After flowers fade, the bracts remain showy, but if the old spikes are removed another crop of fresh flowers develops. Oblong, 3-inch-long, gray-green leaves make a nice contrast to the stalks of rich-colored flowers.

Size: 1½ to 3 feet tall; spreads to 3-foot-wide clumps.

Light: Full sun to light shade.

Soil and Moisture: Fertile to average, moist soil; moderate moisture best, but tolerates drought once established.

Salvia x *superba* 'East Friesland'

Planting and Propagation: Plant container-grown plants in spring, spacing 2 to 3 feet apart. Divide in early spring every four or five years, being careful with woody base.

Special Care: Cut back hard after each flush of flowers to encourage repeat bloom. Tall types may need staking in hot areas.

Pests and Diseases: Usually pest free.

Climate: Zones 4–7. Best with cool nights; performs poorly in heat and humidity.

Cultivars: 'Blue Hill,' true blue flowers, 1½ feet tall; 'Blue Queen' ('Blakonigin'), violet-blue, 1½ feet tall; 'East Friesland' ('Oestfriesland'), deep purple, 1½ feet tall; 'May Night' ('Mainacht'), deep indigo-blue, early blooming, 1½ feet tall; 'Rose Queen,' rose-pink, 2 feet tall; 'Rose Wine,' mauve-pink, 2 feet tall; 'Miss Indigo,' violet, 2½ feet tall.

Garden Use: Outstanding vertical effect and purple color in informal and formal gardens.

Sanguinaria canadensis
BLOODROOT

This beloved early spring wildflower has the charming habit of enfolding its rounded leaves about its flower stalks as they close up at night. Pure white with a tuft of showy yellow stamens in their centers, the solitary 3-inch-wide flowers rise directly from the ground on 6-inch-tall stalks. Lasting but a few days before the petals drop, each flower folds up at night like hands praying, opening during sunny days. More flowers appear, however, with the bloom period lasting about two weeks. The lobed, blue-green leaves have a round outline and emerge directly from the ground, growing to 1 foot across after flowers fade. Plants go dormant in early summer. The rootstalks exude an orange-red sap; hence, the common name.

Size: 3 to 6 inches tall; 8 inches wide.

Light: Full sun in spring, followed by summer shade cast by deciduous trees.

Soil and Moisture: Fertile, humus-rich, moist, acid soil; plentiful moisture during growth.

Sanguinaria canadensis 'Multiplex'

Planting and Propagation: Plant bare-root or container-grown plants in spring, spacing 1 foot apart. Divide after leaves yellow, if desired; wear gloves as protection against poisonous sap. Do not dig from the wild; purchase only nursery-propagated plants.

Special Care: Mulch soil well in summer. Will self-sow if happily situated.

Pests and Diseases: Usually pest free.

Climate: Zones 3–9.

Cultivars: 'Multiplex,' showy, long-lasting double flowers resembling waterlilies.

Garden Use: Charming planted in drifts in woodland wildflower and shade gardens.

Santolina chamaecyparissus (S. incana)
LAVENDER COTTON, GRAY SANTOLINA

This odd-looking plant produces mounds of tiny, feathery, woolly, silvery gray leaves with a camphorlike scent. Evergreen in mild winter climates, it forms broad, spreading clumps but is often pruned as a low hedge. All summer, buttonlike yellow flowers bloom profusely across the tops of unpruned plants.

Size: 1 to 2 feet tall; 2 to 6 feet wide.

Light: Full sun.

Soil and Moisture: Average to sandy, well-drained soil; infrequent water. Drought tolerant.

Santolina chamaecyparissus

Planting and Propagation: Plant container-grown plants in spring, spacing 1½ to 2 feet apart. Take cuttings in spring.

Special Care: In early spring in cold climates, prune back to where new growth emerges near woody base. Where evergreen, prune back by one-half to one-third to shape in spring. Shear monthly to maintain as a hedge. Shear off faded flowers after flowering ceases.

Pests and Diseases: Root rot in wet site.

Climate: Zones 6–8; heat tolerant but performs poorly where hot and humid.

Cultivars and Similar Species: 'Compacta,' dwarf form *S. virens* (green santolina), lime-green leaves, pale creamy yellow flowers.

Garden Use: Clip into low hedges as edging for herb or flower gardens or to create intricate knot garden. Use unpruned plants to spill over rock wall.

Saponaria ocymoides
ROCK SOAPWORT

Clusters of bright pink, ¼-inch-wide, five-petaled flowers blanket this fine-textured, mat-forming plant for several weeks in early summer, and sometimes again in late summer. The pointed, oval leaves are 1 inch long, hairy, and semi-evergreen, cloaking the flexible reddish stems. Sap from soapwort

Saponaria ocymoides

roots lathers when mixed with water and was once used to make soap.

Size: 6 inches tall, sprawls to 1 foot wide.

Light: Full sun.

Soil and Moisture: Average to sandy, well-drained soil; moderate water. Drought tolerant once established.

Planting and Propagation: Plant container-grown plants in spring, spacing 1 foot apart. Divide in spring or fall every three years.

Special Care: Cut back hard after flowering to promote bushiness and rebloom. Floppy in fertile soil.

Pests and Diseases: Root rot may be problem in winter-wet site.

Climate: Zones 2–7; performs poorly where hot and humid.

Cultivars and Similar Species: *S. o. alba,* white; *S. o. rubra compacta,* mound forming, deep pink to rose-red. *S.* x *lempergii* 'Max Frei': sprawling but compact to 1 foot tall, clusters of 1-inch-wide pink flowers, Zones 6–8. *S. officinalis* (bouncing Bet): 1 to 3 feet tall, phloxlike clusters of pale pink fragrant flowers in summer, roots invasive, single forms self-sow weedily, double forms are sterile, Zones 2–8.

Garden Use: *S. ocymoides* best in rock garden or planted to cascade over wall or bank. Grow other species in flower borders.

Scabiosa caucasica
PINCUSHION FLOWER, SCABIOUS

Valued for its long-blooming blue flowers that begin appearing in midsummer, pincushion flower produces blossoms until fall. Its lance-shaped, fuzzy, gray-green, basal foliage forms evergreen clumps. Sparse, lobed leaves occur along the slender, flowering stems, which are topped with solitary, flat, 3- to 4-inch-wide flower heads. Many tightly packed flowers with lobed petals and gray-tipped stamens make up the inflorescenses; petals around the outside of the flower head are larger, giving it a lacy frame. Flowers are most commonly light lavender-blue, but deep blue, white, and pink forms are available.

Size: Flower stems 1½ to 2 feet tall; foliage clumps 6 inches tall, 1½ feet wide.

Light: Full sun in the North; part shade in the South.

Soil and Moisture: Fertile, humus-rich, moist soil; plentiful moisture.

Planting and Propagation: Plant container-grown plants in spring, spacing 1 to 2 feet apart. Divide in spring every four years.

Special Care: Remove faded flowers to promote continual bloom. Mulch well in summer.

Scabiosa caucasica

Pests and Diseases: Slugs may be troublesome.

Climate: Zones 3–7; best with cool summers.

Cultivars and Similar Species: 'Kompliment,' deep lavender-blue, 2 feet tall; 'Blue Butterfly,' lavender-blue, blooms from spring until frost, 1 foot tall; 'Perfecta,' light lavender-blue, 1½ to 2 feet tall; 'Fama,' intense sky-blue, 1⅔ feet tall; 'Pink Mist,' rose-pink, 1 foot tall, blooms until frost; *S. c. perfecta alba,* white 1½ to 2 feet tall. *S. atropurpurea* (annual pincushion flower): velvety purple and in mixed colors.

Garden Use: Plant in groups in front of cottage, rock, and informal gardens.

Scutellaria baicalensis
SKULLCAP

This member of the mint family spreads enthusiastically, just like its cousins. The ground-hugging stems turn up at the ends to support the flower spikes and sport rounded, lance-shaped leaves. In midsummer, spikes of 1-inch-long, hooded purple flowers almost smother the plants with rich color.

Size: 1 foot tall; spreads to form clumps 1½ to 2 feet wide.

Light: Full sun.

Soil and Moisture: Average, well-drained, moist soil; plentiful moisture.

Scutellaria baicalensis

Planting and Propagation: Plant bare-root or container-grown plants in spring, spacing 1 foot apart. Divide in spring every few years.

Special Care: Spreads rapidly; may be considered invasive in tidy gardens.

Pests and Diseases: Usually pest free.

Climate: Zones 6–8.

Cultivars: Only species is sold.

Garden Use: Makes good ground cover under taller perennials in informal gardens.

Sedum cauticolum

Sedum cauticolum

This deciduous, ground-hugging sedum features purplish woody stems and round, succulent, 1- to 2-inch-wide, blue-gray leaves. Clusters of starry rose-pink flowers bloom in late summer and fall.

Size: 2 to 4 inches tall; 8 to 10 inches wide.

Light: Full sun.

Soil and Moisture: Average to sandy, well-drained soil; moderate moisture.

Planting and Propagation: Plant bare-root or container-grown plants in spring, spacing 8 inches apart. Divide in spring if becomes crowded.

Special Care: Tolerates moist soil better than other sedums.

Pests and Diseases: Usually pest free.

Climate: Zones 5–9.

Cultivars and Similar Species: x 'Ruby Glow' (hybrid with x 'Autumn Joy'), 1 foot tall but floppy stems, dark ruby-red flowers, red-tinged blue-gray leaves. x 'Vera Jameson' (hybrid of 'Ruby Glow' and *S. maximum* 'Atropurpureum'), purple leaves, pink early fall flowers. *S. spurium:* mat-forming, dense 1-inch semi-evergreen leaves, Zones 3–8; 'Dragon's Blood,' bronze leaves, blood-red summer flowers; 'Tricolor,' red-green-and-white leaves, pink flowers; 'Album Superbum,' white flowers, bronze foliage.

Garden Use: Excellent specimen plants for contrasting colorful foliage and late flowers in rock gardens and borders. *S. spurium* makes good ground cover and edging.

Sedum kamtschaticum

KAMTSCHATKA STONECROP, GOLDEN STONECROP

The pale green stems and succulent, scalloped, 2-inch rounded leaves of this beautiful stonecrop are unbranched and sculptural. Flat clusters of dark orange-yellow flowers top the stems in summer. As these die back, new rosettes of foliage form at their bases.

Size: 4 to 9 inches tall; 1 to 1¼ feet wide.

Light: Full to half sun.

Soil and Moisture: Average to sandy, well-drained soil; moderate moisture. Drought tolerant.

Planting and Propagation: Plant bare-root or container-grown plants in spring, spacing 1 foot apart. Divide in spring or fall.

Special Care: Rake away dead stems and foliage in late fall, being careful not to injure overwintering rosettes.

Pests and Diseases: Usually pest free.

Climate: Zones 3–8.

Cultivars and Similar Species: 'Variegatum,' leaves green and creamy white with pink tinge; *S. middendorffianum,* needlelike red-bronze leaves. *S. acre* (goldmoss sedum): invasive, self-seeding, mat-forming species

Sedum kamtschaticum

with small, pointed leaves and showy yellow flowers in early summer. *S. aizoon* (aizoon stonecrop): yellow summer flowers, 2-inch toothed leaves, 1 to 1¼ feet tall. *S. spathulifolium:* variable with dusty blue or red-tinged evergreen ground-covering leaves, yellow summer flowers.

Garden Use: Wonderful planted in crevices of rock walls, arranged in clusters in rock garden, or planted as bank cover.

Sedum x telephium 'Autumn Joy'

AUTUMN JOY STONECROP

This fashionable plant creates a changing and beautiful sight through much of the year. Its shoots poke through the ground in early spring, creating clusters of whorled, succulent, jade-green leaves. By midsummer, pale green flower heads resembling broccoli top the stems. These turn pale pink in late summer, bright pink in fall, and rose-red with the onset of cold weather. Frost turns the whole plant rusty-bronze, and the sturdy dried stems and seed heads stand all winter, adding an extra dimension to the garden.

Size: 1½ to 2 feet tall and wide.

Light: Full sun best; tolerates half shade.

Soil and Moisture: Average to sandy, well-drained soil; moderate moisture. Drought tolerant.

Planting and Propagation: Plant bare-root or container-grown plants in spring, spacing 2 to 3 feet apart. Divide in spring every four years. Take stem cuttings in early summer.

Special Care: May sprawl in part shade; provide support or pinch in midsummer.

Pests and Diseases: Usually pest free.

Climate: Zones 3–10.

Cultivars and Similar Species: *S. maximum* 'Atropurpureum,' bronze-purple leaves, weakly upright stems, cream-rose flowers. *Sedum spectabile* (showy stonecrop): very similar but 1½ to 2 feet tall, blooms earlier, not as sturdy in winter; 'Brilliant,' light lavender-pink; 'Stardust,' pale pinkish white; 'Meteor,' carmine-red, 1½ feet tall; 'Variegatum,' green-edged creamy yellow leaves, pink flowers.

Garden Use: Mass-plant in New American-style gardens; use as specimens in beds and borders. Attracts butterflies. Dried seed heads are lovely in arrangements.

Sedum x *telephium* 'Autumn Joy'

Sempervivum tectorum 'Mahogany'

Sempervivum tectorum
HENS-AND-CHICKS, HOUSELEEK

A fascinating evergreen succulent native to Europe, hens-and-chicks produces ground-hugging whorls of fleshy, pointed, red-tinged green leaves arranged in flower-shaped rosettes. The large, main rosette (the hen) sends out short stems that produce smaller rosettes (the chicks) tucked close beside. Main rosettes bloom erratically in summer, producing thick, hairy, odd-looking stems topped with compact clusters of starry flowers. After flowering, the main rosette dies, but the growing chicks soon fill in.

Size: Rosette clusters to 6 inches tall; 1 foot wide. Flower stalks 1 to 1½ feet tall.

Light: Full sun to half shade.

Soil and Moisture: Average to poor, well-drained soil; moderate moisture.

Planting and Propagation: Plant bare-root or container-grown plants in spring, spacing 2 feet apart. Remove chicks with a bit of stem attached; will root where planted.

Special Care: Water during dry spells; not drought tolerant even though a succulent.

Pests and Diseases: Crown rot in damp site or wet climates. Rust fungus where humid.

Climate: Zones 3–8.

Cultivars and Similar Species: The species is quite variable with diverse leaf colors and forms; many cultivars and hybrids are listed under a confusing number of duplicate names.

Garden Use: Once grown on cottage roofs to ward off witches and lightning, now best grown in crevices of rock walls and stone steps or in containers.

Senecio aureus
GOLDEN GROUNDSEL

This native wildflower makes wet, open woodland sites its home. In late spring, clusters of golden yellow, ragged daisy-type flowers bloom atop leafless branched stems, bringing hot color to the spring wildflower garden. The dark green, oval- to heart-shaped, toothed leaves are evergreen and form loose clumps beneath the flower stalks. Plants spread rapidly to form impressive stands.

Size: 2 to 3 feet tall; spreads to form 2- to 3-foot-wide clumps.

Senecio aureus

Light: Light shade; full sun in wet site.

Soil and Moisture: Average to humus-rich, moist to wet or boggy soil; provide plentiful moisture.

Planting and Propagation: Plant container-grown plants in spring, spacing 1½ feet apart. Divide in fall when crowded.

Special Care: Readily self-sows; remove faded flower stalks to prevent sowing if desired.

Pests and Diseases: Usually pest free.

Climate: Zones 4–9.

Similar Species: *S. tomentosus* (butterweed), gray leaves, similar flowers, sun-loving, drought tolerant, for meadows.

Garden Use: Plant in groups in naturalistic woodland, shade, or bog gardens.

Sidalcea malviflora
CHECKERBLOOM, PRAIRIE MALLOW

Native to fields and meadows of California and Mexico, checkerbloom resembles a miniature hollyhock, offering loose spikes of silky 1- to 2-inch-wide flowers from mid- to late summer. The five-petaled, dish-shaped flowers are lilac-pink in the species, but improved cultivars come in many beautiful cool shades of pink and red. The clump-forming

Sidalcea malviflora

basal leaves are 3 inches wide and unlobed or shallowly lobed; stem leaves are deeply divided into five to seven fingerlike lobes.

Size: 2 to 5 feet tall; 2 feet wide.

Light: Full sun to light shade.

Soil and Moisture: Humus-rich, fertile, well-drained soil; plentiful moisture.

Planting and Propagation: Plant container-grown plants in spring, spacing 2 feet apart. Divide in fall when centers die out.

Special Care: Cut back faded stalks for repeat bloom. Keep moist; leaves brown quickly under dry conditions.

Pests and Diseases: Japanese beetles troublesome. Rust resistant.

Climate: Zones 5–7; best in cool climate. Poor performance where hot and humid.

Cultivars: 5 feet tall: 'Stark's Hybrids,' mix of pink to lavender-purple. All 2 to 3 feet tall: 'Brilliant,' deep rose; 'Elsie Heugh,' fringed pastel pink; 'Partygirl,' rose-carmine; 'William Smith,' salmon-red; 'Bianca,' white; 'Rosy Gem,' dark rose; 'Sussex Beauty,' satiny pink.

Garden Use: Delicate, vertical effect for borders and naturalistic gardens.

Sisyrinchium striatum
ARGENTINE BLUE-EYED GRASS

Native to Chile, this old-fashioned perennial has gray-green, sword-shaped leaves that rightly label it a member of the iris family. The flowers, however, are more subtle than iris blossoms. Tall spikes bearing clusters of 1-inch-wide, pale yellow, six-petaled, wheel-shaped blossoms with dark yellow throats and purple-striped backs bloom in early summer. The evergreen foliage remains attractive year-round.

Size: 1 to 2 feet tall; 1½ feet wide.

Light: Full sun.

Soil and Moisture: Average, well-drained soil; moderate moisture. Drought tolerant, but looks best if soil stays moist.

Planting and Propagation: Plant bare-root or container-grown plants in spring, spacing 1 foot apart. Divide fleshy roots after flower-

Sisyrinchium striatum

ing, when clumps become crowded.

Special Care: In early spring, clip foliage back to several inches to make way for fresh growth. Self-seeds freely; remove faded flower stems to neaten appearance and prevent sowing if desired.

Pests and Diseases: Not bothered by slugs.

Climate: Zones 4–8; best where cool.

Similar Species: *S. angustifolium* (blue-eyed grass), blue flowers, grassy leaves, 1 to 1½ feet tall.

Garden Use: Plant in groups for best vertical effect in formal and informal gardens. Pastel color combines well with most other colors.

Solidago hybrids
GOLDENROD

Prized in Europe as a late-blooming perennial, native goldenrods have only recently found a place in North American gardens. Wrongly blamed for causing hay fever because they bloom at the same time as ragweed, goldenrod has an ill-deserved bad reputation. Garden-worthy hybrids, mostly bred

Solidaster luteus

in Europe, bring large, feathery plumes of tiny, golden yellow, daisylike blossoms to gardens in late summer and fall. The dark green toothed leaves form handsome clumps. Some types spread aggressively; others are better behaved.

Size: 2 to 3 feet tall; spreads to form 3- to 4-foot-wide clumps.

Light: Full sun.

Soil and Moisture: Average to poor, well-drained soil; moderate moisture. Drought tolerant.

Planting and Propagation: Plant bare-root or container-grown plants in spring, spacing 2 feet apart. Divide every three years to control spreading.

Special Care: May grow rampantly and flop in fertile soil. Usually needs no staking.

Pests and Diseases: Usually pest free.

Climate: Zones 3–9.

Cultivars: Hybrids bred from several native species are compact and floriferous: 'Crown of Rays,' yellow-gold, late summer; 'Golden Dwarf,' golden yellow, 1 foot tall; 'Peter Pan,' bright yellow, 2 feet tall, midsummer and fall;

'Golden Baby,' canary yellow, 2½ feet tall; 'Baby Sun,' clear yellow, midsummer, 1 foot tall. *S. sphacelata* 'Golden Fleece': gold flowers all fall, 1½ feet tall, semi-evergreen heart-shape ground-covering leaves. *S. rugosa* 'Fireworks': arching yellow-gold sprays, 3 to 4 feet tall. *Solidaster luteus:* a hybrid of aster and goldenrod, soft yellow plumes late summer, needs staking, 2 feet tall, Zones 5–9.

Garden Use: Wonderful form and color to combine with ornamental grasses, coneflowers, and asters in fall gardens. Good cut flower.

Stachys byzantina (S. lanata)
LAMB'S-EARS

With leaves the shape, size, and plushness of lamb's ears, this plant's common name is obvious. Forming ground-covering evergreen clumps of thick, 6- to 10-inch-long, silver-furred leaves, lamb's-ears makes an indispensable addition to almost any garden. The summer flower stalks also are silvery white furred with odd looking clusters of magenta flowers tucked at their tops. Some gardeners like the flowers; others cut them off as they form, admiring the plant for its foliage alone.

Stachys byzantina

Size: Foliage clumps 6 inches to 1¼ feet tall; spreads to 2 feet wide. Flower stalks reach 2½ feet tall.

Light: Full sun.

Soil and Moisture: Fertile to poor, well-drained soil; moderate moisture. Drought tolerant.

Planting and Propagation: Plant bare-root or container-grown plants in spring, spacing 1 to 2 feet apart. Divide in spring or fall as needed to control spread.

Special Care: Gently rake out or hand-pull winter-tattered leaves in early spring to make room for new growth. Remove flower stalks as they fade, if not earlier. Avoid overhead watering. May be invasive.

Pests and Diseases: Crown and leaf rot in humid- or wet-summer areas.

Climate: Zones 4–8; tolerates hot, dry sites.

Cultivars: 'Silver Carpet,' nonblooming form, best choice for edging; 'Helen Von Stein,' huge leaves twice as large as species.

Garden Use: Silver foliage combines well with almost any color. Use as edging or border in formal and informal situations and as ground cover under roses and tulips.

Stokesia laevis
STOKES' ASTER

Improved selections of this southeastern wildflower are fashionable, long-blooming garden subjects. Broad, lance-shaped, shiny green leaves with prominent white midribs form attractive evergreen rosettes. Flowering begins in early to midsummer, when the loosely branched, hairy flower stalks bearing 3- to 4-inch-wide, flat, lavender-blue, pink, or white flower heads develop. Flowers have two rows of ragged-toothed petals surrounding fuzzy, creamy white centers. As long as faded stalks are removed, more flower stalks form after the initial flush— extending the bloom season into fall and even winter where the climate is mild.

Size: Flower stalks 1 to 2 feet tall; clumps spread to 1½ feet wide.

Stokesia laevis

Light: Full sun to part shade.

Soil and Moisture: Average to sandy, well-drained, moist soil; moderate moisture.

Planting and Propagation: Plant container-grown plants in spring, spacing 1¼ feet apart. Divide in spring every three or four years.

Special Care: Deadhead regularly to prolong bloom. Provide winter mulch in the North.

Pests and Diseases: Crown rot very troublesome if not well drained in winter.

Climate: Zones 5–9.

Cultivars: 'Blue Danube,' deep blue; 'Klaus Jelitto,' pale blue, 5-inch flowers; 'Wyoming,' very dark blue; 'Silver Moon,' white, 5-inch flowers; 'Rosea,' rosy pink.

Garden Use: Plant in groups in foreground of informal flower gardens.

Thalictrum rochebrunianum
JAPANESE MEADOW-RUE,
LAVENDER MIST

Despite its grand size, Japanese meadow-rue is a delicate-looking perennial that adds lovely fine textures to the garden. The blue-green leaves are cut into rounded, ferny segments and change to attractive golden hues in fall. Arching sprays of small, wispy, dangling flowers on purple-blue stems create a

lavender-violet mist above the leaves in midsummer. The flowers lack petals but consist of showy sepals surrounding a fringe of yellow stamens; other species' flowers resemble powderpuffs, consisting only of colorful stamens. Plants grow slowly into nice-sized clumps.

Size: 3 to 6 feet tall; 3 feet wide.

Light: Full sun to light shade in the North; light shade in the South.

Soil and Moisture: Fertile, humus-rich, moist soil; plentiful moisture.

Planting and Propagation: Plant container-grown plants in spring, spacing 2 to 3 feet apart. Rarely needs division, but plants may be divided in fall to propagate.

Special Care: Cut back flower stalks immediately after blossoms fade to promote rebloom. Do not allow soil to dry in sunny sites. May need individual staking in shaded sites. Provide deep summer mulch.

Pests and Diseases: Powdery mildew sometimes troublesome.

Climate: Zones 4–7.

Cultivars and Similar Species: 'Purple Mist,' deep purple flowers. *T. delavayi* (Yun-

nan meadow-rue): very similar flowers and foliage, 2 to 4 feet tall; 'Hewitt's Double,' longer-lasting flowers. *T. aquilegifolium* (columbine meadow-rue): white, rose-lavender, or purple late-spring powderpuffs, blue-green foliage, 3 feet tall, Zones 4–8; 'Thundercloud,' deep purple; 'White Cloud,' large white flowers. *T. speciosissimum* (dusty meadow-rue): fragrant yellow midsummer powderpuffs, blue-gray leaves, 4 feet tall.

Garden Use: Plant in drifts in back or midground of border, taking care not to hide beautiful foliage.

Thermopsis caroliniana (T. villosa)
SOUTHERN LUPINE, CAROLINA LUPINE

Resembling but not closely related to lupine, the southeastern wildflower offers a two-week display of foot-long spires of yellow, pealike flowers in late spring or early summer. Dense clumps of tall, upright stems cloaked with bright green or blue-green leaves divided into three rounded leaflets

Thalictrum rochebrunianum

Thermopsis caroliniana

look attractive during the first half of the growing year but may become scraggly by midsummer.

Size: 3 to 4 feet tall and as wide.

Light: Full sun in the North; part shade in the South.

Soil and Moisture: Deep, average, well-drained soil; moderate moisture. Drought tolerant.

Planting and Propagation: Plant container-grown plants in spring, spacing 3 feet apart. Deep taproot resents disturbance and does not divide well. Propagate by fresh seed.

Special Care: Remove faded flower spikes immediately to promote possible rebloom. Cut to ground in midsummer if it looks un-attractive. May need staking in shade.

Pests and Diseases: Leafhoppers sometimes troublesome.

Climate: Zones 3–9.

Similar Species: *T. lanceolata* (*T. lupinoides*) similar, 9 inches to 1 foot tall, Zones 2–7.

Garden Use: Dramatic as specimens in borders and naturalistic gardens.

Thymus praecox arcticus
MOTHER-OF-THYME

This aromatic herb forms mats of tiny, dark, elliptical, evergreen leaves that release a minty-herbal scent when crushed. In late spring and early summer, ½-inch-tall spikes of tiny, fragrant, rose-purple flowers completely blanket the foliage and attract bees.

Size: 3 to 6 inches tall; spreads to 2-foot-wide mats.

Light: Full sun.

Soil and Moisture: Average to sandy, well-drained soil; moderate moisture. Drought tolerant.

Planting and Propagation: Plant container-grown plants in spring, spacing 1 to 2 feet apart. Divide in spring or fall.

Special Care: Good drainage essential.

Pests and Diseases: Fungus diseases troublesome in damp sites.

Thymus praecox arcticus 'Coccineus'

Climate: Zones 5–9.

Cultivars and Similar Species: Often misla-beled *T. serpyllum.* 'Coccineus,' reddish purple flowers, foliage bronzes in winter; 'Albus,' white flowers. *T. pseudolanuginosus* (woolly thyme): tiny gray, woolly leaves turn steely purple in winter, mat forming, rose-pink flowers. *T. vulgaris* (common thyme): gray-green leaves, woody stems, favored for cooking. *T. x citriodorus* (lemon thyme): glossy lemon-scented leaves, 6 to 8 inches tall, rose-purple flowers; 'Argenteus,' silver variegated.

Garden Use: Lovely, fragrant paving plant for paths and patios; use as edging or ground cover in herb or rock gardens.

Tiarella cordifolia
ALLEGHENY FOAMFLOWER

A woodland wildflower native up and down the East Coast, Allegheny foamflower is aptly named for foamy clusters of creamy white flower spires. Flowers bloom above the foliage at the tips of straight, wiry stems for four to six weeks beginning in mid-spring. Many woodland wildflowers die to the ground after flowering, but foamflower's sharply toothed leaves (similar to maple tree leaves) are evergreen, often decoratively

Tiarella cordifolia

marked with dark veins or mottling. Plants spread enthusiastically by runners and make a good ground cover.

Size: Foliage clumps to 1 foot tall; flower stalks reach 1½ feet tall. Clumps spread to 2 feet wide.

Light: Light to full shade.

Soil and Moisture: Humus-rich, fertile, moist soil; plentiful moisture.

Planting and Propagation: Plant container-grown plants in spring, spacing 2 to 3 feet apart. Divide every three or four years in spring or fall.

Special Care: May burn in cold, snowless winters; rake away tattered leaves in early spring to make room for new growth. Shear off faded flower spikes if desired.

Pests and Diseases: Usually pest free.

Climate: Zones 3–8.

Cultivars and Similar Species: 'Brandy-wine,' pink-tinged flowers, leaves with wine-red centers. *T. collina* (*T. wherryi*): runner-less, forms clumps; 'Oakleaf,' profuse pink-tinged white flowers for six to eight weeks, new red leaves mature to dark green, turn burgundy in fall and winter.

Garden Use: Spectacular ground cover for shade and woodland gardens; use under taller plants and shrubs. Use clump forms near low woodland wildflowers so they won't overrun them.

Tradescantia x *andersoniana*
SPIDERWORT, VIRGINIA SPIDERWORT

Blooming for about two months from late spring to midsummer, spiderwort produces clusters of three-petaled, 2- to 3-inch-wide, blue, lavender, pink, purple, red, or white flowers at its branch tips. Individual flowers last only one day, but drop off cleanly and are replaced the next day by another open flower. Leaves are bright green, straplike, and somewhat floppy, forming rounded mounds.

Size: 1½ to 2 feet tall; spreads 3 feet wide.

Light: Best in full sun if moist; tolerates light shade but blooms less.

Soil and Moisture: Humus-rich, fertile, well-drained soil.

Planting and Propagation: Divide every three or four years to control spread.

Special Care: Cut back unkempt foliage in midsummer; tidier growth and more flowers result. May need loose staking.

Tradescantia x *andersoniana*

Pests and Diseases: Gray mold fungus may attack flowers; caterpillars may eat leaves.

Climate: Zones 4–9.

Cultivars and Similar Species: A large-flowered hybrid of the wildflower *T. virginiana* and sometimes listed as such. 'Pauline,' orchid-pink; 'Zwanenburg,' deep blue; 'Red Cloud,' cerise-red; 'Snowcap,' white; 'Iris Pritchard,' white with blue eye; 'Purple Dome,' purple; 'James C. Weguelin,' China blue.

Garden Use: Best massed in informal or naturalistic gardens; good in bog garden.

Tricyrtis hirta
TOAD LILY

An unusual, late-blooming shade lover, toad lily clumps are made up of arching unbranched stems that form graceful fans. Soft-haired, olive-green, 3- to 6-inch-long, pointed leaves clasp the stems in orderly fashion. The fall-blooming, 1-inch-wide flowers form clusters of one to three flowers in the leaf axils and stand up on short stems across the tops of the curving stems. The flowers aren't large and showy, but they are eye-catching, resembling small, purple-spotted lavender orchids.

Size: 2 to 3 feet tall; 2 feet wide.

Light: Half sun to light shade.

Soil and Moisture: Humus-rich, fertile, moist soil; plentiful moisture.

Planting and Propagation: Plant bare-root or container-grown plants in spring, spacing 3 feet apart. Divide in early spring while dormant when crowded.

Special Care: Provide deep summer mulch. Do not allow to dry out.

Pests and Diseases: Usually pest free.

Climate: Zones 4–8.

Cultivars and Similar Species: *T. h.* var. *alba*, pure white; 'Miyazaki,' lavender-white flowers spotted purple and black; 'Variegata,' gold-edged leaves. *T. formosana* (Formosa toad lily): spreads into large colonies,

Tricyrtis hirta

amethyst blue-and-white yellow-eyed flowers spotted with red, at ends of arched stems from midsummer to fall, glossy leaves, Zones 6–8; *T. f. amethystina*, lavender-blue with creamy throats and red spots.

Garden Use: Excellent late-blooming plant for shade and woodland gardens. Combines well with wildflowers, ferns, and hostas.

Trollius europaeus
GLOBEFLOWER

Showy and long blooming where conditions are cool and moist but finicky elsewhere, globeflower displays its rounded, lemon-yellow flowers at the tops of tall stems in mid-spring and early summer. Forming bushy mounds, the toothed, dark green leaves are lobed into five parts and remain attractive all summer if the soil remains moist.

Size: 2 feet tall and wide.

Light: Afternoon shade best; full sun only if constantly moist.

Soil and Moisture: Humus-rich, fertile, moist to boggy soil; constant moisture.

Planting and Propagation: Plant bare-root

plants in fall or container-grown plants in spring or fall, spacing 1 foot apart. Division not needed for years but may be performed in early spring or late fall if desired.

Special Care: Deadhead to prolong bloom; cut back foliage if it declines in summer.

Pests and Diseases: Usually pest free.

Climate: Zones 4–7. Best where cool and moist; does not tolerate heat and dryness.

Cultivars and Similar Species: 'Superbus,' flowers more prolifically. *T. ledebourii* (ledebour globeflower): orange flowers. Hybrids: 'Earliest of All,' double orange-yellow, long blooming; 'Commander-in-Chief,' golden yellow; 'Etna,' dark orange, summer; 'Lemon Queen,' double lemon-yellow.

Garden Use: Plant in groups along streams, in bogs, or in other moist, naturalistic garden sites.

Trollius ledebourii

Verbascum x *hybridum*
MULLEIN

These statuesque plants are short-lived perennials grown for their woolly stalks of flowers. Hybrids of several species, this variable group offers the best features of its parents. In mid- and late summer, yellow, white, or pink flowers on tall, silver-furred flower stalks rise above low, bushy clumps of foliage. Depending on the cultivar, the foot-long leaves may be gray-green or silvery gray, and the flower stalks may be branched or unbranched

Size: Flower stalks 3 to 5 feet tall above 2-foot-tall and -wide foliage clumps.

Light: Full sun.

Soil and Moisture: Average to sandy, well-drained soil; moderate moisture.

Planting and Propagation: Plant container-

Verbascum x hybridum

grown plants in spring, spacing 3 feet apart. Propagate by 3-inch-long root cuttings in late winter or early spring.

Special Care: Cut off faded flower stalks to promote rebloom. Hybrids are sterile and do not self-seed as do the species.

Pests and Diseases: Spider mites troublesome in hot climates; crown rot where damp.

Climate: Zones 6–8.

Cultivars and Similar Species: 'Silver Candelabra,' 5- to 7-foot-tall branched stalks, yellow flowers, silver leaves; 'Pink Domino,' soft lavender-pink flowers, late summer, 3 to 4 feet tall; 'Royal Highland,' apricot-yellow, 4 to 5 feet tall; 'Cotswold Queen,' amber to salmon, 5 feet tall. *V. bombyciferum:* biennial, rosettes of downy, silvery white, foot-long leaves, yellow flowers. *V. chaixii:* gray-green leaves, green unbranched stems of red-centered yellow flowers all summer. *V. x h. album:* red-centered white flowers.

Garden Use: Plant in groups for vertical effect in midground of beds and borders.

Verbena bonariensis
BRAZILIAN VERBENA

Tight, rounded, 2-inch clusters of lilac or purple flowers bloom on angular, branched stems from midsummer until frost. The plants are sparse and architectural with a stiff,

Verbena bonariensis

upright habit and a few scattered, small, narrow-toothed leaves with a sandpaper texture.

Size: 3 to 4 feet tall; 1 to 3 feet wide.

Light: Full sun.

Soil and Moisture: Average, well-drained soil; moderate moisture. Drought tolerant.

Planting and Propagation: Plant container-grown plants or sow seeds in place in spring, spacing 1 to 2 feet apart.

Special Care: Self-sows but is not weedy; transplant seedlings in spring. Deadheading is not necessary. Cut back to encourage bushiness, if desired.

Pests and Diseases: Powdery mildew sometimes unsightly.

Climate: Zones 7–9, but reseeds to perpetuate itself in colder climates. Heat tolerant.

Similar Species: *V. rigida* (rigid verbena), very similar but 2 feet tall, Zones 8–10; 'Flame,' bright red, 6 inches tall.

Garden Use: Plant in groups in front of border, despite its height, to create a scrim in front of plants with bolder flowers. Combines beautifully with tall ornamental grasses.

Verbena canadensis

CLUMP VERBENA, ROSE VERBENA

This perennial version of the popular bedding verbena (*V.* x *hybrida*) is native to the East Coast, Southwest, and Mexico. Plants form cascading clumps with creeping stems that root as they grow to form billowing masses of foliage and flowers. Showy circular clusters of small, hot pink or purple flowers blanket the plants from early summer until fall. The wedge-shaped, toothed leaves are evergreen but take on attractive burgundy hues in winter.

Size: 8 inches to 1½ feet tall; 3 feet wide.

Light: Full sun.

Soil and Moisture: Average, well-drained soil; moderate moisture. Drought tolerant.

Planting and Propagation: Plant container-grown plants in spring, spacing 3 feet apart. Divide in spring or fall, every three or four years; take cuttings in spring.

Verbena canadensis

Special Care: Cut back stems hard if plant becomes scraggly or grows out of bounds.

Pests and Diseases: Crown rot and mildew in damp sites; spider mites if too dry.

Climate: Zones 6–10; tolerant of seashore conditions, heat, and drought.

Cultivars and Similar Species: 'Homestead Purple,' dark purple, early blooming; 'Sissinghurst,' deep pink; 'Old Royal Fragrance,' lavender-and-white, fragrant; 'Springbrook,' rose-pink. *V. tenuisecta* (moss verbena): 1 foot tall and spreads widely, finely divided leaves, lilac-lavender flowers, Zones 8–10 (self-sows in colder areas or may be grown as an annual), very heat and drought tolerant; 'Imagination,' violet-blue.

Garden Use: Plant to tumble over walls or slopes or in rock garden. Also works well in containers or as foreground planting.

Veronica latifolia (V. teucrium)

GERMANDER SPEEDWELL,
HUNGARIAN SPEEDWELL

This long-lived, easy-care plant spreads slowly to form a weakly upright spreading mound of 1½-inch-long, somewhat toothed leaves. Deep blue star-shaped flowers blanket the plants for a month in late spring and early summer and may rebloom later in summer.

Unlike most other speedwells, the spikes arise from along the sides of the branches rather than from their tips, creating a fuller, less vertical effect.

Size: Mound 6 to 20 inches tall; spreads 3 to 4 feet wide.

Light: Full sun best; tolerates half shade.

Soil and Moisture: Humus-rich to average, slightly acidic to alkaline soil; moderate to plentiful moisture.

Planting and Propagation: Plant container-grown plants in spring, spacing 2 to 3 feet apart. Divide in early spring or fall every three or four years. Take stem cuttings in summer.

Special Care: Cut back after flowering to neaten and encourage reblooming.

Pests and Diseases: Usually pest free.

Climate: Zones 3–8.

Cultivars and Similar Species: 'Crater Lake Blue,' navy blue, 1 to 1¼ feet tall; 'Trehane,' bright blue flowers, golden foliage, 6 inches tall; 'Royal Blue,' bright blue, 1 foot tall; 'Rosea,' pink, 1 foot tall. *V. repens* (creeping speedwell): fine-textured, light blue flowers, rapidly spreading ground-hugging mat, Zones 5–8. *V. chamaedrys* (germander speedwell): fine-textured, bright blue flowers, rapidly spreading ground cover, to 8 to 10 inches tall.

Garden Use: Pure-blue flowers combine well with pastel yellow, pink, and white flowers.

Veronica latifolia 'Crater Lake Blue'

Veronica longifolia

Veronica spicata incana

Veronicastrum virginicum

Veronica longifolia
SPEEDWELL

This tall, stunning veronica produces foot-long, feather-shaped spikes of tiny, pale lilac-blue, purple, pink, or white flowers for one to two months in early to midsummer. The 4-inch-long, lance-shaped, toothed leaves grow on bushy plants that form a neat clump beneath the flowers.

Size: 2 to 4 feet tall; 2 feet wide.

Light: Full sun.

Soil and Moisture: Humus-rich, well-drained, moist soil; plentiful moisture.

Planting and Propagation: Plant container-grown plants in spring, spacing 2 feet apart.

Special Care: Needs staking only if grown in shade or in overly fertile soil.

Pests and Diseases: Usually pest free.

Climate: Zones 4–8.

Cultivars: 'Blue Giant,' pale blue, 4 feet tall, midsummer to late summer; x 'Sunny Border Blue,' dark violet-blue flowers all summer into fall, rounded leaves, 1½ feet tall; 'Foerster's Blue,' dark blue, 1½ feet tall; 'Rosea,' pink, 3 feet tall. *V. l.* var. *subsessilis:* larger dark blue flowers, later blooming.

Garden Use: Plant in groups for vertical effect in midsummer borders.

Veronica spicata
SPIKED SPEEDWELL

Crowned in late spring and early summer with dense, 1- to 3-foot-long spikes of tiny, pure-blue flowers with long purple stamens, this showy perennial may produce a second flush of bloom later in summer. Cultivars offer flowers in shades of pink, lavender, blue, and white. The evergreen plants form low clumps of scalloped, oval, dark green leaves, but one beautiful form is decorated with woolly, white, feltlike foliage.

Size: 10 inches to 3 feet tall; 2 feet wide.

Light: Full sun best; partial shade tolerated.

Soil and Moisture: Humus-rich to average, well-drained, moist soil; plentiful to moderate moisture.

Planting and Propagation: Plant container-grown plants in spring, spacing 2 feet apart. Divide in early spring or fall every four or five years. Take stem cuttings in summer.

Special Care: Cut back faded flower spikes immediately to promote rebloom.

Pests and Diseases: Root rot in winter-wet sites in the South. Mildew and leafspot occasionally troublesome.

Climate: Zones 3–8.

Cultivars: 'Icicle,' white, 2 feet tall; *V. s. alba,* white, 1¼ feet tall; 'Blue Peter,' dark blue, 1½ feet tall; 'Red Fox,' deep rose-red, 1¼ feet tall, midsummer; 'Blue Fox,' lavender-blue, 1¼ feet tall; 'Blue Charm,' blue-violet, 1½ feet tall. *V. s. incana* (woolly speedwell): silvery white feltlike leaves, sapphire-blue flower spikes, 1 to 2 feet tall, Zones 3–7. Hybrids: 'Minuet,' pale pink flowers, gray-green foliage; 'Barcarolle,' rose-pink, 10 inches tall, gray-green leaves.

Garden Use: Wonderful massed for vertical effect in foreground of beds and borders.

Veronicastrum virginicum (Veronica virginica)
CULVER'S ROOT

In late summer, this tall native plant opens its branched spires of white or very pale lavender-blue flowers, creating a stately, vertical impact. The central spike opens first, followed by the side branches, for a month or more of blossoms. Glossy, dark green, lance-shaped leaves, with toothed edges arranged in dense whorls and held at right angles to the upright stems, create a striking architectural effect. Plants spread slowly to form thick stands.

Size: 4 to 6 feet tall; spreads to form 4-foot-wide clumps.

Light: Full sun best; tolerates half shade.

Soil and Moisture: Fertile, humus-rich, moist soil; plentiful moisture.

Planting and Propagation: Plant bare-root or container-grown plants in spring, spacing 3 to 4 feet apart. Divide well-established clumps in spring or fall.

Special Care: Slow to get established. Needs staking and is less attractive in part shade.

Pests and Diseases: May suffer from root rot in winter-wet sites.

Climate: Zones 3–8.

Cultivars: 'Album,' ivory-white; 'Roseum,' pale pink; 'Albo-roseum,' pale pink.

Garden Use: Use as background specimen in formal border or mass-plant in naturalistic setting near water.

Viola cornuta 'Scottish Yellow'

Viola cornuta
HORNED VIOLET, TUFTED PANSY

Resembling a small pansy, the horned violet is a hardy perennial hailing from the Pyrenees Mountains. The 1- to 1½-inch-wide rounded flowers have five petals, a short spur, and may or may not have pansylike faces. Blossoms form on single stems from the leaf axils, transforming the tufted mounds of egg-shaped leaves into a mass of color

during spring and early summer and again when weather cools in fall.

Size: 5 inches to 1 foot tall and as wide.

Light: Light to part shade; full sun where cool.

Soil and Moisture: Humus-rich, fertile, moist soil; plentiful moisture.

Planting and Propagation: Plant bare-root or container-grown plants in spring, spacing 1 foot apart. Divide in spring or fall.

Special Care: Deadhead regularly to prolong bloom; cut back after first bloom to encourage rebloom in late summer and fall.

Pests and Diseases: Spider mites sometimes troublesome in hot sites; slugs and snails often troublesome.

Climate: Zones 6–9; heat tolerant.

Cultivars and Similar Species: 'Chantreyland,' large faceless apricot flowers; 'Jersey Gem,' bright blue; 'White Perfection,' pure white; 'Cuty,' purple-and-white with face; 'Nellie Britten,' lavender-pink with face; 'Etain,' pastel yellow with lavender edges; 'Arkwright Ruby,' deep red with face; 'Baby Franjo,' light yellow; 'Baby Lucia,' sky blue; 'Lord Nelson,' deep violet; 'Scottish Yellow,' lemon-yellow; 'Ulla Lack,' dark violet; 'Blue Perfection,' sky blue.

Garden Use: Use as edging or foreground plant; combines well with tulips and other spring-flowering bulbs.

Viola labradorica var. *purpurea*
LABRADOR VIOLET

This beautiful native violet is valued for its foliage as well as its flowers. The small, heart-shaped leaves, which grow on short main stems, are deep purple when they first emerge and may lighten in summer. Violet-purple flowers bloom profusely in spring and sporadically throughout the growing season. Spreads rapidly by creeping rootstocks and self-seeding.

Size: 1 to 4 inches tall; 1 foot wide.

Viola labradorica var. *purpurea*

Light: Light to full shade; tolerates full sun if constantly moist.

Soil and Moisture: Humus-rich, fertile, moist soil; plentiful moisture.

Planting and Propagation: Plant bare-root or container-grown plants in spring, spacing 1 foot apart. Divide in fall every three years or when crowded.

Special Care: Self-sows prolifically.

Pests and Diseases: Usually pest free.

Climate: Zones 3–8.

Similar Species: Species has green leaves.

Garden Use: Excellent ground cover for foliage contrast in shade gardens and woodland settings. Tuck into rocks and crevices of shaded rock gardens.

Viola odorata
SWEET VIOLET

Once grown for perfume, the sweet violet produces its fragrant, short-spurred, purple blossoms on long stems that rise directly from the rootstalks. The irregularly shaped flowers are made of five petals marked with dark veins and small beards near the flower's center. Blossoms peak just above the foliage from early to late spring. Semi-evergreen, heart-shaped leaves have bluntly serrated edges and are covered with fine hairs. They

Viola odorata

also arise directly from the creeping root-stalks.

Size: 2 to 8 inches tall; 1¼ feet wide.

Light: Light shade best; tolerates full sun if constantly moist.

Soil and Moisture: Humus-rich, well-drained, moist soil; plentiful moisture.

Planting and Propagation: Plant bare root or container-grown plants in spring, spacing 1 foot apart. Divide in fall when crowded.

Special Care: Self-sown seedlings may become weedy, and creeping plants may be invasive; diligent weeding necessary.

Pests and Diseases: Leaf spot sometimes troublesome.

Climate: Zones 6–9.

Cultivars and Similar Species: 'Black Magic,' black blossoms with yellow eyes; 'Czar,' deep violet; 'White Czar,' pure white; 'Rosina,' mauve-pink; 'Queen Charlotte,' dark blue; 'Royal Robe,' large, long-stemmed, deep violet-blue flowers. *V. cucullata* (marsh violet): heart-shaped hairless leaves, purple-veined bearded petals, clump-forming, Zones 4–9; 'Priceana' (confederate violet), white with deep blue eye; 'Freckles,' pale blue dotted with purple.

Garden Use: Plant in naturalistic settings such as shade and woodland gardens. Makes a pretty cut flower.

Viola tricolor

Viola tricolor
JOHNNY-JUMP-UP

This perky little violet is named Johnny-jump-up because it seeds itself all over the place, jumping up where least expected. The narrow branched stems sport small, heart-shaped leaves and bunches of 1-inch-wide, tricolored purple, blue, and yellow pansy-faced flowers in spring and summer. The plants are short-lived perennials and are often treated as annuals.

Size: 8 inches to 1 foot tall; 4 to 6 inches wide.

Light: Full sun to light shade.

Soil and Moisture: Fertile, humus-rich, moist soil; plentiful moisture.

Planting and Propagation: Sow seeds in place in early spring, or plant nursery-grown seedlings in spring, spacing 1 foot apart.

Special Care: Self-sows but is not weedy; pull out excess or transplant.

Pests and Diseases: Usually pest free.

Climate: Zones 6–9; perpetuates itself by self-sowing in colder climates.

Cultivars and Similar Species: 'Helen Mount,' large, long-blooming flowers.

Garden Use: Charming scattered about bolder flowers in cottage gardens and informal settings; combines well with spring bulbs.

Yucca filamentosa
ADAM'S NEEDLE, NEEDLE PALM

This handsome succulent forms bold rosettes of sharp-pointed, leathery, gray-green, ever-green leaves with a decorative threadlike edging peeling away in curls from the leaf margins. Tall, stout, leafless flower stalks arise in midsummer, exhibiting numerous bold, waxy, white, pendulous, bell-shaped flowers.

Size: Foliage clumps 3 feet tall and wide; flower stalks 5 to 7 feet tall.

Light: Full sun.

Soil and Moisture: Average to sandy, well-drained soil; moderate moisture. Drought tolerant.

Planting and Propagation: Plant container-grown plants in spring or fall, spacing 4 feet apart. Divide in spring, separating offsets from main plant when crowded.

Special Care: Cut off flower stalks after flowers fade.

Pests and Diseases: Rots in winter-wet site.

Climate: Zones 4–10; heat tolerant.

Cultivars: 'Bright Edge,' gold-banded leaf margins; 'Golden Sword,' gold stripe down leaf center; 'Variegata,' leaves striped with cream; 'Ivory Tower,' upright creamy white flowers, gray-green leaves.

Garden Use: Use as bold evergreen architectural accent plant in naturalistic border or rock garden.

Yucca filamentosa 'Bright Edge'

ANNUALS

Blooming almost nonstop for months on end, flowering annuals deliver a lot of bloom for the bucks.

Abelmoschus moschatus

Abelmoschus moschatus
SILK FLOWER

This little sister of hibiscus makes a pretty garden flower in a limited but lovely color range: rose, scarlet, and red, all with white centers. The five-petaled, 3- to 4½-inch-wide flowers bloom freely from July to frost and form attractive seedpods. Deeply lobed, dark green leaves make a striking backdrop. It often self-sows.

Size: 1 to 1½ feet tall; twice as wide.

Light: Full sun best; blooms in part shade.

Soil and Moisture: Fertile soil; plentiful moisture.

Planting and Propagation: Soak seed in tepid water for one hour, then sow outdoors after last frost, when soil is warm. Or sow indoors six to eight weeks earlier, at 75°F. Nursery transplants sometimes available. Space 2 feet apart.

Special Care: Take care that summer heat doesn't dry out soil.

Pests and Diseases: Usually problem free.

Climate: Half-hardy, warm-season annual in Zones 2–11. Thrives in heat and humidity.

Cultivars and Similar Species: 'Mischief,' red; 'Mischief Soft Pink'; 'Pacific Light Pink,' pastel pink; 'Pacific Scarlet,' scarlet. *A. manihot:* pale yellow flowers with dark centers, 5 to 6 feet tall.

Garden Use: Use in informal gardens and containers and as houseplants.

Ageratum houstonianum
FLOSSFLOWER

Gardeners have long treasured ageratum because it is one of the purest blue flowers in the garden. The furry-looking blossoms are now also available in shades of pink and white. The flowers of dwarf types practically hide the rounded dark green leaves. Taller varieties make lovely cut flowers. Flossflower self-sows in warm, moist climates.

Size: Dwarf varieties typically 6 to 8 inches tall, forming a wide cushion; taller types 1 to 2½ feet tall and taller than wide.

Light: Full sun, but best in part shade where summers are hot.

Soil and Moisture: Rich, well-drained soil; plentiful moisture.

Ageratum houstonianum 'Hawaii Royal'

Planting and Propagation: Sow uncovered, inside, at 64° to 70°F, eight to 10 weeks before last frost, or set out nursery transplants after last frost. Space plants 6 to 8 inches apart.

Special Care: Pinch young plants to encourage branching. Shear or pick off unsightly faded flowers.

Pests and Diseases: Southern blight, powdery mildew, two-spotted mite, whitefly, gray mold, and snails troublesome.

Climate: Half-hardy, warm-season annual in Zones 2–11. In warm climates, replant in late summer for fall bloom.

Cultivars: Tall: 'Blue Mink,' powder blue, 1 foot tall; 'Blue Horizon,' mid-blue, 2½ feet tall; 'Capri,' blue-and-white, 1 foot tall. Dwarf to 6 inches tall: 'Pink Powderpuffs,' pale pink; 'Pinky Improved Selection,' dusky pink; 'Hawaii' series, floriferous, compact, comes in 'White,' 'Royal,' and 'Blue.'

Garden Use: Short varieties best at front of border; position taller ones in midground or cutting garden.

Amaranthus caudatus
LOVE-LIES-BLEEDING

Flamboyant ropes up to 1½ feet long of deep red flowers dangle among the large green leaves of this old-fashioned favorite. Variants offer drooping green ropes as well as upright red or green spikes. All bloom from early summer to frost. Red stems and bronzy fall color add end-of-season drama.

Size: 2 to 4 or more feet tall and usually as wide; dwarfs 1 to 2 feet tall.

Light: Full sun best.

Soil and Moisture: Ordinary, well-drained garden soil; keep well watered.

Planting and Propagation: Sow outdoors when soil is warm. In short-season areas, sow indoors at 70° to 75°F, eight to 10 weeks

Amaranthus tricolor

before last frost. Space 1½ to 3 feet apart.

Special Care: Stake in windy sites.

Pests and Diseases: Root rot in too-wet soil; aphid, spider mite, and aster yellows-virus sometimes troublesome.

Climate: Warm-season annual in Zones 2–11.

Cultivars: Tall: 'Love Lies Bleeding,' pendant dark red blossoms; 'Viridis,' pendant green. Dwarf: 'Pygmy Torch,' upright maroon spikes; 'Green Thumb,' upright green spikes.

Garden Use: Dramatic in middle or back of cottage or herb garden.

Amaranthus tricolor
JOSEPH'S COAT

These tall plants create a tropical look from early summer to frost with their large, color-splashed leaves. Although the flowers are tiny, the red, yellow, green, and bronze-patterned foliage provides plenty of color. Try sowing a few seeds in the vegetable garden and adding young, edible leaves sparingly to salads.

Size: 1½ to 5 feet tall; most cultivars are 3 to 4 feet tall and half as wide.

Light: Full sun.

Soil and Moisture: Any soil with moderate moisture; tolerates drought.

Planting and Propagation: Sow indoors, at 70° to 75°F, four to six weeks before last frost, or outdoors when soil warms. Space 1¼ feet apart.

Special Care: Keep area well weeded until small seedlings are established.

Pests and Diseases: Root rot in too-wet soil; aphid, spider mite, and aster yellows-virus can be troublesome.

Climate: Warm-season annual in Zones 2–11; best if nights are over 60°F.

Cultivars: 'Early Splendor,' upper leaves red, lower leaves bronze; 'Joseph's Coat,' yellow, red, and green; 'Illumination,' upper leaves red-and-gold, lower leaves green-and-bronze.

Garden Use: Use as accent in informal or cottage garden or in bed. Good cut flower.

Anethum graveolens
DILL

Feathery dill leaves fill in quickly between slower growing plants in spring, and brighten a garden at summer's end where longer seasons permit a midsummer sowing. Harvest leaves from young herbs for cooking, or allow the tall stems of lacy yellow flowers to form. Flowers make pretty bouquets, but if left uncut, they will produce dill seed, which can be used in pickling. Dill may self-sow.

Size: Most cultivars 2 to 4 feet tall. Bushy when young; tall and narrow as they bloom.

Light: Full sun.

Soil and Moisture: Average garden soil; moderate moisture.

Planting and Propagation: Sow in place in early spring, again in late summer if season permits. Thin to 6 inches apart.

Special Care: Doesn't transplant well. Stake if strong winds threaten plants.

Pests and Diseases: Parsleyworm and carrot weevil may be troublesome.

Climate: Cool-season annual in Zones 2–11. Grow in spring and early fall.

Cultivars: 'Aroma' and 'Dukat' are leafier than average. 'Bouquet,' 3 feet tall; 'Fernleaf,' 1½ feet tall, slow to flower.

Amaranthus caudatus

Anethum graveolens

Garden Use: Herb or cottage gardens. Plant taller types in back of border; use short types as midground filler.

Antirrhinum majus
SNAPDRAGON

Children love to squeeze snapdragon flowers to see the "jaws" open. Some newer types, however, have exchanged their snap for open blossoms, even open double ones. Flowers are purple, red, orange, pink, yellow, and white, or bicolored in dense spikes. Snapdragons bloom summer to frost from a spring planting, early winter to summer when planted in the fall where winters are mild.

Size: Varies from bushy dwarfs 7 inches to 1 foot tall to cutting types that reach 3 feet tall.

Light: Full sun or partial shade.

Antirrhinum majus

Soil and Moisture: Average to rich, well-drained soil; moderate moisture.

Planting and Propagation: Sow seeds at 55° to 75°F inside, uncovered, six to eight weeks before last frost, or buy nursery transplants. In Zones 9–11, plant in fall for winter and spring bloom. Space 6 inches to 1½ feet apart, depending on final size.

Special Care: Stake taller types. Cut back spent stems to stimulate rebloom.

Pests and Diseases: Snapdragon rust (seek resistant types, don't overhead water, and rotate in garden from year to year), downy mildew, aphid, and whitefly are problems.

Climate: Cool-season annual in Zones 2–8. Annual or perennial in Zones 9–11. Needs cool weather when young for best growth.

Cultivars: 'Floral Carpet Mixed,' 6 to 8 inches tall; 'Royal Carpet Mixed,' 8 inches tall; 'Coronette Mixed,' 1½ feet tall; 'Princess with a Red Eye,' red-and-white bicolor, 1⅔ feet tall. Available as mixes or single colors: 'Liberty,' 3 feet tall; 'Rocket,' 3 feet tall; 'Little Darling,' 1 foot tall, trumpet, nonsnap flowers; 'Madame Butterfly,' 2 to 2½ feet tall, double azalea-type flowers.

Garden Use: Use in front to mid-border in formal or cottage gardens or as cut flowers.

Begonia x *semperflorens*
WAX BEGONIA, FIBROUS BEGONIA, BEDDING BEGONIA

Whether called wax, fibrous, or bedding begonia, this popular annual is a willing shade bloomer. Newer types form tight, compact mounds and often have larger flowers, which may be doubles or picotees. Colors include white and shades of pink, peach, and red. The glossy, rounded leaves may be bright green or bronze. Bronze-leaf types tolerate more sun.

Size: Most 6 inches to 1 foot tall and as wide.

Light: Full sun in cool-summer areas; partial to full shade in warm-summer areas.

Soil and Moisture: Fertile, well-drained soil rich in organic matter; moderate moisture.

Planting and Propagation: Press tiny seeds into seedling mix surface and grow indoors, at 61° to 75°F, for four to six months, potting up once. Or purchase nursery transplants. Plant outdoors, 8 inches to 1 foot apart, when soil warms.

Special Care: Can be dug before first frost and brought indoors as houseplant.

Pests and Diseases: Usually problem free, but sometimes two-spotted spider mite, leaf rot, and whitefly cause problems. Root rot if overwatered.

Begonia x *semperflorens*

Climate: Spring to fall annual in Zones 2–8. May be short-lived perennial in Zones 9–11, blooming most of the year.

Cultivars: Many mixes and single colors available. 'Cocktail,' bronze foliage, 6 to 8 inches tall; 'Thousand Wonders,' 6 inches tall; 'Viva,' white, 6 to 8 inches tall; 'Pizzazz,' 10 inches tall, large blossoms; 'Wings,' 1 foot tall, extra-large blossoms; 'Frilly Dilly,' 10 inches to 1 foot tall, frilled petals. 'Bingo' series: bronze foliage, 8 to 10 inches tall, early flowering. 'Encore': deep bronze or green leaves, extra-large flowers, 1 foot tall, bushy, upright.

Garden Use: Use as edging in formal borders and in beds, containers, and shade gardens.

Borago officinalis
BORAGE

The coarse, somewhat prickly leaves of this annual or biennial form a basal rosette from which arises a hollow stalk topped with pure blue, starlike flowers. These open successively in midsummer for a month or more and look especially lovely when backlit by the sun. An herb valued for its flavor and medicinal properties, borage flowers and tiny young leaves can be used in salads and as

Borago officinalis

decoration; borage tea made from the leaves is said to instill courage and good spirits.

Size: 2 to 3 feet tall and half as wide.

Light: Full sun.

Soil and Moisture: Best in fertile, well-drained but moist soil; do not allow to dry.

Planting and Propagation: Sow seeds in spring for next year's blossoms or plant nursery plants in spring; thin to 2 feet apart. May self-sow to perpetuate the stand.

Special Care: Pull out plants after they set and shed seed and begin to yellow. Self-sown plants are more robust than purchased transplants.

Pests and Diseases: Slugs may eat leaves.

Climate: Zones 3–8.

Similar Species: *B. laxiflora,* perennial in Zones 5–9, blue flowers in late spring.

Garden Use: Attractive in herb or cottage garden; use in informal gardens for blue flowers.

Brachycome iberidifolia
SWAN RIVER DAISY

A pretty Australian native, the Swan River daisy offers abundant, delicately fragrant, 1-inch-wide flowers in blue, pink, violet, or white with dark or yellow centers. The flowers are held on branching stems above fine-textured, gracefully sprawling mounds of needlelike leaves. They bloom best in cool weather.

Size: Forms mounds 8 inches to 1½ feet tall and wide.

Light: Full sun.

Soil and Moisture: Rich, well-drained soil; moderate moisture.

Planting and Propagation: Sow indoors, at 60° to 70°F, six weeks before last frost. If winters are mild, sow in garden in early spring. Space plants 6 inches apart.

Special Care: Tends to burn out when weather turns hot; cut back to rejuvenate. Deadheading and successive plantings prolong bloom period in hot areas. Shear spent flowers to extend blooming.

Brachycome iberidifolia

Pests and Diseases: Usually problem free, but occasionally botrytis and aphid.

Climate: Cool-season annual in Zones 2–11.

Cultivars: Mixes provide several colors. 'Splendor' series: 9 inches to 1 foot tall, available in 'Blue,' 'Purple,' and 'White.' 'Blue Star': quilled petals, dark centers.

Garden Use: Mass for informal effect in rock and cottage gardens. Use as edging in formal gardens; allow to cascade from window boxes. Excellent in containers.

Brassica oleracea
FLOWERING CABBAGE AND KALE

These spectacular cabbage-leaf "roses" are at their best as fall weather cools; light frost improves their color. Usually blue-green outer leaves surround white or brightly colored inner ones, but variegated leaves are common. Colors include cream, white, pink, rose-red, and purple. Leaves of ornamental kale are frillier than cabbage. Use the edible leaves to garnish salads.

Size: 1 to 1½ feet tall; 1¼ to 1⅔ feet across.

Light: Full sun.

Soil and Moisture: Average to fertile, well-drained, moist soil; moderate moisture.

Planting and Propagation: Sow in garden in late summer, or inside, at 75° to 80°F,

eight to 10 weeks before last spring frost. Space 1 foot apart. Purchase nursery plants in fall.

Special Care: Inspect regularly for pests.

Pests and Diseases: Imported cabbageworm, cutworms, snails and slugs, and clubroot may be troublesome.

Climate: Tender biennial in Zones 8–10; grow as annual in Zones 2–11. Showy into mild winters.

Cultivars: Many variations, including: 'Osaka,' wavy leaves, red, pink, or white centers; 'Dynasty' mix, semiwaved leaves, rose-red, pink, or white; 'Sparrow' kale, dwarf, 10 inches to 1 foot across; 'Peacock,' feathery, cut-leaf kale.

Garden Use: Plant to replace warm-season annuals for fall and early winter display as edging or carpet bedding or in containers.

Brassica oleracea

Browallia speciosa
AMETHYST FLOWER, STAR FLOWER, SAPPHIRE FLOWER

A charming choice for shady gardens or window boxes, amethyst flower forms low mounds of bright green leaves studded with starry blue, violet, or white flowers. It blooms from late spring through summer where summers are warm. The plant may self-sow.

Size: 1 to 1½ feet tall with equal spread.

Light: Light to partial shade; full sun in cool

Browallia speciosa 'Blue Bells Improved'

areas with mulched, moist soil.

Soil and Moisture: Fertile, well-drained soil rich in organic matter; plentiful moisture.

Planting and Propagation: Sow uncovered, at 64° to 75°F, eight weeks before last frost date; set out after last frost, spacing 8 to 10 inches apart.

Special Care: May be brought inside as a houseplant at summer's end.

Pests and Diseases: Whitefly common; botrytis an occasional problem.

Climate: Warm-season annual in Zones 2–11. May not flower in short, cool summers. May live through mildest winters.

Cultivars: 'Blue Bells,' lavender-blue; 'Marine

Calendula officinalis

Bells,' indigo blue; 'Blue Troll,' clear blue; 'White Bells' and 'Silver Bells,' white. 'Starlight' series: dwarf to 6 inches tall, good basal branching, early and long blooming; 'Blue,' 'Sky Blue.'

Garden Use: Use as edgings, in foreground, and for containers, window boxes, and hanging baskets.

Calendula officinalis
POT MARIGOLD

This easy-to-grow annual is a pot herb often found in cottage or herb gardens. The 2- to 4-inch-wide, daisy-type flowers are often double and bloom on sturdy, branched stems with small, straplike leaves. Long available in orange and bright yellow, newer hues now include white, cream, pale yellow, and apricot. The petals are edible in soup or salad.

Size: 1 to 2 feet tall; 10 inches to 1¼ feet wide.

Light: Full sun.

Soil and Moisture: Poor to rich, well-drained soil; moderate moisture.

Planting and Propagation: Sow in garden early spring to midsummer in Zones 3–8; fall to spring in Zones 9–11. May be sown inside, at 70°F, six to eight weeks before planting outdoors. Set out 10 inches to 1¼ feet apart. Often self-sows.

Special Care: Remove spent blossoms to prolong bloom period.

Pests and Diseases: Powdery mildew, leaf spot, smut, cabbage looper, and aphid may be troublesome.

Climate: Cool-season annual in Zones 2–11. Larger blossoms in cool weather.

Cultivars: 'Fiesta Gitana,' mixed, 9 inches to 1 foot tall; 'Bon Bon,' mixed or single colors, 1 foot tall; 'Pacific Beauty,' mixed, 1½ feet tall; 'Art Shades,' mixed includes apricot and cream, 2 feet tall; 'Touch of Red,' mixed, with red picotee, 1⅓ to 1½ feet tall.

Garden Use: Front to midground in borders, cottage, herb, or cutting gardens.

Callistephus chinensis

Callistephus chinensis
CHINA ASTER, ANNUAL ASTER

The native Chinese plant produces single, purple, daisylike flowers, but breeders have created blue, pink, peach, red, and white semidouble and double flowers with shapes varying from spidery to pompon. The midsummer-into-fall flowers are fine for cutting, but plants do not rebloom if cut.

Size: 6 inches to 3 feet tall. Dwarfs are as wide as they are tall; tall plants are 1 foot or more wide.

Light: Full sun or light shade.

Soil and Moisture: Rich, well-drained, neutral to basic soil; moderate moisture.

Planting and Propagation: Sow in place when frost danger is past, or inside, at 55° to 64°F, six weeks earlier. Thin to 6 inches to 1 foot apart.

Special Care: Replant every few weeks for continuous bloom. Stake tall types.

Pests and Diseases: Wilt diseases and aster yellows-virus common; destroy affected plants, seek resistant types, and rotate planting location. May also get aphid, mealybug, rust, and gray mold.

Climate: Warm-season annual in Zones 2–11.

Cultivars: Wilt resistant: 'Ostrich Plume,' 1½ feet tall; 'Pastel Mixed,' 2½ feet tall; 'Dwarf Queen' and 'Carpet Ball,' 8 to 10 inches tall. New and unusual are: 'All Change,' bicolor pompons, 1¼ to 1½ feet tall; 'Florette Champagne,' quilled, pale pink, 1⅗ to 2 feet tall.

Garden Use: Use dwarfs for edging; taller ones in middle of border or cutting beds.

Campanula medium
CANTERBURY BELLS

Really a biennial, Canterbury bells can be sown early indoors to stimulate bloom in midsummer of the same year, acting as an annual. New early types classify as true annuals. The large blue, lilac, pink, or white bells pack tall stems above a basal rosette of wavy-edged, slightly hairy leaves. Semidouble and double blossoms are available.

Size: 1 to 4 feet tall; half as wide.

Light: Full sun; light shade where summers are hot.

Soil and Moisture: Rich, well-drained soil; even, plentiful moisture.

Planting and Propagation: Sow indoors, uncovered, at 64° to 70°F, six to eight weeks before late-spring transplanting, or use nursery starts. May also be sown outdoors in midsummer for bloom the following spring.

Special Care: Mulch late-sown seedlings, or overwinter in cold frame. Apply summer mulch to cool roots. Stake tall forms.

Pests and Diseases: Leaf spot, powdery mildew, stem rot, crown rot, aphid, and slugs troublesome.

Climate: Grow as hardy, cool-season annual or biennial in Zones 2–11.

Cultivars and Similar Species: 'Cup and Saucer,' mixed colors, semidouble, 2½ feet tall; 'Dwarf Bedding Mixture,' 1¼ to 1½ feet tall; 'Russian Pink,' 1¼ feet tall, true annual. The related *C. pyramidalis* reaches 4 feet tall, has smaller flowers.

Garden Use: Good choice for borders and cutting beds. Use dwarfs in containers and rock gardens.

Campanula medium

Capsicum annuum
ORNAMENTAL PEPPER

Grown for their brightly colored fruits, not their tiny white flowers, this annual bears round or pointed upright peppers nestled among dark green, oval, pointed leaves. The fruits start out pale green and turn various colors, including yellow, orange, red, purple, or black. Plants often show several fruit colors at once; the show lasts from midsummer to frost. Fruits are edible, but often very hot.

Size: Usually 8 to 20 inches tall and as wide.

Light: Full sun to partial shade.

Capsicum annuum

Soil and Moisture: Rich soil, high in organic matter; even moisture.

Planting and Propagation: Sow indoors, at 64° to 75°F, eight to 10 weeks before last frost, or buy transplants. Plant 8 inches to 1 foot apart when ground has warmed.

Special Care: Can be potted for indoor holiday decoration.

Pests and Diseases: Those common to peppers in your area.

Climate: Warm-season annual in Zones 2–9; perennial in Zones 10–11. Heat tolerant.

Cultivars: 'Holiday Cheer,' round fruit; 'Candelabra,' red fruit in spikes; 'Aurora,' yellow fruit.

Garden Use: Unusual plants for hot color in front of border, as edging, and in containers.

Catharanthus roseus
(Vinca rosea)
MADAGASCAR PERIWINKLE, VINCA

One of the most reliable annuals in hot summers, this spreader produces white, light or deep pink, and bicolored flowers, including white with a red eye. The glossy dark green leaves provide a handsome setting for the 1½-inch-wide phloxlike blossoms, which bloom from May until frost.

Size: 4 inches to 2 feet tall and as wide or wider.

Catharanthus roseus

Light: Full sun or partial shade.

Soil and Moisture: Any well-drained soil. Withstands drought; does better if kept moist.

Planting and Propagation: Use nursery plants, or sow indoors, at 70° to 75°F, eight to 12 weeks before last frost. Space 8 inches to 1½ feet apart.

Special Care: Shear plants in midsummer to late summer to force new growth and additional blossoms.

Pests and Diseases: Slugs are the only serious problem.

Climate: Annual in Zones 2–8; perennial in Zones 9–11. Thrives in heat.

Cultivars: 'Carpet' series, 4 inches tall, 2 feet wide; 'Pretty In' series, 12 to 14 inches tall, large flowers; 'Cooler' series, 6 to 8 inches tall and wide, good where cool.

Garden Use: Excellent as annual ground cover; use as edging, in middle to front of border, and in containers and hanging baskets.

Celosia cristata
COCKSCOMB

Cockscomb flowers come in two forms: plumes resembling colorful hat feathers or convoluted velvety crests resembling a cock's comb. Both bloom in white, gold, pink, and shades of red and maroon, and are available in dwarf, medium, and tall forms. Plants tol-

Celosia cristata 'Pink Tassel'

erate high temperatures, bloom from midsummer to frost, and make excellent cut or dried flowers.

Size: 4 inches to 3 feet tall; as wide as tall.

Light: Full sun.

Soil and Moisture: Rich, fertile soil; moderate moisture.

Planting and Propagation: Sow outdoors, barely covered, when soil is warm, or indoors, at 64° to 75°F, four weeks before last frost. Set out before plants bloom; space 4 inches to 1½ feet apart.

Special Care: Harden off transplants well before planting out.

Pests and Diseases: Spider mite sometimes troublesome; root rot after transplanting if too wet.

Climate: Warm-season annual in Zones 2–11.

Cultivars: Crested: 'Toreador' and 'Fireglow,' both red and 1⅔ feet tall; 'Jewel Box Mixed,' 5 to 9 inches tall. Plumed: 'Century Mixed,' 2 feet tall; 'Geisha,' 10 inches tall, and 'Kimono,' mixed or single colors, 4 to 6 inches tall.

Garden Use: Formal and informal gardens, containers, and cutting beds.

Centaurea cineraria and Chrysanthemum ptarmiciflorum
DUSTY MILLER, SILVER LACE

The common name dusty miller refers to several similar-looking plants grown for their lovely, silvery gray, felt-covered leaves. Leaves of *Centaurea cineraria* are bluntly lobed, while those of *Chrysanthemum ptarmiciflorum* are lacier. Both enhance the colorful flowers of other plants when tucked between or planted in a drift.

Size: 6 inches to 1½ feet tall and as wide.

Light: Full sun.

Soil and Moisture: Average to rich, well-drained soil; moderate moisture.

Planting and Propagation: Sow uncovered indoors, at 75° to 80°F, 10 weeks before last

frost, or use nursery starts. In Zones 10–11, set out in fall. Space 1 to 1½ feet apart.

Special Care: Remove flower stems in bud stage; cut back to keep compact.

Pests and Diseases: Root rot common in wet soil; aphid, downy mildew, aster yellows-virus, and rust sometimes a problem.

Climate: *C. cineraria*, half-hardy annual in Zones 2–4; perennial in Zones 5–11, but best replanted each year and treated as annual. *Chrysanthemum ptarmiciflorum*, annual in Zones 2–11. Both prefer warm weather.

Cultivars and Similar Species: 'Cirrus,' less lobed than species; 'Silverdust,' 7 inches tall, more finely cut. *Chrysanthemum ptarmiciflorum* 'Silver Lace,' 7 inches tall, lacy.

Garden Use: Plant in groups in beds and borders to form bold contrasts; use as edging or in window boxes and containers.

Centaurea cineraria 'Silverdust'

Centaurea cyanus
BACHELOR'S BUTTON, CORNFLOWER

Bright blue cornflowers often provide the blue in a Fourth of July bouquet, but they also bloom in mixtures that combine blue with white, pink, and purple. The 1½-inch-wide flowers stand out vividly against their gray-green stems and small, narrow leaves. Cornflowers often self-sow.

Size: 1 to 3 feet tall; half as wide.

Light: Best bloom occurs in full sun.

Centaurea cyanus

Soil and Moisture: Best in sandy loam with moderate moisture; tolerates poor soil and drought.

Planting and Propagation: Sow in garden after last frost, or indoors, at 60° to 76°F, four weeks earlier for summer bloom. Sow in garden in late summer or fall for spring bloom. Space 6 inches to 1¼ feet apart.

Special Care: Deadhead after first flush of bloom to prolong bloom period.

Pests and Diseases: Aphid can sometimes be serious.

Climate: Biennial grown as warm-season annual in Zones 2–8; cool-season annual in warmer parts of Zone 9 and in Zones 10–11.

Cultivars: 'Blue Boy,' 2 to 3 feet tall, blue; 'Jubilee Gem,' 1 foot tall, deep blue, dense; 'Polka Dot,' 1¼ feet tall, white, blue, crimson.

Garden Use: Delicate plant for weaving with other flowers in borders, cottage gardens, and meadow plantings; good cut flower.

Cheiranthus cheiri
WALLFLOWER

Wallflowers are not drab and unattractive garden bystanders, but perky flowers that grow well in the cracks of garden walls. Where prolonged cool spring or summer weather permits, they offer clusters of fragrant, ⅓- to 1-inch-wide, single or double blossoms in white, bright yellow, orange, bronze, red, and purple. They are fine in bouquets.

Size: 9 inches to 2 feet tall; mounded or sprawling.

Light: Full sun or light shade.

Soil and Moisture: Average soil with very good drainage; keep moist.

Planting and Propagation: Sow indoors, at 65° to 75°F, in midwinter. Pot once, harden in cold frame, and set out after last frost. Where winter is mild, sow outside from late summer to fall for winter or spring bloom. Or purchase nursery plants in spring.

Special Care: Pinch tips of young plants to increase bushiness.

Pests and Diseases: Cabbage clubroot, white rust, botrytis, aphid, and beetles sometimes troublesome.

Climate: Biennial grown as annual in cold-winter climates; may live a few years where winters are mild. Cold triggers bloom; cool, damp weather prolongs it.

Cultivars and Similar Species: 'Bedder' series, mixed and single colors, 10 inches tall; 'My Fair Lady,' soft colors, 1 foot tall; 'Blood Red' and 'White Dame,' 1¼ feet tall.

Garden Use: Use in cutting gardens, in rock gardens, and on walls; as path edging or front of border planting. Excellent ground cover for spring bulbs.

Cheiranthus cheiri

Clarkia amoena
(Godetia amoena)
GODETIA, SATIN FLOWER

Godetia's subtly sweet-scented flowers can be red, purple, dark or light pink, peach, or white, with many bicolors. The 2- to 4-inch-wide, satiny, cup-shaped blossoms are upturned at the top of the stiff plant, mostly hiding the narrow leaves, and providing a solid mass of color in a garden or a bouquet. It blooms for weeks during cool weather.

Size: 8 inches to 2½ feet tall; may be bushy or narrow.

Light: Full sun or light shade.

Soil and Moisture: Poor, well-drained soil; moderate moisture.

Planting and Propagation: Best sown in place in early spring. In mild-winter areas, sow in fall as well, and where summers are cool, sow again in late spring. Thin to 6 inches to 1 foot apart.

Special Care: Some are basal branching; others are bushier if pinched while small.

Pests and Diseases: Aster yellows-virus, stem rot, and rust sometimes troublesome.

Climate: Hardy, cool-season annual in Zones 2–11. Needs cool, humid days and nights.

Clarkia amoena

Cultivars: 'Satin' series, 1½ feet tall; 'Grace' series, both in mixed and single colors, 2½ feet tall; 'Azalea-flowered Mix,' 1¼ feet tall, doubles and semidoubles, 'Double White,' 1¼ to 1⅔ feet tall.

Garden Use: Pretty in rock garden or as edging for border; cut flower garden.

Clarkia unguiculata (C. elegans)
FAREWELL-TO-SPRING

Frilly, 1- to 2-inch-wide puffs of color bloom along the stems of this festive, spring-blooming annual amid small, narrow leaves. Try them in groups under taller, upright flowers such as foxglove. The red, pink, purple, white, or creamy yellow flowers are good for cutting. Most available strains are double flowered.

Size: 1 to 4 feet tall; bushy or spreading.
Light: Full sun or light shade.
Soil and Moisture: Poor to average, well-drained soil; moderate moisture.
Planting and Propagation: Best sown in place in early spring, or in fall where winters are mild. Thin to 9 inches apart.

Clarkia elegans 'Royal Bouquet'

Special Care: Pinching young plants encourages bushiness. Stake if not grown in self-supporting groups.
Pests and Diseases: Aster yellows-virus, stem rot, and rust.
Climate: Hardy, cool-season annual in Zones 2–11. Needs cool, humid days and nights.
Cultivars and Similar Species: 'Royal Bouquet Mixed,' 2 feet tall; 'Apple Blossom,' apricot-pink with white, 3 to 4 feet tall. *C. pulchella:* similar plant, mixed colors, 1 foot tall. *C. concinna* (red ribbons): lobed pink or red flowers, 9 inches to 1 foot tall.
Garden Use: Plant in middle to back of border, in rock garden, or in cutting bed.

Cleome hasslerana
SPIDER FLOWER

The tall, sturdy stems of spider flower grow taller all summer, tipped from midsummer to frost with 3-inch-wide rounded clusters of pink, purple, or white blossoms. Elongated stamens and, later, long seedpods, give the plants an airy, spidery appearance. Leaves are large and have seven lobes. It makes a wonderful cut flower, although some people dislike the flower's odor, which may be unpleasant up close but is not overpowering.

Size: Usually 3 to 4 feet tall; 1 foot wide. May reach 5 to 6 feet tall.
Light: Full sun or partial shade.
Soil and Moisture: Average to rich soil; moderate to plentiful moisture.
Planting and Propagation: Chill seed overnight and sow in garden after last frost or indoors, at 70° to 75°F, four to six weeks earlier. Set plants 1½ to 2½ feet apart.
Special Care: Stake in part shade or windy locations. Be careful of thorny stems. Often self-sows.
Pests and Diseases: Usually pest free, but sometimes bothered by aphid, leaf spot, and rust.
Climate: Hardy, warm-season annual in Zones 2–11. Tolerates heat if well watered.

Cleome hasslerana

Cultivars: 'Queen' series available in pink, deep pink, purple, or a mix; 'Helen Campbell,' white.
Garden Use: Back of border in informal or cottage gardens. Cutting bed. Group for bushier effect. Underplant with shorter annuals to hide eventually leggy base.

Coleus x hybridus
COLEUS

Coleus' multicolored foliage has made it a favorite houseplant and shade-garden plant. Planted in a large drift, coleus supplies bright color from early summer to frost. The tooth-edged leaves may be broad or narrow, crinkled or flat, and feature simple patterns or harlequin markings in combinations of green, red, pink, yellow, bronze, purple, and almost-black. Named varieties provide mixes or same-patterned leaves.

Size: 6 inches to 2 feet tall; variable width.
Light: Partial to full shade.
Soil and Moisture: Rich, well-drained soil; plentiful moisture.

Coleus x *hybridus* 'Pineapple Beauty'

Planting and Propagation: Sow uncovered indoors, at 65° to 75°F, six to eight weeks before last frost, or buy nursery starts. Space 6 inches to 1 foot apart. Stem cuttings root easily.

Special Care: Some are basal branching; others are bushier if pinched while small. Pinch older plants to reshape; remove blossom spikes early to keep plants attractive.

Pests and Diseases: Sometimes attacked by mites, mealybugs, leaf spots, and damping-off fungus.

Climate: Warm-season annual in Zones 2–11.

Cultivars: Color mixes and single patterns available. 'Rainbow Mix,' 14 inches to 1⅓ feet tall; 'Wizard,' 10 inches to 1 foot tall, mix or singles; 'Fiji Mix,' 1 to 1¼ feet tall, fringed; 'Black Dragon,' 1 foot tall, rose with deep purple edge; 'Scarlet Poncho,' 1 foot tall, red with gold edge.

Garden Use: Use large groups of single color or pattern to avoid busy look. Purple and chartreuse forms, especially, make excellent color contrasts in foliage gardens.

Consolida ambigua (*Delphinium ajacis*)
ROCKET LARKSPUR

An annual cousin of the magnificent perennial delphinium, rocket larkspur bears similar tall stems of spurred blossoms. The blue, white, lilac, pink, or peach flowers emit a light scent and are held above a mass of lacy dark green foliage. At its best where summers are cool, this fine cutting flower is handsome when grouped in a border. It may self-sow.

Size: 9 inches to 4 feet tall.

Light: Full sun or light shade.

Soil and Moisture: Rich, well-drained soil; plentiful moisture, but avoid wetting leaves.

Planting and Propagation: In Zones 9–11, sow in fall for spring bloom. Otherwise, sow in early spring to summer. Chill summer-sown seed seven days before planting. May be started indoors in peat pots, at 60° to 65°F, six to eight weeks before setting outdoors. Space 1 foot apart.

Special Care: May require staking. Cut spent stems for longer bloom.

Pests and Diseases: May be troubled by aphid, leaf miner, mealy bug, and southern

Consolida ambigua

blight; root rot or crown rot can be problem in too-wet soil.

Climate: Hardy, cool-season annual in Zones 2–11. Warm weather shortens bloom period.

Cultivars and Similar Species: 'Giant Imperial' series, mixed or singles, 3 to 4 feet tall; 'Imperial Blue Picotee,' white with blue edge, 3 feet tall; 'Dwarf Hyacinth Flowered Mix,' 1 foot tall, double.

Garden Use: Use in cottage or informal garden, as filler among bulbs, and in cut-flower garden.

Coreopsis tinctoria

Coreopsis tinctoria (*Calliopsis bicolor*)
GOLDEN COREOPSIS, CALLIOPSIS

This airy prairie wildflower has finely cut leaves and 1- to 2-inch-wide daisylike blossoms, which may be golden yellow or yellow banded with red, mahogany, or maroon. The effect is meadowy, and it mixes well with the equally informal cornflower in cottage gardens, meadows, and bouquets.

Size: 1 to 3 feet tall; spreads as wide. Cultivated forms shorter than species.

Light: Full sun.

Soil and Moisture: Poor to average soil; light soil best. Moderate moisture.

Planting and Propagation: Best sown in

garden after danger of frost is past. May be sown indoors, at 70° to 75°F, six to eight weeks earlier. May self-sow.

Special Care: Stems may break in strong wind; stake tall types or interplant with sturdier plants. Cut spent flowers to prolong bloom period. Easy to grow except in heavy clay or shade.

Pests and Diseases: Leaf spot, rust, virus, aphid, and cucumber beetle sometimes a problem.

Climate: Hardy, warm-season annual in Zones 2–11. Heat tolerant.

Cultivars: 'Golden Crown,' yellow with deep red centers, 2 feet tall; 'Dwarf Mixed,' shades of bright yellow, red, and mahogany, 1 to 1¼ feet tall.

Garden Use: Use in informal, cottage, meadow, or cut-flower gardens.

Cosmos bipinnatus
COSMOS

This airy, informal plant is one of the easiest annuals to grow. The satiny, 3- to 4-inch-wide, yellow-centered, daisy-type blossoms may be bright magenta, shades of rose, pink, white, or bicolored. It's a good cut flower, and cutting prolongs its bloom period, which can last from July to frost. The plants often self-sow.

Size: Older types, 3 to 6 feet tall; newer strains, 2 to 3 feet tall.

Light: Full sun.

Soil and Moisture: Poor to average, well-drained soil. Overfertilizing inhibits blooming. Somewhat drought tolerant.

Planting and Propagation: Sow outdoors in spring when soil is warm, or indoors, at 68° to 86°F, six weeks before last frost. Space 1 to 1½ feet apart.

Special Care: For best blooming, pinch out plant tips when they're about 1½ feet tall. In windy locations, stake or interplant with sturdier plants.

Pests and Diseases: Usually pest free, but sometimes troubled by bacterial wilt, pow-

Cosmos bipinnatus

dery mildew, aster yellows-virus, aphids, and mites.

Climate: Half-hardy, warm-season annual in Zones 3–10.

Cultivars: In short-season areas, plant early blooming 'Sensation' and 'Early Wonder' series. 'Purity,' white, 3 to 4 feet tall; 'Gloria,' 5-inch flowers, pink-red, 3 to 4 feet tall; 'Seashells,' white, pink or two-toned, 3½ feet tall; 'Red Versailles,' fiery red, 4 feet tall; 'Imperial Pink,' deep rose-pink, 3 to 4 feet tall; 'Sonata' series, early flowering in white or mix, bushy, 2 feet tall.

Garden Use: Informal or cottage gardens or meadow plantings. Taller versions shine in back of border or cutting garden. Use dwarfs in middle of border or in containers.

Cosmos sulphureus
YELLOW COSMOS

This charming cousin of *C. bipinnatus* blooms in vibrant shades of gold, yellow, orange, and scarlet. The 2- to 3-inch-wide flowers aren't as good for cutting because they tend to quickly shatter.

Size: Full-size types can reach 7 feet tall. Newer strains may be 3 to 4 feet tall or 1-foot-tall dwarfs.

Light: Full sun.

Cosmos sulphureus

Soil and Moisture: Poor to average, well-drained soil. Overfertilizing inhibits blooming. Somewhat drought tolerant.

Planting and Propagation: Sow outdoors in place in spring when soil is warm. Does not transplant well. Thin or space plants to 1 to 1½ feet apart.

Special Care: For best blooming, pinch out plant tips when they're about 1½ feet tall. In windy locations, stake or interplant with sturdier plants.

Pests and Diseases: Usually pest free.

Climate: Half-hardy, warm-season annual in Zones 2–11. Very heat tolerant.

Cultivars: 'Bright Lights,' in mixed shades of yellow, orange, and red, 3 feet tall; 'Ladybird' series, mixed or singles, with 1½- to 2-inch flowers, 1 foot tall; 'Sunny Gold' or 'Sunny Red,' 12 to 14 inches tall.

Garden Use: Ideal for informal gardens and meadow plantings.

Cynoglossum amabile
CHINESE FORGET-ME-NOT

This hardy biennial is usually grown as a late-spring- and early summer-blooming annual for its dense sprays of small sky-blue flowers. Flowers are usually blue, but pink and white forms are sometimes seen. The blossoms resemble forget-me-nots but lack their yellow or white eye. Plants are rangy

Cynoglossum amabile

with downy gray-green leaves. The sticky seeds hitchhike on gardeners' clothing to outposts all over the garden. Self-sows readily to become a permanent garden fixture.

Size: 1½ to 2 feet tall.

Light: Full sun.

Soil and Moisture: Average to fertile, well-drained soil rich in organic matter; moderate to ample moisture.

Planting and Propagation: Sow in garden in fall or in spring as soon as ground can be worked, thinning or transplanting to 8 inches to 1 foot apart.

Special Care: Pull out plants after they finish blooming. Cutting off faded flower stalks reduces self-seeding and promotes side branching and more flowers.

Pests and Diseases: May get mildew if water-stressed.

Climate: Zones 2–9; blooms longest where cool. Winter annual in warmest climates.

Cultivars and Similar Species: 'Firmament,' shorter and with darker blue flowers than species, to 1¼ feet tall. *C. nervosum* (hound's tongue): perennial in Zones 4–8, coiled sprays of blue flowers for a month in spring, 2 feet tall.

Garden Use: Provides electric blue color in summer; wonderful scattered through informal plantings and cottage gardens. Arrange low plants in front of Chinese forget-me-not to hide somewhat gangly plants.

Dahlia x *hybrida*

ANNUAL DAHLIA

These shorter versions of tuberous dahlias are also tender perennials, but because they bloom the first summer from seed they are used as annuals. Blossoms are smaller than their gigantic cousins but come in the same brilliant colors—every color but blue—and include single, semidouble, double, and collarette dahlia flower forms.

Size: 1 to 2 feet tall; about half as wide.

Light: Full, or at least half-day sun.

Soil and Moisture: Fertile, moist soil.

Planting and Propagation: Sow indoors, at 68° to 85°F, six to eight weeks before last frost. In areas with long growing seasons, seed may be sown outdoors in place. Plant 1 foot apart.

Special Care: Pinch tips early in season for bushier plants. Cut spent flowers for longer bloom.

Pests and Diseases: Occasionally aphid, powdery mildew, and spider mite. In the West, earwigs may eat flowers and foliage.

Climate: Cool-season annual in Zones 3–11. May not thrive in very hot summer weather.

Cultivars: 'Mignon Silver,' white, 1¼ to 1⅔ feet tall. Mixed colors: 'Rigoletto,' 13 inches tall; 'Redskin,' 14 inches tall, reddish foliage; 'Collarette Dandy,' 1⅔ to 2 feet tall; 'Sunny' series, available in red, rose, or yellow.

Garden Use: Formal or informal gardens in foreground or midground. Grow in cutting bed or containers.

Datura metel

DOWNY THORN APPLE, HORN-OF-PLENTY

Dramatic, 7-inch-long tubular flowers with a sweet, heavy perfume and broad 8-inch-long leaves characterize this native of India. Although blossoms are usually white, some cultivars bear violet, yellow, or a mixture of

Dahlia x *hybrida*

Datura metel

blue, yellow, and red flowers. Plants grow best in warm weather, blooming in late summer and into fall. All parts are poisonous if eaten.

Size: 3 to 5 feet tall; usually sprawls widely.

Light: Full sun.

Soil and Moisture: Rich soil; moderate moisture.

Planting and Propagation: Sow indoors in midwinter, at 62° to 64°F, and plant two or three weeks after last frost; or purchase transplants in spring.

Special Care: Use support made of bamboo stake tripod for taller, less sprawling plant.

Pests and Diseases: Sometimes bothered by thrip and aphid.

Climate: Tender, warm-season annual in Zones 3–11.

Cultivars: 'Alba,' white; 'Aurea,' yellow; 'Huberana,' blue, yellow, and red. Similar: *D. meteloides,* short-lived perennial in mild-winter areas; sometimes wintered indoors in cold-winter areas.

Garden Use: Use as garden accent—singly, in small groups, or in containers.

Dianthus chinensis
CHINA PINK

China pink's charming, 1- to 2-inch-wide, lightly scented flowers cover the low mounds of grassy blue-green leaves from late spring to frost. Blossoms have fringed petals and may be white, pink, coral, red, crimson, or purple and often are intricately patterned bicolors. It may self-sow.

Size: 6 inches to 1 foot tall; spreads to 1½ times as wide.

Light: Full sun to light shade.

Soil and Moisture: Average, well-drained, neutral to alkaline soil; moderate moisture. Tolerates poor soil and drought.

Dianthus chinensis 'Colour Magic'

Planting and Propagation: Sow outdoors after last frost or indoors, at 70° to 75°F, eight to 10 weeks before last frost. In mild-winter areas, sow outdoors in fall.

Special Care: Blossoms are usually self-cleaning, but shearing in midsummer rejuvenates heat-stressed plants.

Pests and Diseases: Root rot in heavy, wet soil; spider mites in dry climates.

Climate: Hardy, cool-season annual in Zones 2–11; tolerates light frost.

Cultivars: 'Queen of Hearts,' scarlet-red. Mixes of mostly solid colors: 'Charms,' 6 to 8 inches tall; 'Princess,' 8 to 10 inches tall. Solids and picotees: 'Telstar,' dark red eyes, 8 to 10 inches tall; 'Strawberry Parfait,' rose with scarlet centers, 8 inches tall, early bloomer; 'Raspberry Parfait,' blush pink with crimson centers, 8 inches tall, early bloomer. Solid and bicolor mix: 'Splendor Mixed,' 8 to 10 inches tall. 'Flash' series: pink or mix, very heat tolerant.

Garden Use: Use low types as edging in cottage gardens, as focal points in rock gardens, or in containers. Use taller types in cutting bed.

Diascia barberae
TWINSPUR

This uncommon but lovely South African annual looks particularly nice on a rock wall. Clusters of rose-pink, deep pink, or coral flowers bloom from summer to frost on slender stems with small, glossy, toothed, dark green leaves. Each flower has curved spurs on the backs of the two lower petals, and a yellow throat blotched with green. The prostrate stems root as they go.

Size: 1 foot tall; sprawling.

Light: Full sun; part shade where summers are hot.

Soil and Moisture: Average, well-drained soil; moderate moisture.

Planting and Propagation: Sow, uncovered, indoors, at 61° to 64°F, six to eight weeks before last frost or in garden after last

Diascia barberae

frost. Space plants 6 inches apart. Stem cuttings root easily to increase the number of plants during the growing season.

Special Care: Grow seedlings at 55°F to avoid leggy plants. Do not deadhead, but sheer back to encourage repeat bloom.

Pests and Diseases: Usually pest free.

Climate: Cool-season annual in Zones 2–11.

Cultivars: 'Pink Queen,' rose-pink flowers, 6-inch-wide clusters.

Garden Use: Excellent in rock gardens or spilling over edge of wall or containers.

Dyssodia tenuiloba
(Thymophylla tenuiloba)
DAHLBERG DAISY, GOLDEN FLEECE

A delicate-looking plant with a mass of ½- to 1-inch-wide, bright yellow daisies blanketing the finely divided dark green leaves, Dahlberg daisy hails from Texas and Mexico. Its perky blossoms continue from summer through fall and into early winter where mild temperatures permit. The plant self-sows.

Size: 6 inches to 1 foot tall; widely sprawling.

Light: Full sun.

Soil and Moisture: Any well-drained soil. Allow soil to dry between waterings.

Planting and Propagation: Purchase nursery plants, or sow, uncovered, at 65° to 70°F, indoors six to eight weeks before last frost. Where winters are mild, sow in garden in

Dyssodia tenuiloba

Eschscholzia californica

Euphorbia marginata

fall, or set out transplants in fall or early spring, spacing 6 inches apart.

Special Care: Takes four months to flower from seed; may prove difficult to start indoors. Needs no deadheading.

Pests and Diseases: Usually pest free.

Climate: Tender annual in Zones 2–11. May overwinter, but generally looks scruffy after winter. Drought and heat tolerant.

Cultivars and Similar Species: Only species is commonly sold.

Garden Use: Plant in rock garden, on walls, in cracks in paths, and in containers.

Eschscholzia californica
CALIFORNIA POPPY

The 2-inch-long, satiny, funnel-shaped blossoms of California poppy wave atop long, nearly bare stems above finely cut gray-green leaves. Wild versions are gleaming orange, yellow, or bicolored; new selections include cream, crimson, pink, and violet—some with fluted or double petals. California's state flower blooms in summer from a spring sowing or in spring if sown in fall. Flowers close in shade or on overcast days. It self-sows.

Size: 8 inches to 2 feet tall; often sprawling.

Light: Full sun to partial shade.

Soil and Moisture: Sandy, nonacid soil; rich soil inhibits bloom. Ample moisture until past seedling stage, then drought tolerant.

Planting and Propagation: Sow in garden in fall or early spring. Thin to 6 inches.

Special Care: Cut spent flowers to prolong blooming.

Pests and Diseases: Usually pest free; sometimes bacterial blight, leaf mold, powdery mildew, and aster yellows-virus.

Climate: Hardy, cool-season annual in Zones 2–11.

Cultivars and Similar Species: Single colors: 'Orange King'; 'Milky White'; 'Purple-violet'; 'Mikado,' crimson-orange. Mixes: 'Ballerina' and 'Mission Bells,' semidouble and double. 'Thai Silk': pink shades or mixed, 8 to 10 inches tall with fluted petals. Similar: *E. caespitosa* 'Sundew,' yellow, 6 to 10 inches tall, scented.

Garden Use: Charming in rock gardens, cottage gardens, and low meadow plantings.

Euphorbia marginata
SNOW-ON-THE-MOUNTAIN

Grown mainly for its showy, green-and-white variegated foliage, snow-on-the-mountain also has clusters of small flowers at the stem tips, which bloom among white, papery bracts.

Size: 8 inches to 3 feet tall; bushy.

Light: Full sun to part shade.

Soil and Moisture: Any well-drained soil; best in poor, light soil with moderate moisture. Tolerates drought.

Planting and Propagation: Sow in garden as soon as ground can be worked, or indoors, at 70° to 75°F, six to eight weeks before last frost. Thin to 1 foot apart.

Special Care: The milky sap can irritate skin and eyes; wear gloves to transplant or trim. Before adding to bouquets, dip cut ends in boiling water. Self-sows, sometimes aggressively and may become weedy.

Pests and Diseases: Relatively pest free.

Climate: Half-hardy, warm-season annual in Zones 2–11. Heat tolerant.

Cultivars: The species *E. marginata*, 2 feet tall, is commonly available, as well as dwarf 'Summer Icicle,' 1½ feet tall, and 'White Top,' 3 feet tall.

Garden Use: Plant in border behind shorter, bright colored flowers. Bushy ones will mask stem bases, which become bare as plant matures.

Eustoma grandiflora
(Lisianthus russellianus)
PRAIRIE GENTIAN, LISIANTHUS

Since the early 1980s, when Japanese growers released a mixed color selection of this native American wildflower, prairie gentian has become popular for its beauty and abili-

Eustoma grandiflora

ty to last as a cut flower. The upturned, cup-shaped blossoms, to 3½ inches across, may be single or double, white, pale yellow, pink, violet, blue, or bicolored. Gray-green leaves meet in pairs on the stems.

Size: 6 inches to 2⅓ feet tall; half as wide.
Light: Full sun to partial shade.
Soil and Moisture: Average, well-drained soil. Keep moist.
Planting and Propagation: Sow, uncovered, indoors, at 68° to 77°F, three months before last frost, or purchase nursery transplants. Space 6 inches apart.
Special Care: Some are basal branching; others are bushier if pinched while small. Remove faded flowers.
Pests and Diseases: Usually pest free, but occasionally root rot or leaf spot.
Climate: Biennial grown as half-hardy annual in Zones 2–11. Prefers warm weather.
Cultivars: 'Double Eagle Mixed,' 1½ to 2 feet tall, blossoms to 3 inches across. Mix or single color series: 'Echo,' 2 feet tall, includes some picotees; 'Flamenco,' heat tolerant, includes some colored-rim types. Dwarfs: 'Mermaid,' 6 to 8 inches tall; 'Little Bell Mixed,' 9 inches tall, silver-veined leaves, double.
Garden Use: Plant in groups in informal gardens or containers. Excellent cut flower.

306

Felicia amelloides
BLUE DAISY, BLUE MARGUERITE

This eye-catcher features flowers with blue petals and yellow centers on slender stems above a mound of small, oval dark green leaves. Flowers close at night and on overcast days.
Size: 1 to 3 feet tall; 2 to 5 feet wide if untrimmed.
Light: Full sun.
Soil and Moisture: Fertile, well-drained soil. Drought tolerant; better with moisture.
Planting and Propagation: Set out nursery plants in spring in cold-winter areas, in fall where winters are mild. Or sow indoors, at 55° to 60°F, 10 to 12 weeks before last frost. Plant 9 inches to 1 foot apart.
Special Care: Pinch, shape, and deadhead frequently. Prune to control spread. Cut spent flowers often to prolong bloom.
Pests and Diseases: Usually pest free, but aphid, beech scale, scab, or caterpillars occasionally troublesome.
Climate: Cool-season annual in Zones 7–8; short-lived perennial in Zones 9–11, but hard to keep looking good after a year.

Felicia amelloides 'Astrid Thomas'

Cultivars and Similar Species: Dark blue: 'George Lewis,' 'Midnight,' 'Rhapsody in Blue.' Medium blue: 'San Luis,' 'San Gabriel,' 'Santa Anita.' Dwarf: 'Astrid Thomas,' stays open at night, 1 to 1¼ feet tall. Similar: *F. bergerana,* abundant ½-inch turquoise-blue flowers, 6 to 8 inches tall.
Garden Use: Effective in rock gardens, cascading over walls and embankments, and in window boxes and containers. Combines well with yellow flowers. Good cut flower.

Fuchsia x *hybrida*
FUCHSIA, LADY'S EAR DROPS

Fuchsia is a tropical shrub with flowers so fanciful that one old name for them is lady's ear drops. The prominent stamens and pistil dangle through the ring of petals that is framed by decorative, backswept sepals. Sepals and petals may be white, pink, red, or purple, and often are two different colors. A shrub where mild winters permit, fuchsia is grown as an annual elsewhere.
Size: 1 to 2 feet tall when grown as annual.
Light: Light shade or sun.
Soil and Moisture: Average, neutral to acid,

Fuchsia x *hybrida*

well-drained soil. Plentiful moisture; do not allow to dry out, especially in summer.

Planting and Propagation: Set out nursery plants in spring, or use plants grown from softwood cuttings taken in summer. Some seed is available; sow indoors at 70° to 75°F; expect germination in three to 13 weeks.

Special Care: Pinch tips of young plants to increase bushiness. Protect from drying wind.

Pests and Diseases: Fuchsia mite, spider mite, whitefly, and aphid sometimes troublesome, especially on water-stressed plants.

Climate: Annual in Zones 2–8; perennial in Zones 9–11. Cool, humid weather best.

Cultivars: Purchased seeds and seedlings are often mixed in color, flower form, and habit. Cuttings are used to reproduce the many named varieties.

Garden Use: Often grown in hanging baskets or as standard in containers. Use as temporary low shrub in mild climates.

Gaillardia pulchella
ANNUAL BLANKET-FLOWER

A homespun flower of the American prairie, annual blanket-flower looks right at home in informal gardens. Flowers are 2 to 3 inches across, yellow, gold, cream, red, or crimson, often with bicolored petals, and have dark red centers. Newer double types resemble bright pompons and grow on more compact plants. This excellent cutting flower blooms from late spring to frost.

Size: 10 inches to 2 feet tall; often sprawling.

Light: Full sun.

Soil and Moisture: Best in poor, sandy soil kept moderately dry. Drought tolerant.

Planting and Propagation: Sow in garden after last frost, or indoors, at 70° to 75°F, four to six weeks before last frost. Barely cover seeds. Thin to 1 foot apart.

Special Care: Does poorly in cold, heavy soil. Deadhead to prolong bloom.

Pests and Diseases: Leaf spot, powdery mildew, rust, and aphid sometimes are troublesome.

Gaillardia pulchella 'Red Plume'

Climate: Half-hardy, warm-season annual in Zones 2–11.

Cultivars: Species is single, to 2 feet tall, with solid or bicolored petals. 'Double Mixed,' cream, gold, crimson, and bicolors, 2 feet tall; 'Red Plume,' red pompon, 12 to 14 inches tall; 'Yellow Plume,' yellow pompon, 12 to 14 inches tall.

Garden Use: Use in meadow gardens, informal borders, cutting beds, and containers.

Gazania rigens
GAZANIA

Brightly splashed flowers stand on single stems above these mat-forming plants. Flowers are 2½- to 5-inch-wide daisies. Older types are solid yellow, orange, red, or bronze with black dots at each petal base. Newer ones may be boldly striped or ringed with contrasting colors. Flowers close at night, and most kinds close on dull days. The lobed leaves, which form a low mat, may be silvery on the undersides or both sides.

Size: Mats of leaves 6 to 9 inches tall; flower stems 6 inches to 1 foot tall.

Gazania rigens

Light: Full sun best; tolerates light shade.

Soil and Moisture: Poor to average, well-drained soil. Tolerates drought.

Planting and Propagation: Grow from nursery plants or sow inside, at 68° to 86°F, seven to nine weeks before last frost. Space 6 to 10 inches apart.

Special Care: Can be overwintered as cuttings from favorite plants.

Pests and Diseases: Crown rot troublesome if overwatered.

Climate: Tender annual in Zones 2–8; perennial in Zones 9–11. Best in dry, hot climates where it blooms from three to four months after seeding until frost; blooms year-round in mild areas.

Cultivars: 'Mini Star,' solids, including beige and pink, 2½-inch flowers, 8 to 9 inches tall; 'Sundance,' mixed darker colors and a red-and-yellow-striped form, 5-inch flowers, 1 foot tall; 'Sunshine,' rings and stripes, 4-inch flowers, 6 inches tall; 'Daybreak,' 8 inches tall, opens earlier in day, large blossoms. 'Chansonette Mix': 10 inches tall, compact, and early flowering.

Garden Use: Makes good ground cover. Use for edging or in containers.

Gerbera jamesonii

Gomphrena globosa

Gerbera jamesonii
GERBERA DAISY, TRANSVAAL DAISY

This dramatic South African daisy makes an excellent cut flower and looks pretty in containers and cottage gardens. The 4-inch-wide blossoms may be cream, yellow, peach, pink, red, or subtle variations of these hues, as well as bicolored. Flowers appear, one to five at a time, on bare stems rising above a basal rosette of lobed leaves.

Size: Leaf rosette 9 to 10 inches high; flower stems 8 inches to 1½ feet tall.

Light: Full sun; partial shade where summers are hot. Cool nights favor blooming.

Soil and Moisture: Fertile soil with good drainage; even moisture.

Planting and Propagation: Set out nursery transplants or sow seeds when soil has warmed. Space 1 to 1¼ feet apart.

Special Care: Take care not to bury crown or plant will die.

Pests and Diseases: Gray mold, aphid, whitefly, thrip, and leaf miner are sometimes troublesome.

Climate: Cool-season annual in Zones 3–7; perennial in Zones 8–10 if well drained.

Cultivars: Many mixed-color strains, including 'California,' 'Blackheart,' which has dark

308

centers, and 'Happipot,' 6-inch dwarf. Dwarf series, mixed or single colors: 'Rainbow'; 'Festival.'

Garden Use: Rock garden or cutting garden. Dwarfs are attractive in border.

Gomphrena globosa
GLOBEFLOWER, GLOBE AMARANTH

This easy-to-grow everlasting adds a strong green presence to a border. It forms a dense, bushy plant sprinkled with colorful cloverlike flowers. The 1-inch flower balls, formed of papery bracts, may be purple, red, lavender, pink, or white and are fine for cutting or for dried bouquets.

Size: 8 inches to 2 feet tall; 1 foot wide.

Light: Full sun.

Soil and Moisture: Poor to average, well-drained soil; sandy soil best. Moderate moisture, but tolerates drought.

Planting and Propagation: Soak seed for one to four days, then sow in garden after last frost or indoors, at 70° to 75°F, six to eight weeks before last frost. Space 10 inches to 1¼ feet apart.

Special Care: Taller varieties may need staking. Cut when partly open for drying, and hang in a shady place.

Pests and Diseases: Occasionally aphid, two-spotted spider mite, and red spider mite troublesome.

Climate: Half-hardy, warm-season annual in Zones 2–11. Grows best in hot, dry locations, but tolerates humidity.

Cultivars and Similar Species: 'Buddy' series, purple or white, 6 to 8 inches tall. All 1½ to 2 feet tall: 'Lavender Lady,' lavender-pink; 'Strawberry Fayre,' light red; 'Innocence,' white; 'Professor Plum,' purple; 'Amber Glow,' light orange; 'Blushing Bride,' pale salmon-pink.

Garden Use: Charming in cottage or informal gardens. Cut flower beds.

Gypsophila elegans
ANNUAL BABY'S BREATH

Treasured for the contrast that the airy sprays of dainty blossoms add to bouquets of larger flowers, annual gypsophila also brings lightness to a garden bed or rock garden. Most commonly seen in white, it also is available in pink or carmine, either in mixes or alone. The narrow stems and small, linear leaves are gray-green. The life cycle is brief, only five or six weeks, so you need to resow every couple of weeks for continuous bloom. Flowers may be dried for everlasting bouquets.

Gypsophila elegans

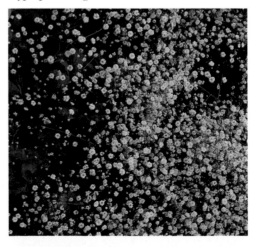

Size: 8 inches to 2 feet tall; upright and bushy.

Light: Full sun.

Soil and Moisture: Average to poor, well-drained, alkaline soil; moderate moisture.

Planting and Propagation: Sow in place every two to four weeks, early to mid-spring, or indoors, at 70° to 80°F, four or five weeks earlier. In mild-winter areas, also sow in fall. Set 1 foot apart.

Special Care: Let plants grow through mesh or low cages for support.

Pests and Diseases: Usually pest free.

Climate: Cool-season annual in Zones 2–11.

Cultivars: 'Covent Garden,' white, 1½ feet tall; 'Giant White,' 1½ feet tall, flowers 25 percent larger; 'Rose,' pale rose, 2 feet tall; 'Crimson,' bright crimson, 2 feet tall.

Garden Use: Grow in informal gardens, cracks in walls, and cutting beds.

Helianthus annuus
SUNFLOWER

While the tall sunflowers grown for their edible seeds make a striking appearance, newer, lower ornamental types offer more garden-worthy sizes, colors, and forms. Flowers vary from a few inches to more than a foot across and are borne singly or in groups on sturdy

Helianthus annuus

stems clothed in large heart-shaped leaves. Most have showy dark centers with bright yellow, cream, orange, maroon, or bicolored petals.

Size: 2 to 12 feet tall; 1 to 3 feet wide.

Light: Full sun.

Soil and Moisture: Poor to average, well-drained soil; provide ample moisture.

Planting and Propagation: Sow in garden after last frost, or indoors, at 68° to 86°F, four to six weeks before last frost. Space 1 to 3 feet apart, depending on size.

Special Care: Stake taller types. To save seed, wrap head in paper bag until mature.

Pests and Diseases: Verticillium wilt, powdery mildew, and beetles may be troublesome. Squirrels may break tall stems.

Climate: Hardy, warm-season annual in Zones 2–11. Thrives in heat.

Cultivars: 'Mammoth,' 12 feet tall, edible seeds; 'Sunburst,' mixed colors, 4-inch heads, 4 feet tall; 'Italian White,' cream and pale yellow, 4-inch heads, 4 feet tall; 'Sunspot,' yellow, 10-inch heads, 1½ to 2 feet tall; 'Sunbeam,' 5 feet tall, green centers. 'Teddy Bear': dwarf, double, golden-orange, 6-inch heads.

Garden Use: Informal and cottage gardens; temporary hedge or screen and cutting beds.

Helichrysum bracteatum
STRAWFLOWER

Strawflower's 1- to 2-inch-wide double blossoms bloom in clusters on narrow plants. They are pretty in the garden, as cut flowers, or in dried arrangements. These easy-to-grow plants bloom in shades of orange, pink, yellow, red, white, bronze, and purple, from July until the first hard frost. Flowers close up at night when young, then dry in place.

Size: 1 to 4 feet tall; 6 to 10 inches wide.

Light: Full sun.

Soil and Moisture: Average to sandy, well-drained, alkaline soil kept on the dry side; drought tolerant.

Helichrysum bracteatum

Planting and Propagation: In long-season areas, sow outdoors after last frost. Elsewhere, sow indoors, at 70° to 75°F, six to eight weeks before last frost. Space 8 to 10 inches apart. May self-sow.

Special Care: Stake taller forms. For dried flowers, cut before central yellow eye is visible, strip leaves, wire stems, and hang in warm, dry room.

Pests and Diseases: Aster yellows-virus and aphids may be troublesome.

Climate: Half-hardy, warm-season annual in Zones 2–11.

Cultivars: 'Monstrosum,' mixed and single colors, 3 to 4 feet tall; 'Pastel Mixed,' 3 to 4 feet tall; 'Bright Bikini Mix,' 10 inches to 1 foot tall, bushy and showy; 'Frosted Sulphur/Silvery Rose,' pale silvery yellow and pink, 2½ to 3 feet tall.

Garden Use: Use in cottage or cutting garden.

Heliotropium arborescens
HELIOTROPE

A tropical shrub grown as an annual, heliotrope is best loved for its intoxicating vanillalike scent. The flowers are borne in dense heads 1 to several inches across, from early summer to frost, and may be purple, deep blue, lavender, or white. The leaves are deeply veined, lance-shaped, and dark green. Heliotrope can be potted for overwintering inside.

Size: 1 to 2 feet tall and as wide.

Light: Full sun; afternoon shade where summers are hot.

Soil and Moisture: Rich to average, well-drained soil; moderate moisture, but not drought tolerant.

Planting and Propagation: Set out purchased plants when weather has settled, or sow seed indoors, at 65° to 75°F, 10 to 12 weeks earlier. Space 1 foot apart.

Special Care: Overwatering decreases scent.

Pests and Diseases: Aphid, thrip, mealybug, and gray mold sometimes troublesome.

Climate: Half-hardy annual in Zones 2–9; can be carried through with some protection in Zone 10. Perennial in Zone 11.

Cultivars and Similar Species: 'Marine,' violet-purple, scentless, 1½ feet tall. 'Dwarf Marine': 14 inches tall. *H.* x *peruvianum:* lavender to purple, some with white eyes, 1½ to 2 feet tall.

Garden Use: Use in cottage gardens or informal borders, containers, and cutting beds.

Hypoestes phyllostachya
POLKA-DOT PLANT

This colorful tropical perennial has been grown for years as a foliage houseplant but has recently gained popularity as a garden annual. Older forms have small, pointed, dark green leaves spotted and streaked with pink polka dots. Newer strains have more color and less green, being splashed all over with white, pink, rose, or maroon.

Size: 8 inches to 2 feet tall; spreading.

Light: Light shade.

Soil and Moisture: Rich, moist, well-drained soil; plentiful moisture.

Planting and Propagation: Sow indoors at 70° to 75°F, 10 to 12 weeks before soil is warm. Space 8 to 10 inches apart.

Special Care: Pinch to encourage branching and to shape; pinch out flower buds.

Heliotropium arborescens "Marine"

Pests and Diseases: Sometimes gray mold.

Climate: Warm-season annual in Zones 3–10; perennial in Zone 11.

Cultivars: 'Confetti' series, mixed or single, in burgundy, pink, rose, or white, 1½ to 2 feet tall; 'Splash Select' series, pink, rose, or white, 8 to 10 inches tall.

Garden Use: Colorful ground-covering plant for shade gardens; plant to tumble over edge of containers.

Iberis umbellata
ANNUAL CANDYTUFT

This graceful annual offers a mass of tiny flowers borne in 2-inch, dome-shaped clusters. The floral palette includes white, pink, rose, red, lavender, and purple. Flowers may be so profuse as to completely hide the small, narrow, dark green leaves. Cutting prolongs the bloom period.

Size: 6 inches to 1 foot tall; spreads up to 1½ times its height.

Light: Full sun; part shade where hot.

Soil and Moisture: Average, well-drained soil; keep moist, especially when warm.

Planting and Propagation: Sow outdoors after last frost, thin to 1 foot apart. In mild-winter areas, sow in fall. Thin to 6 inches to 1 foot apart.

Special Care: Blooms most in spring and

Hypoestes phyllostachya 'Rose Splash Select'

Iberis umbellata

early summer; shear off spent flower heads to encourage reblooming.

Pests and Diseases: Aphid, scale, and diamond-back moth may be troublesome.

Climate: Cool-season annual in Zones 2–11. Best with sunny days and cool nights.

Cultivars and Similar Species: 'Fairy Mixed,' mixed pastels, 6 to 9 inches tall; 'Flash Mixed,' mixed brights; 9 inches to 1 foot tall; 'Cream Flash,' creamy white, 9 inches to 1 foot tall. Similar: *I. amara*, rocket candytuft, elongated spikes of fragrant white blossoms; 'Pinnacle,' 1¼ to 1½ inches tall.

Garden Use: Use in informal or cottage gardens; plant densely for annual ground cover. Use dwarfs in rock garden. May be used in annual meadow garden.

Impatiens balsamina
BALSAM

A Victorian favorite, balsam tucks its blossoms between the leaves along its stems, adding more as the stems elongate. Newer forms are showier, with flowers held further from the stems or higher on the plant. The 1- to 3-inch-long flowers are usually double, in white or shades of pink, rose, salmon, scarlet, yellow, or purple; some are bicolored. The bright green leaves are 6 inches long, pointed, and deeply serrated. Balsam blooms from early summer to frost.

Size: 1 to 3 feet tall; almost as wide.

Light: Full sun where summers are cool; shade in warm-summer areas.

Soil and Moisture: Rich, sandy loam; plentiful moisture, especially when hot.

Planting and Propagation: Sow indoors, uncovered, at 70° to 75°F, four to six weeks before last frost. Plant outdoors two weeks after last frost, spacing 8 inches to 1½ feet apart. May self-sow.

Special Care: Remove spent flowers to prolong bloom period. To better show flowers, pinch taller forms to increase bushiness, and strategically pinch off leaves.

Pests and Diseases: Occasionally two-spotted spider mite, thrip, and damping off.

Impatiens balsamina

Climate: Warm-season annual in Zones 2–11.

Cultivars: 'Tom Thumb Mix,' 8 inches to 1 foot tall, bushy, top flowering; 'Double Camellia-flowered Mix,' 1⅓ to 2⅓ feet tall; 'Double Strawberry,' red-and-white bicolor; 'Blackberry Ice,' purple-and-white bicolor; 'Peppermint Extra Double,' red with white spots, 2 feet tall.

Garden Use: Lovely in cottage garden or informal border.

Impatiens wallerana
IMPATIENS, BUSY LIZZIE

Admired for the carpets of care-free color it produces in the shade, impatiens is the number-one rated annual. Intensive breeding brings a myriad of varieties, including types that branch basally and need no pinching, ones that form a blanket of self-cleaning blossoms, and ones with better sun tolerance—as well as new colors. The 1- to 2-inch-wide, open-faced blossoms have spurred petals and come in white, pink, rose, red, peach, salmon, orange, lavender, or purple and may be bicolored. A few produce double, roselike blossoms. Leaves are usually bright green, but some types are bronze.

Size: 6 inches to 1¼ feet tall; 10 inches to 1½ feet wide.

Light: Part or full shade; tolerates full sun in cool-summer areas.

Soil and Moisture: Rich, sandy loam; plentiful moisture, especially when hot.

Planting and Propagation: Use nursery transplants or sow indoors, lightly covered, at 70° to 75°F, 10 to 12 weeks before last frost. Set 10 inches to 1¼ feet apart. Some types come true only from cuttings.

Special Care: If plants don't branch enough, pinch tips. Wilting at midday usually means too much sun, not too little water.

Pests and Diseases: Occasionally two-spotted spider mite, thrip, and damping off.

Climate: Tender perennial grown as warm-season, half-hardy annual in Zones 2–11.

Impatiens wallerana 'Accent Pink'

Perennial in Zone 11 and in mild parts of Zone 10.

Cultivars: 'Super Elfin' series, 11-color mix and single colors, 6 to 10 inches tall, excellent in deep shade. 'Accent' series: 4 to 8 inches tall, 2-inch blossoms, 15 colors and five bicolors called 'Accent Star' series; 'Rosette Hybrid Mix,' 1½ to 1⅔ feet tall, doubles. 'Deco' series: red, orange, purple, or scarlet with bronze foliage. 'Blitz' series: 12 to 14 inches tall, 2-inch flowers. 'Dazzler' series: 8 to 10 inches tall, excellent shade performer, more than 15 colors, including 'Cranberry' and 'Sky Blue' (pale lavender). 'Confection' series: doubles and semidoubles, light pink, orange, red, rose, or mixed, 1 to 2 feet tall.

Garden Use: Best planted in single-color groups in shade gardens, window boxes, or containers. Combines with ferns, hostas, and other shade-loving foliage plants. Pastel colors stand out best in shade.

Impatiens x hybrida
NEW GUINEA IMPATIENS

Introduced in the 1970s, these striking plants bear 3- to 4-inch vivid red, orange, pink, coral, purple, lavender, or white single, spurred flowers on bushy plants that thrive in sunny sites. As a bonus, the leaves are usual-

Impatiens x *hybrida*

ly bronze, bicolored, or even tricolored with green, bronze, yellow, orange, or red stripes and splashes.

Size: 1 to 2 feet tall; forms wide mound.

Light: Full sun to light shade.

Soil and Moisture: Rich, well-drained soil; plentiful moisture.

Planting and Propagation: Best started from nursery transplants or stem cuttings. Sow seed uncovered, indoors, 10 weeks before last frost. Space 1 to 1⅓ feet apart.

Special Care: Pinch leggy plants. Plants can be wintered indoors in a sunny window.

Pests and Diseases: Cyclamen mite, thrip, and red spider mite may be troublesome.

Climate: Warm-season annual in Zones 2–10. Blooms year-round in frost-free climates. Performs best in cool summers.

Cultivars: From cuttings: 'Sunshine' series, compact plants; 'American Indian,' large, abundant flowers; 'Vista,' large flowers. 'Celebration': large, abundant flowers. As seed: 'Spectra' series, 10 to 14 inches tall in mixes of various flower and leaf colors; 'Sweet Sue,' red-tinged dark foliage, intense tangerine flowers. 'Tango': huge, glowing orange flowers, dark green leaves, 2 feet tall.

Garden Use: Site carefully because color combinations can be overpowering. Good in containers, window boxes, and gardens.

Ipomoea tricolor
MORNING GLORY

The showy, tubular flowers of this much-loved vine bloom in abundance among heart-shaped leaves from midsummer to frost. Flowers open in the morning, close by mid-afternoon, lasting but one day each. *I. tricolor* blossoms are purplish blue with white throats and red tips on the buds. More common is the hybrid 'Heavenly Blue.' Other hybrids and species are white, pink, red, purple, lavender, chocolate, or bicolored.

Size: Vining to 8 to 10 feet long.

Light: Full sun.

Soil and Moisture: Poor to average, well-drained soil; moderate moisture.

Planting and Propagation: Nick seed coat or soak 24 hours, then sow in garden after last frost. Space 6 inches to 1 foot apart.

Special Care: Provide trellis, fence, or dead tree for climbing. Self-sows, but seedlings are inferior. Seed poisonous.

Pests and Diseases: Canker, leaf spot, and rust sometimes troublesome.

Ipomoea tricolor

Climate: Cool-season annual in Zones 2–11.

Cultivars and Similar Species: 'Heavenly Blue,' sky blue, white center, 5-inch flowers; 'Tricolor Mix,' blue, rose, and pink; *I. purpurea,* mixed, indigo, maroon, and white, 2- to 2½-inch flowers; 'Early Call Mix,' red, blue, pink, chocolate, and violet, 4-inch flowers, good in short-summer areas. *I.* x *nil:* 'Scarlet O'Hara,' red; 'Scarlet Star,' deep pink-and-white bicolor. *I. alba* (moonflower): huge, white, fragrant, night-blooming flowers.

Garden Use: Use to decorate fences, trellises, mailboxes, and lampposts.

Iresine herbstii
BLOOD LEAF, BEEFSTEAK PLANT

This amaranth relative was a popular bedding plant grown for its colorful leaves in Victorian gardens; now it is more commonly grown as a houseplant. The 1- to 2-inch-long leaves are rounded and sometimes notched at the tips. They may be purple-red with red veins, or green or bronze with yellow veins. Inconspicuous small white flowers may appear during summer. The plants are bushy when young, but tend to trail when older.

Size: Usually 1½ feet tall in gardens.

Light: Full sun for best leaf color.

Soil and Moisture: Average, well-drained soil; plentiful moisture. Tolerates wet site.

Iresine herbstii

Kochia scoparia var. *trichophylla*

Lantana camara 'Samantha'

Planting and Propagation: Generally started from stem cuttings; purchase nursery transplants in spring. Space 6 to 8 inches apart.

Special Care: Pinch to shape and promote branching and to remove blossoms.

Pests and Diseases: Smut can sometimes be problem.

Climate: Tropical perennial grown as an annual in Zones 2–9; large evergreen shrub in warm parts of Zones 10–11.

Cultivars and Similar Species: 'Jepson,' brownish-purple with red veins; 'Aureo-reticulata,' green with yellow veins; *I. lindenii,* red, pointed.

Garden Use: Use for foliage contrast in beds, borders, and containers.

Kochia scoparia var. *trichophylla (K. childsii)*
SUMMER CYPRESS, BURNING BUSH

Grown as a small annual shrub, summer cypress has dense, feathery green foliage that turns bright red in early fall. The foliage is lovely in arrangements and keeps its color when dried. The tiny flowers are insignificant but can cause hayfever.

Size: 2 to 3½ feet tall; almost as wide.

Light: Full sun.

Soil and Moisture: Average, well-drained soil; moderate moisture. Drought tolerant.

Planting and Propagation: Soak seeds 24 hours, then sow uncovered in garden after last frost. In short seasons, sow uncovered, indoors, at 70° to 75°F, eight weeks before last frost, using peat pots. Space 8 inches apart for hedge; otherwise, 1½ to 2 feet apart.

Special Care: Shear to maintain pleasing shape. May reseed too profusely in mild-winter climates; pull out plants before seeds ripen or hoe out extra seedlings.

Pests and Diseases: Leaf hoppers occasionally troublesome.

Climate: Half-hardy, warm-season annual in Zones 2–11. Tolerates heat.

Cultivars: 'Childsii,' lighter green, no fall color. 'Acapulco Silver': green foliage speckled white, deep purple in fall, 3½ feet tall. 'Evergreen': no fall color.

Garden Use: Use as annual shrub or hedge. Plant three to five together as filler or accent.

Lantana camara
LANTANA

Lantana has 1½-inch-wide flat domes of small flowers arranged in a pinwheel. Flowers start out yellow, turn orange or red, and finally become lavender, sometimes showing all colors at once. The many varieties include ones with only white, orange, or yellow flowers, and others with multicolored heads such as red-and-yellow and lilac-and-white. Lantana is a popular houseplant and blooms nonstop in gardens from late spring to frost.

Size: 1½ to 4 feet tall; wide spreading.

Light: Full sun.

Soil and Moisture: Average to rich, neutral to acid, well-drained soil; moderate moisture.

Planting and Propagation: Set out nursery plants in spring, or sow indoors, at 70° to 75°F, eight to 10 weeks earlier. Where season is long, sow in garden. Space 1 foot apart.

Special Care: Cut back to shape if needed.

Pests and Diseases: Sometimes troubled by whitefly, aphid, caterpillars, mealy bug, and mites.

Climate: Tropical shrub grown as annual in Zones 2–8; may survive winter in Zone 9. Perennial in Zones 10–11.

Cultivars and Similar Species: Many available as nursery plants. Seed is most likely 'Camara Mixed Hybrids,' dwarf strain, to 1½ feet tall, mixed color combinations. Similar: *I. montevidensis,* trailing, purple flowers; a parent in many *L. camara* hybrids.

Garden Use: Excellent ground cover in informal gardens. Graceful trailer for containers and window boxes.

Lathyrus odoratus
SWEET PEA

Short, bushy, or tall, climbing sweet peas bear clusters of 1-inch-long, pea-type flowers on long stems amid gray-green leaves. Most, though not all, are highly fragrant and make wonderful cut flowers. The blossoms may be white, pink, peach, creamy yellow, lavender, blue, red, purple, or bicolored. Sweet peas bloom beginning in winter where mild and elsewhere in early spring, lasting into summer where cool. New heat-resistant types bloom longer.

Size: Bushy forms, 1 to 3 feet tall; climbers, 3 to 8 feet tall on trellis.

Light: Full sun.

Soil and Moisture: Fertile, well-drained soil. Ample moisture; do not allow to dry.

Planting and Propagation: Sow in deeply dug soil high in organic matter in early spring. Where winters are mild, sow in winter or fall. Where summers are cool, sow again in mid-spring. Thin bushy types 6 inches to 1 foot apart; climbers to 4 inches apart.

Special Care: Provide netting, string supports, or trellis. Mulch ground to keep roots cool. Remove spent blossoms immediately to encourage rebloom. Feed heavily.

Pests and Diseases: Sometimes troubled by powdery mildew in warm weather; anthracnose, black root rot, aphid, and two-spotted spider mite occasional problems.

Climate: Hardy, cool-season annual in Zones 2–11. Dies out with onset of hot weather.

Cultivars and Similar Species: Climbers: 'Spencer' strain, many colors, some well scented; 'Royal Family,' heat tolerant, fragrant. Bushy: 'Bijou Mix,' to 1 foot tall, heat tolerant; 'Cupid,' mixed colors, 6 inches tall, 1½ foot spread, very fragrant.

Garden Use: Decorative on trellis or fence in cottage or informal gardens. Good cut flower.

Lavatera trimestris
TREE MALLOW, ANNUAL MALLOW

Tropical hibiscus shares its splendor with this annual cousin, which grows rapidly to 2 to 4 feet tall and bears stalks of 4-inch flowers. The single blossoms are pale to deep pink or white, with a silvery sheen and dark veins. The small leaves resemble maple leaves. In cool summers, tree mallow blooms from early summer to frost, providing splashy garden color and lasting reasonably well as a cut flower.

Size: Typically 3 to 4 feet tall; dwarfs 2 feet tall.

Light: Full sun.

Soil and Moisture: Sandy loam; moderate moisture.

Planting and Propagation: Best sown in garden in early spring because it resents transplanting. Or sow indoors at 70°F, six to eight weeks earlier, in peat pots. Space 1½ to 2 feet apart.

Special Care: Stake tall varieties. Remove spent blossoms to prolong bloom period. Pull out any self-sown seedlings.

Lathyrus odoratus

Lavatera trimestris

Pests and Diseases: Usually pest free.

Climate: Hardy, cool-season annual in Zones 2–11. Performs poorly where hot and dry.

Cultivars: 'Loveliness,' deep rose pink, 3 to 4 feet tall; 'Silver Cup,' rich pink, 2 feet tall, well branched; 'Mont Blanc,' white, 1¾ feet tall; 'Pink Beauty,' pale pink, 2 feet tall.

Garden Use: Use for vertical effect in borders. Include in cutting garden.

Limonium sinuatum

Limonium sinuatum
STATICE

One of the most useful flowers for fresh and dried arrangements, statice produces branched stems densely packed with papery blue, rose, lavender, red, salmon, yellow, or white bracts. The tiny white flowers, nestled in the bracts, fade fast, but the bracts remain showy. The lobed leaves form a ground-hugging rosette; stems are nearly leafless but have flat wings.

Size: 1 to 3 feet tall; 6 inches to 1¼ feet wide.

Light: Full sun.

Soil and Moisture: Deep, sandy loam; allow to dry between waterings.

Planting and Propagation: Sow outdoors after last frost, or indoors, in peat pots, at 70°F, eight to 10 weeks before last frost. Space 1 to 1½ feet apart.

Special Care: Cut often to increase blooming. Cut when flowers have just opened.

Pests and Diseases: Rust and leaf spot sometimes troublesome.

Climate: Half-hardy annual in Zones 2–11.

Cultivars: 'Fortress,' single colors and mix, 2 feet tall; 'Mixed Art Shades,' pastel colors, 2½ feet tall; mix of 'Sunset Shades,' orange, gold, rose, amber, and apricot, 2 feet tall; 'Azure,' purest blue, 2 feet tall.

Garden Use: Dwarf, bushy forms in borders, rock gardens, and seaside gardens; tall types in cutting beds.

Linaria maroccana
TOADFLAX

Toadflax's delicate flower spikes resemble miniature snapdragons and provide the garden with both jewel-bright and subtle hues. The flowers may be white, cream, pink, red, yellow, bronze, gold, orange, red, purple, or lavender, and are frequently bicolored. Unless summers are cool, this spring-blooming plant yields to summer's heat by July. If not crowded by weeds or grasses, it self-sows.

Size: 6 inches to 2 feet tall; narrow to bushy.
Light: Full sun or light shade.
Soil and Moisture: Average, well-drained soil; moderate moisture.
Planting and Propagation: Sow in garden in spring as soon as ground thaws. In mild-winter areas, sow in fall for bloom in late winter. Thin to 6 inches to 1 foot apart.
Special Care: Weed young plants carefully. Shear after first flush for rapid rebloom.
Pests and Diseases: Usually pest free.
Climate: Hardy, cool-season annual in Zones 2–11. Best with cool nights.
Cultivars: 'Fairy Lights,' 8 inches to 1 foot tall, mixed colors; 'Northern Lights,' 1 to 2 feet tall, pink, purple, white, and yellow mix.
Garden Use: Lovely in informal, cottage, and naturalistic gardens; plant in rock gardens, in wall cracks, and as bulb cover.

Lobelia erinus
EDGING LOBELIA

A small plant best known for its vivid blue flowers, edging lobelia now also comes in pale blue, lilac, rose, and white. The tiny flowers are borne on thin stems in dense clusters amid narrow green or bronze-green

Linaria maroccana 'Fairy Bouquet'

leaves. If high temperatures or humidity do not cause their decline, the plants bloom from spring to hard frost, and much of the year where winters are mild. Lobelia is poisonous if eaten.

Size: 3 to 8 inches tall; as wide or wider.
Light: Full sun or part shade.
Soil and Moisture: Light, fertile soil rich in organic matter; keep moist.
Planting and Propagation: Set out nursery plants after last frost or sow indoors, at 70° to 75°F, 10 to 12 weeks earlier. May sow outdoors when soil thaws. Space seedling clusters 6 inches apart.

Lobelia erinus

Special Care: Pinch when young to promote branching. Shear after first bloom. May die out in hot weather if soil dries.
Pests and Diseases: Occasionally rust and leaf spot cause problems.
Climate: Tender perennial treated as hardy, cool-season annual in Zones 2–11.
Cultivars and Similar Species: 'Crystal Palace,' intense blue, bronze leaves, 6 inches tall; 'Cambridge Blue,' sky blue, 4 inches tall; 'Sapphire,' blue with white eye; 'String of Pearls,' mixed, 4 inches tall; 'Cascade' series, trailing in mix or single colors—ruby, blue, crimson, and lilac.
Garden Use: Use trailers to cascade from hanging baskets, containers, or walls. Plant compact forms as edging or in rock gardens.

Lobularia maritima
(Alyssum maritimum)
SWEET ALYSSUM

Blooming six weeks after seeding and continuing until hard frost, sweet alyssum quickly forms a sweet-scented white, cream, lavender, rose, or purple carpet of flowers. The dainty, 1-inch-wide rounded flower heads all but hide the small, linear, gray-green leaves. Sweet alyssum self-sows readily, but seedlings tend to be taller and not true to color, so some gardeners hoe them out.

Lobularia maritima

Size: 3 to 6 inches tall; up to 2 feet wide.

Light: Full sun or light shade.

Soil and Moisture: Average to poor, well-drained soil; moderate moisture.

Planting and Propagation: Sow in garden, uncovered, in early spring; thin to 4 inches apart. Or sow indoors, at 65° to 70°F, four to six weeks earlier. Or purchase plants, spacing seedling clusters 8 inches apart.

Special Care: Elongates and may stop blooming in hot weather; shear to reinvigorate and promote more flowers.

Pests and Diseases: Downy mildew and caterpillars sometimes cause problems.

Climate: Half-hardy, cool-season annual in Zones 2–9; perennial in Zones 10–11.

Cultivars: 'Carpet of Snow,' white, 3 to 4 inches tall; 'Snow Crystals,' larger white flowers, 4 inches tall, heat tolerant; 'Violet Queen,' deep violet; 'Rosie O'Day,' deep rose, 3 to 4 inches tall. 'Oriental Night': purple, 3 to 4 inches tall; 'Apricot Shades,' apricot to buff, 3 to 4 inches tall.

Garden Use: Excellent paving and rock garden plant. Use to edge bed, underplant tall flowers, or cascade from container.

Lupinus texensis
TEXAS BLUE-BONNET

A pretty wildflower that deserves more use in gardens, Texas blue-bonnet produces spires of ⅜-inch, vivid blue-and-white flowers. The leaves are typical lupine—composed of five to six leaflets forming a rounded outline. Blue-bonnets bloom from summer through fall from a spring sowing in cool climates, from spring until weather turns hot in hot climates. Seeds are poisonous.

Size: 1 foot tall and as wide.

Light: Full sun or light shade.

Soil and Moisture: Poor to average soil; moderate moisture.

Planting and Propagation: Sow indoors, at 55° to 70°F, eight to 10 weeks before last frost. In mild-winter areas, sow outdoors in fall. Set plants, or thin to 1 foot apart.

Lupinus texensis

Special Care: If planted too closely, branching and blooming suffers.

Pests and Diseases: Leaf blight, leaf spot, crown rot, powdery mildew, and rust may cause problems.

Climate: Half-hardy, cool-season annual in Zones 2–11. Blooms best in cool weather.

Cultivars: The species is often included in wildflower seed mixes. 'Pixie Delight': hybrid, flowers in white and various pastel shades, 1 to 1½ feet tall.

Garden Use: Use in meadow, cottage, and informal plantings.

Matthiola incana
STOCK

Grown for its strong, sweet-and-spicy scent, stocks are old-fashioned cut flowers. Double-flower forms offer solid spires of blossoms, while single-flower types are wispy. Both bloom in white, pink, rose, lavender, purple, cream, red, and bicolors. The straplike, gray-green leaves cloak the bottom of the plants.

Size: Column types reach 3 feet tall; dwarf bedding types reach 1¼ feet tall. Both types spread 1 foot.

Light: Full sun or light shade.

Soil and Moisture: Moderately rich, well-drained soil. Keep moist; don't overwater.

Planting and Propagation: In Zones 3–8, sow seed of dwarfs indoors, at 70°F, eight weeks before last frost. Space 9 inches to 1¼ feet apart. In Zones 9–11, set plants outdoors in late fall. Column types need five-month growing season below 65°F.

Special Care: Won't bloom if warmer than 65°F. Fertilize weekly. To select for doubles, cool to 45°F after germination and in several weeks transplant light-green seedlings, discarding dark ones, which will be single.

Pests and Diseases: Root rot if overwatered; downy mildew, powdery mildew, leaf spot, springtail, and diamond-back moth may cause problems.

Climate: Biennial grown as half-hardy spring annual in Zones 3–8; as winter annual in Zones 9–11.

Cultivars: 'Giant Imperial,' single or mixed colors, 2½ feet tall, branched; 'Trysomic Ten Week,' 1½ feet tall, blooms early; 'Cinderella,' single or mixed colors, 8 to 10 inches tall; 'Midget,' 8 to 10 inches tall, heat tolerant.

Garden Use: Use column types in cut-flower garden; use dwarf types in cottage garden.

Matthiola incana 'Column Mix'

Melampodium paludosum

Melampodium paludosum
MELAMPODIUM, BLACK-FOOT DAISY

This bushy, free-flowering little plant produces small, daisy-type flowers with golden yellow petals and orange centers. The plant is self-branching and self-cleaning, needing no deadheading or pinching. Light green leaves are rough to the touch and perfectly set off the flowers. The plant blooms abundantly from early summer until frost.

Size: 1 to 1½ feet tall and wide.

Light: Full sun.

Soil and Moisture: Average to poor soil on the dry side. Drought tolerant.

Planting and Propagation: Sow seed indoors at 70°F six to eight weeks before last frost date. Plant outdoors after soil has warmed, spacing 8 inches apart. Seed may be sown outdoors when warm. Take cuttings in midsummer. May self-sow.

Special Care: Overfeeding decreases flowers and causes leafy growth.

Pests and Diseases: Slugs in damp areas; occasionally aphid and red spider mite.

Climate: Half-hardy, warm-season annual in Zones 2–11. Thrives in heat.

Cultivars: 'Medallion,' 1½ feet tall, gold.

Garden Use: Plant in groups as path edging or in informal or rock gardens. Good in containers and window boxes.

Mimulus x *hybridus*
MONKEY FLOWER

Wild ancestors of this pretty little flower live beside streams and springs, so it is no surprise that it thrives in cool, moist gardens. The two-lipped flowers may be yellow, red, rose, cream, or orange, often bicolored with patterns and spots of a darker color. Blossoms are up to 2 inches wide, borne above succulent, medium green leaves. Monkey flowers provide welcome color in shade from late spring to frost.

Size: 6 to 10 inches tall; 9 inches wide.

Light: Partial to full shade.

Soil and Moisture: Fertile, organic, well-drained soil. Keep moist with plentiful water; do not allow soil to dry.

Planting and Propagation: Sow uncovered, indoors, at 70° to 75°F, no earlier than four weeks before 13-hour days, or outdoors in early spring. Space 6 inches apart.

Special Care: Mulch to keep roots cool and soil moist. If drought stops flowering, cut back and fertilize to reinvigorate.

Pests and Diseases: Aphid and whitefly may be troublesome.

Climate: Grow as hardy annual in Zones 2–8 and cool part of Zone 9; perennial in warm part of Zone 9 and in Zones 10–11.

Cultivars: 'Calypso,' many colors and bicolors, 9 to 10 inches tall; 'Mystic,' mixed colors, spotted, 7 inches tall, most heat tolerant; 'Malibu,' solid colors, singles or mixed, 6 to 8 inches tall.

Garden Use: Use in shade garden beside stream or pond or in moist garden site.

Mirabilis jalapa
FOUR-O'CLOCK

This bushy plant bears bright, tubular flowers that don't open until late afternoon, then remain open all night, exuding a rich fragrance. From midsummer until frost, they bloom in party colors: red, rose, pink, salmon, yellow, or white, often mottled or

Mimulus x *hybridus*

Mirabilis jalapa

striped. When the flowers aren't open, attention shifts to the glossy, pointy leaves, which are similar to pepper leaves.

Size: 1 to 3 feet tall and as wide.

Light: Full sun; tolerates light shade.

Soil and Moisture: Average, well-drained soil; best with plentiful moisture, but drought tolerant.

Planting and Propagation: Sow indoors at 70°F, six to eight weeks before last frost, or outside after last frost. Space 1 to 1½ feet apart.

Special Care: To overwinter in Zones 6–7, apply winter mulch or dig roots and store in cool spot, in damp peat moss.

Pests and Diseases: Usually trouble free but sometimes root rot and rust.

Climate: Annual in Zones 2–5; perennial in Zones 6–11, with winter protection in Zones 6–7.

Cultivars: Available only in unnamed mixes.

Garden Use: Use as mass planting in beds or as temporary shrub or hedge.

Moluccella laevis
BELLS-OF-IRELAND

This unusual plant provides a reliable source of striking green spires for the back of the border, cutting, or drying to a pale beige for winter arrangements. The tiny, fragrant, white or pale pink flowers are not very showy themselves, but are set like clappers in rows of apple-green bells, creating an eye-catching whole.

Size: 2 to 3 feet tall; one to several stems, each 6 to 8 inches wide.

Light: Full sun.

Soil and Moisture: Average, well-drained soil; moderate moisture.

Moluccella laevis

Planting and Propagation: Sow outdoors, uncovered, in very early spring (fall in mild-winter areas) or indoors, at 55° to 60°F, eight to 10 weeks before last frost. Set 1 foot apart.

Special Care: Protect from strong wind. Hang cut stalks indoors in darkness to dry.

Pests and Diseases: Usually pest free but somtimes troubled by crown rot in wet sites.

Climate: Hardy, warm-season annual in Zones 2–11. Best in warm summer weather.

Cultivars and Similar Species: Usually only species is available.

Garden Use: Use for middle of border and cutting beds.

Nemesia strumosa
NEMESIA

Easy to grow where the growing season is cool, nemesia provides a solid mass of color and a sweet scent. The two-lipped flowers are available in white, red, blue, and orange, as well as in mixes. Mixes may contain all pastels, all brights, or combinations of both, and in addition to the above colors, pink, mauve, lavender, purple, gold, and yellow flowers. The 1-inch blossoms are often bicolored or even tricolored.

Size: 7 inches to 1½ feet tall; often wider than tall.

Light: Full sun to part shade.

Soil and Moisture: Fertile, well-drained, nonalkaline soil; plentiful moisture.

Planting and Propagation: Sow in garden after last frost or indoors, at 55° to 70°F, eight to 10 weeks earlier. In mild-winter areas, sow in late summer for fall or winter bloom. Set 6 inches apart.

Special Care: Pinch plants when 6 inches tall to encourage branching.

Pests and Diseases: Aphids, snails, and slugs may cause problems.

Climate: Half-hardy, cool-season annual in Zones 2–11; replant for fall and winter bloom in Zones 10–11.

Cultivars: 'Mello White,' 7 to 9 inches tall; 'Blue Gem,' light blue, 8 to 10 inches tall;

'Mello Red and White,' red-and-white bicolor, 7 to 9 inches tall; 'Carnival Mix,' brights, 9 inches to 1 foot tall; 'Tapestry,' pastels, 10 inches tall.

Garden Use: Use in cottage and informal gardens, as spring bulb cover, and in window boxes and containers.

Nicotiana alata (N. affinis)
FLOWERING TOBACCO

This showy relative of commercial tobacco brings vertical spires of unusual colored flowers to the garden. The blossoms are 2- to 3-inch-long tubes with 1- to 2-inch-wide flared faces. Colors include white, cream, rose, red, purple, buff-salmon, wine, pink,

Nemesia strumosa

Nicotiana alata 'Nicki Pink'

chartreuse, and chocolate. Flowers of the species open only from late afternoon until morning and are fragrant; modern hybrids remain open all day and may be scentless.

Size: 1 to 3 feet tall; 8 inches to 1¼ feet wide.

Light: Light shade; full sun where humid.

Soil and Moisture: Fertile, well-drained soil high in organic matter; moderate moisture.

Planting and Propagation: Sow barely covered, outside, after last frost, or inside, at 68° to 86°F, six to eight weeks earlier. Set 8 inches to 1 foot apart.

Special Care: Provide plenty of water when weather is hot. Remove spent flower stalks.

Pests and Diseases: Sometimes troubled by whitefly, tobacco budworm, aphid, and virus.

Climate: Warm-season annual in Zones 2–9; perennial in Zones 10–11. Heat tolerant.

Cultivars: 'Nicki' series, 1¼ to 1½ feet tall, free flowering, mix or singles, light scent. 'Domino' series: 12 to 14 inches tall, bushy, fragrant, open all day, weather tolerant, mix or singles, white eyes; 'Sensation,' color range, 4 feet wide, open all day. 'Starship' series: 10 inches to 1 foot tall, compact, early flowering, several colors including 'Lemon-Lime.' 'Breakthrough Mix': 10 inches to 1 foot tall, nonhybrid, fragrant, open all day; 'Lime Green,' 2½ feet tall; 'Daylight White,' 1¾ feet tall.

Garden Use: Excellent vertical effect in gardens and containers. Good cut flower.

Nicotiana sylvestris
GREAT-FLOWERING TOBACCO

Bold, tropical-looking leaves form a vase-shaped rosette at the base of this dramatic annual. Tall, branched stems bear more leaves and starbursts of narrow, white, tubular flowers, each 4 to 5 inches long and tipped with a ½-inch-wide flared face. Up to 50 flowers form from one set of buds. Although the blossoms remain open all day, they do not release their sweet, heavy fragrance until evening. Blooms from midsummer to frost.

Nicotiana sylvestris

Size: 2 to 6 feet tall; 1½ to 2 feet wide.

Light: Light shade best; full sun if moist.

Soil and Moisture: Fertile, well-drained soil high in organic matter; moderate moisture.

Planting and Propagation: Sow, uncovered, in garden after last frost, or indoors, six to eight weeks earlier. Space 1 to 3 feet apart.

Special Care: May need staking where windy.

Pests and Diseases: Sometimes troubled by whitefly, tobacco budworm, aphid, and virus.

Climate: Tender perennial grown as warm-season annual in Zones 2–9. May overwinter in Zones 10–11.

Cultivars: Only species is available.

Garden Use: Dramatic used in border background; valued for height and late-season flowers.

Nicotiania langsdorfii
GREEN-FLOWERED TOBACCO

Airy sprays of chartreuse bells on wiry stems above refined, narrow leaves make this plant a beautiful garden novelty. Inside each bell are surprising blue anthers. Hummingbirds are very fond of the flowers. The plant blooms from early summer to frost and has long-lasting flowers when cut.

Size: Usually 3 to 4 feet tall; may reach 5 feet tall.

Light: Light shade best; full sun if humid.

Nicotiania langsdorfii

Soil and Moisture: Fertile, well-drained soil; moderate moisture.

Planting and Propagation: Sow uncovered, outdoors, after last frost, or indoors, at 68° to 86°F, six to eight weeks earlier. Space 1 to 2 feet apart.

Pests and Diseases: Sometimes troubled by whitefly, tobacco budworm, aphid, and virus.

Climate: Warm-season annual in Zones 2–9. May live over in Zones 10–11.

Cultivars: Only species is available.

Garden Use: Excellent for blending brighter flower colors. Plant in groups in front of dark burgundy or dark green foliage plants for stunning effect. Nice cut flower.

Nierembergia hippomanica violacea
CUPFLOWER

This little-known annual deserves wider planting. Forming mounds of needlelike 1-inch-long leaves, plants are covered with upward-facing, 1-inch, cup-shaped violet or white flowers from summer through fall. The effect is delicate and enchanting.

Size: 6 inches to 1 foot tall and as wide.

Light: Full sun; light shade where hot.

Soil and Moisture: Fertile, humus-rich, well-drained soil; plentiful moisture.

Planting and Propagation: Sow seed indoors, uncovered, eight to 10 weeks before last frost date. Transplant to garden, spacing 8 inches apart.

Nierembergia hippomanica violacea 'Purple Robe'

Special Care: Needs no deadheading.
Pests and Diseases: Usually pest free.
Climate: Cool-season annual in Zones 3–8; perennial in Zones 9–11.
Cultivars and Similar Species: 'Purple Robe,' deep purple-blue with yellow eye; 'Mount Blanc,' white flowers. *N. repens:* creeping and rooting at nodes, white to lilac, 2-inch flowers with yellow throats, heat tolerant; use in rock garden.
Garden Use: Excellent edging. Plant in drifts around taller plants.

Nigella damascena
LOVE-IN-A-MIST

A halo of thin, branched filaments surrounding each lovely 1½-inch-wide flower and the airy, finely divided leaves inspired this plant's common name. Flowers are commonly light blue, but also come in white, pink, and purple. The flowers make reasonably good cut flowers. The feathery seedpods are excellent for drying, and the seeds have a spicy flavor that is good in baking.
Size: 1 to 2½ feet tall and as wide.
Light: Full sun.
Soil and Moisture: Sandy loam or gravely soil; excellent drainage. Moderate moisture.
Planting and Propagation: Sow in garden

320

in early spring and in fall. Thin to 8 inches to 1¼ feet apart.
Special Care: Stake taller varieties with pea stakes. Deadheading prolongs bloom but delays seedpods. Short lived, but if days are cool, resow to prolong the show. For arrangements, cut stems with dried leaves as seedpods dry and split open. Readily self-sows.
Pests and Diseases: Usually problem free.
Climate: Hardy, cool-season annual in Zones 2–11. Dies out quickly in hot weather.
Cultivars: 'Miss Jekyll,' light sky blue, 1½ inches tall; 'Persian Jewels,' mixed lavender-blue, pink, and white, 1¼ inches tall. 'Dwarf Moody Blue': 6 to 8 inches tall, semidouble, compact.
Garden Use: Attractive in cottage gardens and as cover for spring bulbs. Cut flower.

Ocimum basilicum
SWEET BASIL

Besides being a delicious culinary herb, basil acts as an attractive foliage plant in ornamental gardens. Pinch out basil's flower buds when you grow it for harvesting, but let the graceful spires of small, white or rose-pink flowers remain in ornamental plantings. Foliage varies dramatically from tiny leaves on globe-shaped plants to bold, scalloped, or crinkled ones on tall stems. Leaf color may be bright emerald green or deep, dusky purple. All are wonderfully aromatic.
Size: 9 inches to 2 feet tall; 9 inches to 1½ feet wide.
Light: Full sun.
Soil and Moisture: Rich soil; provide plentiful moisture.
Planting and Propagation: Sow indoors, at 70°F, eight weeks before soil is warm, or outdoors after soil has warmed. Or use nursery transplants. In long, warm-summer areas, resow in midsummer. Set 9 inches to 1 foot apart.
Special Care: Pinch several times when young to encourage branching.

Nigella damascena

Pests and Diseases: Often troubled by slugs and snails.
Climate: Warm-season annual in Zones 2–11.
Cultivars and Similar Species: 'Mini,' 9 inches to 1 foot tall, small green leaves, white flowers; 'Anise' or 'Thai,' 1 to 1½ feet tall, young leaves purple, flowers pink; 'Green Ruffles,' 1 to 1½ feet tall, green ruffled leaves, white flowers; 'Purple Ruffles,' deep purple ruffled leaves, pink flowers.
Garden Use: Use miniature forms as edging, or purple leaf forms for contrast in borders, containers, and herb gardens.

Ocimum basilicum

Papaver rhoeas
CORN POPPY, SHIRLEY POPPY, FLANDERS POPPY

Corn poppies add waving splashes of color to gardens and meadows from mid-June to early August. They readily reseed. The species has four black- or white-spotted scarlet petals in a 2-inch-wide, cup-shaped blossom on downy, wiry stems clad with ferny, blue-green leaves. Cultivars have large flowers in red, purple, pink, white, pastel blue, lavender, and apricot. The strain called Shirley Poppy has white petal edges and pink centers in shadings from red to apricot, in singles and doubles.

Size: 1 to 3 feet tall; 6 inches to 1 foot wide.
Light: Full sun.
Soil and Moisture: Poor to average, very well-drained soil; moderate moisture.
Planting and Propagation: In mild-winter areas, sow in garden in fall or very early spring. Elsewhere, sow outdoors in early spring and thin to 9 inches to 1 foot apart.
Special Care: For bouquets, cut just before bud opens; sear cut stem with a match.
Pests and Diseases: Occasionally aphid, whitefly, bacterial blight, downy mildew, and leaf spot.
Climate: Hardy annual in Zones 2–11.

Papaver rhoeas

Cultivars and Similar Species: 'Shirley Mix,' pink, white, rose, salmon, crimson, usually double, 2 feet tall; 'Mother of Pearl,' pastel shades, 10 to 14 inches tall. *P. commutatum:* red with black splotch. *P. nudicaule:* perennial, often grown as fall-planted biennial or annual.
Garden Use: Use in informal and meadow gardens.

Pelargonium peltatum
IVY GERANIUM

The trailing stems of ivy geranium are studded with glossy bright green leaves shaped like ivy. Long-stemmed clusters of double red, pink, burgundy, lavender, or white flowers top plants from summer until frost, unless subjected to high heat and humidity.

Size: Stems 2 to 3 feet or more long, trailing.
Light: Partial shade in hot climates; full sun in cool climates.
Soil and Moisture: Fertile, well-drained soil; moderate moisture. Drought tolerant.
Planting and Propagation: Propagated by cuttings; purchase transplants in spring.
Special Care: Remove faded blossom clusters to prolong bloom period.
Pests and Diseases: Occasionally bacterial leaf spot, oedema, pythium, gray mold, spi-

Pelargonium peltatum

der mite, and geranium bud worm.
Climate: Tender perennial grown as annual in Zones 2–9; overwinters in Zones 10–11. Best in warm weather, but high heat with humidity causes decline.
Cultivars: 'Beauty of Eastbourne,' cerise; 'Salmon Queen,' light pink; 'Amethyst,' lavender; 'Snow Queen,' double white; 'Comtesse de Gray,' pink, semidouble; 'Galilee,' cherry pink; 'Sugar Baby,' dwarf bright pink. 'Balcon' series: single flowered, heat tolerant.
Garden Use: Excellent cascading from containers, hanging baskets, and window boxes.

Pelargonium species

Pelargonium species
SCENTED GERANIUMS

Scented geraniums are loved for their fruit- or floral-scented leaves. There are 50 or more types—the popular ones smell like orange, rose, mint, lemon, or coconut. Most have small, unshowy flowers. Many kinds trail, making them attractive in hanging baskets. The scented leaves may be used in sachets, potpourris, or cooking.
Size: Varies by species. Most 1 to 1½ feet

321

tall in containers; some to several feet in gardens.
Light: Full sun; light shade in hot areas.
Soil and Moisture: Fertile, well-drained soil; moderate moisture.
Planting and Propagation: Stem cuttings are easiest; some may be started from seed.
Special Care: Pinch to encourage branching.
Pests and Diseases: Occasionally bacterial leaf spot, pythium, gray mold, geranium bud worm, aphid, spider mites, rust, and bacterial wilt.
Climate: Tender perennials grown as annuals in Zones 2–9. Plants overwinter in Zones 10–11.
Cultivars and Similar Species: *P. tomentosum*, peppermint scent, velvety leaves, trailing; *P. graveolens*, rose scent; *P. x fragrans*, nutmeg scent; *P. grossularioides*, coconut scent; *P. crispum*, lemon scent, crinkled leaves.
Garden Use: Plant in garden or containers in herb and cottage gardens. May be overwintered as houseplants.

Pelargonium x *domesticum*
MARTHA WASHINGTON GERANIUM, REGALS

This is the showiest geranium, with huge clusters of 2-inch-wide white, pink, red, lavender, or purple blossoms blotched with a darker color on the upper petals. The 2- to 4-inch-wide, heart- to kidney-shaped leaves have attractive wavy edges. Flowers appear in spring, continuing as long as nights remain below 60°F.
Size: To 1½ feet tall as annuals; to 3 feet tall as perennials. Bushy or somewhat spreading.
Light: Full sun where cool; light shade in hot-summer areas.
Soil and Moisture: Fertile, well-drained soil; moderate moisture.
Planting and Propagation: Purchase nursery plants. Plant in spring, 2 feet apart. Propagate by stem cuttings.
Special Care: Pinch growing tips of young

Pelargonium x *hortorum* 'Orbit Hot Pink'

plants to promote branching. Cut spent blossoms to extend bloom period.
Pests and Diseases: Occasionally whitefly, spider mite, bacterial leaf spot, pythium, and gray mold.
Climate: Annual in Zones 2–9; perennial in Zones 10–11. Requires cool nights, 59°F or lower, to bloom well.
Cultivars: 'Allure,' cameo pink with red center; 'Bollero,' pink with black center; 'Crystal,' white with vermilion center; 'Granada,' apricot with white eye; 'Lily,' violet-red with dark purple throat; 'Candy,' pink with purple and lavender splotches.
Garden Use: Excellent container plant.

Pelargonium x *hortorum*
ZONAL GERANIUM

Few annuals are simultaneously as neat and exuberant as zonal geraniums. The clusters of 2- to 2½-inch flowers form bright balls above tidy rounded leaves. Flowers may be white, red, salmon, pink, lavender, orange, peach, bicolored, or even speckled. The leaves are softly hairy, often "zoned" with

brown, yellow, red, or white rings. Cutting-grown cultivars are husky tetraploids with double flowers. Seed-grown cultivars have single flowers and are less stocky. These geraniums bloom from early summer to mid-fall, year-round in mildest climates.
Size: To 1½ feet tall as annuals; to 3 feet tall as perennials. Erect or somewhat spreading.
Light: Full sun; light shade where hot.
Soil and Moisture: Fertile, well-drained soil; moderate moisture.
Planting and Propagation: Purchase plants, or sow seed indoors, at 55° to 65°F, three months before last frost. Set 1 to 1½ feet apart.
Special Care: Pinch growing tips of young plants to promote branching. Cut spent blossom stalks to extend bloom period.
Pests and Diseases: Occasionally bacterial leaf spot, pythium, gray mold, geranium bud worm, aphid, whitefly, spider mite, rust, and bacterial wilt.
Climate: Tender perennial grown as annual in Zones 2–9; overwinters in Zones 10–11.
Cultivars: Seed-grown: 'Orbit' series, 1 to 1⅓ feet tall, basal branching, many colors, zoned leaves; 'Elite Series,' wide color range, compact, basal branching; 'Ringo Series,' intense leaf zone, range of colors, almost dwarf; 'Breakaway,' salmon or red, 9 to 10 inches

Pelargonium x *domesticum*

tall, spreading form for hanging baskets; 'Softly, Softly Mix,' pastels, 1 to 1¼ feet tall. Cutting-grown: 'Tango,' orange-red, dark foliage; 'Forever Yours,' scarlet; 'Sincerity,' semidouble scarlet; 'Appleblossom,' pastel pink; 'Springtime Irene,' deep salmon; 'Snowwhite,' semidouble, white; 'Cherry Blossom,' soft rose with white center.

Garden Use: Use in cottage gardens, informal borders, containers, and window boxes, and as houseplants.

Penstemon x gloxinioides
BORDER PENSTEMON,
BEARDED TONGUE

English plant breeders created this beautiful flower by hybridizing two wildflowers, one from cool regions of Mexico and another from Midwestern prairies. Reminiscent of snapdragons, the plant has tall stalks, densely packed with nodding, bell-shaped, 2-inch blossoms in brilliant pink, red, purple, and lavender with white throats.

Size: Foliage clumps 6 inches to 1 foot tall; flower stalks 2 to 3 feet tall.

Light: Full sun to light shade.

Penstemon x gloxinioides

Soil and Moisture: Fertile, moist soil; ample moisture.

Planting and Propagation: Sow seed indoors, uncovered, at 60°F, eight to 10 weeks before last frost date. Plant outdoors when soil is warmed, spacing 1 to 1½ feet apart. May be overwintered as cuttings in cool greenhouse or cold frame. In mild areas, plant in fall.

Special Care: Cut back after main bloom to encourage reblooming.

Pests and Diseases: Root rot in heavy, wet soil; sometimes aphid.

Climate: Tender perennial used as half-hardy, cool-season annual in Zones 2–11.

Cultivars: Color seed mixes available; single colors are cutting propagated.

Garden Use: Use for vertical effect, in informal borders; excellent cut flower.

Pentas lanceolata
EGYPTIAN STAR-CLUSTER

This greenhouse plant has recently made a garden entrance, as the result of innovative breeding that generated dwarf plants perfect for bedding. Clusters of star-shaped flowers

Pentas lanceolata 'Dwarf Mix'

in pink, lilac, red, white, and some bicolors decorate plants all summer and fall. Woody stems are somewhat trailing and feature broad, pointed, hairy leaves with prominent veins.

Size: Greenhouse types 3 feet tall and as wide or wider. Dwarfs to 6 inches tall, 1 foot wide.

Light: Full sun.

Soil and Moisture: Fertile, well-drained, organic soil; plentiful moisture.

Planting and Propagation: Purchase nursery plants or propagate from cuttings. Seed is very slow; sow, uncovered, indoors, at 70° to 75°F, three to four months before ground is warm. Space 1 foot apart in garden.

Special Care: Pinch tips as the plant grows to increase branching.

Pests and Diseases: Occasionally troubled by whitefly.

Climate: Tender perennial grown as annual in Zones 4–8; overwinters in Zones 9–11.

Cultivars: From seed: 'Cheers,' medium pink blossoms, 6 inches tall; 'Cranberry,' rich rose-pink, 6 inches tall; 'Dwarf Mix,' cool colors. From cuttings: 'Starburst,' bicolored dark and light pink; 'Pink Profusion,' medium pink; 'Ruby Glow,' red.

Garden Use: Excellent in containers, mixed borders, and cottage gardens.

Perilla frutescens
PERILLA, BEEFSTEAK PLANT, SHISO

Strongly resembling coleus, and used as a culinary herb in Japan and Korea, perilla is also handsome enough to grow as an ornamental. Most commonly grown is the purple-leaf form, valued for the excitement its dark color and metallic sheen brings to a flower garden. Small white or red-tinged blossoms appear on the upper stems when the plant is mature. If you like the spicy scent and flavor of perilla, try seasoning a salad with a teaspoon or two of chopped young leaves.

Size: To 3 feet tall; 1 to 1¼ feet wide.

Light: Full sun or partial shade.

Perilla frutescens

Petroselinum crispum

Petunia x *hybrida* 'Plum Crazy Madness'

Soil and Moisture: Average to rich, well-drained soil; moderate moisture.

Planting and Propagation: Refrigerate seed in moist peat moss for 1 week. Then sow in garden after last frost, or indoors, at 65° to 75°F, six to eight weeks before last frost. Space 6 inches to 1 foot apart. Stem cuttings root easily.

Special Care: Pinch to encourage branching. Often reseeds.

Pests and Diseases: Usually pest free.

Climate: Tender, warm-season annual in Zones 2–11. Prefers warm weather.

Cultivars: Species has green leaves. 'Atropurpurea': purple leaves. 'Crispa' and 'Laciniata': purple, crinkled or fringed.

Garden Use: Use for foliage contrast in informal, herb, and fragrance gardens.

Petroselinum crispum
PARSLEY

Valued as a culinary herb, parsley makes a wonderful ornamental because of its intense emerald-green leaves. Low mounds of curled or moss-leaf types (*P. c.* 'Crispum') work best as edging or tucked between low bedding plants such as pansies or marigolds. Flat-leaf, or Italian, parsley (*P. c.* 'Neapolitanum'),

324

which grows taller and more openly, looks attractive in informal borders. Cut sprigs to use as a garnish, or chop leaves for cooking.

Size: 6 inches to 1¼ feet tall; 1¼ feet wide.

Light: Full sun or part shade.

Soil and Moisture: Fertile, well-drained soil; plentiful moisture.

Planting and Propagation: Use nursery plants, set out after last frost, or sow indoors at 60°F, 10 to 12 weeks earlier. Seed takes three weeks or more to germinate. Sow outdoors in fall for spring germination. Space 6 inches to 1 foot apart.

Special Care: Pull out and replace overwintered plants; they produce few leaves.

Pests and Diseases: Parsley worm often troublesome.

Climate: Biennial grown as half-hardy annual in Zones 2–11. Best in cool weather. May be grown year-round in warmer parts of Zone 9 and in Zones 10–11.

Cultivars: *P.c.* 'Crispum,' 'Extra Curled Dwarf,' 'Moss Curled,' 10 inches to 1 foot tall; 'Paramount,' 6 inches tall; 'Decora,' resists heat. *P.c.* 'Neapolitanum': 'Italian Dark Green,' 1 to 1¼ feet tall.

Garden Use: Use in herb and ornamental gardens, as edging, or in containers; excellent combined with white or pastel flowers.

Petunia x hybrida
PETUNIA

Well-grown petunias provide color from early summer to frost. The fragrant, funnel-form flowers bloom in white and shades of salmon, pink, red, magenta, lavender, purple, and, rarely, yellow. Flowers may be picoteed, striped, or dark veined. Doubles, resembling carnations, are best suited to containers. Multiflora types are vigorous with numerous 2-inch, smooth-edged blossoms that recover well from rain. Grandiflora types have fewer, but larger, ruffled or fringed blossoms, to 4 to 5 inches across, and are not weather resistant. Floribunda types are a cross between the two, with profuse 3-inch blossoms and good rain recovery.

Size: 8 inches to 1½ feet tall and as wide or wider.

Light: Full sun.

Soil and Moisture: Fertile to poor, well-drained soil; moderate moisture. Tolerates alkalinity.

Planting and Propagation: Set out nursery plants when warm, or sow uncovered, indoors, at 70° to 80°F, 10 to 12 weeks earlier. In Zones 10–11, plant in fall. Space 6 inches to 1 foot apart.

Special Care: Avoid in-bloom nursery starts. Pinch when 6 inches tall, remove spent flowers, and shear after first bloom flush.

Pests and Diseases: Whitefly, botrytis, pythium, aster yellows-virus, and ozone damage sometimes troublesome.

Climate: Tender perennial grown as summer annual in Zones 2–8; winter annual in deserts of Zones 9–11. Performs poorly above 90°F.

Cultivars: Multifloras: 'Merlin' series, solid colors and picotees; 'Joy' series, clear colors and bicolors; 'Plum' series, dark veined, includes the bright yellow 'Summer Showers'; 'Carpet' series, compact, basal-branching, 2-inch flowers in pink, plum, red, rose, white, and mixed; 'Blue Lace,' mid-blue with violet veins; 'Flame,' soft coral-orange with gold throat. Grandifloras: 'Dreams' series, disease-resistant, 4-inch flowers in clear, bright colors—midnight (violet-blue), pink, red, white, and mixed. 'Supercascade' series: more compact, trailing, in many colors; 'Ultra' series, solids and stripes, compact and branched; 'Magic' and 'Super Magic' series, heavy bloom, compact, branched plants. Floribundas: 'Madness' series, solids or dark veined and striped, doubles and singles.

Garden Use: Use grandifloras in containers and hanging baskets or to cascade over walls; use other types in beds and borders.

Phlox drummondii
ANNUAL PHLOX

Breeders have turned this deep rose, 1½-foot-tall Texas wildflower into a low plant with large clusters of white, pink, red, blue, lavender, purple, salmon, and, rarely, yellow flowers. Blossoms often are bicolored with dark or light eyes. The lightly scented flowers form mounds of color and are long lasting when cut.

Size: Dwarfs 6 to 8 inches tall and spreading; tall types 1¼ to 1½ feet tall and upright.

Light: Full sun.

Soil and Moisture: Average to fertile, well-drained soil; moderate moisture.

Phlox drummondii 'Dwarf Beauty Blue'

Planting and Propagation: Sow in garden in very early spring, or indoors, at 55° to 65°F, eight to 10 weeks before last frost. Sow outdoors in fall for winter and spring bloom in mild climates. Space 6 inches apart.

Special Care: Water early in day, at ground level, to prevent disease. Remove spent flowers to stimulate rebloom. May decline in hot weather, but revives when cooler.

Pests and Diseases: Leaf spot, powdery mildew, rust, beetles, and two-spotted mite may cause problems.

Climate: Half-hardy, cool-season annual in Zones 2–11.

Cultivars: 'Brilliant' series, 1⅔ feet tall, eyed; 'Twinkle,' often bicolored, star shaped, 6 inches tall; 'Promise Pink,' semidouble pink, 8 to 10 inches tall. 'Dwarf Beauty' series: mixed or single colors, bushy, 6 inches tall

Garden Use: Use in informal and cottage gardens, containers, and cutting gardens.

Portulaca grandiflora
MOSS ROSE

Few annuals have the firecracker brightness of the reds, oranges, yellows, purples, and pinks of moss rose. The petals reflect the sun with a lustrous sheen that makes even white ones glow. The lush 2-inch blossoms make a surprising contrast to the sparse, ground-hugging plants with their narrow, succulent, dull green leaves. Older kinds opened at noon and closed at dusk and on overcast days; new types remain open longer. The plant flourishes in dry, hot sites that deter most flowers. May self-sow.

Size: 4 to 8 inches tall; spreads to 2 feet.

Light: Full sun.

Soil and Moisture: Average, well-drained soil; sandy soil best. Allow to dry between waterings. Drought tolerant.

Planting and Propagation: Sow outdoors, uncovered, after last frost, or indoors, at 70° to 80°F, four to six weeks earlier. Space 1 foot apart.

Special Care: Once established, water only when plants seem near wilting.

Pests and Diseases: Aphid, thrip, and white rust sometimes troublesome.

Climate: Half-hardy, warm-season annual in Zones 2–11. Best in hot, sunny climates.

Cultivars: 'Sundial' series, mix or singles, flowers remain open longer, 5 inches tall; 'Sundance Mix,' flowers open even when overcast, 6 inches tall; 'Minilaca Mix,' 4 inches tall, upright.

Garden Use: Excellent in dry sites as ground cover, in rock gardens, and in paving.

Portulaca grandiflora 'Sundial Peppermint'

Ricinus communis
CASTOR OIL PLANT, CASTOR BEAN

Rapidly growing from seed to a person's height, castor oil plant makes a dramatic summer show. The large leaves have five to 11 lobes, and measure 1 to 3 feet across. Foliage may be green, green-and-white, blue-gray, or various shades of reddish purple and brown. Flowers are usually insignificant, although the stems and spiny pods may be colorful. Some gardeners remove the pods because the seeds are poisonous.

Size: 3 to 6 or more feet tall; three-fourths as wide.

Light: Full sun.

Soil and Moisture: Rich, deep, well-drained soil; moderate moisture.

Planting and Propagation: Soak seeds 24 hours, then sow 1 inch deep outdoors in warm soil, or indoors, at 70° to 75°F, six weeks earlier. Space 3 to 4 feet apart.

Special Care: Do not plant where young children might eat seeds. Do not nick seeds. Sap may cause allergic reaction.

Pests and Diseases: Bacterial leaf spot and bacterial wilt may be troublesome.

Ricinus communis 'Zanzibarensis'

Climate: Tropical perennial grown as warm-season annual in Zones 2–7; perennial in Zones 8–11. Thrives in heat and moisture.

Cultivars: 'Sanguineus,' bronze stems, red leaves; 'Impala,' young growth is maroon, 3 to 4 feet tall; 'Zanzibarensis,' green leaves, white veins.

Garden Use: Use for tropical look and architectural foliage in gardens; makes a quick screen or hedge.

Salpiglossis sinuata
PAINTED TONGUE

A beautiful flower with fairly exacting needs, painted tongue bears flowers in unusual colors: dusky shades of purple, mahogany, rose, red, maroon, yellow, or orange, with contrasting veins, sometimes in striking herringbone patterns. Petunia-shape blossoms appear in loose clusters above dark green, lance-shaped leaves from midsummer to frost.

Size: 1 to 3 feet tall and upright.

Light: Full sun.

Soil and Moisture: Average, nonacidic, very well-drained soil; moderate moisture.

Salpiglossis sinuata

Planting and Propagation: Sow indoors, uncovered (but keep dark), at 70° to 80°F, eight weeks before last frost. Space 8 inches to 1 foot apart.

Special Care: Pinch tips of growing plants to increase bushiness. Stake taller types. Soil must not dry out or be soggy.

Pests and Diseases: Botrytis may be troublesome in damp weather; fusarium and verticillium wilt may attack plants.

Climate: Half-hardy annual in Zones 2–10. May overwinter in frost-free areas. Damaged by wind and heavy rains. Needs fairly cool weather with good sun; suffers when humid.

Cultivars: 'Splash,' 2 feet tall, early; 'Casino Mix,' 1½ to 2 feet tall, basal branching; 'Splendissima,' 8 inches to 1 foot tall, good where humid.

Garden Use: Use in midground of borders, in cutting beds, and in containers.

Salvia farinacea
MEALY-CUP SAGE

Narrow spires of small, deep violet-blue, light blue, or white flowers bloom all summer on leafless stems held above mounds of gray-green, straplike foliage. The short, whitish hairs covering much of the plant give it a mealy surface. Cut the flowers for bouquets or drying, and enjoy this plant's sturdy good looks in your garden.

Size: 1¼ to 3 feet tall; bushy.

Light: Full sun; light shade in the South and Southwest.

Soil and Moisture: Average, well-drained soil; moderate moisture.

Planting and Propagation: Sow indoors, uncovered, at 75°F, 10 to 12 weeks before last frost, or in garden in warm soil if summer is long and hot. Space 1 foot apart.

Special Care: Pinch older varieties to encourage branching.

Pests and Diseases: Damping off, leaf spot, rust, aphid, stalk borer, and leafhopper occasionally troublesome.

Salvia farinacea 'Victoria'

Climate: Tender perennial grown as annual in Zones 2–7; perennial in Zones 8–11. Best in warm weather; poor in low humidity.

Cultivars and Similar Species: 'Victoria,' violet-blue, 1½ feet tall, uniform; 'Blue Bedder,' deep blue, 2 feet tall; 'Porcelain,' white, 1¼ to 1½ feet tall; 'Silver White,' white flowers, silvery foliage, 1½ feet tall.

Garden Use: Excellent for spiky shape in formal and informal gardens, containers, and cutting beds.

Salvia splendens
RED SALVIA, SCARLET SAGE

Despite its common name, this popular sage is now available not only in the familiar scarlet, but also in white, pink, dusky purple, and lavender. The 1½-inch-long flowers bloom from summer to frost on wide spires held above heart-shaped, medium to dark green leaves. This plant is commonly used for mass bedding but is less gaudy when used to accent a mixed border or in containers to brighten a patio. Although a poor cut flower, it attracts hummingbirds.

Size: 6 inches to 3 feet tall; half to three-fourths as wide.

Salvia splendens 'Fuego'

Light: Full sun; partial shade for pastels.

Soil and Moisture: Average, well-drained soil; plentiful moisture.

Planting and Propagation: Sow uncovered, indoors, at 75°F, six to eight weeks before last frost. Space 6 inches to 1 foot apart.

Special Care: Remove entire flower spikes as they fade to stimulate more flowers.

Pests and Diseases: Damping off, leaf spot, rust, aphid, stalk borer, and leafhopper occasionally troublesome.

Climate: Half-hardy summer annual in Zones 2–10; spring or fall annual in Zones 9–11.

Cultivars: Bright red: 'Red Fire,' 1 foot tall; 'Fuego,' scarlet, early blooming, 8 inches tall; 'St. John's Fire,' 1 foot tall. 'Red Hot Sally': deep red, 10 inches to 1 foot tall, compact, and stocky. 'Laser Purple': 10 inches to 1 foot tall, resists fading. 'Phoenix Mix': 1 to 2 feet tall, includes salmon, pink, cream, lilac, and red. 'Empire Series': 1 to 1¼ feet tall, well branched, dark salmon, light salmon, lilac, deep purple, red, white, or mixture.

Garden Use: Plant in groups in borders for spiky shaped. Use reds carefully; try with green-flowered plants and foliage.

Salvia viridis (S. horminum)
PAINTED SAGE

An unusual source of annual color for the garden, painted sage is loved for the spikes of large, pretty bracts that grow behind each tiny flower. These may be pink, blue, or white, often veined with deeper color or green. Being bracts, they remain showy long after the actual blossoms fade, often lasting all summer. Spikes are excellent in fresh or dried bouquets.

Size: 10 inches to 1½ feet tall; bushy.

Light: Full sun.

Soil and Moisture: Average, well-drained soil; moderate moisture. Drought tolerant.

Planting and Propagation: Garden-sown seedlings catch up with those sown indoors, so best to sow in garden two weeks before last frost, thin to 8 inches apart.

Special Care: Reseeds, but never weedy.

Pests and Diseases: Damping off, leaf spot, rust, aphid, stalk borer, and leafhopper occasionally troublesome.

Climate: Hardy annual in Zones 2–11.

Cultivars: 'Pink Sunday,' pink, 1½ feet tall; 'Oxford Blue,' violet-blue, 1½ feet tall; 'Claryssa,' 1½ feet tall, well branched, large bracts in singles (blue, deep pink, and white) or mixed.

Garden Use: Attractive massed in informal and cottage gardens, in herb gardens, and in containers.

Salvia viridis

Sanvitalia procumbens
CREEPING ZINNIA

Cheerful miniature zinnia flowers in orange, gold, or lemon-yellow with black-purple centers bloom all summer on this ground-hugging plant. Flowers are ½ to 1 inch across, and leaves are about 2 inches long. A popular rock garden and ground-cover annual, creeping zinnia also performs in a hanging basket. The blossoms fall invisibly when spent, making it an easy-care annual.

Size: 4 to 8 inches tall, trailing to 1 foot or more.

Light: Full sun or part shade.

Soil and Moisture: Average, well-drained soil; moderate moisture. Drought tolerant.

Planting and Propagation: Sow, uncovered, in garden after last frost. Or sow indoors in individual peat pots, at 70°F, six to eight weeks earlier. Space 4 to 6 inches apart.

Special Care: Avoid overhead watering. Performs poorly in wet soil.

Pests and Diseases: Somewhat resistant to zinnia mildew.

Climate: Warm-season annual in Zones 2–11. Tolerates heat and high humidity.

Sanvitalia procumbens

Cultivars and Similar Species: 'Gold Braid,' gold, 4 inches tall; 'Mandarin Orange,' vivid orange, 4 inches tall; 'Yellow Carpet,' lemon-yellow, 4 inches tall.

Garden Use: Use as edging in informal and cottage gardens; use in rock gardens, wall plantings, and hanging baskets.

Schizanthus pinnatus
BUTTERFLY FLOWER, POOR MAN'S ORCHID

These ferny-leaf plants make splendid drifts of airy pink, lavender, white, salmon, yellow, or purple spikes. Closer inspection reveals the intricate patterns on each 1½-inch flower—the stripes, blotches, and yellow markings that give it the name butterfly flower. Blossoms last about six weeks; sow every few weeks for succeeding spring and summer bloom periods in cool-summer areas. Good cut flower.

Size: 1 to 4 feet tall; nearly as wide.

Light: Full sun where cool; light shade where summers are warm.

Soil and Moisture: Fertile, very well-drained organic soil; moderate moisture.

Planting and Propagation: Sow indoors,

Schizanthus pinnatus

uncovered (but keep dark), at 60° to 75°F, 12 weeks before last frost. Or make succession sowings in garden in spring; in fall in mild-winter areas. Set 8 inches to 1 foot apart.

Special Care: Pinch young plants, and pinch again several times to increase bushiness. Protect brittle stems from wind.

Pests and Diseases: Anthracnose, damping off, and leafhopper may cause problems.

Climate: Cool-season annual in Zones 2–8; winter annual in Zones 9–11. Best in North, mountain areas, and coastal California.

Cultivars: 'Disco,' 1 to 1¼ feet tall; 'Angel Wings,' 1 foot tall, 10 inches wide; 'Star Parade,' 6 to 9 inches tall, 8 inches wide.

Garden Use: Charming in informal gardens, cutting beds, and containers.

Tagetes erecta
AFRICAN MARIGOLD

Mexican in origin, these big, bold marigolds have long been called African marigolds, although some catalogs more aptly call them American marigolds. The carnationlike blossoms are 3 to 6 inches across, yellow, pale yellow, gold, or orange, and, rarely, creamy white. Deeply cut, dark green pungent foliage provides a nice contrast. The plant blooms from summer through light fall frosts. Afro-French hybrids (between *T. erecta* and *T. patula*) are generally shorter, with profuse, long-lasting, large blossoms in all of the above colors, plus red and red-and-yellow bicolors. These triploid plants are not bothered by heat and humidity and do not set seed, so they need no deadheading to keep on blooming.

Size: 1 to 3 feet tall; 1 to 2 feet wide.

Light: Full sun; part shade in hot-summer areas of the South and Southwest.

Soil and Moisture: Fertile to average, well-drained, sandy loam; moderate moisture.

Planting and Propagation: Sow indoors, at 65° to 75°F, four to six weeks before last frost. In long-summer areas, sow outdoors after frost. Set 1 to 2 feet apart.

Tagetes erecta 'Excel Primrose'

Tagetes patula

Tagetes tenuifolia 'Lemon Gem'

Special Care: Pinch young plants to encourage branching and more bloom. Avoid overhead watering, which can rot blossoms. Deadhead to prolong blooming of nonhybrids. Remove faded blossoms of triploids to improve appearance.

Pests and Diseases: Botrytis, root rot, fusarium wilt, leaf spot, rust, Japanese beetle, and slugs may be troublesome.

Climate: Warm-season annual in Zones 2–11. Flowering slows when hot and humid.

Cultivars and Similar Species: 'Toreador,' rich orange, 2½ feet tall; 'Inca Mixed,' orange, bright yellow, tangerine, and gold, 1 foot tall; 'Excel,' gold, orange, primrose (pale yellow), yellow, or mix, 14 inches to 1⅓ feet tall; 'Climax,' 2½ to 3 feet tall; 'Snowdrift,' white, 22 inches tall, give afternoon shade. Afro-French hybrids: 'Solar,' 12 to 14 inches tall, 3-inch blossoms, gold, lemon, orange; 'Zenith,' 1¼ to 1½ feet tall, 2½- to 3-inch blossoms in yellow, orange, or red-and-yellow bicolor.

Garden Use: Group in midground of formal and informal gardens.

Tagetes patula
FRENCH MARIGOLD

These easy-to-grow, fine-leaf beauties are small, low plants with 2-inch-wide single or double flowers that are usually bright yellow or gold and bicolored with red or mahogany. Some flower types are flat headed with shin-

gled petals; others are crested with a prominent central tuft of petals surrounded by flat petals, or single with five petals surrounding a central button. Blooms from early summer through light frosts.

Size: 6 inches to 1½ feet tall and as wide.

Light: Same as *T. erecta.*

Soil and Moisture: Same as *T. erecta.*

Planting and Propagation: Same as *T. erecta,* except space 6 to 10 inches apart.

Special Care: Same as *T. erecta.*

Pests and Diseases: Same as *T. erecta.*

Climate: Same as *T. erecta.*

Cultivars: Singles: 'Disco' series, 1 foot tall, 2-inch blossoms in golden yellow, yellow-and-mahogany, bronze-and-russet, and red. Broad petaled: 'Aurora' series, 10 inches to 1 foot tall, 3-inch double blossoms in orange-and-red, gold-yellow, light yellow, gold, or mixed; 'Sophia' series, 1 foot tall, double yellow, orange, red, or the red-and-gold; 'Safari' series, self-cleaning and disease-resistant, 1 foot tall, 3-inch blooms in yellow, scarlet, orange, light yellow, maroon-and-gold, and red-and-gold. Dwarf Crested: 'Hero' series, 10 inches to 1 foot tall, 3-inch blossoms in yellow, orange, red, gold, red-and-gold, yellow, maroon-and-orange, yellow-and-mahogany, or mixed; 'Boy' series, 8 to 10 inches tall, 1½-inch flowers in gold, orange, yellow, or yellow-and-maroon; 'Little Devil' series, flat crested 1½-inch double flowers, early flowering, in orange, yellow, yellow-and-maroon,

and mixed; 'Bonanza' series, deep colors, 10 inches to 1 foot tall, 2-inch flowers in orange, gold, yellow, and bicolors.

Garden Use: The 6-inch-tall dwarf types make excellent edging annuals. Use taller ones in cutting beds and containers.

Tagetes tenuifolia
SIGNET MARIGOLD

Signet marigolds are delicate-looking plants with mounds of feathery foliage and masses of ¾-inch-wide single blossoms in colors and bicolors similar to those of French marigolds. Less commonly grown than African or French marigolds, these dainty plants are favored by sophisticated designers.

Size: 6 inches to 1 foot tall and as wide.

Light: Same as *T. erecta.*

Soil and Moisture: Same as *T. erecta.*

Planting and Propagation: Same as *T. erecta,* except space 6 to 10 inches apart.

Special Care: Deadhead to prolong bloom. Try edible petals in a salad.

Pests and Diseases: Same as *T. erecta.*

Climate: Same as *T. erecta.*

Cultivars: 'Gem' series, 9 inches tall; 'Lemon,' 'Gold,' 'Tangerine'; 'Paprika,' red edged gold, 6 inches tall; 'Starfire,' mix of orange and orange with gold edge.

Garden Use: Dainty plants for cottage and herb gardens, front of border, window boxes, and containers.

Thunbergia alata 'Susie Orange with Black Eye'

Thunbergia alata
BLACK-EYED SUSAN VINE

This annual vine quickly can cover a fence in a sheltered corner with its 1- to 2-inch-wide, five-petaled blossoms that bloom from mid-summer until frost. Flowers are most often yellow or orange with startling dark eyes. Also available are blossoms in white and buff, and ones without dark eyes. The plant climbs by twining and holds the flowers well away from 3-inch-long, arrow-shaped leaves.

Size: Vining to 6 to 10 feet high.
Light: Full sun or light shade.
Soil and Moisture: Fertile, well-drained soil; plentiful moisture.
Planting and Propagation: Sow indoors, at 70° to 75°F, six to eight weeks before last frost. In mild-winter areas, sow in garden in early spring. Space 1 to 1½ feet apart.
Special Care: Provide support for climbing.
Pests and Diseases: Red spider mite and aphids sometimes cause problems.
Climate: Warm-season annual in Zones 2–9; perennial in Zones 10–11. Light frost kills top but not roots. Avoid reflected heat.
Cultivars: 'Susie' series, orange or yellow with dark eyes, or mixed with and without dark eyes; 'Angel Wings,' 2-inch white flowers, yellow centers, lightly fragrant.
Garden Use: Use for bold color on fence or wall, as screen or ground cover, and in containers and hanging baskets.

Tithonia rotundifolia
MEXICAN SUNFLOWER

The dahlialike blossoms of this dramatically tall, heat-tolerant annual bloom from mid-summer to frost and attract butterflies. Once available only in fiery red-orange with yellow undersides and yellow centers, the 2½- to 3½-inch-wide flowers now also come in deep chrome yellow. The leaves are large, velvety, and often deeply lobed.

Size: Newer varieties 2 to 4 feet tall. Species grows to 5 or more feet tall and half as wide.
Light: Full sun.
Soil and Moisture: Average to poor, well-drained soil; light to moderate moisture.
Planting and Propagation: Sow in garden after last frost, or indoors in peat pots, covered lightly, at 70°F, six to eight weeks earlier. Space 2 to 3 feet apart.
Special Care: Stake in windy sites. For cut flowers, sear stem ends in flame, and plunge into warm water. Do not overfertilize.
Pests and Diseases: Slugs and snails may be troublesome.
Climate: Half-hardy, warm-season annual in Zones 2–11. Heat tolerant.
Cultivars: 'Torch,' orange-red, 2½ feet tall; 'Goldfinger,' 2 to 2½ feet tall; 'Yellow Torch,' chrome yellow, 3 to 4 feet tall.
Garden Use: Use in back of border in informal and cottage gardens. Good cut flower.

Tithonia rotundifolia

Torenia fournieri
WISHBONE FLOWER

In a relatively cool, lightly shaded corner of an otherwise warm garden, this pretty annual forms rounded mounds of 1-inch-long, funnel-shaped blossoms from spring to frost. Usually bicolored in shades of blue and purple, the flowers now come in pink, burgundy, and white, all with pale or white throats and yellow-spotted lower petals. The wishbone is the pair of arching stamens at each flower's center. Foliage turns reddish purple in fall. Often self-sows.

Size: 8 inches to 1 foot tall and as wide.
Light: Light shade; full sun where day temperatures are below 75°F.
Soil and Moisture: Fertile soil high in organic matter; plentiful moisture.
Planting and Propagation: Sow indoors, uncovered, at 70° to 75°F, 10 to 12 weeks before last frost. Space 6 to 8 inches apart.
Special Care: Thrives in high humidity.
Pests and Diseases: Root rot sometimes a problem in wet soil.
Climate: Warm-season annual in Zones 5–11.
Cultivars: Species, 1 foot tall, sky blue marked white and yellow; 'Clown' series, 8 to 10 inches tall, single colors and mix in burgundy, pink, lavender, white marked with purple and pink. 'Pink Panda,' 4 to 8 inches

Torenia fournieri 'Blue Panda'

tall, white marked rose-pink; 'Blue Panda,' 4 to 8 inches tall, light blue marked deep purple-blue.

Garden Use: Excellent as edging in formal and informal gardens; use in containers.

Tropaeolum majus
NASTURTIUM

Either tidy and dwarf or exuberantly trailing, nasturtiums bring the garden a cheerful combination of nearly round 1- to 4-inch-wide leaves and bright, 2½-inch-wide flowers. The spurred blossoms are single, semidouble, or double in orange, yellow, gold, scarlet, mahogany, carmine, and sometimes bicolors. Leaves and blossoms are edible; they have a peppery taste.

Size: Dwarfs 6 inches to 1 foot tall, mounded; trailers 1½ feet high, trailing or climbing 6 feet or more.

Light: Full sun to part shade.

Soil and Moisture: Average to poor, well-drained, sandy soil; tolerates drought.

Planting and Propagation: Best started in garden. Sow after last frost. In mild-winter areas, sow in fall for winter and spring bloom. Often self-sows.

Special Care: Don't fertilize. Rich soil makes leaves taller than flowers.

Pests and Diseases: Aphid, leaf spot, aster yellows-virus, cabbage looper, and two-

Tropaeolum majus

spotted mite may be troublesome.

Climate: Cool-season annual in Zones 2–11.

Cultivars: Dwarf: 'Double Dwarf Jewel,' 1 foot tall, mixed; 'Whirlybird,' 6 to 10 inches tall, very showy, upward facing, spurless blossoms in seven rich colors or mixed; 'Empress of India,' 2 feet tall, dark scarlet, blue-green leaves; 'Alaska,' 6 to 10 inches tall, mixed flower colors, white-splashed leaves. Trailing: 'Climbing Mixed,' 6 to 8 feet tall, all colors; 'Parks Fragrant Giants,' varied colors, fragrant; 'Gleam,' 3 feet tall, semitrailing, semidouble, and double, all colors.

Garden Use: Use trailers as bank covers, in hanging baskets, and on trellises. Use dwarf varieties as edging in informal, cottage, and herb gardens.

Verbena x hybrida
VERBENA

Verbena has charmed many generations of gardeners with its 2- to 3-inch-wide domed heads of small, fragrant, white-eyed blossoms. It blooms early summer to frost, in white, red, purple, blue, lavender, and a new peach. Leaves are dark green and lance shaped with serrated edges.

Size: 6 inches to 1 foot tall; up to twice as wide.

Light: Full sun; light shade where hot.

Soil and Moisture: Fertile, very well-drained soil; moderate moisture. Drought tolerant.

Planting and Propagation: Sow indoors, uncovered (but keep dark), at 65° to 70°F, 12 to 14 weeks before last frost. Improve germination by sowing in moist medium, then not watering again until germination begins. Space 1 to 1½ feet apart.

Special Care: Pinch young plants to encourage branching. Remove spent blooms.

Pests and Diseases: Bacterial wilt, mildew, aphid, blister beetle, caterpillar, whitefly, thrips, and mites sometimes cause problems.

Climate: Half-hardy, warm-season annual in Zones 2–11; perennial in Zones 9–11.

Cultivars: Upright: 'Blue Lagoon,' blue, 9

Verbena x *hybrida*

inches tall, mildew resistant; 'Derby,' mix, eyed, 10 inches tall; 'Armour' series, early flowering, balled heads. Spreading: 'Peaches and Cream,' peach-pink and cream, 8 inches tall; 'Sparkle,' mix, some eyed, 6 inches tall; 'Trinidad,' rose-pink, eyeless; *V. tenuisecta* 'Imagination,' violet, 2 feet tall and wide spreading, ferny leaves, perennial in Zones 8–10, sold as annual.

Garden Use: Use as ground cover and in rock gardens, wall cracks, and containers.

Viola x wittrockiana
PANSY

The familiar flat-faced pansy flower comes in an ever-growing array of single colors, bicolors, and tricolors that include white, yellow, peach, cream, mahogany, red, orange, pink, lavender, purple, blue, and almost-black. The blossoms range from 2 to 7 inches across. Pansies need cool weather; heat-tolerant types extend bloom somewhat.

Size: 4 to 9 inches tall and as wide.

Light: Full sun to part shade.

Soil and Moisture: Fertile, well-drained, organic soil; plentiful moisture.

Planting and Propagation: Set out nursery plants several weeks before last frost. Or sow indoors, at 65° to 70°F, 10 to 12 weeks earlier. In mild-winter areas, also plant in fall for winter bloom. Space 4 to 6 inches apart.

Viola x *wittrockiana*

Special Care: Mulch to cool roots and prolong blooming. Remove spent flowers.

Pests and Diseases: Anthracnose, crown rot, downy mildew, botrytis, leaf spot, powdery mildew, and slugs may be troublesome.

Climate: Hardy, cool-season annual in Zones 2–11; winter annual in Zones 9–11.

Cultivars: 'Imperial' series, mostly bicolors, many pastels, 6 inches high; 'Crystal Bowl' series, solid colors, 7 inches tall, heat tolerant; 'Super Chalon Giants Mix,' deep, rich bicolors and tricolors, ruffled; 'Floral Dance,' many bicolors and tricolors, 6 to 9 inches tall, cold hardy. 'Universal,' best for winter flowering, 11 colors; 'Bingo Series,' enormous upward-facing flowers, many colors; 'Rally Series,' upward-facing flowers, good winter annual in the South.

Garden Use: Use as companion to spring bulbs in informal and cottage gardens; excellent in containers and cutting beds.

Zinnia angustifolia (Z. linearis)

NARROW-LEAF ZINNIA

Short and sweet, narrow-leaf zinnia is a delightfully sprawling plant quickly gaining in popularity because of its easy-care nature. Perky 1- to 2½-inch-wide single blossoms in burnished yellow, orange, or white, with prominent orange centers bloom freely all

332

Zinnia angustifolia

summer, blanketing the narrow dark green leaves with brilliant color.

Size: To 1 foot tall; sprawling.

Light: Full sun; part sun in hottest areas.

Soil and Moisture: Moderately fertile, nonalkaline, well-drained soil; best with regular moisture although drought tolerant.

Planting and Propagation: Best sown in garden after last frost. Sow indoors in peat pots, at 75° to 80°F, six weeks earlier. Set 6 inches to 1 foot apart.

Special Care: Avoid wetting leaves. Needs no deadheading.

Pests and Diseases: Sometimes mildew.

Climate: Warm-season annual in Zones 2–11; thrives on heat.

Cultivars: 'Star' series: 'Orange'; 'White'; 'Starbright Mix,' orange, white, and gold; 'Classic Orange,' orange; 'Classic White,' creamy white.

Garden Use: Easy-care plant for informal gardens, cottage gardens, and containers.

Zinnia elegans

COMMON ZINNIA

Zinnia, sturdy and bright, blooms steadily in warm gardens from early summer to frost. Plants and flowers vary from dwarf to tall, with blossoms from 1 to 6 inches across. Most are double, and these may be pompons or cactus flowered. Blossoms now include all

the colors of the rainbow, in brilliant hues and pastels. Some types are bicolored, streaked, and speckled with other colors.

Size: 6 inches to 3 feet tall. Some bushy; others upright and narrow.

Light: Full sun; part sun in hottest areas.

Soil and Moisture: Fertile, well-drained soil; water regularly.

Planting and Propagation: Best sown in garden after last frost. Sow inside in peat pots, at 75° to 80°F, six weeks earlier. Set 6 inches to 1 foot apart.

Special Care: Avoid wetting leaves. Cut often to encourage blooming. Strip off leaves before adding to arrangements.

Pests and Diseases: Mildew-prone, although many cultivars are now mildew-resistant; bacterial wilt, alternaria, powdery mildew, root and stem rot, Japanese beetle, and mites may be troublesome.

Climate: Warm-season annual in Zones 2–11.

Cultivars: 'Thumbelina,' 6 to 10 inches tall, 1½- to 2-inch flowers; 'Peter Pan,' 10 inches to 1 foot tall, 4-inch flowers; 'Splendor,' 22 inches tall, 5-inch flowers; 'Peppermint Stick Mix,' 2 feet tall, streaked bicolors; 'Cut and Come Again,' 2 feet tall, well-branched. 'Dreamland' series: 4-inch flowers in bright colors, compact, 10 inches to 1 foot tall.

Garden Use: Plant in masses in foreground or mid-ground of borders, cottage gardens, and cutting beds.

Zinnia elegans 'Dreamlands Mix'

BULBS

Blooming mostly in spring before perennials and annuals make a display, bulbs bring welcome color to an otherwise bare garden.

Acidanthera murielae

Acidanthera murielae
ABYSSINIAN GLADIOLUS,
PEACOCK ORCHID

More graceful than the florist gladiolus, this Ethiopian native has curving rather than stiff flower stems. The exotic-looking creamy white flowers are 3 to 4 inches wide with chocolate, maroon, or red stars at their throats. They bloom for two months in late summer and fall. Plant where their glowing, butterflylike flowers and pleasant fragrance can be enjoyed in the evening.

Size: 2½ to 3½ feet tall.

Light: Full sun.

Soil and Moisture: Deeply prepared, well-drained soil; abundant moisture.

Planting and Propagation: Plant corms 4 to 6 inches deep and 6 inches apart after last frost. In Zone 6 and colder, start in cold frame or indoors in peat pots one month before last frost.

Special Care: Protect from wind. Remove spent flowers to promote continued bloom.

Pests and Diseases: Thrips, bacterial scab, and mosaic virus sometimes troublesome.

Climate: Cold hardy in Zones 7–11. In Zones 3–6, dig corms in fall when leaves turn yellow, and store at 60° to 68°F. In Zone 7, apply winter mulch or dig and store corms.

Similar Species: *A. bicolor,* 1½ to 2 feet tall, white with chocolate star.

Garden Use: Plant in groups of 12 or more in fragrance garden or in formal borders. Excellent in containers and cutting beds.

Agapanthus hybrids
LILY OF THE NILE, AFRICAN LILY

Agapanthus is a handsome, easy-care plant that blooms throughout the summer. Dome-shaped clusters of 1- to 6-inch-wide blue or white lilylike flowers bloom atop bare stems, high above thick clumps of straplike leaves. Evergreen types are frost-tender; grow them in containers and overwinter indoors.

Size: 1 to 5 feet tall, depending on cultivar.

Light: Full sun in the North; part shade where summers are hot.

Soil and Moisture: Fertile, well-drained, moist soil; abundant moisture during growth.

Agapanthus hybrid

Planting and Propagation: Plant tuberous roots just under soil surface, 1 to 2 feet apart.

Special Care: Blooms best when undisturbed for several years or if pot bound.

Pests and Diseases: Snails and slugs troublesome; stem rot if overcrowded.

Climate: Evergreen types hardy in Zones 8–11; deciduous types to Zone 7 with winter mulch.

Cultivars and Similar Species: Evergreen: *A. orientalis* and *A. africanus* are often confused. The first reaches 5 feet tall; the second, 3 feet tall. Both are available in blue and white. Popular evergreen hybrids include 'Rancho White,' white, 2 feet tall; 'Peter Pan,' deep blue, 1½ feet tall; 'Lilliput,' porcelain blue, 1½ feet tall; 'Albidus,' white, 3 feet tall. Deciduous: 'Headbourn Hybrids,' 3 feet tall, mixed shades of blue with occasional white, or as selections such as 'Bressingham Blue,' amethyst-blue.

Garden Use: Mass-plant in borders where cold hardy; in containers where tender. Use dwarfs for edgings. Excellent in cutting beds and as houseplants.

Allium aflatunense
PERSIAN ONION

Similar to *A. giganteum* but with smaller flower heads and a less massive appearance, Persian onion bears 2- to 4-inch-wide spherical clusters of small violet flowers on bare stems. The low, straplike leaves decline as the plant blooms in late spring to early summer, so place it among plants with summer foliage. Persian onion makes an excellent cut or dried flower.

Size: 2½ to 5 feet tall.

Light: Sun or light shade.

Soil and Moisture: Sandy, well-drained, moderately fertile soil; abundant moisture.

Allium aflatunense 'Purple Sensation'

Planting and Propagation: Plant bulbs in fall, 5 to 8 inches deep and 10 inches apart. Divide when become crowded and blooming diminishes.

Special Care: Divide only when crowded.

Pests and Diseases: Rodents may eat bulbs.

Climate: Zones 4–8.

Cultivars: 'Purple Sensation,' deep violet, 2 to 3 feet tall; 'Lucille Ball,' hybrid with larger deep violet flowers, 3 feet tall.

Garden Use: Plant in groups of five or more in borders and rock gardens. Include in cut-flower garden.

Allium caeruleum (*A. azureum*)
BLUE GLOBE ONION

One of the few bulbs that offers true blue blossoms, blue globe onion features 1- to 2-inch-wide, pale to cornflower blue flower heads from early summer to midsummer. The narrow, three-sided leaves form attractive bushy clumps in spring but decline as the plant blooms. The dried seed heads remain handsome for months and are useful in arrangements.

Size: 1 to 3 feet tall.

Light: Sun or light shade.

Soil and Moisture: Sandy, moderately fertile soil; abundant moisture during growth.

Planting and Propagation: Plant bulbs in fall, 4 to 6 inches deep and 10 inches apart. Divide when become crowded and blooming diminishes.

Special Care: Divide only when crowded.

Pests and Diseases: Rodents may eat bulbs.

Climate: Zones 2–7; best with hot, dry summers.

Cultivars: Only species is sold.

Garden Use: Plant where summer foliage from other plants masks leaves. Looks good in borders and rock gardens combined with pastel pink and yellow blossoms.

Allium giganteum
GIANT ONION

This tallest of the commonly planted alliums produces ground-hugging clusters of 2-inch-wide blue-green leaves, from which arise tall, bare flower stalks topped by 4- to 6-inch-wide globe-shaped flower heads. The spheres of small, tightly packed reddish purple flowers make unusual cut flowers, which may be air-dried for winter bouquets. When the blossoms appear in early summer, the leaves are declining.

Size: Most 3 to 4 feet tall; some more than 5 feet tall.

Light: Sun or part shade.

Soil and Moisture: Sandy, well-drained, moderately fertile soil; abundant moisture.

Planting and Propagation: Plant bulbs in fall, 4 to 6 inches deep and 1 to 1½ feet apart. Divide when crowded and blooming diminishes.

Special Care: May need staking.

Pests and Diseases: Rodents may eat bulbs.

Climate: Zones 4–8.

Cultivars and Similar Species: 'Globemaster,' hybrid with 10-inch-wide flower heads, attractive foliage during and after blooming. *A. christophii* (star-of-Persia): 6-inch- to 1-foot-wide heads of silvery lilac star-shaped flowers, 1 to 2½ feet tall. *A. karataviense:* 3- to 5-inch-wide round heads of pink or purplish white blossoms, 6 to 10 inches tall, broad gray-green leaves; use in rock gardens or containers.

Garden Use: Dramatic shape when massed in midground or background of borders where foliage is masked. Include in cut-flower garden.

Allium caeruleum

Allium giganteum 'Globemaster'

Allium moly

LILY LEEK

Sunny yellow, star-shaped, ¾-inch blossoms in 3-inch-wide heads top this charming and useful allium. Each plant has two leaves, ½ inch to 2 inches wide and 1 foot long, which remain green throughout the bulb's late-spring and early summer bloom period. The plant spreads and self-sows to form wide clumps, a feature some cherish and others find disagreeable.

Size: 6 inches to 1½ feet tall.

Light: Full sun to light shade.

Soil and Moisture: Sandy, moderately fertile soil; abundant moisture.

Planting and Propagation: Plant bulbs in fall, 4 inches deep and 3 to 4 inches apart.

Special Care: Remove seed heads to prevent self-sowing, if desired. Divide when crowded and blooming diminishes.

Pests and Diseases: Rodents may eat bulbs.

Climate: Zones 4–8.

Cultivars and Similar Species: *A. flavum,* similar but taller, with bell-shaped yellow flowers.

Garden Use: Charming in between paving stones, tucked into rock gardens, and massed in low ground-cover plantings. Use in cut-flower gardens. Interplant with pink *A. ostrowskianum* and white *A. neapolitanum.*

Allium neapolitanum.

DAFFODIL GARLIC

This spring-blooming white-flowered allium possesses a light, sweet fragrance. The ¾-inch star-shaped flowers have rosy stamens and are borne in loose 2- to 3-inch-wide domed heads. Daffodil garlic makes an excellent cut flower and container plant.

Size: 8 inches to 1 foot tall.

Light: Full sun.

Soil and Moisture: Heavy to average or sandy, moderately fertile soil; provide abundant moisture.

Planting and Propagation: Plant bulbs in fall, 4 to 6 inches deep and 4 inches apart.

Divide when become crowded and blooming diminishes.

Special Care: Best with year-round mulch to reduce soil temperature fluctuations. Spreads aggressively where adapted and may be invasive; deadhead to prevent seeding.

Pests and Diseases: Rodents may eat bulbs.

Climate: Zones 6–8; mulch heavily in winter in Zone 6. Where not hardy, grow in containers and overwinter inside.

Similar Species: 'Grandiflorum,' 3-inch flower heads. *A. tuberosum* (garlic chive): fragrant white flowers midsummer to late summer, semi-evergreen, flat grassy leaves used in cooking, Zones 5–8.

Garden Use: Charming in borders, rock garden, cutting beds, and containers.

Allium schoenoprasum

CHIVE

The common chive used in cooking looks beautiful in a flower border when decorated by its numerous 1-inch spheres of small,

Allium moly

Allium tuberosum

Allium schoenoprasum

tightly packed lavender flowers. The leaves are bright green, upright, narrow, and tubular, forming dense clumps beneath the slightly taller flower heads. If you don't use any pest control treatments forbidden on vegetables in your flower bed, you can eat both leaves and blossoms.

Size: To 1 foot tall.

Light: Full sun.

Soil and Moisture: Sandy, well-drained, moderately fertile soil; abundant moisture.

Planting and Propagation: Plant seed or transplants in spring; plant in fall where winters are mild. Divide when crowded and blooming diminishes.

Special Care: Avoid harvesting leaves during and just after blooming. To avoid a sheared look, harvest leaves by cutting only some of them 1 inch from ground. Use flowers pulled apart into individual blossoms in salads.

Pests and Diseases: Usually pest free, but aphids sometimes attack.

Climate: Zones 4–8.

Similar Species: Also eaten as chives: *A. tuberosum* (garlic chive); see *A. neapolitanum.*

Garden Use: Use as specimens in borders and herb gardens, or as edging.

Allium senescens glaucum
FALL LILY LEEK

A. senescens is a variable species native across Europe and Asia. The *"glaucum"*, which comes from the Asian end of its range, is the preferred garden choice because its low, twisted leaves are an attractive gray-green. The small flower clusters are made up of lilac-pink flowers with bright yellow anthers. Unlike most alliums, the foliage of this valuable late-summer and fall bloomer looks attractive all summer.

Size: 1 to 1⅓ feet tall.

Light: Full sun to part shade.

Soil and Moisture: Sandy, moderately fertile soil; abundant moisture during growth.

Planting and Propagation: Plant bulbs in fall, 5 inches deep and 8 to 10 inches apart. Divide when crowded and blooming diminishes.

Special Care: May be weedy if allowed to set seed; deadhead to avoid self-sowing.

Pests and Diseases: Rodents may eat bulbs.

Climate: Zones 3–7.

Similar Species: Other summer and fall bloomers include: *A. cernuum*, 12 to 14 inches tall, deep pink, pendulous blossoms; 'Early Dwarf,' 6 to 8 inches tall; *A. minor alba*, 1¼ feet tall, white flowers; *A. thunbergii*, 2 feet tall, 1-inch heads of pinkish purple blossoms with long, orange anthers; 'Ozawa,' shorter than species, larger flower heads; 'Alba,' white with yellow anthers, green centers. Both 'Ozawa' and 'Alba' are hardy to Zone 4 and have seed heads that remain attractive through winter.

Garden Use: Plant in groups in rock gardens and informal plantings; especially handsome with gray stone or gravel.

Allium sphaerocephalum
DRUMSTICK ALLIUM,
DRUMSTICK CHIVE

This ornamental onion produces eye-catching, egg-shaped, 2-inch-wide reddish purple flower heads on slender stalks in early summer to midsummer. The green flower buds give the heads a bicolored appearance, and long stamens add an airy feel. The blossoms dry in place to produce a long-lasting effect. Leaves, which are semicylindrical and hollow, are much shorter than the flower stalks.

Size: Flower stalks to 3 feet tall.

Light: Full sun to light shade.

Soil and Moisture: Sandy, moderately fertile soil; abundant moisture during growth.

Planting and Propagation: Plant bulbs in fall, 6 inches deep and 6 inches apart. Divide when crowded and blooming diminishes.

Special Care: Divide every five years.

Pests and Diseases: Rodents may eat bulbs.

Climate: Zones 3–9.

Allium senescens glaucum

Allium sphaerocephalum

Cultivars: Only species is sold.

Garden Use: Midground of borders, meadow gardens, and cutting beds. Plant in groups for best effect. Fine for cut or dried flowers.

Amaryllis belladona
(Brunsvigia rosea)
BELLADONA LILY, NAKED LADY

The startling sight of bare flower stems rising directly from the ground without any leaves in sight accounts for this plant's risque common name: naked lady. The 1½- to 2-foot-long leaves are green from fall to early spring but wither away before the rosy pink or white lilylike flowers bloom in late summer or fall. Four to 12 sweetly fragrant, trumpet-shaped, 3- to 6-inch-long blossoms form a cluster atop each stem

Size: 2 to 3 feet tall.

Light: Full sun.

Soil and Moisture: Fertile, deep, well-drained soil; moderate moisture best. Drought tolerant.

Planting and Propagation: In Zones 9–11, plant bulbs in fall with tops 1 to 2 inches below soil surface; in Zones 5–8, plant 6 to 9 inches deep. Divide just after blooming if crowded.

Special Care: Leave undisturbed as many years as possible.

Pests and Diseases: Usually pest free.

Climate: Cold hardy in Zones 6–11; may survive in Zone 5 in protected location and if deeply planted and mulched.

Similar Species: Hybrids with *Crinum* (x *Amarcrinum* or *Crinodonna*) have evergreen foliage in mild climates, if watered, and 3- to 4-foot stems of fragrant pink blossoms. Hardy to Zone 7, or to Zone 6 with mulch. Good in containers, as crowded roots foster bloom.

Garden Use: Plant in groups in mid-border, where other plants mask their bare bases in summer, but allow sun to strike and warm soil where they grow. Attractive combined with ornamental grasses in meadows or New American-style landscapes.

Amaryllis belladona

Anemone blanda
GRECIAN WINDFLOWER

A common wildflower of lands bordering the Mediterranean Sea, the wild *Anemone blanda* has sky-blue flowers. Garden varieties bloom in sky blue and dark blue, white, pink, or red for a month beginning in early spring. The wheel-shaped 2-inch-wide flowers have numerous narrow silky petals surrounding clusters of yellow stamens. Each plant bears one or two low, finely divided leaves that last through spring. Spreads readily.

Size: 6 inches to 1 foot tall.

Light: Full sun to light shade from deciduous trees in spring; avoid exposure to midday sun in hot climates.

Soil and Moisture: Fertile, well-drained soil; abundant moisture during growth, with drier conditions during summer dormancy.

Planting and Propagation: In fall, soak tubers overnight in warm water, then plant 2 to 3 inches deep and 4 to 6 inches apart. In Zone 5 or colder, plant in spring.

Special Care: In very wet summer climates, dig when dormant and store until fall.

Pests and Diseases: Tubers decay if soil is too moist after bloom.

Climate: Zones 4–8. Apply heavy mulch in Zones 4–5; spreads best in Zones 4–7.

Cultivars and Similar Species: Popular large-flowered cultivars include 'Blue Star,' dark blue; 'Blue Shades,' mixed blues; 'Pink Star,' light pink; 'White Splendor,' bright white. *A. coronaria* (poppy anemone): 6 inches to 1½ feet tall, 2- to 5-inch red, pink, blue, or white flowers, dark-centered, sometimes double blossoms, Zones 6–9; 'De Caen Hybrids,' singles in mix or separate colors.

Garden Use: Plant in groups of two dozen or more under trees and shrubs or along walks. Allow to naturalize in woodland and rock gardens.

Anemone blanda

Arisaema triphyllum
JACK-IN-THE-PULPIT

The charming spring flowers of this woodland wildflower line a tall stalk (spadix) that rests inside a hooded cup (spathe), creating the so-called Jack-in-the-pulpit. Green with faint white or purple stripes, the hooded cup is surrounded by several three-part leaves that rise directly from the ground. The leaves usually remain all summer, and the stalks ripen into a showy wand of bright red berries in fall.

Size: 1 to 3 feet tall; 1½ feet wide.
Light: Light shade.
Soil and Moisture: Moist to wet, fertile, humus-rich, slightly acid soil.
Planting and Propagation: Plant container-grown plants in spring, or plant corms 6 inches deep in fall. Do not dig from the wild.
Special Care: Easy in proper location.
Pests and Diseases: Usually pest free.
Climate: Zones 4–9.

Arisaema triphyllum

Similar Species: *A. sikokianum* (Japanese Jack-in-the-pulpit), very showy with silver-green leaves, dark purple hood, and white-tipped spadix.
Garden Use: Use in wildflower, bog, or shade garden, where it will naturalize.

Begonia x *tuberhybrida*
TUBEROUS BEGONIA

Offering spectacular summer and fall blossoms in shady gardens, tuberous begonias thrive in areas with warm, humid days and cool nights. The flowers are as much as 6 inches wide and are white, yellow, red, and shades of peach and pink. They may be bicolored or picoteed. Blossoms come in single or several distinctive double forms, including rose, camellia, carnation, and ruffled. The glossy, succulent leaves point in the direction that blossoms will face.

Size: 1 to 1½ feet tall; often trailing.
Light: Light to medium shade.

Begonia x *tuberhybrida*

Soil and Moisture: Humus-rich, fertile, moist soil. Provide extra fertilizer and abundant moisture during bloom; gradually withhold both for a few weeks as plants go dormant in late fall.
Planting and Propagation: Plant tuberous roots at soil level, indented side up, indoors in early spring. Move outdoors after nights are above 50°F. Or plant in place, barely covered, 1 to 1¼ feet apart, when nights are warm.
Special Care: Remove spent flowers to neaten and prevent disease. Where tender, dig tubers after they die back and store in dry peat over winter, at 40° to 50°F.
Pests and Diseases: Whiteflies, mealybugs, powdery mildew, and gray mold troublesome.
Climate: Cold hardy in Zones 10–11; grow as tender bulb in other zones.
Similar Species: Numerous cultivars. 'Non-Stop' series: easy to grow, large rose-form double flowers in various colors.
Garden Use: Very showy in hanging baskets and containers and massed in shady borders.

Brodiaea coronaria
TRIPLET LILY

West Coast wildflowers include many species of Brodiaea: small, charming plants with grassy leaves and loose heads of small trumpet-shaped flowers. *B. coronaria* is the most common, with 1½-inch-long, dark blue flowers in late spring or summer. Best adapted to areas with mild, wet winters and dry summers, triplet lilies need special care where winters are very cold or summers are very wet.

Size: 1 to 1½ feet tall.
Light: Full sun.
Soil and Moisture: Best in sandy or gritty soil with abundant moisture until after blooming ceases.
Planting and Propagation: Plant bulbs in fall or early spring, 4 to 6 inches deep and 3 to 5 inches apart. Divide in fall, if crowded.

Brodiaea coronaria

Special Care: Where summers are very wet, dig and store in peat after blooming and foliage dies back. Where not hardy, overwinter in pots; plant outdoors in early spring.
Pests and Diseases: Mice may eat corms, or corms may decay if drainage is poor.
Climate: Zones 8–11; to Zone 6 with winter protection.
Similar Species: *Triteleia laxa* (*Brodiaea laxa*), deep blue-purple flowers; 'Queen Fabiola,' deep violet.
Garden Use: Mass in informal gardens, meadow gardens, and rock gardens.

Bulbocodium vernum
SPRING MEADOW SAFFRON

Native to the Alps and southern European mountains, this hardy plant asks little for its contribution to the garden. Crocuslike lavender-pink, chalice-shaped blossoms with a satiny sheen emerge in late winter and earliest spring, followed by strap-shaped leaves. The plants are dormant in summer.
Size: Flowers to 4 inches tall; leaves reach 5 to 6 inches high.
Light: Full sun or light shade.
Soil and Moisture: Sandy, well-drained soil; keep moist until leaves die down.

Planting and Propagation: Plant corms in early fall, 4 inches deep and 3 to 4 inches apart.
Special Care: Divide every three or four years.
Pests and Diseases: Usually pest free.
Climate: Zones 3–11.
Similar Species: Usually only species is sold. Similar to, but distinct from, *Crocus* and *Colchicum*.
Garden Use: Plant in groups under shrubs, in rock garden, along path, or in flower border where noticeable from indoors.

Caladium x *hortulanum*
FANCY-LEAVED CALADIUM

Grown for its wildly patterned tropical-looking foliage, fancy leaved caladium lives up to its name. Its 6-inch- to 2-foot-long arrowhead-shaped leaves often show little or no green, being various combinations of pink, rose, red, or white with green edges or centers. The pink flowers are insignificant and rarely noticed.
Size: 1 to 3 feet tall.
Light: Light to deep shade.
Soil and Moisture: Humus-rich, well-drained, moist, acid to neutral soil; plentiful moisture.
Planting and Propagation: Plant tubers in garden, 2 inches deep, knobby side up, 1 to 1½ feet apart, when nights are above 60°F, or begin indoors six to eight weeks earlier.
Special Care: Store dormant tubers at 40°F in dry peat; overwinter containerized plants indoors as houseplants, or allow to go dormant in their pots.
Pests and Diseases: Snails and slugs often troublesome.
Climate: Zones 10–11; tender elsewhere.
Cultivars: Available as color mixtures or in dozens of named cultivars with predictable leaf colors and patterns. 'Postman Joyner,' green-edged red; 'Little Miss Muffet,' red-speckled white, dwarf; 'Candidum,' green-veined white; 'Rose Bud,' bright pink and

Bulbocodium vernum

green edged with white; 'White Queen,' white with pink central veins and green outer veins.
Garden Use: Plant in single-type drifts in shade gardens, or use in containers indoors or out.

Caladium x *hortulanum*

Camassia leichtlinii
CAMAS

Producing tall spikes of 20 to 40 blue or creamy white 1- to 1½-inch-wide spidery flowers in late spring and early summer, camas adds meadowy charm to a garden. The grasslike leaves, which are much shorter than the spikes, die back soon after flowers fade, so locate where foliage of other plants covers plant bases.

Size: 2 to 4 feet tall.

Light: Full sun to light shade.

Soil and Moisture: Fertile to heavy, moisture-holding soil; abundant moisture.

Planting and Propagation: Plant bulbs in fall, 4 inches deep and 6 inches apart. Needs no division for years.

Special Care: Plant where slowly spreading bulb clumps can be undisturbed for years.

Pests and Diseases: Usually pest free.

Climate: Hardy in Zones 3–11.

Cultivar and Similar Species: 'Blue Danube,' blue; 'Alba,' creamy white. Similar: *C. quamash* (*C. esculenta*), 20 to 40 blue or

Camassia leichtlinii

white flowers, 2 to 3 feet tall; *C. cusickii*, 30 to 100 pale blue blossoms, 2 to 3 feet tall.

Garden Use: Plant in groups in midground of borders or in naturalistic meadow, woodland, and streamside gardens. Combine with daylilies or hostas to hide bare spot.

Canna x *generalis*
CANNA LILY

Boldly dramatic in both flower and foliage, canna lily brings a lush tropical appearance to a garden. Big, broadly lance-shaped leaves vary from deep green to bronzy red or purple, or may be variegated green-and-yellow. Clusters of 4- to 5-inch-wide orchidlike or gladioluslike blossoms appear atop the tall plants from midsummer to frost and may be white, cream, yellow, peach, pink, orange, red, or bicolored. The flowers fade too quickly for cutting, but the leaves are useful in arrangements.

Size: 1½ to 6 feet tall.

Light: Full sun.

Soil and Moisture: Adaptable, but humus-rich, well-drained, moist soil best. Water well in dry weather, but avoid overwatering.

Planting and Propagation: In Zones 7–11, plant rhizomes in garden in spring, 2 to 4 inches deep and 1 to 2 feet apart; divide every three or four years. Elsewhere, start indoors in peat pots a month before nights stay above 50°F, then plant outdoors.

Special Care: In Zones 8–10, leave in ground over winter; elsewhere, dig and store over winter above 40°F in dry peat.

Pests and Diseases: Snails, slugs, leaf-feeding insects, leaf-rolling caterpillars, and bacterial bud rot troublesome.

Climate: Zones 9–11; to Zone 7 with winter mulch. Thrives in heat and humidity.

Cultivars: Pfitzer's Dwarfs, 2½ feet tall, green leaves; 'Chinese Coral,' coral-pink; 'Primrose Yellow,' soft yellow; 'Salmon-Pink,' bright salmon-pink; 'Scarlet Beauty,' early blooming scarlet. 'Seven Dwarfs,' mixed colors, 1½ feet tall. 'Red King Humbert': purple-red foliage,

Canna x *generalis*

scarlet blossoms, 7 feet tall. 'Wyoming': light orange flowers, bronze-red foliage, 5 to 6 feet tall. 'Striatus': yellow-streaked leaves, orange flowers.

Garden Use: Best used in groups of single color to give bushy, tropical effect in borders or as accent plantings near pools and in large containers.

Chionodoxa luciliae
GLORY-OF-THE-SNOW

First discovered blooming at the snow's edge in the mountains of Asia Minor, glory-of-the-snow is among the earliest flowers to bloom in the garden, opening soon after the snow crocus. Each plant has two or three ribbon-like dark green leaves and several arching stems of as many as 10 star-shaped flowers arranged in a loose spike. The blossoms are usually bright blue to lavender-blue with white centers, but they may be pink or white.

Size: 3 to 6 inches tall.

Light: Full sun; light shade in hot-summer areas.

Soil and Moisture: Humus-rich, fertile, well-drained soil. Abundant moisture while growing; less when dormant.

Planting and Propagation: Plant bulbs in fall, 2 to 3 inches deep and 1 to 3 inches apart. Divide, during dormancy, only when crowded.

Chionodoxa luciliae

Clivia minata

Special Care: If conditions are favorable, plants self-sow vigorously. Do not mow foliage for six weeks after blooming.

Pests and Diseases: Nematodes may destroy bulbs; chipmunks and mice may eat bulbs.

Climate: Hardy in Zones 4–9; best in cooler climates.

Cultivars: 'Alba,' white; 'Rosea,' pink; 'Gigantea,' larger leaved, violet-blue; 'Pink Giant,' larger leaved, pink.

Garden Use: Plant in groups of 50 or more in rock gardens or under shrubs. Allow to naturalize in lawn or meadow.

Clivia minata

CLIVIA, KAFFIR LILY

Clivia adds flashes of brilliant color to shady garden sites in warm climates. Rounded clusters of 12 to 20 two-inch-long rich orange, red, yellow, or white funnel-shaped flowers form on stems held above dense clumps of arching, straplike, dark green, evergreen leaves. Flowers bloom in late winter and spring, followed by showy red berries. Because clivia blooms best when roots are crowded, it is often grown as a container plant and wintered indoors or, where hardy, left outside all year long.

Size: 2 feet tall.

Light: Part to full, but not deep, shade.

Soil and Moisture: Average, well-drained soil. Abundant moisture while blooming; less when not in bloom.

Planting and Propagation: Transplant from containers anytime; plant tuberous roots immediately after bloom period, setting just below soil surface, 1 to 1½ feet apart.

Special Care: Leave undisturbed for years.

Pests and Diseases: Snails and slugs may be troublesome.

Climate: Zones 9–11. Often grown as container plants in colder zones.

Cultivars: The most common strain is orange with yellow centers. Search to locate other colors.

Garden Use: Mass in midground of shady borders and under trees; use in containers.

Colchicum autumnale

AUTUMN CROCUS, MEADOW SAFFRON

Resembling a long-stalked crocus without leaves (*Crocus* has three stamens; *Colchicum* has six), this spectacular fall bloomer produces its 4-inch-long, chalice-shaped, pink, pale lavender, or white flowers in early to mid-fall. The blooming plant has no leaves; flowers arise in clusters directly from the ground. Leaves are coarse-looking with prominent veins, making unsightly clusters in spring when most bulbs are blooming. Corms may bloom without being planted and sometimes are used as decorations.

Size: 6 to 8 inches tall.

Light: Full sun to light shade.

Soil and Moisture: Average, very well-drained soil; abundant moisture when actively growing.

Planting and Propagation: Plant corms before they bloom in midsummer to late summer, 3 to 4 inches deep, 4 to 6 inches apart. To increase, divide after three or four years, when dormant; otherwise leave undisturbed. Plants may self-sow.

Special Care: All plant parts poisonous. Corms allowed to bloom unplanted survive if planted but may be weakened temporarily.

Pests and Diseases: Usually pest free.

Climate: Zones 5–9.

Cultivar and Similar Species: 'Waterlily,' 6 inches tall, lavender-pink, waterlilylike double. *C. a. album:* white, 3 inches tall. *C. a. plenum:* lilac, double peony form. *C. byzantium:* very large rosy lilac flowers, leaves emerge after flowers fade and overwinter. *C. speciosum:* raspberry-lilac, fragrant, later blooming, Zones 3–9. *C. cilicicum:* star-shaped, fragrant, deep rosy lilac, later blooming, leaves grow in autumn.

Garden Use: Plant where unattractive leaves are unnoticed and won't mask spring bloomers. Excellent massed in low ground cover; use in rock garden or under shrubbery in mixed borders.

Colchicum autumnale

Convallaria majalis

Convallaria majalis
LILY-OF-THE-VALLEY

Valued for its delicious fragrance and dainty form, lily-of-the-valley is popular in bridal bouquets and as a charming, low-maintenance ground cover. The broad green leaves resemble tulip leaves but remain attractive until late summer. Slender stems emerge in mid-spring to bear 12 to 20 tiny, waxy-white, bell-shaped flowers.

Size: 6 to 10 inches tall; wide spreading.
Light: Light shade; sun in cool-summer areas.
Soil and Moisture: Humus-rich, acid to neutral, moist soil. Apply manure or compost in late fall.
Planting and Propagation: Plant rhizomes in fall or early spring 1 to 2 inches deep, 4 to 6 inches apart. Divide when leaves yellow in fall or late summer when stands become crowded.
Special Care: Creeping rootstocks spread to form thick stands and may be invasive. Foliage yellows early if soil dries.
Pests and Diseases: Stem rot and leaf spots sometimes troublesome.

Climate: Best in Zones 3–7; performs poorly in milder climates.
Cultivars: 'Rosea,' light pink; 'Plena,' double-flowered white.
Garden Use: Best used as ground cover in naturalistic garden, under shrubs, or in woodland or shade garden. Excellent cut flower.

Crocosmia x crocosmiiflora (Tritonia x crocosmiiflora)
MONTBRETIA

A valuable plant for its brilliant late-summer and early fall blossoms, montbretia is an old garden favorite from South Africa. Its sword-shaped gladioluslike leaves measure up to 3 feet long and form upright to slightly arching clumps. Leafless branched flower stems carry curving spikes of numerous lilylike orange, red, gold, yellow, and sometimes bicolored 1½- to 3-inch-wide flowers. The spikes make attractive long-lasting cut flowers.

Size: 1½ to 3 feet tall.
Light: Full sun or light shade.
Soil and Moisture: Average to humus-rich, well-drained soil; drought tolerant, but best with moderate moisture.

Crocosmia x crocosmiiflora 'Lucifer'

Planting and Propagation: Plant corms in spring, 2 inches deep and 3 inches apart. Where hardy, divide corms every third spring.
Special Care: Where not hardy, cut frosted tops, dig with soil attached, dry in shade, and store at 55° to 65°F in dry peat.
Pests and Diseases: Usually pest free.
Climate: Zones 6–10.
Cultivars: 'Emily McKenzie,' orange with deep red central stars; 'Jenny Bloom,' deep yellow; 'Lucifer,' scarlet, hardy to Zone 5 with winter mulch.
Garden Use: Use as accent in midground of hot color border, or mass in meadow gardens and with ornamental grasses.

Crocus chrysanthus
SNOW CROCUS

Snow crocuses are smaller than Dutch hybrid crocuses, but bloom earlier and produce more flowers per corm. The species has bright orange flowers and bronze markings on the petal exteriors; hybrids may be white, cream, yellow, blue, and purple, and are often bicolored. The fragrant, long-lasting blossoms appear in late winter, at the same

Crocus chrysanthus 'Princess Beatrix'

time as the narrow, upright, spiky leaves, which elongate after blooming then die down. Corms increase rapidly.

Size: Flowers 3 to 4 inches tall; leaves to 10 inches high.

Light: Full sun to light shade from deciduous trees.

Soil and Moisture: Sandy to average, well-drained, acid to neutral soil. Requires moisture during growth; tolerates it when dormant but best in summer-dry site.

Planting and Propagation: Plant corms in fall, 2 to 5 inches deep and 2 to 3 inches apart. Divide only when crowded and during dormancy.

Special Care: For earliest bloom, plant where sun warms soil in late winter. Where naturalized in lawn, do not mow leaves until at least six weeks after blooming.

Pests and Diseases: Rodents may eat corms.

Climate: Hardy in Zones 3–11; best performance in Zone 7 or colder.

Cultivar and Similar Species: 'Prinz Claus,' white inside, purple blotched outside; 'Lady Killer,' white inside, deep purple edged white outside; 'Blue Ribbon,' light blue; 'Purity,' white; 'Advance,' yellow inside, lavender outside; 'E. A. Bowles,' lemon yellow with bronze veins; 'Princess Beatrix,' pale blue with yellow bases. *C. tomasinianus:* lilac-mauve; 'Barr's Purple,' large lavender-blue.

Garden Use: Plant in groups of 50 or more for best effect in fronts of borders and rock gardens; naturalize in lawn or meadow.

Crocus sativus
SAFFRON CROCUS

The large forked scarlet stigmas of this showy flower are the source of saffron, the world's most expensive spice. It takes at least six flowers to season one recipe. The 4-inch-long, fragrant, lilac-purple blossoms appear in autumn, along with short, spiky leaves, which elongate after blooming and last through winter. Corms are often available from sources that sell herbs.

Light: Full sun to light shade.

Soil and Moisture: Fertile, well-drained soil; moderate moisture when growing.

Planting and Propagation: Plant corms in summer, 4 to 6 inches deep and 4 to 6 inches apart. Divide every one to three years when leaves die in spring, and replant in improved soil.

Special Care: To harvest saffron, pick stigmas, which protrude from top of flower, when flowers open; let dry, and store in plastic or glass vial.

Pests and Diseases: Usually not bothered by rodents.

Climate: Zones 6–8; Zone 5 with protection. Best with long, hot summer.

Similar Species: *C. s.* var. *cartwrightianus albus,* white, rare. *C. medius,* similar.

Garden Use: Plant in groups in rock gardens, along walks, and in foreground of borders and beds where will be appreciated.

Crocus speciosus
FALL CROCUS

Pretty and easy to grow, fall crocus is less commonly sold than some autumn-blooming crocuses, but well worth seeking out. The long-stalked, 5- to 6-inch-long blossoms are lavender-blue with showy scarlet stigmas; cultivars come in blue, lavender, white, and bicolors. Blossoms appear in succession from late summer through early autumn; the 1-foot-long, 4-inch-wide leaves appear in spring and die back by summer.

Size: Flowers to 6 inches tall.

Light: Sun or light shade.

Soil and Moisture: Average, well-drained soil; abundant moisture when growing.

Planting and Propagation: Plant in midsummer, 4 to 6 inches deep and 3 inches apart. Divide only when crowded.

Special Care: Plants multiply quickly by seed and offsets. Corms and seeds are poisonous. Flops if planted too shallowly.

Pests and Diseases: Not bothered by rodents.

Crocus sativus

Crocus speciosus

Climate: Zones 4–8.

Cultivar and Similar Species: Cultivars may be difficult to locate. *C. goulimyi:* pale lavender with white throat, mid- to late fall. *C. kotschyanua* (*C. zonatus*): pale lilac with dark veins, yellow throat.

Garden Use: Plant in groups in meadow, rock, or woodland gardens; interplant in low ground covers in mixed borders.

Crocus x *vernus*

Crocus x *vernus*
DUTCH CROCUS

Dutch crocus hybrids are the most common and largest crocuses. These early spring bloomers come in white, yellow, and various shades of lavender and violet, often streaked or veined in a contrasting color. Flowers have satiny petals and bright orange stamens and measure up to 4 inches tall and 3 inches wide when open. The leaves, which appear before or along with the flowers, are 2 to 8 inches long, upright, narrow, and dark green with central white stripes.

Size: Flowers 3 to 4 inches tall; leaves 8 inches long.

Light: Full sun to light shade.

Soil and Moisture: Average to very well-drained soil. Moderate moisture while growing; drier during dormancy.

Planting and Propagation: Plant corms in fall, 5 inches deep and 2 to 3 inches apart. Divide during dormancy only when crowded and blooming diminishes.

Special Care: Mulch in coldest winters.

Pests and Diseases: Rodents may eat corms; birds may damage flowers.

Climate: Zones 3–8; best with cold winters.

Cultivars: 'Peter Pan,' white; 'Pickwick,' silvery white with violet stripes; 'Yellow Mammoth,' golden yellow; 'Purpurea,' purple; 'Queen of the Blues,' blue; 'Remembrance,'

344

silvery purple; 'Jean d'Arc,' pure white.

Garden Use: Naturalize in lawns or under trees and shrubs, or plant in groups of 25 or more in borders and rock gardens.

Cyclamen coum
WINTER CYCLAMEN

Winter cyclamen is dormant in summer, produces overwintering leaves in fall, and blooms for several weeks beginning anywhere from December to April, depending on the climate. The rounded leaves are solid green or spotted silver with red-purple undersides. The dainty ¾-inch flowers have swept-back petals and resemble butterflies hovering over the foliage on leafless stalks. Blossoms may be purplish magenta, crimson, or white, with a purple blotch.

Size: 3 to 6 inches tall.

Light: Light shade.

Soil and Moisture: Humus-rich, well-drained soil; plentiful moisture during growth.

Planting and Propagation: Plant container-grown plants in spring or fall; plant tubers during dormancy, smooth side up, 1 inch deep and 6 to 8 inches apart.

Special Care: Best if undisturbed for years and allowed to self-sow. After bloom ends, top-dress with 1 inch of compost or leaf mold. Do not divide; reproduces by seed. Endangered in the wild; purchase only nursery-propagated plants.

Pests and Diseases: Cyclamen mites serious; leaf spot less so. Gray mold troublesome in humid weather.

Climate: Zones 7–9; possibly to Zone 5 with mulch or snow cover. Best where summers are dry and nights are cool.

Cultivars: Various selections with silver-marbled leaves. 'Album': white flowers.

Garden Use: Locate where small plants and winter foliage can be appreciated in rock garden, under shrubs, or along path; naturalize under high-branched trees in woodland or shade gardens for winter ground cover.

Cyclamen coum

Cyclamen hederifolium (*C. neapolitanum*)
HARDY CYCLAMEN

This late-summer- to fall-blooming hardy cyclamen may not bloom much its first year or two, but mature tubers can produce up to 50 flowers at a time. Located where they are undisturbed for a long time, corms produce a bounty of 1-inch, dark-eyed pink or white flowers with swept-back petals. Leaves are heart-shaped but more pointed than winter cyclamen, measure up to 5½ inches across, and are silver-marbled. They begin to appear with or soon after the flowers, lasting all winter and spring.

Size: 3 to 6 inches tall.

Cyclamen hederifolium

Light: Light shade.

Soil and Moisture: Humus-rich, well-drained soil; plentiful moisture during growth.

Planting and Propagation: Plant container-grown plants in spring or fall; or plant tubers during dormancy, smooth side down with tops at soil surface, 6 inches to 1 foot apart.

Special Care: Best if undisturbed for many years and allowed to self-sow. After bloom ends, top-dress with 1 inch of compost or leaf mold. Do not divide corms; plant reproduces by seed.

Pests and Diseases: Cyclamen mites serious; leaf spot less so. Gray mold troublesome during humid weather.

Climate: Zones 7–9; possibly to Zone 5 with winter mulch or snow cover. Best where summers are relatively dry and nights are cool.

Similar Species: *C. purpurescens*, shade-loving, fragrant, ¾-inch pink to magenta flowers from midsummer to late summer.

Garden Use: Locate where can be seen along paths or in rock gardens, or naturalize in woodland or shade gardens.

Dahlia x *pinnata*
DAHLIA

One of the garden's most luxuriant flowers, dahlia offers late-summer to early fall blossoms in every color but blue. Breeding transformed the original Mexican daisy-form flower into a variety of double forms, including ball-shaped pompons to spiky-petaled cactus-flower types. Flowers are borne at the tops of branched stems and vary from several inches across to dinner-plate size. The dark green compound leaves make bushy plants.

Size: 1 to 7 feet tall.

Light: Full sun; midday shade in hot summer areas.

Soil and Moisture: Fertile, humus-rich, well-drained soil; abundant moisture.

Planting and Propagation: Plant tuberous roots horizontally in 6-inch-deep holes, under 3 to 4 inches of soil, in spring after soil has warmed. Divide stored roots two to four weeks before planting, and set in moist sand. As shoots grow, gradually add 3 inches more soil. Space small types 1 to 2 feet apart; larger ones 3 to 4 feet apart. Usually grown from tuberous roots, but seeds started indoors in early spring bloom in one season and can be propagated from roots in subsequent years.

Special Care: Stake tall types at planting with 5-foot stout stakes placed 2 inches from growth eye end of tubers. Tie loosely when 2 feet tall. For cut flowers, strip leaves from lower stems; dip ends in boiling water for one second before arranging.

Pests and Diseases: Potato leafhopper, mites, European corn borer, beetles, aphids, slugs, snails, virus diseases, and powdery mildew may be troublesome.

Climate: In Zones 8–11, if soil is well-drained and unfrozen, plant may be left in ground over winter, or dug. In colder zones, dig after dieback or first frost and store, undivided, where cool in dry sand or peat.

Cultivars: Hundreds of named cultivars. Specialty nurseries offer many, and local dahlia societies often sell tubers.

Garden Use: Depending on size, locate in groups in front to back of formal borders. Excellent in cutting garden.

Eranthis hyemalis
WINTER ACONITE

Often blooming on the edge of the melting snow, winter aconite's satiny 1- to 2-inch yellow flowers announce winter's end. Each plant bears a single stem with a ruff of lobed leaves ringing a single 1-inch-wide buttercup-like flower. Ground-hugging lobed basal leaves develop right after the blossoms, going dormant by summer.

Size: 2 to 8 inches tall.

Light: Full sun to part shade.

Soil and Moisture: Average to humus-rich, well-drained, moist soil; plentiful moisture even during summer dormancy.

Dahlia x *pinnata*

Planting and Propagation: Plant tubers 3 inches deep and 3 inches apart in late summer or early fall after soaking overnight in warm water. Divide after three or more years by breaking tubers into pieces.

Special Care: Plant tubers where they will not be disturbed for a long time. Plants self-sow freely and may invade lawns.

Pests and Diseases: Usually pest free.

Climate: Zones 3–7; best where cold.

Similar Species: *E. cilicia*, 2½ inches tall, bronzy leaves, blooms a bit earlier.

Garden Use: Plants work best in large groups and when allowed to naturalize in naturalistic setting.

Eranthis hyemalis

Erythronium americanum
DOG-TOOTH VIOLET, FAWN LILY, ADDER'S-TONGUE, TROUT LILY

In mid-spring, this native woodland wild-flower produces solitary, 2-inch-long, yellow, lilylike flowers with swept-back petals. These nod on leafless stems above ground-hugging leaves, which are mottled with pale green, darker green, and purplish brown. The tubers form stolons that enlarge the planting year after year.

Size: 6 inches to 1 foot tall.

Light: Light to medium shade from deciduous trees.

Soil and Moisture: Humus-rich soil kept moist during growing season; drier in late summer and fall.

Planting and Propagation: Plant corms in early fall, 6 inches deep and 4 to 6 inches apart. Rarely needs division.

Special Care: Plant where it will be undisturbed for a long time.

Pests and Diseases: Usually pest free.

Erythronium denscanis

Climate: Zones 3–8; performs poorly in hot, dry summers.

Similar Species: *E. californicum*, cream to white flowers, banded inside with yellow or orange. *E. denscanis*, white, pink, or purple flowers, mottled leaves, needs more sun; 'Lilac Wonder,' large lilac. *E. tuolumense* 'Pagoda': vigorous hybrid with one to four sulfur-yellow flowers per stem, Zones 5–8.

Garden Use: Naturalize in woodland or shade gardens; use as specimen in shaded rock gardens.

Freesia hybrids
FREESIA

Freesia's sweet, light fragrance is one of the most powerful of floral scents, although not every modern hybrid is fragrant. Each leafless flower stem is sharply angled below the one-sided row of up to eight trumpet-shaped flowers, causing blossoms to point upward. Flowers may be white, yellow, orange, pink, lavender, red, purple, or bicolored. The two-ranked, sword-shaped leaves precede the flowers and die back after blooming.

Size: 1 to 1½ feet tall.

Light: Sun or part shade.

Soil and Moisture: Average, well-drained soil. Abundant moisture during growth; drier during summer dormancy.

Planting and Propagation: In Zones 9–11, plant corms in fall, 2 inches deep and 2 to 4 inches apart. Elsewhere, purchase corms specially treated to bloom in midsummer and plant in spring.

Special Care: When grown indoors, freesias do best at 68° to 72°F during the day and 55° to 60°F at night.

Pests and Diseases: Mosaic virus can be serious; remove infected plants.

Climate: Zones 9–11; in colder zones lift corms and overwinter in cool, dark place.

Similar Species: Telecote hybrids, large flowers, very fragrant, in 'Multi-Rainbow Mix.' Single colors: 'Matterhorn,' white; 'Golden Melody,' rich yellow; 'Oberon,' strawberry-

Freesia hybrids

red with yellow throat; 'Talisman,' soft orange and pink; 'Adonis,' double-flowered, rose-pink, cream throat; 'Silvia,' rich blue-violet, semidouble. *F. alba* (*F. refracta alba*): white-flowered, strongly scented parent of modern hybrids, naturalizes well in suitable climates.

Garden Use: Arrange in single-color groups in front or midground of borders. Force as indoor plant. Excellent cut flower.

Fritillaria imperalis
CROWN IMPERIAL

Blooming just about daffodil time, crown imperial is an unusual-looking plant whose crownlike arrangement of flowers and foliage accounts for its common name. A tightly packed whorl of nodding 4-inch orange, red, or yellow blossoms topped by a spiky cap of green leaves forms a crownlike effect at the top of the stout stems. These are bare below the flowers, then covered to the ground with whorled, wavy-edged leaves that release a skunklike odor if crushed.

Size: 2 to 4 feet tall.

Light: Full sun to part shade.

Soil and Moisture: Humus-rich, fertile, well-drained soil. Regular moisture during growth; less while dormant.

Fritillaria imperalis

Planting and Propagation: Plant bulbs as soon as available in fall, 4 to 6 inches deep and 8 inches to 1 foot apart. Tip bulbs slightly to keep water from puddling in their tops. Divide every four to six years when dormant, if desired.

Special Care: Apply deep mulch in fall.

Pests and Diseases: Leaf spot and mosaic virus sometimes troublesome.

Climate: Zones 5–8.

Cultivars: 'Aurora,' orange-yellow; 'Lutea Maxima,' yellow; 'Rubra Maxima,' red.

Garden Use: Plant in groups of a dozen or more to grow out of lower leafy plants such as hostas or ornamental grasses to hide conspicuous dying foliage in summer.

Fritillaria meleagris
CHECKERED LILY, GUINEA-HEN TULIP

This graceful European wildflower produces its unusual 2-inch-long bell-shaped blossoms in early spring. The flowers, which dangle from wiry stems, may be white or purple with a delicate two-tone brown or wine checkered pattern. Each plant has a few 3- to 6-inch-long, blue-green grasslike basal leaves with a few smaller leaves scattered along the flowering stems.

Size: 1 to 1½ feet tall.

Fritillaria meleagris

Light: Full sun or part shade.

Soil and Moisture: Fertile, humus-rich, very well drained soil; moderate moisture.

Planting and Propagation: Plant bulbs as soon as available in fall, 3 to 4 inches deep and 3 to 4 inches apart. Tip bulbs slightly to keep water from puddling in their tops.

Special Care: Be careful not to weed out delicate foliage.

Pests and Diseases: Usually pest free.

Climate: Zones 3–8; not well-adapted to hot, dry summers or frostless winters.

Cultivars and Similar Species: 'Alba,' white. In Pacific Northwest, choose better-adapted West Coast natives: *F. lanceolata*, brownish purple, checkered greenish yellow; *F. recurva*, scarlet.

Garden Use: Plant in drifts for best visibility in rock, meadow, and woodland gardens. White flowers show up best.

Galanthus nivalis
SNOWDROP

Not even a light snowfall stops snowdrops from showing off their nodding white bells. Blooming in late winter and early spring, when little else is in flower, the ½-inch flowers appear on single slender stems above two or three short, thin, gray-green leaves.

Green marks tip the three inner petals; the longer outer ones are pure white. Bulbs spread to form dense stands of flowers and foliage, which die back in early summer.

Size: Leaves 3 to 8 inches tall; flower stems 4 to 10 inches tall.

Light: Full sun or part shade.

Soil and Moisture: Fertile, well-drained, constantly moist soil.

Planting and Propagation: Plant bulbs 4 inches deep and 2 to 3 inches apart. Move or divide as flowers are fading, not when dormant as with most bulbs.

Special Care: Do not mow foliage until at least six weeks after blooming.

Pests and Diseases: Usually pest free. May rot in winter-wet southern sites.

Climate: Zones 3–8; performs best in cold-winter climates.

Cultivar and Similar Species: 'Flore Pleno,' double. *G. elwesii* (giant snowdrop): 1½ inch earlier-blooming flowers, 1 foot stems, wider leaves, Zones 4–8; better adapted to mild-winter areas

Garden Use: Plant in groups of at least 25. Snowdrops make charming drifts in lawns and woodland gardens and share stage prettily with winter aconites.

Galanthus nivalis

Gladiolus x *hortulanus*

Gladiolus x *hortulanus*
GLADIOLUS

A popular cut flower, gladiolus offers tall, tightly packed spikes of beautiful ruffled flowers with contrasting throats. The 2½- to 6-inch-wide blossoms open in sequence from the bottom up, all facing the same way. They come in solids or bicolors in all hues but true blue. Blooming about two months after they are planted, gladiolus can be planted for blooming in late spring, summer, or fall. Each plant has one flower stem and a few sword-shaped leaves.

Size: 3 to 6 feet tall.

Light: Full sun.

Soil and Moisture: Average to humus-rich, well-drained soil. Provide plentiful moisture from shoot emergence until blooming ends, then reduce.

Planting and Propagation: Plant corms after soil warms, beginning in midwinter in mild-winter areas and early summer in the North, 4 to 6 inches deep and 4 to 6 inches apart. Stagger plantings at two-week intervals to produce flowers for cutting over a long season. Separate cormels from mother corms when digging, and replant in nursery bed to mature.

Special Care: Stake plants, or mound earth to 6 inches around stems when 1 foot tall.

348

Remove faded flower stalks immediately. Leave three or four leaves if cutting flowers to allow corms to mature for next year.

Pests and Diseases: Thrips, spider mites, aphids, bacterial scab, mosaic virus, gray mold, corm rots, rust, and corn borer can be serious. Obtain clean stock, rotate site, and clean up debris.

Climate: Zones 8–11; tender elsewhere, but best if stored over winter in all climates.

Cultivars and Similar Species: Cultivars too numerous to list. *G. nanus* (hardy gladiolus): 1½ to 2 feet tall, white, red, pink, salmon, and bicolors; Zones 5–11 (to Zone 3 with winter protection). *G. byzantinus* (byzantine gladiolus): 2 feet tall, maroon, pink, white, or two-tone pinkish purple with white strips; Zones 7–11 (often hardy to Zone 5 with winter protection).

Garden Use: Single plants or rows look stiff, but makes pleasing vertical effect if grouped in drifts among other plants.

Hyacinthoides hispanica (*Endymion hispanicus, Scilla hispanica,* and *S. campanulata*)
WOOD HYACINTH, SPANISH BLUEBELLS

Botanists have tossed this pretty shade-loving bulb from name to name. Although it is now called *Hyacinthoides hispanica,* catalogs may sell it by earlier names. The 1-inch-wide glossy green straplike leaves develop into vase-shaped clusters in early spring and are joined from late spring into early summer by sturdy spikes of 12 to 15 blue, pink, or white, ¾-inch bell-shaped flowers. Wood hyacinth increases when well situated both by self-sowing and by offsets. Plants go dormant by midsummer.

Size: 1 to 1⅔ feet tall; 1 foot wide.

Light: Half sun to light or full shade.

Soil and Moisture: Fertile, well-drained, acid to neutral soil. Plentiful moisture from fall until blossoms fade, then drier.

Planting and Propagation: Plant bulbs in fall, 3 to 6 inches deep (deeper in cold winter areas), 4 to 6 inches apart. Divide during dormancy only if crowded.

Special Care: Plant where will be undisturbed. Cut off faded flowers, and remove foliage as it becomes unsightly.

Pests and Diseases: Usually pest free.

Climate: Zones 4–8.

Cultivars and Similar Species: 'Excelsior,' deep blue; 'Blue Queen,' porcelain blue; 'Rosabelle,' pink; 'White City,' white. *H. non-scriptus/Scilla non-scriptus* (English bluebell): gracefully arching fragrant, violet-blue flowers, 8 inches to 1 foot tall, Zones 5–8. See also *Scilla siberica*.

Garden Use: Allow to naturalize in woodland or shade gardens.

Hyacinthus orientalis
DUTCH HYACINTH

Blooming in mid-spring, Dutch hyacinths are treasured for their showy flowers and their heady fragrance, which permeates the garden with one of the sweetest and strongest scents of any flower. Colors include pastel or vivid shades of yellow, pink, salmon, orange, blue,

Hyacinthoides hispanica 'Blue Queen'

violet, and white. The 1-inch-long tubular blossoms open to star-shaped faces and are tightly packed around a 6- to 10-inch stem. Leaves are ¾ inch wide and straplike, forming a stiff whorl beneath the flower stalk.

Size: Flower stems 1 to 1½ feet tall.

Light: Full sun or light shade.

Soil and Moisture: Humus-rich, well-drained, acid to neutral soil; plentiful moisture during growth and bloom.

Planting and Propagation: In Zones 3–7, plant bulbs in early fall, 4 to 6 inches deep and 6 to 9 inches apart. In Zones 8–11, refrigerate bulbs for nine weeks and plant in mid- to late fall.

Special Care: Plants persist but multiply slowly and revert to open blooming habit after first year. Replace each year or when flowers are no longer pleasing.

Pests and Diseases: Fungal and bacterial rot may be serious; do not plant in infected soil for three years. Aphids may be troublesome.

Climate: Zones 3–7; elsewhere special treatment is required. Winter-mulch in Zones 3–4. Poorly adapted where little or no freezing cold but can treat as annual.

Cultivars: 'L'Innocence,' white; 'Mont Blanc,'

Hyacinthus orientalis 'Gypsy Queen'

white; 'City of Haarlem,' yellow; 'Lemon Queen,' yellow; 'Pink Pearl,' pink; 'Anna Marie,' pink; 'Wedgewood,' light blue; 'Delft Blue,' medium blue; 'Blue Jacket,' dark purple-blue; 'Gypsy Queen,' light orange.

Garden Use: Best in informal drifts with underplanting of pansies or smaller bulbs to soften stiff appearance. Force for indoor bloom in pots or in water.

Hymenocallis narcissiflora (*H. calathina* and *Ismene calathina*)
SPIDER LILY, PERUVIAN DAFFODIL

The 3- to 5½-inch-wide very fragrant blossoms of this tender tropical stand out in warm-climate borders. The flowers may be white, striped with green, almost pure white, or yellow. Their complex structure resembles a daffodil with spidery back petals and arching stamens. The flower stalk, bearing two to five flowers, appears in early summer to midsummer, followed by six to eight straplike leaves, each 2 inches wide and 2 feet long.

Size: 2 feet tall.

Light: Full sun or light shade.

Hymenocallis narcissiflora

Soil and Moisture: Fertile, humus-rich, well-drained soil. Plentiful moisture while growing; taper off in summer dormancy.

Planting and Propagation: Plant bulbs 3 to 5 inches deep and 1 foot apart in early winter where hardy and after last spring frost elsewhere.

Special Care: Where tender, dig as leaves yellow. Suspend upside down to dry; do not cut off roots.

Pests and Diseases: Usually pest free.

Climate: Zones 8–11; treat as tender bulb elsewhere, digging and overwintering in dry peat at 70°F—cooler winter temperatures inhibit flowering the next season.

Cultivars and Similar Species: 'Advance,' white, traces of green in throat; 'Sulfur Queen,' yellow. Similar: *Pancreatium maritimum* (sea daffodil), fragrant 3-inch white flowers, evergreen leaves.

Garden Use: Lovely planted as accent in midground of borders and in containers.

Ipheion uniflorum (*Triteleia uniflora* and *Brodiaea uniflora*)
SPRING STARFLOWER

This early spring bloomer spreads rapidly to form great drifts of fragrant, pale blue, 1- to 1½-inch stars with bright orange stamens. Each flowering stem bears only one flower, but each bulb produces several stems over several weeks. The narrow, flattish leaves emerge in fall or spring, die back in early summer, and when crushed emit an oniony odor. Starflower blooms best when crowded.

Size: 6 to 8 inches tall.

Light: Full sun or part shade.

Soil and Moisture: Average, well-drained soil. Plentiful moisture during active growth; drier during summer dormancy.

Planting and Propagation: Plant bulbs in midsummer to late summer, 2 to 3 inches deep and 3 to 6 inches apart. Lift after flowering to divide.

Special Care: May be invasive.

Ipheion uniflorum

Iris bucharica

Light: Full sun.

Soil and Moisture: Average to rich, well-drained soil. Moderate moisture while growing; dry during summer dormancy.

Planting and Propagation: Plant bulbs in fall, 3 to 4 inches apart and 3 to 4 inches deep. Divide only when overcrowding reduces vigor.

Special Care: In wet-summer areas, most may decline in a few years, but some may adapt and thrive.

Pests and Diseases: Bulb scab sometimes troublesome. Birds may destroy blossoms.

Climate: Hardy in Zones 5–9; poorly adapted to wet-summer areas.

Cultivars and Similar Species: 'Joyce,' sky blue; 'Natascha,' ivory with yellow blotch; 'Violet Beauty,' deep purple; 'Harmony,' royal-blue; 'J. S. Dyt,' reddish purple. *Iris danfordiae* (Danford iris): green-marked yellow blossoms in late winter.

Garden Use: Plant in groups of 10 or more in rock gardens or under shrubs along walk.

Iris reticulata

Pests and Diseases: Snails and slugs sometimes troublesome.

Climate: Hardy in Zones 7–9; to Zone 5 with winter mulch.

Cultivars: 'Wisely Blue,' large deep blue blossoms.

Garden Use: Allow to naturalize in lawns and woodland and shade gardens.

Iris bucharica

BOKHARA IRIS

The most common of the Juno irises—ones with thick, fleshy roots attached to their bulbs—this mid-spring bloomer bears a single flower stem with five to seven fragrant 3- to 4-inch flowers. Creamy white, with a patch of yellow on each fall (the three drooping petals), blossoms stand just above bold, 2-inch-wide arching leaves, which are glossy above and whitish beneath and fade away by midsummer.

Size: Leaves 8 inches to 1 foot tall; flower stems 1 to 1½ feet tall.

Light: Full sun.

Soil and Moisture: Fertile, well-drained soil. Keep moist during growth and blooming; completely dry during summer dormancy.

Planting and Propagation: Plant bulbs with their attached fleshy roots in fall, 4 inches deep and 4 to 6 inches apart.

Special Care: Do not apply overhead water. Gravel mulch helpful.

Pests and Diseases: Usually pest free.

Climate: Hardy in Zones 5–8 on East Coast, to Zone 11 in the West; not well adapted where summers are wet or cool.

Similar Species: *I. magnifica,* seven blossoms per stem, lilac standards, white falls with orange blotches.

Garden Use: Plant in drifts in dry, sunny borders and rock gardens.

Iris reticulata

RETICULATED IRIS

Sometimes blooming with snow surrounding its feet, this little bulb's violet-scented blossoms make a welcome display in late winter and early spring. Each plant bears a single, 3-inch, orange-splashed, purple blossom. Leaves, which are short when flowers bloom but elongate later, are narrow, four-angled, and upright, disappearing by summer.

Size: Leaves to 1½ feet high; flowers 3 to 8 inches tall.

Iris x *xiphium*

Leucojum aestivum 'Gravetye Giant'

Iris x *xiphium*
DUTCH IRIS

Treasured as garden and cut flowers for their long stems and handsome blossoms, hybrid Dutch iris bear one or two 4- to 5-inch flowers atop a single stem. The beardless mid spring and early summer blossoms may be blue, white, yellow, orange, bronze, or bicolored, often with contrasting blotches on the lower petals. The narrow, almost round leaves grow in winter and die back in midsummer.

Size: Flower stems 1½ to 2 feet tall; leaves to 2 feet tall.

Light: Full sun.

Soil and Moisture: Humus-rich, well-drained soil. Regular moisture during growth; less or none after leaves die.

Planting and Propagation: Plant bulbs in fall, 3 to 5 inches deep and 4 to 6 inches apart. Divide after blooming, setting small bulbs in nursery bed to mature.

Special Care: When dividing, replant immediately. In Zones 3–5, treat as tender bulb.

Pests and Diseases: Bulb rots, aphids, mosaic virus (spread by aphids) troublesome.

Climate: Hardy in Zones 7–11; to Zone 6 with winter mulch.

Cultivars: 'Casablanca,' white; 'Lemon Queen,' two shades of yellow; 'Ideal,' lobelia blue; 'Professor Blaauw,' violet-blue; 'Purple Sensation,' deep violet-purple, small yellow blotch.

Garden Use: Plant in drifts in midground of borders and in cut-flower gardens.

Leucojum vernum
SPRING SNOWFLAKE

Flowering two weeks later than similar-looking snowdrops (*Galanthus nivalis*), spring snowflake produces numerous stalks of several violet scented, bell shaped, ¾-inch white flowers. Each of the blossom's six equal-length petals is tipped with a green spot. (Only three of snowdrops' petals have green tips, and lengths are not even.)

Size: Leaves to 10 inches long; flower stalks about 1 foot tall.

Light: Full sun to part shade.

Soil and Moisture: Humus-rich, well-drained soil; regular moisture all year, especially while growing and blooming.

Planting and Propagation: Plant bulbs in fall, 3 to 5 inches deep and 8 to 10 inches apart. Do not divide for at least three years.

Special Care: May leave undisturbed for many years.

Pests and Diseases: Usually pest free.

Climate: Zones 3–9; better in the South than snowdrops.

Similar Species: *L. aestivum* (summer snowflake), late spring to early summer, 1 to 1½ feet tall, two to eight blossoms per stem; Zones 4–9; 'Gravetye Giant,' 1- to 1½-inch flowers, 1½ feet tall.

Garden Use: Excellent bulb for mixed borders and interplanting with later-blooming perennials. Naturalize in meadow, woodland, or New American-style garden.

Lilium Asiatic hybrids
ASIATIC HYBRID LILY

Asiatic lilies bring bright splashes of color to the early summer garden. Plants bear up to twenty 4- to 6-inch-wide flowers with flat or recurved petals. Flowers may be white, yellow, orange, pink, red, or combinations, often with small dark spots. Most face upward, but some face outward or downward. Upward-facing types, which include the popular Mid-Century Hybrids, are ideal for beds that will be viewed from an adjacent path or a second-story window. Outward-facing and pendant types show their faces from across the garden.

Size: 2 to 6 feet tall; varies by cultivar.

Light: Best with tops in full or part sun and lower stems shaded by other plants.

Soil and Moisture: Deep, fertile, humus-rich, very well-drained soil. Regular moisture during growth and blooming; do not allow to go completely dry, even when dormant.

Planting and Propagation: Plant bulbs in fall, before first frost, or when available in spring, 4 to 6 inches deep and 1 to 1½ feet apart. Divide in late summer when plants are going dormant.

Special Care: Stake with individual stakes. Spread 1 inch of organic matter around shoots in spring. Cut stems just below lowest

Lilium Asiatic hybrid

spent flower; when leaves die, cut just above ground to mark location. Excellent cut flower, but removing leaves weakens plants.

Pests and Diseases: Moles and mice may damage bulbs. Other common problems include aphids, gray mold, viruses, and bulb rots.

Climate: Best in Zones 4–8, east of the Rocky Mountains.

Cultivars: Upward: 'White Swallow,' pure white, a few dark spots, 3 feet tall; 'Snowy Owl,' white, black-spotted, 4 feet tall; 'Dreamland,' golden yellow with apricot centers, 3 to 4 feet tall; 'Malta,' lavender-pink, 2 to 3 feet tall; 'Cream Puff,' ivory, a few tiny spots, 2 feet tall; 'Lemon Custard,' pastel yellow, dark dotted lines, 2 to 3 feet tall; 'Corsica,' pink with pink-spotted ivory centers, 3 feet tall; 'Connecticut Yankee,' bright yellow with golden centers, unspotted, 2 to 3 feet tall; 'Enchantment,' nasturtium-red, dark spots, 3 feet tall. Outward: 'Sally,' orange-pink, burnt-orange center, 6 feet tall; 'Sunny Twinkle,' golden yellow, many black spots, 3 feet tall. Pendant: 'Red Velvet,' deep red, 4 feet tall.

Garden Use: Plant in groups of three or more in midground of formal borders and meadow gardens.

Lilium Oriental hybrid

Lilium Oriental hybrids
ORIENTAL HYBRID LILIES

Richly scented, voluptuously formed Oriental lilies bloom mainly in white and shades of pink and ruby red. Yellow is rare, although some have a yellow or coral band along the length of each swept-back petal. Many have dark spots, bands of a second color or a white picotee edge, and ruffled petal edges. Flower size varies from 6 inches to 1 foot across. Oriental hybrids bloom mainly in August, although a few newer, short hybrids bloom in late June or July.

Size: 2 to 7 feet tall; mostly 3 to 5 feet tall.

Light: Tops in full sun to light shade; bottoms shaded by other plants.

Soil and Moisture: Fertile, humus-rich, deep, well-drained soil. Regular moisture during growth and bloom; do not allow to dry completely, even when dormant.

Planting and Propagation: Plant bulbs in fall, before first frost, or when available in spring, 4 to 6 inches deep and 1 to 1½ feet apart. Divide in late summer when going dormant.

Special Care: Stake individual stems. Cut stems just below lowest spent flower; when leaves die, cut stems just above ground to mark location. Cutting creates wonderful bouquets, but removal of leaf-bearing stem weakens plants.

Pests and Diseases: Rodents may damage bulbs. Other common problems include aphids, gray mold, viruses, and root and bulb rots.

Climate: Zones 5–8.

Cultivars and Similar Species: Bowl-shaped: 'Fine Art,' pure white with a touch of yellow in center, 3 feet tall, July. Flat-faced: 'Casa Blanca,' pure brilliant white, 4 to 5 feet tall, August. 'Imperial' series: pinks and reds, 5 to 7 feet tall, August. 'Journey's End,' magenta-rose with red stripes, 4 to 5 feet tall, August to September. Backswept: 'Everest,' white, 4 to 5 feet tall, August; 'Jamboree,' crimson with silver margins, 5 to 6 feet tall, August. Upward: 'Stargazer,' deep crimson with crimson-spotted white edges, 2 to 3 feet tall, July to August. Dwarfs: 'Mona Lisa,' white with pink pots; 'Mr. Ed,' pink with pink-dotted white edges; 'Mr. Sam,' white dotted red. *L. aurantum* (gold-band lily): white with gold bands and red spots. *L. speciosum* 'Rubrum' (rubrum lily): white and crimson, very fragrant.

Garden Use: Plant in groups of three or more in midground to background of borders and meadows.

Lilium x *auralianense*
AURELIAN, TRUMPET, OR OLYMPIC HYBRID LILIES

Derived from several Asiatic species, aurelian hybrid lilies offer up to 20 splendid variously shaped blossoms atop tall stems whorled with narrow leaves. Blooming in July and

Lilium x *auralianense*

August, between the earlier Asiatic and the later Oriental hybrids, these fragrant flowers are 6 to 8 inches long and up to 8 inches wide. Colors include white, greenish white, orange, yellow, peach, pink, or purple, often with yellow throats or maroon stripes.

Size: 3 to 8 feet tall; mostly 4 to 6 feet tall.

Light: Best with tops in full or part sun with bases shaded by other plants.

Soil and Moisture: Deep, fertile, humus-rich, very well-drained soil. Regular moisture during growth and bloom; do not allow to completely dry, even when dormant.

Planting and Propagation: Plant bulbs in fall, before first frost, or when available in spring, 4 to 6 inches deep, 1 to 1½ inches apart. Divide in late summer when going dormant.

Special Care: Stake with individual stakes. After blooming, cut stems just below lowest spent flower; when leaves die, cut stem just above ground, to mark location. If blossoms are cut with many leaves, plants may die or fail to bloom the next year.

Pests and Diseases: Rodents may damage bulbs. Slugs, snails, aphids, gray mold, viruses, and bulb rot sometimes troublesome.

Climate: Best in Zones 4–7; in Zones 9–10, dig bulbs and refrigerate for at least eight weeks before spring planting. Not well adapted to dry heat, but may perform if mulched heavily and grown in moist shade.

Cultivars and Similar Species: Trumpet: 'Black Dragon,' white inside, maroon reverse; 'Golden Splendor,' buttercup yellow, maroon stripes on reverse; 'Pink Perfection,' deep pink. Bowl-shaped: 'Moonlight,' chartreuse-yellow, scented in evening; 'Heart's Desire,' cream to white, golden orange center. Pendant: 'Golden Showers,' yellow, tinged maroon on reverse; 'Thunderbolt,' deep apricot-orange. Sunburst: 'Bright Star,' white with orange-gold centers.

Garden Use: Plant in groups of three or more in midground or background of borders or meadows.

Lycoris squamigera
(Amaryllis hallii)

RESURRECTION LILY, NAKED LADIES, HURRICANE LILY, MAGIC LILY

In late summer, resurrection lily bears a ring of fragrant, rose-lilac, trumpet-shaped flowers, each 3 inches long, around the top of its leafless flower stems. The leaves, 9 inches to 1 foot long and 1 inch wide, don't appear until flowers fade, then remain green until spring. Bulbs are dormant in summer and multiply freely, forming handsome clumps.

Size: Leaves to 1 foot tall, 2 feet wide; flower stems 1½ to 2 feet tall.

Light: Full sun.

Soil and Moisture: Humus-rich, well-drained soil. Regular moisture while growing; on the dry side while dormant.

Planting and Propagation: Plant bulbs mid-summer to late summer, 5 to 6 inches deep and 6 inches apart. Divide bulbs during dormancy, only when crowded.

Special Care: Tolerates some summer water, if soil dries quickly. Bloom increased by crowding, so container culture is successful. Protect container plants from freezing.

Pests and Diseases: Root and bulb rot if overwatered; otherwise no special problems.

Lycoris squamigera

Climate: Zones 5–9; best with some winter chill.

Similar Species: *L. radiata* (spider lily), red with spidery stamens, Zones 8–10; to Zone 6 with winter protection. *L. aurea* (golden spider lily): yellow with spidery stamens, Zones 9–11. Similar: *Nerine*, frost-tender, smaller, several pink-flowered species.

Garden Use: Plant in groups in midground of borders and naturalistic gardens; combines well with ornamental grasses. Looks best if interplanted with other plants whose foliage hides the naked stems.

Muscari botryoides
GRAPE HYACINTH

This diminutive bloomer naturalizes easily in most gardens, putting on a pretty show of tiny, intense blue, urn-shaped flowers, packed 20 to 40 to a stem, for a month or more from early to mid-spring. The grasslike leaves emerge with the flowers in spring and last all summer. The plants, with their grape-like clusters of buds and flowers, make charming drifts under daffodils and tulips and may be cut for small bouquets.

Size: 1 foot tall; usually 6 to 8 inches tall.

Light: Full sun to light shade.

Muscari botryoides 'Blue Spike'

Soil and Moisture: Average to poor, well-drained soil; regular to plentiful moisture all year.

Planting and Propagation: Plant bulbs in fall, 3 inches deep and 3 to 5 inches apart. Divide and transplant just after blooming.

Special Care: Spreads by seeding and increasing bulbs.

Pests and Diseases: Usually pest free.

Climate: Zones 2–8.

Cultivars and Similar Species: 'Album,' white. *M. armeniacum:* white-tipped cobalt-blue flowers, very similar to *M. botryoides,* but blooms a bit later and leaves appear in fall and overwinter, Zones 4–8; 'Blue Spike,' double, sterile; 'Heavenly Blue,' clear deep blue. *M. azureum:* bright blue, dense spikes. *M. comosum:* light and dark blue flowers in tassellike clusters.

Garden Use: Plant in groups of 50 or more as border edging, in woodland, rock, or meadow gardens; combine with daffodils, tulips, and Dutch hyacinths. Overwintering foliage of *M. armeniacum* may look messy but serves as marker for other bulbs.

Narcissus hybrids
TRUMPET AND LARGE-CUP DAFFODILS

Garden hybrid daffodils are among the cheeriest flowers, blooming in early spring before tree leaves emerge. The classic blossom is the long-trumpeted yellow such as 'King Alfred,' but many variations such as long-cup, short-cup, split-cup, and double abound. Colors include white, pale to bright yellow, and bicolors or tricolors with orange-red, peach, or pink. The strap-shaped leaves emerge before the flower stems and are usually somewhat shorter. The sweetly fragrant blossoms make excellent cut flowers.

Size: 14 inches to 1⅔ feet tall.

Light: Full sun to light shade in spring from deciduous trees. Pink-flowered types retain color best in part shade.

Soil and Moisture: Humus-rich, well-drained, neutral to slightly acid soil. Regular moisture when growing and blooming; drier during summer dormancy.

Planting and Propagation: In cold-winter areas, plant bulbs in late summer to early fall, 6 to 8 inches deep and 4 to 6 inches apart. In areas with warm falls and mild winters, plant in November.

Special Care: Do not remove foliage until it yellows. Do not braid foliage as is sometimes advised to increase tidiness. Cut off faded flowers.

Pests and Diseases: Root and bulb rot, mosaic virus, and narcissus bulb fly occasionally troublesome. Usually not eaten by rodents.

Climate: Zones 3–9; not well-adapted where summers are wet.

Cultivars: The flat petals are called the perianth; the trumpet or cup, the corona. (Color code: perianth/corona.) Trumpet: 'King Alfred,' yellow/yellow, 1⅓ to 1⅔ feet tall; 'Mt. Hood,' opens creamy yellow, turns white, 1⅓ feet tall; 'Spellbinder,' sulfur yellow/white, 1⅓ to 1½ feet tall. Large cup: 'Accent,' white/salmon-pink, 14 inches to 1⅓ feet tall; 'Rosy Wonder,' white/pink, 1⅓ to 1½ feet tall, often two flowers per stem; 'Daydream,' pale yellow/white, 14 inches to 1⅓ feet tall; 'Carlton,' yellow/yellow, naturalizes well, 1½ to 1⅔ feet tall; 'Ice Follies,' creamy white/light yel-

Narcissus 'Carlton'

low, naturalizes well, 16 to 19 inches tall. Short cup: 'Barret Browning,' creamy white/orange, 1⅓ feet tall, early. Double: 'Cheerfulness,' white/creamy yellow, 14 inches to 1⅓ feet tall; 'Ice King,' opens creamy yellow, turns white, 1⅓ to 1½ feet tall.

Garden Use: Plant in groups of 10 or more in borders, woodlands, and meadows. Interplant with daylilies or hostas to hide fading foliage. Allow to naturalize under deep-rooted deciduous trees.

Narcissus jonquilla
JONQUIL

Jonquils are the most fragrant of the narcissus, bearing small, sweet-scented, golden yellow small-cupped flowers, up to six on a stem in early spring. Leaves are very narrow, rushlike, and dark green. Jonquils like hot summer weather and are more likely than most narcissus to thrive in the South.

Size: 1 foot tall.

Light: Full sun to light shade.

Soil and Moisture: Humus-rich, well-drained, neutral to slightly acid soil. Regular moisture when growing and blooming; drier during summer dormancy.

Planting and Propagation: In cold-winter areas, plant bulbs in late summer to early fall,

Narcissus jonquilla

6 to 8 inches deep and 4 to 6 inches apart. In areas with warm falls and mild winters, plant in November.

Special Care: Do not remove foliage until it dies back. Do not tie it in knots. Remove faded flowers.

Pests and Diseases: Root and bulb rot, mosaic virus, and narcissus bulb fly sometimes troublesome. Usually not eaten by rodents.

Climate: Zones 4–9 in the East; to Zone 11 in the West.

Cultivars: (Color code: perianth/corona.) 'Suzy,' yellow/deep orange, 1⅓ feet tall; 'Bell Song,' creamy white/pink, 1⅓ feet tall; 'Baby Moon,' pale yellow/pale yellow, 7 inches tall; 'Pipit,' light yellow/white, 7 inches tall.

Garden Use: Plant in groups of 10 or more in borders and rock gardens.

Narcissus triandrus
ANGEL'S TEARS

Native to Portugal and Spain, this wild narcissus bears several white to pale yellow flowers per stem and blooms in late spring, after most other narcissus are finished. The narrow leaves are about a foot long. Cultivars share the species' delicate, medium to long trumpeted form and may be white, yellow, or bicolored.

Size: 10 inches to 1½ feet tall.

Light: Full sun to light shade.

Soil and Moisture: Humus-rich, well-drained soil. Regular moisture when growing and blooming; drier in summer dormancy.

Planting and Propagation: In cold-winter areas, plant bulbs in late summer to early fall, 5 to 6 inches deep and 6 to 8 inches apart. In areas with warm falls and mild winters, plant in November.

Special Care: Do not remove foliage until it yellows. Do not braid foliage. Remove faded flowers.

Pests and Diseases: Root and bulb rot, mosaic virus, and narcissus bulb fly sometimes troublesome. Usually not eaten by rodents.

Narcissus triandrus 'Hawera'

Climate: Hardy in Zones 4–9; to Zone 11 in the West.

Cultivars: 'Thalia' (orchid narcissus), pure white with up to five pendant, lightly fragrant blossoms per stem, 1½ feet tall; 'Ice Wings,' ivory-white, scented, 1 foot tall; 'Hawera,' lemon-yellow, very fragrant, 10 inches tall; 'Liberty Bells,' soft yellow, 12 to 14 inches tall; 'Tuesday's Child,' clear white and yellow, 14 inches to 1⅓ feet tall.

Garden Use: Plant in groups of 12 or more in midground of borders and in groundcover plantings; naturalize in woodland, meadow, or rock gardens.

Narcissus x cyclamenius
CYCLAMEN DAFFODIL

One parent of these charming hybrid daffodils is *N. cyclamenius,* a 4- to 8-inch-tall species with long, bright yellow trumpets and perianth segments that flare backward. Hybrids are generally taller and come in various colors and combinations; all have recurved perianths and long trumpets. They are the first daffodils to open, blooming from late winter through early spring, and bear one blossom per stem.

Size: 5 inches to 1⅓ feet tall; mostly 10 inches to 1 foot tall.

Light: Full sun to light shade.

Soil and Moisture: Humus-rich, well-drained, neutral to slightly acid soil. Regular moisture when growing and blooming; drier during summer dormancy.

Planting and Propagation: In cold-winter areas, plant bulbs in late summer to early fall, 5 to 8 inches deep and 3 to 6 inches apart. In areas with warm falls and mild winters, plant in November.

Special Care: Do not remove foliage until it dies back. Do not braid foliage. Remove faded blossoms.

Pests and Diseases: Root and bulb rot, mosaic virus, and narcissus bulb fly occasionally troublesome. Usually not eaten by rodents.

Climate: Zones 6–9 in the East; to Zone 11 in the West.

Cultivars: (Color code: perianth/corona.) 'February Gold,' yellow/yellow, 1 foot tall, good naturalizer; 'February Silver,' white/yellow fading white, 1 foot tall; 'Tête-à tête,' yellow/yellow, 5 to 7 inches tall, two flowers per stem, not as swept back; 'Jack Snipe,' white/yellow, 8 to 10 inches tall; 'Jenny,' white/white, 10 inches tall; 'March Sunshine,' yellow/orange, 10 inches tall; 'Peeping Tom,' golden yellow/golden yellow, 10 inches tall.

Garden Use: Plant in groups of 10 or more along walkways and in borders, woodlands, and rock gardens.

Narcissus x cyclamenius 'Jack Snipe'

Narcissus x *poeticus*

Narcissus x *poeticus*
PHEASANT'S-EYE NARCISSUS,
POET'S NARCISSUS

This sweetly fragrant mid- to late-spring-blooming narcissus bears one flower to a stem. The perianth is purest white, surrounding a very short, pale yellow cup edged in red. Cultivars retain the white perianth but feature variously colored coronas. Leaves are narrow and blue-green.

Size: 1 to 1½ feet tall.

Light: Full sun to light shade from deep-rooted deciduous trees.

Soil and Moisture: Humus-rich, well-drained neutral to slightly acid soil. Regular moisture when growing and blooming; drier during summer dormancy. Adapts better to poorly drained soil than most *Narcissus.*

Planting and Propagation: In cold-winter areas, plant bulbs in late summer to early fall, 6 to 8 inches deep and 4 to 6 inches apart. In areas with warm falls and mild winters, plant in November.

Special Care: Do not remove foliage until it dies back. Do not braid foliage. Remove faded blossoms.

Pests and Diseases: Root and bulb rot, mosaic virus, and narcissus bulb fly sometimes troublesome. Usually not troubled by rodents.

Climate: Zones 4–9 in the East; to Zone 11 in the West.

Cultivars: (Color code: perianth/corona.) 'Actaea,' white/yellow with red edge, flowers 3 inches across, 1⅓ to 1½ feet tall; 'Pheasant's Eye' ('Poeticus Recurvus'), white/yellow, edged with green, orange centers, 14 inches tall.

Garden Use: Front to midground in border, woodland, meadow, and rock gardens and in containers.

Narcissus x *tazetta*
TAZETTA NARCISSUS,
PAPERWHITE NARCISSUS

Hybrids *N.* x *tazetta* share a heady fragrance, small shallow-cupped flowers borne several to a stem, and a tall, slender grace. Flower color varies from white to deep yellow, with a smooth or ruffled shallow corona, which is orange or the same color as the perianth. The bright white tazetta hybrid 'Paperwhite' is commonly forced in winter to bring sweetly scented flowers indoors to the winter-weary.

Size: 1 to 1⅔ feet tall.

Light: Full sun to light shade in spring from deciduous deep-rooted trees.

Soil and Moisture: Humus-rich, well-drained soil. Regular moisture when plant is growing and blooming; drier during summer dormancy.

Planting and Propagation: Plant bulbs in fall, 3 to 5 inches deep and 6 to 8 inches apart.

Special Care: Do not remove foliage until it dies back. Do not tie in knots. Remove faded flowers.

Pests and Diseases: Root and bulb rot, mosaic virus, and narcissus bulb fly occasionally troublesome. Usually not eaten by rodents.

Climate: *N. tazetta* to Zones 7–11; some cultivars to Zone 5. Poorly adapted where summers are wet. Better in the South than many

Narcissus x *tazetta* 'Geranium'

Narcissus because does not need long, cold dormant period.

Cultivars: (Color code: perianth/corona.) 'Paperwhite,' white/white, 1⅓ feet tall; 'Grand Soleil d'Oro,' yellow/orange, 1⅓ feet tall; 'Minnow,' pale yellow/yellow, 8 to 10 inches tall; 'Geranium,' white/orange, 15 to 17 inches tall; 'White Pearl' white/white; 'Cragford,' white/orange, 12 to 14 inches tall.

Garden Use: Plant in groups of 10 or more in borders, woodlands, meadows, and rock gardens. Interplant with hostas or daylilies to hide fading foliage.

Polianthes tuberosa
TUBEROSE

These old garden favorites are more commonly found in a florist's shop than a garden. With at least four months of warm summer weather, however, it's easy to grow these headily fragrant flowers. Several flower spikes—made up of some 30 waxy white, 2½-inch-long, single or double, tubular flowers—appear from a fountain of grassy leaves in late summer and fall.

Size: Basal leaves to 1½ feet tall; flower stems 2½ to 3½ feet tall.

Light: Full sun.

Soil and Moisture: Fertile, humus-rich, acid to neutral, well-drained soil. Water once at planting. After shoots emerge, water regularly during growth and bloom; taper off when foliage declines.

Planting and Propagation: Plant rhizomes in spring, after last frost, no more than 1 or 2 inches deep and 4 to 8 inches apart. Or start indoors, four to six weeks before warm nights begin. Divide offshoots in fall when digging, but divisions may not rebloom for one or two years.

Special Care: In short-season areas, start indoors, or grow outdoors in containers kept inside until spring and protected during early fall frosts. Where temperatures fall below 20°F, dig rhizomes, dry for two weeks, and store in cool place in dry peat.

Pests and Diseases: Aphids may damage buds.

Climate: Zones 8–11; elsewhere, treat as tender bulb, although usually dug and wintered inside even where hardy.

Cultivars: 'The Pearl,' double flowers, 1¼ feet tall; 'Everblooming,' to 3½ feet tall, single, longer-lasting cut flower.

Garden Use: Use in groups in midground of formal borders and in cut-flower gardens and containers.

Polianthes tuberosa

Puschkinia scilloides

Puschkinia scilloides (P. lebanotica)
STRIPED SQUILL

Resembling a pale version of Siberian squill, these pale milky blue or white, ½- to 1-inch-wide bell-shaped flowers get their color from blue stripes running through the petals. Plants bear a single flower stem with a cluster of up to eight spicily fragrant blossoms in late winter or early spring. Two ½-inch-wide, 6-inch-long basal leaves appear with the flowers and die back in early summer.

Size: 4 to 8 inches tall.

Light: Full sun or part shade.

Soil and Moisture: Average, well-drained soil. Regular moisture while growing and blooming; much drier during summer dormancy.

Planting and Propagation: Plant bulbs in early fall, 3 to 4 inches deep and 3 inches apart.

Special Care: Divide only if bulbs become overcrowded.

Pests and Diseases: Usually pest free.

Climate: Zones 4–9. Best where winters have freezing weather and summers are not wet.

Cultivars and Similar Species: Variable; read descriptions to check exact coloration of selection you buy. *P. s.* var. *libanotica:* smaller purple-blue flowers. *Scilla tubergeniana:* similar flowers on several 5-inch flower stems per plant.

Garden Use: Plant groups of these small charmers where they can be seen close up, or plant large drifts to admire at greater distance in mixed borders, along paths, and in rock gardens.

Ranunculus asiaticus
PERSIAN BUTTERCUP

Modern hybrid Persian buttercups display their elegant partly to fully double flowers for up to four months beginning in spring as long as the weather remains cool. When the weather turns warm, plants decline. The 2- to 5-inch-wide blossoms appear one to four to a stem, in white, yellow, orange, pink, and red, including numerous subtle variations and bicolors. The compound, toothed leaves form a good-looking bushy clump.

Size: 10 inches to 2 feet tall.

Light: Full sun or very light shade.

Soil and Moisture: Humus-rich, fertile, well-drained soil. Water well at planting. After

Ranunculus asiaticus

shoots emerge, water regularly during growth and bloom. Taper off in summer dormancy.

Planting and Propagation: Plant tuberous roots from fall to spring in Zones 8–11; elsewhere in spring. If roots seem dry, soak for several hours before planting. Place roots prongs down, 2 inches deep and 8 to 10 inches apart. Rots if planted during warm weather.

Special Care: May be dug, dried, and wintered in dry peat at 50° to 55°F, but usually rhizomes are discarded and fresh ones bought each year.

Pests and Diseases: Mildew where air circulation is poor. Overwatering yellows foliage.

Climate: Zones 8–11; but here and elsewhere usually treated as tender bulb. Best adapted to long, cool springs.

Cultivars: 'Tecalote,' 3-inch blossoms, bright and pastel colors, some picotees, 1 to 1¼ feet tall, sold as single or mixed colors.

Garden Use: Plant in groups in front to midground of spring borders and rock gardens; excellent in containers.

Scilla siberica
SIBERIAN SQUILL

Dark, pure blue, Siberian squill forms wonderful eye-catching drifts in late winter and early spring, blooming soon after snowdrops. The nodding ½-inch flowers have flared petals, and although only three to five form to a flower stem, each plant makes three or four stems. The straplike leaves, which emerge with the flowers, are ½ inch wide, up to 6 inches long, and die back in summer.

Size: 4 to 6 inches tall.

Light: Full sun to light shade.

Soil and Moisture: Plant bulbs in fertile, well-drained, acid to neutral soil. Keep moist from fall until plant declines after blooming; drier during dormancy.

Planting and Propagation: Plant bulbs in fall, 3 to 4 inches deep and 4 inches apart.

Special Care: Plant where it will be undisturbed for a long time. Readily reseeds.

Pests and Diseases: Bulbs rot easily in storage; plant only healthy bulbs.

Climate: Zones 2–8.

Cultivars: 'Spring Beauty,' large flowers, 6 inches tall, but multiplies more slowly than the species because it makes fewer seeds. *S. s.* var. *alba:* white.

Garden Use: Plant in groups of 50 or more in mixed borders and rock gardens. Naturalize in lawns, woodlands, and meadows.

Sternbergia lutea
WINTER DAFFODIL

Looking much like a large, deep yellow crocus, *Sternbergia* adds its surprising blossoms to the fall garden. Each bulb sends up one to several flower stems, each bearing a single 1½-inch-long chalice-shaped blossom that opens to a six-pointed star. The ¾-inch-wide leaves emerge with or just after the flower stems and last through winter.

Size: Flower stems 4 to 9 inches tall; leaves 8 inches to 1 foot high.

Light: Full to half sun.

Soil and Moisture: Average, well-drained soil. Moderate moisture during growth; drier during summer dormancy.

Planting and Propagation: Plant bulbs in midsummer to late summer, 4 inches deep and 6 inches apart. Divide in summer if crowded.

Scilla siberica

Sternbergia lutea

Special Care: Best in hot, dry summer site. Endangered in its native Iran, plant only nursery-propagated bulbs.

Pests and Diseases: Bulb rot if drainage is poor.

Climate: Zones 6–11.

Cultivar: 'Major,' larger blossoms.

Garden Use: Plant in groups in front of borders and under shrubs, in rock gardens, and on slopes where drainage is good.

Tigridia pavonia
TIGER FLOWER

Blooming in brilliant hot colors, tiger flowers make a strong statement in the summer garden. Each 3- to 6-inch-wide flower is a widely flared, upward-facing tube with three large and three small petals. The small petals and

Tigridia pavonia

the bases of the larger ones are speckled with bright or dark spots, while edges of the large petals are solid. The palette includes red, orange, yellow, pink, cream, and white. Each blossom lasts one day, but flowers open on the branched stems over many weeks from midsummer to late summer. The ridged leaves form an attractive fan beneath the blossoms.

Size: 1½ to 2½ feet tall.

Light: Full sun; part shade best in hot-summer climates.

Soil and Moisture: Fertile, humus-rich, well-drained soil. Regular moisture during growth and blooming; none when foliage yellows.

Planting and Propagation: Plant corms in spring, 2 to 4 inches deep and 4 to 8 inches apart. Where hardy, divide every three or four years.

Special Care: Reseeds where hardy. May need staking.

Pests and Diseases: Gophers and red spider mites may be troublesome.

Climate: Zones 7–11; elsewhere, treat as tender bulb.

Cultivars: Usually sold in mix of colors.

Garden use: Plant in groups in formal and informal gardens, using hot-colored types carefully.

Trillium grandiflorum
GREAT WHITE TRILLIUM

Unquestionably one of the showiest woodland wildflowers native to the East Coast, great white trillium displays its lovely flowers for three or four weeks in early to mid-spring. The 2- to 3-inch-wide flowers are solitary, opening atop a slender 3- to 4-inch-long stalk that arises from the joint formed by three oval, pointed, 3- to 6-inch-long leaves. The upward-facing flowers are made up of three wavy, pointed petals backdropped with three pointed green sepals. They open white and gradually fade to pink. Red berries follow the blossoms, and the foliage dies down in summer if soil dries.

Trillium grandiflorum

Size: 1½ to 2 feet tall; forms 2-foot-wide colonies.

Light: Full sun in spring followed by light shade cast by deciduous trees.

Soil and Moisture: Humus-rich, fertile, moist, neutral to acid soil; plentiful moisture.

Planting and Propagation: In spring, plant rhizomes 4 inches deep, or plant container-grown plants, spacing 2 feet apart. Do not dig up or purchase wild plants. Division not necessary, but roots of mature clumps may be separated when dormant. Seeds may be sown directly in the garden when fresh.

Special Care: Keep moist and well mulched.

Pests and Diseases: Usually pest free.

Climate: Zone 4–9.

Cultivars and Similar Species: 'Flore-pleno,' double, very showy. *T. erectum* (purple wake robin): deep maroon flowers, needs acid soil.

Garden Use: Magnificent wildflower for naturalizing in shade and woodland gardens.

Tuhlbaghia violacea
SOCIETY GARLIC

This native of eastern Cape Province in South Africa forms loose, rounded heads of up to twenty ¾-inch-wide, purplish violet flowers on slender bare stems held well above the

Tuhlbaghia violacea

large clumps of arching evergreen leaves. Blossoms appear mainly in spring and summer, but when well-adapted, flowers occur throughout the year. When bruised, the leaves smell of onions. Although the flowers are long lasting when cut, the onion odor limits their usefulness.

Size: Leaves to 1 foot long; flower stems to 2 feet tall.

Light: Full sun or light shade.

Soil and Moisture: Average, moisture-retaining, well-drained soil; best with regular moisture.

Planting and Propagation: Plant container-grown plants anytime; or plant bulbs with tops at soil surface, 8 inches to 1 foot apart.

Special Care: May be used as culinary herb instead of chives.

Pests and Diseases: Usually pest free.

Climate: Zones 9–11; to Zone 8 with winter mulch. Where not hardy, dig and store in cool area after foliage dies, or plant in large container and keep indoors in winter.

Cultivars and Similar Species: 'Silver Lace,' white-striped leaves. *T. fragrans:* fragrant, lavender-blue, 1 to 1½ feet tall.

Garden Use: Use as edging or ground cover in mixed borders; good container plant.

Tulipa batalinii
BOKHARA TULIP

This diminutive wildflower from Central Asia just north of Afghanistan is buff yellow with a yellow-gray blotch at the base of each petal, but cultivars come in shades of yellow, bronze, and red. The 2-inch-long cups have blunt, sometimes notched petals that stay upright in a perfect tulip form. The leaves are narrow and grasslike, forming along with the mid-spring blossoms.

Size: 4 to 6 inches tall.
Light: Full sun to light shade.
Soil and Moisture: Fertile, humus-rich, well-drained soil. Regular moisture during growth and blooming; dry off when leaves die back.
Planting and Propagation: Plant in fall, 3 to 6 inches deep and 3 to 6 inches apart.
Special Care: Remove faded flowers.
Pests and Diseases: Usually pest free.
Climate: Zones 4–8. Where summers are wet, dig dormant bulbs and store at 65° F. until time to plant in fall.
Cultivars and Similar Species: 'Bright Gem,' golden yellow, flushed orange; 'Bronze Charm,' bronze; 'Red Jewel,' red;

'Yellow Jewel,' lemon-yellow. Similar: *T. linifolia*, red, bluish base, pointed petals, red-edged leaves, 5 to 10 inches tall.
Garden Use: Plant in groups in rock gardens and in fronts of borders.

Tulipa clusiana
CANDYSTICK TULIP, LADY TULIP

This appealing tulip species is especially easy to grow in mild winter areas with hot, dry summers, where it often naturalizes. The graceful, fragrant blossoms are rosy-red and white on the outside, with reddish purple bases, opening to reveal a white interior. When fully opened, the flowers are star-shaped. Leaves are narrow and few, folded lengthwise.

Size: 12 to 14 inches tall.
Light: Full sun best
Soil and Moisture: Fertile, humus-rich, well-drained soil. Regular moisture during growth and blooming; dry off when leaves die back.
Planting and Propagation: Plant bulbs in fall, 4 to 7 inches deep and 3 to 6 inches apart.
Special Care: Easy to grow and spreads by

stolons if well situated. Cut off faded flowers.
Pests and Diseases: Usually pest free.
Climate: Adapted in Zones 4–8 in the East; to Zone 11 in the West. Where summers are wet, dig dormant bulbs and store at 65° F. until time to plant in fall.
Cultivars and Similar Species: *T. c.* var. *chrysantha*, crimson outside, deep yellow inside, 6 inches tall; *T. c.* var. *stellata*, yellow blotch inside.
Garden Use: Plant in groups in rock gardens and in fronts of borders.

Tulipa pulchella
DWARF TAURUS TULIP

A diminutive native of Asia Minor, the dwarf Taurus tulip is painted red to purple on the inside of the petals with a bluish basal blotch, and gray or green on the reverse of the petals. Cultivars come in violet, violet-pink, and white. The 1½-inch blossoms are usually solitary and open into flat stars on sunny days. Flowers bloom early, from a base of two or three strap-shaped leaves.

Size: 4 to 6 inches tall.
Light: Full sun best.

Tulipa batalinii 'Bright Gem'

Tulipa clusiana

Tulipa pulchella violaceae 'Persian Pearl'

Soil and Moisture: Fertile, humus-rich, well-drained soil. Regular moisture during growth and blooming; dry off when leaves die back.

Planting and Propagation: Plant in fall, 3 inches deep and 3 to 6 inches apart. Divide during dormancy only if crowded.

Special Care: Remove faded flowers. Cut back foliage only when yellow.

Pests and Diseases: Usually pest free.

Climate: Zones 5–8. Where summers are wet, dig dormant bulbs and store at 65°F until fall planting. Mulch in cold climates.

Cultivars and Similar Species: *T. p. humilis* (*T. humilis*), bright rose-pink, yellow base; *T. p. violacea,* violet-purple petals, black base, crocus-shaped blossoms, 4 inches tall; 'Persian Pearl,' rosy red inside, silvery gray outside, 6 inches tall. Similar: *T. bakeri,* large wine-purple flowers with yellow bases, 4 to 6 inches tall; 'Lilac Wonder,' lavender-pink, large lemon-yellow base.

Garden Use: Plant in groups in rock gardens, at fronts of borders, and under shrubs.

Tulipa x *hybrida*

HYBRID TULIPS

Among the most familiar spring flowers are hybrid tulips with their elegant, long-stemmed, cup-shaped blossoms. As they age, the egg-shaped flowers open into wide bowls on sunny days, closing at night. The usually 2- to 3-inch-deep flowers may be single or double, fringed, pointed, or ruffled, blooming in mid- to late spring. They come in all colors but true blue. Some are streaked, blotched with basal stars, or picoteed. The broad gray-green leaves are generally much shorter than the blossoms. Modern hybrids are classified by bloom time (early, mid-, or late in the tulip season) as well as by flower type.

Size: 10 inches to 2½ feet tall.

Light: Full sun or light shade; leans toward light that isn't overhead.

Soil and Moisture: Fertile, humus-rich, well-drained soil. Regular moisture during growth and blooming; drier when leaves die back.

Planting and Propagation: In Zones 3–7, plant bulbs in early fall, 5 to 6 inches deep (10 inches to 1 foot deep to encourage rebloom in subsequent years) and 4 to 6 inches apart. In Zones 8–11, refrigerate bulbs for eight weeks at 45°F, then plant in mid- to late fall, 6 to 8 inches deep.

Special Care: Most hybrid tulips do not rebloom well after first year, so they are often treated as annuals even where hardy. To encourage reblooming in subsequent years, plant deeply, fertilize with nitrogen during leaf growth, and allow foliage to die back naturally. For bouquets, cut as bud is about to open, split stem, and cure in water in cool, dark place for two to eight hours with stems tightly wrapped in clear wrap to keep them upright. If treating as annual, pull plants after flowers fade; otherwise, deadhead, then cut back leaves only when foliage yellows.

Pests and Diseases: Fire (a disease similar to gray mold), mosaic virus, aphids, gophers, mice, and deer may be troublesome.

Climate: Zones 4–7. In Zones 8–11, use as annual, or dig bulbs when dormant and refrigerate in moist peat at 40° to 45°F until late-fall planting.

Cultivars: Early-Single: 'Couleur Cardinal,' dark red, 13 inches tall; 'Dr. An Wang,' lilac-blue, 1⅓ feet tall; 'General De Wet,' warm orange, fragrant, 13 inches tall. Early-Double: 'Schoonord,' white, light fragrance, 1 foot tall; 'Abba,' bright red, 12 to 14 inches tall. Mid-season, Triumph: 'Apricot Beauty,' salmon and apricot, green at base, 1½ feet tall; 'Bastogne,' red, light fragrance, 1½ feet tall; 'Boccherini,' dark periwinkle-blue, slight scent, 1⅔ feet tall; 'Hans Anrud,' deep lilac, 22 inches tall; 'Orange Wonder,' warm orange, fragrant, 1½ feet tall; 'White Dream,' white, 1⅔ feet tall. Late, Lily-Flowered: 'Ballerina,' apricot-tangerine, fragrant, 2 feet tall; 'West Point,' primrose-yellow, 23 inches tall; 'White Triumphator,' white, 26 inches tall. Late, Darwin and Cottage: 'Blue Aimable,' lilac-blue,

Tulipa x *hybrida* 'Blue Heron'

touches of lavender, 26 inches tall; 'Georgette,' butter-yellow, red edge, several to a stem, 1½ feet tall; 'Sweet Harmony,' pastel yellow, white edge, 2 feet tall. Mid-season, Darwin Hybrids: 'Burning Heart,' white, flamed red, 2⅓ feet tall; 'General Eisenhower,' red, 26 inches tall; 'Golden Apeldoorn,' golden yellow, black-and-green base, 2 feet tall; 'Holland's Glory,' orange-scarlet, 26 inches tall; 'Jewel of Spring,' primrose-yellow, red edge, 2 feet tall. Late, Parrot: 'Blue Parrot,' lilac-blue, streaked lavender, 26 inches tall; 'White Parrot,' white, streaked green, 25 inches tall. Late, Double and Peony: 'Maravilla,' violet, 22 inches tall; 'Mount Tacoma,' white, 23 inches tall; 'Angelique,' pale pink, lighter edged, 22 inches tall.

Garden Use: Plant in groups in midground of borders and beds; excellent in cut-flower gardens. Combine with hostas to camouflage unsightly dying foliage.

Tulipa sylvestris

Tulipa sylvestris
FLORENTINE TULIP

This pretty mid-spring-blooming species tulip adapts better than most tulips to mild-winter areas. The 2-inch-long fragrant yellow blossoms, often borne several to a stem, are nodding while in bud but upright when open. Red or green tinges the backs of the petals. The straplike leaves are nearly as tall as the flower stems and ridged.

Size: 6 inches to 1 foot tall.

Light: Full sun or light shade.

Soil and Moisture: Fertile, humus-rich, well-drained soil. Regular moisture during growth and blooming; drier when leaves die back.

Planting and Propagation: Plant bulbs in fall, 4 to 6 inches deep and 3 to 6 inches apart.

Special Care: Cut off faded flowers; cut back leaves only when yellow.

Pests and Diseases: Usually pest free.

Climate: Zones 4–10.

Similar Species: *T. saxatilis,* also well suited to mild-winter areas, forms bulbs at ends of

362

stolons, fragrant rosy lilac flowers with yellow bases, one to three per stem, 1 foot tall, thrives in poor soil and hot-summer climates. **Garden Use:** Plant in groups in rock gardens and fronts of borders.

Tulipa tarda (T. dasystemon)
KUENLUN TULIP

This tulip grows almost like a ground cover, with bright green flat leaves and flowers that open to flat stars. Petals are yellow with white edges on the inside, white with hints of green and sometimes red on the outside. The 2-inch blossoms open several to a stem in early spring. Bulbs form on ends of stolons and spread where well sited.

Size: 4 to 6 inches tall.

Light: Best in full sun.

Soil and Moisture: Fertile, humus-rich, well-drained soil. Regular moisture during growth and blooming; drier when leaves die back.

Planting and Propagation: Plant bulbs in fall, 5 to 6 inches deep and 3 to 6 inches apart.

Special Care: Cut off faded flowers. Do not remove foliage until yellow.

Pests and Diseases: Usually pest free.

Climate: Zones 4–8.

Cultivars: Only species is sold.

Garden Use: Plant in groups in rock gardens, under shrubs, and in fronts of borders.

Tulipa tarda

Tulipa kaufmanniana

Tulipa kaufmanniana
WATER LILY TULIP

Water lily tulips are hybrids of *T. kaufmanniana,* which shares its short stature, very early bloom period, and water-lily-shaped blossoms with its offspring. The petals of the species open into wide stars on sunny days and are creamy white inside, with golden yellow bases and bright carmine exteriors. Blossoms of cultivars may be 3 inches across in shades of yellow, mauve-pink, deep red, violet, and creamy white, often with a contrasting base, edge, or reverse. The leaves are broad and low spreading, in one case striped with white. This easy-care tulip naturalizes more readily than most.

Size: 4 to 10 inches tall.

Light: Full sun best.

Soil and Moisture: Fertile, humus-rich, well-drained soil. Regular moisture during growth and blooming; drier when leaves die back.

Planting and Propagation: Plant bulbs in fall, 3 to 6 inches deep and 3 to 6 inches apart.

Special Care: Cut off faded flowers. Allow foliage to turn yellow before removing.

Pests and Diseases: Usually pest free.

Climate: Zones 3–8.

Cultivars: 'Cherry Orchard,' scarlet, lemon-yellow base inside, 8 inches tall; 'Heart's Delight,' pink with pale pink edges outside, pale pink with lemon-yellow base inside, 6 inches tall; 'Alfred Cortot,' deep scarlet, white-striped leaves, 6 inches tall; 'Gaiety,' violet edged in creamy white, creamy white interior, 4 inches tall; 'Shakespeare,' carmine exterior, salmon with yellow base interior. *T. greigii,* similar to *T. kaufmanniana,* but blooms a bit later, gray-green leaves striped with maroon: 'Red Riding Hood,' red, black base; 'Perlina,' rose with lemon-yellow base; 'Cape Cod,' apricot edged yellow, black base.

Garden Use: Plant in groups in rock gardens and in fronts of borders.

Zantedeschia aethiopica
CALLA LILY

A large subtropical plant related to Jack-in-the-pulpit, calla lily shares that flower's unusual form. Tiny petalless flowers decorate the yellow spike, around which furls a graceful, showy, cone-shaped bract. The bract may be white, creamy white, or marked with green. The plant's large, arrow-shaped, glossy dark green leaves emerge in late winter, and the slightly longer flower stems bear solitary 6- to 8-inch flower heads from early spring into early summer. Where hardy, the plants naturalize and sometimes become weedy.

Size: 1½ to 4 feet tall.

Light: Full sun or part shade.

Soil and Moisture: Average to humus-rich, well-drained to wet soil. Ample moisture while growing and blooming; tolerates year-round wetness.

Planting and Propagation: Where hardy, plant rhizomes in fall through early spring, 2 to 3 inches deep, and at least 1 foot apart. In cold-winter areas, rhizomes may be sprouted indoors and planted out after last frost.

Special Care: Cut off faded flower stalks.

Pests and Diseases: Leaf spots may be troublesome; remove affected leaves. Virus,

Zantedeschia aethiopica

spread by sucking insects, and snails and slugs can cause problems.

Climate: Zones 9–11; best overwintered as container plant elsewhere. Rhizome may be dug and stored in peat, but it is never quite dormant, so it doesn't store well.

Cultivars and Similar Species: 'Hercules,' larger than species, broad, recurved, bracts; 'Green Goddess,' bracts green toward tips; 'Childsiana,' 1-foot-tall, heavy-blooming dwarf. Similar: *Z. pentlandii,* deep yellow bracts, 1⅓ to 1½ feet tall; 'Golden Mikado Lily,' a choice cultivar. Also available: hybrid callas in various shades of pink, lavender, and orange, usually 1½ to 2 feet tall, often with spotted leaves.

Garden Use: Plant in groups in midground to background of borders and naturalistic gardens. Excellent in boggy or damp sites and around garden ponds.

Zephranthes atamasco
RAIN LILY

The rain lily earned its name from its habit of bursting into bloom right after a rain. Several species are summer to autumn bloomers, but the most hardy is *Z. atamasco,* a native of the Southeast that blooms for a month or more beginning in early spring. The dainty white or purple-tinged, 3-inch, six-pointed,

Zephranthes atamasco

starlike flowers are borne singly on slender stems above dark green, narrow, grasslike leaves.

Size: To 1 to 1½ feet tall.

Light: Full to part shade.

Soil and Moisture: Average, well-drained soil. Alternate periods of wet and dry soil stimulates flowering; best if drier for two months after blooming. Tolerates some moisture while dormant; never should be bone-dry.

Planting and Propagation: Plant bulbs in fall where hardy, in spring in colder areas, 1 to 2 inches deep and 3 to 4 inches apart.

Special Care: Divide when number of blossoms declines. Bulbs are poisonous.

Pests and Diseases: Usually pest free.

Climate: Zones 7–11. Where not hardy, treat as tender bulb, storing in moist sand, or overwinter in container, keeping moist.

Similar Species: *Z. candida,* 2-inch white flowers, summer to fall, evergreen foliage, Zones 9–11. *Z. grandiflora* (zephyr lily): 3-inch pink to red flowers in spring and summer, Zones 9–11. *Z. rosea* (Cuban zephyr lily): 1-inch rose-red flowers in late summer and fall, Zones 9–11.

Garden Use: Naturalize in moist, open woodlands and shade gardens. Plant in groups in borders. Excellent container plant.

ROSES

The perfumed flowers of the romantic old garden roses or the elegant modern hybrids round out a garden.

Alba rose 'Semi Plena'

ALBA ROSES

Alba roses are among the oldest known roses in cultivation, originating about 200 A.D. *R. alba*, as it sometimes is called, probably arose in Eastern Europe from a chance hybrid of a damask rose and a local wild rose. The Romans brought the alba rose to Britain, where herbalists used it for medicinal purposes and included it in their apothecary gardens. Later, hybrids were developed in France and Holland.

Noted for their strong, rich rose attar perfume, the refined-looking, semidouble or double flowers of alba roses open flat and may be white or shades of pink. The blossoms appear in early summer and are set off against lovely blue-green foliage. Showy rose hips develop on cultivars with the fewest petals. Growing taller than those of other old roses, the stout stems are studded with a scattering of thorns.

Size: Upright and slender; 4 to 6 feet tall.
Light: Full sun to half shade.

Soil and Moisture: Tolerates poor soil, but performs best in fertile, moist site.
Planting: Plant bare-root or container-grown plants in spring.
Pruning: Little pruning needed; remove old canes of mature shrubs every year or so immediately after flowering for best blooms.
Special Care: Easily grown.
Pests and Diseases: Very disease resistant.
Climate: Very cold hardy, Zones 3–9.
Cultivars: 'Semi Plena,' white, semidouble, cultivated for perfume; 'Celestial,' delicate pink, semidouble; 'Félicité Parmentier,' pink fading to cream, double, green button center; 'Queen of Denmark,' soft rose-pink, double.
Garden Use: Use in background of flower border or as hedge because of height. Train as climber on fences or pillars.

BOURBON ROSES

One of the few repeat-flowering old roses, the first bourbon rose originated during the early 1800s as a chance hybrid between a damask rose and an 'Old Blush' China rose. The seedling was found in a hedgerow on a

Bourbon rose 'Madame Isaac Pereire'

farm on L'Ile de Bourbon, a French possession off the African Coast in the Indian Ocean. A French botanist sent this unique rose to King Louis Phillipe's gardener in France, who hybridized it.

These Victorian roses, with their heady fragrance, feature globular flowers that open to buttonlike centers nestled between the neatly interlocked petals. Colors include white, pink, and purple. Intermittent blossoms follow the profuse spring bloom; some cultivars bloom almost constantly. Leaves and stems resemble modern roses, but flowers, scent, and overall growth are definitely characteristic of old-fashioned roses.

Size: 5 to 6 feet tall; varies from bushy to spreading.
Light: Full sun.
Soil and Moisture: Fertile, well-drained soil rich in organic matter. Keep well watered.
Planting: Plant own-root (nongrafted) shrubs in spring.
Pruning: Prune mature plants when dormant, shortening main branches by one-third and others by two-thirds. Deadhead and encourage repeat bloom by cutting back laterals by one-third. Remove old wood at ground level every few years.
Special Care: Fertilize after each blooming to encourage repeat flowering.
Pests and Diseases: Suffers from black spot more frequently than other old roses.
Climate: Zones 6–9; colder with protection.
Cultivars and Similar Species: 'Boule de Neige,' little white flowers all summer; 'Zéphirine Drouhin,' deep rose-pink, thornless, train as climber; 'Madame Isaac Pereire,' dark raspberry-purple, intense fragrance; 'Louise Odier,' warm pink.
Garden Use: Use strong, vigorous shrubs as specimens or hedges. Peg procumbent types to ground or train on pillars, which encourages greater flowering.

Canadian rose 'William Baffin'

CANADIAN ROSES

This group of diverse roses, which includes shrubs and climbers, was bred by the Canadian Department of Agriculture to withstand Canada's tough growing conditions. No other modern roses equal the Canadian roses for cold hardiness and long season of bloom. Hybrid teas and other bush roses cannot withstand Canadian winters, except in coastal British Columbia and Nova Scotia and the borders of the Great Lakes, and then only with elaborate winter protection. The Canadian roses flourish where others freeze, blooming with abandon through the summer.

Size: Large shrubs or climbers; height varies according to cultivar.

Light: Full sun.

Soil and Moisture: Fertile, moist, well-drained soil high in organic matter. Keep well watered and mulched.

Planting: Plant bare-root or container-grown plants in spring. Don't plant grafted plants; insist on own-root (nongrafted) specimens to ensure cold hardiness.

Pruning: Prune according to type of rose, cutting out deadwood in spring.

Special Care: Needs no winter protection. If an exceptionally cold winter kills rose to ground, it will regrow from roots. Climbers do not need winter protection.

Pests and Diseases: Generally resistant to black spot and powdery mildew.

Climate: Zones 2/3–8.

Cultivars: Shrubs: 'Cuthbert Grant,' red; 'Morden Armorette,' dark pink; 'Morden Blush,' light pink; 'Henry Hudson,' light pink; 'J. P. Connell,' yellow. Climbers: 'John Cabot,' red; 'William Baffin,' dark pink; 'Louis Jolliet,' pink.

Garden Use: Excellent garden shrubs for Canada and northern U.S.

CENTIFOLIA ROSES

These sumptuous roses, sometimes called cabbage roses because their whorled petals and lush, rounded blossoms resemble cabbage heads, were immortalized in Dutch Master paintings and Victorian fabrics and wallpapers. Like most old-fashioned roses, they flower but once a year, producing very fragrant, luxurious flowers on arched, thorny branches. Cabbage roses may be pink, rose, violet, or, rarely, white.

Size: 4 to 6 feet tall; upright to bushy plants. Some are arching.

Light: Full sun.

Soil and Moisture: Fertile, well-drained, moist soil; keep well watered and mulched.

Planting: Plant bare-root or container-grown plants in spring.

Pruning: Prune out old wood immediately after flowering if needed; blooms best on older wood.

Special Care: Clip off faded blossoms.

Pests and Diseases: Susceptible to black spot and mildew. Plant in full sun; avoid wetting foliage.

Climate: Zones 3–9; winter protection in Zones 3–4.

Centifolia rose 'Paul Ricault'

Cultivars: 'Tour de Malakoff,' purple-crimson, arching stems; 'De Meaux,' light rose, compact dwarf plant; 'Paul Ricault,' deep rose-pink, opening flat; 'Juno,' blush pink; 'Fantin-Latour,' clear pink, opens flat.

Garden Use: Use in mixed border or cottage garden; train types with long, flexible canes to pillars, arches, or fences.

CHINA AND TEA ROSES

China roses arrived in France on trading ships from the Orient during the late 1700s and sparked an immediate enthusiasm. These were the first continuous-flowering roses seen in Europe. Their clusters of small fragrant flowers darken alluringly instead of fading as they age.

Tea roses, so named because their foliage smells like tea or because they were shipped in tea crates, arrived from China in the 1830s. These continuous-flowering roses with high-centered buds and large flowers stirred excitement because they bloomed in colors not yet seen: yellow, red, and apricot-orange.

China rose 'Old Blush'

Neither type can survive cold winters. They make admirable plants for gardens in Texas, southern California, and the Deep South, blooming almost year-round. China and tea roses are parents of modern roses.

Size: Most are small, bushy plants, 3 to 4 feet tall; some are lanky and cascade to 7 feet tall.

Light: Full sun.

Soil and Moisture: Fertile, moist, well-drained soil best; drought tolerant.

Planting: Plant bare-root or container-grown plants in spring.

Pruning: Cut back by one-third when out of bloom to encourage new growth; prune to shape and remove deadwood.

Special Care: Thrives on neglect, but pinch off faded flowers to prevent hip formation and encourage abundant bloom.

Pests and Diseases: Disease resistant.

Climate: China roses, Zones 6–10; tea roses, Zones 7–10.

Cultivars and Similar Species: China: 'Old Blush,' semidouble, pink; 'Louis Phillipe,' deep crimson, double; 'Madame Laurette Messimy,' salmon pink, semidouble. Tea:

'Fortune's Double Yellow,' apricot-yellow-pink blend, climber; 'Marie van Houtte,' cream to yellow; 'Monsieur Tillier,' copper to pink; 'Sombreuil,' creamy white. Noisette: clusters of constantly blooming, fragrant, pastel flowers; Zones 8–10.

Garden Use: Prune severely to maintain as small shrubs, or train as climbers on pillars or fences.

DAMASK ROSES

The heavenly scented *R. damascena*, a descent of *R. gallica*, originated in the Far East during Biblical times and was brought to Europe by the Crusaders in the middle of the 13th century. Most damask roses bloom once in early summer, but those derived from the autumn damask, a natural sport that reblooms in fall, will repeat bloom.

Damask roses produce sprays of very fragrant flowers noted for their rich damask perfume, a source of attar of roses. Blossoms come in clear shades of pink or white and may be semidouble to double. Foliage is light green. Stems are thorny and may bend under the flowers' weight.

Damask rose 'Madame Hardy'

Size: Larger and taller than gallicas, reaching 4 to 6 feet tall. Lax growth.

Light: Full sun.

Soil and Moisture: Fertile, well-drained, moist soil; keep well watered and mulched.

Planting: Plant bare-root or container-grown plants in spring.

Pruning: Thin old canes every few years immediately after blooming. Cut back hard every five years or so to reinvigorate.

Special Care: Easy to maintain.

Pests and Diseases: Double blossoms may hang onto bush and rot; best to immediately clip off faded flowers.

Climate: Zones 4–9; winter protection in Zone 4.

Cultivars: 'Madame Hardy,' pure white double with green button center; 'La Ville de Bruxelles,' lavender-pink, large, flat, double; 'Autumn Damask,' repeats in fall, one of few early old roses that reblooms.

Garden Use: Peg floppy lateral branches of cascading types to ground or low fence to encourage profuse bloom.

ENGLISH ROSES

Introduced in the early 1970s by British nurseryman David Austin, this new group of roses combines the wide color range and continuous flowering of modern roses with the heady fragrance, sumptuous flower form, and attractive shrub character of old-fashioned roses. These revolutionary roses came from hybridizing modern climbers, floribundas, and hybrid teas with the two oldest roses known to antiquity—gallica and damask roses.

Although not strictly a class of old garden roses because they originated so recently, the English roses can be considered old-fashioned roses for purposes of garden design. Their graceful growth habit makes them wonderful plants to include in a mixed border or cottage garden, but unlike old roses, they bloom all summer and fall. Several

English rose 'Graham Thomas'

dozen varieties are available in England; fewer are available here.

Size: Bushy plants; 3 to 6 feet tall.

Light: Full sun to part shade.

Soil and Moisture: Fertile, moist soil; keep well watered and mulched.

Planting: Plant bare-root or container-grown plants in spring.

Pruning: Prune for shape, removing weak, twiggy, and old unproductive wood. Cut remainder back by one-third to one-half when dormant.

Special Care: Remove faded blossoms by cutting above first five-leaflet leaf.

Pests and Diseases: Foliage generally resists diseases. Usual rose insect pests can be troublesome.

Climate: Zones 4/5–9. Various types behave differently in different regions; too new to evaluate.

Cultivars: 'Abraham Darby,' apricot; 'Charmian,' rose-pink; 'Constance Spry,' pink, blooms once; 'Cottage Rose,' pink; 'Fair Bianca,' white; 'Gertrude Jekyll,' bright pink; 'Graham Thomas,' yellow; 'Heritage,' soft pink; 'Mary Rose,' medium pink; 'Red Coat,' scarlet, single; 'Wenlock,' crimson; 'Othello,' deep crimson edging to purple and mauve.

Garden Use: Excellent in shrub borders, cottage gardens, or fragrance gardens. Cultivars with pliable arching canes can be trained to pillars and arches.

FLORIBUNDA ROSES

Derived from crossing hybrid teas with polyantha roses, floribunda roses combine the best qualities of the two groups: high-centered blossoms borne in profuse clusters from early summer through fall. Flowers come in all colors and most are single (five to 12 petals) or semidouble (13 to 25 petals; some are double (25 to 45 petals), and some are fragrant.

Decorative floribundas produce masses of clustered 2- to 3-inch flowers in bursts from early summer through fall. Large-flowered floribundas are compact plants with larger, long-stemmed flowers that rival hybrid tea blossoms.

Size: Compact 2- to 3-foot-tall bushes.

Light: Full sun.

Floribunda rose 'Fashion'

Soil and Moisture: Fertile, well-drained, moist soil; keep well watered and mulched.

Planting: Plant bare-root or container-grown plants in spring with bud union 2 inches below soil level to encourage own roots.

Pruning: Pruning not as critical as with hybrid teas; cut back canes to within 6 inches of ground every three years to renew vigor. Remove any suckers from understock.

Special Care: Easier to care for than hybrid teas. Fertilize twice monthly during blooming season; withhold fertilizer one month before frost. When cutting flowers and deadheading, make cut just above first five-leaflet leaf below entire cluster for best reblooming. Winter protection needed in cold climates.

Pests and Diseases: Slightly more resistant than hybrid teas; pesticide program needed.

Climate: Slightly more cold hardy than hybrid teas, Zones 5–9; winter protection in Zones 5–6.

Cultivars: Decorative: 'Betty Prior,' hot pink, single; 'Europeana,' dark crimson; 'Rose Parade,' pink; 'Bahia,' orange; 'Fashion,' coral-pink; 'Vogue,' coral. Large-flowered: 'Cherish,' pink; Apricot Nectar,' apricot; 'Saratoga,' white; 'Angel Face,' mauve.

Garden Use: Attractive in formal or mixed border; good as hedge or mass planting.

GALLICA ROSES

The oldest known cultivated rose is *R. gallica officinalis*, a rose prized by the ancient Greeks and Romans. The Crusaders brought the apothecary's rose, as it was called, to England and France, where it was used for medicinal purposes, including preventing the plague. Petals of these very fragrant flowers retain their perfume even when dried. This rose and its cultivars, bred by the Dutch and the French, were popular until the age of the modern rose.

Gallica roses have light green foliage and bloom once in early summer, producing single or semidouble flowers followed in autumn by a profuse number of showy

Gallica rose 'Rosa Mundi'

round red hips. Double-flowered forms do not produce rose hips. Flowers, which may be crimson, pink, purple, lavender, and even striped, bloom mostly on old wood. These attractive shrubs have nearly thornless branches and become showier with age.

Size: Dense and compact; 3 to 5 feet tall and wide. New canes grow upright; older ones arch outward, forming vaselike shape.

Light: Full sun.

Soil and Moisture: Tolerates poor, gravelly soil, but fertile conditions best.

Planting: Plant bare-root or container-grown plants in spring. Own-root (nongrafted) plants form thickets; grafted ones will not.

Pruning: Thin out old wood of mature plants immediately after blooming to encourage new growth for next year's flowers.

Special Care: Do not prune faded flowers.

Pests and Diseases: Disease resistant.

Climate: Zones 4–9.

Cultivars: *R. g. officinalis,* pink-red, semidouble with yellow centers; 'Charles de Mills,' dark crimson-maroon, double; 'Rosa Mundi,' semidouble, pale pink, striped crimson; 'Cardinal de Richelieu,' dark purple, small, double; 'Belle de Crécy,' bright pink changing to lavender, double.

Garden Use: Use as low hedges, in mixed borders, or in cottage or herb gardens.

GRANDIFLORA ROSES

Representing the best characteristics of its parent hybrid tea and floribunda roses, the first grandiflora rose, 'Queen Elizabeth,' was introduced in 1954. Now several colors are widely grown. The long-stemmed, hybrid-tea-like flowers form abundant clusters from early summer through fall on tall bushes. Flowers are midway in size between hybrid teas and floribundas.

Size: 5 to 6 feet tall.

Light: Full sun.

Soil and Moisture: Fertile, well-drained, moist soil; keep well watered and mulched.

Planting: Plant bare-root or container-grown plants in spring. Usually grafted to hardy rootstock.

Pruning: Remove all but five strongest canes in spring just after buds break, and cut laterals back to three buds. Remove suckers.

Special Care: Fertilize twice monthly during blooming season; withhold fertilizer one month before frost. Cut fresh or faded flower

Grandiflora rose 'Love'

clusters just above first five-leaflet leaf for best reblooming.

Pests and Diseases: Same as for hybrid teas; continual pest control program needed.

Climate: Slightly more cold hardy than hybrid teas; Zones 5/6–9. Winter protection in Zones 5–6.

Cultivars: 'Queen Elizabeth,' pink; 'Sundowner,' copper; 'Love,' red with white reverse; 'Prominent,' orange; 'Arizona,' bronze; 'John S. Armstrong,' red.

Garden Use: Use as background plants in flower border, or plant behind hybrid teas in rose beds.

HYBRID MUSK ROSES

These musk-scented shrub roses were bred in England by the Rev. Joseph Pemberton in the early 1900s. He crossed a number of popular hybrids to create this new class noted for its profusion of large clusters of highly scented flowers that resemble a long-lost musk rose ancestor (*R. moyesii*). Bearing single or semidouble flowers in shades of pink, apricot, or yellow, hybrid musks bloom heavily in spring and fall with scattered blossoms in between.

Size: 4 to 6 feet tall, with arching canes.

Light: Full sun to part shade.

Soil and Moisture: Fertile, well-drained, moist soil; keep well watered and mulched.

Planting: Plant bare-root or container-grown plants in spring.

Pruning: Cut out older canes when dormant. Clip off faded blossoms, cutting laterals back by one-third.

Special Care: Fertilize twice a month, and keep well watered for repeat bloom.

Pests and Diseases: Disease resistant.

Climate: Most are hardy only to Zones 6–9; some cultivars are more cold hardy.

Cultivars: 'Belinda,' rose-pink with white center, single; 'Ballerina,' pink with white centers, single; 'Bubble Bath,' pink, double; 'Cornelia, apricot-copper, double; 'Daybreak,'

Hybrid musk rose 'Belinda'

primrose yellow, double; 'Felicia,' pink, single; 'Moonlight,' creamy white, semidouble.
Garden Use: Attractive shrubs for landscape use; train arching types as climbers or peg canes to ground to encourage spreading into ground cover.

HYBRID PERPETUAL ROSES

These stunning roses were all the rage when first introduced to Victorian gardens because they were the first large-flowered roses that bloomed repeatedly. Hybrid perpetual roses feature very large, fully double, rounded flowers at the ends of their canes. The very fragrant blossoms bloom in spring and again in fall.

Representing the last breakthrough on the way to developing modern hybrid tea roses, hybrid perpetual roses enjoyed only a short popularity before hybrid teas eclipsed their beauty. These fine, cold-hardy, fragrant roses deserve to be rediscovered by today's gardeners.

Size: Upright and narrow; 3 to 5 feet tall.

Light: Full sun.
Soil and Moisture: Fertile, moist, well-drained soil high in organic matter.
Planting: Plant bare-root or container-grown plants in spring.
Pruning: Prune during dormancy by removing old wood and cutting main stems no more than one-half and lateral branches to one-third their length. Prune again after first flowering to encourage repeat bloom.
Special Care: Easy care.
Pests and Diseases: Suffers from black spot.
Climate: Very cold hardy; Zones 4–9.
Cultivars: 'Reine des Violettes,' purest purple of all roses, almost thornless; 'Baroness Rothschild,' soft pink, cup-shaped; 'Général Jacqueminot,' cherry-red, double, yellow center; 'Androisée de Lyon,' deep pink with purple and violet; 'Granny Grimmetts,' velvety red, double; 'Baronne Prevost,' deep rose-pink touched with lilac; 'Enfant de France,' silvery pink, double; 'Magna Charta,' pink.
Garden Use: Best trained to pillars or along low fences.

Hybrid perpetual rose 'Reine de Violettes'

Hybrid tea rose 'Tiffany'

HYBRID TEA ROSES

'La France,' the first hybrid tea rose, was introduced by a French breeder in 1867. This startling new plant, which featured a silvery pink blossom with deep pink reverse, marked the era of the modern rose. Hundreds, perhaps thousands, of cultivars exist today, making it the world's most popular rose.

Representing perfection in flower form, blossoms of hybrid tea roses have characteristic high-centered, tapered buds that gently unfold into double flowers of 20 to 50 petals. Colors may be bold reds, purples, oranges, and golds or delicate pastels and whites—every color but blue. Flowers form singly at the tips of long stems. Fragrance depends on the cultivar.

Unfortunately, the perfection in flower form is not equalled by the plant itself. Bushes grow leggy with sparse foliage and host a number of insects and diseases.

Size: 2½ to 5 feet tall.
Light: Full sun.

Soil and Moisture: Fertile, well-drained, moist soil. Keep deeply watered and mulched; do not allow to dry out.

Planting: Plant bare-root or container-grown plants in spring with bud union at or below soil surface, depending on climate.

Pruning: Remove all but three to five strongest canes in spring just after buds break. Prune remaining canes back to 1 to 2 feet tall, cutting to an outward-facing bud. Remove any suckers from understock.

Special Care: Fertilize twice monthly during blooming season; withhold fertilizer one month before frost. When cutting flowers, make cut just above first five-leaflet leaf for best reblooming. Winter protection needed in cold climates. Even well-grown plants seldom live more than 10 years.

Pests and Diseases: Aphids, spider mites, Japanese beetles, and rose chafers may be serious. Powdery mildew, black spot, and rust may defoliate bushes; worse where foliage gets wet. Continual pest control program needed for high-quality flowers.

Climate: Zones 5–9, depending on cultivar; winter protection in Zones 5–6.

Large-flowered climbing rose 'Madame Grégoire Staechelin'

Cultivars: Hundreds of cultivars. Most popular are: 'Peace,' yellow edged pink; 'Mr. Lincoln,' red; 'Double Delight,' red blend; 'Garden Party,' white with lavender edge; 'Tropicana,' orange-red; 'Tiffany,' medium pink blending to yellow; 'Royal Highness,' pink; 'First Prize,' pink.

Garden Use: Grown for exhibition blooms or cut flowers rather than garden appearance. Bushes not attractive. Plant in formal beds and camouflage bottoms of leggy plants with low hedges or other plants.

LARGE-FLOWERED CLIMBING ROSES

These elegant roses are usually sports of modern bush varieties of the same name with long, supple canes that can be trained to fences or trellises. Climbing roses do not really climb, because they can't entwine, nor do they have twining tendrils, so you'll need to tie them to supports. Large-flowered climbers usually bloom heavily once in spring and sporadically through fall.

Size: 7 to 10 feet tall.

Light: Full sun.

Soil and Moisture: Fertile, well-drained, moist soil; keep mulched and well watered.

Planting: Plant bare-root or container-grown roses in spring.

Pruning: Remove oldest and weakest canes at their bases while dormant, leaving a total of five to eight newest, strongest canes. Cut side branches back to three buds.

Special Care: Cut faded flowers as for hybrid teas. Tie canes to trellis, pillar, arch, or fence; horizontal canes produce the most flowers. Fertilize twice monthly until one month before frost. To overwinter in cold climates, partially dig up roots, tilt plant, lay canes on ground, and bury with soil.

Pests and Diseases: Same as for hybrid teas.

Climate: Zones 5–9; best in warmer zones where they can reach greater heights. Winter protection in Zones 5–7.

Meidiland rose 'Alba'

Cultivars: 'Climbing Peace,' yellow and pink; 'Climbing Golden Dawn,' yellow; 'New Dawn,' silvery pink; 'Elegance,' yellow; 'Madame Grégoire Staechelin,' shell pink; 'Climbing American Beauty,' red; 'Don Juan,' red; 'America,' coral pink; 'Blaze Improved,' red; 'White Dawn,' white.

Garden Use: Elegant trained to adorn walls, pillars, or trellises.

MEIDILAND ROSES

This recently developed group of French-bred shrub and ground-cover roses are promoted as excellent landscape plants. They look stunning covering a bank or weeping over a wall, displaying sprays of pretty flowers in bursts from early summer through fall. They are not, however, maintenance-free plants. As with almost all roses, good soil, full sun, and plenty of water and fertilizer produce the best flowers.

Size: Hedge types reach 3 to 4 feet tall and 2 to 3 feet wide; ground-cover types spread 5 to 6 feet across with arching canes 2 to 3 feet tall.

Light: Full sun.

Soil and Moisture: Fertile, well-drained, moist soil; keep well watered and mulched.

Planting and Propagation: Plant bare-root or container-grown plants in spring. Space ground-cover types 3 to 4 feet apart.

Pruning: Cut back every few years to renew.

Special Care: Remove sprays of faded flowers to encourage rebloom; remove deadwood.

Pests and Diseases: May suffer from blackspot and usual pests, despite contrary claims.

Climate: Zones 4–9.

Cultivars: Hedges: 'Bonica,' double, fragrant, pale pink blossoms; 'Meidiland Pink,' pink, single, white centers. Ground covers: 'Alba,' tiny, white, double flowers in profuse clusters; 'White Meidiland,' large, white, double flowers in clusters; 'Scarlet Meidiland,' deep red, double; 'Pearl Meidiland,' very pale pink, double; 'Red Meidiland,' red, single, white centers.

Garden Use: Ground-cover types make excellent bank covers; train to weep over walls. Use bushes as hedges or specimens.

MINIATURE ROSES

Growing no more than 1½ feet tall and wide with diminutive flowers and leaves to match, miniature roses seem like tiny versions of their big sisters. Indeed, the flowers of some miniatures have high centers, like hybrid tea roses; others produce sprays of decorative blossoms like floribundas. These petite beauties are becoming more and more popular, with new cultivars available every year.

Size: 6 inches to 1½ feet tall.

Light: Full to half sun.

Soil and Moisture: Fertile, well-drained, moist soil; keep well watered and mulched.

Planting: Plant bare-root or container-grown roses in spring; needs at least 1 cubic foot of soil if grown in container.

Pruning: Prune when dormant, removing all but six strong new canes and cutting these back by half.

Miniature rose

Special Care: Fertilize twice monthly until a month before frost. Keep container plants well watered. Prune off faded blossoms.

Pests and Diseases: Same as hybrid teas, but spider mites especially troublesome.

Climate: Zones 5–9; winter protection in Zones 5–6.

Cultivars: 'Child's Play,' white with pink edges; 'Small Miracle,' white; 'Jitter Bug,' orange; 'New Beginning,' orange-red; 'Pinstripe,' red-and-white; 'Charm Bracelet,' golden yellow; 'Cartwheel,' pink-and-white; 'Little Sizzler,' dark red.

Garden Use: Delightful in window boxes or containers and as edging for flower border or formal rose garden.

MOSS ROSES

Moss roses, named for the eye-catching mossy spines covering their flower buds and stem tips, were favorites of Empress Josephine, Napoleon's wife. These roses, hybridized between 1850 and 1870, originated as mutations of centifolia and autumn damask roses. The mossy spines vary from soft to bristlelike and emit a resinous fragrance; the cabbage-shaped flowers emit a rich fragrance. Although most moss roses bloom abundantly only once a year, autumn brings attractive red hips set off against the mossy stem tips.

Size: More stiff and upright than centifolia roses; to 6 feet tall.

Light: Full sun.

Soil and Moisture: Fertile, well-drained, moist soil; keep well watered and mulched.

Planting: Plant bare-root or container-grown plants in spring.

Pruning: Prune as for centifolias.

Special Care: Easy care.

Pests and Diseases: Blossoms susceptible to botrytis blight fungus; avoid wetting flowers and foliage.

Climate: Zones 4–9.

Cultivars: 'Comtesse de Murinais,' rich pink changing to white; 'Salet,' bright pink, rebloomer; 'Perpetual White Moss,' white double, rebloomer; 'Maréchal daVoust,' mauve turning purple; compact shrub; 'Hunslet Moss,' rose-pink.

Garden Use: Cottage garden.

Moss rose 'Maréchal daVoust'

Polyantha rose 'The Fairy'

POLYANTHA ROSES

These low-growing, compact shrubs originated in the late 19th century as hybrids between *R. multiflora*, an American rose with clusters of prolific small blossoms, and *R. chinensis*, a tender Chinese rose with repeat bloom. Polyanthas feature dense clusters of dainty white, pink, orange, red, or yellow flowers borne in waves from late spring through fall. They have neat, fine-textured leaves and make excellent low-maintenance landscape plants for the front of a mixed border or cottage garden.

Size: Compact plants up to 2 feet tall.
Light: Full sun.
Soil and Moisture: Fertile, well-drained, moist soil; keep well watered and mulched.
Planting: Plant bare-root or container-grown plants in spring.
Pruning: Cut off faded flower clusters by pruning lateral branches back about one-third their length for repeat bloom.
Special Care: Keep well watered, and fertilize twice monthly for repeat bloom.

Pests and Diseases: Not badly troubled by insects and diseases.
Climate: Zones 4–9; winter protection in Zone 4.
Cultivars and Similar Species: 'The Fairy,' pink; 'Margo Koster,' salmon-orange; 'China Doll,' pink-and-white; 'Cécile Brünner,' pale pink; 'Nathalie Nypels,' rose-pink. Climbers: 'Climbing Cécile Brünner'; 'Climbing Margo Koster.'
Garden Use: Good for low hedges; use in mixed border or cottage garden.

PORTLAND ROSES

Also called the damask perpetual, these roses descended from a single, red, repeat-flowering rose with damask ancestry, which was found around 1800 at the Duchess of Portland's estate in England. This rose was sent to Andre DuPont, gardener to Empress Josephine and Emperor Napoleon, and he named it 'Duchess of Portland.' Numerous hybrids, which became parents of the hybrid perpetual roses, soon followed.

Portland roses feature blossoms on short stems with foliage closely nestled just beneath the flowers. Their garden value lies in their repeat show of richly fragrant, old-rose-type blossoms.

Portland rose 'Jacques Cartier'

Size: Shorter than damasks; to 4 feet tall.
Light: Full sun.
Soil and Moisture: Fertile, well-drained, moist soil; keep well watered and mulched.
Planting and Propagation: Plant bare-root or container-grown plants in spring.
Pruning: Prune mature plants when dormant, shortening main branches by one-third and others by two-thirds. Deadhead and encourage repeat bloom by cutting back laterals about one-third. Remove older wood at ground level every few years.
Special Care: Fertilize regularly to encourage repeat bloom. Keep well watered.
Pests and Diseases: Usually disease and pest resistant.
Climate: Zones 5–9.
Cultivars: 'Comte de Chambord,' bright pink changing to mauve; 'Jacques Cartier,' rich pink with green eye; 'Sidonie,' rose-pink; 'Delambre,' red.
Garden Use: Compact plants suited to small gardens and mixed borders.

RAMBLER ROSES

A rambling rose's untamed look and profusion of fragrant flowers brings romance to any garden. Bouquets of small blossoms open in breathtaking profusion, putting on a show for several weeks in early summer or midsummer. Although they don't actually climb, the long, pliable canes can easily be coaxed to clamber over an archway, along a fence, or up and over a roof. Some types can be encouraged to scale a tree, where their thorns help hold them in place.

Size: 20 to 50 feet tall.
Light: Full sun.
Soil and Moisture: Fertile, moist, well-drained soil high in organic matter. Keep mulched and well watered.
Planting: Plant container-grown or bare-root plants in spring.
Pruning: Blooms on year-old wood; cut off flowering canes at base immediately after blooming and tie up new growth.

Rambling rose 'Goldfinch'

Special Care: Tie or secure to support. Fertilize before and after blooming.

Pests and Diseases: Powdery mildew may be troublesome if air circulation is poor.

Climate: Multiflora ramblers, Zones 5/6–9; wichuraiana ramblers, Zones 4–9; sempervirens ramblers, Zones 6–9; noisette ramblers, Zones 7–10.

Cultivars: Wichuraiana: 'Etain,' salmon-pink; 'Ethel,' lilac-pink; 'Lady Gay,' rose-pink; 'Jersey Beauty,' yellow, single. Multiflora: 'Goldfinch,' golden aging to cream; 'Apple Blossom,' pastel pink; 'Bobbie James,' creamy white, semidouble; 'Bleu Magenta,' deep purple-blue aging to violet; 'Trausendschon,' pink, semidouble; 'Veilchenblau,' purple-violet aging to lilac-blue. Sempervirens: 'Princess Louise,' creamy blush pink; 'Félicité et Perpétue,' pink buds opening creamy. Noisette: 'Claire Jacquier,' yellow, repeats; 'Madame Alfred Carrière,' pearl pink, continuous.

Garden Use: Delightful in cottage garden trained on fences, arbors, trellises, or arches. Can be trained to scramble over roof of house or shed or into tree.

REDLEAF ROSE

Unusual for a rose, this beautiful shrub is grown more for its foliage than for its flowers. The leaves of the redleaf rose (*Rosa glauca* syn. *R. rubrifolia*) are a dusky gray-purple with reddish edges and a silvery sheen along the veins, making a striking accent amid garden greenery. The small, single rose-pink blossoms have starry white centers and sparkle against the dark leaves for two months in spring and early summer. In fall, the foliage turns orange and scarlet, accompanied by eye-catching clusters of cranberry-size red hips.

Size: Vase-shaped; 6 to 8 feet tall and wide.

Light: Full sun.

Soil and Moisture: Plant in fertile, well drained soil rich in organic matter.

Planting: Plant bare-root or container-grown shrubs in spring.

Pruning: Blooms on old wood. Prune out oldest canes after blooming.

Special Care: Easy to maintain.

Pests and Diseases: Disease free.

Climate: Zones 2–8.

Cultivars: 'Carmenetta,' larger flowers.

Garden Use: Use for foliage color contrast in shrub or mixed borders; elegant with pink, blue, and lavender flowers.

RUGOSA ROSES

Among the most beautiful and certainly the toughest of the shrub roses, *R. rugosa* and its cultivars produce fragrant flowers all summer. The large single or semidouble flowers may be pink, rose-red, or white and feature prominent clusters of yellow anthers in their centers. These ripen into large, glossy red rose hips that cling to the stout, thorny stems from fall well into winter. The crinkled texture of the disease-resistant leaves gives them wonderful garden impact, especially when they turn brilliant shades of orange to gold in autumn.

Redleaf rose

Rugosa rose

R. rugosa, sometimes called the beach rose, is native to Japan and Siberia but has naturalized along North America's eastern seaboard. Many cultivars are available, and the species has been used extensively in hybridizing modern shrub roses.

Size: 4 feet tall; 6 feet wide. Stout, arching canes.

Light: Full sun.

Soil and Moisture: Tolerates poor, dry soil.

Planting and Propagation: Usually grown on own roots. Plant container-grown plants in spring, summer, or fall. May be grafted, but best to purchase nongrafted plants.

Pruning: Cut out 3- or 4-year-old canes each fall. Remove suckers from grafted plants.

Special Care: Easy to maintain. Do not remove faded flowers if hips are desired.

Pests and Diseases: Foliage of species is highly disease resistant; some cultivars susceptible to black spot. Japanese beetles and aphids may be troublesome.

Climate: Zones 2–9. Tolerates wind and salt-spray.

Cultivars: 'Blanc Double de Coubert,' double, white, no hips, considered finest white landscape rose; 'Frau Dagmar Hastrup,' 2 to 3 feet tall, silvery pink; 'Therese Bugnet,' deep red changing to rosy pink, very fragrant, red winter stems; 'Pink Grootendorst,' clusters of small pink flowers with unique pinked edges; 'Hansa,' double, reddish purple.

Garden Use: Excellent seaside and xeriscape plant. Beautiful in mixed borders. Attractive year-round.

SHRUB ROSES

This catchall category includes large-flowered, tall, bushy modern roses that don't fit neatly into other categories. Most, however, are tough performers whose repeat bloom, cold hardiness, and ease of care make them ideal roses for low-maintenance gardens.

Size: Tall to low growing, depending on type and cultivar.

Light: Full sun.

Soil and Moisture: Fertile, well-drained, moist soil; keep mulched and well watered.

Planting: Plant bare-root or container-grown shrubs in spring.

Pruning: Remove deadwood yearly. Cut back and thin canes every few years to renew.

Special Care: Easy to maintain.

Shrub rose 'Fred Loads'

Pests and Diseases: Generally disease resistant, although insects may be troublesome.

Climate: Zones 4/5–9, depending on particular cultivar.

Cultivars: 'Carefree Beauty,' pink, semidouble; 'Golden Wings,' yellow, single; 'Sparrieshoop,' light pink, single; 'Fred Loads,' orange, single; 'Dortmund,' red, single, climber; 'Nearly Wild,' pink, single. See also entries for Rugosa, Meidiland, Canadian, English, and Hybrid Musk roses.

Garden Use: Excellent for mass plantings or in shrub and mixed borders.

TREE ROSES

Elegant tree roses are actually standards featuring an eye-level ball of foliage and flowers atop a tall, straight stem. These creations come from grafting a bush-type rose to a tall, sturdy trunk and rootstock. Almost any type of rose can be made into a standard, but typically hybrid teas, grandifloras, and floribundas are used.

Size: To 5 feet tall.

Tree rose

Light: Full sun.

Soil and Moisture: Fertile, well-drained, moist soil; keep mulched and well watered.

Planting: Plant container-grown plants in spring with bud union at or below soil surface, depending on climate. May be planted in decorative pots or in ground.

Pruning: Prune out selected oldest and weakest canes when dormant, keeping symmetrical shape. Remove suckers from trunk.

Special Care: Stake trunk to keep it straight. Where temperatures fall below 28°F, protect graft union in winter by partially digging up plant, tipping it over and laying it on the ground, and burying it with soil until spring.

Pests and Diseases: Same as for hybrid teas.

Climate: Zones 5–9; needs winter protection in Zones 5–7.

Cultivars: Almost any bush-type rose can be made into tree rose.

Garden Use: Use in formal settings as focal point or to frame entrance. Often planted in containers.

ORNAMENTAL GRASSES

Rustling and swaying in the wind, ornamental grasses bring graceful movement and architectural beauty to a garden.

Briza media
QUAKING GRASS,
RATTLESNAKE GRASS

The flowers of this small, clump-forming, cool-season evergreen grass resemble rattlesnake tails. Opening luminescent green and faintly striped with purple in spring and maturing to golden seed heads in summer, the tiny flower spikelets shake and quiver delightfully in the slightest breeze, but shatter by summer's end. Flower stalks rise above the dense clumps of soft-to-the-touch linear leaves. Cut flowers at various stages of maturity for both green and tan flowers for fresh and dried arrangements.

Size: 1- to 1½-foot-tall leaf clumps; flowers 1 foot taller.
Light: Full sun to part shade.
Soil and Moisture: Average to poor, moist to wet soil; becomes coarse in fertile soil.
Planting and Propagation: Plant container-grown plants in spring, spacing 2 feet apart, or sow seeds. Divide in spring or fall.
Special Care: Remove tattered flower heads. If looks ragged, cut back to several inches from ground in summer to renew.

Briza media

Pests and Diseases: Usually pest free.
Climate: Zones 4–8; tolerates heat with regular water.
Similar Species: *B. maxima* (annual quaking grass), 2 to 3 feet tall, loose quaking spikes of large, light green spikelets in early summer; naturalize in meadows or use in cut-flower gardens.
Garden Use: Individual plants not very interesting; best used as ground cover in meadow or naturalistic garden or in cut-flower garden.

Calamagrostis acutiflora 'Stricta'
FEATHER REED GRASS

This stiffly upright, cool-season clump grass changes alluringly through the seasons. Spring brings a fountain of light green leaves, which by early summer are topped with tall, feathery pink inflorescences. These change to light purple and by midsummer ripen into golden wheatlike sheaves. The sterile seed heads remain attractive into fall, when the green leaves turn gold, and stand through winter.

Size: 3 to 4 feet tall; 2 to 3 feet wide.

Calamagrostis acutiflora 'Stricta'

Carex morrowii

Light: Best in full sun; tolerates half shade.
Soil and Moisture: Average to heavy, well-drained to wet soil.
Planting and Propagation: Plant container-grown plants in spring, spacing 3 feet apart.
Special Care: Cut back in late winter.
Pests and Diseases: Foliage rust disease an occasional problem.
Climate: Zones 5–9.
Cultivars and Similar Species: 'Karl Foerster,' 5 to 6 feet tall, blooms two weeks earlier.
Garden Use: Handsome, very stiff specimen in formal gardens; mass-plant in New American-style landscape, as screening, or around ponds.

Carex morrowii
JAPANESE SEDGE GRASS

Forming a dense, arching mound of stiff ½-inch-wide leaves, this plant thrives in shade, remaining evergreen or semi-evergreen through most winters to add texture and color to the dull months. Flowers are insignificant, tucked among the leaves in summer. Variegated forms with gold or white stripes are most popular.

375

Size: 1 to 1½ feet tall; 2 to 3 feet wide.
Light: Light to full shade.
Soil and Moisture: Fertile to average, well-drained, moist soil; plentiful moisture.
Planting and Propagation: Plant container-grown plants in spring, spacing 3 feet apart. Divide clumps in spring.
Special Care: Hand-pull winter-tattered leaves from clumps; do not cut back.
Pests and Diseases: Usually pest free.
Climate: Zones 5–9.
Cultivars: 'Variegata,' green with thin white leaf margins; 'Goldband,' gold-striped leaf edges, Zones 7–9; 'Aureo-variegata,' broad creamy-yellow-striped edges, floppy leaves with tips curling under.
Garden Use: Variegated forms especially nice in shade gardens; use as specimen or plant as ground cover in shade gardens.

Carex stricta 'Bowles Golden'
BOWLES GOLDEN GRASS

Sending up light green shoots in spring, this charming cool-season plant brings welcome greenery to shady sites. The narrow upright leaves cascade at their tips, creating a loose vase-shaped mound of cascading foliage that turns luminous golden green or chartreuse with narrow green margins in summer.

Carex stricta 'Bowles Golden'

Brightest yellow of all the grasses, Bowles golden grass retains its color until a heavy frost. Flowers are not showy.
Size: 1⅓ feet tall and wide.
Light: Light to full shade; more shade needed in the South than in the North.
Soil and Moisture: Humus-rich, well-drained to wet soil; plentiful moisture.
Planting and Propagation: Plant container-grown plants in spring, spacing 1 to 1½ feet apart. Divide in spring or fall.
Special Care: Cut back dried leaves.
Pests and Diseases: Usually pest free.
Climate: Zone 5–9.
Cultivars and Similar Species: *C. buchananii* (leatherleaf sedge), fine-textured cinnamon-bronze leaves; interesting contrast to green or blue plants; Zones 6–9.
Garden Use: Creates effect of sunlight in shade garden. Makes excellent companion to gold-variegated hostas. Does well in wet sites beside pond or stream.

Chasmanthium latifolium (Uniola latifolia)
NORTHERN SEA OATS, WILD OATS

This warm-season native grass forms graceful, bamboolike, vase-shaped clumps of light to dark green foliage, which change to copper in fall and bleach to tan in winter. Arching spikes of flat, nodding flowers and seedheads look decorative and rustle in the wind. They start out purple-tinged green in mid- to late summer and finally age to bronze in winter. Makes a lovely cut flower for fresh and dried arrangements.
Size: 2 to 3 feet tall and wide.
Light: Part shade best.
Soil and Moisture: Fertile to poor, well-drained to wet soil; best with moderate to plentiful moisture, but tolerates drought.
Planting and Propagation: Sow seeds or plant container-grown plants in spring, spacing 1½ feet apart. Divide in spring when crowded.
Special Care: Reseeds but is not weedy.

Chasmanthium latifolium

Becomes light yellow-green in too much sun. Leaf tips brown if too dry.
Pests and Diseases: Usually pest free.
Climate: Zones 5–9. Good seashore plant.
Cultivars: Only species is sold.
Garden Use: Excellent in flower gardens or massed in meadows or along sides of streams. Include in cut-flower gardens.

Cortaderia selloana 'Pumila'
DWARF PAMPAS GRASS

A midget compared to the species, this smaller-growing selection of a normally 10-foot-tall-and-wide species fits better in most gardens. Its razor-edged evergreen leaves form dense weeping mounds that are topped in

Cortaderia selloana

autumn with flamboyant shaggy plumes of creamy white flowers that resemble huge feather dusters. Flowers remain showy into winter.

Size: Foliage 3 feet tall; flowers reach 4 to 6 feet tall.

Light: Full sun to part shade.

Soil and Moisture: Fertile, well-drained soil; moderate to plentiful moisture.

Planting and Propagation: Plant container-grown plants in spring, spacing 5 feet apart. Divide with axe in early spring if needed.

Special Care: Cut flowers for arrangements when freshly opened to avoid shattering. May rot in winter-wet site. Cut back winter-damaged leaves or thin out old foliage in spring, wearing protective clothing.

Pests and Diseases: Usually pest free.

Climate: Zones 8–10; to Zone 7 in protected site. Use as annual elsewhere.

Cultivars: 'Argentea,' silver plumes, 9 to 12 feet tall; 'Carminea Rendatleri,' pink plumes, 8 to 9 feet tall; 'Silver Comet,' variegated, 6 to 8 feet tall, Zones 7–10.

Garden Use: Use as specimen in large-scale garden. Eye-catching near water and where struck from behind by sunlight.

Deschampsia caespitosa
TUFTED HAIR GRASS

This cool-season grass features low hummocks of dark green, rough-textured, very narrow pleated leaves. One of the earliest-blooming grasses, tufted hair grass sends up numerous stems of delicate airy inflorescences that form a mist of silky green above the foliage in late spring. Flowers turn yellow to gold, then bronze or purple as ripening progresses. Seed heads often remain ornamental into late winter. Leaves are evergreen in mild climates, turn russet in winter in cool climates.

Size: Foliage 1 to 3 feet tall; flowers 2 to 3 feet taller.

Light: Full sun to part shade.

Soil and Moisture: Average to fertile, well-drained to damp soil; best with moderate moisture.

Planting and Propagation: Sow seeds or plant container-grown plants in spring, spacing 3 feet apart. Divide in spring or fall.

Special Care: Cut back flower stalks when unsightly or in late winter; rake out winter-tattered foliage. May brown in hot, dry sites in summer. Flowers last longest if protected from winter wind.

Pests and Diseases: Rabbits may eat plants.

Climate: Zones 3–9; flowers showiest in cool zones.

Cultivars: 'Bronzeschleier' ('Bronze Veil'), bronze-yellow seed heads; 'Goldschleier' ('Golden Veil'), bright yellow seed heads.

Garden Use: Elegant used in drifts against dark background in borders and shade gardens. Use as ground cover in moist sites.

Elymus arenarius 'Glaucus'
BLUE WILD RYE, BLUE LYME GRASS

Spreading by rhizomes to form stands of bright blue-gray leaves, blue wild rye creates a beautiful long-lasting accent in a flower garden. It's the largest of the blue-colored grasses and valued as a colorful foliage plant. The sturdy warm-season plant looks attractive all year, changing in late fall and winter from blue to yellow to bright beige in cold climates but remaining evergreen or semi-evergreen in mild areas. The beige flowers that sometimes appear in summer are insignificant.

Size: 1 to 2 feet tall; 2 to 3 feet wide.

Light: Full sun to light shade.

Soil and Moisture: Heavy to sandy, dry to wet soil; spreads less aggressively in heavy or dry soil.

Planting and Propagation: Plant bare-root or container-grown plants in spring, spacing 3 to 5 feet apart. Divide in spring, as needed, to control growth.

Special Care: Plant in bottomless container sunk in ground to control spread in flower gardens. Mow or cut back in spring, even where evergreen, to stimulate brightly colored new growth.

Pests and Diseases: Usually pest free.

Climate: Zones 3–10; tolerates hot, dry sites and seashore conditions.

Cultivars and Similar Species: Often mislabeled *E. glaucus*, a less invasive blue species native to California but rarely available, or sold simply as *E. arenarius*.

Garden Use: Use as specimen in flower garden; combines well with pink, white, pastel yellow, and purple flowers. Mass-plant for erosion control on banks and at seashores.

Deschampsia caespitosa

Elymus arenarius 'Glaucus'

Festuca ovina 'Elijah Blue'

Festuca ovina 'Glauca' (*F. cinerea, F. glauca,* and *F. arvernensis*)
BLUE FESCUE, BLUE SHEEP'S FESCUE

This petite cool-season grass is everyone's favorite, because it forms cute hedgehoglike mounds of fine-textured, pale silvery blue leaves. Its perfect symmetry and neat appearance gives blue fescue a pleasing character that endures throughout the year because the foliage is evergreen, retaining its lovely color through winter. Tall stalks of fine-textured green flowers, which age to tan, wave above the foliage in summer.

Size: 6 inches to 1 foot tall and wide.

Light: Full sun.

Soil and Moisture: Average to poor, well-drained soil; moderate moisture. Best in low-fertility soils; tolerates drought.

Planting and Propagation: Plant container-grown plants in spring, spacing 1 foot apart. Divide every three years in spring or fall to prevent dead centers and maintain best foliage color.

Special Care: May rot in winter-wet site or if heavily mulched in summer. Cut back to 3 to 4 inches in late winter.

Pests and Diseases: Crown rot if heavily mulched in summer.

Climate: Zones 4–9, but best in cool regions; suffers in heat and humidity.

Cultivars: 'Elijah Blue,' icy blue, retains color through summer heat, 10-inch mounds; 'Solling,' blue-gray in spring and summer, red-brown in fall and winter, 8 inches tall, no

378

---

flowers; 'Bluefinch,' 6 to 8 inches tall, fine-textured; 'Tom Thumb,' silver-blue in spring, green in summer, 4 inches tall, ground cover; 'Sea Urchin,' silvery-blue-gray, medium textured, 1 foot tall. *F. amethystina* (sheep's fescue): blue-green, fine-textured, 1-foot mounds with 1½- to 2½-foot-tall flowers; 'Superba,' showy flowers.

Garden Use: Combines well with pastel pink, yellow, or white flowers, and purple foliage. Use as edging, as ground cover, or in rock gardens.

Hakonechloa macra (*Phragmites macra*)
JAPANESE WIND GRASS, HAKONE GRASS

This low, slow-spreading, cool-season grass displays elegant, bright green, bamboolike leaves that cascade toward the light from short, wiry stems. Sprays of dainty flowers bloom among the leaves in late summer and fall, adding a soft mist around the leaves. Foliage turns an alluring pinkish red in fall and bleaches to bright tan in winter. The golden-variegated cultivar is even more beautiful and more widely grown.

Size: 1 to 2 feet tall.

Light: Light to half shade.

Soil and Moisture: Humus-rich, fertile, well-drained, moist soil; plentiful moisture.

Planting and Propagation: Plant container-grown plants in spring, spacing 1½ feet apart. Divide in spring when crowded.

Special Care: Foliage burns in too much sun. Cut back dried foliage in late winter.

Pests and Diseases: Usually pest free.

Climate: Zones 4–9, with winter protection in colder zones.

Cultivars: 'Aureola,' bright yellow to creamy white foliage streaked with green, leaves burn in too much sun, Zones 6–9.

Garden Use: Excellent planted to weep over rocky slope or beside waterfall. Use as specimen or ground cover in shade, rock, and woodland gardens. Combines well with hostas.

Hakonechloa macra 'Aureola'

Helictotrichon sempervirens
BLUE OAT GRASS

Resembling a larger, bolder blue fescue, blue oat grass forms spiky, metallic-blue hummocks of sharp-pointed leaves. Attractive blue-gray one-sided flowers on wiry stems dance above the leaves in early summer and dry to golden tan by midsummer. This cool-season grass remains evergreen in mild climates and is semi-evergreen in cold climates.

Size: Foliage 1 to 1½ feet tall; flowers 1 to 2 feet taller.

Helictotrichon sempervirens

Light: Full sun to part shade.

Soil and Moisture: Fertile, humus-rich, moist, well-drained soil; moderate moisture.

Planting and Propagation: Sow seeds or plant container-grown plants in spring, spacing 3 feet apart. Divide in spring if centers become bare.

Special Care: Rake out winter-tattered leaves in early spring.

Pests and Diseases: Root rot in wet site or heavy soil. Rust fungus in too much shade.

Climate: Zones 4–8; best in cooler regions. Performs poorly in areas with high summer rainfall and humidity.

Cultivars: Only species is sold.

Garden Use: Nice contrasting color and texture as specimen in flower or rock garden; also works well mass planted.

Imperata cylindrica 'Red Baron'
JAPANESE BLOOD GRASS

The narrow, upright grassy leaves of Japanese blood grass emerge green with red tips in spring, and gradually become redder. By summer they create a stunning two-tone effect. Autumn transforms the foliage to flaming scarlet until frost turns it bronze and winter bleaches it straw colored. This warm-

Imperata cylindrica 'Red Baron'

season grass does not bloom and spreads slowly by rhizomes to form attractive light-catching clumps.

Size: 1 to 2 feet tall and wide.

Light: Best color in full sun; grows well in light to part shade but is less red. Provide some midday shade in hot regions.

Soil and Moisture: Fertile, humus-rich, well-drained, moist soil; plentiful moisture.

Planting and Propagation: Plant container-grown plants in spring, spacing 1 to 2 feet apart. Divide in spring if crowded.

Special Care: Reversions to all-green should be pulled immediately because they spread aggressively and are pernicious weeds. Performs poorly in hot, dry sites or heavy, wet soil.

Pests and Diseases: Usually pest free.

Climate: Zones 5–9; perhaps to Zone 4 with winter protection.

Cultivars: This is only cultivar.

Garden Use: Plant in ribbons in front of border or rock garden where sunlight strikes foliage from behind or side.

Milium effusum 'Aureum'
GOLDEN WOOD MILLET

This cool-season evergreen grass forms loose clumps of bright yellow-green leaves topped with a sparkling cloud of tiny golden yellow flowers in early summer. New spring growth is bright yellow and becomes yellow-green with maturity.

Size: Foliage clumps 1 to 1½ feet tall; flowers 1 to 1½ feet taller.

Light: Light shade best; tolerates full shade.

Soil and Moisture: Fertile, humus-rich, moist soil; plentiful moisture.

Planting and Propagation: Sow seeds or plant container-grown plants in spring, spacing 2 to 3 feet apart. Divide when clumps become crowded, in spring.

Special Care: May self-sow; select the most golden seedlings to propagate.

Pests and Diseases: Usually pest free.

Milium effusum 'Aureum'

Climate: Zones 6–8; may die in hot summer weather or hot regions.

Cultivars and Similar Species: Green species form is less eye-catching but makes a pretty, somewhat taller plant.

Garden Use: Plant as specimen or in group to brighten shade gardens and borders. Useful on edge of woodland.

Miscanthus sinensis
EULALIA GRASS, SILVER GRASS

This outstanding warm-season grass brings gardeners a wealth of showy cultivars valued for both foliage and flowers. Leaves of the species, which are 1 inch wide and dark green with a white midrib, form huge vase-shaped clumps. Inflorescenses begin in late summer as drooping, purple-tinged fans. These open to long, silky spikelets that mature after frost to dazzling curly plumes of silvery hairs. The foliage and plumes bleach to the color of dried corn husks and stand proudly through winter's ice and snow. Cultivars are variations on the theme, featuring narrower leaves, variegated foliage, excellent fall color, or more silvery flowers in a variety of sizes.

Size: 3 to 15 feet tall; 3 to 8 feet wide.

Light: Full sun best; flops with shade.

Soil and Moisture: Average to heavy soil; moderate to wet conditions. Drought tolerant.

Planting and Propagation: Plant bare-root or container-grown plants in spring, spacing

Miscanthus sinensis

3 to 6 feet apart, according to size. Divide every five or more years, when centers become bare and plants flop open.

Special Care: Drought resistant, but leaf tips may burn. Cut back to ground in late winter with hedge shears or weed-whacker.

Pests and Diseases: Usually pest free.

Climate: Zones 4–9.

Cultivars: 'Condensatus,' broad leaves, white midribs, bronze seed heads, 6 to 8 feet tall; 'Gracillimus' (maiden grass, Japanese silver grass), 3 to 4 feet tall, very silvery plumes, narrow leaves with white midrib, vase-shaped; 'Morning Light,' very narrow leaves with thin white edges that make the leaves appear gray-green, very silvery plumes, 4 feet tall; 'Silver Feather,' 6 to 7 feet tall, silvery-white early plumes; 'Zebrinus' (zebra grass), wide leaves banded horizontally with gold, tolerates wet soil, floppy; 'Strictus' (porcupine grass), gold horizontal bands, more stiffly upright; 'Graziella,' wide leaves with broad silver midribs, deep burgundy fall color, 4 to 5 feet tall; 'Variegatus,' wide leaves with creamy white vertical stripes, 5 to 6 feet tall, floppy, tolerates some shade; 'Cosmopolitan,' wide white stripes, 6 to 7 feet tall, nonfloppy; 'Purpurascens' (flamegrass), 4 to 5 feet tall, narrow foliage turns orange-red in fall in sun, salmon, pink, or gold in part shade, early blooming, needs moisture.

Garden Use: Use as specimen in mixed borders; mass-plant in New American-style gardens or as screen. Excellent with evergreen background. Be sure to allow enough space.

380

Molinia caerulea

MOOR GRASS, PURPLE MOOR GRASS

Upright to slightly arching light green leaves form neat mounds that turn brilliant bright yellow or orange-yellow in fall. The slender spikes of purplish flowers rise over the plants, forming a see-through mist in summer that turns tawny and remains effective through fall. Moor grass is not effective in winter because the leaves shatter and drop to the ground with the first heavy rains.

Size: Foliage 1½ feet tall, 2 feet wide; flowers 1 to 2 feet taller and arch 3 to 4 feet wide.

Light: Full sun; light shade in the South.

Soil and Moisture: Fertile, humus-rich, moist, well-drained, acid soil; plentiful water.

Planting and Propagation: Plant container-grown plants in spring, spacing 3 feet apart. Rarely needs division.

Special Care: Slow to establish; may not bloom for several years.

Pests and Diseases: Leaf spots if too humid and moist; provide air circulation.

Climate: Zones 4–8; good seashore plant.

Cultivars and Similar Species: 'Variegata,' cascading green leaves with creamy yellow stripes, 1 to 1½ feet tall, purple flowers 6 inches to 1 foot above, foliage longer lasting

Molinia caerulea 'Skyracer'

in winter. *M. c. arundinacea* (tall moor grass): gray-green foliage to 2 to 3 feet tall, flowers 3 to 4 feet above, Zones 5–8; 'Skyracer,' flower stalks to 8 feet tall, fine texture; 'Windspiel,' golden flowers.

Garden Use: Use as specimen or in mass planting in borders and rock gardens; best with dark background.

Ophiopogon planiscapus 'Nigrescens'

BLACK MONDO GRASS

Not a true grass, but resembling ornamental grasses in appearance and behavior, this unusual foliage plant is a standout in any garden, especially when contrasted with brighter flowers and foliage. It forms slowly spreading clumps of purple leaves that are so dark they are almost black. Pink-tinted white flowers bloom on short spikes among the leaves in midsummer, followed by clusters of black berries.

Size: 6 inches tall; 1 foot wide.

Light: Full sun to part shade.

Soil and Moisture: Fertile, humus-rich, moist soil; plentiful moisture.

Planting and Propagation: Plant bare-root or container-grown plants in spring, spacing

Ophiopogon planiscapus 'Black Knight'

1 foot apart. Divide in spring only when crowded.

Special Care: Slow growing.

Pests and Diseases: Usually pest free.

Climate: Zones 6–9.

Cultivars and Similar Species: *O. japonicus* (dwarf mondo grass), fine-textured green leaves, lilac flowers, excellent ground cover; Zones 7–9.

Garden Use: Use to contrast with light green, chartreuse, or blue-gray foliage plants. Makes good edging or paving plant.

Panicum virgatum
SWITCH GRASS

This deep-rooted native prairie grass makes an excellent display in fall and winter. Its blue-green leaves form an upright to narrow fountain, which turns bright yellow in autumn. Some cultivars become red in autumn. An airy cloud of dark purple or pink flowers, which ripen to straw-yellow, floats over the plants in midsummer. The dried grass persists well through winter, standing as a buff-colored spray of leaves.

Size: Foliage 3 to 6 feet tall; flowers 2 feet above.

Light: Full sun best; may flop in shade.

Soil and Moisture: Average to sandy, well-drained soil. Moderate moisture, but tolerates drought.

Planting and Propagation: Plant bare-root or container-grown plants in spring, spacing 3 feet apart.

Special Care: May need staking in shade. Cut back in late winter.

Pests and Diseases: Usually pest free.

Climate: Zone 5–9; heat tolerant.

Cultivars: 'Haense Herms' (red switch grass), 3 to 4 feet tall, good red fall color; 'Rotstrahlbusch' (red rays switch grass), best red fall color; 'Strictum' (tall switch grass), blue leaves, 5 to 6 feet tall; 'Heavy Metal,' stiff, upright, metallic blue leaves, 4 to 5 feet tall.

Panicum virgatum 'Heavy Metal'

Garden Use: Use as specimen in flower border; very effective, especially in winter and fall, mass planted in naturalistic garden and along water.

Pennisetum alopecuroides
FOUNTAIN GRASS

One of the most useful grasses for including in flower gardens and mixed borders, fountain grass is a warm-season grass that looks wonderful throughout most of the year. The fine-textured, glossy green leaves form a dense, wide-spreading symmetrical mass that remains green well into fall and briefly changes to rose, apricot, or gold before bleaching to bright almond in winter. In late summer or fall, 9-inch-long foxtaillike plumes, which open green and mature to rosy silver, purple, or white, stand out just above the foliage all over the plant. The flowers shatter by the end of fall, but the leaves remain attractive.

Size: 2 to 4 feet tall and wide.

Light: Full sun in the North; full sun to light shade in the South.

Soil and Moisture: Average to fertile, well-drained, moist soil; moderate to plentiful moisture. Tolerates drought in cool climates.

Planting and Propagation: Sow seed in spring or fall, or plant bare-root or container-grown plants in spring, spacing 2½ to 3 feet apart. Divide in spring or fall if center flops open, usually every five to 10 years.

Special Care: Cut back dried foliage in late

winter. May self-seed and be invasive in natural landscape in moist, mild climates.

Pests and Diseases: Usually pest free.

Climate: Zones 5–9.

Cultivars and Similar Species: 'Hameln,' compact to 2 feet tall and wide, Zones 5–8; 'Little Bunny,' miniature to 1 foot tall and wide; 'Cassian,' foliage to 10 inches tall, flowers to 2 feet tall; 'Moudry,' iridescent stiff black foxtails, late blooming, 1-inch-wide leaves, Zones 7–9; 'National Arboretum,' improved 'Moudry.'

Garden Use: Use as specimen in mixed borders; mass-plant for meadowlike effect and around water. Especially useful for adding volume to empty winter garden.

Pennisetum alopecuroides

Pennisetum orientale
ORIENTAL FOUNTAIN GRASS

From summer into fall, this showy long-blooming fountain grass becomes a mound of silky pink 4-inch-long foxtails, which mature to creamy light brown before shattering in late fall. The fine-textured blue-green leaves form a dense, mounded clump that turns yellow-brown in autumn and bleaches to an effective straw color for winter.

Size: 1 to 2 feet tall and wide.

Light: Full sun to part shade.

Pennisetum orientale

Soil and Moisture: Fertile, humus-rich, well-drained soil; plentiful moisture.

Planting and Propagation: Plant container-grown plants in spring, spacing 2 feet apart. Divide in spring only when dead centers develop, because resents division.

Special Care: Cut back dried foliage to 6 inches from ground, no lower, in late winter.

Pests and Diseases: Usually pest free.

Climate: Zones 7–9; tolerates seashore conditions if moist.

Cultivars: Only species is sold.

Garden Use: Elegant grass for small gardens. Use as specimen or mass-plant.

Pennisetum setaceum 'Rubrum' (*P. s.* 'Atrosanguineum')
PURPLE FOUNTAIN GRASS

This tender warm-season grass is valued for its arching clumps of magnificent burgundy-bronze leaves and 1-foot-long, reddish purple foxtails, which bring a long season of color to mixed borders. The leaves are evergreen to semi-evergreen where the plant is hardy; elsewhere they bleach to straw-colored in winter but look attractive until spring.

Size: 3 to 4 feet tall; 2 to 2½ feet wide.

Light: Full sun to light shade.

Soil and Moisture: Humus-rich to sandy, moist to dry soil; best with good soil and moderate water.

Planting and Propagation: Plant container-grown plants in spring, spacing 2 feet apart.

Special Care: Remove winter-killed plants in early spring. Flops in too much shade. Plants are usually sterile and rarely self-sow.

Pests and Diseases: Usually pest free.

Climate: Zones 8–10; grow as annual elsewhere. Adapts to seashore gardens.

Cultivars: The species has green leaves and pink-tinged flowers; may self-seed aggressively and is a pest in the Southwest. 'Burgundy Giant,' 1-inch-wide leaves, to 6 to 7 feet tall.

Garden Use: Often used as bedding plant along with flowering annuals. Makes beautiful accent in perennial border. Combines well with pink, blue, and pale yellow blossoms. Wonderful in containers combined with other annuals. Excellent cut flower.

Phalaris arundinacea var. *picta*
RIBBON GRASS, GARDENER'S GARTERS

This rapidly spreading grass features longitudinally striped green-and-white leaves that produce a beautiful flash of white in the garden. May remain evergreen in mild climates but turns beige with the first frost in cold climates. The lacy white flowers are not significantly showy.

Size: 3 feet tall and wide spreading.

Light: Part to full shade.

Soil and Moisture: Average to poor or heavy soil. Tolerates wet to standing shallow water; also tolerates drought.

Planting and Propagation: Plant bare-root or container-grown plants in spring, spacing 2 to 3 feet apart. Divide rhizomes every few years in spring to keep in bounds; sprouts from any tiny piece of root left in ground.

Special Care: Extremely invasive; needs impenetrable underground barrier, such as concrete or fiberglass, to keep in place in tidy gardens, or plant in bottomless container, or choose noninvasive form. If becomes tattered during growing season, cut back to 4 inches from ground. Cut back dried stems in

Pennisetum setaceum

late winter. Weed out nonvariegated reversions.

Pests and Diseases: Usually pest free.

Climate: Zones 5–9; to Zone 3 with snow cover. Heat tolerant. Good seashore plant.

Cultivars: 'Tricolor,' pink-white-and-green; 'Luteo-picta,' creamy gold and green; 'Dwarf Garters,' pink-tinged green-and-bright-white leaves, 1 to 1¼ feet tall, more upright and noninvasive, good in flower gardens; 'Feesey's Variety,' 1½ to 2 feet tall, spreading, pink in spring, almost snow-white in summer.

Garden Use: Makes excellent ground cover where invasive nature is not a problem. Use 'Dwarf Garters' in mixed borders in formal and informal settings.

Phalaris arundinacea var. *picta*

FERNS

Ferns bring cool greenery and fine texture to shady sites, flourishing where many other plants fail.

Adiantum pedatum

Adiantum pedatum
MAIDENHAIR FERN

There's no mistaking this magnificent fern for any other, for its fronds grow in an unusual pattern, forming layered rounded fans 1 to 2 feet across and parallel to the ground. The translucent, bright green wedge-shaped leaflets grow on wiry, shiny black stems, which further add to the fern's allure. Rusty brown fiddleheads emerge in early spring, and the plant spreads slowly by rhizomes to form large patches.

Size: 2 to 2½ feet tall.
Light: Deep to light shade.
Soil and Moisture: Deep, humus-rich, fertile, lightly acid to slightly alkaline, moist soil; plentiful moisture.
Planting and Propagation: Plant container-grown plants in spring, spacing 2 to 3 feet apart. Divide in early spring when fiddleheads are visible.
Special Care: Loses color and vigor in too much sun or in poor soil. Protect from wind.
Pests and Diseases: Slugs may be troublesome.

Climate: Zones 3–8.
Similar Species: *A. capillus-veneris* (southern maidenhair, rosy maidenhair), leaflets arranged in slender pattern, excellent ground cover; Zones 7–8.
Garden Use: Graceful fern for shade and woodland gardens; elegant in shaded formal gardens.

Athyrium filix-femina
LADY FERN

Perhaps the most common wild fern, lady fern makes a graceful addition to a wildflower or shade garden, spreading by rhizomes to colonize large areas. Its delicate-looking 2- to 3 foot-long feathery fronds are twice divided and emerge from the rhizomes at 6-inch to 1-foot intervals. Varying from light to dark green, the leaves have red or green stems and feature characteristic crescent-shaped spore cases arranged in a herringbone pattern on the undersides of the fertile fronds.

Athyrium filix-femina

Size: 2 to 3 feet tall and wide.
Light: Best in light shade; tolerates full sun if constantly moist.
Soil and Moisture: Humus-rich, moist, neutral to slightly acid, well-drained, moist soil; plentiful moisture.
Planting and Propagation: Plant container-grown plants in spring, spacing 2 to 3 feet apart. Divide in spring just as fiddleheads are visible.
Special Care: May become tattered by summer's end if exposed to too much heat and wind. Keep well mulched and constantly moist.
Pests and Diseases: Fungus disease may attack plant bases; avoid watering at night. Slugs and snails may eat foliage.
Climate: Zones 2–8.
Cultivars: Leaf shape and height may vary according to native habitat. 'Cristata' (crested lady fern): contorted (crested) leaflets create fluffy-textured effect.
Garden Use: Best used in naturalistic shade or woodland gardens because of wandering habit.

Athyrium niponicum pictum (A. goeringianum pictum)
JAPANESE PAINTED FERN

This outstanding fern brings subtle color to the shade garden with its maroon-splashed silvery gray leaves. The gracefully tapered fronds are 1 to 1½ feet long and feature maroon midribs. This Asian fern spreads slowly by rhizomes.

Size: 1 to 2 feet tall; spreads to form clumps 2 to 3 feet across.
Light: Part to full shade.
Soil and Moisture: Humus-rich, neutral to slightly acid, moist, well-drained soil; plentiful moisture.

Athyrium niponicum pictum

Planting and Propagation: Plant container-grown plants in spring, spacing 2 feet apart. Divide in late spring when fiddleheads emerge or in fall.

Special Care: Emerges late, but new growth continues to appear until late summer. Keep well watered during summer drought to prolong beauty through fall.

Pests and Diseases: Usually pest free.

Climate: Zones 3–9.

Cultivars: None other sold.

Garden Use: Gorgeous planted with blue flowers and blue-leaf hostas.

Dennstaedtia punctilobula
HAY-SCENTED FERN, BOULDER FERN

Spreading rapidly in open locations, this fine-textured fern gives off a fresh sweet scent when brushed against. The lacy, bright to light green fine-textured leaves are 2 feet long and 8 inches wide, tapering at the tips and broader at the bases. This sun-tolerant native fern grows around boulders in fields where the mower can't touch it or colonizes clear-cut areas in forests.

Size: 2 to 3 feet tall; spreads to form large colonies.

Light: Part shade best; tolerates full sun if constantly moist.

Soil and Moisture: Humus-rich to average, well-drained, moist soil; plentiful moisture.

Planting and Propagation: Plant container-grown plants in spring, spacing 2 to 3 feet apart. Divide rhizomes in early spring when fiddleheads are visible.

Special Care: Aggressiveness can be controlled with mowing in lawns or fields.

Pests and Diseases: Usually pest free.

Climate: Zones 3–8.

Cultivars: Only species is available.

Garden Use: Looks lovely planted around boulders and at bases of stone walls. Use as ground cover to stabilize banks and along edges of large-scale woodland gardens.

Dryopteris marginalis
MARGINAL SHIELD FERN,
LEATHER WOOD FERN

The fronds of this leathery-textured evergreen native fern grow from a central crown, forming a tidy individual plant that does not spread. Dark blue-green and twice cut, the fronds are 10 inches to 1¼ feet long. During late summer or early fall, a crown of tightly coiled brown croziers forms just above the ground at the base of the fronds and over-winters until the new fronds unfurl in spring.

Size: 2½ feet tall.

Light: Light to full shade.

Dennstaedtia punctilobula

Soil and Moisture: Deep, humus-rich, moist to wet soil; plentiful moisture.

Planting and Propagation: Plant container-grown plants in spring, taking care to keep crown at same level it was growing, spacing 2 to 3 feet apart. Separate small crowns from side of large crown in early spring, if desired.

Special Care: Keep heavily mulched. Remove old brown foliage underneath new growth if desired, but helps hold mulch on slopes. Protect from winter sun and wind.

Pests and Diseases: Usually pest free.

Climate: Zones 3–8.

Similar Species: *D. spinulosa* var. *intermedia* (spinulose wood fern), 2½ feet tall, twice- or thrice-cut fronds, nearly evergreen.

Garden Use: Fronds are cut for flower arrangements. Dark green leaves look very attractive in fall and winter gardens. Plant in shade and woodland gardens.

Matteuccia pensylvanica (M. struthiopteris)
OSTRICH FERN

The bright green, feathery, twice-cut fronds of the ostrich fern arise from a central crown, forming an imposing tall vase. Leaves may be 4 or more feet long and are widest at the middle. Resembling ostrich feathers, fertile fronds emerge in the plant's center in mid-

Dryopteris marginalis

Matteuccia pensylvanica

Onoclea sensibilis

summer and are half as long as the infertile fronds. They are shiny bronze-green, eventually turning brown, and remain standing and attractive all winter. Ostrich fern spreads aggressively by underground runners, sending up vase-shaped clusters of leaves from its far-flung rhizomes.

Size: 3 to 4 feet tall; 2 to 3 feet wide.
Light: Half sun to light shade; more sun tolerant than many ferns.
Soil and Moisture: Humus-rich, slightly acid, moist soil; constant plentiful moisture. Tolerates wet or swampy sites.
Planting and Propagation: Plant container-grown plants in spring, spacing at least 4 feet apart. Divide in spring every few years to control spread.
Special Care: Emerges late; take care not to injure. Leaves scorch if soil dries. Spreads aggressively.
Pests and Diseases: Usually pest free.
Climate: Zones 2–9.
Cultivars: Only species is available.
Garden Use: Naturalize in moist woodlands, along streams and ponds, or in bog gardens. Spreads too exuberantly for small gardens.

Onoclea sensibilis
SENSITIVE FERN, BEAD FERN

The triangular-shaped 1- to 2-foot-long fronds of this native fern are only once-cut and have toothed margins, giving them a coarse appearance unlike most ferns. The light green to yellow-green leaves are sensitive to cold and turn brown with the lightest frost, accounting for the fern's common name. Fertile fronds are attractive, dark brown, rattlelike spore cases, which make interesting additions to dried arrangements. This fern spreads aggressively by underground runners.

Size: 1 to 2 feet tall; wide spreading.
Light: Full sun where damp or wet; light shade elsewhere.
Soil and Moisture: Humus-rich, acid soil; constantly moist or wet to marshy conditions.
Planting and Propagation: Plant container-grown plants in spring, spacing 2 to 3 feet apart. Divide in spring or fall to control spread.
Special Care: Spreads rapidly where moist.
Pests and Diseases: Usually pest free.
Climate: Zones 3–8.
Cultivars: Only species is available.
Garden Use: Naturalize in wet spots or along streams and ponds where spreading is acceptable.

Osmunda cinnamomea
CINNAMON FERN

This statuesque native fern forms elegant, slow-spreading, vase-shaped clumps. Uncurling from woolly white croziers, fertile fronds develop in early spring, emerging green, then withering and turning cinnamon brown. Soon after the fertile fronds appear, a ring of bright green twice-cut infertile fronds expands around the fertile fronds. Turning orange-yellow in fall with the first frost, cinnamon fern boasts the best fall color of any fern.

Size: 2 to 5 feet tall; half as wide.
Light: Full sun in wet to swampy or constantly damp soil; part, light, or full shade in drier but moist conditions.
Soil and Moisture: Humus-rich, acid, moist soil; constant, plentiful moisture.
Planting and Propagation: Plant container-grown plants in spring, spacing 3 feet apart.
Special Care: Spreads slowly.
Pests and Diseases: Usually pest free.
Climate: Zones 4–9.
Similar Species: *O. claytoniana* (interrupted fern), very similar but fertile dark green leaflets that wither and turn brown form along portions of leaf stalks, interrupting the infertile leaflets; tolerates deeper shade.
Garden Use: Elegant, formal shape works well in moist flower borders and foundation plantings, as well as naturalistic sites.

Osmunda cinnamomea

Osmunda regalis
ROYAL FERN

The branched foliage of this magnificent fern consists of rounded leaflets resembling leaves of the honey locust tree. Measuring 3 to 4 feet long and 1 to 2 feet wide, the fronds are twice-cut and open wine-red, maturing to blue-green. Flowerlike clusters of brown spore-bearing structures appear at the tops of the fronds in midsummer. Spreads slowly.

Size: 3 to 6 feet tall; 2 feet wide.

Light: Full sun to open shade in wet or constantly damp soil; shade in drier but moist conditions.

Soil and Moisture: Humus-rich, very acid soil. Wet to boggy site best; tolerates moist garden conditions.

Planting and Propagation: Plant container-grown plants in spring, spacing 3 feet apart. Divide when center becomes bare in spring.

Special Care: Grows tallest with wet conditions.

Pests and Diseases: Usually pest free.

Climate: Zones 3–9.

Cultivars: Only species is available.

Garden Use: Eye-catching planted in groups in bog gardens, along stream sides, and in moist naturalistic gardens.

Polystichum acrostichoides
CHRISTMAS FERN

This easy-to-grow native fern forms an individual cluster of once-divided 1- to 2-foot long, 4-inch-wide leathery fronds. The foliage emerges light green in early spring, maturing to dark green. It remains green all winter, but flattens to the ground under snow cover. Spores form on the undersides of the leaflets.

Size: 1 to 2 feet tall; 2½ feet wide.

Light: Part to light shade; more sun in constantly moist site.

Soil and Moisture: Average to humus-rich, neutral, well-drained soil. Best in moist conditions but tolerates some dryness.

Osmunda regalis

Planting and Propagation: Plant container-grown plants in spring, spacing 2½ feet apart. Divide clumps with multiple crowns when crowded.

Special Care: Needs good drainage. Remove old brown foliage as new growth emerges, if desired.

Pests and Diseases: Usually pest free.

Climate: Zones 3–9.

Cultivars: 'Crispum,' ruffled leaves; 'Incisum,' deeply cut leaflets.

Garden Use: Plant on slopes in open shade where soil drains too fast for other ferns. Lovely in shade and woodland gardens as well as borders.

Polystichum munitum
WESTERN SWORD FERN

Resembling a large, stiff Christmas fern, the western sword fern features erect, once-divided, rough-textured fronds. The evergreen fronds of this West Coast native grow from 1 to 5 feet long and 2 to 10 inches wide, making a dramatic appearance.

Size: 2 to 4 feet tall.

Light: Part to light shade.

Soil and Moisture: Humus-rich, well-drained, moist soil; plentiful moisture.

Polystichum acrosticoides

Planting and Propagation: Plant container-grown plants in spring, spacing at least 3 feet apart; divide in fall when multiple crowns appear crowded.

Special Care: Cut off old brown foliage in spring. Keep well mulched and moist.

Pests and Diseases: Usually pest free.

Climate: Zones 5–8.

Cultivars: None.

Garden Use: Use as focal point in garden or mass-plant in naturalistic setting.

Polystichum munitum

BEST PERENNIALS AND BIENNIALS FOR THE NORTHEAST

Achillea filipendulina (fern-leaf yarrow)
Achillea x 'Moonshine' (moonshine yarrow)
Aconitum spp. (monkshoods)
Alcea rosea (hollyhock)
Alchemilla mollis (lady's mantle)
Anaphalis triplinervis (three-veined pearly everlasting)
Anemone x *hybrida* (Japanese anemone)
Aquilegia canadensis (American columbine)
Aquilegia x *hybrida* (hybrid columbine)
Arabis caucasica (wall rock cress)
Armeria maritima (sea pink, thrift)
Artemisia spp. (mugworts)
Aruncus dioicus (goat's beard)
Asclepias tuberosa (butterfly weed)
Aster novi-belgii x *novae-angliae* (Michaelmas daisy, fall aster)
Aster x *frikartii* (Frikart's aster)
Astilbe spp. (astilbes)
Aubrieta deltoidea (rock cress)
Aurinia saxatilis (basket-of-gold)
Baptisia australis (blue wild indigo)
Boltonia asteroides (white boltonia)
Brunnera macrophylla (Siberian bugloss)
Caltha palustris (marsh marigold)
Campanula spp. (bellflowers)
Centaurea montana (mountain bluet)
Cerastium tomentosum (snow-in-summer)
Chelone spp. (turtle-heads)
Chrysanthemum nipponicum (nippon daisy, Montauk daisy)
Chrysanthemum weyrichii (miyabe)
Chrysanthemum x *morifolium* (chrysanthemum, garden mum)
Chrysanthemum x *rubellum* (hybrid chrysanthemum)
Cimicifuga simplex (Kamchatka bugbane)
Coreopsis verticillata (threadleaf coreopsis)
Corydalis lutea (yellow corydalis)
Dianthus spp. (pinks)
Dicentra eximia (fringed bleeding heart)
Dicentra spectabilis (common bleeding heart)
Dictamnus albus (gas plant)
Digitalis spp. (foxgloves)
Doronicum caucasicum (leopard's bane)

Echinacea purpurea (purple coneflower)
Echinops ritro (globe-thistle)
Epimedium spp. (barrenworts)
Erigeron x *hybridus* (fleabane)
Eryngium spp. (sea hollies)
Eupatorium fistulosum (Joe-Pye weed)
Euphorbia epithymoides (cushion spurge)
Filipendula spp. (queen-of-the-prairies)
Galium odoratum (sweet woodruff)
Geranium spp. (cranesbills, geraniums)
Gypsophila paniculata (baby's breath)
Helenium autumnale (sneezeweed)
Heliopsis helianthoides scabra (false sunflower)
Helleborus niger (Christmas rose)
Helleborus orientalis (Lenten rose)
Hemerocallis hybrids (daylilies)
Hesperis matronalis (dame's rocket, sweet rocket)
Heuchera spp. (coralbells)
Hosta species and hybrids (hostas)
Iberis sempervirens (edging candytuft)
Iris cristata (crested iris)
Iris ensata (Japanese iris)
Iris hybrida (bearded iris)
Iris siberica (Siberian iris)
Lamium maculatum (spotted dead nettle)
Lavandula angustifolia (lavender, English lavender)
Liatris spicata (spike gayfeather, blazing star)
Ligularia stenocephala (golden ray)
Lobelia cardinalis (cardinal flower)
Lobelia siphilitica (big-blue lobelia)
Lychnis coronaria (rose campion)
Lythrum salicaria (purple loosestrife)
Macleaya cordata (plume poppy)
Monarda didyma (bee-balm, oswego tea)
Myosotis scorpioides (forget-me-not)
Nepeta x *faassenii* (catmint)
Origanum vulgare 'Aureum' (golden oregano, golden marjoram)
Paeonia lactiflora (Chinese peony, garden peony)
Papaver nudicaule (Iceland poppy)
Papaver orientale (Oriental poppy)
Penstemon barbatus (beard-tongue)
Phlox spp. (phloxes)
Physostegia virginiana (obedient plant, false dragonhead)
Platycodon grandiflorus (balloon flower)

Polemonium caeruleum (Jacob's ladder)
Polygonatum biflorum (small Solomon's seal)
Polygonatum odoratum 'Variegatum' (variegated fragrant Solomon's seal)
Polygonum bistorta (knotweed, snake-weed, European bistort)
Potentilla tabernaemontani (spring cinquefoil)
Primula japonica (Japanese primrose)
Primula veris (cowslip primrose)
Pulmonaria spp. (lungworts)
Pulsatilla vulgaris (pasque flower)
Ratibida pinnata (yellow coneflower)
Rudbeckia fulgida (orange coneflower)
Rudbeckia nitida (shining coneflower)
Salvia x *superba* (hybrid blue salvia, hybrid sage)
Sanguinaria canadensis (bloodroot)
Saponaria ocymoides (rock soapwort)
Scabiosa caucasica (pincushion flower, scabious)
Sedum spp. (stonecrops)
Sempervivum tectorum (hens-and-chicks, houseleek)
Solidago hybrids (goldenrod)
Stachys byzantina (lamb's-ears)
Tiarella cordifolia (Allegheny foamflower)
Tradescantia x *andersoniana* (spiderwort, Virginia spiderwort)
Tricyrtis hirta (toad lily)
Trollius europaeus (globeflower)
Veronica spp. (speedwells)
Viola labradorica var. *purpurea* (Labrador violet)

BEST PERENNIALS AND BIENNIALS FOR THE MID-ATLANTIC

Acanthus spinosus var. *spinosissimus* (spiny bear's breeches)

Achillea filipendulina (fern-leaf yarrow)

Achillea millefolium (common yarrow)

Achillea x 'Moonshine' (moonshine yarrow)

Aconitum spp. (monkshoods)

Ajuga reptans (bugleweed, carpet bugle)

Alcea rosea (hollyhock)

Alchemilla mollis (lady's mantle)

Amsonia tabernaemontana (willow amsonia)

Anaphalis triplinervis (three-veined pearly everlasting)

Anemone x *hybrida* (Japanese anemone)

Aquilegia canadensis (American columbine)

Aquilegia flabellata (hybrid columbine)

Aquilegia vulgaris (granny's bonnet)

Aquilegia x *hybrida* (hybrid columbine)

Arabis caucasica (wall rock cress)

Armeria maritima (sea pink, thrift)

Artemisia x 'Powis Castle' (Powis castle mugwort)

Aruncus dioicus (goat's beard)

Asclepias tuberosa (butterfly weed)

Aster novi-belgii x *novae-angliae* (Michaelmas daisy, fall aster)

Aster x *frikartii* (Frikart's aster)

Astilbe spp. (astilbes)

Aubrieta deltoidea (rock cress)

Aurinia saxatilis (basket-of-gold)

Baptisia australis (blue wild indigo)

Begonia grandis (hardy begonia)

Bergenia spp. (bergenias)

Boltonia asteroides (white boltonia)

Caltha palustris (marsh marigold)

Campanula spp. (bellflowers)

Centranthus ruber (red valerian)

Ceratostigma plumbaginoides (leadwort)

Chelone lyonii (pink turtle-head)

Chrysanthemum nipponicum (nippon daisy, Montauk daisy)

Chrysanthemum parthenium (feverfew)

Chrysanthemum x *morifolium* (chrysanthemum, garden mum)

Chrysanthemum x *rubellum* (hybrid chrysanthemum)

Chrysanthemum x *superbum* (shasta daisy)

Chrysanthemum weyrichii (miyabe)

Chrysogonum virginianum (goldenstar)

Cimicifuga simplex (Kamchatka bugbane)

Coreopsis verticillata (threadleaf coreopsis)

Corydalis lutea (yellow corydalis)

Dianthus spp. (pinks)

Dicentra spp. (bleeding hearts)

Dictamnus albus (gas plant)

Digitalis purpurea (foxglove)

Doronicum caucasicum (leopard's bane)

Echinacea purpurea (purple coneflower)

Echinops ritro (globe-thistle)

Epimedium spp. (barrenworts)

Erigeron x *hybridus* (fleabane)

Eryngium spp. (sea hollies)

Eupatorium coelestinum (mist flower, hardy ageratum)

Eupatorium purpureum (Joe-Pye weed)

Euphorbia epithymoides (cushion spurge)

Filipendula rubra (queen-of-the-prairie)

Galium odoratum (sweet woodruff)

Gaura lindheimeri (white gaura)

Geranium spp. (hardy geraniums)

Hedyotis caerulea (bluets, quaker ladies)

Helenium autumnale (sneezeweed)

Helianthus angustifolius (fall sunflower, swamp sunflower)

Heliopsis helianthoides scabra (false sunflower)

Helleborus orientalis (Lenten rose)

Hemerocallis hybrids (daylilies)

Hesperis matronalis (dame's rocket, sweet rocket)

Heuchera spp. (coralbells)

Hibiscus moscheutos (rose mallow, swamp mallow)

Hosta species and hybrids (hostas)

Iberis sempervirens (edging candytuft)

Iris spp. (irises)

Kniphofia uvaria (red-hot poker, torchlily)

Lamium maculatum (spotted dead nettle)

Lavandula angustifolia (lavender)

Liatris spicata (spike gayfeather)

Liriope muscari (blue lilyturf)

Lupinus hybrids (lupine)

Lychnis flos-jovis (flower-of-Jove)

Lychnis chalcedonia (Maltese cross)

Lysimachia nummulara (moneywort, creeping Jenny, creeping Charley)

Lysimachia punctata (yellow loosestrife, circle flower)

Lythrum salicaria (purple loosestrife)

Macleaya cordata (plume poppy)

Mazus reptans (mazus)

Myosotis scorpioides (forget-me-not)

Nepeta x *faassenii* (catmint)

Oenothera spp. (evening primroses and sundrops)

Omphaloides verna (blue-eyed Mary, navel seed)

Paeonia lactiflora (Chinese peony, garden peony)

Papaver orientale (Oriental poppy)

Penstemon barbatus (common beard-tongue)

Perovskia atriplicifolia (Russian sage)

Phlox spp. (phloxes)

Platycodon grandiflorus (balloon flower)

Polygonatum biflorum (small Solomon's seal)

Polygonatum odoratum 'Variegatum' (variegated fragrant Solomon's seal)

Primula japonica (Japanese primrose)

Primula veris (cowslip primrose)

Primula x *polyantha* (polyanthus primrose)

Pulmonaria spp. (lungworts)

Pulsatilla vulgaris (pasque flower)

Rodgersia aesculifolia (fingerleaf rodgersia)

Rudbeckia fulgida (orange coneflower)

Rudbeckia nitida (shining coneflower)

Salvia officinalis (garden sage)

Salvia x *superba* (hybrid blue salvia, hybrid sage)

Sanguinaria canadensis (bloodroot)

Saponaria officinalis (bouncing Bet)

Scabiosa caucasica (pincushion flower, scabious)

Sedum spp. (stonecrops)

Senecio aureus (golden groundsel)

Solidago hybrids (goldenrod)

Stachys byzantina (lamb's-ears)

Stokesia laevis (Stokes' aster)

Thalictrum spp. (meadow-rues)

Thermopsis caroliniana (southern lupine, Carolina lupine)

Tiarella cordifolia (Allegheny foamflower)

Tradescantia x *andersoniana* (spiderwort, Virginia spiderwort)

Tricyrtis hirta (toad lily)

Verbena bonariensis (Brazilian verbena)

Verbena canadensis (clump verbena, rose verbena)

Veronica spp. (speedwells)

Viola spp. (tufted pansies, violets)

Yucca filamentosa (Adam's needle, needle palm)

BEST PERENNIALS AND BIENNIALS FOR THE SOUTH

Ajuga reptans (bugleweed, carpet bugle)
Alstroemeria aurantiaca (Peruvian lily)
Amsonia tabernaemontana (willow amsonia)
Anemone x *hybrida* (Japanese anemone)
Aquilegia canadensis (American columbine)
Aquilegia x *hybrida* (hybrid columbine)
Artemisia ludoviciana var. *albula* (white sage, wormwood)
Artemisia 'Valerie Finnis'
Artemisia x 'Powis Castle' (Powis castle mugwort)
Aster x *frikartii* (Frikart's aster)
Astilbe x *arendsii* (astilbe)
Baptisia australis (blue wild indigo)
Boltonia asteroides (white boltonia)
Artemisia 'Valerie Finnis'
Chrysanthemum nipponicum (nippon daisy, Montauk daisy)
Chrysanthemum x *rubellum* (hybrid chrysanthemum)
Chrysanthemum x *superbum* (shasta daisy)
Chrysogonum virginianum (goldenstar)
Cimicifuga racemosa (snake-root)
Coreopsis grandiflora (coreopsis)
Coreopsis verticillata (threadleaf coreopsis)
Dianthus barbatus (sweet William)
Dianthus gratianopolitanus (cheddar pink)
Dianthus plumarius (cottage pink)
Dicentra cucullaria (Dutchman's breeches)
Dicentra eximia (fringed bleeding heart)
Echinacea purpurea (purple coneflower)
Epimedium spp. (barrenworts)
Gaillardia x *grandiflora* (blanket-flower)
Gaura lindheimeri (white gaura)
Helianthus angustifolius (fall sunflower)
Heliopsis helianthoides scabra (false sunflower)
Helleborus orientalis (Lenten rose)
Hemerocallis hybrids (daylilies)
Heuchera spp. (coralbells)
Hibiscus moscheutos (rose mallow)
Hosta species and hybrids (hostas)
Iberis sempervirens (edging candytuft)
Iris cristata (crested iris)
Iris ensata (Japanese iris)
Iris pseudacorus (yellow flag iris)
Iris siberica (Siberian iris)
Iris versicolor (blue flag iris)
Lamium maculatum (spotted dead nettle)
Liatris spicata (spike gayfeather)
Linum perenne (blue flax)
Liriope muscari (blue lilyturf)
Lobelia spp. (cardinal flowers)
Myosotis scorpioides (forget-me-not)
Oenothera speciosa (showy evening primrose, Mexican evening primrose)
Oenothera tetragona (common sundrops)
Paeonia lactiflora (Chinese peony, garden peony)
Perovskia atriplicifolia (Russian sage)
Phlox divaricata (wild blue phlox)
Phlox maculata (wild sweet William, spotted phlox)
Phlox paniculata (garden phlox)
Phlox pilosa ozarkana (downy phlox)
Phlox stolonifera (creeping phlox)
Phlox subulata (moss pink)
Physostegia virginiana (obedient plant)
Platycodon grandiflorus (balloon flower)
Polygonatum odoratum 'Variegatum' (variegated fragrant solomon's seal)
Rudbeckia fulgida (orange coneflower)
Rudbeckia hirta (black-eyed Susan, gloriosa daisy)
Salvia x *superba* (hybrid blue salvia, hybrid sage)
Sanguinaria canadensis (bloodroot)
Saponaria officinalis (bouncing Bet)
Sedum spectabile (showy stonecrop)
Sedum x *telephium* 'Autumn Joy' (autumn joy stonecrop)
Senecio aureus (golden groundsel)
Stachys byzantina (lamb's-ears)
Stokesia laevis (Stokes' aster)
Thalictrum aquilegifolium (columbine meadow-rue)
Thermopsis caroliniana (southern lupine)
Tiarella cordifolia (Allegheny foamflower)
Tradescantia x *andersoniana* (spiderwort)
Tricyrtis hirta (toad lily)
Verbena bonariensis (Brazilian verbena)
Veronica spicata (spiked speedwell)
Veronicastrum virginicum (culver's root)
Viola odorata (sweet violet)
Viola tricolor (Johnny-jump-up)

BEST PERENNIALS AND BIENNIALS FOR THE SOUTHWEST

Acanthus spinosus var. *spinosissimus* (spiny bear's breeches)
Achillea filipendulina (fern-leaf yarrow)
Achillea tomentosa (woolly milfoil)
Achillea x 'Moonshine' (moonshine yarrow)
Alstroemeria aurantiaca (Peruvian lily)
Anthemis tinctoria (golden marguerite)
Aquilegia chrysantha (golden columbine)
Aquilegia x *hybrida* (hybrid columbine)
Centranthus ruber (red valerian)
Chrysanthemum coccineum (painted daisy, pyrethrum)
Coreopsis verticillata (threadleaf coreopsis)
Dianthus barbatus (sweet William)
Dianthus plumarius (cottage pink)
Gaillardia x *grandiflora* (blanket-flower)
Galium odoratum (sweet woodruff)
Gaura lindheimeri (white gaura)
Hemerocallis hybrids (daylilies)
Heuchera sanguinea (coralbells)
Iberis sempervirens (edging candytuft)
Iris ensata (Japanese iris)
Kniphofia uvaria (red-hot poker)
Lavandula angustifolia (lavender)
Lavandula stoechas (Spanish lavender)
Liatris spicata (spike gayfeather)
Limonium perezii (sea lavender)
Linum perenne (blue flax)
Oenothera missouriensis (Ozark sundrops, Missouri primrose)
Oenothera speciosa (showy evening primrose)
Penstemon barbatus (beard-tongue)
Perovskia atriplicifolia (Russian sage)
Petrorhagia saxifraga (tunic flower)
Phlomis russeliana (sticky Jerusalem sage)
Santolina chamaecyparissus (lavender cotton, gray santolina)
Sedum x *telephium* 'Autumn Joy' (autumn joy stonecrop)
Stachys byzantina (lamb's-ears)
Verbena canadensis (clump verbena)
Yucca filamentosa (Adam's needle)

BEST PERENNIALS AND BIENNIALS FOR THE GULF COAST AND COASTAL PLAINS

Achillea millefolium (common yarrow)
Amsonia tabernaemontana (willow amsonia)
Aquilegia chrysantha (golden columbine)
Asclepias tuberosa (butterfly weed)
Coreopsis grandiflora (coreopsis, tickseed)
Echinacea purpurea (purple coneflower)
Eupatorium coelestinum (hardy ageratum)
Gaillardia x *grandiflora* (blanket-flower)
Hemerocallis hybrids (daylily)

Iris ensata (Japanese iris)
Iris pseudacorus (yellow flag iris)
Iris siberica (Siberian iris)
Iris versicolor (blue flag iris)
Liriope muscari (blue lilyturf)
Oenothera speciosa (showy evening primrose, Mexican evening primrose)
Phlox maculata (wild sweet William, spotted phlox)
Phlox paniculata (garden phlox)

Physostegia virginiana (obedient plant, false dragonhead)
Rudbeckia fulgida (orange coneflower)
Salvia greigii (autumn sage)
Salvia leucantha (Mexican bush sage)
Salvia farinacea (mealy-cup sage)
Tradescantia x *andersoniana* (spiderwort, Virginia spiderwort)
Verbena canadensis (clump verbena, rose verbena)

BEST PERENNIALS AND BIENNIALS FOR THE MIDWEST

Acanthus spinosus var. *spinosissimus* (spiny bear's breeches)
Alcea rosea (hollyhock)
Amsonia tabernaemontana (willow amsonia)
Anemone x *hybrida* (Japanese anemone)
Aquilegia x *hybrida* (hybrid columbine)
Arabis caucasica (wall rock cress)
Artemisia x 'Powis Castle' (Powis castle mugwort)
Asclepias tuberosa (butterfly weed)
Aster novi-belgii x *novae-angliae* (Michaelmas daisy, fall aster)
Aster x *frikartii* (Frikart's aster)
Astilbe chinensis var. *pumila* (dwarf Chinese astilbe)
Aurinia saxatilis (basket-of-gold)
Baptisia australis (blue wild indigo)
Bergenia cordifolia (heart-leaf bergenia)
Boltonia asteroides (white boltonia)
Campanula glomerata (clustered bellflower)
Centranthus ruber (red valerian)
Chrysanthemum nipponicum (nippon daisy, Montauk daisy)
Chrysanthemum parthenium (feverfew)
Chrysanthemum x *morifolium* (chrysanthemum, garden mum)
Chrysanthemum x *rubellum* (hybrid chrysanthemum)
Coreopsis grandiflora (coreopsis, tickseed)
Coreopsis verticillata (threadleaf coreopsis)
Corydalis lutea (yellow corydalis)
Dianthus gratianopolitanus (cheddar pink)
Dicentra spectabilis (common bleeding heart)

Dictamnus albus (gas plant)
Echinacea purpurea (purple coneflower)
Echinops ritro (globe-thistle)
Epimedium spp. (barrenworts)
Eryngium amethystinum (amethyst sea holly)
Eupatorium fistulosum (Joe-Pye weed)
Euphorbia epithymoides (cushion spurge)
Filipendula rubra (queen-of-the-prairie)
Gaillardia x *grandiflora* (blanket-flower)
Gaura lindheimeri (white gaura)
Geranium spp. (hardy geraniums)
Gypsophila paniculata (baby's breath)
Helenium autumnale (sneezeweed)
Helianthus angustifolius (fall sunflower)
Heliopsis helianthoides scabra (false sunflower)
Hemerocallis hybrids (daylily)
Hesperis matronalis (dame's rocket)
Heuchera spp. (coralbells)
Hosta species and hybrids (hostas)
Iberis sempervirens (edging candytuft)
Iris hybrida (bearded iris)
Iris siberica (Siberian iris)
Lamium maculatum (spotted dead nettle)
Liatris spicata (spike gayfeather)
Linum perenne (blue flax)
Lunaria annua (money-plant, honesty)
Lychnis coronaria (rose campion)
Lythrum salicaria (purple loosestrife)
Macleaya cordata (plume poppy)
Nepeta x *faassenii* (catmint)
Oenothera speciosa (showy evening primrose, Mexican evening primrose)
Oenothera tetragona (common sundrops)
Paeonia lactiflora (Chinese peony, garden peony)

Papaver orientale (Oriental poppy)
Penstemon barbatus (beard-tongue)
Perovskia atriplicifolia (Russian sage)
Phlox maculata (wild sweet William)
Phlox paniculata (garden phlox)
Phlox subulata (moss pink)
Physostegia virginiana (obedient plant)
Platycodon grandiflorus (balloon flower)
Potentilla tabernaemontani (spring cinquefoil)
Pulsatilla vulgaris (pasque flower)
Ratibida pinnata (yellow coneflower)
Rudbeckia fulgida (orange coneflower)
Rudbeckia nitida (shining coneflower)
Salvia x *superba* (hybrid blue salvia, hybrid sage)
Scabiosa caucasica (pincushion flower, scabious)
Sedum spp. (stonecrops)
Sempervivum tectorum (hens-and-chicks)
Sidalcea malviflora (checkerbloom, prairie mallow)
Solidago hybrids (goldenrod)
Stachys byzantina (lamb's-ears)
Thermopsis caroliniana (southern lupine, Carolina lupine)
Tiarella cordifolia (Allegheny foamflower)
Tradescantia x *andersoniana* (spiderwort, Virginia spiderwort)
Veronica spp. (speedwells)
Viola labradorica var. *purpurea* (Labrador violet)
Viola tricolor (Johnny-jump-up)
Yucca filamentosa (Adam's needle, needle palm)

BEST PERENNIALS AND BIENNIALS FOR THE PLAINS AND ROCKY MOUNTAINS

Acanthus spinosus var. *spinosissimus* (spiny bear's breeches)
Achillea filipendulina (fern-leaf yarrow)
Achillea millefolium (common yarrow)
Achillea tomentosa (woolly milfoil)
Achillea x 'Moonshine' (moonshine yarrow
Ajuga reptans (bugleweed, carpet bugle)
Alchemilla mollis (lady's mantle)
Anaphalis cinnamomea (pearly everlasting)
Anemone x *hybrida* (Japanese anemone)
Anthemis tinctoria (golden marguerite)
Aquilegia caerulea (Rocky Mountain columbine)
Aquilegia chrysantha (golden columbine)
Arabis caucasica (wall rock cress)
Armeria maritima (sea pink, thrift)
Artemisia schmidtiana 'Silver Mound' (silvermound mugwort)
Asclepias tuberosa (butterfly weed)
Asphodeline lutea (Jacob's-rod, king's-spear)
Aster novi-belgii x *novae-angliae* (Michaelmas daisy, fall aster)
Aubrieta deltoidea (rock cress)
Aurinia saxatilis (basket-of-gold)
Baptisia australis (blue wild indigo)
Belamcanda chinensis (blackberry lily)
Brunnera macrophylla (Siberian bugloss)
Campanula carpatica (Carpathian bellflower)
Campanula poscharskyana (Serbian bellflower)
Centaurea macrocephala (Armenian basket flower)
Centranthus ruber (red valerian, Jupiter's beard)
Cerastium tomentosum (snow-in-summer)
Chrysanthemum coccineum (painted daisy)
Chrysanthemum nipponicum (nippon daisy, Montauk daisy)
Chrysanthemum weyrichii (miyabe)
Chrysanthemum x *morifolium* (chrysanthemum, garden mum)

Chrysanthemum x *superbum* (shasta daisy)
Coreopsis grandiflora (coreopsis, tickseed)
Coreopsis verticillata (threadleaf coreopsis)
Delphinium x *elatum* (delphinium)
Dianthus deltoides (maiden pink)
Dianthus gratianopolitanus (cheddar pink)
Dianthus plumarius (cottage pink)
Dicentra spectabilis (common bleeding heart)
Dictamnus albus (gas plant)
Digitalis grandiflora (yellow foxglove)
Echinacea pallida (pale coneflower)
Echinacea purpurea (purple coneflower)
Echinops ritro (globe-thistle)
Erigeron x *hybridus* (fleabane)
Eupatorium coelestinum (mist flower, hardy ageratum)
Geranium sanguineum (bloody cranesbill)
Geum quellyon (geum, Chilean avens)
Gypsophila paniculata (baby's breath)
Gypsophila repens (creeping baby's breath)
Heliopsis helianthoides scabra (false sunflower)
Hemerocallis hybrids (daylilies)
Heuchera sanguinea (coralbells)
Iberis sempervirens (edging candytuft)
Iris hybrida (bearded iris)
Iris siberica (Siberian iris)
Kniphofia uvaria (red-hot poker, torchlily)
Lavandula angustifolia (lavender, English lavender)
Leontopodium alpinum (edelweiss)
Liatris spicata (spike gayfeather, blazing star)
Limonium latifolium (sea lavender, statice)
Linum perenne (blue flax)
Lupinus hybrids (lupine)
Lysimachia punctata (yellow loosestrife, circle flower)
Lythrum salicaria (purple loosestrife)
Monarda didyma (bee-balm, oswego tea)
Monarda fistulosa (wild bergamot)
Myosotis scorpioides (forget-me-not)
Nepeta x *faassenii* (catmint)
Oenothera missouriensis (Ozark sundrops)
Oenothera speciosa (showy evening primrose, Mexican evening primrose)
Oenothera tetragona (common sundrops)

Paeonia lactiflora (Chinese peony, garden peony)
Penstemon barbatus (common beard-tongue)
Perovskia atriplicifolia (Russian sage)
Petrorhagia saxifraga (tunic flower, coat flower)
Phlox maculata (wild sweet William, spotted phlox)
Phlox paniculata (garden phlox, summer phlox)
Phlox subulata (moss pink)
Physostegia virginiana (obedient plant, false dragonhead)
Platycodon grandiflorus (balloon flower)
Polygonum bistorta (snakeweed, knotweed)
Potentilla tabernaemontani (spring cinquefoil)
Pulmonaria spp. (lungworts)
Rudbeckia fulgida (orange coneflower)
Salvia argentea (silver sage)
Salvia officinalis (garden sage)
Salvia x *superba* (hybrid blue salvia, hybrid sage)
Saponaria ocymoides (rock soapwort)
Sedum spp. (stonecrops)
Sempervivum tectorum (hens-and-chicks, houseleek)
Solidago hybrids (goldenrods)
Stachys byzantina (lamb's-ears)
Thalictrum aquilegifolium (columbine meadow-rue)
Thymus spp. (thymes)
Veronica spp. (speedwells)
Viola labradorica var. *purpurea* (Labrador violet)
Yucca filamentosa (Adam's needle, needle palm)

BEST PERENNIALS AND BIENNIALS FOR THE PACIFIC NORTHWEST

Acanthus spinosus var. *spinosissimus* (spiny bear's breeches)

Achillea filipendulina (fern-leaf yarrow)

Achillea millefolium (common yarrow)

Achillea x 'Moonshine' (moonshine yarrow)

Aconitum spp. (monkshoods)

Ajuga reptans (bugleweed, carpet bugle)

Alchemilla mollis (lady's mantle)

Anaphalis triplinervis (three-veined pearly everlasting)

Anemone x *hybrida* (Japanese anemone)

Angelica archangelica (wild parsnip, cow parsnip, archangel)

Aquilegia x *hybrida* (hybrid columbine)

Arabis caucasica (wall rock cress)

Armeria maritima (sea pink, thrift)

Artemisia spp. (mugworts)

Asclepias tuberosa (butterfly weed)

Asphodeline lutea (Jacob's-rod, king's spear)

Aster x *frikartii* (Frikart's aster)

Aubrieta deltoidea (rock cress)

Aurinia saxatilis (basket-of-gold)

Begonia grandis (hardy begonia)

Belamcanda chinensis (blackberry lily)

Bellis perennis (English daisy)

Bergenia spp. (bergenias)

Boltonia asteroides (white boltonia)

Campanula spp. (bellflowers)

Centaurea montana (mountain bluet)

Centranthus ruber (red valerian, Jupiter's beard)

Cerastium tomentosum (snow-in-summer)

Ceratostigma plumbaginoides (leadwort, plumbago)

Chrysanthemum coccineum (painted daisy)

Chrysanthemum x *morifolium* (chrysanthemum, garden mum)

Chrysanthemum x *rubellum* (hybrid chrysanthemum)

Chrysanthemum x *superbum* (shasta daisy)

Coreopsis verticillata (threadleaf coreopsis)

Corydalis lutea (yellow corydalis)

Crambe cordifolia (colewort)

Cynara cardunculus (cardoon)

Delosperma cooperi (hardy iceplant)

Delphinium x *elatum* (delphinium)

Dianthus spp. (pinks)

Dicentra formosa (western bleeding heart)

Dicentra spectabilis (common bleeding heart)

Digitalis purpurea (foxglove)

Echinacea purpurea (purple coneflower)

Echinops ritro (globe-thistle)

Epimedium spp. (barrenworts)

Erigeron x *hybridus* (fleabane)

Eryngium amethystinum (amethyst sea holly)

Euphorbia epithymoides (cushion spurge)

Filipendula spp. (queen-of-the-prairie)

Gaura lindheimeri (white gaura)

Geranium spp. (hardy geraniums)

Geum quellyon (geum, Chilean avens)

Gypsophila paniculata (baby's breath)

Helenium autumnale (sneezeweed)

Helianthus angustifolius (fall sunflower, swamp sunflower)

Heliopsis helianthoides scabra (false sunflower)

Helleborus spp. (Lenten roses)

Hemerocallis hybrids (daylilies)

Hesperis matronalis (dame's rocket)

Heuchera spp. (coralbells)

Iberis sempervirens (edging candytuft)

Iris hybrida (bearded iris)

Iris siberica (Siberian iris)

Lamium maculatum (spotted dead nettle)

Lavandula stoechas (Spanish lavender)

Liatris spicata (spike gayfeather)

Ligularia stenocephala (golden ray)

Limonium latifolium (sea lavender, statice)

Linum perenne (blue flax)

Liriope muscari (blue lilyturf)

Lobelia siphilitica (big-blue lobelia)

Lupinus hybrids (lupine)

Lychnis chalcedonia (Maltese cross)

Lychnis coronaria (rose campion)

Lysimacchia nummulara (moneywort, creeping Jenny, creeping Charley)

Lythrum salicaria (purple loosestrife)

Malva alcea (hollyhock mallow)

Mazus reptans (mazus)

Monarda didyma (bee-balm, oswego tea)

Myosotis scorpioides (forget-me-not)

Nepeta x *faassenii* (catmint)

Omphaloides verna (blue-eyed Mary)

Origanum vulgare 'Aureum' (golden oregano, golden marjoram)

Paeonia lactiflora (Chinese peony, garden peony)

Papaver nudicaule (Iceland poppy)

Penstemon barbatus (common beard-tongue)

Perovskia atriplicifolia (Russian sage)

Phlomis russeliana (sticky Jerusalem sage)

Phlox paniculata (garden phlox, summer phlox)

Phlox subulata (moss pink)

Physostegia virginiana (obedient plant, false dragonhead)

Platycodon grandiflorus (balloon flower)

Polemonium caeruleum (Jacob's ladder)

Polygonatum odoratum 'Variegatum' (variegated fragrant Solomon's seal)

Polygonum bistorta (snakeweed, knotweed)

Potentilla tabernaemontani (spring cinquefoil)

Primula x *polyantha* (polyanthus primrose)

Pulmonaria spp. (lungworts)

Pulsatilla vulgaris (pasque flower)

Rodgersia aesculifolia (fingerleaf rodgersia)

Rudbeckia fulgida (orange coneflower)

Rudbeckia nitida (shining coneflower)

Ruta graveolens (rue)

Salvia officinalis (garden sage)

Salvia pratensis (meadow sage, meadow clary)

Salvia x *superba* (hybrid blue salvia, hybrid sage)

Saponaria ocymoides (rock soapwort)

Scabiosa caucasica (pincushion flower, scabious)

Sedum spp. (stonecrops)

Sidalcea malviflora (checkerbloom, prairie mallow)

Sisyrinchium striatum (Argentine blue-eyed grass)

Solidago hybrids (goldenrod)

Stachys byzantina (lamb's-ears)

Stokesia laevis (Stokes' aster)

Thalictrum spp. (meadow-rues)

Verbascum x *hybridum* (mullein)

Verbena bonariensis (Brazilian verbena)

Verbena canadensis (clump verbena, rose verbena)

Veronica spp. (speedwells)

Viola cornuta (horned violet, tufted pansy)

Viola labradorica var. *purpurea* (Labrador violet)

Viola odorata (sweet violet)

Viola tricolor (Johnny-jump-up)

Yucca filamentosa (Adam's needle, needle palm)

MAIL-ORDER SOURCES

Although it's usually best to purchase container-grown plants from your local nursery or garden center, if you can't find the varieties you're looking for locally, you can order them by mail. The following nurseries are just a few that sell plants through the mail.

ANNUALS

Ed Hume Seeds, Inc.
P.O. Box 1450
Kent, WA 98032
(plants for the Pacific Northwest)

Hastings
2350 Cheshire Bridge Road
P.O. Box 4274
Atlanta, GA 30313
(plants for the South)

Nichols Garden Nursery
1190 North Pacidic Highway
Albany, Oregon 97321
(herbs and rare seeds)

Park Seed Co., Inc.
P.O. Box 46
Greenwood SC 29648-0046

Stokes Seeds, Inc.
P.O. Box 548
Buffalo, NY 14240-0548

Thompson & Morgan
P.O. Box 1308
Jackson NJ 08527

W. Atlee Burpee Co.
300 Park Ave.
Warminister PA 18974

BULBS

B & D Lilies
330 P Street
Port Townsend, WA 98368

Bakker of Holland
U.S. Reservation Center
Louisiana, MO 63353-0050

The Daffodil Mart
Rt. 3, Box 794
Gloucester, VA 23061

Dutch Gardens
P.O. Box 200
Adelphia, NJ 07710

Ed Hume Seeds, Inc. (see above)

Jackson & Perkins
P.O. Box 1028
Medford, OR 97501

John Scheepers, Inc.
R.D. 6
Phillipsburg Road
Middletown, NY 10940

Messelaar Bulb Co., Inc.
P.O. Box 269
County Road, Rt. 1-A
Ipswich, MA 01938

McClure & Zimmerman
108 West Winnebago St.
P.O. Box 368
Friesland, WI 53935

Michigan Bulb Co.
1950 Waldorf, NW
Grand Rapids, MI 49550

Nancy Wilson Species & Miniature Narcissus
571 Woodmont Ave.
Berkeley, CA 94708

Oakwood Daffodils
2330 West Bertrand Road
Niles, MI 49120

Peter De Jager Bulb Co.
P.O. Box 2010
South Hamilton, MA 01982

Quality Dutch Bulbs
P.O. Box 225
Hillsdale, NJ 07642

Smith & Hawken
25 Corte Madera
Mill Valley, CA 94941

Ty Ty Plantation Bulb Co.
P.O. Box 159
Ty Ty, GA 31795

Van Bourgondien Bros., Inc.
P.O. Box A
245 Farmingdale Road
Babylon, NY 11702

Vandenberg
One Black Meadow Road
Chester, NY 10918

Wayside Gardens
One Garden Lane
Hodges, SC 29695

White Flower Farm
P.O. Box 50
Rt. 63
Litchfield, CT 06759-0050

Wyatt-Quarles Seed Co.
P.O. Box 739
Garnder, NC 27529
(plants for the South)

PERENNIALS

Anderson Iris Gardens
22179 Keather Ave., North
Forest Lake, MN 55025

Andre Viette Farm and Nursery
Rt. 1, Box 16
Fishersville, VA 22939

Appalachian Gardens
P.O. Box 82
Waynesboro, PA 17268

Bluestone Perennials
7211 Middle Ridge Road
Madison, OH 44057

Borbeleta Gardens
15980 Canby Ave.
Rt. 5
Faribault, MN 55021

Busse Gardens
Rt. 2, Box 238
Cokato, MN 55321-9426

Cal Dixie Iris Gardens
14115 Pear St.
Riverside, CA 92504

Charles Kelm & Son Nursery
Rt. 1, Box 197
Penny Road
South Barrington, IL 60010

The Crownsville Nursery
P.O. Box 797
Crownsville, MD 21032

Daylily World
P.O. Box 1612
Sanford, FL 32771

Ed Hume Seeds, Inc.
(see above)

Fieldstone Gardens, Inc.
620 Quaker Lane
Vassalboroa, ME 04989-9713

Garden Place
6780 Hershey Road
P.O. Box 388
Mentor, OH 44061-0388

Greenwood Nursery
5595 East 7th, #490
Long Beach, CA 90804

Heritage Gardens
One Meadow Ridge Road
Shenandoah, IA 51601

Holbrook Farm and Nursery
P.O. Box 368
115 Lance Road
Fletcher, NC 28732

Inter-State Nurseries
P.O. Box 208
Hamburg, IA 51640

Jackson & Perkins
(see above)

Kimberly Garden
R.R. 1, Box 44G
Lisle, NY 13797-9732

Klehm Nursery
P.O. Box 197
Penny Road, Rt. 5
South Barrington, IL 60010

Lamb Nurseries
101 East Sharp Ave.
Spokane, WA 99202

Lee Bristol Nursery
P.O. Box 5
Gaylordville, CT 06755-0005

Milaeger's Gardens
4838 Douglas Ave.
Racine, WI 53402-2498

Montrose Nursery
East King Street
P.O. Box 957
Hillsborough, NC 27278

Native Gardens
5737 Fisher Lane
Greenback, TN 37742
(wildflowers)

Oak Hill Gardens
P.O. Box 25
Dundee, IL 60118-0025

Oakes Daylilies
Monday Road
Corryton, TN 37721

Park Seed Co., Inc.
(see above)

Plant Delights Nursery
9241 Sauls Road
Raleigh, NC 27603

Porter & Son
1510 East Washington
P.O. Box 104
Stephensville, TX 76401

Sandy Mush Herb Nursery
Rt. 2, Surrett Cove Road
Leicester, NC 28748
(herbs)

Shady Oaks Nursery
700 19th Ave., NE
Waseca, MN 56093

Siskiyou Rare Plant Nursery
2825 Cummings Road
Medford, OR 97501

Solomon Daylillies
105 County Club Road
Newport, News, VA 23606

Springbrook Gardens Inc.
6776 Heisley Road
P.O. Box 388
Mentor, OH 44061

Sunny Border Nurseries
1709 Kensington Road
P.O. Box 483
Kensington, CT 06037

Thompson & Morgan
(see above)

Wayside Gardens
(see above)

White Flower Farm
(see above)

Woodlanders, Inc.
1128 Colleton Ave.
Aiken, SC 29801
(native plants)

Wright Iris Nursery
6583 Pacheco Pass Highway
Gilroy, CA 95020

Wyatt-Quarles Seed Co.
(see above)

ROSES

Antique Rose Emporium
Rt. 5, Box 143
Brenham, Texas 77833

Heirloom Old Garden Roses
24062 N.E. Riverside Dr.
St. Paul, OR 97137

Heritage Rose Gardens
40350 Wilderness Road
Branscomb, CA 95417

Jackson & Perkins
(see above)

Roses of Yesterday & Today
802 Brown's Valley Road
Watsonville, CA 95076

Wayside Gardens
(see above)

White Flower Farm
(see above)

FERNS

Fancy Fronds Nursery
1911 4th Avenue West
Seattle, WA 98119
(206) 284-5332)

ORNAMENTAL GRASSES

Andre Viette Farm and Nursery
Rt. 1, Box 16
Fishersville, VA 22939

Kurt Bluemel, Inc.
2740 Greene Lane
Baldwin, MD 21013

THE USDA PLANT HARDINESS MAP
OF NORTH AMERICA

ZONE 1
ZONE 2
ZONE 3
ZONE 4
ZONE 5
ZONE 6
ZONE 7
ZONE 8
ZONE 9
ZONE 10
ZONE 11

SPRING FROST DATES

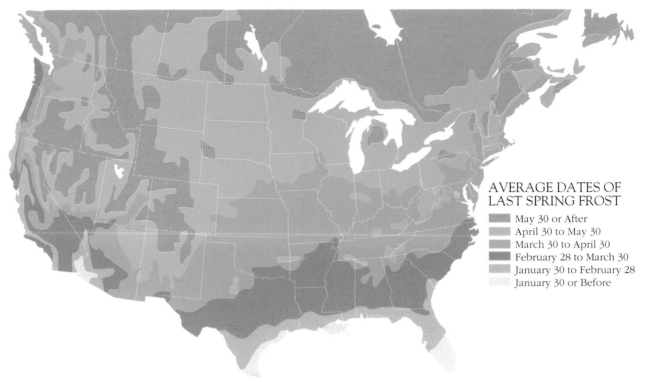

**AVERAGE DATES OF
LAST SPRING FROST**

- May 30 or After
- April 30 to May 30
- March 30 to April 30
- February 28 to March 30
- January 30 to February 28
- January 30 or Before

AUTUMN FROST DATES

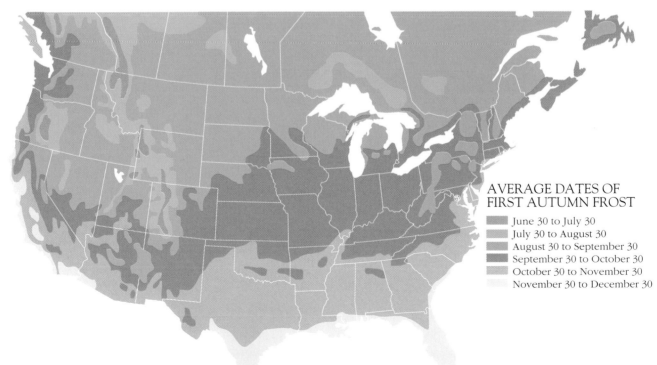

**AVERAGE DATES OF
FIRST AUTUMN FROST**

- June 30 to July 30
- July 30 to August 30
- August 30 to September 30
- September 30 to October 30
- October 30 to November 30
- November 30 to December 30

GENERAL INDEX

Annuals
buying, 17
cutting back, 27–28
deadheading, 27
easy-care, 121
encyclopedia, 292–332
feeding, 28
general information, 10–12
high-maintenance, 121
pinching, 27
planting and care, 27-28

Backgrounds, 56–57
Bare-root plants, 21
Beds and borders, creating, 42–43
Biennials
encyclopedia, 202–291
general information, 13
Bog gardens, 166–171
Borders
color schemes for, 102
creating, 42–43
double, 102–103
easy-care, 110–113
English, 100–103
herbaceous, 101–102
mixed, 110–113
Brick patterns, 86
Bulbs
buying, 17
deadheading, 30
dividing, 31
encyclopedia, 333–363
feeding, 30
general information, 12–13
planting and care, 28-31
storing, 31
tender, 31
Butterfly gardens, 142, 146–150
Buying plants, 16–17

Clean-up chores, 39
Color in garden, 49–52, 102
Color scheme gardens, 172–179
Color schemes
analogous, 176
complementary, 175
cool, 182
hot, 180
monochromatic, 184
Color sequence, 52
Color temperature, 177
Color wheel, 50, 174
Companion plants, 53, 115, 116
Composting, 37–38
Container gardens, 86
Containers, 19
Contrast, creating, 46–47
Cottage gardens, 71–76
Country gardens, 64–97
cottage gardens, 71–76
cutting gardens, 77–82
easy-care patio gardens, 83–87
fragrance gardens, 88–91
herb gardens, 67–70
rose gardens, old-fashioned, 92–97
Cutting back plants, 24–25, 27–28
Cutting gardens, 77–82

Deadheading plants, 10, 24–25, 27, 30
Dividing plants, 25–26, 31
Double borders, 102–104
Dried flowers, 80
Drifts, 45–46

Easy-care gardens, 83–87, 123–124
Easy-care patio gardens, 83–87
Edging, 36–37, 44–45
English borders, 100–109
Everlastings, 80

Fall garden clean-up, 39
Feeding, 15–16, 28, 30, 32, 38
Fences, 56
Ferns, 14, 383–386
Fertilizing, 15–16, 28, 30, 32, 38
Flowering shrubs, 9
Focal points, 60
Foliage, 52, 55
Formal rose gardens, 114–117
Fragrance gardens, 88–91
Frost date maps, 395

Gardener profiles, 70, 76, 82, 104, 105, 129, 135, 142, 186
Garden plans
blue-and-yellow, 178
bog, 170
butterfly, 150
cottage, 75
cutting, 81
double border, 108
easy-care island bed, 120
easy-care mixed border, 113
easy-care patio, 87
English border, 109
formal rose, 117
fragrance, 90
herb, 69
hot color, 181
hot, dry, 165
hummingbird, 151
New American, 134
old-fashioned rose, 97
pink, 179
rock, 141
shade, 160, 161
white, 185
woodland wildflower, 128
Gardens
bog, 166–171
butterfly, 142, 146–150
color scheme, 172–179
cottage, 71–76
cutting, 77–82
double borders, 102–104
easy-care patio, 83–87
English borders, 100–109
fragrance, 88–91
herb, 67–70
hot, dry, 162–165
hummingbird, 143–146, 151
island beds, 118–121
mixed borders, 110–113
New American, 130–135
rose, old-fashioned, 92–97, 114–117
rock and wall, 136–142
shade, 154–161
woodland, 124–129
Garden shape, 42–44
Garden size, 42
Garden style, 56
Growing conditions, 60
Gulf Coast and Coastal Plains, best plants for, 390

Hardening off, 21
Hardiness Zone Map, 394
Hedges, 57
Herbaceous borders, 101–102
Herb gardens, 67–70
Hot, dry gardens, 162–165
Hummingbird gardens, 143–146, 151

Impact, achieving, 53
Interplanting, 53
Island flower beds, 118–121

Lighting, 18
Long-blooming perennials, 54
Long-lasting plants, 54, 79

Mail-order plant sources, 393
Mid-Atlantic, best plants for, 388
Midwest, best plants for, 390

Mixed borders, 110–113
Monochromatic color schemes, 184
Mulching, 35–36

Naturalistic gardens, 122–151
butterfly gardens, 142, 146–150
hummingbird gardens, 143–146, 151
New American gardens, 130–135
rock and wall gardens, 136–142
woodland gardens, 124–129
New American gardens, 130–135
Northeast, best plants for, 387

Old-fashioned rose gardens, 92–97
Ornamental grasses
cutting back, 24–25
deadheading, 24, 25
dividing, 25–26
encyclopedia, 375–382
general information, 14
pinching, 24–25
planting and care, 21–22
staking, 22, 23

Pacific Northwest, best plants for, 392
Paths, 58
Patio garden plan, 87
Patio gardens, 83–87
Paving plants, 85
Perennials
bare-root, 21
buying, 16–17
container-grown, 22
cutting back, 24–25
deadheading, 24, 25
dividing, 25–26
easy-care, 121
encyclopedia, 202–291
general information, 10
high-maintenance, 121
long-blooming, 54
pinching, 24–25
planting and care, 10, 21–26
staking, 22, 23
transplanting, 21
Pest control, 39
Pinching, 24–25, 27
Pink garden plan, 179
Pink garden plant lists, 179, 194–195
Plains and Rocky Mountains, best plants for, 391
Plant combinations, 53
Plant lists
blue flowers, 190–191
blue or blue-gray leaves, 187
bog garden, 169
bronze foliage, 199
butterfly garden, 149
companion plants for formal rose gardens, 116
coral flowers, 196–197
cottage garden, 73, 74, 75
crimson (purplish red) flowers, 198–199
cutting garden, 79, 80, 81
drought-tolerant, 164
easy-care, 121
English border, 106
everlastings, 80
fragrance garden, 90, 91
golden foliage, 187
gold flowers, 192–193
gray foliage, 197
herb garden, 67, 69
high-maintenance, 121
hummingbird garden, 145
lavender flowers, 190–191
long-blooming, 54
long-lasting, 54, 79
magenta-pink flowers, 194–195
New American garden, 132–133
old-fashioned, 74
orange flowers, 196–197
patio garden, 83–87
paving, 85
pink flowers, 194–195
purple flowers, 190–191

Plant lists (continued)
purple foliage, 199
red flowers, 198–199
rock and wall garden, 140
rose flowers, 194–195
scarlet (orange-red) flowers, 196–197
self-sowing flowers, 73
self-sowing herbs, 73
silver foliage, 197
spikes and spires, 48
variegated gold-and-green leaves, 187
variegated green-and-white foliage, 187
wet sites, 169
white flowers, 185, 188–189
wildflowers, 127
yellow flowers, 192–193
Plants, buying, 16–17
Plants, self-sowing, 73
Plants, shapes and sizes of, 49
Plants, sharing, 16
Plants, staking, 22–23
Poorly drained sites, 166–169
Preparing the soil, 15–16, 19
Problem-site gardens, 152–171
bog gardens, 166–171
hot, dry gardens, 162–165
shade gardens, 154–161
Pruning roses, 32-33

Rock and wall gardens, 136–142
Rose gardens, 92–97, 114–117
Roses
bare-root, 31
companions, 115
encyclopedia, 364–374
feeding, 32
general information, 12
pest control, 39
pinching, 24–25, 27
planting and care, 31–35
pruning, 32–33, 34
winter care, 34

Seed, starting plants from, 18–21
Seedlings, transplanting, 20
Selecting plants, 16-17
Self-sowing plants, 73
Shade gardens, 154–161
Shape of garden, 42–44
Shape of plants, 49
Size of garden, 42
Size of plants, 49
Soil for containers, 19
Soil preparation, 15–16, 19
South, best plants for, 389
Southwest, best plants for, 389
Sowing seeds, technique for, 19
Spikes and spires, plants with, 48
Staking plants, 22–23
Starting plants from seed, 18–21
Storing bulbs, 31
Style, 56–57

Temperature, color, 177
Texture, 42, 46–47
Three seasons of bloom, 52
Trading plants, 16
Traditional gardens, 98–121
double borders, 102–104
English borders, 100–109
island beds, 118–121
mixed borders, 110–113
rose gardens, formal, 114–117
Transplanting seedlings, 20

Views, incorporating, 57

Wall gardens. See Rock and wall gardens
Walls, 56
Watering, 38–39
Weeding, 36
Wildflowers, 126
Winter protection, 34, 39
Woodland gardens, 124–129

PLANT INDEX

'Abba,' 361
'Abbey's Violet,' 248
'Abbotswood Rose,' 255
Abelmoschus manihot, 292
Abelmoschus moschatus, 292
'Abo-roseum,' 290
'Abraham Darby,' 367
Abyssinian gladiolus. See *Acidanthera murielae*
Acanthus mollis, 164, 197, 202
Acanthus spinosus var. *spinosissimus,* 202, 388, 389, 390, 391, 392
Acanthus spp., 106, 132
'Acapulco Silver,' 313
'Accent,' 311, 354
'Accent Deep Pink,' 195
'Accent Lavender,' 161, 191
'Accent Lavender Blue,' 191
'Accent Orange,' 196
'Accent Orange Star,' 196
'Accent Pink,' 160, 311
'Accent Star' series, 311
'Accent White,' 113, 189
'Accord Blue Notch,' 191
Achillea filipendulina, 79, 80, 121, 181, 192, 202, 387, 388, 389, 391, 392
Achillea millefolium, 67, 69, 80, 87, 188, 192, 194, 196, 198, 203, 388, 390, 391, 392
Achillea spp., 106, 132, 149, 164
Achillea taygetea, 183, 203
Achillea tomentosa, 85, 192, 197, 203, 389, 391
Achillea x 'Coronation Gold,' 54, 203
Achillea x 'Moonshine,' 54, 120, 165, 181, 192, 197, 203, 387, 388, 389, 391, 392
Acidanthera bicolor, 333
Acidanthera murielae, 91, 333
Aconitum carmichaelii, 75, 79, 97, 204
Aconitum fischeri. See *Aconitum carmichaelii*
Aconitum napellus, 204
Aconitum spp., 48, 74, 107, 121, 127, 159, 190, 387, 388, 392
Aconitum x *cammarum,* 204
'Actaea,' 356
'Activity,' 190
'Adam,' 260
Adam's needle. See *Yucca filamentosa*
Adder's tongue. See *Erythronium americanum*
Adiantum capillus-veneris, 383
Adiantum pedatum, 14, 127, 128, 383
'Adonis,' 346
'Adrian Bloom,' 233
'Advance,' 343, 349
African lily. See *Agapanthus* hybrids
African marigold. See *Tagetes erecta*
Agapanthus, 182
Agapanthus africanus, 191, 333
Agapanthus hybrids, 159, 333
Agapanthus orientalis, 333
Ageratum houstonianum, 116, 148, 149, 189, 191, 292
'Aglaya,' 226
Aizoon stonecrop. See *Sedum aizoon*
Ajuga genevensis, 204
Ajuga pyramidalis, 204
Ajuga reptans, 48, 85, 97, 116, 132, 157, 160, 190, 204, 388, 389, 391, 392
Ajuga spp., 106
'Alaska,' 49, 81, 103, 120, 226, 331
'Alba,' 188, 209, 215, 218, 219, 220, 221, 223, 228, 230, 233, 235, 238, 241, 242, 245, 250, 254, 255, 259, 262, 266, 304, 336, 339, 340, 341, 347, 370, 371
Alba Plena,' 266
Alba roses, 92, 364
'Alba-variegata,' 187
'Albidus,' 333
'Albo-marginata,' 41, 187
'Albo-roseum,' 290
'Album,' 188, 189, 241, 271, 290, 344, 354
'Album Superbum,' 280
'Albus,' 231, 285
Alcea rosea, 13, 48, 74, 75, 107, 145, 149, 150, 192, 194, 198, 204, 387, 388, 390
Alchemilla alpina, 205

Alchemilla mollis, 67, 90, 91, 92, 99, 159, 161, 205, 387, 388, 391, 392
Alchemilla spp., 106, 116, 132
Alchemilla vulgaris, 205
'Alert,' 90
'Alesia,' 188
'Alexander's White,' 247
'Alfred Cortot,' 363
'All Change,' 297
Allegheny foamflower. See *Tiarella cordifolia*
'Allen Bush,' 226
Allium, 53, 131
Allium aflatunense, 79, 80, 81, 120, 134, 191, 333, 334
Allium azureum, 191. See also *Allium caeruleum*
Allium caeruleum, 334
Allium cernuum, 336
Allium christophii, 191, 334
Allium flavum, 335
Allium giganteum, 29, 191, 334
Allium karataviense, 334
Allium minor alba, 336
Allium moly, 183, 193, 335
Allium neapolitanum, 335
Allium ostrowskianum, 335
Allium schoenoprasum, 66, 67, 69, 80, 335
Allium senescens glaucum, 191, 336
Allium sphaerocephalum, 191, 336
Allium spp., 133, 140, 149, 164
Allium thunbergii, 336
Allium tuberosum, 335, 336
'Allure,' 322
'Alma Potschke,' 54, 194, 212
'Alpha,' 194, 267
Alstroemeria aurantiaca, 79, 205, 389
Alyssum, sweet, 27, 45, 46, 84, 105. See also *Lobularia maritima*
Alyssum maritimum, 315
Alyssum saxatile. See *Aurinia saxatilis*
Amaranthus caudatus, 198, 292, 293
Amaranthus tricolor, 293
Amaryllis belladonna, 79, 91, 195, 337
Amaryllis hallii. See *Lycoris squamigera*
'Amazing Grace,' 268
'Ambassador,' 199
'Amber Glow,' 308
'Amber Queen,' 91
'America,' 91, 370
American columbine. See *Aquilegia canadensis*
'American Indian,' 312
'Amethyst,' 213, 237, 321
Amethyst flower. See *Browallia speciosa*
Amethyst sea holly. See *Eryngium amethystinum*
Amsonia angustifolia, 206
Amsonia montana, 206
Amsonia salicifolia, 206
Amsonia tabernaemontana, 104, 106, 121, 178, 206, 388, 389, 390
Anaphalis cinnamomea, 80, 106, 140, 206, 391
Anaphalis margaritacea, 206, 391
Anaphalis triplinervis, 87, 188, 197, 206, 387, 388, 392
Anchusa azurea, 190, 207
'Androisee de Lyon,' 369
Anemone blanda, 29, 189, 191, 195, 337
Anemone coronaria, 337
Anemone japonica. See *Anemone* x *hybrida*
Anemone pulsatilla. See *Pulsatilla vulgaris*
Anemone tomentosa, 207
Anemone vitifolia, 194
Anemone x *hybrida,* 55, 74, 75, 107, 108, 109, 113, 121, 132, 149, 150, 159, 179, 183, 185, 188, 194, 207, 387, 388, 389, 390, 391, 392
Anethum graveolens, 67, 73, 91, 149, 293
'Angel Face,' 91, 367
Angelica archangelica, 67, 107, 132, 188, 207, 392
Angelica atropurpurea, 208
'Angelique,' 109, 179, 195, 361
'Angel Pink,' 195
'Angel's Blush,' 255
Angel's tears. See *Narcissus triandrus*
'Angel Wings,' 328, 330
'Anise,' 320
'Anna Marie,' 195, 349
'Anne Arundel,' 194, 246
Annual aster. See *Callistephus chinensis*

Annual baby's breath. See *Gypsophila elegans*
Annual blanket-flower. See *Gaillardia pulchella*
Annual candytuft. See *Iberis umbellata*
Annual dahlia. See *Dahlia* x *hybrida*
Annual mallow. See *Lavatera trimestris*
Annual monkey flower. See *Mimulus* x *hybridus*
Annual phlox. See *Phlox drummondii*
Annual pincushion flower. See *Scabiosa caucasica atropurpurea*
Anthemis tinctoria, 54, 121, 163, 164, 192, 208, 389, 391
Antirrhinum majus, 48, 73, 79, 81, 121, 145, 149, 189, 191, 192, 195, 196, 198, 293
'Apeldoorn,' 75
'Aphrodite,' 213
Apothecary rose, 92. See also *Rosa gallica officinalis*
'Apple Blossom,' 97, 300, 373
'Appleblossom,' 154, 194, 203, 268, 323
Apple mint. See *Mentha suaveolens*
'Apricot Beauty,' 197, 235, 361
'Apricot Nectar,' 367
'Apricot Shades,' 316
Aquilegia canadensis, 127, 192, 196, 208, 387, 388, 389
Aquilegia caerulea, 188, 208, 248, 391
Aquilegia chrysantha, 192, 209, 389, 390, 391
Aquilegia flabellata, 87, 209, 388
Aquilegia spp., 140, 145, 151
Aquilegia vulgaris, 74, 75, 209, 388
Aquilegia x *hybrida,* 51, 54, 87, 106, 108, 113, 157, 178, 179, 181, 190, 192, 194, 198, 208, 387, 388, 389, 390, 392
Arabis albida. See *Arabis caucasica*
Arabis aubrietioides, 209
Arabis caucasica, 91, 149, 188, 209, 387, 388, 390, 391, 392
Arabis procurrens, 209
Arabis spp., 140
Archangel. See *Angelica archangelica*
'Arendsii,' 204
'Argentea,' 377
'Argenteus,' 285
Argentine blue-eyed grass. See *Sisyrinchium striatum*
Arisaema sikokianum, 169, 338
Arisaema spp., 171, 169
Arisaema triphyllum, 127, 128, 338
'Arizona,' 91, 368
'Arkwright Ruby,' 290
Armenian basket flower. See *Centaurea macrocephala*
Armeria maritima, 54, 85, 106, 140, 149, 164, 188, 194, 209, 387, 388, 391, 392
'Armour,' 331
'Armour Purple,' 191
'Aroma,' 293
Artemisia, 96, 116, 182
Artemisia absinthium, 210
Artemisia ludoviciana, 80, 107, 197, 209, 389
Artemisia schmidtiana, 44, 106, 108, 116, 178, 185, 197, 210, 391
Artemisia spp., 132, 387
Artemisia stelleriana, 115, 197, 209
Artemisia x 'Powis Castle,' 210, 388, 389, 390
Artemisia x 'Valerie Finnis,' 109, 210, 389
'Art Shades,' 296
Aruncus aethusifolius, 210
Aruncus dioicus, 107, 121, 169, 170, 188, 210, 387, 388
Aruncus spp., 127, 132
Aruncus sylvester. See *Aruncus dioicus*
Asclepias tuberosa, 79, 106, 121, 145, 149, 150, 164, 192, 196, 211, 387, 388, 390, 391, 392
Asiatic hybrid lily. See *Lilium* Asiatic hybrids
Asphodeline lutea, 41, 48, 106, 175, 211, 391, 392
Aster, 22, 24, 87
Aster azureus, 190
Aster novi-belgii x *novae-angliae,* 54, 79, 81, 107, 108, 109, 121, 178, 188, 190, 194, 198, 211, 387, 388, 390, 391
Aster spp., 149
Aster x 'Alma Potschke,' 54, 81, 212
Aster x *frikartii,* 54, 107, 108, 132, 134, 178, 183, 190, 212, 387, 388, 389, 390, 392
Aster x 'September Ruby,' 54, 212

Astilbe, 25, 26, 53, 55, 213
Astilbe chinensis, 90
Astilbe chinensis var. *pumila,* 106, 159, 194, 212, 390
Astilbe simplicifolia, 106, 159, 194, 212
Astilbe spp., 121, 132, 149, 169, 387, 388
Astilbe taquetii, 48, 87, 107, 159, 160, 194, 213
Astilbe x *arendsii,* 45, 79, 99, 106, 154, 159, 161, 177, 188, 194, 198, 213, 389
'Astolat,' 230
'Astrid Thomas,' 306
Athyrium filix-femina, 127, 383
Athyrium goeringianum pictum, 14, 154, 383
Athyrium niponicum pictum, 14, 383
'Atropurpurea,' 199, 204, 268, 324
'Atropurpureum,' 109, 238, 280, 281
'Atrosanguineum,' 179, 223, 382
Aubrieta deltoidea, 85, 139, 140, 149, 190, 214, 387, 388, 391, 392
'August Glory,' 54, 251
August lily. See *Hosta plantaginea*
'August Moon,' 161, 187
'Aurea,' 187, 206, 256, 277, 304
'Aurea Pura,' 192, 240
Aurelian lilies. See Lilium
Aurelian hybrid lilies. See *Lilium* x *auralianense*
Aurelian trumpet lilies. See Lilium
'Aureola,' 161, 187, 378
'Aureo-marginata,' 187
'Aureo-reticulata,' 313
'Aureo-variegata,' 91, 187, 376
'Aureum,' 91, 263, 379, 392
Aurinia saxatilis, 74, 106, 109, 139, 140, 141, 149, 150, 164, 165, 178, 192, 197, 214, 387, 388, 390, 391, 392
'Aurora,' 297, 329, 347
'Auten's Pride,' 194
'Autumn Beauty,' 120
Autumn crocus. See *Colchicum autumnale*
'Autumn Damask,' 366
'Autumn Glory,' 198, 275, 276
'Autumn Joy,' 53, 54, 80, 87, 130, 134, 135, 150, 165, 280, 281, 389
Autumn joy stonecrop. See *Sedum* x *telephium*
Autumn sage. See *Salvia greigii*
'Autumn Snow,' 247
'Autumn Sun,' 276
'Avalanche,' 90, 214
'Avignon,' 197
'Awkwright Ruby,' 290
Azalea, 112, 113, 142, 146, 158
'Azalea-flowered Mix,' 300
'Azure,' 314
'Azurea,' 273
'Azure Blue,' 237
'Azure Fairy,' 237
Azure grape hyacinth. See *Muscari azureum*
Azure monkshood. See *Aconitum carmichaelii*

'Baby Cole,' 54, 240
'Baby Franjo,' 290
'Babylon,' 199
'Baby Lucia,' 290
'Baby Moon,' 355
Baby's breath, 49. See also *Gypsophila paniculata*
'Baby Sun,' 227, 283
'Baby White,' 250
Bachelor's button. See *Centaurea cyanus*
'Bahia,' 367
'Balcon,' 321
'Ballerina,' 197, 305, 361, 368
Balloon flower, 24, 25, 104. See also *Platycodon grandiflorus*
Balsam. See *Impatiens balsamina*
Baptisia alba, 188, 215
Baptisia australis, 48, 106, 121, 132, 134, 149, 178, 190, 214, 387, 388, 389, 390, 391
'Barbara Bush,' 117
Barberry, 96
'Barcarolle,' 289
'Baroness Rothschild,' 369
'Baronne Prevost,' 369
Barrenwort, 10. See also *Epimedium* x *youngianum*
'Barrett Browning,' 354

Basil. See *Ocimum basilicum*
'Barr's Purple,' 343
'Bartered Bride,' 238
Basket-of-gold. See *Aurinia saxatilis*
'Bastogne,' 199, 361
'Bath's Pink,' 194, 232
Beach rose. See *Rosa rugosa*
Beach wormwood. See *Artemisia stelleriana*
'Beacon,' 203
'Beacon Silver,' 194, 250
Beach wormwood, 115, 210. See also *Artemisia stelleriana*
Bead fern. See *Onoclea sensibilis*
Bearded iris, 196. See also *Iris hybrida*
Bearded tongue. See *Penstemon* x *gloxinioides*
Beard-tongue. See *Penstemon barbatus*
Bear's breeches. See *Acanthus*
'Beauty of Cobham,' 260
'Beauty of Eastbourne,' 321
'Beauty of Grallagh,' 208
'Beauty of Livermore,' 196, 264
'Bedder,' 299
Bedding begonia. See *Begonia* x *semperflorens*
Bee-balm, 67. See also *Monarda didyma*
Beech fern, 123
'Beedham's White,' 250
Beefsteak plant, 182. See *Iresine herbstii* and *Perilla frutescens*
'Bee's Flame,' 199, 253
Begonia, wax, 45
Begonia evansiana. See *Begonia grandis*
Begonia grandis, 107, 159, 160, 194, 215, 388, 392
Begonia spp., 29
Begonia x *semperflorens,* 121, 159, 189, 195, 198, 294
Begonia x *tuberhybrida,* 159, 193, 195, 197, 199, 338
'Beidermeier Hybrids,' 208
Belamcanda chinensis, 106, 164, 196, 215, 391, 392
'Belinda,' 368
Belladona lily. See *Amaryllis belladona*
Belladonna delphinium. See *Delphinium* x *belladonna*
'Bella Vista,' 197
'Belle de Crecy,' 368
Bellflower, 24. See also *Campanula carpatica*
Bellis perennis, 44, 74, 75, 106, 188, 216, 392
'Bellona,' 91
Bells-of-Ireland. See *Moluccella laevis*
'Bell Song,' 355
'Bennington White,' 188
Berberis thunbergii, 113
Bergenia cordifolia, 87, 106, 179, 194, 216, 390
Bergenia crassifolia, 216
Bergenia purpurascens, 216
Bergenia spp., 10, 132, 169, 388, 392
'Berggarten,' 277
'Bertie Ferris,' 196
Bethlehem sage. See *Pulmonaria saccharata*
'Betty Prior,' 113, 367
'Beverly Sills,' 194
'Bewitched,' 79
'Bianca,' 282
'Bicolor,' 204
Bicolor monkshood. See *Aconitum carmichaeli*
'Big Blue,' 190
Big–blue lobelia. See *Lobelia siphilitica*
Big-leaf ligularia. See *Ligularia dentata*
'Big Red,' 199
'Bijou Mix,' 314
'Bingo,' 294, 332
'Bingo Red,' 198
Bishop's hat. See *Epimedium* x *youngianum*
'Blackberry Ice,' 311
Blackberry lily. See *Belamcanda chinensis*
'Black Dragon,' 90, 301, 353
Black-eyed Susan, 130. See also *Rudbeckia hirta* and *Thunbergia alata*
Black-foot daisy, 193, 317
'Blackheart,' 308
'Black Knight,' 230, 380
'Black Magic,' 291
Black mondo grass. See *Ophiopogon planiscapus*
'Blakonigin,' 278
'Blanc Double de Coubert,' 90, 91, 374
Blanket-flower. See *Gaillardia* x *grandiflora*

'Blaze,' 199
'Blaze Improved,' 370
Blazing star. See *Liatris spicata*
Bleeding heart. See *Dicentra spectabilis*
'Bleu Magenta,' 373
'Blitz,' 311
'Blitz Red,' 198
Bloodleaf. See *Iresine herbstii*
'Blood Red,' 198, 231, 299
Bloodroot. See *Sanguinaria canadensis*
Bloody cranesbill. See *Geranium sanguineum*
'Blue,' 292, 295, 296
'Blue Aimable,' 178, 191, 361
'Blue Balsam,' 259
Bluebeard shrub. See *Caryopteris*
'Blue Bedder,' 327
Bluebells, Virginia, 182. See also *Mertensia virginica*
'Blue Bells,' 296
'Blue Bells Improved,' 191, 296
'Blue Bird,' 190, 230
'Blue Blazer,' 191
'Blue Boy,' 190, 267, 299
'Blue Boy Double,' 191
'Blue Brilliant,' 190
'Blue Butterfly,' 54, 190, 231, 279, 301
'Blue Cadet,' 187
'Blue Cascade,' 191
'Blue Charm,' 49, 182, 190, 289
'Blue Chips,' 109
'Blue Clips,' 178, 218
Blue daisy. See *Felicia amelloides*
'Blue Danube,' 190, 284, 340
'Blue Diadem,' 191
'Blue Diamond,' 252
Blue-eyed Mary. See *Omphaloides verna*
Blue fescue, 44. See also *Festuca ovina*
'Bluefinch,' 378
Blue flag iris. See *Iris versicolor*
Blue flax. See *Linum perenne*
'Blue Fox,' 289
'Blue Fountains,' 230
'Blue Gardenia,' 220
'Blue Gem,' 318
'Blue Giant,' 289
Blue globe onion. See *Allium caeruleum*
'Blue Gown,' 190
Blue grape hyacinth. See *Muscari armeniacum*
'Blue Heron,' 361
'Blue Hill,' 278
'Blue Horizon,' 292
'Blue Improved,' 191
'Blue Jacket,' 175, 185, 191, 349
'Blue Jay,' 190
'Blue Joy,' 191
'Blue Lace,' 191, 325
'Blue Lagoon,' 190, 331
Blue lilyturf. See *Liriope muscari*
'Blue Lisa,' 191
Blue lungwort. See *Pulmonaria angustifolia*
Blue lyme grass. See *Elymus arenarius*
'Blue Mammoth,' 52
Blue marguerite. See *Felicia amelloides*
'Blue Mink,' 292
'Blue Moon,' 91, 113, 178, 190, 249
'Blue Mound,' 276
Blue oat grass. See *Helictotrichon sempervirens*
'Blue Panda,' 113, 191, 330, 331
'Blue Parrot,' 191, 361
'Blue Pearl,' 190, 191, 269
'Blue Perfection,' 290
'Blue Peter,' 254
'Blue Picotee,' 191
'Blue Queen,' 191, 278, 348
'Blue Ribbon,' 191, 343
'Blue Ridge,' 190, 268
'Blue Shades,' 191, 337
Blue sheep's fescue. See *Festuca ovina*
'Blue Showers,' 191
'Blue Skies,' 191
'Blue Spike,' 176, 191, 353, 354
'Blue Spire,' 191, 265
'Blue Splendor,' 191
'Blue Springs,' 230
'Blue Staccato,' 191
'Blue Star,' 113, 191, 295, 337
'Blue Stocking,' 190, 260
'Bluestone,' 54
'Blue Troll,' 191, 296
Bluets. See *Hedyotis caerulea*

Blue wild indigo. See *Baptisia australis*
Blue wild rye. See *Elymus arenarius*
'Blue Wonder,' 261
'Blushing Bride,' 308
'Bobbie James,' 373
'Boccherini,' 191, 361
Bocconia cordata. See *Macleaya cordata*
Bokhara iris. See *Iris bucharica*
Bokhara tulip. See *Tulipa batalinii*
'Bollero,' 322
Boltonia, 104. See also *Boltonia asteroides*
Boltonia asteroides, 107, 108, 132, 179, 188, 194, 216, 387, 388, 389, 390, 392
'Bonanza,' 198, 329
'Bon Bon,' 180, 296
'Bon-bon Orange,' 196
'Bonfire,' 264
'Bonica,' 371
'Bonn,' 213
Borage, 182. See also *Borago officinalis*
Borago laxiflora, 295
Borago officinalis, 67, 69, 73, 149, 191, 294
Border penstemon. See *Penstemon* x *gloxinioides*
'Borisii,' 242
Bottle gentian. See *Gentiana andrewsii*
Boulder fern. See *Dennstaedtia punctilobula*
'Boule de Neige,' 364
Bouncing Bet. See *Saponaria officinalis*
'Bountiful,' 54, 233
'Bouquet,' 293
'Bouquet Rose,' 179, 195, 269
Bourbon roses, 91, 93, 96, 97, 364
Boxwood, 57, 70, 99, 100, 101, 103, 114, 115
'Boy,' 329
Brachycome iberidifolia, 85, 97, 121, 140, 141, 164, 165, 191, 295
Branched bugbane. See *Cimicifuga ramosa*
'Brandywine,' 285
Brassica oleracea, 295
'Bravado,' 236
Brazilian verbena. See *Verbena bonariensis*
'Breakaway,' 322
'Breakthrough Mix,' 319
'Bressingham Blue,' 333
'Bressingham Hybrids,' 246
'Bressingham Ruby,' 216
'Bressingham Spire,' 204
'Bressingham White,' 216
'Bridal Veil,' 161, 188, 214
'Bridget Bloom,' 194, 246
'Bright Bikini Mix,' 309
'Bright Edge,' 291
'Bright Eyes,' 109, 179, 182, 194, 267
'Bright Gem,' 120, 141, 176, 193, 360
'Bright Lights,' 302
'Bright Orange Daybreak,' 196
'Bright Star,' 54, 113, 194, 236, 353
'Bright Yellow Daybreak,' 192
'Brilliant,' 231, 243, 281, 282, 325
'Brio,' 197
'Bristol Fairy,' 242
Briza maxima, 375
Briza media, 80, 375
'Broadway,' 91
Brodiaea coronaria, 191, 338, 339
Brodiaea laxa, 339
Brodiaea uniflora. See *Ipheion uniflorum*
'Bronze Beauty,' 204
'Bronze Charm,' 360
Bronze-leaf cardinal flower. See *Lobelia* x *speciosa*
'Bronze Elegance,' 213
'Bronzeschleier,' 377
'Bronze Veil,' 377
Browallia speciosa, 73, 121, 189, 191, 295
'Bruce's White,' 188, 268
'Brunette,' 199, 227
Brunnera macrophylla, 106, 190, 217, 387, 391
Brunsvigia rosea. See *Amaryllis belladonna*
'Bubble Bath,' 368
Buddleia, 43, 113, 146, 183
'Buddy,' 308
Bugbane. See *Cimicifuga ramosa*
Bugleweed, 96, 182. See also *Ajuga reptans*
Bugloss, Italian, 182
Bulbocodium vernum, 140, 339
'Bunny Puff,' 189

'Burgundy,' 240
'Burgundy Giant,' 382
'Burgundy Glow,' 96, 97, 160, 182, 204
Burning bush. See *Kochia scoparia* var. *trichophylla*
'Burning Heart,' 361
Busy lizzie. See *Impatiens wallerana*
'Butter and Sugar,' 181, 192, 249
Butterfly bush, 146. See *Buddleia*
Butterfly flower. See *Schizanthus pinnatus*
Butterfly weed. See *Asclepias tuberosa*
'Butterpat,' 192, 243
'Butterscotch,' 193
Butterweed. See *Senecio tomentosus*
'Buttery Orange,' 197
'Buzz Bomb,' 196

'Caesar,' 249
'Caesar's Brother,' 87, 104, 190, 249
Caladium x *hortulanum,* 159, 339
Calamagrostis acutiflora, 133, 134, 375
Calamint. See *Calamintha nepeta*
Calamintha grandiflora, 217
Calamintha nepeta, 91, 106, 164, 217
Calamintha nepetoides, 217
Calendula officinalis, 67, 73, 79, 164, 180, 192, 196, 296
'California,' 308
California poppy. See *Eschscholzia californica*
Calla lily. See *Zantedeschia aethiopica*
Calliopsis. See *Coreopsis tinctoria*
Calliopsis bicolor, 301
Callistephus chinensis, 79, 121, 191, 296
Bowles golden grass. See *Carex stricta*
'Bowles Golden,' 133, 159, 187, 376
'Calypso,' 317
'Camara Mixed Hybrids,' 313
Camas. See *Camassia leichtlinii*
Camassia cusickii, 340
Camassia esculenta, 340
Camassia leichtlinii, 48, 127, 191, 340
Camassia quamash, 340
'Cambridge,' 249
'Cambridge Blue,' 87, 191, 315
'Cambridge Scarlet,' 54, 151, 198, 260
'Cameliard,' 194
Campanula carpatica, 54, 85, 87, 106, 109, 140, 141, 178, 188, 190, 218, 391
Campanula elantines var. *garganica,* 219
Campanula garganica, 106, 218
Campanula glomerata, 74, 97, 106, 113, 178, 219, 390
Campanula lactiflora, 97, 107, 219
Campanula medium, 48, 195, 297
Campanula persicifolia, 48, 74, 75, 87, 107, 219
Campanula portenschlagiana, 54, 97, 116, 140, 141, 220
Campanula poscharskyana, 54, 220, 391
Campanula pyramidalis, 297
Campanula spp., 121, 387, 388, 392
Canadian roses, 365
'Candelabra,' 297
'Candidum,' 339
'Candy,' 322
Candystick tulip. See *Tulipa clusiana*
'Candy Stripe,' 268
Candytuft, edging, 10, 103. See also *Iberis sempervirens*
Canna lily, 46, 340
Canna x *generalis,* 48, 133, 145, 193, 195, 197, 199, 340
Canterbury bells. See *Campanula medium*
'Cape Cod,' 197, 363
'Capri,' 191, 292
Capsicum annuum, 297
'Cardinal de Richelieu,' 368
Cardinal flower. See *Lobelia cardinalis*
Cardoon. See *Cynara cardunculus*
'Carefree Beauty,' 374
Carex buchananii, 376
Carex morrowii, 133, 159, 187, 375
Carex stricta, 133, 159, 187, 376
'Carlton,' 120, 134, 181, 354
'Carmenetta,' 373
'Carmina,' 194, 198, 271
'Carmine,' 198
'Carminea Rendatleri,' 377
'Carmine Rose,' 195

'Carnival,' 264
'Carnival Mix,' 318
Carolina lupine, 104. See also *Thermopsis caroliniana*
Carolina phlox. See *Phlox carolina*
'Carousel,' 225
Carpathian bellflower. See *Campanula carpatica*
'Carpet,' 298, 325
'Carpet Ball,' 297
Carpet bugle. See *Ajuga reptans*
'Carpet of Snow,' 87, 189, 316
'Carpet White,' 185, 189
'Cartwheel,' 117, 371
Caryopteris, 43
'Casa Blanca,' 81, 89, 109, 185, 352
'Casablanca,' 189, 351
'Cascade,' 214, 315
'Casino Mix,' 326
'Cassian,' 381
'Castle Pink,' 195
'Castle Scarlet,' 196
'Castle Yellow,' 192
Castor bean, 46. See also *Ricinus communis*
Castor oil plant. See *Ricinus communis*
Catharanthus roseus, 121, 189, 195, 297
'Catherine Woodbury,' 113, 194
Catmint, 95, 115. See also *Nepeta mussinii* and *Nepeta x faassenii*
Catnip. See *Nepeta cataria*
'Cattleya,' 214
'Cavalier,' 198
'Cecile Brunner,' 372
'Celebration,' 312
'Celestial,' 364
Celosia cristata, 48, 79, 80, 81, 121, 180, 181, 192, 195, 196, 198, 298
Celosia spicata, 195
Centaurea cineraria, 55, 87, 132, 298
Centaurea cyanus, 73, 79, 81, 191, 298, 299
Centaurea macrocephala, 192, 221, 391
Centaurea montana, 54, 74, 75, 107, 178, 190, 220, 387, 392
Centifolia roses, 91, 93, 97, 365
Centranthus ruber, 54, 74, 75, 91, 107, 108, 185, 187, 188, 194, 221, 388, 389, 390, 391, 392
'Century Mixed,' 298
'Century Red,' 198
'Century Yellow,' 180, 192
Cerastium biebersteinii, 222
Cerastium tomentosum, 74, 85, 106, 116, 140, 164, 165, 188, 190, 197, 221, 387, 391, 392
Ceratostigma plumbaginoides, 54, 106, 116, 132, 222, 388, 392
Ceratostigma willmottianum, 222
'Cerise Queen,' 203
Chamaemelum nobile, 67, 74, 91, 222
Chamomile, 89. See also *Chamaemelum nobile*
'Champagne Bubbles,' 264
'Chandelier,' 254
'Chansonette Mix,' 307
'Chantreyland,' 196, 290
'Charles de Mills,' 92, 368
'Charm,' 198
'Charm Bracelet,' 371
'Charmian,' 367
'Charms,' 304
Chasmanthium latifolium, 80, 133, 159, 376
'Chatelaine,' 194, 254
'Chater's,' 205
'Chater's Yellow,' 192
'Chatterbox,' 194, 246
Checkerbloom. See *Sidalcea malviflora*
Checkered lily. See *Fritillaria meleagris*
Cheddar pink. See *Dianthus gratianopolitanus*
'Cheerfulness,' 120, 354
'Cheerio,' 264
'Cheers,' 195, 323
Cheiranthus cheiri, 91, 140, 192, 196, 299
Chelone glabra, 107, 170, 223
Chelone lyonii, 194, 222, 388
Chelone obliqua, 223
Chelone spp., 169, 387
'Chequers,' 250
'Cherish,' 79, 367
Cherry tree, 148
'Cherry Blossom,' 195, 323
'Cherry Cheeks,' 109, 194

'Cherry Orchard,' 197, 363
'Cherry Queen,' 195
'Cherry Ripe,' 198
'Cherry Splash,' 246
'Chicago Braves,' 244
'Chief Justice,' 198
'Childsiana,' 363
'Childsii,' 313
'Child's Play,' 371
Chilean avens. See *Geum quellyon*
China aster. See *Callistephus chinensis*
'China Boy,' 264
'China Doll,' 196, 218, 372
'China Glow,' 195
China pink, 11. See also *Dianthus chinensis*
China roses, 93, 365, 366
Chinese astilbe. See *Astilbe chinensis*
'Chinese Coral,' 340
Chinese delphinium. See *Delphinium grandiflorum*
Chinese forget-me-not. See *Cynoglossum amabile*
Chinese peony. See *Paeonia lactiflora*
Chinese trumpet lilies. See *Lilium*
Chionodoxa luciliae, 29, 87, 178, 191, 195, 340, 341
Chive, 66, 67. See also *Allium schoenoprasum*
'Chocolate,' 259
Christmas fern, 14. See also *Polystichum acrostichoides*
'Christmas Marvel,' 91
Christmas rose. See *Helleborus niger*
Chrysanthemum, 22, 24, 26, 88, 224
Chrysanthemum coccineum, 194, 198, 223, 389, 391, 392
Chrysanthemum maximum, 188. See also *Chrysanthemum x superbum*
Chrysanthemum nipponicum, 188, 223, 387, 388, 389, 390, 391
Chrysanthemum pacificum, 224
Chrysanthemum parthenium, 54, 74, 75, 79, 81, 107, 113, 163, 187, 188, 224, 388, 390
Chrysanthemum ptarmiciflorum, 298
Chrysanthemum weyrichii, 106, 120, 179, 188, 194, 224, 387, 388, 391
Chrysanthemum x morifolium, 79, 81, 90, 91, 106, 121, 188, 192, 194, 196, 198, 224, 387, 388, 390, 391, 392
Chrysanthemum x rubellum, 54, 87, 107, 113, 179, 192, 194, 225, 387, 388, 389, 390, 392
Chrysanthemum x superbum, 79, 81, 103, 107, 153, 225, 388, 389, 391, 392
'Chrysler Imperial,' 91
Chrysogonum virginianum, 54, 106, 121, 127, 128, 158, 181, 192, 226, 388, 389
Cicuta maculata, 208
Cimicifuga racemosa, 107, 127, 199, 227, 389
Cimicifuga ramosa, 107, 227
Cimicifuga simplex, 107, 132, 188, 226, 387, 388
Cimicifuga spp., 48, 54, 121, 159, 160, 169
'Cinderella,' 108, 316
'Cinderella Pink,' 195
Cinnamon fern. See *Osmunda cinnamomea*
Circle flower. See *Lysimachia punctata*
'Cirrus,' 298
'Citrina,' 249
'Citrinum,' 109, 165, 178, 214
'City of Haarlem,' 90, 181, 193, 349
'Claire Jacquier,' 373
'Clara Curtis,' 113, 179, 194, 225
Clarkia amoena, 73, 91, 299
Clarkia concinna, 300
Clarkia elegans, 300
Clarkia pulchella, 300
Clarkia unguiculata, 300
'Claryssa,' 327
'Classic Orange,' 332
'Classic White,' 120, 189, 332
Clematis, 72, 81, 104, 116
Clematis maximowiziana, 75
Clematis x hybrida, 151
Clematis x jackmanii, 75
Cleome, 46

Cleome hasslerana, 73, 75, 79, 121, 132, 148, 149, 164, 165, 179, 195, 300
'Climax,' 329
'Climbing America,' 117

'Climbing American Beauty,' 117, 370
'Climbing Cecile Brunner,' 97, 372
'Climbing Crimson Glory,' 91
'Climbing Golden Dawn,' 370
'Climbing Margo Koster,' 372
'Climbing Mixed,' 331
'Climbing Peace,' 370
Climbing roses, 94, 117
Clivia. See *Clivia minata*
Clivia minata, 193, 197, 341
'Cloth of Gold,' 192
Clover, 148
'Clown,' 330
'Clown Blue,' 191
'Clown Violet,' 191
Clump verbena. See *Verbena canadensis*
Clustered bellflower. See *Campanula glomerata*
Coat flower. See *Petrorhagia saxifraga*
'Cobham Gold,' 226
'Coccineus,' 285
Cockscomb. See *Celosia cristata*
'Cocktail,' 294
'Coerulea,' 220
Cohosh. See *Cimicifuga racemosa*
Colchicum autumnale, 195, 341
Colchicum byzantium, 341
Colchicum cilicicum, 341
Colchicum speciosum, 341
Coleus. See *Coleus x hybridus*
Coleus x hybridus, 51, 159, 187, 199, 300
Colewort. See *Crambe cordifolia*
'Collarette Dandy,' 303
'Colour Magic,' 79, 304
Columbine, 55. See also *Aquilegia* entries
Columbine meadow-rue. See *Thalictrum aquilegifolium*
'Column Mix,' 316
'Commander-in-Chief,' 287
Common bleeding heart. See *Dicentra speciabilis*
Common lungwort. See *Pulmonaria officinalis*
Common monkey flower. See *Mimulus guttatus*
Common monkshood. See *Aconitum carmichaelii*
Common sundrops. See *Oenothera tetragona*
Common thyme. See *Thymus vulgaris*
Common yarrow. See *Achillea millefolium*
Common zinnia. See *Zinnia elegans*
'Compacta,' 115, 277, 278
'Compacta Plena,' 242
'Compactum,' 113, 214
'Compliment,' 190
'Compliment Scarlet,' 253
'Comte de Chambord,' 372
'Comtesse de Gray,' 321
'Comtesse de Murinais,' 371
'Condensatus,' 380
Coneflower. See *Rudbeckia* entries
Coneflower, pale. See *Rudbeckia pallida*
'Confection,' 311
'Confetti,' 310
'Confetti Burgundy,' 199
'Connecticut Yankee,' 177, 178, 181, 193, 352
Consolida ambigua, 48, 73, 79, 145, 149, 191, 301
'Constance Spry,' 367
Convallaria majalis, 74, 75, 79, 81, 91, 159, 189, 342
'Cooler,' 298
'Coral and Gold,' 196
Coralbells, 44, 96, 103, 182. See also *Heuchera anguinea*
'Coral Cloud,' 246
'Coral Eye,' 268
'Coral Flash,' 87, 196
'Coral Isle,' 196
'Corallina,' 249
'Coral Plume,' 257
'Corbett,' 192, 208
Coreopsis, 10, 25, 46, 49, 104, 180, 227
Coreopsis grandiflora, 54, 79, 81, 192, 227, 389, 390, 391
Coreopsis lanceolata, 227
Coreopsis rosea, 106, 116, 194, 227
Coreopsis spp., 107, 149
Coreopsis tinctoria, 149, 192, 196, 301

Coreopsis verticillata, 53, 54, 55, 87, 108, 113, 132, 134, 150, 163, 164, 165, 178, 181, 192, 228, 387, 388, 389, 390, 391, 392
'Cori,' 238
'Cornelia,' 368
Cornflower, 182. See also *Centaurea cyanus*
Corn poppy. See *Papaver rhoeas*
'Coronation Gold,' 203
'Coronette Mixed,' 294
'Corsica,' 195, 352
Corsican mint, 89. See *Mentha requienii*
Cortaderia selloana, 133, 376
Corydalis cheilanthifolia, 228
Corydalis lutea, 54, 121, 140, 141, 149, 159, 192, 228, 387, 388, 390, 392
'Cosmopolitan,' 380
Cosmos. See *Cosmos bipinnatus*
Cosmos bipinnatus, 73, 75, 79, 81, 149, 164, 189, 195, 302
Cosmos spp., 11, 12, 132
Cosmos sulphureus, 164, 192, 196, 302
Cotinus, 47
'Cotswold Queen,' 287
Cottage pink. See *Dianthus plumarius*
'Cottage Rose,' 367
'Couleur Cardinal,' 199, 361
'Country Club,' 245
'Covent Garden,' 309
Cow parsnip. See *Angelica archangelica*
Cowslip primrose. See *Primula veris*
Crab apple, 51, 73, 112
'Cragford,' 356
Crambe, 49
Crambe cordifolia, 107, 132, 149, 188, 197, 229, 392
Crambe maritima, 229
'Cranberry,' 311, 323
'Cranberry Cove,' 198
Cranesbill. See *Geranium* entries
'Crater Lake Blue,' 178, 190, 288
'Cream Flash,' 310
'Cream Puff,' 193, 352
Creeping Charley. See *Lysimachia nummulara*
Creeping foamflower, 127
Creeping Jacob's Ladder. See *Polemonium reptans*
Creeping Jenny. See *Lysimachia nummulara*
Creeping phlox, 127. See also *Phlox stolonifera*
Creeping zinnia. See *Sanvitalia procumbens*
'Cresendo Hybrids,' 272
Crested iris. See *Iris cristata*
Crested lady fern, 383
'Crimson,' 309
'Crimson Brocade,' 198, 212
'Crimson Charm,' 198
'Crimson Elegance,' 195
'Crimson Glory,' 91
'Crimson Pygmy,' 113
'Crimson Shadow,' 198
'Crimson Star,' 87, 198, 236
Crinum, 337
'Crispa,' 90, 199, 324
'Crispum,' 324, 386
'Cristata,' 383
Crocosmia x crocosmiiflora, 48, 133, 181, 193, 197, 342
Crocus, 13, 29, 30, 53, 131
Crocus achroleuces, 189
Crocus chrysanthus, 133, 140, 141, 161, 189, 191, 193, 342
Crocus goulimyi, 343
Crocus kotschyanus, 343
Crocus medius, 343
Crocus sativus, 67, 140, 189, 343
Crocus speciosus, 140, 343
Crocus spp., 29, 164, 165
Crocus tomasinianus, 343
Crocus x vernus, 74, 75, 87, 97, 113, 133, 134, 140, 181, 185, 189, 191, 193, 344
Crocus zonatus, 343
'Croftway Pink,' 90, 179, 194, 260
Crown imperial. See *Fritillaria imperalis*
'Crown of Rays,' 283
'Crusader,' 196
'Crystal,' 322
'Crystal Bowl,' 332
'Crystal Bowl Orange,' 175, 197
'Crystal Bowl Primrose,' 193
'Crystal Bowl White,' 189
'Crystal Palace,' 191, 315

399

Culver's root. See *Veronicastrum virginicum*
'Cum Laude,' 191
'Cup and Saucer,' 297
Cupflower. See *Nierembergia hippomanica violacea*
'Cupid,' 314
'Curly Girl,' 276
'Curly Pink,' 91
'Cushion Blue,' 190
Cushion spurge. See *Euphorbia epithymoides*
'Cut and Come Again,' 332
'Cuthbert Grant,' 365
'Cuty,' 290
Cyclamen coum, 140, 195, 344
Cyclamen daffodil. See *Narcissus* x *cyclamenius*
Cyclamen hederifolium, 140, 195, 344
Cyclamen neapolitanum. See *Cyclamen hederifolium*
Cyclamen purpurescens, 345
Cynara cardunculus, 132, 197, 229, 392
Cynoglossum amabile, 191, 303
Cynoglossum nervosum, 303
'Czar,' 291

Daffodil, 13, 28, 53, 131, 158. See also *Narcissus* entries
Daffodil garlic. See *Allium neapolitanum*
Dahlberg daisy. See *Dyssodia tenuiloba*
Dahlia, 23, 30. See also *Dahlia* x *pinnata*
Dahlia x *hybrida,* 149, 192, 196, 198, 303
Dahlia x *pinnata,* 79, 145, 193, 195, 197, 199, 345
Daisies, 49, 72
'Dalli,' 196
Dalmatian bellflower. See *Campanula portenschlagiana*
Damask rose, 91, 92, 93, 366. See *Rosa* x *damascena*
Dame's rocket, 88. See also *Hesperis matronalis*
Danford iris. See *Iris danfordiae*
'Dan Juan,' 91
'Dark Crimson,' 198
'Darkest of All,' 237
'Dark Opal,' 199
Darwin hybrid tulip. See *Tulipa* entries
'Dasher Orange,' 197
'Dasher Pink,' 195
Datura metel, 91, 303
Datura meteloides, 304
'David,' 188
'Davidii,' 212
'Dawn Glow,' 195
'Daybreak,' 307, 368
'Daydream,' 354
'Daylight White,' 319
Daylily, 25, 26, 28, 29, 53, 89. See also *Hemerocallis* hybrids
'Dazzler,' 311
'Dazzler Orange,' 196
'Dazzler Pink,' 195
'Dazzler Red,' 198
'Dazzler Scarlet,' 196
'Dazzler White,' 189
'De Caen Hybrids,' 337
'Deco,' 311
'Decora,' 324
'Deco Red,' 198
'Deep Purple,' 79
'Deep Red,' 199
'Deep Regards,' 196
'Deep Salmon,' 196
'Delambre,' 372
'Delaware Valley White,' 113
'Delft Blue,' 191, 349
Delosperma congestum nubigenum, 230
Delosperma cooperi, 140, 141, 164, 192, 229, 392
Delphinium, 10, 22, 25, 182, 230
Delphinium ajacis. See *Consolida ambigua*
Delphinium grandiflorum, 188, 190
Delphinium x *belladonna,* 230
Delphinium x *elatum,* 48, 51, 65, 79, 81, 107, 108, 121, 188, 190, 194, 230, 391, 392
'De Meaux,' 365
Dendranthema grandiflorum. See *Chrysanthemum* x *morifolium*

Dendranthema weyrichii. See *Chrysanthemum weyrichii*
Dendranthema x *rubella.* See *Chrysanthemum* x *rubellum*
Dennstaedtia punctilobula, 384
*Derby,' 331
Deschampsia caespitosa, 133, 377
'Desdemona,' 196, 252
'Deutschland,' 188, 213
'Diamond,' 188, 214, 252
'Diamond Anniversary,' 245
'Diamont Yellow,' 193
Dianthus barbatus, 13, 45, 74, 75, 77, 79, 145, 151, 190, 194, 196, 198, 231, 389
Dianthus caryophyllus, 232
Dianthus chinensis, 11, 90, 91, 140, 149, 195, 196, 198, 304
Dianthus deltoides, 74, 231, 194, 197, 198, 391
Dianthus gratianopolitanus, 194, 197, 231, 389, 390, 391
Dianthus plumarius, 108, 141, 194, 232, 389, 391
Dianthus spp., 84, 91, 106, 140, 149, 387, 388, 392
Dianthus x *allwoodii,* 232
Diascia barberae, 304
Dicentra cucullaria, 233, 389
Dicentra eximia, 54, 106, 121, 127, 128, 158, 159, 160, 188, 194, 233, 387, 389
Dicentra formosa, 233, 392
Dicentra spectabilis, 74, 75, 79, 106, 121, 151, 159, 179, 188, 194, 233, 387, 390, 391, 392
Dicentra spp., 145, 388
Dictamnus albus, 107, 121, 188, 194, 233, 387, 388, 390, 391
Digitalis ambigua, 192
Digitalis grandiflora, 234, 391
Digitalis lutea, 234
Digitalis purpurea, 48, 65, 74, 75, 79, 159, 160, 175, 188, 194, 234, 388, 392
Digitalis spp., 107, 145, 387
Digitalis x *mertonensis,* 151, 194, 235
Dill. See *Anethum graveolens*
'Dirigo Ice,' 190, 266
'Disco,' 328, 329
'Disco Belle,' 246
'Disco Belle Red,' 198
Dittany of Crete. See *Origanum dictamnus*
Dog-tooth violet. See *Erythronium americanum*
Dogwood, 112, 153
Dollar–plant. See *Lunaria annua*
'Domino,' 319
'Domino Pink with White Eye,' 195
'Domino Red,' 198
'Domino Salmon Pink,' 195
'Don Juan,' 370
'Doris Cooper,' 194
Doronicum caucasicum, 192, 235, 387, 388
Doronicum orientale. See *Doronicum caucasicum*
'Dortmund,' 91, 374
'Double Blue,' 65, 269
'Double Camellia-flowered Mix,' 311
'Double Delight,' 370
'Double Dwarf Jewel,' 331
'Double Eagle Mixed,' 306
'Double Mixed,' 307
'Double Strawberry,' 311
'Double White,' 300
'Douglas Baader,' 195
'Dover Orange,' 206
Downy amsonia. See *Amsonia angustifolia*
Downy phlox. See *Phlox pilosa*
Downy thorn apple. See *Datura metel*
'Dr. An Wang,' 191, 361
'Dragonfly,' 208
'Dragon's Blood,' 199, 280
'Dreamland,' 193, 195, 332, 352
'Dreamland Pink,' 195
'Dreamlands Mix,' 332
'Dreams,' 325
'Dresden China,' 216
'Dropmore,' 207
'Dropmore Hybrid,' 261
'Dropmore Purple,' 257
'Dropmore Scarlet,' 151
Drumstick allium. See *Allium sphaerocephalum*
Drumstick chive. See *Allium sphaerocephalum*
Dryopteris marginalis, 127, 169, 170, 384

Dryopteris spinulosa var. *intermedia,* 384
'Dubloon,' 264
'Duchess of Portland,' 372
'Dudley Neville Variegated,' 214
'Duet,' 79
'Dukat,' 293
'Dunnet's Dark Crimson,' 198
'Duro,' 223
Dusty miller. See *Centaurea cineraria* and *Senecio cineraria*
Dutch crocus. See *Crocus* x *vernus*
Dutch hyacinth, 30, 175, 182. See also *Hyacinthus orientalis*
Dutch iris. See *Iris* x *xiphium*
Dutchman's breeches. See *Dicentra cucullaria*
'Dwarf Beauty,' 325
'Dwarf Beauty Blue,' 325
'Dwarf Bedding Mixture,' 297
'Dwarf Blue Midget,' 191
Dwarf Chinese astilbe. See *Astilbe chinensis* var. *pumila*
'Dwarf Cinderella Red,' 198
'Dwarf Garters,' 382
Dwarf goat's beard. See *Aruncus aethusifolius*
'Dwarf Hyacinth Flowered Mix,' 301
'Dwarf Marine,' 310
'Dwarf Mix,' 323
'Dwarf Mixed,' 302
Dwarf mondo grass. See *Ophiopogon japonicus*
'Dwarf Moody Blue,' 320
Dwarf pampas grass. See *Cortaderia selloana*
'Dwarf Queen,' 297
Dwarf taurus tulip. See *Tulipa pulchella*
'Dwarf White Bedder,' 189
'Dynamo White,' 189
'Dynasty,' 295
Dyssodia tenuiloba, 85, 87, 121, 192, 304, 305

'E. A. Bowles,' 343
'Earliest of All,' 287
'Early Call Mix,' 312
'Early Dwarf,' 336
'Early Splendor,' 293
'Early Sunrise,' 54, 227
'Early Wonder,' 302
'East Friesland,' 277, 278
'E.C. Buxton,' 54, 208
Echinacea pallida, 236, 391
Echinacea purpurea, 53, 54, 79, 103, 107, 113, 132, 140, 164, 165, 184, 185, 188, 194, 235, 387, 388, 389, 390, 391, 392
Echinacea tennesseensis, 236
Echinops ritro, 54, 79, 80, 81, 107, 109, 132, 149, 164, 178, 184, 190, 197, 236, 387, 388, 390, 391, 392
'Echo,' 306
'Echo Pink,' 195
Edelweiss. See *Leontopodium alpinum*
Edging candytuft, 10, 103. See also *Iberis sempervirens*
Edging lobelia. See *Lobelia erinus*
'Edulus Superba,' 194
Egyptian star-cluster. See *Pentas lanceolata*
'Eleanor Parry,' 248
'Elegance,' 91, 370
'Elegans,' 113, 160, 187
'Elfin Pink,' 194, 265
'Elfin White,' 189
'Elijah Blue,' 120, 378
'Elite Pink,' 195
'Elite Red,' 196
'Elite Series,' 327
'Elite White,' 189
'Elsie Heugh,' 194, 282
Elymus arenarius, 133, 187, 377
Elymus glaucus, 377
'Emerald Blue,' 178, 190, 268
'Emerald Pink,' 194, 268
'Emily McKenzie,' 342
'Emotion,' 248
'Empire Red,' 199
'Empire Series,' 327
'Empress of India,' 199, 331
'Enchantment,' 197, 351, 352
'Encore,' 294
'Encore Light Pink,' 195
'Encore Pink,' 195
'Encore Pink 'n' Bronze,' 195

'Encore Red,' 198
'Encore Red/Bronze,' 198
Endrew's geranium. See *Geranium endressii*
Endymion hispanicus. See *Hyacinthoides hispanica*
'Enfant de France,' 369
English daisy. See *Bellis perennis*
English ivy, 157
English lavender. See *Lavandula angustifolia*
English roses, 12, 94, 96, 366, 367
Epimedium grandiflorum, 237
Epimedium pinnatum, 237
Epimedium roseum, 237
Epimedium spp., 106, 159, 161, 387, 388, 389, 390, 392
Epimedium x *rubrum,* 237
Epimedium x *versicolor,* 192, 237
Epimedium x *youngianum,* 132, 236
Eranthis cilicia, 29, 345
Eranthis hyemalis, 29, 193, 345
'Erfurt,' 91
Erigeron speciosus. See *Erigeron* x *hybridus*
Erigeron x *hybridus,* 106, 149, 188, 190, 237, 387, 388, 391
Eryngium alpinum, 237
Eryngium amethystinum, 80, 107, 132, 164, 197, 237, 390, 392
Eryngium bourgatii, 237
Eryngium giganteum, 237
Eryngium spp., 149, 387, 388
Erythronium americanum, 126, 127, 128, 193, 346
Erythronium californicum, 346
Erythronium denscanis, 346
Erythronium tuolumense, 346
Eschscholzia caespitosa, 305
Eschscholzia californica, 58, 73, 85, 140, 141, 164, 192, 196, 198, 305
'Essex Witch,' 232
'Etain,' 290, 373
'Ethel,' 373
'Etna,' 198, 214, 287
Eulalia grass. See *Miscanthus sinensis*
Eupatorium coelestinum, 159, 188, 190, 238, 388, 390, 391
Eupatorium fistulosum, 107, 109, 132, 149, 169, 170, 194, 199, 238, 387, 390
Eupatorium maculatum, 238
Eupatorium purpureum, 238, 388
Euphorbia epithymoides, 238, 387, 388, 390, 392
Euphorbia marginata, 73, 140, 189, 305
Euphorbia myrsinites, 239
Euphorbia palustris, 239
Euphorbia polychroma, 164, 165, 192. See also *Euphorbia epithymoides*
'Europa,' 213
European bistort. See *Polygonum bistorta*
'Europeana,' 367
Eustoma grandiflora, 79, 186, 190, 192, 195, 305
'Eva Cullum,' 54, 194, 267
'Evangeline,' 108
'Evenglow,' 223
'Evening Glow,' 216
'Eventide,' 178, 190, 212
'Everblooming,' 357
'Everest,' 352
'Evergreen,' 313
Evolvulus, 182
'Excel,' 329
'Excelsior,' 191, 348
Exbury azalea, 112
'Excel Primrose,' 329
'Excelsior Hybrids,' 235
'Extra Curled Dwarf,' 324

'Fair Bianca,' 367
'Fairy Bouquet,' 315
'Fairy Lights,' 315
'Fairy Mixed,' 310
Fairy primrose. See *Primula malacoides*
'Falcon Blush Pink,' 195
Fall aster. See *Aster novi-belgii* x *novae-angliae*
Fall astilbe. See *Astilbe taquetii*
'Fall Classic,' 197
Fall crocus. See *Crocus speciosus*
Fall lily leek. See *Allium senescens glaucum*
Fall sunflower. See *Helianthus angustifolius*

False dragonhead. See *Physostegia virginiana*
False indigo. See *Baptisia alba pendula*
False sunflower. See *Heliopsis helianthoides scabra*
'Fama,' 279
'Fanal,' 99, 154, 194, 198, 214
Fan columbine. See *Aquilegia flabellata*
Fancy-leaved caladium. See *Caladium* x *hortulanum*
'Fantin-Latour,' 365
Farewell-to-spring. See *Clarkia unguiculata*
'Fashion,' 91, 367
'Fastigiata,' 194, 258
'Favour,' 190
Fawn lily. See *Erythronium americanum*
Featherleaf rodgersia. See *Rodgersia pinnata*
Feather reed grass. See *Calamagrostis acutiflora*
'February Gold,' 113, 355
'February Silver,' 355
'Feesey's Variety,' 382
'Felicia,' 369
Felicia amelloides, 140, 149, 191, 306
Felicia bergerana, 306
'Felicite et Perpetue,' 373
'Félicité Parmentier,' 364
'Fernleaf,' 293
Fernleaf peony. See *Paeonia tenuifolia*
Fern-leaf yarrow. See *Achillea filipendulina*
'Festival,' 308
'Festival Orange,' 196
'Festiva maxima,' 188
Festuca, 162
Festuca amethystina, 187, 378
Festuca arvernensis. See *Festuca ovina*
Festuca cinerea. See *Festuca ovina*
Festuca glauca. See *Festuca ovina*
Festuca ovina, 120, 133, 178, 187, 378
Feverfew. See *Chrysanthemum parthenium*
Fibrous begonia. See *Begonia* x *semperflorens*
'Fiesta Gitana,' 296
'Fiji Mix,' 301
Filipendula hexapetala, 239
Filipendula palmata, 239
Filipendula rubra, 107, 108, 121, 132, 169, 194, 239, 388, 390
Filipendula spp., 387, 392
Filipendula ulmaria, 187, 239
Filipendula vulgaris, 239
'Finale,' 212
'Fine Art,' 352
Fingerleaf rodgersia. See *Rodgersia aesculifolia*
'Fire,' 214, 255
'Fire-candle,' 257
'Fireglow,' 198, 298
'Fire King,' 196, 203
'Fire Opal,' 196, 242
'Fireworks,' 54, 262, 283
'Firmament,' 269, 303
'First Prize,' 370
'Flame,' 288, 325
'Flame Carpet,' 196
Flamegrass, 380
'Flamenco,' 306
'Flamingo Feather,' 195
'Flamingo Purple,' 195
Flanders poppy. See *Papaver rhoeas*
'Flare,' 196
'Flash,' 304
'Flash Fire,' 257
'Flash Mixed,' 310
Fleabane. See *Erigeron* x *hybridus*
'Floral Carpet Mixed,' 294
'Floral Dance,' 332
'Floral Showers Purple,' 191
Florentine tulip. See *Tulipa sylvestris*
'Flore-plena,' 232
'Flore-Plena,' 243
'Flore-pleno,' 239
'Flore Pleno,' 347
'Flore-Pleno,' 218, 222
'Florepleno,' 211, 359
'Florette Champagne,' 297
Floribunda roses, 32, 94, 114, 367
'Floristan White,' 87, 251
Flossflower. See *Ageratum houstonianum*
Flower-of-Jove. See *Lychnis flos-jovis*
Flowering cabbage. See *Brassica oleracea*
Flowering kale. See *Brassica oleracea*
Flowering tobacco, 27. See *Nicotiana alata*

'Fluffy Ruffles,' 199
Foamflower. See *Tiarella*
Foamy bells. See *Heucherella tiarelloides*
'Foerster's Blue,' 190
'Forever Yours,' 196, 323
Forget-me-not, 182. See also *Myosotis scorpioides*
Formosa toad lily. See *Tricyrtis formosana*
'Fortress,' 314
'Fortune's Double Yellow,' 366
Fountain grass. See *Pennisetum alopecuroides*
'Fountain White,' 189
Four-o'clock. See *Mirabilis jalepa*
Foxglove, 22. See also *Digitalis*
'Foxy,' 235
'Fragrant Cloud,' 91
Fragrant Solomon's seal. See *Polygonatum odoratum*
'France,' 187
'Francis Williams,' 187
'Franz Schubert,' 267
'Frau Dagmar Hastrup,' 91, 374
'Freckle Face,' 215
'Freckles,' 291
'Fred Loads,' 87, 374
'Freedom,' 246
'Freesey's Variety,' 382
Freesia. See *Freesia* hybrids
Freesia alba, 346
Freesia hybrids, 79, 91, 193, 197, 346
Freesia refracta alba, 346
French marigold. See *Tagetes patula*
Frikart's aster. See *Aster* x *frikartii*
'Frilly Dilly,' 294
Fringed bleeding heart. See *Dicentra eximia*
Fringed loosestrife. See *Lysimachia ciliata*
Fritillaria imperialis, 29, 74, 75, 133, 193, 197, 346, 347
Fritillaria lanceolata, 347
Fritillaria meleagris, 140, 191, 347
Fritillaria persica, 191
Fritillaria recurva, 347
'Frosted Sulphur/Silvery Rose,' 309
Fuchsia, 144. See *Fuchsia* x *hybrida*
Fuchsia x *hybrida,* 145, 306
'Fuego,' 327
'Fuji Pink,' 194, 269
'Fuji White,' 185, 188, 269
'Fuller's White,' 188, 266

'Gaiety,' 204, 363
Gaillardia aristata, 240
Gaillardia pulchella, 79, 140, 149, 164, 192, 307
Gaillardia x *grandiflora,* 54, 149, 192, 196, 239, 389, 390
'Galahad,' 188, 230
Galanthus elwesii, 347
Galanthus nivalis, 74, 75, 159, 160, 347
Galanthus spp., 29
Galaxy hybrids, 203
'Galilee,' 321
Galium odoratum, 67, 74, 90, 91, 97, 116, 127, 158, 188, 240, 387, 388, 389
'Gallery Hybrids,' 255
'Gallery Yellow,' 192
Gallica roses, 68, 92, 367, 368
Gardener's garters. See *Phalaris arundinacea* var. *picta*
Garden mum. See *Chrysanthemum* x *morifolium*
'Garden Party,' 370
Garden sage. See *Salvia officinalis*
'Gardenview Red,' 198, 260
Gargano bellflower. See *Campanula garganica*
'Garnet,' 245
Gas plant, 10. See also *Dictamnus albus*
'Gateway,' 238
Gaura lindheimeri, 54, 107, 132, 164, 165, 240, 388, 389, 390, 392
'Gay Butterflies,' 211
Gayfeather, 49, 53. See also *Liatris spicata*
Gazania. See *Gazania rigens*
Gazania rigens, 140, 192, 196, 307
'Geisha,' 298
'Gem,' 329
'Gene Wild,' 194
'General De Wet,' 91, 197, 361
'General Eisenhower,' 199, 361

'General Jacqueminot,' 369
Gentiana andrewsii, 241
Gentiana asclepiadea, 241
Gentiana septemfida lagodechiana, 241
Gentiana spp., 241
Gentians. See *Gentiana* spp.
'George Lewis,' 306
'Georgette,' 193, 361
Geranium, 11, 182
'Geranium,' 90, 356
Geranium, scented, 89. See also *Pelargonium* species
Geranium endressii, 54, 194, 241
Geranium himalayense, 183, 190, 241
Geranium platypetalum, 87, 97, 190, 241
Geranium pratense, 183, 241
Geranium sanguineum, 54, 113, 141, 194, 241, 391
Geranium spp., 106, 116, 140, 387, 388, 390, 392
Geranium x 'Johnson's Blue,' 241
Gerbera daisy. See *Gerbera jamesonii*
Gerbera jamesonii, 79, 193, 196, 198, 308
German catchfly. See *Lychnis viscaria*
German chamomile. See *Matricaria chamomilla*
Germander speedwell. See *Veronica latifolia*
'Gertrude Jekyll,' 97, 367
Geum. See *Geum quellyon*
Geum chiloense, 41. See also *Geum quellyon*
Geum quellyon, 140, 192, 196, 198, 242, 391, 392
Giant allium, 53. See also *Allium giganteum*
Giant coneflower. See *Rudbeckia maxima*
'Giant Dark Blue,' 191
'Giant Hybrids,' 223
'Giant Imperial,' 301, 316
'Giant Light Blue,' 191
Giant onion. See *Allium giganteum*
'Giant Pacific Hybrid,' 108
'Giant White,' 309
'Gibbsoni,' 199
'Gigantea,' 178, 341
'Ginko Craig,' 160, 187
'Ginger,' 259
Gladiolus, 78. See also entries below
Gladiolus byzantinus, 348
Gladiolus hybrids, 48, 193, 197, 199
Gladiolus nanus, 348
Gladiolus spp., 29
Gladiolus x *hortulanus,* 79, 81, 145, 195, 348
'Glamour,' 194
Glauca, 133, 178, 187, 378
'Glaucus,' 133, 187, 377
'Gleam,' 331
Globe amaranth. See *Gomphrena globosa*
Globeflower. See *Gomphrena globosa* and *Trollius europaeus*
'Globemaster,' 334
Globe-thistle. See *Echinops ritro*
'Gloria,' 302
Gloriosa daisy. See *Rudbeckia hirta*
Glory-of-the-snow, 53. See also *Chionodoxa luciliae*
'Glow,' 198, 214
'Glowing Rose,' 264
'Gnome,' 251
Goat's beard. See *Aruncus dioicus*
'Goblin,' 196, 240
Godetia. See *Clarkia amoena*
Godetia amoena. See *Clarkia amoena*
'Gold,' 329
'Goldband,' 134, 376
'Gold Banded,' 187, 253
'Gold Bound,' 248
'Gold Braid,' 193, 328
'Gold Coin,' 193
'Gold Drop,' 276
'Gold Edger,' 187, 247
'Golden Apeldoorn,' 193, 361
'Golden Baby,' 283
'Golden Ball,' 224
'Golden Bikini,' 193
Golden columbine. See *Aquilegia chrysantha*
Golden coreopsis. See *Coreopsis tinctoria*
'Golden Crown,' 302
'Golden Dwarf,' 283
Golden feather. See *Chrysanthemum parthenium aureum*
'Golden Fleece,' 283

Golden fleece. See *Dyssodia tenuiloba*
'Golden Glow,' 276
'Golden Goblin,' 192, 240
Golden groundsel. See *Senecio aureus*
'Golden Harvest,' 193
Golden marguerite. See *Anthemis tinctoria*
'Golden Melody,' 91, 120, 346
'Golden Mikado Lily,' 363
'Golden Orange,' 197
'Golden Plume,' 244
'Golden Promise,' 264
Golden ray, 131. See also *Ligularia stenocephala*
Goldenrod. See *Solidago* hybrids
'Golden Showers,' 193, 228, 353
'Golden Splendor,' 193, 353
Golden spotted nettle. See *Lamium maculatum*
Goldenstar. See *Chrysogonum virginianum*
Golden stonecrop. See *Sedum kamtschaticum*
'Golden Sword,' 187, 291
'Golden Temple,' 90
'Golden Veil,' 377
'Golden Wings,' 373
Golden wood millet. See *Milium effusum*
'Golden Yellow Festival,' 193
'Goldfinch,' 373
'Goldfinger,' 330
'Goldfink,' 227
'Gold Green-heart,' 244
'Goldilocks,' 275
Goldmoss sedum. See *Sedum acre*
'Gold Plate,' 203
'Goldquelle,' 276
'Goldschleier,' 377
'Gold Standard,' 187
'Goldsturm,' 10, 54, 81, 121, 134, 150, 181, 192, 275
Gomphrena globosa, 80, 132, 191, 195, 198, 308
Gooseneck loosestrife. See *Lysimachia clethroides*
'Grace,' 300
'Gracillimus,' 47, 134, 380
'Graham Thomas,' 90, 91, 94, 367
'Granada,' 322
'Grandiflora Blue,' 220
'Grandiflorum,' 335
Grandifolia roses, 94, 368
'Grand Soleil d'Oro,' 356
'Granny Grimmetts,' 369
Granny's bonnet. See *Aquilegia vulgaris*
Grape hyacinth, 30, 182. See also *Muscari botryoides*
Grape-leaf anemone. See *Anemone vitifolia*
'Gravetye Giant,' 351
Gray santolina. See *Santolina chamaecyparissus*
'Graziella,' 380
Great-flowering tobacco. See *Nicotiana sylvestris*
Great Solomon's seal. See *Polygonatum commutatum*
Great white trillium. See *Trillium grandiflorum*
Grecian windflower, 195. See also *Anemone blanda*
Green and gold. See *Chrysogonum virginianum*
Green-eyed coneflower. See *Rudbeckia laciniata*
Green-flowered tobacco. See *Nicotiania langsdorfii*
'Green Goddess,' 363
'Green Ruffles,' 320
Green santolina. See *Santolina virens*
'Green Thumb,' 293
Greigii tulips. See *Tulipa greigii*
'Greynog Gold,' 252
'Grootendorst,' 96
Guinea-hen tulip. See *Fritillaria meleagris*
Gypsophila elegans, 308
Gypsophila paniculata, 47, 79, 80, 81, 107, 153, 188, 194, 242, 387, 390, 391, 392
Gypsophila repens, 140, 242, 391
Gypsophila spp., 164
'Gypsy Queen,' 197, 349

'Hadspen Blue,' 187
'Haense Herms,' 381
'Hakone Blue,' 269

Hakonechloa macra, 159, 161, 187, 378
Hakone grass. See *Hakonechloa macra*
'Halo Yellow,' 215
'Hameln,' 381
'Hansa,' 374
'Hans Anrud,' 191, 361
'Happipot,' 308
'Happy,' 257
'Happy Returns,' 54, 192, 245
Hardy ageratum. See *Eupatorium coelestinum*
Hardy begonia. See *Begonia grandis*
Hardy cyclamen. See *Cyclamen hederifolium*
Hardy geranium. See *Geranium sanguineum*
Hardy iceplant. See *Delosperma cooperi*
'Harmony,' 350
'Harrington's Pink,' 194, 212
'Harvest Moon,' 264
'Haunting Melody,' 245
'Hawaii,' 292
'Hawaii Hybrid,' 191
'Hawaii Royal,' 292
'Hawera,' 355
Hay-scented fern. See *Dennstaedtia punctilobula*
'Headbourn Hybrids,' 333
Heart-leaf bergenia. See *Bergenia cordifolia*
'Heart's Delight,' 363
'Heart's Desire,' 353
'Heavenly Blue,' 113, 151, 178, 182, 190, 191, 312, 354
'Heavy Metal,' 381
Hedyotis caerulea, 127, 242, 388
'Heidi,' 194, 209
'Heidi Cherry Blossom,' 195
'Heidi Yellow,' 192
'Helen Campbell,' 300
'Helen Elizabeth,' 264
Helenium autumnale, 107, 121, 181, 192, 196, 243, 387, 388, 390, 392
'Helen Mount,' 291
'Helen Von Stein,' 283
Helianthus angustifolius, 107, 164, 192, 243, 388, 389, 390, 392
Helianthus annuus, 132, 164, 193, 309
Helianthus spp., 149
Helianthus x *multiflorus*, 243
Helichrysum bracteatum, 80, 149, 164, 193, 309
Helictotrichon sempervirens, 120, 133, 187, 378
Heliopsis helianthoides, 54, 103, 107, 164, 192, 244, 387, 388, 389, 390, 391, 392
Heliotrope, 88. See also *Heliotropium arborescens*
Heliotropium arborescens, 79, 132, 149, 183, 309, 310
Heliotropium x *peruvianum*, 310
'Hella Lacy,' 190, 212
Helleborus foetidus, 244
Helleborus niger, 188, 244, 387
Helleborus orientalis, 156, 157, 244, 387, 388, 389
Helleborus spp., 54, 79, 106, 121, 158, 159, 161, 392
'Hello Yellow,' 192, 211
Hemerocallis, 26, 87, 90, 91, 108, 109, 113, 120, 121, 131 146, 161, 162
Hemerocallis fulva, 74, 75, 159, 196, 245
Hemerocallis hybrids, 54, 89, 107, 132, 134, 149, 150, 181, 192, 194, 196, 198, 244, 387, 388, 389, 390, 391, 392
Hemerocallis lilioasphedelus, 74
'Hennie Graafland,' 213
'Henry Hudson,' 365
'Henry's White,' 188
Hens-and-chicks. See *Sempervivum tectorum*
'Hensol Harebell,' 208
Herbaceous perennials, 10
'Herbstsonne,' 276
'Hercules,' 363
'Heritage,' 91, 97, 367
'Herman's Pride,' 41, 187, 250
'Hero' series, 329
Hesperis matronalis, 41, 74, 88, 90, 91, 107, 149, 150, 175, 185, 194, 245, 387, 388, 390, 392
Heuchera americana, 245
Heuchera micrantha, 55, 87, 97, 179, 106, 108, 132, 199, 245
Heuchera sanguinea, 106, 194, 198, 246, 389, 391

Heuchera spp., 116, 140, 145, 151, 387, 388, 389, 390, 392
Heuchera x *brizoides*, 246
Heucherella tiarelloides, 194, 246
'Hewitt's Double,' 284
Hibiscus, 25, 86. See also *Hibiscus moscheutos*
Hibiscus moscheutos, 107, 120, 132, 169, 194, 198, 246, 388, 389
Hibiscus palustris. See *Hibiscus moscheutos*
'Hidcote,' 97, 190, 250
'Highlight Coral,' 196
'Highlights,' 262
'High Society,' 91
Hiamalayan cranesbill. See *Geranium himalayense*
'Hime Murasaki,' 269
'Holiday Cheer,' 297
'Holland's Glory,' 361
Hollyhock, 148. See also *Alcea rosea*
Hollyhock mallow. See *Malva alcea*
Holly, Japanese, 57, 101, 115
'Home Fires,' 126, 194, 268
'Homeland,' 231
'Homestead Purple,' 190, 288
Honesty. See *Lunaria annua*
Honeysuckle, 72, 146
'Honeybells,' 151
'Honorine Jobert,' 108, 185, 188, 207
'Hope,' 192
Horned violet. See *Viola cornuta*
Horn–of–plenty. See *Datura metel*
Horsemint. See *Monarda punctata*
Hosta, 26, 28, 29, 52, 53, 55, 133, 151, 157, 158, 161, 187, 246. See also entries below
Hosta, siebold, 47
Hosta lancifolia, 161
Hosta plantaginea, 87, 90, 91, 154, 188
Hosta sieboldiana, 113, 123, 160, 187
Hosta species and hybrids, 41, 48, 52, 53, 107, 121, 132, 145, 159, 160, 246, 387, 388, 389, 390
'Hot Ember,' 26, 196
'Hotline Red,' 151
Hound's tongue. See *Cynoglossum nervosum*
Houseleek. See *Sempervivum tectorum*
Houstonia caerulea. See *Hedyotis caerulea*
'Huberana,' 304
Hungarian speedwell. See *Veronica latifolia*
'Hunslet Moss,' 371
Hurricane lily. See *Lycoris squamigera*
'Husker Red,' 265
'Hyacinth,' 214
Hyacinth, Dutch, 30, 175, 182. See also *Hyacinthus orientalis*
Hyacinth, grape, 30, 182. See also *Muscari botryoides*
Hyacinthoides hispanica, 153, 159, 160, 189, 191, 195, 348
Hyacinthoides non-scriptus, 348
Hyacinthus orientalis, 48, 74, 90, 91, 109, 113, 120, 181, 185, 189, 191, 193, 195, 197, 348
Hybrid blue salvia. See *Salvia* x *superba*
Hybrid chrysanthemum. See *Chrysanthemum* x *rubellum*
Hybrid columbine. See *Aquilegia* x *hybrida*
Hybrid musk roses, 88, 368, 369
Hybrid perpetual roses, 93, 96, 369
Hybrid sage. See *Salvia* x *superba*
Hybrid tea roses, 12, 32, 81, 93, 94, 97, 117, 269
Hybrid tulips. See *Tulipa* x *hybrida*
Hydrangea quercifolia, 113
Hymenocallis calathina. See *Hymenocallis narcissiflora*
Hymenocallis narcissiflora, 349
'Hyperion,' 89, 90, 91, 120, 161, 181, 192
Hypoestes phyllostachya, 187, 199, 310
Hyssop, 99

Iberis amara, 310
Iberis sempervirens, 106, 109, 116, 120, 140, 141, 149, 188, 247, 387, 388, 389, 390, 391, 392
Iberis umbellata, 140, 149, 310
'Iceberg,' 79, 91
'Ice Follies,' 161, 354
'Ice King,' 354
Iceland poppy. See *Papaver nudicaule*
'Ice Wings,' 189, 355

'Icicle,' 108, 188, 289. See *Veronica* x *spicata*
'Ideal,' 191, 351
'Ideal Crimson,' 198
'Ideal Pink,' 195
Ilex crenata, 115
'Illini-charm,' 249
'Illini Red,' 198
'Illumination,' 293
'Imagination,' 191, 288, 331
'Impala,' 193, 326
Impatiens, 45, 112, 157. See *Impatiens wallerana*
Impatiens balsamina, 311
Impatiens wallerana, 73, 75, 113, 121, 159, 160, 161, 189, 191, 195, 196, 198, 311
Impatiens x *hybrida*, 311
Imperata cylindrica, 133, 134, 199, 379
'Imperial,' 332, 352
'Imperial Blue Bell,' 191
'Imperial Blue Picotee,' 301
'Imperial Frosty Rose,' 195
'Imperial Pink,' 195, 302
'Imperial Pink Shades,' 195
'Inca Mixed,' 329
'Incisum,' 386
'Indian Carpet,' 231
'Indian Spring,' 205
'Indian Summer,' 198
'Indigo Blue,' 261
'Innocence,' 308
Interrupted fern. See *Osmunda claytoniana*
'Intrigue,' 79, 91
Ipheion uniflorum, 349, 350
Ipomoea alba, 312
Ipomoea purpurea, 145, 312
Ipomoea tricolor, 149, 151, 191, 312
Ipomoea x *nil*, 312
Iresine herbstii, 312–313
Iresine lindenii, 313
Iris, 77, 177
Iris bucharica, 350
Iris cristata, 87, 106, 127, 128, 188, 190, 247, 387, 389
Iris danfordiae, 140, 193, 350
Iris ensata, 107, 169, 170, 188, 190, 248, 387, 389, 390
Iris hybrida, 41, 79, 81, 107, 164, 165, 188, 190, 192, 194, 196, 248, 387, 390, 391, 392
Iris kaempferi. See *Iris ensata*
Iris magnifica, 350
Iris pallida, 187
'Iris Pritchard,' 286
Iris pseudoacorus, 169, 170, 192, 248, 389, 390
Iris pumila, 249
Iris reticulata, 29, 133, 140, 141, 189, 191, 350
Iris siberica, 87, 104, 107, 108, 109, 113, 121, 169, 178, 181, 185, 188, 190, 192, 249, 387, 389, 390, 391, 392
Iris spp., 388
Iris versicolor, 169, 248, 389, 390
Iris x *germanica*, 175
Iris x *xiphium*, 189, 191, 193, 351
'Ise,' 248
Ismene calathina. See *Hymenocallis narcissiflora*
'Isphahan,' 92
Italian alkanet. See *Anchusa azurea*
Italian bugloss, 182. See also *Anchusa azurea*
'Italian Dark Green,' 324
'Italian White,' 309
'Ivory Floradale,' 189
'Ivory Tower,' 188, 291
'Ivory Towers,' 230
Ivy geranium. See *Pelargonium peltatum*

Jack-in-the-pulpit. See *Arisaema triphyllum*
Jackman clematis. See *Clematis* x *jackmanii*
'Jack Snipe,' 355
Jacob's ladder. See *Polemonium caeruleum*
Jacob's–rod. See *Asphodeline lutea*
'Jacob Styer,' 188
'Jacques Cartier,' 372
'Jamboree,' 352
'James C. Weguelin,' 286
'James Kelway,' 223
'Janet Fish,' 274
'Jan Van Leeuwen,' 188

Japanese anemone. See *Anemone* x *hybrida*
Japanese blood grass. See *Imperata cylindrica*
Japanese holly, 57, 101, 115
Japanese iris. See *Iris ensata*
Japanese meadow-rue. See *Thalictrum rochebrunianum*
Japanese painted fern. See *Athyrium niponicum pictum*
'Japanese Pink,' 194
Japanese primrose. See *Primula japonica*
Japanese sedge grass. See *Carex morrowii*
Japanese silver grass, 380
Japanese wind grass. See *Hakonechloa macra*
'Jean d'Arc,' 344
'Jean Davis,' 194, 250
'Jenny,' 198, 355
'Jenny Bloom,' 34, 193, 342
'Jenny Sue,' 245
'Jepson,' 313
'Jersey Beauty,' 373
'Jersey Gem,' 87, 190, 290
'Jewel Box Mixed,' 298
'Jewel Mixed,' 197
'Jewel of Spring,' 193, 361
'Jitter Bug,' 371
'Joan Elliot,' 113, 178, 219
Joe-Pye weed. See *Eupatorium fistulosum*
'John Burch,' 253
'John Cabot,' 365
Johnny-jump-up. See *Viola tricolor*
'John S. Armstrong,' 368
'Johnson's Blue,' 190, 241
Jonquil. See *Narcissus jonquilla*
Joseph's coat, 293
'Journey's End,' 352
'Joy,' 325
'Joyce,' 350
'J.P. Connell,' 365
'J. S. Dyt,' 350
'Jubilee Gem,' 191, 299
'June Bride,' 246
Juniperus squamata, 113
'Juno,' 365
Jupiter's beard. See *Centranthus ruber*

'Kabitan,' 187
'Kablouna Gold,' 192
Kaffir lily. See *Clivia minata*
'Kagari Bi,' 248
Kale. See *Brassica oleracea*
Kamchatka bugbane. See *Cimicifuga simplex*
Kamchatka stonecrop. See *Sedum kamtschaticum*
'Kansas,' 198
Kansas gayfeather. See *Liatris pycnostachya*
'Karat,' 244
'Karen Gray,' 198
'Karl Foerster,' 375
'Kathleen,' 91
'Kathryn Morley,' 94
'Kevin Floodlight,' 193
'Kimono,' 298
'Kimono Cream,' 181
'Kimono Orange,' 196
'Kimono Red,' 198
'Kimono Rose,' 195
'Kimono Yellow,' 192
'King Alfred,' 354
King's–spear. See *Asphodeline lutea*
'Kito,' 216
'Klaus Jelitto,' 190, 284
'Kneiffii,' 170, 210
Kniphofia uvaria, 48, 107, 145, 192, 196, 249, 388, 389, 391
'Knob Hill,' 194
Knotweed. See *Polygonum bistorta*
'Kobold,' 179, 251
Kochia childsii. See *Kochia scoparia* var. *trichophylla*
Kochia scoparia var. *trichophylla*, 313
Koelera glauca, 187
'Kompliment,' 279
'Kristall,' 187, 209
'Krossa Regal,' 187
Kuenlun tulip. See *Tulipa tarda*
Labrador violet. See *Viola labridorica* var. *purpurea*
'Laciniata,' 324
'Lacy Sails,' 191

'Lacy Snowflake,' 188
'Lady Baltimore,' 246
'Ladybird,' 302
'Ladybird Orange,' 196
'Ladybird Yellow,' 192
Lady fern. See *Athyrium filix-femina*
'Lady Gay,' 75, 373
'Lady in Red,' 199
'Lady Killer,' 343
'Lady Mary,' 266
Lady's ear drops. See *Fuchsia* x *hybrida*
Lady's mantle. See *Alchemilla mollis*
'Lady Strathedon,' 192, 242
Lady tulip. See *Tulipa clusiana*
'La France,' 369
Lagerstrommea, 186
'Lambrook Silver,' 210
Lamb's-ears, 29, 44, 96, 103, 116, 182. See also
Stachys byzantina
Lamiastrum galeobdolon, 41, 187, 250
Lamium maculatum, 87, 106, 116, 159, 160,
187, 194, 197, 250, 387, 388, 389, 390, 392
Lamium maculatum aureum, 187, 250
Lantana. See *Lantana* entries
Lantana camara, 51, 313
Lantana montevidensis, 191, 313
Lantana spp., 140, 145, 149
'Lapsley,' 262
Large-cup daffodils. See *Narcissus* hybrids
Large-flowered climbing roses, 33, 34, 370
'Laser Purple,' 327
Lathyrus odoratus, 71, 79, 91, 121,
195, 313
'Lavandula,' 259
Lavandula angustifolia, 48, 54, 66, 67, 69, 80,
90, 91, 97, 106, 116, 164, 188, 190, 194, 197,
250, 387, 388, 389, 391
Lavandula officinalis. See *Lavandula
angustifolia*
Lavandula spica. See *Lavandula angustifolia*
Lavandula stoechas, 250, 389, 392
Lavandula verna. See *Lavandula angustifolia*
Lavatera trimestris, 48, 149, 195, 314
Lavender, 44, 67, 68, 99, 115, 250. See also
Lavandula angustifolia
'Lavender Charm,' 54
Lavender cotton, 99, 115. See also *Santolina
chamaecyparissus*
'Lavender Lady,' 250, 308
'Lavender Lassie,' 97
Lavender mist. See *Thalictrum
rochebrunianum*
'La Ville de Bruxelles,' 93, 366
Leadwort, 182. See also *Ceratostigma
plumbaginoides*
Leather bergenia. See *Bergenia crassifolia*
Leatherleaf sedge. See *Carex buchanaii*
Leather wood fern. See *Dryopteris marginalis*
'Lemon,' 329
'Lemon Custard,' 193, 352
Lemon daylily. See *Hemerocallis lilioasphedelus*
'Lemon Gem,' 113, 120, 329
'Lemon Lime,' 193, 319
'Lemon Lollipop,' 54
'Lemon Queen,' 193, 287, 349, 351
'Lemon Rocket,' 192
Lemon thyme. See *Thymus* x *citriodorus*
Lenten rose. See *Helleborus orientalis*
Leontopodium alpinum, 140, 197, 250, 391
Leopard's bane. See *Doronicum caucasicum*
'Le Reve,' 195
Leucanthemum x *superbum*. See
Chrysanthemum x *superbum*
Leucojum aestivum, 153, 159, 351
Leucojum vernum, 351
Liatris, 131, 162. See also *Liatris spicata*
Liatris aspera, 251
Liatris callilepis. See *Liatris spicata*
Liatris pycnostachya, 251
Liatris scariosa, 120, 188, 251
Liatris spicata, 10, 48, 87, 107, 164, 165, 179,
194, 251, 387, 388, 389, 390, 391, 392
'Liberty,' 294
'Liberty Bells,' 355
'Liberty Lavender,' 191
'Liberty Light Pink,' 195
'Liberty Pink,' 195
'Liberty Yellow,' 192, 193
'Light of Loddon,' 244
'Light Salmon,' 196

Ligtu hybrids, 206
Ligularia dentata, 196, 252
Ligularia przewalskii, 252
Ligularia spp., 48, 131, 159, 161, 192
Ligularia stenocephala, 107, 132, 181, 251,
387, 392
Lilac, 146
'Lilac Queen,' 203
'Lilac Wonder,' 346, 361
Lilies, 47. See also *Lilium* entries
Lilium, 47, 81, 90, 108, 109, 177, 181, 193, 197
Lilium Asiatic hybrids, 29, 351
Lilium aurantium, 352
Lilium canadense, 169, 170
Lilium candidum, 74
Lilium hybrids, 79, 91
Lilium longifolium, 74, 179, 193, 195, 197
Lilium martagon, 159
Lilium Oriental hybrids, 29, 89, 352
Lilium rubrum, 123
Lilium speciosum, 352
Lilium spp., 91, 149
Lilium x *auralianense*, 352
'Lilliput,' 333
'Lily,' 322
Lily, 22, 49, 53, 112
Lily leek. See *Allium moly*
Lily of the nile. See *Agapanthus* hybrids
Lily-of-the-valley. See *Convallaria majalis*
Lilyturf. See *Lipiope muscari*
Lilyturf, variegated, 44
'Lime,' 259
'Lime Green,' 319
Limonium latifolium, 79, 80, 107, 164, 190, 252,
391, 392
Limonium perezii, 252, 389
Limonium sinuatum, 80, 193, 314
Linaria macroccana, 193, 315
Linaria vulgaris, 192
'L'Innocence,' 189, 349
Linum perenne, 54, 107, 190, 252, 389, 390,
391, 392
'Lipoma,' 195
Liriope muscari, 87, 106, 113, 159, 160, 161,
187, 190, 255, 388, 389, 390, 392
Lisianthus. See *Eustoma grandiflora*
Lisianthus russellianus, 305
'Little Bell Mixed,' 306
'Little Boy Blue,' 232
'Little Bunny,' 381
'Little Darling,' 294
'Little Devil,' 329
'Little Gem,' 247
'Little John,' 207
'Little Maid,' 247
'Little Miss Muffet,' 339
'Little Princess,' 226
'Little Sizzler,' 371
Lobelia, 182
Lobelia cardinalis, 48, 107, 121, 145, 151, 169,
170, 198, 253, 387
Lobelia erinus, 85, 87, 116, 121, 140, 145, 151,
189, 191, 195, 315
Lobelia fulgens, 253
Lobelia siphilitica, 48, 107, 190, 253,
387, 392
Lobelia splendens, 253
Lobelia spp., 389
Lobelia vedraiensis, 254
Lobelia x *gerardii*, 254
Lobelia x *speciosa*, 199, 253
Lobularia, 162
Lobularia maritima, 11, 73, 75, 84, 85, 87, 116,
121, 140, 141, 149, 159, 189, 315
Locust tree, 148
'Loddon Anna,' 219
'Loddon Gold,' 243
'Loddon Royalist,' 207
'Lodon Grove Blue,' 266
'Longin,' 265
Lonicera x *brownii*, 151
'Lord Baltimore,' 120, 198, 246
'Lord Nelson,' 290
'Louise Odier,' 97, 364
'Louis Jolliet,' 365
'Louis Phillipe,' 366
'Love,' 368
Love-in-a-mist. See *Nigella damascena*
Love Lies Bleeding, 293

Love-lies-bleeding, 198. See *Amaranthus
caudatus*
'Loveliness,' 194, 272, 314
'Lucifer,' 181, 197, 342
'Lucille Ball,' 117, 334
'Lucky Number,' 195
Lunaria annua, 73, 75, 80, 159, 188, 190, 194,
254, 390
Lungwort, 182. See also *Pulmonaria* entries
Lupine. See *Lupinus* hybrids
Lupinus hybrids, 41, 48, 79, 107, 108, 121, 190,
192, 194, 198, 254, 388, 391, 392
Lupinus texensis, 316
Lupinus x *hybridus*, 175
'Lutea,' 206
'Lutea Maxima,' 193, 347
'Lutea Splendens,' 192
'Luteo-picta,' 382
'Luxuriant,' 54, 233
Lychnis chalcedonia, 74, 107, 196, 255,
388, 392
Lychnis coronaria, 74, 188, 194, 255, 387,
390, 392
Lychnis flos-cuculi, 255
Lychnis flos-jovis, 255, 388
Lychnis splendens flore-plena, 255
Lychnis viscaria, 255
Lychnis x *haageana*, 255
Lycoris aurea, 353
Lycoris radiata, 197, 353
Lycoris squamigera, 74, 87, 91, 113, 159,
195, 353
Lysimachia ciliata, 257
Lysimachia clethroides, 107, 149, 188, 256
Lysimachia nummulara, 85, 192, 256, 388, 392
Lysimachia punctata, 127, 192, 256, 388, 391
Lythrum salicaria, 107, 195, 257, 387, 388, 390,
391, 392
Lythrum virgatum, 107, 257

Macleaya cordata, 107, 257, 387, 388, 390
Macleaya microcarpa, 257
Madagascar periwinkle, 12. See also
Catharanthus roseus
'Madame Alfred Carriere,' 373
'Madame Butterfly,' 294
'Madame Hardy,' 97, 366
'Madame Isaac Pereire,' 219, 364
'Madame Grégoire Staechelin,' 96, 370
'Madame Laurette Messimy,' 366
'Madness,' 325
Madonna lily. See *Lilium candidum*
'Magic,' 325
'Magic Fountains,' 230
Magic lily. See *Lycoris squamigera*
'Magna Charta,' 97, 369
'Magnificum,' 235
'Magnus,' 53, 103, 113, 194, 236
'Mahogany,' 120, 260
Maiden grass, 47, 380
Maidenhair fern. See *Adiantum pedatum*
Maiden pink. See *Dianthus deltoides*
'Mainacht,' 278
'Majestic,' 253
'Major,' 358
'Malibu,' 317
'Malta,' 195, 352
Maltese cross. See *Lychnis chalcedonia*
Malus floribunda, 113
Malva alcea, 48, 107, 194, 258, 392
Malva moschata, 258
'Mammoth,' 209
'Mandarin Orange,' 328
'Maravilla,' 108, 176, 361
'March Sunshine,' 355
'Marconi,' 226
'Maréchal daVoust,' 97, 371
'Margaret,' 205
'Margarete,' 113, 194, 207
'Margery Fish,' 274
'Marie Ballard,' 212
Marigold, 11, 27, 88, 193. See also *Calendula
officinalis* and *Tagetes* entries
'Marine,' 88, 183, 310
'Marine Bells,' 191, 296
Marginal shield fern. See *Dryopteris marginalis*
'Margo Koster,' 372
'Marie van Houtte,' 366

Marjoram, golden. See *Origanum Vulgare*
'Marshall's Delight,' 194, 260
Marsh marigold. See *Caltha palustris*
Marsh violet. See *Viola cucullata*
Martha Washington geranium. See
Pelargonium x *domesticum*
'Mary Rose,' 12, 91, 96, 97, 367
'Mary Stoker,' 87, 192, 225
'Matin Bells,' 151, 198, 246
Matricaria. See *Chrysanthemum parthenium*
Matricaria chamomilla, 222
'Matterhorn,' 346
'Matsumoto Blue,' 191
'Matsumoto Light Blue,' 191
Matteuccia pensylvanica, 384
Matteuccia struthiopteris, 128, 169, 384
Matthiola incana, 48, 79, 91, 193, 195, 198, 316
'Mawson's Variety,' 273
'Max Frei,' 279
'Maxistar,' 192
'May Night,' 54, 108, 183, 278
'Mazur,' 274
Mazus. See *Mazus reptans*
Mazus reptans, 169, 170, 190, 258, 388, 392
'McKana Giant,' 208
'McKana Hybrid,' 54, 208
Meadow clary. See *Salvia pratensis*
Meadow saffron. See *Colchicum autumnale*
Meadow sage. See *Salvia pratensis*
Mealy-cup sage. See *Salvia farinacea*
'Medallion,' 193, 317
'Medio-picta,' 158, 187
'Meidiland Pink,' 371
Meidiland roses, 370, 371
Melampodium. See *Melampodium paludosum*
Melampodium paludosum, 132, 140, 193, 317
'Mello Red and White,' 318
'Mello White,' 318
'Melody Orange,' 175
'Melody Pink Shades,' 195
'Melody White,' 189, 318
'Melody White with Blotch,' 189
'Melody Yellow,' 193
Mentha requienii, 85, 259
Mentha spicata, 259
Mentha spp., 91
Mentha suaveolens, 67, 187, 258
Mentha x *piperita*, 67, 69, 259
'Menton,' 195
'Merlin,' 325
'Merlin Pink,' 195
'Merlin Red,' 199
'Merlin White,' 189
'Mermaid,' 306
'Mermaid Pink,' 195
Mertensia virginica, 106, 124, 127, 128, 151,
190, 259
'Meteor,' 108, 109, 179, 195, 281
Mexican bush sage. See *Salvia leucantha*
Mexican evening primrose. See *Oenothera
speciosa*
Mexican lobelia, 253
Mexican phlox. See *Phlox mesoleuca*
Mexican sunflower. See *Tithonia rotundifolia*
Michaelmas daisy. See *Aster novi-belgii* x
novae-angliae
'Midget,' 316
'Midget Rose,' 195
'Midnight,' 306
'Midnight Hour,' 190
'Midnight Madness,' 191
'Mignon Silver,' 303
'Mikado,' 305
'Mildred May,' 188
Milium effusum, 379
Milkweed, 148
Milky bellflower. See *Campanula lactiflora*
'Milky White,' 305
'Miller's Crimson,' 198, 271
'Millstream Daphne,' 194
Mimulus cardinalis, 196, 260
Mimulus guttatus, 145, 169, 260
Mimulus x *hybridus*, 151, 169, 170, 260, 317
'Minarette,' 255
'Mini,' 320
Miniature roses, 115, 117, 371
'Mini Blue,' 71
'Minilaca Mix,' 325
'Mini Star,' 307
'Ministar Tangerine,' 196

'Minnow,' 356
Mint, Corsican, 89
Mints. See *Mentha* spp.
'Minuet,' 194, 289
Mirabilis jalapa, 73, 145, 164, 317
'Misato Purple,' 269
Miscanthus sinensis, 14, 43, 47, 80, 131, 133, 134, 135, 178, 181, 185, 187, 379
'Mischief,' 292
'Mischief Soft Pink,' 292
'Miss Indigo,' 278
'Mission Bells,' 305
'Miss Jekyll,' 320
'Miss Lingard,' 54, 97, 113, 185, 188, 267
Missouri primrose. See *Oenothera missouriensis*
'Miss Willmott's Ghost,' 237
Mist flower. See *Eupatorium coelestinum*
'Misty Blue,' 191
'Mixed Art Shades,' 314
Miyabe. See *Chrysanthemum weyrichii*
'Miyazaki,' 286
'Moerheim Beauty,' 196, 243
Molinia caerulea, 133, 380
Moluccella laevis, 48, 73, 80, 318
'Mona Lisa,' 352
'Monarch Mix,' 240
Monarda didyma, 54, 67, 74, 75, 90, 91, 107, 120, 121, 145, 149, 150, 151, 179, 188, 190, 194, 198, 260, 387, 391, 392
Monarda fistulosa, 69, 260, 391
Monarda punctata, 260
'Monch,' 54, 178, 190, 212
'Mondragon,' 197
Money-plant. See *Lunaria annua*
Moneywort. See *Lysimachia nummulara*
Monkey flower. See *Mimulus* x *hybridus*
Monkshood, 182. See also *Aconitum* spp.
'Monsieur Tillier,' 366
'Monstrosa,' 216
'Monstrosum,' 309
Montauk daisy. See *Chrysanthemum nipponicum*
'Mont Blanc,' 185, 189, 349
Montbretia. See *Crocosmia* x *crocosmiiflora*
'Moody Blues,' 230
'Moonbeam,' 53, 54, 55, 87, 104, 113, 165, 178, 180, 181, 228
Moonflower, 72. See also *Ipomoea alba*
'Moonlight,' 208, 353, 369
'Moonlight Wave,' 188
'Moon of Nippon,' 185, 188
Moonshine yarrow. See *Achillea* x 'Moonshine'
Moor grass. See *Molinia caerulea*
'Morden Armorette,' 365
'Morden Blush,' 365
'Morden Pink,' 195, 257
'Morden's Gleam,' 257
'Moriah,' 190, 248
'Morning Blush,' 216
Morning glory, 27, 72, 182. See also *Ipomoea tricolor*
'Morning Light,' 43, 187, 380
'Moss Curled,' 324
Moss pink. See *Phlox subulata*
Moss rose, 91, 371. See also *Portulaca grandiflora*
'Mother of Pearl,' 321
Mother-of-thyme. See *Thymus praecox arcticus*
'Moudry,' 381
Mountain bluet. See *Centaurea montana*
'Mount Blanc,' 189, 320
'Mount Tacoma,' 381
Mountain mantle. See *Alchemilla alpina*
'Mr. Ed,' 352
'Mr. Lincoln,' 79, 91, 117, 370
'Mr. Sam,' 352
'Mrs. Bradshaw,' 196, 242
'Mrs. Eileen,' 197
'Mrs. Kendall Clarke,' 97, 182, 190, 241
'Mrs. Moon,' 151, 187, 273, 274
'Mt. Everest,' 87, 188, 212
'Mt. Fuji,' 54, 188, 267
'Mt. Hood,' 108, 185, 189, 354
'Mt. St. Helens,' 198
Mullein. See *Verbascum* x *hybridum*
'Multiplex,' 218, 278
'Multi-rainbow Mix,' 346
'Munroe's White,' 253
'Munstead,' 54

'Munstead Dwarf,' 90, 190, 250
'Munstead Purple Giant,' 254
'Munstead Variety,' 273
Muscari armeniacum, 191, 354
Muscari azureum, 191, 354
Muscari botryoides, 74, 189, 191, 353, 354
Muscari comosum, 354
Muscari spp., 29, 48, 176
Musk mallow. See *Malva moschata*
Musk roses, 91, 368, 369
'My Castle,' 198, 254
'My Fair Lady,' 261, 299
Myosotis alpestris, 261
Myosotis palustris. See *Myosotis scorpiodes*
Myosotis scorpioides, 44, 74, 116, 190, 260, 387, 388, 389, 391, 392
Myosotis sylvatica, 73, 99, 159, 169, 170, 261
'Mystic,' 317

Naked ladies. See *Lycoris squamigera*
Naked lady. See *Amaryllis belladona*
'Nana,' 210, 228, 271
'Nanho Purple,' 113
Narcissus, 29, 134, 181, 185
Narcissus cyclamenius, 113, 355
Narcissus hybrids, 79, 81, 108, 189, 195, 197, 354
Narcissus jonquilla, 90, 91, 120, 354
Narcissus spp., 133, 160, 161, 193
Narcissus triandrus, 97, 189, 355
Narcissus x *cyclamenius*, 140, 355
Narciussus x *hybrida*, 120
Narcissus x *poeticus*, 74, 75, 87, 356
Narcissus x *tazetta*, 91, 356
Narrow-leaf zinnia. See *Zinnia angustifolia*
Nasturtium, 11, 27, 148. See also *Tropaeolum majus*
'Natascha,' 189, 350
'Nathalie Nypels,' 372
'National Arboretum,' 381
Navel seed. See *Omphaloides verna*
'Neapolitanum,' 324
'Nearly Wild,' 374
Needle palm. See *Yucca filamentosa*
'Nellie Britten,' 179, 194, 290
'Nelly Moser,' 81
Nemesia. See *Nemesia strumosa*
Nemesia strumosa, 196, 318
Nepeta cataria, 70, 261
Nepeta gigantea, 261
Nepeta mussinii, 70, 261
Nepeta spp., 146, 164
Nepeta x *faassenii*, 54, 67, 91, 95, 97, 99, 106, 116, 163, 165, 190, 197, 261, 387, 388, 390, 391, 392
Nerine, 353
'New Beauty,' 115
'New Beginning,' 371
'New Dawn,' 91, 370
'New Day,' 79
New Guinea impatiens. See *Impatiens* x *hybrida*
'Newport Pink,' 45, 194, 231
'Nicki,' 319
'Nicki Red,' 120, 198
'Nicki White,' 87
Nicotiana affinis. See *Nicotiana alata*
Nicotiana alata, 48, 87, 89, 91, 120, 175, 182, 189, 193, 195, 198, 318
Nicotiana spp., 145, 146
Nicotiana sylvestris, 48, 120, 132, 151, 189, 319
Nicotiania langsdorfii, 48, 132, 319
Nierembergia hippomanica violacea, 140, 141, 189, 191, 319
Nierembergia repens, 320
Nigella damascena, 73, 79, 80, 82, 116, 132, 140, 164, 191, 320
'Nigrescens,' 133, 199, 380
'Nikko,' 248
'Niobe,' 151
Nipponanthemum nipponicum. See *Chrysanthemum nipponicum*
Nippon daisy. See *Chrysanthemum nipponicum*
'Niveum,' 237
'Noble Maiden,' 254
'Noblesse,' 195
Noisette roses, 93
'Non-stop,' 338

'Non-stop Copper,' 197
'Non-stop Pink,' 195
'Non-stop Red,' 199
'Non-stop Rose Pink,' 195
'Non-stop White,' 189
'Non-stop Yellow,' 193
'Nora Barlow,' 179, 194, 209
'Nora Leigh,' 187, 267
'Northern Lights,' 315
Northern sea oats. See *Chasmanthium latifolium*
'Norwich Canary,' 193

'Oakleaf,' 285
Obedient plant. See *Physostegia virginiana*
'Oberon,' 346
Ocimum basilicum, 67, 69, 73, 91, 132, 179, 199, 320
Oenothera berlandieri, 164, 165. See also *Oenothera speciosa*
Oenothera fruticosa. See *Oenothera tetragona*
Oenothera missouriensis, 262, 389, 391
Oenothera rosea, 262
Oenothera speciosa, 54, 106, 194, 261, 389, 390, 391
Oenothera spp., 54, 388
Oenothera tetragona, 99, 107, 108, 181, 182, 192, 262, 389, 390, 391
'Oestfriesland,' 278
'Ohio Glow,' 260
'Old Blush,' 364, 366
Old garden roses, 32, 34, 92–96, 101
'Old Royal Fragrance,' 288
'Ole,' 79
'Olympiad,' 79
Olympic hybrid lilies. See *Lilium* x *auralianense*
'Omega,' 54, 267
Omphaloides verna, 190, 262, 388, 392
Onoclea sensibilis, 112, 385
'Opal,' 237
Ophiopogon japonicus, 381
Ophiopogon planiscapus, 133, 199, 380
'Orange,' 259, 332
'Orange Appeal,' 196
'Orange Bedder,' 196
'Orange Brilliant,' 197
'Orange Cascade,' 197
Orange coneflower. See *Rudbeckia fulgida*
'Orange Elite,' 197
'Orange King,' 196, 197, 305
'Orange Maxim,' 197
'Orange Perfection,' 196, 267
'Orange Prince,' 196, 197
'Orange Queen,' 87, 196
'Orange-scarlet Sonnet,' 196
'Orange Star,' 181, 197
'Orange Sun,' 197
'Orange Tiger,' 197
'Orange with Eye,' 197
'Orange Wonder,' 197, 361
'Orbit,' 322
'Orbit Appleblossom,' 195
'Orbit Hot Pink,' 322
'Orbit Pink,' 195
'Orbit Rose,' 197
Oregano, golden, 67. See also *Origanum vulgare*
'Oregon Rainbows,' 264
'Oriental,' 198
Oriental fountain grass. See *Pennisetum orientale*
Oriental hybrid lilies, 88. See also *Lilium* Oriental hybrids
Oriental lily. See *Lilium*
'Oriental Night,' 316
Oriental poppy, 49, 177. See also *Papaver orientale*
Origanum dictamnus, 263
Origanum vulgare 'Aureum,' 67, 69, 91, 263, 387, 392
'Orion,' 195
Ornamental grasses, 9, 14, 52, 53. 375-382, 393
Ornamental pepper. See *Capsicum annuum*
'Osaka,' 295
Osmunda cinnamomea, 125, 127, 128, 161, 169, 170, 385
Osmunda claytoniana, 385
Osmunda regalis, 127, 171, 169, 386

Ostrich fern. See *Matteuccia pensylvanica*
'Ostrich Plume,' 297
Oswego tea. See *Monarda didyma*
'Othello,' 91, 97, 198, 252, 367
'Oxford Blue,' 191, 327
Oxlip. See *Primula elatior*
Ozark sundrops. See *Oenothera missouriensis*
'Ozawa,' 336

'Pacific Beauty,' 296
'Pacific Giants,' 272
'Pacific Light Pink,' 292
'Pacific Scarlet,' 292
'Padparadja,' 197
Paeonia lactiflora, 25, 74, 75, 79, 81, 90, 91, 107, 108, 121, 179, 185, 188, 194, 196, 263, 387, 388, 389, 390, 391, 392
Paeonia tenuifolia, 263
'Pagoda,' 346
Painted daisy. See *Chrysanthemum coccineum*
Painted sage. See *Salvia viridis*
Painted tongue. See *Salpiglossis sinuata*
'Palace Purple,' 44, 55, 87, 96, 97, 106, 108, 132, 179, 182, 199, 245
Pale coneflower. See *Echinacea pallida* and *Rudbeckia pallida*
'Pale Moon,' 208
'Palona Carmine,' 199
'Palona Deep Rose,' 195
'Palona Light Blue,' 191
'Palona White,' 189
'Palona White with Eye,' 189
Pancreatium maritimum, 349
Panicum virgatum, 133, 381
Pansy, 17, 105, 175. See also *Viola* x *wittrockiana*
'Pantaloons,' 188, 233
Papaver commutatum, 321
Papaver nudicaule, 193, 195, 196, 264, 321, 387, 392
Papaver orientale, 107, 120, 121, 181, 188, 194, 196, 198, 264, 387, 388, 390
Papaver rhoeas, 73, 196, 198, 321
Papaver spp., 79, 164
'Paper Doll,' 117
'Paper Moon,' 189
'Paper White,' 189
'Paperwhite,' 356
Paperwhite narcissus. See *Narcissus* x *tazetta*
'Papillon,' 249
'Paprika,' 196, 203, 329
'Paradise,' 79
'Paramount,' 324
'Parker's Variety,' 203
'Parks Fragrant Giants,' 331
Parsley. See *Petroselinium crispum*
'Partygirl,' 194, 282
'Pascali,' 79
Pasque flower. See *Pulsatilla vulgaris*
'Pastel Mixed,' 297, 309
'Paul Bunyan,' 245
'Pauline,' 286
'Paul Ricault,' 97, 365
'Peace,' 79, 117, 370
'Peach Blossom,' 45, 177, 194, 214
'Peaches and Cream,' 87, 197, 331
Peach-leaf bellflower. See *Campanula persicifolia*
'Peacock,' 295
Peacock orchid. See *Acidanthera murielae*
'Pearl Meidiland,' 371
Pearly everlasting. See *Anaphalis triplinervis*
'Peeping Tom,' 355
Pelargonium crispum, 322
Pelargonium graveolens, 322
Pelargonium grossularioides, 322
Pelargonium peltatum, 108, 145, 195, 321
Pelargonium spp., 67, 91, 321, 322
Pelargonium tomentosum, 69, 322
Pelargonium x *domesticum*, 198, 321, 322
Pelargonium x *fragrans*, 322
Pelargonium x *hortorum*, 79, 121, 145, 189, 195, 196, 199, 322
'Pembina,' 190, 249
'Penelope,' 88, 90, 91
Pennisetum, 162
Pennisetum alopecuroides, 53, 80, 87, 133, 134, 381
Pennisetum orientale, 133, 381

Pennisetum setaceum, 51, 133, 179, 199, 382
'Penny's Worth,' 54, 192
Penstemon barbatus, 48, 143, 190, 194, 265, 387, 388, 389, 390, 391, 392
Penstemon digitalis, 265
Penstemon spp., 145
Penstemon x *gloxinioides*, 323
Pentas lanceolata, 195, 323
Peony, 10, 25, 49, 78. See also *Paeonia lactiflora*
Peppermint. See *Mentha* x *piperita*
'Peppermint Cooler,' 189
'Peppermint Extra Double,' 311
Peppermint geranium. See *Pelargonium tomentosum*
'Peppermint Stick Mix,' 332
'Perfecta,' 179, 194, 216, 242, 279
Perilla. See *Perilla frutescens*
Perilla frutescens, 73, 90, 91, 132, 183, 199, 323, 324
'Perlina,' 363
Perovskia atriplicifolia, 48, 54, 90, 91, 107, 132, 164, 165, 178, 190, 197, 265, 388, 389, 390, 391, 392
'Perpetual White Moss,' 371
'Perry's Blue,' 190, 249
'Perry's Variety,' 208
'Perry's White,' 188, 249
Persian buttercup. See *Ranunculus asiaticus*
Persian catmint. See *Nepeta mussinii*
Persian fritillaria. See *Fritillaria persica*
'Persian Jewels,' 320
Persian onion. See *Allium aflatunense*
'Persian Pearl,' 360, 361
Peruvian daffodil. See *Hymenocallis narcissiflora*
Peruvian lily. See *Alstroemeria aurantiaca*
'Peter Pan,' 87, 185, 189, 283, 332, 333, 344
'Peter Pan Flame,' 199
'Peter Pan Gold,' 193
'Peter Pan Orange,' 197
'Peter Pan Pink,' 195
'Petite,' 232
Petrorhagia saxifraga, 140, 265, 389, 391
Petroselinum crispum, 67, 69, 73, 149, 150, 324
Petunia. See *Petunia* x *hybrida*
Petunia x *hybrida*, 79, 87, 91, 97, 121, 145, 149, 150, 179, 185, 191, 193, 195, 196, 199, 324
'Pfitzeri,' 196, 249
'Pfitzer's Crimson Beauty,' 199
Pfitzer's Dwarfs. See *Canna* x *generalis*
Phalaris arundinacea var. *picta*, 133, 187, 382
'Pheasant's Eye,' 356
Pheasant's-eye narcissus. See *Narcissus* x *poeticus*
Phlomis cashmeriana, 266
Phlomis russeliana, 107, 178, 192, 266, 389, 392
Phlomis viscosa. See *Phlomis russeliana*
Phlox carolina, 97, 107, 267
Phlox, creeping, 127. See also *Phlox stolonifera*
Phlox decussata. See *Phlox paniculata*
Phlox divaricata, 112, 126, 127, 128, 158, 188, 190, 266, 389
Phlox, downy. See *Phlox pilosa*
Phlox drummondii, 91, 121, 145, 149, 150, 189, 191, 195, 196, 199, 325
Phlox, garden, 10, 25, 47, 182. See *Phlox paniculata*
Phlox maculata, 54, 113, 185, 188, 194, 266, 389, 390, 391
Phlox mesoleuca, 268
Phlox nivalis, 268
Phlox paniculata, 47, 54, 74, 75, 79, 81, 90, 91, 107, 109, 121, 179, 182, 184, 187, 188, 190, 194, 196, 198, 267, 389, 390, 391, 392
Phlox pilosa, 127, 128, 194, 266, 389
Phlox spp., 149, 387, 388
Phlox stolonifera, 126, 127, 128, 159, 160, 188, 190, 194, 266, 389
Phlox subulata, 74, 84, 106, 140, 141, 178, 188, 190, 194, 268, 389, 390, 391, 392
Phlox, wild blue, 112, 124. See also *Phlox divaricata*
Phlox x *chattahoochee*, 266
'Phoenix Mix,' 337
Phragmites macra. See *Hakonechloa macra*
Physostegia virginiana, 48, 54, 107, 108, 179, 185, 187, 188, 195, 268, 387, 389, 390, 391, 392

'Pickwick,' 344
'Picotee Red,' 199
'Piedmont Gold,' 187
'Pierre,' 226
'Pimpernel,' 197
'Pinafore Pink,' 194, 267
Pincushion flower. See *Scabiosa caucasica*
'Pineapple Beauty,' 51, 301
'Pink Beauty,' 179, 194, 204, 217, 231, 314
'Pink Bomb,' 179, 194, 224
'Pink Bouquet,' 194, 269
'Pink Carpet,' 195
'Pink Champion,' 195
'Pink Charm,' 195
Pink coreopsis. See *Coreopsis rosea*
'Pink Daisy,' 194
'Pink Dawn,' 274
'Pink Domino,' 287
'Pink Dreams,' 195
'Pink Fairy,' 194, 242
'Pink Flamingo,' 253
'Pink Frost,' 248
'Pink Giant,' 195, 341
'Pink Grootendorst,' 374
'Pinkie,' 195
'Pink Impression,' 195
'Pink Jewel,' 237
'Pink Lavender Appeal,' 194
'Pink Loveliness,' 272
'Pink Mist,' 279
'Pink Pagoda,' 194
'Pink Panda,' 195, 330
'Pink Parfait,' 79
'Pink Pearl,' 109, 195, 349
'Pink Perfection,' 195, 353
'Pink Pewter,' 250
'Pink Powderpuffs,' 292
'Pink President,' 195
'Pink Profusion,' 323
'Pink Queen,' 304
'Pink Ridge,' 268
Pinks. See *Dianthus* entries
'Pink Star,' 195, 242, 337
'Pink Sunday,' 327
'Pink Tempo,' 195
'Pink Tiger,' 179, 195
Pink turtle-head. See *Chelone lyonii*
'Pinky Improved Selection,' 292
'Pinnacle,' 310
'Pinstripe,' 371
'Pinto Red,' 199
Pinto Salmon Orange,' 196
'Pipit,' 355
'Pixie Delight,' 316
'Pizzazz,' 194
Platycodon, 162
Platycodon grandiflorus, 54, 65, 97, 107, 109, 121, 177, 178, 179, 185, 188, 190, 194, 269, 387, 388, 389, 390, 391, 392
'Playboy,' 79, 193
'Plena,' 342
'Plum,' 325
Plumbago. See *Ceratostigma plumbaginoides*
'Plum Blue,' 191
Plume poppy. See *Macleaya cordata*
'Plum Purple,' 191
'Poeticus Recurvus,' 356
Poet's narcissus. See *Narcissus* x *poeticus*
'Polaris,' 226
Polemonium caeruleum, 87, 106, 127, 159, 190, 269, 387, 392
Polemonium reptans, 269
Polianthes tuberosa, 48, 74, 79, 90, 91, 356, 357
'Polka,' 274
'Polka Dot,' 299
Polka-dot plant. See *Hypoestes phyllostachya*
Polyantha roses, 71, 94, 372
Polyanthus primrose. See *Primula* x *polyantha*
Polygonatum biflorum, 125, 127, 128, 270, 387, 388
Polygonatum commutatum, 270
Polygonatum odoratum 'Variegatum,' 187, 270, 387, 388, 389, 392
Polygonum bistorta, 48, 107, 194, 270, 387, 391, 392
Polystichum acrostichoides, 60, 127, 128, 156, 386
Polystichum munitum, 386

Poor man's orchid. See *Schizanthus pinnatus*
Poppies. See *Papaver* entries
Poppies, Oriental, 49
'Porcelain,' 189, 327
Porcupine grass, 380
Portland roses, 93, 96, 372
Portulaca grandiflora, 73, 85, 164, 193, 195, 196, 325
'Postman Joyner,' 339
Potentilla tabernaemontani, 140, 271, 387, 390, 391, 392
Potentilla verna, 192. See *Potentilla tabernaemontani*
Pot marigold, 11. See also *Calendula officinalis*
'Potsford White,' 271
'Pouffe,' 219
'Powder Blue,' 191
'Powderpuff Mix,' 205
'Powis Castle,' 190
'Prairie Dawn,' 265
'Prairie Dusk,' 190, 265
'Prairie Fire,' 265
Prairie gentian. See *Eustoma grandiflora*
Prairie mallow. See *Sidalcea malviflora*
'Prairie Night,' 260
'Prelude Pink,' 195
'Prelude Scarlet,' 198
'President Lincoln,' 198
'Pretty In,' 298
'Pretty Polly,' 246
'Priceana,' 291
'Pride of Dusseldorf,' 209
'Prime Time Blue,' 191
'Prime Time Light Blue,' 191
Primrose. See *Oenothera speciosa*
'Primrose Beauty,' 192, 249
Primroses, Japanese, 60
'Primrose Yellow,' 340
Primula acaulis, 272
Primula elatior, 272
Primula japonica, 60, 169, 170, 171, 188, 194, 198, 271, 387, 388
Primula malacoides, 272
Primula obconica, 272
Primula spp., 121, 149, 159, 171
Primula veris, 74, 106, 156, 161, 192, 271, 387, 388
Primula vulgaris, 272
Primula x *polyantha*, 106, 192, 194, 198, 272, 388, 392
'Prince of Orange,' 101, 196
'Princess,' 304
'Princess Beatrix,' 342, 343
'Princess Charmante,' 197
'Princess Crimson,' 198
'Princess Louise,' 373
'Princess with a Red Eye,' 294
'Prinz Claus,' 189, 343
'Prisom Salmon Halo,' 196
Privet, 101
'Professor Blaauw,' 191, 351
'Professor Kippenburg,' 190, 212
'Professor Plum,' 308
'Progress,' 90
'Prominent,' 368
'Promise Pink,' 325
'Prosperity,' 237
Prunella grandiflora, 272, 273
Prunella x *webbiana*, 106, 190, 194, 272
Pulmonaria alba, 273
Pulmonaria angustifolia, 273
Pulmonaria longifolia, 273
Pulmonaria officinalis, 74, 75, 273, 274
Pulmonaria rubra, 273
Pulmonaria saccharata, 159, 187, 188, 273
Pulmonaria spp., 106, 145, 190, 387, 388, 391, 392
Pulsatilla vulgaris, 106, 140, 164, 190, 198, 274, 387, 388, 390, 392
'Pumila,' 90, 133, 212, 376
'Purity,' 189, 247, 302, 343
'Purple,' 295
'Purple Buddy,' 191
Purple coneflower, 53, 104. See also *Echinacea purpurea*
'Purple Crown,' 190, 260
'Purple Dome,' 190, 212, 286
'Purple Flame,' 241

Purple fountain grass. See *Pennisetum setaceum*
'Purple Gem,' 190, 214
'Purple Joy,' 191
'Purple Lance,' 213
Purple-leaf bugbane. See *Cimicifuga ramose* var. *atropurpurea*
Purple-leaf coralbells. See *Heuchera micrantha*
Purple-leaf Labrador violet. See *Viola labradorica* var. *purpurea*
Purple-leaf sage, 67
Purple loosestrife, 10. See also *Lythrum salicaria*
'Purple Loveliness,' 190, 272
'Purple Mist,' 284
Purple moor grass. See *Molinia caerulea*
'Purple Robe,' 191, 320
'Purple Ruffles,' 320
'Purple Sensation,' 134, 191, 334, 351
'Purple Splendor,' 191
'Purple Star,' 191
'Purple Violet,' 305
Purpurascens, 135, 380
Purpurea, 191, 199, 216, 277, 344
'Purpureus,' 194, 234
'Purpurkerze,' 213
Puschkinia lebanotica. See *Puschkinia scilloides*
Puschkinia scilloides, 191, 357
'Pygmy Torch,' 29
Pyrethrum. See *Chrysanthemum coccineum*

'Quakeress,' 237
'Quakeress White,' 188, 237
Quaker ladies. See *Hedyotis caerulea*
Quaking grass. See *Briza media*
'Queen,' 300
Queen-Anne's lace, 148
'Queen Charlotte,' 109, 194, 207, 291
'Queen Elizabeth,' 79, 91, 368
'Queen Fabiola,' 191, 339
'Queen of Denmark,' 97, 364
'Queen of Hearts,' 196, 304
'Queen of the Blues,' 191, 344
Queen-of-the-meadow. See *Filipendula ulmaria*
Queen of-the-prairie. See *Filipendula rubra*
'Queen Victoria,' 199, 253

Ragged robin. See *Lychnis flos-cuculi*
'Rainbow,' 308
'Rainbow Crimson,' 198
'Rainbow Mix,' 301
Rain lily. See *Zephranthes atamasco*
'Rally Series,' 332
Rambler rose, 372, 373
'Rancho White,' 333
Ranunculus asiaticus, 193, 199, 357
'Raspberry Parfait,' 90, 304
'Raspberry Queen,' 194, 264
Ratibida pinnata, 107, 192, 274, 387, 390
Rattlesnake grass. See *Briza media*
'Rauhreif,' 255
'Reckless,' 198
'Red,' 198
'Red and White Music,' 198
'Red Baron,' 133, 134, 199, 379
'Red Beauty,' 198
'Red Bells,' 274
'Red Bird,' 199
'Red Cascade,' 214
'Red Cloud,' 286
'Red Coat,' 367
'Red Dreams,' 199
'Red Emperor,' 199
'Redfield Hybrids,' 271
'Red Fire,' 327
'Red Flame,' 264
'Red Fox,' 120, 198, 289
'Red-gold Hybrids,' 181, 196, 243
Red-hot poker. See *Kniphofia uvaria*
'Red Hot Sally,' 199, 327
'Red Jewel,' 199
'Red King Humbert,' 199, 340
Redleaf rose, 373. See also *Rosa glauca*
'Red Light,' 198
'Red Madness,' 199
'Red Meidiland,' 371

'Red Night,' 199
'Red Plume,' 307
Red rays switch grass, 381
Red ribbons. See *Clarkia concinna*
'Red Riding Hood,' 199, 363
'Red Rocket,' 198
Red salvia. See *Salvia splendens*
'Red Sentinel,' 213
'Red Shades,' 199
Red switch grass, 381
'Resholt,' 220
'Redskin,' 303
'Red Splendor,' 199
'Red Star,' 198
Red valerian. See *Centranthus ruber*
'Red Velvet,' 199, 352
Red velvet coleus. See *Coleus* x *hybridus*
'Red Versailles,' 302
'Red Wings,' 198, 242
Regals. See *Pelargonium* x *domesticum*
'Reine des Violettes,' 97, 369
'Remembrance,' 191, 344
Resurrection lily. See *Lycoris squamigera*
Reticulated iris. See *Iris reticulata*
'Rhapsody in Blue,' 306
'Rheinland,' 194, 213
Rhododendron, 76, 111, 142
Ricinus communis, 132, 199, 326
Ribbon grass. See *Phalaris arundinacea*
   var. *picta*
'Rigoletto,' 303
'Ringo Series,' 322
'Robert,' 257
'Robinson's Hybrids,' 223
'Robustissima,' 194, 207
Rock cress. See *Aubrieta deltoidea*
'Rocket,' 294
Rocket larkspur. See *Consolida ambigua*
'Rocket Pink,' 195
Rock soapwort. See *Saponaria ocymoides*
Rocky Mountain columbine. See *Aquilegia caerulea*
Rodgersia aesculifolia, 107, 274, 388, 392
Rodgersia pinnata, 170, 199, 275
Rodgersia podophylla, 275
Rodgersia spp., 55, 169, 275
Rodgersia superba, 275
Roman chamomile. See *Chamaemelum nobile*
'Romance White,' 189
'Rosabella,' 209
'Rosabelle,' 195, 348
Rosa alba semi-plena, 92
Rosa damascens, 366
Rosa gallica, 67, 69, 92, 366, 367
Rosa glauca, 113
Rosa hybrids, 81, 121
'Rosalinde,' 267
Rosa moyesii, 368
'Rosa Mundi,' 97, 368
Rosa rugosa, 67, 90, 96, 373
Rosa x *alba*, 92
Rosa x *damascena*, 67, 92, 93, 366
'Rose,' 309
'Rosea,' 194, 203, 215, 221, 242, 261, 262, 284, 288, 341, 342
'Rose Bud,' 339
Rose campion. See *Lychnis coronaria*
'Rose City,' 179, 194
'Rose Elegance,' 195
'Rose Elf,' 194, 265
'Rose Fountain,' 195
'Rose Future,' 230
'Rose Garden,' 195
Rose mallow, 46. See also *Hibiscus moscheutos*
Rosemary, 67, 68, 89, 99
'Rose Parade,' 367
'Rose Queen,' 179, 195, 232, 237, 278
'Rosette,' 265, 266
'Rosette Hybrid Mix,' 311
'Roseum,' 161, 194, 223, 236, 237, 290
'Roseum Superbum,' 257
Rose verbena. See *Verbena canadensis*
'Rose Wine,' 278
'Rosie O'Day,' 316
'Rosina,' 194, 291
'Rosy Clouds,' 195
'Rosy Gem,' 282
'Rosyln Carter,' 91
Rosy maidenhair, 383
'Rosy Wonder,' 354

'Rote Funten,' 199
'Rotstrahlbusch,' 381
'Royal,' 292
'Royal Banner,' 248
'Royal Blue,' 190, 207, 214, 288
'Royal Blue Compact,' 261
'Royal Bouquet Mixed,' 300
'Royal Carpet Mixed,' 294
'Royal Castle,' 249
'Royal Family,' 314
Royal fern. See *Osmunda regalis*
'Royal Gold,' 193
'Royal Highland,' 287
'Royal Highness,' 370
'Royal Purple,' 47, 190, 253
'Royal Red,' 214
'Royal Robe,' 291
'Roy Davidson,' 273
'Rubra,' 234, 259
'Rubra Maxima,' 347
'Rubrum,' 51, 243, 352, 382
'Ruby Glow,' 323, 280
'Ruby Mound,' 198
Rudbeckia fulgida, 10, 54, 79, 81, 107, 121, 132, 133, 134, 150, 153, 164, 181, 192, 275, 387, 388, 389, 390, 391, 392
Rudbeckia hirta, 180, 275, 389
Rudbeckia laciniata, 54, 275
Rudbeckia maxima, 274
Rudbeckia nitida, 107, 150, 181, 192, 275, 387, 388, 390, 392
Rudbeckia spp., 131, 146, 149
Rue. See *Ruta graveolens*
'Ruffled Pink,' 195
Rugosa roses, 68, 373, 374
'Russell Hybrid Blue,' 108
'Russell Hybrids,' 254
'Russell Hybrid Yellow,' 192, 254
'Russian Pink,' 297
Russian sage. See *Perovskia atriplicifolia*
'Rustic Colors,' 180, 275
Ruta graveolens, 67, 91, 106, 116, 187, 197, 276, 392

'Safari,' 329
Saffron crocus. See *Crocus sativus*
Sage, 67, 70. See also *Salvia* entries
'Salet,' 371
'Sally,' 352
'Salmon Beauty,' 203
'Salmon-Pink,' 340
'Salmon Queen,' 321
'Salome,' 195
Salpiglossis sinuata, 326
Salvia, 11, 104, 105
Salvia argentea, 197, 276, 391
Salvia azurea var. *grandiflora*, 277
Salvia coccinea, 195, 199
Salvia farinacea, 11, 48, 51, 79, 81, 97, 151, 178, 185, 189, 191, 326, 327, 390
Salvia greigii, 277, 390
Salvia haematodes. See *Salvia pratensis*
Salvia horminum. See *Salvia viridis*
Salvia leucantha, 277, 390
Salvia nemorosa. See *Salvia* x *superba*
Salvia officinalis, 66, 67, 69, 90, 91, 187, 199, 276, 388, 391, 392
Salvia pratensis, 132, 190, 277, 392
Salvia pitcheri, 277
Salvia splendens, 48, 144, 145, 151, 196, 199, 327
Salvia spp., 48, 149
Salvia viridis, 48, 80, 191, 327
Salvia x *superba*, 48, 54, 106, 107, 108, 183, 190, 277, 387, 388, 389, 390, 391, 392
'Samantha,' 51
'Sandra,' 196, 267. See *Phlox paniculata*
'San Gabriel,' 306
'*Sanguinaria canadensis*, 127, 128, 278, 387, 388, 389
'Sanguineus,' 326
'San Luis,' 306
'Santa Anita,' 306
Santolina, 162
Santolina chamaecyparissus, 91, 106, 116, 164, 165, 197, 278, 389
Santolina incana. See *Santolina chamaecyparissus*
Santolina virens, 278

Sanvitalia procumbens, 121, 132, 140, 149, 164, 193, 196, 328
'Saphyr,' 252
Saponaria ocymoides, 106, 140, 149, 164, 165, 194, 278, 387, 391, 392
Saponaria ocymoides, 279
Saponaria officinalis, 74, 90, 91, 279, 388, 389
Saponaria rubra, 406
Saponaria x *lempergii*, 279
'Sapphire,' 191, 261, 315
Sapphire flower. See *Browallia speciosa*
'Sapphire Hills,' 190
'Saratoga,' 91, 367
'Sargeant Pepper,' 117
Sassafras, 148
'Satin,' 300
Satin flower. See *Clarkia amoena*
Scabiosa atropurpurea, 279
Scabiosa caucasica, 54, 106, 140, 141, 149, 190, 279, 387, 388, 390, 392
Scabious. See *Scabiosa caucasica*
'Scarlet Beauty,' 151, 196, 231, 340
'Scarlet Charms,' 196
'Scarlet Emperor,' 199
'Scarlet Flame,' 197, 268
'Scarlet Meidiland,' 371
Scarlet monkey flower. See *Mimulus cardinalis*
'Scarlet O'Hara,' 198, 312
'Scarlet Poncho,' 301
Scarlet sage. See *Salvia splendens*
'Scarlet Star,' 312
Scented geranium, 89. See also *Pelargonium*
   species
Schizanthus pinnatus, 79, 149, 328
'Schooley's Yellow,' 265
'Schoonord,' 361
Scilla campanulata. See *Hyacinthoides hispanica*
Scilla hispanica. See *Hyacinthoides hispanica*
Scilla non-scriptus, 348
Scilla siberica, 74, 113, 140, 191, 348, 358
Scilla tubergeniana, 357
'Scottish Yellow,' 192, 290
Scutellaria baicalensis, 140, 164, 190, 279
Sea daffodil. See *Pancreatium maritimum*
Sea holly. See *Eryngium amethystinium*
Sea kale. See *Crambe maritima*
Sea lavender. See *Limonium latifolium*
Sea pink. See *Armeria maritima*
'Seashells,' 302
'Sea Urchin,' 378
Sedum acre, 85, 280
Sedum aizoon, 280
Sedum cauticolum, 140, 195, 280
Sedum kamtschaticum, 140, 192, 280
Sedum maximum, 280, 281
Sedum middendorffianum, 280
Sedum spathulifolium, 140, 280
Sedum spectabile, 74, 107, 108 109, 179, 195, 281, 389
Sedum spp., 121, 130, 149, 150, 164, 387, 388, 390, 391, 392
Sedum spurium, 199, 280
Sedum x *telephium*, 53, 54, 80, 87, 132, 134, 135, 165, 280, 389
Sedum x 'Vera Jameson,' 132, 165, 179, 183, 195, 199, 280
Self-heal. See *Prunella* x *webbiana*
'Semi Plena,' 97, 364
Sempervivum tectorum, 164, 281, 387, 390, 391
Senecio aureus, 125, 192, 281, 388, 389
Senecio cineraria, 197, 302, 319
Senecio tomentosus, 282
'Sensation,' 223, 302, 319, 364
Sensitive fern. See *Onoclea sensibilis*
Sentinel, 197
'September Charm,' 179, 194, 207
'September Glory,' 251
'September Ruby,' 212
Serbian bellflower. See *Campanula poscharskyana*
'Seven Dwarfs,' 340
'Shakespeare,' 363
Shasta daisy, 22, 26. See also *Chrysanthemum* x *superbum*
'Shawnee Chief,' 198
Sheep's fescue. See *Festuca amethystina*
'Sheer Bliss,' 97
'Shell Pink,' 97, 109, 179, 194, 250, 269
'Shenandoah Sky,' 248

'Sherwood Purple,' 190, 268
Shining coneflower. See *Rudbeckia nitida*
'Shining Sceptre,' 196
'Shirley Mix,' 321
Shirley poppy. See *Papaver rhoeas*
Shiso. See *Perilla frutescens*
'Show Star,' 193
'Showstopper Red,' 198
Showy evening primrose. See *Oenothera speciosa*
Showy stonecrop. See *Sedum spectabile*
Shrub roses, 12, 374
Siberian bugloss. See *Brunnera macrophylla*
Siberian draba. See *Draba sibirica*
Siberian iris. See *Iris sibirica*
Siberian squill, 182. See also *Scilla siberica*
Sidalcea malviflora, 48, 54, 107, 149, 194, 282, 390, 392
'Sidonie,' 372
Siebold hosta, 47
Signet marigold. See *Tagetes tenuifolia*
Silk flower. See *Abelmoschus moschatus*
'Silver Ball,' 224
'Silver Beauty,' 204
'Silver Bells,' 296
'Silver Brocade,' 115
'Silver Candelabra,' 287
'Silver Carpet,' 55, 90, 108, 113, 134, 185, 283
'Silver Comet,' 197
'Silver Cup,' 314
'Silver Dragon,' 187
'Silverdust,' 298
'Silver Dust,' 55, 87, 197
'Silver Edge,' 109, 190, 249
Silver-edged Japanese sedge grass. See *Carex morrowii*
'Silver Feather,' 380
Silver grass. See *Miscanthus sinensis*
'Silver King,' 80, 120, 197, 210
'Silver Lace,' 87, 298, 359
Silver lace. See *Centaurea cineraria*
'Silver Light,' 216
'Silver Moon,' 284
'Silvermound,' 44, 106, 108, 178, 185, 197, 210
Silvermound mugwort. See *Artemisia schmidtiana*
'Silver Queen,' 210, 241
Silver sage. See *Salvia argentea*
'Silver White,' 11, 185, 189, 327
'Silvery Sunproof,' 253
'Silvia,' 346
'Sincerity,' 323
'Sir John Falstaff,' 267
'Sir Lancelot,' 198
'Siskiyou,' 262
'Sissinghurst,' 288
'Sissinghurst White,' 188, 274
Sisyrinchium angustifolium, 282
Sisyrinchium striatum, 41, 107, 175, 282, 392
'Six Hills Giant,' 99, 116, 261
'Skating Party,' 188
Skullcap. See *Scutellaria baicalensis*
'Sky Blue,' 296, 311
Sky blue prairie aster. See *Aster azureus*
'Sky Joy,' 191
'Skyracer,' 380
'Small Miracle,' 117, 371
Small Solomon's seal. See *Polygonatum biflorum*
Smokebush, 96. See *Cotinus*
Snake-root. See *Cimicifuga racemosa*
Snakeweed. See *Polygonum bistorta*
Snapdragon, 78. See also *Antirrhinum majus*
Sneezeweed. See *Helenium autumnale*
'Sneezy,' 189
'Snow,' 255
'Snowball,' 113, 188, 224
'Snowbank,' 217
'Snow Cap,' 188, 209
'Snowcap,' 226, 286
'Snow Country,' 189
Snow crocus. See *Crocus chrysanthus*
'Snow Crystals,' 316
'Snowdrift,' 113, 188, 233, 329
Snowdrop, 30. See also *Galanthus nivalis*
'Snowflake,' 188, 247, 261, 268
'Snow Flurry,' 188
Snow-in-summer, 53. See also *Cerastium tomentosum*
'Snow Lady,' 226